DANCEHALL

Sound Culture
SERIES

SERIES EDITOR

Sonjah Stanley Niaah

ADVISORY BOARD

Carolyn Cooper
Julian Henriques
David Katz
Deborah Thomas
Jo-Anne Tull

Word, sound and power. This is the definition of the musical vibrations of Jamaican music. The music of Jamaica influences and has been influenced by countless other music forms throughout the Caribbean and worldwide. At the intersection of creation, production, consumption and globalization of Jamaican music, and from an interdisciplinary perspective, Sound Culture begins a long overdue focus on the history and evolution of sounds, tracing the movement from mento to ska and on to rocksteady, reggae, dub, nyabinghi, dancehall and the various styles of reggae fusion. The series covers all Caribbean music that intersects with Jamaican sounds, and artists in the region who work within the musical genres from Jamaica. It examines those who have blended their national musical forms with Jamaica's and acknowledges that, in addition to shaping culture, social relations, economics and politics, Jamaican music has influenced popular cultural production internationally. In particular, reggae has resonated with the disenfranchised and marginalized all over the world, its rhythm and melody appealing to soul rebels from Japan to South Africa, and Croatia to New Zealand. Sound Culture is intended as a record of the colossal impact that Jamaica has had on the planet through its musical vibrations.

DANCEHALL

A Reader on Jamaican Music and Culture

Edited by

Sonjah Stanley Niaah

The University of the West Indies Press
Jamaica • Barbados • Trinidad and Tobago

The University of the West Indies Press
7A Gibraltar Hall Road, Mona
Kingston 7, Jamaica
www.uwipress.com

A catalogue record of this book is available from the National Library of Jamaica.

ISBN: 978-976-640-750-6 (paper)
978-976-640-751-3 (Kindle)
978-976-640-752-0 (ePub)

Cover design by Rebecca Meek
Text design by Robert Harris
Set in Minion Pro 11/15 x 30

Supported by the CHASE Fund, Jamaica

Printed in the United States of America

Contents

Contents

Part 9: Tribute to Bogle

Acknowledgements and Permissions

THE IDEA FOR THIS ANTHOLOGY EMERGED IN CONVERSATION with Bibi Bakare-Yusuf around 2003, when I was about to complete my PhD in cultural studies. We saw the need to afford students, researchers, writers and music enthusiasts the opportunity to access seminal and emerging works on dancehall in one place. The idea germinated over a few years, with a call for abstracts being circulated internationally resulting in submissions from a wide range of scholars and emerging researchers. We are indebted to those who have held this project in their consciousness from the outset. Most of all, I am indebted to Bibi for helping to conceptualize this project and for her own chapter, which forms part of the collection.

I want to acknowledge the tremendous support of Erin C. MacLeod, who served as managing editor on the project. Being there from the beginning, she has worked assiduously to see this project materialize. Thank you for your support, guidance and focus Erin. Thanks also to the reviewers of the manuscript, and the University of the West Indies Press for its unwavering confidence in this project. As the first in the newly created Sound Culture Series, this publication constitutes many firsts and it is my hope that its effects will be far-reaching for students and scholars globally.

Thanks are due to many other persons who made this anthology possible. Their enthusiasm, guidance, insight and encouragement are highly appreciated.

Some of the articles and extracts of articles in this collection have been previously published. Permission granted by the following copyright holders is gratefully acknowledged:

Bibi Bakare Yusuf, "Fabricating Identities: Survival and the Imagination in Jamaican Dancehall Culture", in *Fashion Theory* 10, no. 4, pp. 461–83, reprinted by permission of Bibi Bakare Yusuf, © Taylor and Francis 2015.

Louis Chude-Sokei, "Post-Nationalist Geographies: Rasta, Ragga, and Reinventing Africa", in *African Arts* 24, no. 4, pp. 215–27, reprinted by permission of Louis Chude-Sokei, © MIT Press Journals 1994.

Robin Clarke, "Tommy Lee as 'Uncle Demon': Contemporary Cultural Hybridity in Jamaican Dancehall", in *ReggaeStories: Jamaican Musical Legends and Cultural Legacies*, edited by Donna P. Hope (Kingston: University of the West Indies Press), pp. 45–65, reprinted by permission of the University of the West Indies Press, © the University of the West Indies Press 2018.

Carolyn Cooper, "Slackness Hiding from Culture: Erotic Play in the Dancehall", in *Noises in the Blood: Gender and the "Vulgar" Body of Jamaican Dancehall* (Durham, NC: Duke University Press), pp. 136–73, reprinted by permission of Carolyn Cooper, © Carolyn Cooper 2020. This essay was also previously published in two parts in two 1990 issues of *Jamaica Journal* 22, no. 4 (pp. 12–31) and 23, no. 1 (pp. 44–52). The version in this volume is an edited and revised piece.

Nadia Ellis, "Out and Bad: Toward a Queer Performance Hermeneutic in Jamaican Dancehall", in *Small Axe* 15, no. 2, pp. 7–23, reprinted by permission of Duke University Press, © Duke University Press 2011.

Julian Henriques, "A Caribbean Taste of Technology: Creolization and the Ways of Making of the Dancehall Sound System", in *Technosphere*, April (online: https://technosphere-magazine.hkw.de/p/A-Caribbean-Taste-of-Technology-Creolization-and-the-Ways-of-Making-of-the-Dancehall-Sound-System-45C2uWd9N3ion4Dk92z03c), reprinted by permission of Julian Henriques, © Julian Henriques 2017.

Donna Hope, "Fashion Ova Style: Dancehall's Masculine Duality", in *Man Vibes: Masculinities in the Jamaican Dancehall* (Kingston: Ian Randle), pp. 124–42, reprinted by permission of Donna Hope, © Donna Hope 2010.

Dennis Howard, "Dancehall Political Patronage and Gun Violence: Political Affiliations and the Glorification of Gun Culture", originally pubished in *Jamaica Journal* 32, no. 3, pp. 8–15, reprinted by permission of Dennis Howard, © Institute of Jamaica 2010.

Peter Manuel and Wayne Marshall, "The Riddim Method: Aesthetics, Practice and Ownership in Jamaican Dancehall", in *Popular Music* 25, no. 3, pp. 448–62, 466–70, reprinted by permission of Cambridge University Press, © Cambridge University Press 2006.

Joe Pereira, "Gun Talk and Girls' Talk: The DJ Clash", in *Caribbean Studies* 27, nos. 3/4, pp. 208–23, reprinted by permission of Joe Pereira, © Caribbean Studies 1994.

Andrea Shaw, "Born in Chanel, Christen in Gucci: The Rhetoric of Brand Names and Haute Couture in Jamaican Dancehall", in *Archipelagos of Sound: Transnational Caribbeanities, Women and Music*, edited by Ifeona Fulani (Kingston: University of the West Indies Press), pp. 171–90 reprinted by permission of the University of the West Indies Press, © the University of the West Indies Press 2012.

Tracey Skelton, "Ghetto Girls/Urban Music: Jamaican Ragga Music and Female Performance", in *New Frontiers of Space, Bodies, and Gender*, edited by Rosa Ainely (London: Routledge), pp. 142–54, reprinted by permission of Tracey Skelton, © 1998 Routledge.

Sonjah Stanley Niaah, "Bogle ah di Order fi di Day: Dance and Identity in Jamaican Dancehall", in *LT1: Gender and Sexuality in Jamaica*, edited by Sachiyo Morimoto (Zentsūji, Japan: Mighty Mules), pp. 87–109, reprinted by permission of Sonjah Stanley Niaah, © Sonjah Stanley Niaah 2008.

Marvin Sterling, "Soundsystem Culture in Japan", in *Babylon East: Performing Dancehall, Roots Reggae, and Rastafari in Japan* (Durham, NC: Duke University Press), pp. 65–78, reprinted by permission of Duke University Press, © Duke University Press 2010.

Norman C. Stolzoff, "Murderation: The Question of Violence in the Sound System Dance", in *Social and Economic Studies* 47, no. 1, pp. 55–64, reprinted by permission of *Social and Economic Studies,* © Sir Arthur Lewis Institute of Social and Economic Studies 1998.

Krista Thompson, "Video Light: Dancehall and the Aesthetics of Spectacular Unvisibility in Jamaica", in *Shine: The Visual Economy of Light in African Diasporic Aesthetic Practice* (Durham, NC: Duke University Press), pp. 126–44, reprinted by permission of Duke University Press, © Duke University Press 2015.

Lena Delgado de Torres, "Egúngún in Disguise: The Jamaican Nine Night Ceremony", in *Journal of American Rootwork* 1, no. 1, to be published in Summer 2018, reprinted by permission of Lena Delgado de Torres, © American Rootwork Association 2018.

Garth White, "The Development of Jamaican Popular Music, Part 2. Urbanization of the Folk: The Merger of Traditional and the Popular in Jamaican Music", in *ACIJ Research Review* 1 (Kingston: African-Caribbean Institute of Jamaica), pp. 3–15, 24–36, reprinted by permission of the Institute of Jamaica, © Institute of Jamaica 1984.

Every effort has been made to trace copyright holders of material reproduced in this volume. Any rights that are not acknowledged here will be acknowledged in future printings if notice is given to the publisher, the University of the West Indies Press.

Notes and references in the extracts have been brought into conformity with the balance of the anthology. Authors and editors have made some alterations to material to adhere to length requirements.

Introduction

SONJAH STANLEY NIAAH

THE ORIGINS OF WHAT IS TODAY REFERRED TO AS "DANCEHALL" go back to mid-nineteenth century Jamaica, before the international community had heard of reggae or any of the other musical genres that have made the island a worldwide musical juggernaut. The dancehall has always been and continues to be a space of celebration (Stanley Niaah 2004). It is a location where communities come together to dance to music played by sound systems, the mobile discotheques which are the backbone of Jamaican music, providing entertainment in Kingston, throughout the countryside and increasingly in what can be referred to as the "dancehall diaspora".

From these spaces a range of different musics have been developed, from mento to ska and rocksteady to reggae and dub to dancehall. Dancehall has moved from referencing a place for enjoyment to being both a genre of music as well as a culture. The Jamaican genre of reggae has received significant treatment in multiple works, be they scholarly books or more popular, non-academic publications. This anthology, however, is the first work to bring together thinking about this multifaceted concept of dancehall from the perspectives of history, sociology, cultural studies, geography, anthropology, ethnomusicology and more.

Dancehall culture is vibrant and dynamic, a demonstration of the richness and resilience that is Jamaican creativity. Over the past decades, it has presented the world with innovations in music production and fashion design and illustrated the expression of politics, sexuality, spirituality, community, and both sexual and gender identity. Dancehall is entertainment and competition, lifestyle and novelty. However, given that many of the prevailing sentiments about dancehall point to slackness (meaning vulgarity), violence and debased values, dancehall has been persecuted as much as it has been praised. There have been complaints in local papers over the years, with but one recent example being a 2015 article in one of Jamaica's national newspapers, the *Gleaner*, stating "Dancehall Is the Source of Evil" (Thompson 2015). There have also been reactions and protests locally and internationally against moral codes expressed in dancehall's lyrics, particularly around same-sex relationships. This has led to *Time* magazine's infamous characterization of Jamaica as the "most homophobic place on earth" (Padgett 2006). While there are changing attitudes, what is clear is that dancehall music and culture have become easy avenues through which we can read the pulse of Jamaican sensibilities around a variety of everyday cultural norms.

So as to encompass the kaleidoscope of attitudes, opinions and ideas about dancehall, this collection brings together scholarship from the early days of analysis of the genre in the 1980s to recent work presented at the Global Reggae Conference under the theme "Dancehall, Music and the City" in 2017. The reggae studies conferences have been the source for published works, including Carolyn Cooper's edited collection of work from the 2008 conference, *Global Reggae* (2013), and *International Reggae: Current and Future Trends in Jamaican Popular Music* (2013), edited by Donna Hope. This anthology takes account of what could be referred to as both positive and negative perspectives and does not shy away from discussions of controversies surrounding dancehall as space, genre and culture. In addition, this anthology has been divided into the following sections, each providing relevant focus on the many attributes of dancehall that will allow for a broad understanding.

EARLY REFLECTIONS

Though dancehall is the most recent development in Jamaica's musical history, there has been scholarship on the subject since the early 1980s. Beginning with Garth White's seminal 1984 essay, one that has not been widely available until this publication, the history of what is now referred to as dancehall is told. White provides an outline of dancehall's predecessors and influences, not just musically but also in terms of dance itself. Carolyn Cooper, who was the first scholar to take the lyrics of dancehall seriously, demonstrates her approach and a means of reading the poetic significance in the music. For Cooper, slackness is not a barrier to cultural understanding, but actually part of the culture itself.

In this section, there is also Norman C. Stolzoff, anthropologist and scholar, who completed ethnographic work on dancehall sound system culture. His chapter provides insight on the sound system dance and looks at the role of violence in the dancehall space. Complementing this is work on lyrical clashes from Joe Pereira. Pereira's analysis of the "talk" of dancehall performers – alternately referred to as "DJs" or "deejays" – asks questions about lyrical content that edges toward violence and slackness.

NEGOTIATION, URBAN SPACE AND EXPERIENCE

As dancehall is an expression of a space, a space that is produced, as Henri Lefebvre would see it, by society and community (1991), this section deals with the creation and negotiation of the dancehall space, beginning with Louis Chude-Sokei's "Post-Nationalist Geographies: Rasta, Ragga and Reinventing Africa" that looks at the shift from the universal themes of reggae in the 1970s (promoted internationally by Bob Marley) to the much more spatialized and individualized focus of dancehall. Instead of a complete move away from cultural consciousness, Chude-Sokei argues for the specificity of the Africanness of the dancehall space. Still focused on space, but from a different perspective, Zachary J.M. Beier provides an archaeological view of one specific space that has been transformed through dancehall music: Kingston's historically significant Fort

Rocky. This fort in the Port Royal region is the first declared entertainment zone in the Kingston Metropolitan Area, as part of the modern era of cultural industries' regulatory frameworks and reforms.

Anna Kasafi Perkins takes a wider view of Kingston as a whole, as expressed through Jamaican popular music, with specific focus on the ways in which dancehall has shaped Kingston and vice versa. The final two chapters in this section deal with other influences of dancehall and the negotiation of space and experience. Robin Clarke describes how dancehall artist Tommy Lee has brought together a range of influences to develop his Caribbean, urban-gothic character of "Uncle Demon", and Dennis Howard illustrates the ways in which the reality of politics and crime impact and are described by dancehall artists.

ENGAGEMENT, SPECTACLE AND THE LANGUAGE OF PERFORMANCE

The interaction between dancehall artists and the interaction between sound systems and their audience, or "massive", are key to the environment that is the dancehall. Notably, the dancehall is a space in which the "massive" is as much spectator as performer. One of the most significant elements of any sound system event in Kingston (and internationally) is the role of the "video man", a person hired to record the proceedings. The camera takes into account not only performances but the entirety of the dancehall event, from fashion and dancing to the comments of the sound system MC and those in attendance. This section underlines this dynamic phenomenon, beginning with Krista Thompson's work on the role of the video light and spectatorship.

The dancehall provides opportunities for audiences to involve themselves in many ways, and Joshua Chamberlain's work on civic engagement and the sound clash demonstrates a different type of involvement on a broader, community-based level. Rival sound systems have competed using both the power of their sound as well as the content of the music they play. Chamberlain describes this phenomenon and how it also allows for the development of civic culture through the clash. Rounding out the section is Audene S. Henry's look at the language of the sound clash: communication between sound systems as well as communication between audience and sound system.

SEXUAL POLITICS AND AESTHETICS

Given dancehall's reputation for discussions of sex and sexuality, there is a need to include some of the important research and commentary on these topics, as well as the issue of gender. It is also important to review and expand the conception of dancehall as a simplistic and monolithically homophobic space. Nadia Ellis motions toward a different way of seeing the role of queerness in dancehall by thinking about how to interpret certain forms of masculinities in dancehall. So too does Donna Hope, who provides an analysis of male identity as it functions in the dancehall space. Hope's contribution to this volume looks specifically at how dancehall shapes the image of the man in Jamaica.

Turning to women's identities, Tracey Skelton discusses the performance of femininity and Agostinho Pinnock focuses on Tanya Stephens to illustrate the discourse of and around women in the genre.

SOUND SYSTEM, RIDDIM AND PRACTICE

Of course, dancehall is music, and this music is heard, primarily on sound systems. This section looks at the actual sound of dancehall, beginning with Julian Henriques's look at the sound system as creolized cultural form. Henriques is known for his analysis of the sound system and the dancehall as sound event. His work connects sound system practice with systems of understanding and discursive practices. This is complemented by the three other chapters in this section, including Peter Manuel and Wayne Marshall's thorough analysis of the practice of making dancehall. They describe how the system of "riddims" (the instrumental foundations of dancehall music that are used and reused by vocalists and recreated by producers) is shaped by and shapes dancehall music. Both Erin C. MacLeod and Ray Hitchins discuss the phenomenon of riddims from the same starting point: the sleng teng. MacLeod looks at the derisive discourse surrounding the riddim and Hitchins takes a musicological look at the development of dancehall music, specifically the use of technology in the creation of riddim.

RITUAL, CELEBRATION, SPACE

Dancehall is rooted in history, but it is also rooted in spirituality. The three chapters in this section take the sacred as a starting point. Sonjah Stanley Niaah's work, from the perspective of social and cultural geography, investigates dancehall event practice as ritual. Yes, the space is that of celebration, of music and dance and fashion – but there is a specific process to the dance. By enumerating different dance events, Stanley Niaah illustrates the commonalities and the ritualized nature of dancehall culture. Lena Delgado de Torres and Kate Lawton continue in this vein. De Torres turns to the funereal ritual of the Nine Night, underlining its relation to Yorùbá-based ancestral worship and the relationship of these older cultural practices to the present popular culture of dancehall. Lawton also connects ancestral practices with dancehall by drawing a comparison between the spiritual practice of obeah and the present-day conception of "bad mind", a much discussed concept in dancehall lyrics.

ADORNMENT, EMBODIMENT AND STYLE

Fashion and style are huge elements of dancehall. There is some discussion of fashion in the section dealing with sexuality and gender identity, but these three chapters demonstrate how dress shapes both dancehall and its participants. Bibi Bakare-Yusuf views fashion as a survival tactic, a means of shoring up identity. "H" Patten's work is on dance style and how it reflects both community and self-perception. Dealing with the pressure to sport international brands is Andrea Elizabeth Shaw. Her work on the discourse of luxury fashion brands in the dancehall and in dancehall lyrics illustrates how colonial hierarchies continue in dancehall.

THE DANCEHALL TRANSNATION

Dancehall is, of course, an international phenomenon, with artists from Africa to Europe to Asia to Australia and across the Americas all versioning and voicing riddims and attempting to express themselves in a dancehall style. All chapters in the section turn to dancehall sound, culture and practice in a difference space. Marvin Sterling provides insight into the role of the sound system in Japan and how Japanese culture has connected with dancehall. Andrea Hollington turns to the African continent to investigate the development of dancehall in Zimbabwe. Bruno Barboza Muniz, on the other side of the globe, draws connections between Jamaican sound system culture and Brazilian funk, asking questions about appropriation, authenticity and originality. The idea and impact of international audiences is discussed by Larisa Kingston Mann, who wonders about the result of dancehall's circulation through the wide range of technological platforms now available.

TRIBUTE TO BOGLE

As a final addition to the anthology, this tribute provides not only a fitting eulogy for the famed dancer Bogle but also an understanding of the importance of dance in the dancehall. The desire to remember those who have contributed to dancehall is also the purpose of this anthology. This tribute represents the first of what could be many tributes to those who have helped to develop dancehall, and this collection is itself a tribute to the many who have been at the foundation of dancehall practice and scholarship. But as dancehall – the space, music, style, dance and lifestyle – moves forward, there will always be a need to continue the analysis of this dynamic part of Jamaican culture. This is but one collection and a long overdue one.

REFERENCES

Cooper, Carolyn, ed. 2013. *Global Reggae*. Kingston: University of the West Indies Press.

Hope, Donna, ed. 2013. *International Reggae: Current and Future Trends in Jamaican Popular Music*. Kingston: Ian Randle.

Lefebvre, Henri. 1991. *The Production of Space*. Translated by Donald Nicolson-Smith. Oxford: Blackwell.

Padgett, Tim. 2006. "The Most Homophobic Place on Earth?" *Time*, 12 April. http://content.time.com/time/world/article/0,8599,1182991,00.html.

Stanley Niaah, Sonjah. 2004. "Kingston's Dancehall: A Story of Space and Celebration". *Space and Culture* 7, no. 1: 1102–18.

Thompson, Tyrone. 2015. "Devil in the Music – 'Dancehall is the Source of Evil'". *Gleaner*, 4 June. http://jamaica-gleaner.com/article/lead-stories/20150604/devil-music-dancehall-source-evil.

PART 1
EARLY REFLECTIONS

CHAPTER 1
The Development of Jamaican Popular Music*

GARTH WHITE

SOUND SYSTEM AND DANCE: "THE BLUES RUSH"

The individuals who in the late 1930s decided to build sound systems probably had no idea that their hobby would have a long-term significance. By the early 1950s what had started out as a friendly favour – playing at an acquaintance's house-party – was beginning to be a regular Saturday night's work. As the idea caught on, working class areas and the shanty towns of the unemployed became the scene of many a dance. Prior to this, there had of course been dances (meant here as occasions where dances are for pleasure and not for ritual purposes), with music supplied by small bands of mento and calypso musicians. These were held mostly in the rural areas.

In the urban areas, similar functions increasingly saw the use of bigger bands more and more influenced by music from the United States. The earlier socials were held nowhere nearly as regularly as these "blues dances" to which we are referring came to be.[1]

The later urban popular dance bands provided music for middle-class audiences in nightclubs and to some extent were middle-of-the-road bands that shifted their emphasis musically depending on the make-up of their audiences. Their repertoire would include mento, calypso, merengue, but mostly ballads, swing and progressive jazz. From as early as 1924, reliable observers noted that the earlier folk forms were losing their grip somewhat on the black masses (cf. Bethwick 1929, 209, 223). This was the result of the interplay of factors like increasing urbanization, the growth of national and international transport and communication systems and greater migration and emigration by Jamaican labourers. Those who travelled to work on the canal in Panama, or on the Costa Rican, Cuban or US plantations, tended upon return to settle in the rapidly growing urban areas, associating the old rural base with hardship and lack of opportunity and showing a preference for the more cosmopolitan atmosphere of the city. That which

*Previously published in *ACIJ Research Review* 1 (1984): 3–15, 24–36.

by the 1940s had almost completely supplanted the country band – the urban popular band – reflected these developments. Sonny Bradshaw in reply to questions as to the bands existing at this time explained that "You have to divide it into two categories. You had to divide it between the road bands and the society bands."

> Interviewer: Society bands?
> Bradshaw: The society bands at the time were say, Whylie Lopez, Ivy Graydon, George Alberga and about two or three others.
> Interviewer: Where did they play?
> Bradshaw: Well Ivy Graydon used to play at Camp[2] mostly, and the more higher social parties – you know, that sort of thing, private and otherwise . . . the nightclubs were reserved for the road bands. We were playing for the ordinary people.

Examples of road bands would be those of Sonny Bradshaw, Val Bennette, Baba Motta, Barber Mac, Roy Coburn, Eric Deans and Redver Cook to name a few.[3] Some of these bands, wanting to appear more sophisticated and accomplished, would scoff at calypso and sought to master the new instruments in American big band style. Bradshaw informs us that

> bands in those days used to play what they called stock arrangements, arrangements brought from America which were recorded by the name bands as sort of water-down arrangements of the real thing. . . . Woody Herman used to be very popular at that time, Stan Kenton and the Count Basie series. They used to play the Count Basie series. . . . Ellington music which was more difficult, people used to be afraid to attempt.

Mento musicians became less and less able to find work in the city. Bradshaw describes some: "There was a set of musicians who used to hang out on Princess Street. They used to call them Princess Street musicians. Most of them didn't play in the organised bands: they were free lancers and they used to take all the country jobs like country fairs and things out of town, for all the Kingston people are too sophisticated to want to listen to them."[4] Some of the sophisticated bands still played the occasional calypso or mento, especially for tourists who "used to want to hear this". The majority of the city-based musicians, however, "didn't want to play calypso, we felt this was a downgrade thing . . . we used to play one calypso set every night at twelve o'clock, or one o'clock, after the intermission and that's it. Nobody come and ask you for a calypso after that." As Gordon points out, "While 'swing' music was the popular music of the expatriate and local predominantly white, upper classes and the coloured middle class, in the absence of any other widely popular form of music and the relative unpopularity of the traditional music, it also served as musical entertainment for the black 'lower' classes of Kingston" (1968, 10). Musical favourites across class lines were standards like "Stardust", "Stormy Weather" and "Begin the Beguine". After this short swing interlude the various bands gave way to the sound system as the primary means of musical entertainment.

There were many factors leading to the relative eclipse of the road bands by the sound system. For one, the music played, largely rhythm and blues, as an Afro-Western music readily found an audience among the black masses. Quite the contrary to an early ultra-nationalist view that R&B was the result of crass US commercialism and that its popularity reflected continuing dependence on external sources, its history and subsequent role and use in Jamaica confirm that it really maintained a continuity with the earlier Jamaican folk music. One can easily identify similarities. "African rhythm prominent, harmony essentially European, a melodic fusion . . . it is important to note that in the blending process the African rhythmic foundation absorbs and transforms the European elements" (Keil 1966, 30; see also Waterman 1952, 207–18). They were both Afro-Western. R&B found a ready audience in the Jamaican masses. There really was no disjunction at all, their acceptance being the "product of the social changes in Jamaica which brought the black working class originally engaged in rural agricultural relations into new urban relations and into relations with black Americans, a significantly different kind of relation than the upper classes of the society had with agencies and persons of the dominant white American society. This . . . was reflected in the differing forms of musical activity which they adopted" (Gordon 1968, 2). Because the R&B artists dealt with black life they became both the symbolic and the real representatives of the black man in the street. Second, the sound system was a less expensive form of entertainment. As veteran band leader Sonny Bradshaw explained: "the sound systems started coming in. And this brought about a decline in road band business. Because you could hire a sound-system for five pounds, and at that time the road bands were just coming into money, demanding fifty pounds to one hundred pounds on special occasions. So people decided to use soundsystems" (Gordon 1968, 12). Also, the "sound" could play non-stop and produce music of a technically higher quality for larger crowds.

A sound system of the Jamaican type uses powerful amplifiers to drive recorded music through a number of speakers. In the early World War II years, a fifty-watt amplifier was probably a rarity. Two of the legendary sound operators, Clement "Sir Coxsone" Dodd and Duke Reid, describe how they entered the field. Dodd's mother owned a grocery shop:

> We had a very big murphy radio. So at that time man like Billy Eckstine was singing and was very popular here so what I did was bought me a Garrard changer, plug it in the radio, make an extension box from our room to the front of the shop. On account of that we had to open late and my mother did a lot of business . . . and since then Roy White had a big enough amplifier playing by his shop because he did cabinet making, so he had that form of music out there for the boys from that area who would come and stand and listen to all the new top tunes and stuff like that. But when I went to the States now and saw all the different amplifiers that they had I realize you would get more volume, so as to cover a bigger crowd. (Gordon 1968, 11)

Duke Reid started in a similar way. He had joined the Jamaica Constabulary in 1943:

> In 1946 we got regrading monies and I was transferred in Sav-la-mar. And out of that regrading monies I bought a mercury radio which I still have. I love music and I bought quite a lot of records. And from that I take these records to my house and I play them. The people love them and I start to make Saturday night parties. From this I figured that I had a sound then I would be able to . . . you know . . . make some money. (Gordon 1968, 11–12)

As the entertainment form gained in popularity and the need to outplay rival systems arose, more and more powerful systems were developed. The initial spur to develop ways of reproducing music in which every instrument was fully present was provided by the type of music preferred. The US black R&B and the Jamaican mento and calypso all had a very active bass line, among other things. Other music paled beside them when placed under the scrutiny of sound system reproduction. An ordinary radio gramophone like the wind-up Victrola or the "embryonic" systems of the early Coxsone or Duke Reid did not do justice to the heavy strides and suspension of the black bass player. They also could not throw out sound to accommodate a crowded house, yard or lawn. In the hubbub of the "Coney Island" or holiday fair, a person who desired to dance manifested a willingness not only to hear the music but literally to feel it. Bass notes like thunder, with the objects in the yard where the dance is held resounding in sympathy; a drum roll, lick or snap requires the impact of an event when played through a Jamaican sound system. One three-minute R&B standard takes on the aspect of an epic with the high frequency instruments and voices in the piece coming through loud and clear from horns perched atop the bass boxes, on high stands and secured in mango or lignum vitae trees growing in the yard.

The low-frequency instruments are produced with such resonance through "bass reflex" speaker boxes that it is almost possible to dance to the sympathetic "buzz-buzz" of the zinc fence or glass windows in the dancehall. The sound system became so powerful that a promoter in choosing a hall did not really need to consider the length of its "reverberation period".

One of the earliest recognizable sound systems was that employed by one "Fats Waller" to provide music for his clients as proprietor of the Blue Mirror club located near the city's centre on West Street. Other more mobile systems like Wauldron, Goodies, Nick's, Dean's, Tom the Great Sebastian, Duke Reid, Doc's, Grannums, Sir Coxsone's Downbeat, Smith's, Teddy's, V-Rocket, Sky-Rocket, Admiral Cosmic, Roderick, Count Piah the Blueblaster, Lord Coo's, Count John the Lion, Sinclair the Lion and Little Wonder soon mushroomed and were regularly playing for a potentially large and appreciative set of patrons. Although many of the sound operators may have had their sets as a playing hobby and were regularly employed in one occupation or other, there were many others more properly seen as small businessmen. As a type they were not dissimilar to shopkeepers and launderers and some of the better-off higglers with their two-sided nature – one foot in the camp of labour, the other in that of capital. An unemployed person, more often than not because of some windfall or as a result of combining with others, could conceivably own a set. The majority of operators were, however, small owners. Some of them were to combine their ownership of systems with the running of liquor stores which could advance goods to dance promoters on a kind of consignment, hire-purchase basis. A few of them were to branch out further and build studios for recording artists: they could thus provide their systems with exclusive "hard tunes" and also satisfy some of the demand for records by local audiences. Most of these studio operators became more and more capitalistic in their methods and in their relations with singers and musicians.

Many of the sound operators were identified by residential area and when playing outside of this locale would be seen as representatives of the home base. One would thus hear of Count Piah of Four Roads, Doc Apollo and Heatwave, Sinclair from Fletcher's Land, Duke Reid and Coxsone, Nick's the Champ, Dean's and others from the city's centre and west end, Hylton and Milton from West Street, Admiral Cosmic from Shady Grove in the Papine area, and so on.

While some of their patrons no doubt enjoyed the ballads of a Nat Cole, Perry Como or Patti Page and the barber-shop harmonizing of the Mill's Brothers and the Inkspots, their preference at a dance was definitely for the "harder" R&B. Some controversy has developed around the question of whether these blues patrons were really exposed to mento. Certainly a system like that of Howell's, which was a rurally based system, played many mento pieces. In the urban areas the preponderance of R&B cannot be contested, but there was effective exposure to mento. First, many of the patrons of blues dances had rural backgrounds and connections and would very likely have heard live mento bands – the greater proportion of the formal live music that the urban masses heard in the immediate post-war period was mainly of the swing type but the rural populace still sported quite a few mento aggregations. Also of note here is the fact that cult, Revivalist and other related religious forms together contributed perhaps only slightly less to the earlier music experience of the black folk, urban or rural. Second, some of the earliest locally produced recorded music for popular consumption was mento or calypso. Thirdly, some of these mento tunes were aired nationally, although some were banned as dealing none too subtly with sexual themes. Observers who scoff at the influence of mento have perhaps forgotten the popularity of tunes like "Day de Light (and I Wanna Go Home)", "Woman Smarter", "What Is Catty (Big Boy Ask)", "Penny Wheel", "Dry Weather House", "Give Me Back Mi Shillin (wid de Lion pon It)", "Jamaican Gal", "Night Food", "Dunno What to Say the Monkey Won't Do", "Naughty Flea", "Water the Garden", "Hold im Joe" and many others. While the Trinidadian calypsos were played quite regularly on radio, admittedly they were used less frequently on the sound system circuit; but even here one can remember popular tunes and artists. The standards of a "Kitchener", the "Rio Batucada", and other instrumentals of Fitz Vaughan Bryan and other Trinidadian bands were popular for many years. Also deserving some consideration is the fact that even the R&B field produced some "calypsoesque" renditions – "When You Dance" by the Turbans, the instrumentals "South Way Mambo", Nat Cole's "When Rock and Roll Comes to Trinidad", Ray Johnson's "Calypso Joe", and Harry Belafonte's "Mama Looka Booboo" are ready examples.

As the playing-out field became more competitive, the systems proliferated. It was common in the urban, deprived areas to find two or three top systems vying for active support in the same neighbourhood on a Saturday night. Some owners had more than one set (Coxsone Dodd had six: "two may be in the country and four in Town [Kingston]"). For any one set their arsenal may have included a 200- to 500-watt amplifier, anything between six to twelve sizeable speaker boxes containing 18-inch woofers, a couple of 15s and 12s, smaller 10s in smaller boxes or "hanging boxes", and between two and six horns of the public address type. Part of the larger pattern of social and cultural influences diffusing to rural areas is evidenced by the appearance of smaller sets in Spanish Town and Montego Bay.[5] The operators of the system tried everything to get the edge over rivals. Some of them, rather than relying solely on the efforts of sailors, visitors and returning farm workers, themselves travelled regularly to the United States, procuring tunes, particularly R&B, attempting on return to "beat down" a competitor with a "hard tune". Labels were scratched out to make the task of obtaining a copy difficult for a competitor.

THE DANCE AS INSTITUTION

Some dances, house parties and later "sessions" were put on by an individual or a group trying to generate funds in order to meet household expenses or rent.[6] Others were put on by popular promoters – "regulars" in ghetto slang. The popularity of these regulars often did not so much depend on economic strength as on the strength of face-to-face relationships in the ghettos. It was not uncommon to see a plumber, a "pants-length" vendor, a factory worker and a dressmaker idealized artistically on a commercial poster advertising a proposed dance. People like "Hepo", "Sealie", "Danny as Foot", "Frankie White", "Trevor as Fish", "P. Son as Papa Son from Uptown" and "Lord Comic" were among the early promoters. Dances with titles like "Jumping Sonata" or "Woodchoppers Ball", or seasonal events like Christmas, Easter or Emancipation Day jamborees, were regular yearly promotions. Native ways of speech, of dress, of other modes, possibly more related to level of material well-being than to particular cultural preference – although the latter's influence cannot be ignored – were to thrive in this atmosphere of spontaneous, "uncontrived" creativity.

The sound systems' growing popularity saw the emergence of supporting "followers". The low-income areas of Kingston became more linked as the systems moved around. Many youths learned about many areas after being first acquainted with their dancehalls – from Shady Grove in the northeast to Back-to in the west, Gold Coast and Club Monaco and Palm Beach in the east, to Silver Slipper in the Cross Roads area. From Tower Hill to Kencot to Constant Spring, the dancehalls were popularized. Mutual benefit and friendly society halls acquired new fame – Forest's Hall, Jamaica Success Club, Jubilee Tile Garden, King's Lawn, Barbeque, Live Wire Club and Chocomo Lawn. Famous halls like Marcus Garvey's Liberty Hall took on renewed significance.[7]

In this form of social recreation, a range of styles existed. The middle-class birthday or house party may have been similar in some cases to the lower-class subcultural dance, especially when the hosts' occupation and income level was not far above that of the upper reaches of the working class. Generally, however, similar middle-class occasions followed a more conventional black bourgeois pattern. There would usually be a smaller number of people attending and a smaller, less powerful record-playing system. Only the bigger occasions, staged by the likes of private associations and charities within this class at one of the then existing nightclubs like Bournemouth or Glass Bucket (the later name for the older White Elephant), with orchestras and bands like those of Eric Dean's, Baba

Motta, Mapletoft Poulle, Ivy Graydon, George Alberga and Whylie Lopez providing the music, saw any crowds that could equal in size the fairly typical subcultural case. The middle class public entertainment seems to have entered a low phase and nightclub life of this sort generally declined. In their heyday, not infrequently, dress requirements were imposed and participation was possible, oftentimes only on the basis of fairly formal invitation. Food provided ranged from conventional sandwiches and liquor to more substantial chicken or mutton dishes and choice liquors. This was often provided free but a position lower on the income scale may have forced an "aspirant" host or hostess to charge a small sum for refreshments and, of course, charity organizations and similar associations would have had their fundraising balls where refreshments were sold.

It is tempting and partly justified to see the more lavish of these entertainments as descendants of the type reported by Stewart and others during the period immediately after slavery. Stewart had observed that "creole negroes" showed a "decided preference for European music" as against the "rude" music of the enslaved people. Writing in 1823, he reported that the instruments of Europe, "its tunes, its dances are now pretty generally adopted, by the young creoles, who indeed sedulously copy their masters and mistresses in everything. A sort of subscription balls are set on foot, and parties of both sexes assemble and dance country dances to the music of a violin, tambarines, etc." (1823, 272; see also Beche 1825, 9).

These more public slave entertainments utilized both African and European music and "like the Christmas 'John Canoe' processions" should be distinguished from the "more intransigent 'cult' observances of slaves that were necessarily secret, or at any rate private, and which centred around the drum" (Brathwaite 1973a, 227). While not as studiously European as the earlier "middle-class" balls, the dances of the middle class in the 1940s and 1950s were somewhat Anglophile or sought to imitate the North American counterpart.

As distinct from the middle-class function, the blues dance, the subcultural form, was extremely informal even while at times being spectacular. At no time did it forcibly sanction any mode of conduct. A seemingly spontaneous code developed. A "hustler", slick and cool, may trade moves with a barefooted boy in tattered clothes. "All" were invited – the "strictly by invitation" injunction on most posters and cards promoting the dance was used with wry humour since almost anyone "passing through" could pay a small sum and gain entrance. Food offered on sale usually involved a curry mutton dish with the popularly locally produced beer and stout and an assortment of soft carbonated beverages almost exclusively used as liquid refreshment by the promoters. Additionally, itinerant peanut vendors and a "cane man" almost automatically appeared as the dance got underway. Another often "own account" service was provided by a "mother" or a "daughter" (the popular term then was "sister"), who took up a position at the gate entrance with oranges or roasted or boiled corn. Thus a social function less dependent on foreign imports for consumption than its middle-class or "polite society" counterpart was encouraged. In time, while retaining these features and its accessibility, the subcultural dance could get even more "roots", as the current saying goes, including formerly esoteric modes and practices of the Rastafari movement – wood-roots as drinks and "ital" food (dishes made out of local produce without salt or meat but oftentimes balanced by the provision of almost the whole range of peas and beans). Soups of "cow-cod" or "mannish-water",[8] even an "ital" variant, would also sometimes be offered, and, of course, locally produced music on record came to supplant US R&B.

An important difference then between the conventional middle-of-the-road parties and the subcultural dance was that the latter involved a wider range of persons and was attended by a larger number. Because of this, one would be more likely to see a midnight show featuring a popular band or group of musicians at the dance than at the party, although the cost of a band would normally be more easily shouldered by a middle-class host. Of course, as we have noted, middle-class formal associations may have put on big dances with large bands featured. Some of the music these bands played was a distinguishably local take on American material, with largely swing and ballad primarily used. The use of bands in the subcultural case in the sound system era – featuring more music derived from native experience – reached a tremendous high in the early and middle 1960s, with the activities of the Count Ossie Drummers and the Skatellites band, and is to be distinguished from earlier road band activity.

Attitudes toward occasions such as these varied both between the classes and within them. Some of these attitudes have remained constant over time, others have changed with the times. At first, as we have seen, the lower and middle classes were fairly differentiated in their attitude toward the more "rootsy" dances. Even within these broad groups, nevertheless, attitudinal differences could be met. Thus as time went on, many middle-class youths, mostly male, but with increasing frequency some daughters of the struggling lower bourgeoisie and even of gentry, would participate in these occasions. In other instances, across class lines many alleged Christians ostensibly showed no interest, although the working class and peasant Revivalist churches sang and rocked to religious "clap-hand" music whose rhythm was often close to that of the blues and Jamaican secular folk music. Even among Rasta as a group, there were differences, at the time, in the value assigned these functions by some adherents. Thus an older Rasta of the generation of the 1930s and 1940s may have viewed popular dances, parties and nightclubs as the same thing, places where "women ketch man" or "man get black up" through alcohol consumption and therefore, in the main, places to be shunned. One of this type would still in all likelihood be appreciative of and even committed to the music played at the dance, extolling the virtue of the emerging local greats (more so as some of them were Rastafarians) and placing positive value on the cultural form. His weight would be put, however, on the side of the scale, which, in the building of the code of conduct, frowned on overindulgence and enthusiasm carried to the point of boisterousness on a social occasion.

Younger brethren can be found who hold a similar position now and, more generally, the view is that as an important setting for the movement retaining, strengthening and building African and indigenous ways that are worth keeping, and as a vehicle of this "roots" culture, the dance is to be supported. There were also, of course, members of the lower classes who were uncommitted to the tenacious retention and development of local culture. They simply enjoyed the music and naturally, because of their class position, came into contact with its expressions and were carried along by popular currents. This may have restricted their support for attending stage shows or buying records for home play or just "punching" tunes in a jukebox, but they may have also attended dances at fairs, if not those held in the heart of the ghettos. Despite attitudinal differences and differences in the evaluation placed on the form by different sections and groups within society, by the mid-1960s, the dance as a social event straddled the island, penetrating the middle class and providing the setting for many musical experiments.

"DEEJAY AT THE CONTROLS!"

The dance produced a particular type of disc jockey. It was also the prime medium for the young recording industry. In the case of the disc jockey, while a few of them could be compared to the American radio disc jockey, the two roles were different in many respects and led to remarkable differences in usage and style. The sound system disc jockey did not operate out of a fixed studio in a relatively impersonal relationship with his audience. He could spontaneously create rhymes and comments to fit the music and did so not only in the intervals between the playing of his selection but while the music was being reproduced. As subsequently noted by numerous commentators, disc jockeying became a kind of folk art and came to wield much influence on many young Jamaican poets. The sound system deejay does not restrict himself to the mouthing of "sweet nothings", although "nonsense" verses with a rhythmic intent are often, even mainly, used by some. He often quite boldly ventures opinions on popular issues. Sometimes the mood is light-hearted, and humorous couplets of verses ridiculing a competitor or criticizing someone or some situation are spoken over the rhythm. This reminds one of the prime features of calypso and even of earlier forms, namely the songs of ridicule used in Africa. Roberts points out that "a common social use of music in Africa is to satirize people who have broken social rules. This function has carried over to the New World" (Roberts 1972, 66).

At times, a mystical-religious or radical message is delivered. In most cases the tenor of such commentary is decidedly at the black nationalist level of consciousness and so far only a few have attempted to deal with class conflict. The rhythmic talking was, of course, added to the regular duties performed by the deejay such as spinning the records, advertising future dances and "outings" and "toasting" rival systems. What began as routine service – spinning records – has developed to the stage where big systems in the "Grand Tradition" may hire disc jockeys who just speak. In time they would also be recorded.

Probably the earliest deejay to receive mass acclaim in the urban poor areas was Matchuki of the early Blue Mirror. He was later to join Sir Coxsone's forces. His early rivals would be Roy Chance, Minstick of Tom's and Willie Penny of Dean's. Later examples in the early period, which takes us up to the mid-1960s, were King Stitt, Cuttings, Count Foot and Prince Ruff. King Stitt or Sir Coxsone's Roundbeat received almost country-wide acclaim in the poorer districts. In the later 1960s and early 1970s when the style was being extensively recorded, others like U-Roy, Al Capone, Scotty, Lizzy,

Prince Jazzbo and Big Youth emerged. To U-Roy, one-time deejay of Sir Coxsone then King Tubby's and Soul Attorney and lately of Sturgav, must go the credit of winning truly national attention. The style has now become sufficiently established, and many recordings are done in the style by those who may not be disc jockeys for a regularly playing sound system. Also, producers seeking to benefit from the popularity of the style recorded much material which is poorly conceived. A listener or dancer could not give a balanced judgement of the style were he or she to take these last recordings as a typical and representative indication of usual content and worth.

COMMERCIAL CONSIDERATIONS

To understand the birth of the local recording industry, one has to go back to the days of some of the early system operators who had attempted to regularize relationships with American record outlets. At the time, no regular commercial channel existed linking US record distributors to local outlets, so the sound system operators therefore developed informal and irregular channels of supply:

> Among these were returning migrants and visitors to the US. The relative lack of information about records and the irregular commercial linkage with the rhythm and blues market was closely related to the pattern of acquisition and "shielding" which marked sound-system competition. The practice of scratching out labels from the records was made precisely because communication and contact with the States are irregular. It also made possible the acquisition of old records which rivals could not trace. (Gordon 1968, 18)

Thus was encouraged effective demand for those "hard" R&B tunes on the part of smaller up-and-coming systems and enthusiastic dance patrons who could afford to buy these records for home use.

As the demand for records generally increased, the formal agencies and stores importing records gradually took over the importing function. Because the commercial class involved here comprised Jamaican whites, fair coloured, Jewish and Lebanese people, their choice of record to import tended to reflect the by now extremely tiresome "white bias". Although there was a great demand for black R&B, the radio station of the period (1950–59), Radio Jamaica, and the importing companies dealt almost exclusively with the tunes of Tin Pan Alley and the American Hit Parade.[9] This misplaced emphasis in the circumstances would seem even more determined in the days of rock and roll (1954–59) and was to impel the sound operators to try to produce their own music for dance patrons. From such an interest, the modern local recording industry began.

THE DANCE REVISITED

A typical dance then would be frequented by a range of persons but predominantly black workers and the unemployed – roughly the "people", as these constitute the overwhelming majority of the society. For these, at certain times, say on Friday, Saturday, Sunday or even Monday night, a dance was a social event attended for relaxation. Acute muscular energy is channelled and seeks outlet in dance expression. In a "seemingly unorganised pantomime, which in reality is extremely systematic" can be seen "the huge effort of a community to exorcise itself, to liberate itself, to explain itself" (Fanon 1965, 44).

In the early 1950s when the dance was taking hold as a social practice, in addition to local steps and the waltz, which in its many international variations can almost be described as perennial and universal, many black American dance steps like the shuffle, bebop and jitterbug were utilized in the native black's dance repertoire. This was a continuing feature. These moves were carried by returning farm workers, US sailors and black visitors to the island. As in the case of music making specifically, there is much in the experience of the black poor in the countries of the Western Hemisphere to inspire expressive artistic creations understandable in and relevant to different situations, despite geographical separation, and which would cross national boundaries, the way made easier by the growth in travel and the international system of communication.

As far as dance moves were concerned, one can note that the relative increase in influence of the United States as distinct from the British Isles in the economic area was matched by a similar shift on the dance floor. In fact, Afro-American music from the United States was to be responsible for the vast majority of the so-called dance crazes that swept the world, and even where the craze did not take the same form, the music and dance of the blacks would still have great influence. These styles at first met with mainstream outcry of no uncertain kind. The modern waltz, which probably could have been distinguished from the nineteenth century Austrian example, was denounced by middle- and upper-class circles in the United States as scandalous, indecent and vulgar. Many of the older generation of which these classes were chiefly constituted were also shocked by the turkey trot, the tango, the bunny hug and the foxtrot. The foxtrot, which came to be danced in most capitals, at the time was "judged 'indecent' by a New York court and banned in Japan, even in the state brothels, on the grounds of immorality. Mayor John Fitzgerald Kennedy (grandfather of president John F. Kennedy) banned all turkey trots, bunny hugs and everything else danced to ragtime music and ordered the arrest of anyone caught dancing these steps" ("Dance and Discomania" 1976, 6).

What probably irked these confused guardians of the public morality was the link between some of these dances and sex – but then even walking can sometimes give a suggestion of sexuality. The Roaring Twenties saw dance fads come and go seemingly at will, proving "invulnerable to any legislative restraints" or social pressure from certain quarters. What is sometimes in these discussions called the Jazz Age understandably saw the dominance of black dance styles among others. Dances like the Charleston and the shimmy were to endure into the 1930s and reappear into the late 1950s and early 1960s. Ballroom dancing, as performed by Fred Astaire and Ginger Rogers, was quite popular but did not get the universal response of earlier forms ("Dance and Discomania" 1976, 6–7). Obviously the real home of the blues and related styles, the black ghetto, continued to produce "soulful" moves that coexisted with the white popular moves which were often commercialized versions of black styles.

Two fairly widespread new motions in the 1930s were rhumba and swing. The rhumba was perhaps the best known Cuban rhythm and in a much watered down form (Roberts 1972, 95) was popular in Europe and the United States. It also owed much to the influence of Africa. Swing music, "which was the result of arranged big band jazz" (Jones 1963, 164–65), was still popular during World War II. Count Basie's music during the period, with its "rock-firm four-to-the-bar" (Roberts 1972, 208) rhythm, is a typical example of the authentic black type. White bands like Benny Goodman's had "mastered the swing idiom of big band jazz with varying degrees of authenticity" (Jones 1963, 163). Although it was originally a black music, as was to become a recurring feature, white musicians benefited from the discrimination practised by white radio stations and recording studios against black artists and monopolized studio work. In his favour, it must be noted however that Benny Goodman became the first white band leader to regularly employ blacks on the bandstand.

Similarly, after the war and in the early and mid-1950s, singers like Frank Sinatra, Perry Como, Tony Bennett, Johnny Ray, Frankie Laine and Peggy Lee,[10] whose styles were less rhythmically complex than those of the popular form which was simultaneously growing in popularity among the US black poor, namely rhythm and blues, obtained much more airplay than most black musicians of the time, whatever their calibre.[11] Sinatra claimed that he was influenced by the work of the great Billie Holiday[12] and it is true that she and the earlier "classic" blues singers had developed a performance style somewhat more polished and probably more suited to listening than dance. This kind of music was more to the liking of official society than the dirty R&B. It is R&B, however, in its sophisticated development that saw it overlapping with jazz and gospel and, to a lesser extent, the ballad form and occasionally some Latin American elements, that provided the real basis for subsequent popular dance development in the United States.

The early and mid-1950s ushered in the era of a more commercialized R&B that came to be known as rock and roll. Dance moves to R&B could consist of a single sequence or a combination of different steps. In Jamaica, for example, in the R&B framework an individual could boogie-woogie or shuffle or do the huckleback. Around this time, too, local blacks developed their own "Yank" to R&B. The 1950s and 1960s saw the continued influence of Latin American styles, from the early merengue of Haiti and the Dominican Republic, the mambo – derived from the earlier rhumba – or the cha-cha-cha of Cuba to the samba of Brazil, which was introduced in its Americanized form as the bossa nova.

In the late 1950s in New York and other big capitals, the twist often led to a kind of dance mania that probably can only be put with the dance marathon of the 1920s as examples of sheer obsession. The twist encouraged the establishment of the discotheque, used here in the sense of a club devoted to playing recorded music. There were more inter-class and inter-racial encounters within these clubs than at other occasions of a similar nature in other places, and this facilitated the further creation of dance moves commonly done by a broadened cross-section of the US "young crowd". Other moves first fashioned in the black ghettos were the mashed potato (the latter-day Charleston), hully gully, Watusi and pachanga and the most innumerable proffering of singers like Rufus Thomas. None of these, however, assumed "craze" proportions and with the subsiding of the twist it was not until the "bump" of the mid-1960s that one saw the emergence of a popular dance that came to be practised in the United States on an almost nationwide scale and also gained international usage.

Even taking into account the increase in popularity of forms like white rock, country and western, and blue-eyed soul, it is true to say that it is the black community in the United States that has been mainly responsible for the growth of the current disco form. Of course, commercial interests in the United States were quick to tailor tunes to meet and even to anticipate disco demand. There is often, as a result, much "canning" and consequently cheapening of vital, creative black music. Dance-craze music then is often crassly commercialized. The obvious feature of this brief review of the United States and other dance styles and their radiation outwards is the fact that most of them, even the Cuban contributions, are largely African-inspired or derived from black styles themselves influenced by the song and dance of Africa, thereby showing the thread of continuity in black forms, urban-rural differences and the crossing of national boundaries notwithstanding.

An interesting, long-lived set of moves, which endured the coming and going of the various fads and crazes, was the one involving an encounter between a man and a woman in which the man, while stepping to the music, helps spin the woman regularly around. The local mento, with its suggestive hip moves and "belly rub", often saw the male partners occasionally spinning their female counterparts. In the later move we are discussing, there was male shuffling and improvising and the use of many popular dance moves between and during the woman's turn, which was usually executed at the rate of one in every four beats. It is difficult to say which national component was most important, although the nod should probably be given to the US black scene. This particular routine was to endure for over twenty years – in fact, up until the mid-1960s in Jamaica.

Although black American dance styles very popularly accompanied Afro-American tunes, there was much room for extemporizing; indeed even while utilizing black American steps, the black Jamaican would include an element of his or her own. "Kinesic codes", or body movement, would most of the time be distinctly Jamaican. These features were obvious in the earlier folk forms of Jamaica, religious or secular. While the twentieth century saw the decreasing importance of the earlier cult activity and the gradual adoption of the European denominational religions by many Jamaicans, forms like Kumina, Zion Revival or Pukkumina[13] were still familiar to a majority of the poor. The continuing influence of cult dancing along with that of secular social dances like mento, brukins and gerreh among others, and the singing and dancing games among adults and the young like Maypole, often naturally paved the way for the adoption and adaptation of black moves from the United States. An invaluable part of the resultant common ground was made up of the rhythmic impetus of dancers, ways of holding or carrying the body, the setting up of different movements of the body at the same time and, more generally, the important role dancing played in social activity.

Although one can claim the "distinctly Jamaican" label for some of the dance features of the Jamaican poor right through their history, one is most certainly aware of the susceptibility of the Jamaican populace to influence by outside forms, especially if that "outside form" had familiar elements or elements which could logically be added or developed out of its then present practice. By the late 1920s and early 1930s, the local black poor had not only been exposed to the oftentimes changed ways of returning soldiers (from World War I), farm workers, immigrants and visitors but could also view the latest, "correct" social dances and theatrical forms of the metropolis of the North through the medium of travelling shows and, later, motion pictures. In this manner the tap dancing of Fred Astaire, Ginger Rogers and Bill "Mr Bojangles" Robinson became popular. The dancing of someone like Kid Harold, modelled on the great Bojangles, and the chorus-type dance troupe emerged in this period. Many of the show routines and modern social dances had their origin, it must be remembered, in obscure, poor black areas in the United States. Their international dissemination by white metropolitan commercial interests often led to distortion of the form but the latest "styleit" (Baxter 1970, 205–6) of the local urban poor still reflected a basic underlying understanding of and empathy with the sometimes hidden black source.

The same could be said with perhaps less applicability in the case of the Latin American steps that accompanied the Haitian merengue, the rhumba-mambo and the cha-cha-cha. One of the most African of the cults in Jamaica, Kumina, employs as one of its steps "merengue sideways step; step, close: step, close; etc.". Cult members would also use the "Congo step, moving on the flat of one foot and pushing off with the toe of the other foot". Occasionally, "there are tremendous whirling steps with one dancer facing another" also "forward shuffling steps, with an occasional bending of the knee and a sudden stop with pelvic tilt" (Baxter 1970, 140). Steps with some resemblance could be found in other parts of the Caribbean and Latin America as could, no doubt, the "wheel and turn" of other Jamaican folk forms.

Of course, by the time local music production in the modern idiom was initiated, there were many "strictly" Jamaican "blues" moves and many communities had their localized variant of a move. One of the earliest of the period that this author remembers is one called "shake-a-leg". Another, a kind of proud strut, was termed "going to town", done to tunes like "Times Are Going" by Derrick and Martin. Even "Carolina", which usually featured Rasta runs and leaps, was often danced this way.

Communities in poor districts soon generated "legs" – individuals who best executed the moves through their conceptualizing and improvisation, often expressing in dance the communities' emotive, creative levels. These dancers, famed in the ghettos, were virtually unknown to society. Persons like "Needle" Clifford Strokes, "Persian" the Cat, "Bop" (Mr Legs), "Sparkie", "Pam Pam" and "Baskin" would even be featured at the bigger dances and stage shows. Along with the singers and musicians they need to be seen as "culture-heroes". Many of the young were influenced by these developments so that by the time of the Skatalites, even the middle class may have boasted of having a "legsman", probably the misnamed "black sheep" of a family who had adopted many value-orientations and behaviour patterns of the "lower classes" and divested himself of the snobbery and fear of the class of his parents. The focus, notwithstanding, was centred in the ghettos. On a Saturday night, while picking up bottles at a dance, a small deprived urchin may take time off his chores and execute the moves of a master. Exciting, beautifully timed and sincere, the delicacy and subtlety exhibited by such a youth contrasts sharply with the harsh surrounding ghetto conditions. Another indelible image from this period is of crowd dances with as many people outside as inside and almost everyone moving; unaffected dancing in the streets.

Although officially music does not have the central place in life in Jamaica as it does in Africa, it would still be true to say that it "is an integral part of life-style" of the lower classes. Admittedly, it does not follow the "African-in-Jamaica" in the same way as it does the "African-at-home", who has traditional songs and dances "that are completely necessary to the rituals celebrating each milestone". For example, "the naming of the baby and the appearance of his first tooth are both honoured in song and dance. A child in Dahomey is taught a song which he sings on the loss of his first tooth. The Akan people of Ghana have a special song for the habitual 'bed-wetter', sung by other children at a ritual designed to shame the bed-wetter into drier behaviour" (Warren 1970, 4). These same people also have special drums which are played to "accompany a petty thief while he is paraded through town with whatever he stole in his hands" (Roberts 1972, 5). Local politicians with the intention of using the form of local music without real regard for its content should bear in mind the example of the Bamoun of Cameroon, who have "some eerie and impressive music to be played when a court official is to be hanged" (Roberts 1972, 5). Adherence to old traditions is more prevalent in the rural districts than the urban centres in Africa and the similarities of some dance styles (for example, the High Life of Ghana) and music in the cities of Africa to West Indian and Afro-American forms points to the development, in the field of music at least, of common responses to similar circumstances.

In Jamaica, the attention to ritual shown by African rural areas is not retained as fully but music is used in nearly as regular if not as formal a manner. Thus to celebrate the birth of a son or daughter, victory in a football or cricket match, or the opening of a house, a dance may be held. Or even less formally, the reaching of "age" of a young man may see him fêted at a club or bar accompanied of course by music provided by a jukebox. A man may have just returned from "trouble" and his re-entry into the community may be prefaced by a homecoming dance. These examples must be seen as additional to the recurring promotions of "regulars" and holiday "jamborees" and the music played at stereograms and varieties of "component sets" at home. What should be held in mind also, as is often pointed out, is the striking similarity between "wakes", "set-ups", "nine-nights" and other burial customs with those of Africa and the continent and blacks of the diaspora.

The typical "blues dance" would see a relatively homogenous black lower class group, members ranging between the ages of fifteen and thirty-five, but with some younger and older persons attending quite unaffectedly. This was to change later as older persons grew apprehensive of the growth in social violence and increase in police attention that accompanied the development of the dance in the late-1960s. In the 1950s and early 1960s dance era, a range of moves radiated outward from the American mainland, including Latin sequences and the "rub" (a blend of the older mento "belly rub" and R&B

"soft tune" waltz). At this dance, two "legsman" may trade moves, the others attending showing varying levels of skill but with the majority being more than competent. A group of adolescents may be in a circle, creating new amalgams; a man and a woman may be doing the "boogie woogie", moving quickly and apart except at the first beat in the bar when their hands touch as the male facilitates the spin. Another couple may be dancing slowly, closely, "thighs between thighs, rocking gently, sometimes almost motionless, openly sexual" (McGlashan 1973). This sexuality, however, does not strike one as being forced, frenetic, lascivious or neurotic. Just that for the tune's duration, two people care for each other. One youth may be all by himself – shuffling, or later with the development of "rocksteady" or "reggae", just "rocking". He probably pays no attention to women that night, being quite satisfied just to rock; self-sufficient and wrapped up in music. Even this cool style, with a smaller range of leg movements than the earlier "legs" with its "shuffles", "splits" and "snaps", manifests something peculiarly Jamaican. One observer goes so far as to say that "no other West Indian, let alone European or American Black or White can effectively copy the sinuous, earth-rooted pelvic thrust of the Jamaican dancing the reggae. Only he can maintain a kind of introverted private relationship with the piece of earth on which he dances – alone" (O'Gorman 1972, 51). This view has some truth in it, although it can be claimed that the fluidity of pelvic movement is a characteristic of black popular dancing anywhere. Thus Brathwaite, speaking of black West Indians generally, writes that "what the heart lacked was supplied without hips and the art of our shuffle shoes" (1973b, 22). As he underlines, it is not just hip movement but fairly intricate and nimble "foot-placing". O'Gorman's comparison would be more true of blacks than whites. Colin McGlashan (1973) comments on it in England: "Whites tend to flounce; fast, angular, jerky, hips motionless and everything else flying." O'Gorman herself thinks that the European "is all shoulders and no hips". But her view of the Trinidadian as a type that "dissipates his energy in extrovert movement whose direction is outward and upward" may be a trifle harsh (O'Gorman 1972, 51–52). On the same question, another observer is of the view that the middle and upper classes in Jamaica may take Romantic classical ballet as a "permanent yardstick for all movement patterns". The black masses however, "cannot keep a rigid back" and "may wish to have their movements explode with centrifugal force from the regions of the pelvis rather than through extended arms and legs" (Nettleford 1970, 193–94).

It is interesting to note that the earlier "legs" moves, while involving suggestive hip movement and subtle timing, drew attention to the dancer's nimble and agile legwork. The array of moves of the "legs" period offered a more exciting, scintillating display to the dancer and watcher. Modern moves to the reggae are much less extroverted, more sensuously rhythmical and generally slower. Involving less "virtuosity" than the dance moves of ska, the reggae has encouraged wider participation, as most persons after initial exposure can more closely approximate the ideal. Although there was a commercial version of the "ska" which reduced the level of improvisation and largely consisted of basic hand, arm and foot movement, this author holds that the simplicity of reggae moves has invited the middle classes to attempt, at least, to "look roots" occasionally with more likelihood of success than in the days of ska. One, however, may still be able to identify class membership or background by the ease in performing reggae moves on the part of persons attending dances or sessions at nightclubs.

Also of some interest here is the subtle reflection of the subcultural "mood" in certain dance styles. Thus in the period of economic boom and less unemployment, the most popular moves are generally more easygoing and relaxed. With the rising cost of living, the increasing material dispossession of the masses relative to the dominant strata, and the related increase in crime and terror, the social atmosphere becomes noticeably tense and this "mood" is not cast in conceptual intangibles only but individualized at the level of dance and reflected in more taut shoulder and hip movement. Although, ironically, the whiplash precision and lightning snaps of the ska legsman in the relative calmer era could also be described as explosive and "hot" and paradoxically contrastive to the cool, wary, yet more determined sense of menace in the more aggressive later period. For all the differences in emphases, both styles can be seen as "hot" and "cool". On the part of the "rebels" of the "lower" classes who often originate dance moves and language styles and even patterns of dress – sometimes appropriated from the Rastafarians – that penetrate all but the highest social circles, the dance style becomes more studiously defiant, even at times threatening, in the later period. Yet there is balance of a certain sort, for if the era of individual or "apart" dancing on the part of couples frequently sees a less mobile, more considered projection of potential menace threatening self-assertion than earlier moves, there is still much variety and pauses, rests, hops and sequences used to express joy that can appear at various points. This, in effect, results generally in an engaging combination of tension and relaxation; of tight controlled figures and easy languorous movement. The emphasis usually varies with the mood of the music and the resultant nuances help explain the conflicting descriptions often seen in international comments on Jamaican popular dance moves of today. Additionally, when mixed couples dance together to local music, there is often a maximum of physical contact, the more usual form being the even more relaxed, gently rocking "belly rub", with little foot movement, rather than the somewhat more vigorous "three steps", its counterpart in the Jamaican amalgam of US "souls" moves danced to contemporary US black R&B currently known as "soul music".

In summary, we can itemize the more important effects of the development of sound system and popular dance: it encouraged the development of local electronic expertise; long before the coming of the commercial "component" set, it helped boost the demand for technicians and amplifier specialists; and it continued the tradition of the dance. In the initial stages, it provided the market (along with the jukebox and private collector) for the local music industry and was instrumental in disseminating local effort to a much greater degree than radio.[14] It helped spawned underclass "culture heroes"; it enjoyed a great measure of success in getting the subculture more aware of itself, promoting underclass solidarity through the "intra-group communication" function that is facilitated. It thus succeeded in combining an entertainment function with an educative, acculturative one, making public many views, but most importantly airing the just claims of dissident opinion. Access to other media was very limited to such opinion. It further, in the main, supported the pull to "Africanness" and the revitalization of indigenous ways.

These by no means exhaust the list of contributions, but they suffice in helping to set the stage for an examination of the music proper. This music is now established, although continuing political violence, crime and police "overkill" has sometimes made the dance's existence uncertain. It would be depriving the masses not so much of their "opium" but of one of the few remaining bright spots in lives made harsh and bitter by the continuing legacies of poverty and oppression, inflation and unemployment were the dance to disappear.[15] The spirit, despite the "sufferation", ascends with music, song and dance.

NOTES

1. Earlier in the century country dances may have been held as regularly, if an informant of John Storm Roberts had an experience that was general for his class. Residing in the village of Chatham, St James, he played the guitar and mandolin for country dance groups and "remembered his nostalgia the days when there were dances almost every night, and when every parish had its own way of dancing the lancers and polkas" (Roberts 1972, 128).
2. The garrison at South Camp Road where the island's military forces were headquartered.
3. Other popular road band musician at the time were: Milton McPherson and the Garden Harmonisers, Luther William, Bob White, Ray Cox, Wilton Gaynair, Lance Thelwell.
4. Sonny Bradshaw in interview cited by Gordon (1968, 10).
5. Examples of rurally based systems that were to become as well known as the urban systems were Ruddy's, Wasp and Stereo of Spanish Town, and Quaker City of Montego Bay.
6. A practice which finds parallel in the US black community (cf. Jones 1963, 106, 114, 117).
7. Baxter (1970, 296) reminds us that "Marcus Garvey had been one of the first people in the 1920s to consider the public recreation and entertainment of the poorer people in the Kingston and St Andrew area. Eidleweiss Park was the locale for dances and the projection of new stage talent".
8. "Cow-cod", a thick soup with the scrotum and pizzle of the bull used as meat. "Mannish-water", soup made using the "fifth quarter" of goats.
9. A few R&B artists tended to shade into the rock and roll era and managed to penetrate the largely white international pop scene in attempts to make some money with their product – the virtual "bastardization" of which had made many white performers "overnight millionaires". Black artists like these would include Fats Domino, Little Richard and Ray Charles.
10. Other white balladeers and "songsters" in this mid-1950s period were the Four Aces, Dean Martin, Rosemary Clooney, Julie London, Jo Stafford, Joni James, and the Chordettes. The black artists who came nearest to them as far as radio airplay was concerned, in addition to the New Orleans "rock and rollers", would be the Platters, Tennesse Ernie Ford, Nat Cole, Sammy Davis, Ella Fitzgerald and Billy Eckstine.
11. Black musicians today often complain about similar practices. H.B. Barnum in the August 1975 issue of *Players*, asks "How does one separate rhythm and blues from rock and roll? Or rhythm and blues from pop? A record may have been the top pop record of the year, but if it is done by a Black artist or group, then its listed as rhythm and blues . . . it could sell just as much or more than any pop record, and it could sell to whites, black, green or

whoever wants to buy it, but it is still considered an R&B at the end of the year when that record comes to the attention of the Grammy folk its shifted into the R&B classification. 'Killing Me Softly' was named the Best Rhythm and Blues song of the year." Asked what he thought of the white decision makers in the music industry Barnum adds, "They are in control of the situation and in order not to be straight out biased or wrong they create a situation whereby 'you can get one and I get one', but the one they get has far more power associated with it, because twenty years from now when someone ask what the number one song of the year was, they'll quote the one by the white artist, since the one by the black artist, even though it may well have been more popular, would have been in the R&B category, not the best song category." For a description of the relation between R&B and white capitalism and the evolution of rock and roll see Gillets (1970).

12. Even Billie Holiday suffered at the hands of white commercial interests in the United States.
13. Kumina, Zion Revival, Pukumina – Afro-Euro-Christian cults whose rites and practices include many African or neo-African elements. For brief description of their music use see White (1982). For dances and movement patterns use by these groups and those involved in secular social dances (for example, mento, brukins, gerreh and maypole) see Ryman (1980).
14. Carl Gayle (1976, 33) does not exaggerate when he writes that the system owners-cum-studio operators Duke Reid and Sir Coxsone Dodd "have been responsible for the discovery, development and final recognition in Jamaica of almost every big name in Jamaican music".
15. King Tubby put it graphically in an interview, "Sound-system come in such demand that every weekend if a man naw go to no party or no session is like some pat o'him life gone" (Gayle 1976, 34).

REFERENCES

Baxter, Ivy. 1970. *The Arts of an Island.* Metuchen, NJ: Scarecrow.

Beche, H.T. de la. 1825. *Notes on the Present Condition of the Negroes in Jamaica.* London: Cadell.

Bethwick, Martha. 1929. *Black Roadways: A Study of Jamaican Folk Life.* Chapel Hill: University of North Carolina Press.

Brathwaite, Edward. 1973a. *The Development of Creole Society in Jamaica 1770–1820.* Oxford: Clarendon Press.

———. 1973b. *The Arrivants.* London: Oxford University Press.

"Dance and Discomania". 1976. *Black Music Magazine*, January 1976, 6–7.

Fanon, Frantz. 1965. *The Wretched of the Earth.* New York: Grove Press.

Gayle, Carl. 1976. "Marcus Garvey Meets the Rockers Uptown". *Black Music Magazine*, Febuary, 33.

Gillets, Charlie. 1970. *The Sound of the City.* New York: Outerbridge and Dienstfrey.

Gordon, Derek. 1968. "Notes on the Evolution of Jamaican Popular Music". MA research paper, University of Chicago.

Jones, Leroi. 1963. *Blues People.* New York: William Morrow and Co.

Keil, Charles. 1966. *Urban Blues.* Chicago: University of Chicago Press.

McGlashan, Colin. 1973. "The Sound System", *Sunday Times.* 4 February.

Nettleford, Rex. 1970. *Mirror, Mirror: Identity, Race and Protest in Jamaica.* Kingston: Collins and Sangsters.

O'Gorman, Pam. 1972. "An Approach to the Study of Jamaican Popular Music". *Jamaica Journal* 6, no. 7: 50–54.

Roberts, John Storm. 1972. *Black Music of Two Worlds*. New York: Praeger.

Ryman, Cheryl. 1980. "The Jamaican Heritage in Dance". *Jamaica Journal* 44: 2–24.

———. 1984. "Kumina". *African-Caribbean Institute of Jamaica Research Review* 1: 81–28.

Stewart, James. 1823. *A View of the Past and Present State of the Island of Jamaica*. Edinburgh: Oliver and Boyd.

Warren, Fred, with Lee Warren. 1970. *The Music of Africa. An Introduction*. Englewood Cliffs, NJ: Prentice-Hall.

Waterman, R.A. 1952. "African Influence on the Music of the Americas". In *Acculturation in the Americas*, edited by Sol Tax, 207–18. Chicago: University of Chicago Press.

White, Garth. 1982. "Traditional Musical Practice in Jamaica and Its Influence on the Birth of Modern Jamaican Popular Music". *ACIJ Newsletter* 7 (March): 41–67.

CHAPTER 2

Slackness Hiding from Culture

*Erotic Play in the Dancehall**

CAROLYN COOPER

THE LYRICS OF THE DEEJAYS DEFINE THE FURTHEST extreme of the scribal/oral literary continuum in Jamaica. Unmediated by a middle-class, scribal sensibility, deejay oracy articulates a distinctly urbanized folk ethos.[1] The literariness of this *massive*,[2] popular cultural form is marginalized by its context of performance: the dancehall. The primary function of the deejay's art is to *ram dance-hall an cork party*.[3] Decontextualized, the lyrics often become decidedly limp. To the uninitiated much of the "noise" that emanates from the deejays is absolutely unintelligible. The insistent sing-song of fixed rhythmic structures conspires to obscure meaning; individual words become submerged in a wash of sound. But if you permit your ears to become attuned to this borderline sound and allow for the free play of the intellect, then patterns of meaning cohere and a framework of analysis both sociolinguistic and literary may be constructed.

As Jamaican becomes appropriated by the official culture (for example as "folk heritage", or for "authenticity" in the advertising industry), and as the use of Jamaican in the scribal literary tradition becomes acceptable and conventional, then the rude impulse of the language, formerly manifested in "backward" folk culture, can be seen to now reassert itself in contemporary forms of verbal marronage such as the lyrics of the deejays. This downtown, purely oral art form can be both differentiated from, and situated within, the broader context of the work of *oraliterate* writers like Louise Bennett, Vic Reid and Erna Brodber, for example, who are substantially uptown folk easily commanding the full breadth of the scribal/oral literary continuum. With the deejays there is no presumption of an essentially scribal literary tradition as the context of performance.

The deejay's lyrics interrogate other song traditions – for example, Jamaican folk songs and African American rhythm and blues – with comic (and often ironic) effect.

---

*Previously published in *Jamaica Journal* 22, no. 4 (1989/90): 12–20 and 23, no. 1 (1990): 44–52, and in *Noises in the Blood: Gender and the "Vulgar" Body of Jamaican Dancehall* (Durham, NC: Duke University Press, 1995).

For example, Higgs and Twins' "Jump Up Time" is a dancehall update of a "folk" song, "Evening Time", composed by Barbara Ferland in the 1950s, with lyrics by Louise Bennet:

> Jump an spread out time
> Come everybody better form a line!
> Wi da wuk from mornin,
> Da wuk from mornin,
> Da wuk from nine til five.
> Mek wi rock up fi wi body line
> Mek wi dance an sing,
> Do wi owna ting
> Inna dancehall style

The tune of Red Dragon's "Love Unu" is that of a children's ring game, "There's a Brown Girl in the Ring". The song's derogatory reference to Shaka Zulu modulates, somewhat ironically, into minstrelsy:

> If yu no favour Shaka Zulu
> Seh, tra-la-la-la-la
> If yu no ugly lakka patoo
> Seh, tra-la-la-la-la
> An if yu know yu smile pretty
> Seh, tra-la-la-la-la
> An if yu know yu teet white
> Seh, tra-la-la-la-la

Yellowman's "Waan Mi Virgin" employs the melody of a Revival song for satirical purposes: "Mi alone, mi alone inna di wilderness / Forty days an forty nights inna di wilderness" becomes "Mi no waan, mi no waan weh di man dem nyam an lef / Di man dem walk a mile an a half inna yu gungo walk." The repeated "walk" encodes subtly different meanings: "walk" as both the act of sexual intercourse and the place where it occurs. The primary sex/food metaphor is extended in the identification of the woman's body with both the lush fertility of a bed of gungo peas and the distastefulness of leftover food.[4] Further, "walk" as fowl-run and/or the place in which a gamecock is kept widens the sexual allusiveness of the song. Undomesticated, brazen female sexuality is both desirable (to many men) and threatening (to some), so the ambivalent deejay seeks a virgin. "Waan Mi Virgin" also echoes an earlier mento song, "Mi no waan, mi no waan weh Matty Walla lef / Matty run a mile an a half eena gungo walk", thus suggesting that sexual innuendo is not at all peculiar to the much maligned lyrics of the deejays but is firmly established in Jamaican popular culture. Indeed, a loaded line of the mento song, "Ol lady run a mile an a half an shi tumble down", evokes the evasive/complicit sexuality of the cunning, experienced old woman, a theme that is brilliantly developed in Lovindeer's "Granny Two-Teet".

The sustained narrative and metrical line of Lovindeer's artful compositions, and especially his sensitive handling of double entendre (*pun/aani*[5]), are evidence of his sheer genius and mastery of form. His penchant for *picong* – that Trinidadian art of wicked wit – suggests that he is schooled in the calypso idiom. For example, his signature tune, "Panty Man", parodies Sammy Davis Junior's "The Candy Man":

> Who cyan rock di party?
> Who cyan mek it ram?
> Mek all of di uman kick up an raise deh han?
> Di panty man cyan.

Lovindeer's lyrics illustrate not only his personal genius but the shaping influence of literacy on a predominantly oral verbal art form. Lovindeer composes his lyrics somewhat like Mikey Smith did – responding to vivid expressions heard on the street and then incorporating them into a carefully developed artistic statement. Lovindeer keeps a notebook of ideas to which he refers when he begins to formally compose. The sequential narrative line of his compositions, as distinct from the repetitive, formulaic structures of a Shabba Ranks, for example, seems to be possible only with self-conscious literacy. A comparison of Shabba Ranks's "Trailerload a Girls" and Lovindeer's response "Customs Officer" clearly illustrates these structural differences. This pair of songs also illustrates the general "intertextuality" of dancehall songs. Here the continuity is thematic: Shabba needs a customs officer to clear a trailerload of girls he has imported; Lovindeer is the officer who will do the job, determining appropriate duty based on the cc rating of the engine, the nature of the front-end, bumper and general shock absorbing capacities of the trailer's contents. Lovindeer's sustained use of mechanical imagery to define female anatomy again illustrates his formal training in scribal literature. The intertextuality of dancehall songs is usually rhythmic and melodic, the same basic format being used for a number of songs. Indeed, music is far less important than lyrics in this genre. What is often dismissed as the limiting repetitiveness of dancehall music is more the shaping metrical foundation on which formulaic phrases are constructed.

Further, the deejay's verbal art originates in an inclusivist neo-African folk aesthetic – a carnivalesque fusion of word, music and movement around the centre pole and on the common ground of the dance floor. The deejay's original function of *livelyin up* dance sessions made him a kind of praise poet for his sound system. His status was enhanced by his control of lyrics that *cyaan done*.[6] Dick Hebdige, in "Reggae, Rastas and Rudies", accurately traces the development of the genre, after making the sweepingly wrong generalization that "before 'ska' (the forerunner of reggae) Jamaica had little distinctive music of its own":

> In the 1950's, in West Kingston, R. and B., imported from America, began to attract attention. Men like Duke Reid were quick to recognise the potential for profit and launched themselves as disc-jockeys forming the flamboyant aristocracy of the shantytown slums; the era of the sound system began. Survival in the highly competitive world of the backyard discos, where rival disc-jockeys vied for the title of the "boss-sound", demanded alertness, ingenuity and enterprise; and, as American R. and B. began to lose its original impetus in the late fifties, a new expedient was tried by the more ambitious d-j's [*sic*], who branched out into record

> production themselves. Usually, an instrumental recording was all that was necessary, and the d-j would improvise the lyrics (usually simple and formulaic: "work-it-out, work-it out", etc.) during "live" performances. (1975, 142)

Over time, deejaying evolved from primarily functional talk subject to an economic imperative – *drawin crowd* – to talk as an entertaining end in itself. The deejay is now the star performer, no longer a mere functionary in the sound system business. But in performance the deejays, conscious of lineage, and needing to sell themselves efficiently in an increasingly competitive market, elaborately declare their mastery of the field. For example, Super Cat:

> An anywe mi go,
> Mi a di mike magician
> Mr Cyat on a style an fashion
> An mi come inna di place
> An hol di mike inna mi hand
> Come inna di place an talk,
> An den di session haffi ram
> . . . .
> Cau mi seh dis is di Cyat
> Jah man im jus passin t(h)rough
> An anyweh mi go
> Mi nice up yu revenue.

The literariness of the deejay's art is thus subsumed in the totalizing function of the dance. By contrast, the origins of the work of a neo-oral writer like Louise Bennett, whose poetry seems close in spirit to the pure orality of deejay performance, can be traced to both oral and scribal literary forms. Bennett's creolizing of the inherited ballad form is, initially, an act of conscious literary modelling. Aware of conventional poetic forms that provided a sense of historical context, Bennett becomes a Creole practitioner within an established (English) literary tradition. The poem "Bans a Killin" makes this clear. Jamaican is one of a number of regional dialects of English that must be preserved; Bennett's dialect poems are legitimate regional verse of good pedigree: Chaucer, Burns, Lady Grizel and Shakespeare:

> Dah language weh yuh proud a
> Weh yuh honour an respec –
> Po Mas Charlie, yuh no know seh
> Dat it spring from dialect!
> . . . .
> Yuh wi haffi kill de Lancashire,
> De Yorkshire, de Cockney,
> De broad Scotch and de Irish brogue
> Before yuh start kill me!

> Yuh wi haffi get de Oxford Book
> A English Verse, an tear
> Out Chaucer, Burns, Lady Grizelle [*sic*]
> An plenty a Shakespeare!
> (Bennett 1982, 4–5)

This contextualization of Bennett's work is not intended to detract from the distinctiveness of her accomplishment – inscribing Afro-Jamaican folk culture on the literary imagination – but to underscore its paradoxical conservatism. In a paper entitled "The Decay of Neo-Colonial Official Language Policies: The Case of the English-lexicon Creoles of the Commonwealth Caribbean", Hubert Devonish argues that the firm opposition to the early literary Creole experiments of Bennett in Jamaica and Wordsworth McAndrew in Guyana "forced . . . [them] to take a rather defensive position concerning the Creole language question":

> They ended up stressing the need for the preservation of Creole in its existing roles and functions. There was, at least, a tacit acceptance on their part that, in spite of the expressiveness and efficiency of Creole as a medium of communication, the role of English as the sole official language could not be challenged. This defensive position made it easy, after independence, for the new political elite who had inherited political power to co-opt the work and positions of people like Bennett and McAndrew. In the quest for national symbols to place alongside those of the flag and national anthem, the new political elite occasionally find it necessary to refer to the special place which the 'folk' speech plays as a mark of national identity. But, at best, when the existence of Creole is at all recognised by those who hold political power, this recognition is granted to a symbol and nothing more. (1986, 23–24)

The Creole of the deejays is not preserved "'folk' speech" appropriated by the political/cultural elite. It is a language on the make: *trash an ready.*[7] But if the language of the deejays has not attracted co-optation by the state, the themes of the 1980s recordings nevertheless are characterized by their apparent political conservatism and an overwhelming preoccupation with "slackness". In his study of the cultural politics of race and nation in Britain, *There Ain't No Black in the Union Jack*, Paul Gilroy argues that

> Jamaica's DJs steered the dance-hall side of roots culture away from political and historical themes and towards "slackness": crude and often insulting wordplay pronouncing on sexuality and sexual antagonism. I am not suggesting a simple polarity in which all toasters were agents of reaction and all singers troubadours of revolution. The Jamaican DJ tradition had been as involved in the spread of Rastafari during the late 1960s and early 1970s as recorded *song.* The two aspects of reggae culture interacted and combined in complex fashion. Even as slackness achieved ascendancy there remained popular toasters like Peter Metro and Brigadier Jerry who fought to maintain rhymes with a social content in the dances. However, the role and content of reggae changed markedly after 1980. This shift related to the consolidation of Seaga's regime and the consequent militarization of ghetto life. Both were also expressed in roots music and in the social relations of sound system sub-culture where guns became an increasingly important aspect of the rituals through which the crowd communicated its pleasure to the DJs. (1987, 188)

Yet, paradoxically, though deejay slackness as critiqued by Gilroy is conceived as politically conservative, it can be seen to represent in part a radical, underground confrontation with the patriarchal gender ideology and the pious morality of fundamentalist Jamaican society. In its invariant coupling with culture, slackness is potentially a politics of subversion. For slackness is not mere sexual looseness – though it certainly is that. Slackness is a metaphorical revolt against law and order, an undermining of consensual standards of decency. It is the antithesis of culture. To quote Josey Wales: "Slackness in di backyard hidin, hidin from Culture." Slackness as an (h)ideology of escape from the authority of omniscient culture is negotiated in a coded language of evasive double entendre. Gilroy himself notes, but does not fully explore at the level of politics, "the subversive potential in the ability to switch between the languages of oppressor and oppressed":

> The aesthetics of sound system culture had from its inception been built around the pleasures of using exclusive or specialized language in cryptic coded ways which amused and entertained as well as informed the dancing audience. For example, highly ritualized exchanges between the DJs and the crowd that conveyed appreciation of a particular rhythm (record) or style (sequence of rhymes) frequently involved the systematic corruption of ordinary innocent English words into new forms of public speech. "Massive", "Safe", "Settle", and "Worries" are all words which were playfully endowed with meanings unrelated to those invested in them within the dominant discourse. (1987, 188)

Particularly in reference to the oppositional values slackness/culture, we should add "wicked", which signifies massive approval of the subject thus dubbed. Linguistic innocence in the dancehall is not a virtue.

Eschewing respectability, the deejays operate subversively at the low end of the scale of accepted social propriety. Their privileged subjects are deejaying itself and sexuality. Heterosexuality most often requires a precise listing of body parts, almost exclusively female, and an elaboration of their mechanical function. Homosexuality is gloriously vilified in graphic excremental imagery. Supremacy in deejaying is ritually contested, as in Lecturer's "Well, if a deejay waan fi tes mi, tell im fi come." Verbal and sexual skill are often indistinguishable. Lyrics that *cyaan done* and rough riding rhythms become symbols of sustained sexual potency, as in Beenie Don's "Look (h)ow mi slim, but mi (h)ealthy an (s)trong / Keep pon dem riddim like a dyam stallion." It is not size but technique that determines staying power. Recurring horse racing imagery connotes not only sexual power but also the verbal skill of sports commentators on horse racing, who are able to sustain intelligibility despite an extremely fast-paced delivery that enacts the speed and excitement of the race itself. This kind of skill, as much as the old-fashioned radio deejays' rhymes – "the cool fool with the live jive" – provides models for the deejays' tongue-twisting, ear-bending lines.

The core of the data base for this study is the Derrick's One Stop record shop (Kingston, Jamaica) two-volume collection of thirty-five "Latest Reggae '88"; this is supplemented by Lovindeer's "Panty Man" album and his hit "Wil(d) Gilbert", Yellowman's "Waan Mi Virgin" and "Titty Jump", and Josey Wales's "Culture a Lick" and "Slackness Done".[8] These songs can be grouped thematically into five broad categories: (1) songs that celebrate deejaying itself; (2) dance songs that vigorously invite participants to *wine an push een*; (3) songs of social commentary on a variety of issues, for example, ghetto violence and hunger and (4) songs that focus on sexual/gender relations – by far the largest number in the sample. Some of the songs in this group are clearly inflammatory in intent; Lovindeer and Yellowman are the chief perpetrators. But others, and not just those sung by the female deejays, celebrate the economic and sexual independence of women, thus challenging the conservative gender ideology that is at the heart of both pornographic and fundamentalist conceptions of woman as commodity, virgin and whore. The final group (5) are songs which directly confront the slackness/culture dialectic.

Of the three songs in group five, "Slackness Done" by Josey Wales is the least ambiguous. The opening frame, with its militaristic motif, defines the terms of the deejay's heroic and presumably suicidal mission – cleaning up the dancehall:

> "Colonel Josey Wales!"
> "Yes, Commissioner."
> "I would like yu to go into di dance-hall an clean up all dose slack DJ who is spoilin di kids of today."

(Note the Creole interference in the commissioner's reported English. "Order" is already breaking down as linguistic slackness disarticulates culture.) But the commissioner is not being parodied. The deejay, faced with two mutually hostile orders of responsibility – that of the *massive* who require out-of-order lyrics and that of the commissioner of police, the voice of official morality and social order – simply bows to the censorial authority of state power.

But the sluggish rhythm of the song and the dispirited tone of the reverberating, inebriated first verse suggest that not only slackness but the deejay himself has been done in:

> An yu ever inna dancehall drinkin stout,
> A stout, a stout, a stout,
> Yu dip inna di crate,
> Put di bockle a yu mout,
> Yu mout, yu mout, yu mout,
> An all of a sudden yu bredrin a shout,
> A shout, a shout, a shout,
> Seh di Colonel Josey Wale im deh ya,
> Im deh bout, deh bout, deh bout, deh bout.

After this rather half-hearted start, the colonel, attempting to carry out the commissioner's directive, launches his attack:

> A talkin to di DJ from di street,
> Di street, di street
> Di people in di community cyaan sleep, Lawd.
> Wi goin on like wi live on di rubbish heap
> Life is pretty,

Wi shoulda tek it more smoothly,
Tek it more sweet.
Believe mi, A tell yu
Becau slackness done,
An mi no waan none
Slackness haffi done,
Cau mi no waan none.

The "rubbish heap" image is an accurate representation of how *nice an decent people*[9] in Jamaica view deejay slackness. The *Daily Gleaner* of 13 January 1989 dedicated its page 9 "Letters to the Editor" column to six letters with the following headlines: "'Respect Due' to Reggae Music"; "Unprofessionalism in Local Music"; "Stop, Stop, Now!"; "No!, No! to Slackness"; "To Spurn Indecency"; and "Stance against Slackness". The letter from the chief executive director of King of Kings Promotions, who claims to have "suffered greatly" as a "consciousness" promoter "because the public has gotten so used to reading and hearing about the antics of the slackness merchants" (antics/monkey/jungle/Africa/savage), characterizes the offending deejays as "gutter louts". The event which precipitated this public outcry was the Sting 1988 stage show, attended by an audience of over twenty-five thousand, some of whom, apparently anxious to have the deejays Flourgon and Ninja Man come on stage, pelted off two "singers".

The singer/deejay tension seems rooted in a basic contradiction between the generally sentimental lyrics of the singers and the more earthy particulars of the deejays. Several of the songs in the sample exploit the disparity between the two sensibilities. African American hip-hop, which has clear affinities with deejaying, articulates a similar disengagement from the rhetoric of R&B. In an *Essence* magazine article, Harry Allen characterizes hip-hop thus:

> It exhibits none of the creative listlessness with which much of R & B is currently burdened. Nor does it have the hands-off, gloves-on reverence with which jazz often finds itself draped. Rather than pretending to bourgeois standards of style, or attempting musically to evoke a time dead and gone, as many jazz and R&B artists are wont to do, rappers instead sling the rawest, most realistic insights at your ear. Deejays take your favourite records, cut 'em up, mix 'em around and serve 'em to you on a record platter. Meanwhile their crowds move and shake their bodies in ways that Grandmother once said would definitely get you pregnant or arrested. It all comes together in a whole: funky. Youknowhumsayin? (1989, 78–79; see also Gonzalez and Nelson 1991)

With this frame of reference, it is not surprising to note that Josey Wales offers the sweet, smooth "life is pretty" line as the alternative to slackness on the rubbish heap: "Come my man, tell yu, leave aaf di street / Talk about some lovin an huggin mi frien(d) / Dis slackness business comin to a en(d)." Conversely, Admiral Bailey's "Winey-Winey" energetically denounces "huggin up":

Mi seh huggin up is agains di law
Hi bwoy!

> Wi doan dance like dat anymore
> Mama!
> If yu cyaan do di winey-winey dance
> Hi bwoy!
> Step aside an gi di bubbler a chance.

Winey-winey is to hugging up as deejaying is to singing: the bottom versus the top end of the market. Indeed, when Ninja Man and Flourgon came on stage at the infamous Sting stage show the bottom dropped out of the market.

In his impassioned report of the event in the *Daily Gleaner* (30 December 1988, 6), entertainment columnist Howard McGowan, after decrying the "stoning" of the two singers, though conceding that one of them was "just not up to standard singing so badly off key that the deaf would have had a problem", proceeds to savage the deejays:

> But perhaps the single most distasteful situation came during the clash of male DJs when the worst squalor was presented on stage for lyrics by Ninja Man and Flourgon, ironically two of the leading candidates for the DJ of the Year title, something I will address at another time. So vulgar was this section that the plug was rightly pulled on them saving the ears of the people from the assault on their decency launched by these individuals.

Presumably not all members of the audience were equally grateful for having their ears saved from the "assault"; but the fine distinction drawn between "the people" and "these individuals" reinforces the alienation of the scapegoated deejays from the common fold of humanity. In his "On the Record" column in the *Sunday Gleaner* (1 January 1989, 5), McGowan, in his promised elaboration on the problem of indecent lyrics, proposes a sweeping solution:

> Against this background ON THE RECORD will not be selecting a male or female DJ of the year this year and I have had verbal support from the programmes managers of both RJR and JBC. Further, I have been given the assurance that when the JAMI Nomination Committee meets this week, this body could also consider dropping these categories this year. Rockers say they are willing to go along with the moral majority who spurn indecency, and will therefore not support any DJ awards.

The headline of the piece, "Time for a Stand against 'Dirty Lyrics'", is deliciously suggestive to the dirty-minded deconstructionist, especially when compounded with the following question: "Why, you may ask, the sudden decision to come down so hard on 'dirty lyrics'?" The traitorous signifier at play: *vive la differance!* Harry Allen objects to the fact that

> white music critics and cultural historians are talking about hip-hop and find themselves tossing long, funny words into the air to describe it. Words like *deconstruction, appropriation, iconography* and *recontextualization*. But those words have little to do with the way African-American people live or make music, and hip-hop is no more or less than Black life on black vinyl. Whatever one finds in the community, they'll find in the records. This has a lot to do with why it's so attractive to some people and repulsive to others. (Allen 1989, 114)

Ethnophallogocentricity! "Culture a Lick", also by Josey Wales, suggests more ironic possiblities than the straightforward "Slackness Done". Iconography is appropriated, deconstructed and recontextualized. In the opening frame, personified slackness is addressed in terms that evoke a judge handing down a prison sentence. But the "punishment" is in fact a highly valued commodity – an exit visa: "Now slackness, I am givin you a indefinite multiple to leave Jamaica." Many Jamaicans routinely sweat for a visa, as illustrated in Edward Baugh's wicked "Nigger Sweat". Edward Baugh is not a deejay;[10] but the spirit (and language) of his poem is that of peasant revolt against the magisterial dismissiveness of foreign embassies. The epigraph to "Nigger Sweat" is drily ironic:

> "Please have your passport and all documents out and
> ready for your interview. Kindly keep them dry."
> (Notice in the waiting-room of the U.S. Embassy,
> Visa Section, Kingston, Jamaica, 1982.)
> (Baugh 1988, 50)

Slackness's multiple entry visa allows easy access in and out; it means temporary displacement, not total banishment. And in any case, since the deejays sing of their vaunted successes in Miami, Toronto and London (for they too have multiple entry visas), it is only Jamaica that will suffer the loss of slackness.

The deejay's signalled intention in the first verse of "Culture a Lick" seems honourable despite the fact that it is an implied Other, not the Colonel himself, who now castigates the slack deejay:

> Oh! Tell dem DJ dis
> Tell dem fi stop all di Slackness
> Slackness business big inna Jamaica
> Spoil di youtman an granfader
> All di yout dem a criticize di daughter
> Mus remember wi comin from a modder

But the chorus has multiple resonances that invert the dominant/subdominant relationship of culture to slackness: "Slackness in di backyard hidin, hidin, hidin / Slackness in di backyard hidin, hidin from culture." The repetition of "hidin" suggests dalliance, slackness seductively *lay waitin* culture; but conversely, it also suggests the cowering posture of threatened victim, not predatory villain: culture, the senex, the respectable dirty old man, in pursuit of youthful, female slackness; or slackness, the Don Juan, entrapping virginal, female culture. Further, in melody and parallelism of form, this chorus is identical to a Revival song, "Adam in di garden hidin, hidin, hidin / Adam in di garden hidin, hide imself from God", and also to a children's ring game "Bread in di oven bakin, bakin, bakin / Bread in di oven bakin, bakin til a morning."

The ring game seems to encode rituals of sexual initiation, for the bread baking in the oven becomes in the second verse a sleeping little sister who must be shaken and then awakened in the third verse. The *Oxford English Dictionary* cites a 1753 slang usage of "bread-basket" as the stomach. Rising bread is thus an analogue of pregnancy, as in African American folk speech – "she's got a bun in the oven" – and contemporary British slang usage. Adam, soon to be cast into the backyard, is hiding in the garden because he knows that he is naked. And although he has no bread to rise – unlike Eve who has seduced him into slackness and is edited out of the text – his goose is definitely cooked. The fall from grace is supremely tragic for Adam, but absurdly comic to Eve. For she's the fall guy in the routine and doesn't even blame Adam. Walter Redfern, in his "Introduction" to *Puns,* cites Baudelaire on "the comic sense engendered by the Fall of Man [that] must be exploited in the fight-back towards wholeness. The artist, he said . . . 'is an artist only so long as he is double and faces up to all the implications of his double nature'" (Redfern 1984, 4). Similarly, Herbert Marcuse in *Eros and Civilization* summarizes the existential dilemma in Freudian terms: "The categories in which philosophy has comprehended the human existence have retained the connection between reason and suppression: whatever belongs to the sphere of sensuousness, pleasure, impulse has the connotation of being antagonistic to reason – something that has to be subjugated, constrained. Everyday language has preserved this evaluation: the words which apply to this sphere carry the sound of the sermon or of obscenity" (1966, 159).

Henry Louis Gates Jr's signifying monkey, which is clearly related to that other trickster Anancy, provides a West African model of "wholeness" that transcends the polarities (en)gendered in Western cultures: "Esu is figured as paired male and female statues, which his/her devotees carry while dancing, or as one bisexual figure. Often she holds her breasts in the female figures. Even Esu's sexuality is indeterminate, if unsatiable" (1988, 29). Gates thus privileges Esu as hermeneutic icon, the ambivalent signifier of non-sexist critical discourse:

> Metaphysically and hermeneutically, at least, Fon and Yoruba discourse is truly genderless, offering feminist literary critics a unique opportunity to examine a field of texts, a discursive universe, that escaped the trap of sexism inherent in Western discourse. This is not to attempt to argue that African men and women are not sexist, but to argue that the Yoruba discursive and hermeneutical universes are not. The Fon and the Yoruba escape the Western version of discursive sexism through the action of doubling the double; the number 4 and its multiples are sacred in Yoruba metaphysics. Esu's two sides "disclose a hidden wholeness"; rather than closing off unity, through the opposition, they signify the passage from one to the other as sections of a subsumed whole. Esu stands as the sign of this wholeness. (1988, 30)

These far-reaching correspondences make it clear that the culture/slackness antinomy extends beyond the domain of the half-heartedly suppressed "vulgarity" of the deejay. Its culturally specific manifestations in Jamaica suggest not only the continuity of West African ideological traditions in the diaspora but also the conflict between those traditions and the official Christian morality of the Garden of Eden in which both the suppression of sexuality and the secondariness of woman are institutionalized: Adam (and Eve) hiding from God; versus Esu as the gateway to God.

Chaka Demus's "Back Out" is the most clearly subversive of the three songs in the culture/slackness grouping. It is slackness pure and simple masquerading as culture:

Now all slack it DJ, A waan unu fi run, yu know, cau Culture come fi mek unu run like unu hear news. Now hear dis. Heh, heh, heh! It name
Some man a talk bout dem waan punaani,
Some man a talk bout dem waan puninash,
Some man a talk bout punaani too sweet,
Dem mussi lick it wid dem tongue,
Dem mussi bite it wid dem teet
Is ow dem get fi know
Seh dat punaani too sweet.
Mi seh unu fi back out,
Unu fi back out
All Slackness DJ,
Mi seh unu fi back out.

The playful lingering over the juicy details of *punaani* and *puninash* suggests that the deejay speaks with a forked tongue. Further, the covert reference to homosexuality – backing out as inverted withdrawal – intimates that there are hierarchies of slackness. Heterosexuality, however indulgent its excesses, is infinitely superior to its homosexual variant. Heterosexuality is culture and class; homosexuality is slackness and ass:

Becau Culture come fus
An Slackness come las
Bwoy, ass is ass
And class is class.
Come lissen Chaka Demus
Inna A1 class
Wen mi siddown pon di riddim,
Rasta know mi a di boss

In the cluster of songs that focus on sexual/gender relations, there is a small subgroup in which the homophobic thrust of Jamaican-style machismo is evident in derogatory references to homosexuality and cross-dressing. In Jamaica, cross-dressing is a clear sign of other crosses: taking sleep to mark death. For example, Shabba Ranks's defensively mocking line in "Get Up, Stan(d) Up": "Man inna pants an shirt, no man no hitch up inna frock" ("hitch up" implying a posture of embarrassment); and much more extensively in Lovindeer"s "Mad Puss Tonic" and "Bump Up". The latter, wallowing in the messy details of anal intercourse, protests (perhaps too much) against the double standard of Howard McGowan's "moral majority", who manifest no public outrage at a homosexual beauty contest but lambast the deejay for publicly displaying his fetishistic trademark, a spectacularly oversize red panty almost as wide as Lovindeer is tall: a clear parody of cross-dressing and a simultaneous glorification of what the garment withholds. Note the balancing of "up" and "down" in the first two lines, and the mischievous understatement of line 6:

Now mi did hol up a panty on TV
An half a Jamaica come down pon mi
Deh write letter to newspaper daily
Deh call radio an complain bout mi
Seh mi corruptin di youts of di country
An all because of a red panty
Now dese same people seh nutten to di press
About dis dyam battyman contes.
Deh will fin(d) demselves in a hell ev a mess
If dem support dis kin(d) of slackness.

Alliteration bears the full weight of the deejay's contempt: "Ladies and Gentlemen! The winner of the Mr Gay Mobay is that bouncing batty bwoy from backso, bumpy batty Bombo!" Lovindeer makes no apology for any offence that his scurrilous lyrics may incite. In "Mad Puss Tonic", which also reports (at second hand, of course) on the contest, he simply declares that clean ends justify dirty means: "Yu know seh my lyrics dem lick hot. / Mi a go step pon nuff man corn, but mi no business. / Nasty business call fi nasty lyrics." In an ironic reversal of roles, the deejay becomes the lone prophetic voice in a wilderness of moral woe, crying out against defaulting homosexuals who let the side down, and to neglected women whom the deejay himself is chivalrously moved to service:

Come! Some girls will have to wait in line
Bow! Cause a real man is so hard to fin(d)
(Like me)
Everyday I tell them doan ben(d) down
But they doan listen to my soun(d)
I sing an preach to them a lot
They doan remember they forgot, forgot, forgot.[11]

The sweetly sentimental melody and unsyncopated rhythm of the ironically detached verses that describe, in English, the homosexual happening are counterpointed with the characteristic deejay styling of those verses in Jamaican that deride it:

Some will say that it is their right
To do whatever they like
But if we really should let them
How do we explain it to the children
When they enquire innocently
"Why is that man wearing a brassiere and a panty?"
Come! Mi seh, no put it on,
Doan put it on
....
Im offer yu di panty
Doan put it on
Brassiere an di dress

Doan put it on
Di wig an di perfume
Doan put it on
High heel shoes
Doan put it on

Peter Tosh, in a 1984 *Pulse* magazine interview, criticizing the management of local radio stations for the high percentage of foreign music aired in comparison to reggae, makes a revealing connection between the imported "huggin up" lyrics of popular R&B love songs and male cross-dressing:

> I hear one, two, three, four, five already pon the charts is foreign music. And even if it was even fifty per cent foreign, is still too much. If it was even twenty-five. Me go to America and certain places out there man, fe months you wait fe hear all one reggae, and when them play is like them sorry fe you. Ina my country me haffi a bow fe hear dem foolishness when we hear fe so long? Me hear them things too much and them not saying nothing more than "Darling I love you. I swim the ocean and climb the mountains!" Madness! Ah them things make Merican man wear pantie.[12]

This kind of sentiment that decries the conventions of both heterosexual "romance" and sexual "deviance" as non-indigenous seems to illuminate not only Lovindeer's parodic strategies in "Mad Puss Tonic" but also the ironic framing devices used in several of the songs in the sample that satirize the aberrant "madness" of romantic love. For example, Professor Grizzy and Little Lenny join forces in the combination Sing-J style to caution men against brutalizing women. But the ironic disparity between the two modes – the ethereal sentimentality of the R&B song and the violent specifics of the deejay's lyrics – seems to make a mockery of the entire enterprise:

Now yu, doan brutalize your girl dem way deh man! Yu must treat ar good. Now step up![13]
I'll be your guidin star
My darlin cross my (h)eart
I'll never leave you in the dark
Oh, oh, and I'll be your light
On top of the hill
Love you little darlin, I will never leave you
I'll stay.

. . . . . .

Treat yu lover bad, treat yu lover bad.
Bad, bad, bad, bad, bad, bad
Yu no fi treat yu lover bad
Doan beat ar wid no stick
Doan brutalize ar wid no kick
Shi is someone to ave an to (h)old
Doan kick ar like no ball in no goal
Whisper in my ear then I (h)ear you tell the world

Let me tell you darlin,
You just got to be the lady of my life
Come follow mi now!
So doan give ar no cut
Doan give ar no gun butt.

There is also the unfortunate hesitatation – "Treat yu lover bad" – which does not make it immediately clear that it is the *not* treating bad of the lover that is being affirmed.

"Heartbreaker", by Lady Junie and Tristan Palmer, employs a similar technique of inversion, but here the woman, having once fallen for the smooth lines of the con man singer, is now immunized and offers consolation to similarly seduced women. Lady Junie relates a cautionary tale of distress, within which is embedded an ironic love song. The pattern is repeated in the parable of Devon and Sharon:

Mi a go tell yu bout dis con man weh dem call Devon
Bout dis sexy chick an wa dem call Miss Sharon.
Tell ar ow much im ave cyar, (h)ouse an lan
When shi check im out, yes, im doan own a dyam
Im se:
"Honey, honey, girl I really, really, really, really love you.
Honey, honey, I wanna take care of you
We've been kissin an touchin
An burnin t(h)rough an t(h)rough
Kissin an touchin really turns you on
Let me make love to you" (*rep.*)
Ear ar now, ear ar now, ear ar now:
"No bodder mek love to mi, no mek love to mi
No mek love to mi, an yu no mean i. (*rep.*)
Cause if yu waan fi lef mi, mi seh set mi free
No ask mi fi stay an den mi live in misery.
After all inna mi face it naa grow no tree."

But the potential for irony is not fully developed. Lady Junie's practical advice on basic survival strategies – "So don't yu go mad, no bodder go crazy / Anodder ting doan cry mek im see" and "Go outta street an get anodder smaddy" – also reinforces patterns of economic dependency: "Mek sure yu get one weh ave a degree/ Im gi yu nuff money mek yu feel irie."

In Sugar Minott and Lady G's "Whole Heap a Man", Sugar's seductive lines are trivialized by Lady G's derisive interjections:

Your frien(d)s all say dat you mus(t) dance with me
(Fi wa Sugar?)
An darlin, why won't you let it be?
(It's dat a fac(t)?)

Unmoved by Sugar's sweet talk, Lady G declares her fixed position:

Mi seh mi name is Lady G, an mi no tek brivery [*sic*]
From mi a no willin man, so let it be.
I am a different uman, I doan check fi folly
Yu no bodder tink yu cyan come an hypmotize [*sic*] mi.

Her advice to other women, unlike Lady Junie's somewhat exploitative speculations, affirms a measure of independence:

Mi a go tell yu di trut(h), mi nah go tell yu no lie
No bodder follow dem ya man, dem full up a samfie.
Dem wi bruk yu (h)eart an mek yu cry
No bodder give dem di chance fi get no more blai.[14]

"No more blai" alludes to a long history of female complicity with male *samfie-ness,* from which Lady G carefully distances herself. But there is also an element of coy seductiveness in her flaunted awareness of her desirability; she asserts the woman's right to choose, even if the confusing multiplicity of options inhibits choice. Her teasing indecision is underscored in the rhymes below:

Yes, I'm sorry Sugar Minott, I'm not in di mood
Whole heap a man inna mi life, mi haffi pick an choose.
So man, doan get mi wrong, doan tink I'm rude
Too much man inna mi life fi get mi confuse.

Johnny P's "Gyal Man" and Shelley Thunder's "Yu Man a Rush Mi" approach the problem of *samfie* men from clearly opposing perspectives. Whereas Johnny P simply blames the duplicitous woman for abducting her friend's innocent man – "Now dis one dedicated to all di girl dem we a go roun an tek dem frien(d) man. So young girls, if yu waan to know yu frien(d), introduce ar to yu man, an yu wi know if a yu frien(d)" – Shelly Thunder firmly allocates blame to the compliant, and more often actively seductive man. Her song opens to a chorus of taunting male voices, "Run, gyal, run, di owner fi di man a come!", which, suggestively, parallels the sentiment and form of Chaka Demus's line, "Mi seh run, slackness, run, an mi seh culture it a come!" The fleeing "outside" woman is slackness; the "owner" is culture; and the man is commodified – the rigid, proprietorial respectability of marriage versus the looseness of more fluid sexual arrangements. But Shelly's retort puts both legal and extra-legal affairs in perspective: "Well, no girl suppose fi mek a nex girl haffi run. Cau if it wasn fi your man, yu wouldn get burn!" Seeming to subversively contest the otherness of the "other woman", she narrates a tale that indigenizes the eternal female rivalries replayed in the dilatory drama of the soap opera:

Hear dis ya drama:
Inna mi (h)ouse mi, an mi son an mi daughter
Was two o'clock so mi a watch soap opera
Telephone ring an it mi go answer

Pon di odder en(d) a gyal a scream an a oller
"Mek mi chat to di gyal Shelly Thunder!"
I said, "Who is this?"
Shi seh, "Tell ar Sandra."
I said, "Could you tell me in reference to what?"
Shi seh, "Shi deh wid mi baby fader!
Ow yu mean if a wa?
In im telephone book mi fin(d) ar phone number."
I said, "This is Shelly. Who is yu baby fader?"
Shi seh, "Yu deh wid a man weh name Peter
Im no really want yu, a t(h)rough yu a entertainer.
Im love mi bad, bad, bad, mi im a mad over
Im jus buy mi a (h)ouse an a criss Mazda.
Im seh a business, but im a no Producer
A gwine bruk up yu -- If yu no lef mi lover!"
A seh, "Dibby-dibby gyal, ear ow yu vulgar!
Come aaf a mi phone, an mek mi prosper.
Becau yu man a rush mi, yu man a rush mi
Yu man a rush mi, so yu cyaan blame Shelly."

This is no simple sisterly solidarity against delinquent males. There is a smug superiority and malicious wit in Shelley's contempt for her self-deluding rival. (Note the distancing English initially assumed by the aggrieved Shelly to put the "dibby-dibby gyal" in her place; in the open hostility of the verbal battle the Thunder grandly descends to Jamaican.) Her description of the physical deficiencies of yet another "unfeminine", would-be competitor is full of disdain: "Her foot dem tough like shi did a dig yam / Her muscle dem huge, look big an (s)trong / Like shi use to fling hog pon truck a Portland." For the female deejay, as much as for the male, sexual prowess is an essential element of the kudos of the entertainer. But female sexuality is imaged in terms of the male gaze:[15] "A bwoy stop mi an start a conversation / Im seh mi look nice ave a sexy bottom / Im get goose bump when im see mi iina session." Shelly Thunder's female *persona* is clearly a voiced subjectivity, despite being the object of the male gaze. She approvingly views herself in the flattering light of that gaze while simultaneously voicing her independence from male scrutiny: she reserves the right to choose.

In Johnny P's "Gyal Man", a man is perceived as just one of a number of valuable possessions that successful women display as signs of prosperity. He is a kind of essential accessory for the fashionable woman, somewhat like a handbag:[16]

Yu mus always ave fi yu own man
No mek nobody come a fight up fi no man
Come a talk bout yu a tek fi dem man.
Yu jus hol up yu han, gyal, a no one frock yu ave!
Jump up, gyal, yu no ave no one frock!
Lif up yu foot, gyal, yu no ave no one shoes!
Hol up yu head, yu no ave one hairstyle!

An instructive subtext of Johnny P's song is his respect for the upward social mobility of enterprising women like those cunning characters celebrated by Louise Bennett – ex-domestic servants, perhaps turned higglers, who have ambitiously extricated themselves from traditional drudgery: "Hol up yu head, cau yu nah scour people pot / Hol up yu head cau yu ave ambition / Jump about cau yu full of protential [*sic*]." These women's attention to matters of personal hygiene is one of the social graces that is particularly appreciated in the intimacy of the dance:

Hol up yu han cause yu arm smell good.
Jump up, gyal, yu no frowsy, jump up!
Bounce a gyal weh a frowsy!
Hol up ar han an scent start come up
Dem deh gyal deh, yu know yu cyaan stomach.
Dem deh gyal, dem no bathe, dem wipe up
An come a dancehall, an dem a jump up
An dem a wine up, and dem sweat up
An den di frowsy scent it start come up

The dancehall is the social space in which the smell of female power is exuded in the extravagant display of flashy jewellery, expensive clothes, elaborate hairstyles and rigidly attendant men that altogether represent substantial wealth. In the words of Higgs and Twins's "Jump Up Time":

Lovers hand in hand, single man an uman
Pretty pretty hairdo, nuff style an fashion
Mini skirt, belly skin girls a champion
Di French cut acid dem a seh one.
Dem a bounce, spread out an shake bottom
Di man dem stan up at attention.
Tcho! Six to six an di dance still ram
Five nights a week, everybody a jam.

Inevitably, in a culture of multiple possessions, some women will have more than one man. So there are songs of female inconstancy. Ninja Man's "Tell Me" employs in part the wistful melody and somewhat modified lyrics of a folk song, "Liza Gyal", to sing about lost love and, simultaneously, his skill "roun di microphone":

Everytime mi member fi mi gyal frien(d) Adina
Water come a mi eye
Becau mi love ar to mi (h)eart and mi love ar to mi soul
Mi love ar to mi min(d) an dat, a dat mi control
Roun di microphone mi come fi rackle yu soul
An dis is wat mi givin to di young an di ol
Mi waan yu tell mi, tell mi, tell mi gyal, tell mi
Tell mi why yu love mi an leave mi
Run gone wid di dyam glibity, glamity?

The answer could be that provided in Shabba Ranks's "Cyaan do di Wuk":

> Some man cyan only give yu collaterals
> But where di international work is concern
> Tcho! Sof soap dat.[17]
> Ear mi now girls!
> Yu jus jump aroun if yu man cyan wuk
> Oller out if yu man cyan wuk
> Wine up yu body if yu cyan tek di wuk
> Some man a let aaf di money
> An dem cyaan do di wuk.

This ability to "do di wuk" and "tek di wuk", which separates the men from the boys and the girls from the women, is the heart of slackness. And it is the sexuality of women, much more so than that of men, which is both celebrated and devalued in the culture of the dancehall. The songs in the sample that are simply about *winein* often appeal exclusively to women for approval, using the yardstick of their response as the measure of the song's success as, for example, in Shabba Ranks's "Get Up, Stan(d) Up": "I'm not goin to a circus, I'm not goin to a fair / If is di stage show or di dancehall Shabba Rankin will be dere / Tcho! Time for lyrics di girls waan to hear." Women's enjoyment of sexual and economic independence, as demonstrated in their uninhibited solo *winein* on the dance floor, is most clearly illustrated in Flourgon's "Fret an Worry". The deejay, unintimidated by the women's show of strength, is absolutely confident of his own abilities. He is therefore in a favourable position from which to mock his less fortunate rivals:

> Some a fret an worry, dem a fret an worry
> Seh dem a mad over di girl dem body
> All dem a spen, mi se dem cyaan get i
> Cau di girls dem nowadays a dem no licky-licky.
> Some a fret an worry, dem a fret an worry
> Becau dem cyaan get di girls dem body
> Sexy body Pam an di one Audrey
> Look ow dem a shock out in di party!
> Mi seh some a dem slim, an some a dem fat
> Look ow di girls dem sexy an trash!
> None a dem no live pon no yeye top
> So yu gwan blink none a dem nah go drop.

The erotic wink has been devalued by the women's superior currency – their own. So they can afford to brazenly out-gaze the aspiring man and put him firmly in his place:

> "Wi cyaan come a dance come beg nobody
> An wi nah come a dance come fa nobody
> So who waan chat, an mi seh, mek dem chat chat
> All dem a chat, Lawd wi still hot

Mek dem gwan quint, wi nah drop
None a wi no live pon no eye top.
Cau, inna mi (h)ouse, it haffi trash
Cau mi colour TV mi siddown an watch
Inna one corner yu fin(d) mi wat-not
An mi figurine dem mi cock up on dat
Mi seh two lickle hen an one big cock
Pon di wall a di granfader clock.
Easy Flourgon, dem know seh yu hot
Entime yu come a dance it haffi block."

The "mi cock up" double entendre is wickedly accurate: women made doubly cocky by economic independence, assuming traditionally male privileges of selection, while retaining the conventional woman's right to pick and choose. If we attribute the ambiguous last two lines above not to the self-validating deejay but to the women, then it seems that they themselves accept that their only match is the deejay, whose sexual/lyrical prowess is imaged in the tableau on the what-not.

Lovindeer's "No Pussy Tes(t)", excellent feminist polemics, asserts the woman's right to sexual pleasure as an essential constituent of total health. The song starts off as simple slackness but gradually develops into a critique of the Jamaica Public Service (the electricity company) and health care systems in Jamaica:

Patsy complainin day an night
Seh her pussy doan ha no appetite
Shi use to be so lively an fat
Now shi is jus a lickle mawga cyat.
Well, personally, mi love di lickle pet
So mi tell Patsy fi tek ar to di vet.

The doctor's preliminary investigation raises a number of questions, one of which is about health insurance. Satisfied that the puss is covered, he proceeds with the examination. But before he can "look into" the problem fully the lights go out. In a frustrated orgiastic scene the puss eludes the gaze, to the distress of the owner, the doctor and the deejay:

Di doctor seh, "Lady I'm sorry to say
Yu have to come back anodder day.
Doan blame mi, blame JPS
Dem lock off di light, so no pussy tes(t)."

The song also subversively suggests that the pets of the middle class are likely to have access to much better health care than the vast majority of poor people in Jamaica who have no "health insurance" and are forced to depend on the vagaries of the notoriously inadequate clinic system.

Age is no barrier to sexual pleasure for women. "Granny Two-Teet", also by Lovindeer, is a witty tale of callow youth versus cunning experience:

Mi know a young man dem call Don Juan
Cau when it come to love im a di champion.
Im check every uman, im no partial
Im love ol foot, an im love young gyal.
Now las week-en im go check Beverly
Who live a Shortwood wid ar two-teet granny.
Im drink off a whole quart bottle of sherry
An lickle after dat im get tipsy.
Im seh, "Roses are red and violets are blue,
A gwine mek love to di both a yu."
Beverly seh, "Do wat yu want wid mi
But please doan trouble mi two-teet granny.
Shi ol an feeble an very sickly
So don't yu come come hackle ar body.
Shi ave only two teet in ar mout
Too much hacklin a go mek dem drop out."
Granny jump up seh, "Hush yu mout
Yu doan know wat yu talkin about.
Di man se di two a wi mus get it.
Come out a mi love life, doan romp wid it.
Come Don Juan, no pay ar no min(d)
Come mek mi show yu seh Granny cyan wine.
Nowadays gyal only have so-so mout
Mi experience, deh cyaan get mi out.
Mi got mi two teet, mi two teet, mi two teet (rep.)
Mi temperature jus start to rise
Come mek mi show yu mi panty size.

I know yu will be surprise to see
Mi still ave my glamity.
By the way, one question:
Yu is a Shortwood man?
A doan want yu go deh an feel too shame
Cause I like di man dem from Long Lane."

Granny has risen to the counter-challenge of the omnivorous Don Juan:

"It seems to mi
Yu tek your lovin seriously
Well I gwine love yu tender an hot
For any amount of teet dat yu got."

And she is prepared to do whatever is necessary to prolong sexual pleasure:

Don seh, "Cool off, yu too hot!
Yu figet seh a only two teet yu got?

So done mi done, an mi ready to go."
Granny seh, "Wait! Yu cyaan leave so!
Don Juan mi bwoy, yu mek love sweet,
Hol(d) on lickle mek mi fin(d) more teet.
Mi got two lickle one down in mi jaw corner,
Dentures in mi bureau top drawer
An if yu waan fi come back tomorrow
Mi cousin ave teet mi cyan borrow.
Teet weh mi tief from Sister Mary
Teet weh mi ugly fader dead lef mi
Teet weh drop out from mi was a baby
Teet weh mi tump outa mash mout Daisy
Teet weh mi Aunty sen from foreign
Teet weh mi get from mi dentist bredren."

Don Juan's anxiety about Granny's voracious sexuality (all those teeth!) has its counterpart in the deejay's comical distress, recorded in "Panty Man", after his inadequate confrontation with Miss Fatty, "a big panty gyal". He sheepishly confesses: "water come a mi eyes"; coming at an obviously inappropriate point:

Mi know a big panty gyal dem call Miss Fatty
An long a long time di gyal after mi.
But, t(h)rough mi know my limitation
Bow! Mi no tek on no big panty gyal.
Now one night, mi no know wa get inna mi
Bow! Ow mi decide fi check Miss Fatty.
Shi fling up a piece a wine under mi
Di gyal rackle every bone inna mi body.
Well! Shi will always be mi good frien(d)
But! Intimately? Never again.

Size, size, I have to look mi size
Shi hackle mi body til water come a mi eyes
If deh had a competition
Yu would wid di prize
For di girl wid di biggest panty size.

The melody of the "size" coda, with its hymn-like resonance, underscores the wit of the irreverent lyrics. Miss Fatty's rackling, cutting rather close to the bone, ruffles the cock's feathers. The deejay's hackles are raised in self-defence. What is truly delightful about Lovindeer's wicked compositions is the variable male/female point of view which he assumes. His songs cannot be reduced to simple gynophobia. For even when he appears to be deriding aggressive female sexuality he simultaneously affirms its compelling potency: "mi no know wa get inna mi". The man, out of his depth, may fear that the supernatural has been invoked to overwhelm him. But there is also a sense of conquest in having tested his limitations and surviving to tell the tale.

Women who enjoy the humour and innocuous slackness of songs such as these – and their less subtle variants – are subject to censure under the terms of the prevailing double standard. Thus, Mr McGowan, again: "Let us not fool ourselves, however [*sic*] the fault is not entirely that of the DJs but it lies with a certain section of our society. If females can dance and shout when men stand on stage and give details of sexual exploits with women, then something is very wrong." And a censorial male letter-writer to the *Daily Gleaner* (13 January 1989, 9), on the subject of the Sting stage show:

> A good show, until two DJs . . . displayed their vulgarity, and certain females, if I must call them so, jumped and shouted to their delight to hear certain sections of their body being described most disgracefully. The DJs were urged on by these women who had on the most outrageous outfits that can ever be worn on the face of this earth. Something is definitely wrong. Could it be illiteracy or stupidity?

Explicit in that final question is the slackness/illiteracy equation. A similarly denunciatory letter to the *Daily Gleaner* (13 January 1989, 9) from a young woman inadvertently highlights the contradictions of these simplistic moral generalizations: "The women who dance to this filth do not know better and need to be taught. Many of these women go to church and put on their choir robes and sing Christian hymns." In the conservative discourse of fundamentalist ideology, slackness is thus feminized and censured. Undomesticated female sexuality – erotic marronage – must be repudiated: it has the smell of prostitution.

Lovindeer's complex "Doan Mess wid My Pum-Pum" is an excellent example of a feminist-sounding song about women's sexual independence that seems to quickly degenerate into the old-fashioned rhetoric that tries to keep women in their subservient place as sex objects, available at a fixed market price:

> Well I've been out of crotch now for a long, long time
> So I take an ol frien(d) for a little grin(d).
> Shi said, "I can help yu if yu want to come
> But yu, yu gotta pay mi, freeness days are done.
> Strictly cash I deal with, I doan trus(t) no man
> They are only out to get everything they can."
> The price that shi told mi was very high
> I said, "I only wanna rent it, I doan wanna buy."

But the loaded "trus(t)" – "I doan trus(t) no man" – with its divergent commercial and emotional resonances puts the woman's dilemma clearly into focus. The song is much more than just a mocking deflation of the woman's value/price. It is a disturbing comment on the grim economic conditions in Jamaica that force some women of all social classes to commodify their sexuality: "Shi seh 'I'm a working girl, I doan have a lot/ Pum-pum is the only thing of value that I got.'" And the price of the commodity has to continually escalate to keep up with the rising cost of living. Note the brisk rhythm of the repeated third line, with its sequence of stressed syllables, that enacts the upward march of prices. Sexuality becomes a taxing issue:

Mi check a lickle daughter fi buy a lickle jook
Shi tell mi seh mi money cyan only buy a look.
Mi seh pum-pum price gone up
Tell yu seh di pum-pum price gone up.
An mi seh tings an times dem a get so tight
Up-town girls haffi work at night
Workin to survive
Tell yu seh di pum-pum a keep dem alive.
Deh taxin dis an deh taxin dat
Deh taxin every lickle ting dat wi got
Jook dem wid di pum-pum tax
Im soon jook dem wid di pum-pum tax.
Yu doan have to pay if yu give it free
But if yu use it commercially
Get ready fi di pum-pum tax. (*rep.*)
Except at certain time a di month
Pum-pum taxes pay up front
Batty man haffi pay back tax. (*rep.*)

There's the inevitable stab at the homosexual who is doubly taxed. Menstruation, as universal taboo, turns the woman's natural bodily functions inside out and back to front. "At certain time a di month" woman becomes devaginated, a symbolic batty-man, facilitating the "straight" man's working out of homophobic anxieties. Widened beyond the immediate context of prostitution, the taxing "jook" becomes a provocative metaphor for the government's rapacious desire to muscle in on all forms of small-scale economic activity in the "non-formal" sector: bureaucratic culture seeking to control enterprising slackness.

There are a few songs in the sample in which the commodification of women's sexuality by men assumes truly vulgar proportions: Yellowman's "Waan Mi Virgin" and "Titty Jump". Gilroy identifies Yellowman as the clearest example of the "decline of radical reggae": "After two explicitly political sides chronicling the rise of authoritarian statism in Jamaica – 'Soldier Take Over' and 'Operation Eradication' (the latter a particularly effective version of The Itals' heavy 'Ina Disya Time' rhythm), he opted for the safety of nursery rhymes, animal noises and anti-woman jive talk" (1987, 188–89). "Titty Jump" is the kind of song that draws down the wrath of the righteous and the disdain of the feminist alike. Woman is reduced to a collection of body parts which seem to function independent of her will. This is the crucial difference between "Titty Jump" and, for example, Johnny P's "Wine an Push Een". In the latter, the woman is a whole being actively enjoying her own sexuality. In the former, one part of her anatomy is isolated, and despite its jumping, is a passive, abused object of pleasure for a lecherous voyeur:

Girls, yu cyan do wat di guys do yu know an still be a lady
Titty jump, titty jump, mek mi see yu titty jump!
Some gyal titty stiff like elephant trunk

Some gyal titty stiff like any tree stump
Some gyal titty jump like any bull frog
Wen di brassiere come aaf it favour tread bag.

The tread/money bag image (which includes the transferred meaning of bag as udder) is particularly deflating. Women's sexuality is negatively imaged in terms of the marketplace. The fact that women, and not only higglers, sometimes secrete money in their bosom (a complex symbol of private space where women exercise absolute control of material and sexual resources) is demeaningly extended as the ultimate comic image of woman reduced to undignified, bare essentials. Economic power is the antithesis of sexual power: the money bag is no substitute for the real flesh and blood thing. But the fractured first line of the song can be read ironically: "Girls, yu cyan do wat di guys do yu know" – go through the motions, "an still be a lady" – remain untouched. The "sexual liberation" of woman, her commodification for the pleasure of man, is pure pornography[18] in the most literal sense of the word: "description of life, manners, etc. of prostitutes and their patrons" (*Oxford English Dictionary*).

"Waan Mi Virgin" is not quite as damning as its inflammatory title would suggest. Indeed, read subversively, the song deconstructs itself. It begins: "All special request to di cyat name Audrey, an di cyat call Sandra, an di cyat call Jacqueline, an di cyat call Susie, O.K.?" These "special" requests, going indiscriminately to the feline posse, cannot by their very inclusivity be deemed special. But, perhaps, this is the essential difference in the way that men and women understand the language of mating. Women assume that "special" means "exclusive"; men know that "special" simply means, well, special. Yellowman states his preference for a virgin and proceeds to describe his meeting with a prospective candidate:

Know a gyal from St Elizabeth.
Ask ar weh shi name, an shi name Paulette.
Shi seh, "Mi ave supn weh no man never get."
Mi seh, "Gi mi di virgin, waan di maiden
Gi mi di virgin, waan di virgin
Gi mi di virgin an A gweh tek di maiden
Gi mi di virgin, waan
Mi no waan, mi no waan, weh di man dem nyam an lef."

The elided "di virgin" in the penultimate line, which syntactically compresses what is wanted and what is not, foregrounds the image of woman as object of conflicting desire. Woman is valued for her fleeting virginity and, simultaneously, for her willingness to give it up. Unlike Lovindeer's engulfing Big Panty Gyal, or his lascivious Granny Two-Teet who, Anancy-like, bares her many hidden teeth only when she has securely grabbed a piece of the action, Yellowman's sought-after Virgin is innocently non-threatening.[19] Paulette, herself, in her unsolicited advertisement, seems to passively accede to the commodification of her sexuality, marketing her alleged virginity as scarce goods which she is hoarding until the right buyer comes along. But in the second cycle of the song when the meeting with Paulette is again described (we assume that it is the same Paulette and not another interchangeable virgin of the same name), a somewhat different scenario unfolds. Self-assertive Paulette not only dismisses Yellowman's desperate suit but declares her unwillingness to give in to the man she "deh wid" until she has been appropriately and lengthily wooed:

Becau meet up a gyal las week Satiday
Mi ask ar weh shi name, shi name Paulette.
Mi seh if shi love mi, di gyal seh, "Gu weh!
Cool Yellowman, mi an yu bredrin deh.
But di someting we mi ave, im never get
Di bwoy waan come mek love right away."

Paulette knows the rituals of romance, and/or is simply holding out for a higher price in a seller's market. What is important is that it is she who calls the shots. The frustrated Yellowman continues on his quest; desire, unlike virginity, is a renewable resource.

But even Yellowman's narrow sexism can be viewed somewhat expansively, especially by feminists who theorize the conjunction of gender, class and race, as a "small man" revolt against the institutionalization of working-class female domestic rule and middle-/upper-class male dominance in Jamaican society. For as I suggest in the analysis of representations of female sensibility in the poetry of Louise Bennett, disempowered working-class men cannot be simply stigmatized and dismissed as unqualified "oppressors" of women. Their own oppression by gender-blind classism and notions of matriarchy itself motivates their attempted oppression of women. For example Super Cat's need to "control" a number of women both locally and internationally:

Cau mi se dis is di Cyat it
An im a di wil(d) Apache
An every weh a weh mi go,
An dem a fight over mi.
Ave girl inna yard,
An girl inna broad,
An inna Miami
Ragamuffin Mr Cyat,
Im a di wil(d) Apache.

Cowboys fighting Indians fighting women fighting each other: a chain of disempowerment. The raw sexism of some deejays can thus be seen as an expression of a diminished masculinity seeking to assert itself at the most basic, and often the only, level where it is allowed free play.

Further, the relatively low status of the deejay himself in the mercurial business of record production that is ultimately controlled by the monied producer (as in the movie *The Harder They Come*) can account in part for much of the self-aggrandizing bravado displayed in those songs that celebrate deejaying. For example, Lecturer makes the extravagant claim, as befits his sobriquet, that he is a pen-and-paper deejay:

Daddy Lecturer one di lyrical tongue
An DJ come, an mi nah go run
Pon di groun mi sit down
Wid mi pen an mi paper
Mi write mi lyrics down.
An mi study it, an inna dancehall
Mi fling it down.

The confrontational, throwing-down-the-gauntlet rhetoric of the deejay, imaged in the flinging down of lyrics, suggests not only the deejay's aggressive readiness to defend his honour but also the disposable quality of his throwaway lines.

It is also Lecturer who in "Deejay a Look fi Mi" attempts to put the female deejay in her proper domestic place – away from the male-dominated dancehall. Women should have no business in the dancehall save as ardent fans. The female deejay should become a sleeping beauty, safely resting at home, awaiting the kiss of Don Gorgon Prince Charming:

Charmaine, wa mek yu vex
When mi tell yu seh "go sleep!"
A woman fi sleep
Fi tek out wrinkle an pleat.

Vexed Sister Charmaine is clearly not compliant. Lecturer's attempt to lay the female deejay to rest is clearly an impotent male fantasy given the powerful presence of women in the dancehall as active agents – whether as deejays, disdainful, inaccessible sexual beings or as "fans". Pinchers's account in "Ardent Fan" of the eager response of a female autograph hunter and her admiring friends similarly voices the deejay's desperate need to lionize himself:

So her friends dat stand up,
Dey also did feel di vibe
An upon their faces I saw
The glee an welcome in their eyes.
Dey told mi some come to trill,
But dey ave the confidence
I come to reign.
Cause when I'm in my dance-hall style
Is worries, agony an pain.
They're listenin to my voice
An also feelin my melody
Dat also bring a strong belief
Dat I'm a legend to be.

Shabba Ranks's "No Bodder Dis(respec) Mi" challenges rival deejays to test their skill against his own, recognizing that it is the music itself that gives the socially outcast deejay a measure of respectability:

No bodder dis, Mr Sophistic
Soun(d) a soun(d), ol pan a ol pan
Wi no kill champion, wi raise champion
A di music weh wi play wi gain recognition
An mi bomb up a dance inna Englan.
If it come to Canada,
Yu know seh dat done ram
No bodder dis, doan bodder dis,
I'm tellin yu

Lorna Goodison's "Jah Music (for Michael Cooper)" similarly celebrates the healing power of the underground music that bestows recognition on its creators:

The sound bubbled up
through a cistern one night
and piped its way into
the atmosphere
and decent people wanted
to know
"What kind of ole nayga music is that
playing on the Government's radio?"
But this red and yellow and dark green
sound
stained from travelling underground
smelling of poor people's dinners
from a yard dense as Belgium
has the healing
more than weed and white rum healing
more than bush tea and fever grass cooling
and it pulses without a symphony conductor
all it need is a dub organiser.
(Goodison 1986, 36)

Like Shabba's "No Bodder Dis", "Min(d) Yu Disrespec Mi" by Gregory Isaacs and Josie Wales confims the deejays' need for both respect and respectability, the latter a commodity that is often so splendidly devalued and sardonically deferred to in deejay culture. Indeed, this song validates culture in the old-fashioned, non-elitist sense of the word. It employs biblical injunction – "Honour yu modder, honour yu fader / Dat yu days may be longer" – and proverb – "Wat yu pickin up A put down already / Young bird doan know storm" – to recall a whole way of life, a vanishing rural past in which a folk culture of ritualistic deference to elders is affirmed in the language of proverbial wisdom.

Of the small group of songs classified as (non-sexual) "social commentary", Flourgon and Thriller U's "Peace" is the only one that deals explicitly with political issues. It begins to the accompaniment of simulated gunshots: "Salute di Peace! Cau yu know seh widout peace tings no right." Employing the familiar contrast between the sentimental optimism of the love song and the brutal reality of ghetto life, "Peace" calls judgement on the politicization of violence in Jamaican society:

Ear dem a talk bout love
Mi no see no lovin a gwan
Ear dem a talk bout peace
Mi no see no peace a gwan.
. . . .
Laad, mi seh a pure gun shot,
A pure lootin
Inna one corner
A pure screamin
Up di road, Jahman,
A pure people runnin
Everybody runnin
An hear dem shoutin
"Wi want love, Laad,"
Everyone screamin
A pure gunshot bad bwoy firin
Ear dem a talk bout love

Similarly illustrating that upright folk piety that can coexist unselfconsciously with slackness in the dancehall, Lady G's "No Bad Mind" conflates two biblical references in its plea to "all a di people dem fi live right": "A fool despiseth his father's instruction; but he that regardeth reproof is prudent" (Proverbs 15:5); and "Thy word is a lamp unto my feet and a light unto my path" (Psalm 119:105):

Becau nuff wickedness mi seh inna mankind
Some a tek fi dem daughter to be fi dem wife
Some a go outta street an a tek people life.
Come now, lissen dis a lyrics people if yu wise
Commandment is a lamp an a lamp is a light
Reproof of instruction is di way of life
So done away wid hatred, an done away wid strife
An mek wi pray to di Father day an night.

Papa San's "Watch Mi a Watch Dem", warning against the folly of interfering in other people's business to the detriment of one's own, values the covert wisdom of Anancy:

Yu fi see an blind, yu fi hear an deaf
An no watch people business, a it yu fi lef
An inna fi yu own yu naa put no interes
A fi yu own a spoil t(h)rough yu careless.

He offers a humorous, literal-minded solution to the problem of "watching":

Becau if yu watch man, Poopa San im ave a plan
Jus open yu ears an understan:
Mi a go put dem inna suit like a military man
Buy dem a baton fi cyarry inna dem han
Mek dem walk wid a alstatian [*sic*]
So yu a watchman yu fi dress like one.

Clement Irie's "Hungry No Laugh" makes a serious social statement, employing the dissonant imagery of play: "See food deh! Mi no romp wid it, romp wid i." Personified hunger is a formidable enemy:

Now request to all di people dem who feel hungry an
know wat is hungry. Yu no know, a lot of people don't
know wat is hungry, man, cau dey don't feel it. Now who
feels it, know it. Watch it! Laad a mercy! It name
Hungry no laugh, an Hungry no talk, mi frien(d).
Now inna yu belly bottom Hungry a walk.
....
Becau Hungry is a ting no respec(t) no body
Hungry no partial, modder, neither pikni
So mi sorry for di people who cyan hardly afford it.
Hungry no romp, Hungry no skin
Hungry is a ting weh mash up yu system.
Yes, no frien(d) im too much an mek im get too lovin
Now else im a go tek over yu body system
Mash up yu organ an yu intestine
Yes, yu cyannot see Hungry, but yu only feel im.
Now Hungry mek yu do some very dangerous ting
Like bruk people (h)ouse, shop an kitchen.

"Hungry No Laugh" is an excellent example of the use of metaphor in Jamaican to embody abstraction. Humourless, uncommunicative screw-face Hungry assumes the emaciated form of his victims.

Lovindeer's brilliant "Wil(d) Gilbert" is the classic in this grouping of songs of social commentary, if not in the entire sample. In the opening frame, the hurricane's power – elemental slackness on a grand scale – is acknowledged in the deejay's caution to address Gilbert only in his absence: "Well Gilbert, yu gaan! Aha! Now wi cyan chat behin(d) yu back." This is the cunning of Anancy who can feign great bravery when it is least likely to be challenged. In the opening verse, Lovindeer evokes the bizarre atmosphere of the hurricane in the clever fusion of the real and the surreal:

Water come iina mi room
Mi sweep out some wid di broom
Di lickle daag laugh to see such fun
An di dish run away wid di spoon.

The nursery rhyme dish becomes the satellite dish, bearer of imported, pre-packaged, instant culture. Its alien, flying saucer values, like the strange English nursery rhymes of childhood, are made familiar in the two-way flow of human and media migration: "Dish tek aaf like flying saucer / Di roof migrate widout a visa."

Natural disaster reinforces old barriers of privilege; the wealthy are able to recover much more quickly than the poor. With *their* visas they can fly to Miami for generators and other essential commodities. Not so the exploited deejay, spokesman for the discontented massive:

Mi iina di dark, no light no on ya
An t(h)rough mi no ave no generator
Mi seh, one col(d) beer cos(t) ten dollar.
Mi fish an mi meat spoil in di freezer
A pure bully beef full up mi structure.

But opportunist, looting youth quickly recognize the catastrophe as an act of divine providence. In the spirit of "Hungry No Laugh", *dem doan mek fun fi tief people tings*:

Mi a look someweh safe, dry an warm
Di yout dem a loot in di ragin storm.
Wi tank di Lawd wi never get hurt
Dem seh, "Tank yu, Laad, fa Mr Gilbert.
Cause, yu see mi fridge?
Gilbert gi mi.
Yu see mi colour TV?
Gilbert gi mi.
Yu see mi new stereo?
Gilbert gi mi
Yu see mi new video?
Gilbert gi mi."

The video is the next best thing to the satellite dish.

The inset tale of Knotty Dreadlocks and Mr Chin wittily counterpoints basic Jamaican stereotypes: the Rastaman, emblem of the renunciation of worldly goods; and the Chineyman, symbol of acumen in commercial affairs. Gilbert temporarily levels both:

Knotty Dreadlocks siddown inside
A look ow Gilbert a gwan outside.
When breeze lik down Mr Chin restaurant
Knotty Dread jump up an chant:
"Lik dem Jah, gwan go dwiit,
A dem did gi di Dread pork fi eat.
Juk dem Jah wid storm an tunder
Tear aaf dem roof an bruk dem window."
....

Likle affa dat Gilbert turn back
Lif(t) aaf di roof aaf a Knotty Dread shack
Im seh, "Blouse an skirt, Jah mussa never know
Seh I-an-I live right yasso."

Naturally, in all of this social commentary, Lovindeer must indulge in a little low-key slackness. "Blouse an skirt", old-fashioned, euphemistic swear words, is one of a few references to clothing – "Mi save mi brief, but mi lose mi shirt" – that suggest the inadequacy of the deejay's undergarments to protect his unmentionable private parts from a thorough soaking during the storm: "'Water wet up mi wat's it not.' / 'Yu mean yu wat-not!' / 'No, mi wat's it not!'" The slackness theme is full-blown in Lovindeer's other Gilbert song, "Hell of a Blow-Job".

The culture/slackness antithesis that is reified in the dancehall is one manifestation of a fundamental antagonism in Jamaican society between uptown and downtown, between high culture and low, between literacy and oracy. That the lyrics of the deejays should be identified as an appropriate subject for literary analysis is itself evidence that culture is in hot pursuit of fleet-footed slackness: subjection to analysis is yet another form of containment. But the equivocations of pursuit and capture are transacted in the metathesis "culture hiding from slackness". For marginalized oral discourse, penetrating the rigid boundary of the hegemonic, scribal canon requires that it yield to accommodate the full Creole/English, oral/scribal range of verbal creativity in Jamaica. The literariness of deejay oracy thus declares itself somewhat ambiguously in the loose language of Creole slackness.

NOTES

1. The notable exception is the auspiciously named Lloyd Lovindeer (not a sobriquet), who used to teach English language and literature at Kingston College; a clear case of slackness seducing culture.
2. Deejay term for people in a party, as in Beenie Don's "all a di massive unu get up an dance!", perhaps a folk etymological amelioration of the somewhat pejorative "masses", but also see Gilroy below.
3. Deejay's ritual claim that denotes verbal skill.
4. The *Dictionary of Jamaican English* entry on *nyam* notes that "The source is multiple: both verb (*eat*) and noun (*food*, or specific foods) existed in a number of W Afr languages, and many were brought to Ja. . . . The resulting multiplicity has in the course of time become sorted out so that, in general, NYAM is the verb, NINYAM a noun (food), and NYAAMS a specific food (YAM)." The dictionary notes the negative connotations of the verb: "To eat, esp roughly or voraciously." For an extended analysis of the sex/food homology in another Caribbean popular song tradition see Rohlehr 1988.
5. *Punaani*, *puninash*, *glibity* and *glamity*, all words for female genitalia in deejay culture.
6. As in note 2.
7. Jamaican slang meaning, approximately, "fit and ready" – for consumption, not disposal.

8. Thanks to John Thomas for supplying deejay tapes and commenting on my argument at an early stage of its development. Thomas, who does gardening in the university community where I live, usually works to the accompaniment of dancehall music. After enforced hearing of these songs over several months I decided to give the lyrics more serious attention.
9. Phrase frequently used by the deejay in reference to the audience, as in Red Dragon's "Love Unu": "Now dis one dedicated to all nice an decent people." Read in opposition to the moral majority's contempt for "indecent" lyrics, this phrase encodes divergent decencies.
10. He is professor of English and university orator, University of the West Indies, Mona, Jamaica.
11. "Forgot" becomes "faggot", slang for homosexual.
12. Peter Tosh, interview in Cooper (1984, 15). R&B "Romance" becomes Rastafarian " Ras-mance" and, ultimately, deejay "Rass-mance".
13. Italics indicate the spoken intro to the song.
14. *Samfie* means "cunning"; *blai* means "breaks".
15. For a revisionist, feminist reading of the "male gaze" see Humm (1988, 70): "But the problem with the concept of the 'gaze' hinges, paradoxically, on feminists' expert attention to representation and the male spectator. Feminist criticism has not, as yet, explored the ways in which the representation of sexuality denies women a sexual voice as well as sexual subjectivity." Humm argues that in some film instances "the voices of fascinating and independent women (however problematically presented) won out over the visual construction of spectator relations" (71).
16. I am indebted to Erna Brodber, in conversation, for this analogy.
17. Compare with the proverb "Oman an hood never quarrel"; "hood", Jamaican for "wood" as erect penis. Firmness is clearly at a premium. The inverse relationship between economic and sexual power suggests the compensatory nature of sexual prowess for the economically underendowed man.
18. Despite the notorious problems of definition – what exactly is the difference between pornography and "erotica"? – I use the term because of its decidedly negative connotations. But I am aware of subversive readings of the feminist arguments against commodified sexuality. For example, Gary Day argues in his introduction to *Perspectives on Pornography* (1988, 4) that "feminist attacks on the presentation of sex without love, or sex where women are treated as objects, may perhaps be regarded, at least in part, as an unconscious attempt by feminists to preserve and defend one of the most important sites of subjectivity for women. If this is the case, then there is something profoundly conservative about feminist writing on pornography, for it is implicitly accepting that sex and love are privileged sites for female subjectivity, and the intensity of some feminist attacks on pornography could be said to reflect an unconscious acquiescence in patriarchy's distribution of subject positions. . . . Perhaps the shock of feminism embracing pornography would create a greater potential for radical change than feminism's criticism of it."
19. For a comparable calypso version of "woman as devourer of male sexuality" see Rohlehr (1988, 252): "beneath the condemnation of prostitution lies the fear of castration or emasculation, which is itself a rationalization of male sexual inadequacy"; and "If the precocious young woman was regarded with a mixture of moralizing anxiety, dread and the eager anticipation of the rake on the prowl, the libidinous old woman was regarded with positive horror" (253).

REFERENCES

Allen, Harry. 1989. "Hip-Hop Madness". *Essence*, April, 78–79.

Baugh, Edward. 1984. *A Tale of the Rain Forest.* Kingston: Sandberry Press.

Bennett, Louise. 1982. *Selected Poems.* Edited by Mervyn Morris. Kingston: Sangster's.

Cooper, Carolyn. 1984. Peter Tosh, interview by Carolyn Cooper. *Pulse*, June, 15.

Day, Gary. 1988. Introduction. In *Perspectives on Pornography: Sexuality in Film and Literature*, edited by Gary Day and Clive Bloom, 1–5. London: Macmillan.

Devonish, Hubert. 1986. "The Decay of Neo-Colonial Official Language Policies. The Case of the English-Lexicon Creoles of the Commonwealth Caribbean". In *Focus on the Caribbean*, edited by Manfred Gorlach and John A. Holm, 23–52. Amsterdam: John Benjamins Publishing Co.

Gates, Jr., Henry Louis. 1988. *The Signifying Monkey.* New York: Oxford University Press.

Gilroy, Paul. 1987. *There Ain't No Black in the Union Jack.* London: Hutchinson.

Gonzalez, Michael, and Havelock Nelson. 1991. *Bring the Noise: A Guide to Rap Music and Hip-Hop Culture.* New York: Random House.

Goodison, Lorna. 1986. *I Am Becoming My Mother.* London: New Beacon Books.

Hebdige, Dick. 1975. "Reggae, Rastas and Rudies". In *Resistance through Rituals*, edited by Stuart Hall and Tony Jefferson, 113–30. London: Hutchinson.

Humm, Maggie. 1988. "Is the Gaze Feminist?" In *Perspectives on Pornography: Sexuality in Film and Literature*, edited by Gary Day and Clive Bloom, 69–82. London: Macmillan.

Marcuse, Herbert. 1966. *Eros and Civilization*. First published 1955. Boston: Beacon Press.

Redfern, Walter. 1984. *Puns.* Oxford: Basil Blackwell.

Rohlehr, Gordon. 1988. "Images of Men and Women in the 1930s Calypsoes: The Sociology of Food Acquisition in a Context of Survivalism". In *Gender in Caribbean Development*, edited by Patricia Mohammed and Catherine Shepherd, 232–306. Jamaica: University of the West Indies Women and Development Studies Project.

CHAPTER 3
Murderation
*The Question of Violence in the Sound System Dance**

NORMAN C. STOLZOFF

THE RISING INCIDENCE OF VIOLENCE IN JAMAICA HAS reached a critical point. The consequences of this situation can no longer be ignored; it now demands everyone's attention. Violence and the fear of it have become organizing principles of daily life. Concomitant with the current crisis of urban violence is the prominence of violence in all facets of popular music: in sound system dances, in song lyrics, and in music videos and so on. In response to these circumstances, voices from the government, the press and all sectors of the public sphere are questioning the possible connection between violence in society and these multiple forms of violence in popular music.

The relation between violence in dancehall, in particular, and violence in Jamaican society, in general, is not quickly unravelled. While there is no direct relationship between levels of violence in song lyrics, for example, and the incidence of social violence, there does seem to be some crucial link between the two.

The study of violence in the social sciences has been divided between those who see violence primarily as symbolic (or expressive) versus those who see it as a pragmatic action (or a way to get things done by motivated individuals or groups). There is another division between theorists who view violence as a destructive action carried out by free agents versus those who view it as a systemic phenomenon inherent to institutions and collective ideologies.

I believe that we need a flexible approach in trying to understand violence, one that realizes that violence often destroys our systems of shared meaning. Acknowledging that violence is both sensible and senseless necessitates that we attempt to bridge these two poles in our explanation of it. This position follows the theory that Rene Girard first outlined in his classic book *Violence and the Sacred* (1972), where he postulated that violence both generates social order (through its power to build consensus, make meaning and maintain power relations) and destroys social order (through its power to tear people apart, erase cultural significance and reshape political power). Violence

---

*Previously published in *Social and Economic Studies* 47, no. 1 (1998): 55–64.

has an ambivalent capacity, and this is why it is so easily volatilized, hotly contested and carefully handled in societies.

In this chapter, I discuss the relation of the Jamaican sound system dance to violence. I begin by describing the different types of violence that make up the dance. Next, I offer an analysis that attempts to account for the significance of violence in the dance. I conclude with a comment of the relationship between violence in the dance and violence in the civil sphere.

In performance-entertainment events like the sound system dance, violence takes on many forms. The first form of violence in the dance is a result of the competitive format of the sound system clash. In some instances, the dancehall also becomes an arena of rivalry for the patrons of the dance. We also find violence in the lyrics of many songs ("sound boy" [a rival sound system man] tunes, "matie" [the other woman] tunes, "informer" [a person who informs to the police] tunes, "battyman" [a gay man] tunes and tunes which are sexually violent). Another type of violence is the collective violence of the crowd aimed at informers, batty-men and even the performers themselves. The last form is state violence. This occurs when the police and army come to the dances, harass and prey on the dancehall participants.

THE SOUND SYSTEM DANCE: SPACE OF RIVALRY

The posters which announce upcoming dancehall sessions are often titled with names like "War Zone", "War in the Gulf", "We Come Back with Blood inna We Eye" and "Clash of the Century". While these are not to be taken immediately in their literal sense, they do accurately characterize the dancehall as a place of intense competition and dueling. The featured competition usually takes place between sound systems in the form of a clash. Through the clash the selectors, their DJs and their supporters battle it out for victory. The aim of the clash is to "lock off" the other sound, which is when one set has so thoroughly defeated the other set that the crowd demands that the defeated set stop playing for the night. So the key to winning the clash is getting better crowd support than one's opponents. If one plays a song that "turns over the dance" one gets a "forward", which is when the crowd shouts for the set to go on playing the same tune. When this occurs the selector usually picks up the needle and starts the song back from the beginning. The ability to totally dominate one's opponent is known as "murderation". Anything less than a decisive victory marked by death does not provide for a conclusive ending to the duel, since the judging of most clashes is informally measured by crowd response. And either set can usually claim that they "mashed up the dance". No sound will readily admit to being defeated since this brings disrespect that has both a profound effect on the sound system's popularity and, hence, on its economic viability.

There are basically a combination of four factors that a sound utilizes in its attempt to "kill a sound and its sound boy" (its selector). The first is to have superior sound equipment (or weaponry) which produces a heavier bass and clearer tone than one's competitors. The second is to have a better selection of records (or ammunition) and this is predicated on having specials that the other set cannot play. This is perhaps the factor which has the strongest economic repercussion since dubplates are costing upwards of US$3,300 (circa 1994). The third factor involves the selection of records (or strategy), that is the sequence and timing at which records are played. All things being relatively equal between the top sets, and they usually are to all but the most educated of ears, it is the role of the selector himself – the crucial fourth factor – that swings the crowd his way or another. This involves the tactics the selector employs as the master of the ceremony: that is the verbal dexterity and personal charisma he marshals as he introduces songs, appeals to the crowd, boasts about his sound and "disses" the other sound.

Although the selector uses songs which have a high content of violent lyrics, songs which graphically describe the six million ways he is going to make "drum pan" sound's selectors die, usually the clash remains free of outright physical violence. One of the ways that the clash remains peaceful is by the informal rule that all forms of "dissing", intimidation and violent threat must be in a pre-recorded format. As long as it is on disc, dubplate or digital sample anything one says to another set is fair game and taken as such and this prevents a certain form of spontaneous or contagious violence from entering into the mix. However, in the heat of a closely contested clash, the selector often tries to reinforce the power of his pre-recorded ammunition by making live comments to the other sound. This hurling of invective and the use of other aggressive bodily gestures are what often leads to the eruption of real violence in the dance. Recently, there was a well-publicized occurrence when the selectors of Super D and Stone Love got into a fist fight when all of these factors came into play.

Along with the clashing between the selectors, the participants themselves often get into clashing in the dancehall. Gangs, "modelling posses" (groups of women who employ style and fashion against other similar groups), crews and individuals often use the dancehall as a space of competitive display. While these are not the official entertainment for the night, they sometimes become an integral part of the performance itself. When the tension between these rivalrous entities overflows the banks of friendly competition violence can ensue. Paradoxically, sets like Stone Love which "juggle", that is play tunes of the same "riddim" in unbroken succession, rather than clash, shift the competitive focus away from the sound system to the crowd itself. Stone Love dances at the House of Leo are known for their particularly intense fashion wars. There was an instance in the beginning of 1992, when one of the more notorious crews started a "war" against a rival gang because the selector of a certain sound "bigged-up" the rival crew before his own. This was taken as a sign of disrespect, something which had to be rectified if one's reputation was to be maintained.

So, in this sense, the dancehall is a place where competition is used to gain recognition and to make one's reputation both for performers and the crowd at large. While this can be understood partially in economic and political terms, at some point the competition itself becomes its own motivation. When the rivalry between competitors becomes too intense, when the rules of the game are surpassed, the dancehall often becomes a literal war zone.

LYRICAL VIOLENCE

The content in dancehall lyrics is the most controversial form of violence in the dancehall, perhaps because lyrics themselves are not strictly confined to the parameters of the dancehall. They travel wherever the dance tapes are played. And these cassette tapes are filled with sound boy, gunman, informer, battyman, matie and other misogynistic tunes which rely heavily on violent imagery to convey their message. There is no doubt that the question of violence in the dance is a highly complex affair.

Currently, there is a lot of debate going on in the society about the influence of these lyrics. Some feel that the lyrics are of no importance at all because the music itself tends to dominate the vocal track. Others feel that the individual is an autonomous entity who can be swayed by outside sources only if they choose to be. In support of this view, Cutty Ranks, a veteran top-ranking DJ, said that you can't make a man pick up a gun to shoot someone by telling him to do so unless he wants to. A third group think that the lyrics have a profound conditioning effect even if they do not directly cause someone to commit a particular action.

When we see violent lyrics in their context, as part of a whole network of signs and symbols, we can better comprehend their social impact. That is why it is crucial to understand how they get produced and how they are put to use. Unlike literature, for example, they are consumed in an interactive and sometimes competitive environment. In the dance, songs are rarely played from beginning to end. The selector weaves the songs together to create a text which is larger or smaller than the original. A violent song might be mixed together with a love song. Thus, the meaning of lyrics is tied up in the exchanges that are part of their creation and consumption. How these messages are received and altered by the public is important to understanding the influence of the dancehall. The lyrics are, as Shinehead related to me, "multiconnotational". The meaning of some violent lyrics changes depending on the situation and one's point of view.

For instance, Cutty Ranks has a new song coming out entitled "Gun Disease". He thinks that the song will be a dancehall hit but will be banned from radio play for its hardcore, graphic style of talking about gun violence. Yet its message is not a "gangsta anthem" in the usual sense. He describes to the listener what happens to a person when the gun becomes the centre of his life. The song goes like this:

> Everybody wants to be somebody
> Ask the youth dem whey dem want
> do you want to be a lawyer
> he says no
> do you want to be doctor
> he says no
> do you want a job
> he says no
> so den what do you want
> gi mi one gun, two gun, three gun please
> wave mi gun nuff dem tink mi have gun disease

> 4 gun, 5 gun, 6 gun please,
> me can't hold dem in mi wais
> dem have dem under mi sleeve.
> The M1, mack 10, the bwoy dem naw cease,
> but the tek 9 bring dem to dem to knees.
> I walk with mi gun, talk with mi gun,
> sleep with mi gun, wake up with mi gun,
> bathe with mi gun, dress with mi gun,
> mi no lotion mi gun, mi na powder mi gun,
> mi oil up mi gun, clean up mi gun,
> and if a bwoy try a ting, him life ago dun,
> so give 1 gun, 2 gun, 3 gun please.

After reciting these lyrics to me he offered this interpretation:

> So it's like I am definitely telling you a story. That is not promoting violence. So if you come now and you have two thousand dollars in this hand and you have a machine gun in this hand and you put the two thousand dollar on this side of the table and put the machine gun on this side of the table and ask a little young youth to pick one out of the two of dem. He goin' to pick the machine gun. That is what dem doing. That is things what I see. Him pick de machine gun, because him figure more or less because he can use the machine gun and go around and rob more than two thousand dollars. He can go on one robbery and earn around two thousand. So the gun is more useful to him, that is how him check.

Thus, the popularity of gun lyrics can be attributed to the fact that they are a primary weapon used by selectors in the clash. And they are also relished because they reflect the reality that thousands experience as an everyday reality in uncompromising terms. However, at a certain point, much of the violence in song lyrics goes beyond the mere reflection of social reality. A lot of DJ tunes, especially sound boy tunes cut on dubplate, informer tunes, matie tunes and so on, reflect a deeper sense of cultural value and attitudes. Many dance-goers have told me of instances where a matie tune is playing in the dance and it will incite a woman to attack her alleged matie. There is no doubt that performing and consuming these violent images, like sexual imagery, is pleasurable and generates a sense of power for some of the participants. To be behind the gun, whether it be lyrical or real, provides a certain sense of invulnerability. But dancehall lyrics themselves reveal the inevitable reciprocity of violence when they warn that "who shall ever live by the gun, shall die by the gun".

COLLECTIVE VIOLENCE

The message of some songs combined with the urging of the selector sometimes turns the dancehall into a zone of collective violence. At a certain point in almost every dance the selector will make a speech to the massive where he implores the crowd "all who don't like battyman raise up oonu [your] hand" or "all who think informer fi dead wave oona rag". Or he asks the crowd to symbolically lick two shots against these agents of social disorder. This is then followed by a song that delivers a violent message aimed at these categories of persons. The effect on the crowd is transformative. It is one of the only times that the crowd will react in unison. Especially when there is a clash on between two or more sets, the crowd will not usually get excited as a whole for any particular song, because some participants won't jump for a song as they want to remain loyal to their personal sound. However, these rituals of collective exclusion get a near unanimous response from the crowd. In fact, there is usually some threat either direct or implicit that if one does not participate in the prescribed manner that one is either an informer or a battyman oneself. Because in this circumstance the victim is almost never present, the violence is a symbolic potential rather than a physical reality. Nonetheless, the process of this collective ritual is something similar to hanging someone in effigy. Except in this case even the physical dummy is not present to be sacrificed.

This is one instance when a symbolic form of collective violence, even though it is far removed from actual violence, can be linked to actual violence in other contexts. For instance, at stage shows, it is a common occurrence for the crowd to turn on performers by hurling bottles at them. In these cases the crowd achieves a sense of unity by coming together to express their violence collectively. All of the internal rivalry among the participants themselves is externalized in the figure of the lone victim, who cannot defend himself. In these situations the crowd ceases to behave in an orderly manner. I was in attendance at Mandela Park when chaos broke out both on stage and in the park. It touched off mass panic, a semi-stampede, and one person was shot by the security forces.

So in discussing the collective victimage of absent wrongdoers, something that seems to be harmless symbolic fun, I am arguing it has serious negative social consequences not just for certain categories of despised persons but because it is part of a larger system of dangerous crowd behaviour that can affect anyone. In these situations the crowd acts to terrorize the individual into participating in forms of behaviour that they have no control over. The experience of being in the mob may be pleasurable as long as you are not the one that is turned on.

ZONE OF STATE TERRORISM: POLICE RAIDING

The dance is also a contact zone between the civil sphere and the state where the state often exercises terror. The professionals involved in the sound system dance as well as the patrons who attend the dancehall for entertainment are the targets of violent policing tactics. Even if the police do not usually physically beat or threaten the dancehall participants with guns, they use their power to harass and abuse, to strike fear into the heart and to let everyone know who is in control. I have heard of many instances when the police came to the dance and threatened to lock off the dance even though no one had complained about the noise. They use this opportunity to look for a bribe or to make the public feel their power.

Ricky Trooper, the selector of Killimanjaro Sound System, told me about a Jah Love dance he attended as a youth in Spanish Town. The same day that the dance was held, a policeman was shot. The police broke into the dance, because they felt that the people were celebrating the officer's death. In breaking up the dance, one policeman took the picture of Haile Selassie hanging over the set and broke it over Trooper's head. So the dance is a place where the average citizen has little or no civil rights. The police have free reign to use state sanctioned violence as they wish. A system of equal rights and justice, or law and order, cannot be established on the basis of this sort of conduct.

I share with you a small anecdote. I recently attended a very large, well-publicized dance at the House of Leo, dancehall's most famous venue. There were in excess of two thousand people in the lawn. Shortly before 3:00 a.m., I walked outside the gates to find the security forces conducting a curfew on the dance. The security forces refused to let me leave the area and go to my car. There were at least fifteen armed personal with high powered weaponry and tear gas launchers. I was allowed to go to my car with my friend only after we waited about ten minutes. During this time, I saw people being brought out of the lawn and locked to a flatbed police truck. I later learned that the police were looking for a wanted murderer. To accomplish this they infringed on the rights of hundreds of innocent people, they conducted abusive body searches, they put the lives of many in utter danger. If it was only a matter of apprehending this man, there can be no justification for this sort of policing tactics. If the objective was to terrorize the dancehall public and to create a scenario where naked power reigns, then they accomplished their goals. A week after the raid, I spoke with Janet Lee, daughter of the owner of the House of Leo, and she told me they were never notified that there was going to be a crackdown, yet a foreign video crew was with the police so there must have been some prior information that this operation was going to take place.

CONCLUSION

From everyone I have spoken with there is no doubt that the dancehall has become more violent. People tell me, and I have experienced it myself, that they are afraid to step on somebody's shoe for fear of what the person will do to them. But the dance has no monopoly on this sort of behaviour. This is a condition that one finds almost anywhere crowds gather in Jamaican civil society. Most people I know would rather go to a dance than take a bus ride. I think people are living through an ongoing "loaded situation", where almost anything will send people over the edge into violence. The dance is just one manifestation of this condition. In my mind there is a clear connection between the way that elections are contested and the way that sound clashes are contested, for example. Winning by any means is sanctioned by the political system itself. A society in which martial law prevails will inevitably produce martial art forms.

This is not to say that there is only one trend in the dance or in Jamaican society. Some of the most popular material coming out the dance is strongly nonviolent in nature. I feel that these messages of peace and love, and of "put down the gun" have a positive influence that counteracts much, if not all, of the violent messages. Part of the problem with the reality tunes which decry the state of political violence, "tribal war" and drug violence is that they are for the most part unconnected from social action, from an organized social movement that could effectively seek fundamental changes in the political, legal and economic systems of the country. Perhaps the dance is not the best place to look for protest leading to social change. However, the dancehall could become a more pleasurable atmosphere for everyone if its participants sought to eliminate words and actions that derived entertainment value at the expense of making others into victims.

CHAPTER 4

Gun Talk and Girls' Talk

*The DJ Clash**

JOSEPH PEREIRA

WITH THOUSANDS OF COMPOSERS AND SINGERS, THE JAMAICAN reggae music industry has multiple tendencies in themes and styles. However, the particular style that has come to be labelled *dancehall* shows a marked preference for two themes: violence and sex. Although the latter has been around for some time in popular culture, the former is of more recent vintage and reflects the increasing stress of urban ghettoization.

Hedged around by taboos and notions of morality, sex and *slackness* have been as attractive as they have been vilified by various sectors of the body social. The widespread enterprise of the dominating classes in society to impose notional standards of "decency" and "acceptable behaviour" are complicated in Jamaica by the related association of the Afrocentric culture of the majority classes with negative values, as the dominating groups seek to maintain control over cultural definitions. Labels of "lewdness" and "indecency" – the problematized pelvic thrust – have long been used to try to contain and repress a countervailing value system.

Previously, with restricted outlets for mass communication of popular expression, it was easier for the ruling classes to impose apparent control, but with the proliferation of technology (sound systems, radio stations, production systems and the like), silencing and censorship have had to concede ground to more democratic displays of popular culture and values. Simultaneously, attitudes to sex have been reshaped by a range of mass-media activities ranging from sex advice columns to radio and television talk shows that openly discuss personal sexual practices and problems and related psychological issues. The gender debate and a wider recognition of the proactive rights and potential of women have enhanced this reshaping. Any monolithic notion of morality is therefore constantly subverted. Violence is also redefined from the daily experience of class oppression and undisguised police brutality, particularly among the urban poor. Media images, both fictional and factual, reinforce the everyday experience and inure both eye and ethos as the human being is diminished to but one more material object.

*Previously published in *Caribbean Studies* 27, nos. 3–4 (1994): 208–23.

In a commercially oriented music industry, the market determines to a large extent what is produced. Dancehall is primarily a form of entertainment and is most heavily supported by ghetto and urban working-class communities, for whom violence is an everyday reality and sex one of the few areas in which they have some direct control. In general, it is the males who respond favourably to the lyrics of violence, and as generally women are the most enthusiastic receptors of lyrics of sexuality. These exert a strong influence on the content of the songs. A DJ of the calibre of Lovindeer will conclude: "A DJ might seh 'Cho we nah do noh slackness, we a go do culture.' Well, him can do culture, but it is not commercial. And most of the DJs they do this strictly for the money, the straight economics of it" (Lovindeer 1990, 51). And top DJ Buju Banton advises: "The key to success in the dancehalls is to have the women behind you" (Henry 1992, 3). In his opinion, "Music moves in seasons. There is a season for the gun talk and a season for the girls' talk", and as a result the artist subordinates his own preferences to the market, as he indicates regarding the theme of Caribbean history: "I keep it as a personal thing, because you hardly find people interested in them things right now . . . so you keep them things to yourself and just move with the tide." Similarly, Cobra corroborates regarding gun lyrics: "It's just a style", and sees himself merely "delivering what the crowd needs" (Loebman 1993, 23). Cobra points to the social aspect of dancehall: an appeal to a crowd or to a set of "posses", male and female, rather than to individuals isolated from each other. Crowd dynamics and crowd-play become relevant to the tensions of dancehall and easily facilitate a type of street theatre in which a variety of adjuncts, including movement, dance, voice and costume enhance the efforts of the DJs themselves to create a dramatic fiction. It is germane to this element of theatricality that many of the DJs involve themselves in a language and a style of exaggeration – of larger than life. The musical sound itself is at a volume that physically reverberates through the human structure, becoming like other elements a metaphor of power with its kinetic qualities. The language of the DJ embellishes the theatre of power, where phrases like "big it up", "nuff respect" or "maximum respect" point to rituals of enhancement to negate the devalued place that the dominant social codes would seek to assign to the ghetto, which in itself becomes a signifier of a wider social conflict, expressed in the dancehall notions of "uptown" and "downtown". From the negative code of "masses", dancehall refigures "massives" as a metaphor of power and power-through-size.

Dress has taken on the theatrical dimension of costuming, where it is no longer only the DJ (the stage) who exceeds the ordinary in garb (or arrival on stage). The audience has now developed its own and growing sense of a dancehall fashion, led particularly by the women, but with the men also developing garb with boldness writ large in colour choice and cut, and hairstyles with symbolic or literal messages. Behind the new aesthetics is the project of the class clash. Babsy Grange points out: "The women are proud of showing off their clothes and their bodies and the styles they wear, they do it as a way of defying society and its double standards" (McDonald 1993, 8). These extravagant or "outrageous" hairdos and hair tints or wigs, earrings and other jewellery, revealing netting and lattices, boots and "batty riders" have developed to the point where they have forced an impact on the "mainstream" fashion. Their inherent statements have been aptly analysed by a dancehall fan: "Dressing up in expensive clothes sends a clear message to those who think that ghetto people are the scum of the earth, that they can indeed set the fashion pace" (McDonald 1993, 9). Hence, dancehall fashion designers have attracted significant clienteles locally and internationally, as is the case with Biggy, who distinguishes between "slackness" and "dancehall" fashions: "X-rated a no really dancehall. Dancehall is more a classic thing than X-rated – you have to look sexy still, but the limits that some people carry it, it pass dancehall" ("Big Up" 1993, 6).

In the music, there is a similar line between X-rated and sexy, but the term "X-rated" itself reveals a consciousness of what "others" permit, and that in itself becomes a point of tension and power play, since its transgression defies the generalized authoritarian voice of the notional "society" appropriated by "uptown". The pleasure of the "downtown" classes contests this control in the disguise of morality (the expression of the "vulgar") and legality (gun lyrics and pornophony). Supplementing the seemingly non-ideological lyrics (which have often been rather naively criticized for their lack of "consciousness", meaning the absence of explicit political statement in the traditional expectation) in this assault on a hypocritical moral posturing and its hidden classism, dancehall fans point to the middle and upper classes' own "vulgarities" in their recently developed carnivals and elsewhere, made all the more commonplace by the national televising of the (un) dress and pelvic gyration and thrust.

Most DJs are male, and this shapes the formulation of gender attitudes and relationships in their lyrics, although a few female DJs have complemented or contested that male voice. In the "slacker" dancehall lyrics, the female genitalia and the straightforward sex act are central. The relationship is made out as largely a test of power, using sex as weapon couched in a language of assault and domination: "ram her"; "stab her"; "So wi bus di juice a so di gal beg" (Ninja Kid, "Boom-bye-bye"). There is the obvious link here between sex and violence (yet not as violation, given the explicit compliance of the female persona). Ninja Kid images sexual climax as gunshot through onomatopoeia and metaphor: "buyaka, buyaka, bus juice in har head". Pan Head uses similar imagery. General Pecos proclaims: "kill her wid di rammer" ("Not My Fault"). The female may be a special type of opponent, and the weaponry distinctive, but the language is violence and the objective annihilation.

In this theatrical battle to the death, the male recognizes his risks, which are turned to the enhancement of the ego: "punnany a go kill mi dead" boasts Little Lennie, while "she bruk buddy" is Power Man's appreciation of his adversary. There is a strong element of humour in such confrontations, usually at the expense of the deficient and so reinforcing the ideal of performance. Thus we find Queen Patra teeming up with Squiddly Rankin in "Maaga Man" to ridicule the size of the organ of all fat men and conversely to praise the capabilities of thin men, with advice on how to increase size (size = quality). Correspondingly, the size of the female organ is complimented or ridiculed depending on its ability to accommodate male assaults, providing a sense of egalitarianism between the sexes.

Leading female "hardcore" DJ Patra projects the female as equal in the sexual encounter, every bit as capable as the male: "Man have big hip, ooman have it too, / so come share yours, an mi will share mine wid you" or fearlessly asserting "dere is no position in dis worl' whe mi fraid of" ("Hardcore"). The counterpart to the macho Don is this sexual Queen who images herself as in control of her situations because of her sexuality: "the quality 'im haffi come back quick; / murder mi wrote an mi no tek back mi chat" ("Queen of the Pack"). A space once dominated by the male is now being contested and appropriated by the female both in terms of style and content. The Papa San and Lady G duet indicated this in their humourous "Bun-fi-bun", where stereotypic female fidelity is subverted by the assertion of multiple sexual partners for the female, rejecting the notion of double standards and usurping male privileges. Strong tools of subordination, the shame of self and the sense of guilt are here undermined.

This does not mean that there is not a morality guiding this "slackness". The strongest feature here is the rigid orthodoxy of a heterosexual relationship in which penis and vagina play the lead and sole roles. Oral sex is only fleetingly suggested, and most frequently so by way of denial of this practice of "bowing", attributed to foreign influences. The greatest disapproval is reserved for male homosexuality. Indeed, this has embroiled Shabba Ranks and Buju Banton in international controversies and boycotts. In several songs, one of the techniques for inflating male sexual prowess is to parallel a denounced homosexuality. Little Lennie, in celebrating the female body, takes a biblical approach to homosexuals. He juxtaposes: "dem a devil pickney, down a Hell dem belong" ("Punnany Tegereg"), echoing Capleton's citing of Leviticus: "If the Bible say it is wrong, I can't go against it" (Russell 1993a, 19). Mega Banton simply distances his heterosexuality from their practice: "Whe dem seh dem a defen'? / Cyaan stop mi from love di girl dem; / yu no love ooman, yu have a man intention den / dat simple mean yu an mi a no frien." There are only two choices here in this polarized context: "love ooman" or homosexuality. Heterosexual preference therefore has to be overstated to avoid any doubt. In his hit tune, "Number Two", Terror Fabulous praises his "fabulocious" girl against the tendencies to homosexuality: "Some man a play number two, nuff man a oil an Vaseline now fi true, but I an' I no inna dat it won't do; waan mi fabulocious baby look how yu put di body-mi cyaan resis', so how di hell whole heap a man a switch?"

Male sexuality sees itself threatened by this potentiality of "switch", and so reinforces moral condemnation with violence: "Bang bang in a battyman head. / Homeboys don't condone nasty men, / dem mus' dead" sings Buju Banton in "Boom bye-bye" to the roar of dancehall crowd approval. "Nastiness", then, is beyond the pale of "slackness" and to be denounced by "X-rated" or "hardcore" and shunned in "girls' talk".

While explicit lyrics on sex incur the censorship of the mass-media, "slackness" slips through the back door of double meaning and witty conceit to undermine the discourse of "decency" far more devastatingly. Here, the catchiness of a musical chorus can imprint a risqué image across the listening (and echoing) nation. Such an effect we see in General Degree's "The Pianis", in which the female longs for a particular "musician": "She said she waan di pianis', / she jus' a cry fi di pianis'." A similar wordplay is achieved in the chorus of Buccaneer's "Neighbourhood": "She love her neighbor-hood / her neighbor-hood mek she feel good". In both situations, the male is privileged and the female subordinately dependent on the male for fulfilment, becoming the butt of the humour. Contrast this with the absence of a mediating double meaning in Patra's rawly uncamouflaged "only the dickie can mek mi feel sweet" ("Be Protected"), which gets no airplay for this simple but basic difference.

Perhaps that is why Lovindeer assesses that: "The only thing that is wrong with the slackness in some of these songs nowadays is that it is exposed to children, and to people who don't want to hear it. But in the confines of the dancehall . . . and for the people who go and want to hear this kind of thing, there's nothing wrong with it" (1990, 51). Lovindeer here points to the relativity of moral assumptions and their class-based formulation.

Giving his explanation of the shift toward slackness over the many years of evolving dancehall, Kenneth "Baskin" Scarlett identifies the influence of politics, but that can only be a very partial explanation: "Politics was another thing that changed dancehall. It brought a different human being into the halls of dance. This human being had no love. This human being would talk slackness over the microphone and degrade women, and most people in the dance did not mind."

This final observation raises the problematic which a mere "political" reading cannot satisfy. There is a more hidden type of political motivation: gender politics as containing elements of a wider contention, with the limiting designations of normative behaviour determined by outsiders. Shabba Ranks speaks of similar acceptance in the 1990s: "The women who go to the dancehall . . . do not take offense, because they know it is reality. No disrespect is intended" (Alexander 1993, 19). And lest these are discounted as male perspectives, Patra defends her style, self-tagged "hotness", against interpretations of degrading slackness: "Again is a respect thing, see? Hotness is a vibe, a sexuality thing. We are not dealing with the gutter; we are dealing with the total sexuality of all black women" (Quashie-Morgan 1993, 10).

Examining the evolution of "girls' talk", one can see a shift developing in the 1990s from a male persona anxious to assert control over the female in a direct male-female play of sexual subordination toward a scenario in which the female stands in competition with a rival ("matey"), and male control shifts into a subtler foregrounding of women against women. The format changes from the evocation of a third-person, an often named female, to a direct second-person, a usually unnamed female "you", with its open-ended possibilities for the females in the audience to identify and fantasize, just as they can freely assignate the nameless matey. A new theatrical scenario is created of contrasting female characters whose acceptability is directed by the controlling male DJ voice. The lyrical focus is on the physical (body first and foremost, with waist and "bumper"/bottom as more precise centres of attention, with face completing the basic checklist), and on the material adjuncts – woman as property and propertied.

Compare this with the late 1980s, where direct control is the foreground. In "Wi Run Tings", the DJ speaks for all men ("we") in his introductory assertion: "We rule girls, girls no rule we", and this concern is illustrated by way of a contrastive moral anecdote:

> Know a little yute by di name of Aston
> treat a fi im girl like a gentleman,
> so she start seh im is a saaf man. What!

She cyan do anyting she cyan, like:
come in 12 o'clock an' quarter past one.
But if a girl do mi dat a different fashion,
cho man, she would haffi know seh mi a di don:
we come first an' she come second.

Similarly, General Pecos ("Forget Me Not") distances himself from the man who allows woman to subordinate him, interpreting a one-to-one relationship as a form of male subordination: "Some fall inna di trap an tun house-husban'; mi radda service ooman like a gas station. Dem want a man fi demself, nah share dem tool wid no one: selfishness cause destruction."

The final verse transfers blame to the female for seeking to privatize a public asset (the female is already privatized). Male domestication is seen as a diminution of maleness. The male ego therefore must hold on to the control in determining relationships, as Skull Man advocates in his "No Date or Appointment" open-house approach, where he seeks "someone to have an to hol', / someone to have under control". The female is expected to provide the male his needed sense of power.

By 1993, the persona of the matey becomes well-established in the lyrics, and (drawing in adapted form on a long-standing tendency to misogyny as a route to gender power) she is used as a focus of vilification for qualities designated negative in women, contrasted with the girl in whom positive values are all consolidated in the legitimizing concept of "wifey" (read "fit in the eyes of the male to be wife"). Gospel Fish ("Yu Mi Rate") shows clearly the imposition of a male ordering on the female:

Now wife material: show yu face!
matey: dress back, for dere is no competition.
Watch me!
Gal, ah yu mi rate so yu no haffi fret 'bout yu mate,
from yu stan' up official yu will nyam di weddin' cake.

In this modernized masculine dispensation, the wifey is associated with material well-being: money, living quarters, clothes, transport, overseas travel and so on, while those who share her man as matey are cast in an anonymous frame of material and physical deprivation and illegitimacy. Dugsy Ranks has imaged this counterpoise of qualities neatly in his hit song "Wifee":

Wifee a winna, big sprinta stayah,
yu di man request, mate cyaan tek yu lover;
matey a get lovin all roun a kitchen,
wife honeymoon she tek di plane go a foreign;
matey no ready, tell everybody
she a get di love but a yu get di money; wife
exquisite, everyting yu have it,
no worry unno self 'cause everyting ligit.

> yu a lead, yu a di man 320 Benz,
> matey come in like cyar whe man rent:
> no handle wid care so it mash up an dent;
> wife a di queen inna di man residence,
> mate haffi hitch-up har butt 'roun a fence;
> have yu bank-book an yu independent,
> dem cyaan get yu out because yu stan permanent.

This makes clear how the female is placed and displaced by the male, and who does the requesting, accommodating and legitimizing. It is also clear that the male is consolidating his freedom to enjoy multiple sexual partners and cultivating the privileging of material rewards. Ironically, "wifey" is "independent" at the disposition of the male, who seeks to contain his version of social order by this negotiation of power.

Emerging from the techniques of ridicule used in the matey lyrics is an interesting subset of aesthetic and ideological associations in which lingering negative connotations of Africa absorbed by popular culture from the dominating classes surface. Gospel Fish ("Yu Mi Mate") sings of "ole niggah drop pon dem face" as a part of the insult to matey, while General T.K. ("Nah Gwaan Fi Mate") uses the following comparison in his ridicule: "jump two fence like a African". Another DJ refers mockingly to the "poun' ah livah" lips of the unattractive matey, while Dugsy Ranks exclaims: "Kiss mi neck, she inna dashiki frock" to indicate lack of style and taste. One recalls how Shaka Zulu became a signifier of ugliness in Jamaican popular culture and lyrics after part of the television series was shown. This ambivalence toward Africa is complemented by an equally lingering association of the foreign (read American) as a notional standard of quality. So Hollywood is used in several songs as a signifying reference for beauty. One DJ ascribes the source of quality to the much-privileged "foreign": "gal a mus be foreign yu go accep' di walkin". While Patwa is the standard language of these lyrics, there is an accommodation to long-standing notions of English as a signifier of superiority when Patra makes the shift from Patwa to English in: "Mi no cut-up, cut-up, I can model everytime" ("Queen of the Pack").

Analysing the matey gambit, there is the transparent politics of divide and rule. But in a socio-economic context where the male can provide needed financial support, accommodations are negotiable. The lyrics provide an arena of play, a theatrical space for fictive resolutions of real life dilemmas of choice. Lovindeer indicates:

> They [the women] always think it's somebody else. So they don't take it to mean anything. And the same lyrics that you hear those DJs using, cursing women and all that, that's the same kind of lyrics those women use to curse other women. . . . So the more the DJ can use those kind o' lyrics and describe certain things which these women know about and curse other women with, the more they jump up and shout. Especially if they can point out a woman who might be fooling around with their guy, it done right de so. (1990, 51)

Hence the ritual invitation to "point pon yu matey" allows a theatrical play for working off the rivalries and jealousies within the patriarchal dispensation symbolized in the male DJ.

The antagonistic possibilities between female and "unfaithful" male are deflected to female competing against female, a tactic we see insinuated in Terror Fabulous ("Yu No Catch"): "A no me mek a nex gal come tek her rod, / a di betta property whe di betta gal have." Elsewhere ("Hang on Pon Yu Man"), he locates sole responsibility for the relationship in the female: "cyaan hol' yu man den ooman yu fi gwaan". And exploiting this base of jealousy, the male DJ goads violence female on female in the lyrical play:

Every time yu matey see yu, a yu she waan fight,
rush yu wid ice-pick, rush yu wid knife;
if matey a talk an a run up har mout,
give har one right han' an tump har teet out,
beat har up bad, let di scandal out.

Male on female violence is less socially acceptable than female on female, which is even given comic potential in the context, deflecting responsibility from the male. Some female DJs like Patra are willing to play the male game, and Junie Ranks can boast of routing competitors, but these go only as far as rejecting notions of the passive female. However, other female DJs do not concur with the larger subordinating schema. Hence Lady G choruses: "Some man fi get cuff, fi get cuff, fi get cuff", in response to male deceit, while Lady Saw rings in 1994 with a call for female resistance:

A new year, wid im ooman gal yu nah share,
no mek im tell yu fi try understan',
or else im ooman a go dis di programme.
Sinting wid man whe mi cyaan understan':
dem always waan yu stan wid dem an dem gal,
but mi no cater an mi no give not a damn:
is either me, she, Patsy or Pam.

Independence here does not rest on a bank book in a male dispensation but in a mindset where Lady Saw asserts: "mi star mi own show an run mi program".

In the phallocentric male world view seen in so many DJs, a paradox emerges between power and service: who ultimately determines the satisfaction of service? The DJ sets store by stamina and longevity (natural or assisted). His orgasm is to him the indicator of service. In the hit tune "Twist and Shout", Pliers croons: "an when mi reach [climax] mi will tell yu fi stop". No recognition here of the place of the female climax. Other DJs equate "agony" with female satisfaction, despite its obvious ambiguity. Consider too the DJ's boast: "gal no stop scream when mi give har di potion". A counter-discourse has emerged, however, re(de)fining the signifiers of satisfaction (and if necessary of performance). Hence, Daddy Screw advises: "Some man a mek love to ooman like dem de a Vietnam; / ooman no waan no man fi mek har feel cramp" ("Loverman"). Silver Cat cautions: "dis is makin love, dis is no bullfight". And the duet of Nadine Sutherland and Terror Fabulous proffers in "Action" a more explicit reorientation of sex to female sensibility:

> Bedroom bully she no waan dat yu know,
> she waan a man to caress her up like so.
> Man a mek love to woman like a war dem a go,
> woman a bawl inna agony, a holla out . . .
> Cho! Hardcore lovin' yu mus be insane,
> woman no waan no man fi mek she in pain,
> sweet lovin in de fallin rain,
> sweet lovin a mix up har brain:
> whole heap a lovey-dovey an nuff affection.

Yet even here, the female is imaged as mentally confused by sex, unable to maintain control of the situation, unlike the implicit male.

We have seen how violence overlaps some aspects of "girls' talk" and has been confused with sexual potency by the male, but it has its own distinct history in Jamaican popular music which has influenced this confluence. The lyrical tradition goes back to the "rudies" (1960s), evolved into "ragamuffins" and "dons" (1980s) and now "gangsters". The crucible is the class oppression waged on the have-not classes with the increasing involvement of the police in undisguised violence. Its manifestations include an increasing aggressiveness and insensitivity, a rejection of the authority of "established" society and its symbols and cynicism and "criminal" activities, from drug dealing to robbery and murder. As with sex, a more naked form of the weapon to hand is turned against both immediate community and wider society in demand of a space and respect, as well as material benefits. Buju Banton's "Mr Big Man" succinctly contextualizes the archetypal ghetto youth, now a symbol of a wider working-class male, whose class, gender and economic and political relationships are defined by exploitation. Bereft of a credible political solution, the "gangster" turns from the militancy of "conscious" lyrics to a far more subversive disregard for all values. When Ninjaman affirms on national television with seeming amorality "Mi no kya", he is expressing what had been sung twenty years previously in "Rudie Don't Care", only now at a more intensely meant and shared level.

The increased culture of violence stripped of moral conscience is reflected in the lyrics of current songs. Terror Fabulous proclaims: "Wi no rob plenty money / a pure brains wi jook" ("Gangster Anthem"), where the disarmingly low criminality expressed in the first verse is dramatically displaced by the shock image of the second, with its murder for pleasure. Equally graphic, Bounty Killer tries to capture the outlook of the multiple ghetto gangs of Kingston:

> We a kill bwoy, no show no mercy;
> Spanglers, Seaview, Junglist, Rockfort, T.G.;
> wi no have no mercy, no get wi gun thirsty,
> all inna station mi gun no deh far.

But it is Ninjaman who takes the celebration of anarchic violence to new heights in "My Weapon":

at the age of two mi kill five policeman,

. . . .

when mi rob di bank an kill a woman;

. . . .

yu see di big mag. 10–a mi mek dat one,
as mi mek it me go use it kill a soldier-man.

. . . .

a mi rob di church an kill di pastor-man;
a don't care a damn, mi a hartical badman.

The targets in the lyrics cover various components of the dominant state (law agents, bank, church), and the dead cover not only obvious state authority figures but also others more symbolic of traditional values (woman, pastor). To underscore the absence of any moral base, the singer sings of stealing from his mother and brother, destroying another traditional cohesive social symbol of the family. Yet there is a mediating signifier of play in the obvious fiction from the first verse and its exaggeration, helping us to distance song from reality and singer from criminal, even if the other scenarios are difficult to separate from recent reality.

Echoing the badness of Ninjaman's persona, Beenie Man sets up an awesome self in "Across the Bridge":

gwaan like yu bad, DJ,
yu get buffin',
hear Beenie Man goin' teach the I som'n,
noh disrespect me cause mi no have no pity,
go-on like yu bad an mi will shot all yu granny,
if yu puppa dis, im will get kill and bury.

But once again the apparent brutal disregard for the traditionally revered (granny), ambivalently containing elements of authority to be defied, is mediated by reference to the DJ: the violence is contained at the level of wordplay, a lyrical clash of DJs competing for supremacy as toasters/performers. Even the peripheral language of the sound system scene points to the metaphors of violence, since successful DJs are spoken of as "killing a sound".

Over the years, the language of violence and "gun talk" has been transposed from the street to the stage as a cathartic play and vicarious appropriation of power. From the competitive spirit behind the sound system "clash" comes the lyrical clash of DJs, whose ability as performers is being tested on improvisation and invention, couched in the metaphor of a shoot-out.

As with "girls' talk", exaggeration and self-promotion are necessary devices, as is the vilification of competition. Ninjaman has immortalized the experience in "Border Clash" ("Murder dem, murder dem, inna competition a goin murder dem"), and it was just as popular in the clash of Bounty Killer and Beenie Man at the Sting 1993 concert, with their arsenal of "gun lyrics". It is a ritual that the dancehall crowd demands and sublimates from its violent daily realities, and its participatory acclamation is expressed in equal simulation of violence by live gun salutes or their transmuted onomatopoeic "buyaka, buyaka", "pram, pram" or other symbolic codes such as "flashing up the lighter" or "bun i' down". The names assumed by many of the DJs (General, Major, Rankin', and so on) reflect this mimicry of a society in which the strong are made out to not be wrong.

However, this divide between lyrical play and reality has at times become too blurred, with the gun murder of a number of DJs over time. Recently, the dancehall has begun to question its own impact and the ability to keep play distinct from real practice. This is especially true since the murders of Panhead (October 1993) and Dirtsman (1994), and the result has been a surge of songs against violence coming from the DJs, although mainly those who had been on the fringe of "gun lyrics" and more comfortable with "girls' talk". Hence, Buju Banton's "Murderer" incantation against gun killing. Buju explains: "You see the men dem who a talk the bag a gun lyrics and a kill off the people, dem ya man a fi remember sacrilege pon him house!! Sacrilege pon yu house!! From dem tek the DJ (Panhead) life everybody should clean up dem act" (Russell 1993b, 25). Stitchie, too, in a television interview, expresses the view that the gun lyrics are influencing reality – life is imitating art, not vice versa: "People are taking songs and dramatizing them, living them out. Not only ordinary people but artistes are in danger" ("Morning Time Coffee Guest", JBC-TV, 25 February 1994). Since ordinary people have long been in danger from violence in reality, one must assume that the qualitative shift to a new morality lies in the threat to the artist – a sort of self-preservation that urges: "Man an' man cyan reason" ("Three against War").

But does art have this level of power? Or is it a confusion of the symptom for the cause? Musicians have warned in their lyrics that hunger and poverty must be addressed if violence is to be successfully tackled. To the material is added the emotional need for respect and recognition. In the old interplay of the subjective and objective, it is easier to co-opt the subjective alone and call for new values without material change. To what extent does "girls' talk" deflect the tensions of that violent reality and marginalizing process into a different camouflage of class conflict? Clearly, dancehall is seeking a self-correcting mechanism by which it can both process gender politics and maintain its organic resistance to the dominating culture and discourse without getting itself burned. As sensitive players, the DJs read the shifting moods of their audiences and can "wheel and come again" in their quest to deliver on their prime job of entertaining, even as they mediate and advance popular concerns.

REFERENCES

Alexander, John. 1993. "What Is This Thing Called Dancehall?" *Jammyn* 1, no. 4: 19.

"Big up the King of Fabric". *Lifestyles,* no. 27 (July–August): 6.

Henry, Balford. 1992. "Bonafide Buju Banton". *Lifestyles,* no. 23 (November–December): 3.

Loebman, Lizard. 1993. "DJs Dominate". *Reggae Report* 11, no. 1: 23

Lovindeer, Lloyd. 1990. "Women in Dancehall". *Jamaica Journal* 23, no. 1 (February–April): 51.
McDonald, Paulette . 1993. "The Dancehall Revisited". *Lifestyles,* no. 27 (July–August): 8.
Quashie-Morgan, Caryl. 1993. "Patra, Queen of the Pack". *Reggae Report* 11, no. 1: 10.
Russell, Karie. 1993a. "Capleton, Dancehall Prophet". *Reggae Report* 11, no. 1: 19.
———. 1993b. "Buju Banton: The Bad Bad DJ Don". *Jammyn* 1, no. 6: 25.

PART 2

NEGOTIATION, URBAN SPACE AND EXPERIENCE

CHAPTER 5

Post-Nationalist Geographies

Rasta, Ragga and Reinventing Africa[*]

LOUIS CHUDE-SOKEI

"The whole world is Africa."
—Black Uhuru

"Hear me now raggamuffin: we run all sounds, and we run the nation. So mek we just control the borderline."
—Anonymous pirate deejay

"Ring the alarm, another sound is dying."
—Tenor Saw

BECAUSE "AFRICA" HAS BEEN CALLED UPON TO JUSTIFY so many movements of liberation and exploitation, and because it has functioned not only as a physical reality in the making of Western culture but also as a central concept in the canons of institutional (and revolutionary) knowledge, it is hard to mark a clear space between the layers of discourse and desire, and any Africa which may lie beyond. It is in many ways very difficult to extricate what is said of Africa from what Africa says of itself. Perhaps it is impossible. But if indeed "Africa" spoke, how would it speak and what would it say? What "itself" would it express, and could the sound of that voice be understood by ears still ringing with myth?

After all, a native sound connotes a system of native knowledge, and as Paul Gilroy has so well argued, national and cultural belonging – especially within the various populations of the black diaspora – cannot be fully understood in the realm of literacy and print media. Native knowledge cannot be accurately traced or located in the writings of the literate few. Instead it is articulated in and disseminated by what I call the sound/culture nexus: that discursive space where Africa ceaselessly extends and invents itself in an epistemological matrix coded not in words but in sound. Why sound? Because the discourse in sound is separate from those of the literary, of the *logos*; it is a space

[*]Previously published in *African Arts* 24, no. 4 (1994): 215–27.

independent of the centred semantic structures of science, freed from the objective bias of literacy. It is necessarily the space of oral knowledge, the space of both magic and postmodern technology. Indeed, for this generation within a black diaspora, sound is closer to culture than "race" ever was.

For me, Africa speaks in those shadowy historical moments which go unrecorded, those moments of reflection when diaspora asks the question asked by Harlem poet Countee Cullen in 1925: "What is Africa to me?" But in these moments, the language is opaque, as with all oracular dispensations, and the events which mark them often very threatening. Take for example the stoning of Bunny Wailer. On the level of popular knowledge – as opposed to the towers of "critique" – the stoning of this semi-legendary Rastafarian singer, the last living member of the original Wailers (Bob Marley and Peter Tosh both dying in the 1980s), signifies a crucial moment in diaspora. For you see, Wailer was more than just a singer: he was perhaps the last living symbol of black revolutionary desire from his generation. And his was a generation that helped thrust a mythic "Africa" to the forefront of black popular culture in the West Indies and, via reggae music and Rastafarianism, the world.

His being stoned in Jamaica by this new generation, the raggamuffin generation, signifies that something has radically changed in certain suburbs of the city I call diaspora. Certainly Africa constantly changes, but the meanings of Africa change too; they change and are adapted to fit the local notions of black identity and cultural survival. In this case the "Africa" central to a Rastafarian pan-Africanism has been symbolically dislodged. The generation which celebrated Marcus Garvey as a prophet and Africa as "Zion" has been assaulted by the children birthed by it. This is because new economic and cultural conditions require new gods and symbols; old ones stagnate or become malevolent and repressive. In short, what we have in the raggamuffin/dancehall[1] (sub) cultural movement is a very harsh popular critique of what Africa means to us at this moment in a post/neo/omni-colonial world.

Emerging out of the Seaga-Thatcher-Reagan triumvirate in the 1980s and fuelled by a booming international cocaine trade, ragga stepped boldly onto the diasporan stage as first an overturning of that Rastafarian mythos which celebrated a universalized notion of black racial and cultural identity, an essentialized vision of diaspora which exercised a sort of oppressive control over Jamaican cultural production. In its most sincere moments Rasta fetishized black cultural origins, rooting them in a fixed source of "anciency" called, according to the Old Testament, "Ethiopia". And as the Rastafarian influence in reggae music grew and came to dominate in the 1970s, this obsession became crucially linked to the driving bass and drums of reggae "riddim". The music and its ideology, then, became so fastened to "roots" and ethnic/cultural authenticity that many felt challenged to speak to the raw present of Jamaican ghetto life – that which reggae had once directly addressed. Specificity was lost because of the obsession with global "pan-African" discourses, racial metaphors and religio-political allegories. And the ideology of "roots" did not offer a framework within which to contend with the changing environment of music, multinational capitalism and global communications technology.

The raggamuffin generation then positioned itself as a serious challenge to any attempt to narrate diaspora based on similarities of oppression or pigment. Certainly pan-Africanism has been criticized in the past for some of its racial essentialism, but to criticize the logic of essentialism is not in any way to halt its currency on the street. With the stoning of Bunny Wailer, the much maligned raggamuffin sound/subculture has announced itself as the latest in a long line of exiles to ask Cullen's question and to violently reassess their position within the vagaries of black cultural history. For this generation, the slippages made between race and culture by their forbears have become the space in which new notions of belonging and becoming are asserted.

Where the Rastafarian "Africa" was a cultural commodity available to all those with black skin, one that could be traded across and beyond the Atlantic by Garvey's "Black Star Line" of ships or could be invented in sound by the open metonymic spaces of heavy dub echoes, the signifiers of ragga/dancehall ground themselves firmly in a "blackness" produced out of a specific cultural history. For the Rastafari brethren, "Zion", the promised land of Ethiopia, was both a precolonial utopia and the imminent future of black people who were destined to survive the time span of Babylonian hegemony. With ragga, however, the abstraction of Ethiopia/Africa in what I have elsewhere called the "Discourse of Dread" gives way to Rema, Tivoli Gardens and Jungle, particular "Yard" (Jamaican) realities which do not function as global signifiers of black exile because they are so rooted in the urban myths of Jamaica's postcolonial history. And these signifiers and symbols quite clearly belong to "Yardies" who spend much time carefully "controlling the borderline" which separates one blackness, one idiosyncratic cultural experience, from another.

Rasta-reggae too had moments of specificity in its narratives – for example "Trenchtown" as mythic space, or "Dungle" – but they were always linked directly to some global narrative of black oppression. With raggamuffin sound, which currently dominates the ideologies of Afro-Caribbean youth and black Third World pop/ghetto culture, one is challenged to find references to the mythic signifier of black identity that is Africa. And most important, there is no longing for it. As a matter of fact, the few references in dancehall music to that distant memory of a continent are usually halfhearted attempts to criticize and condemn the present by evoking the moral authority of some always fictitious golden age. The sentiments of raggamuffin music and culture are very different from the nostalgia and longing for "elsewhere" that characterizes much of the kind of reggae and cultural production that comes out of Bob Marley's generation. The "Waiting in Vain", "Back to Africa", "Rasta Waan Go Home" exile narratives have given way to cultural expressions from those who see the new battles as immediate and local – through gun-sights and across dirty inner-city streets. From an aesthetics of exile and absence to an aesthetics of raw, materialistic presence.

Instead of dwelling psychically "elsewhere", the narratives of dancehall feature an exploration and celebration of the microrealities, the obsessive minutiae of Jamaican urban life which holds little meaning for all outsiders. They also investigate the noirish street-level intricacies of a postcolonial underclass navigating a global network of immigrant communities. Outsiders to the culture of ragga (Jamaican and non-Jamaican) tend to find these narratives rude, crude, scatological and "slack". This, however, is what deejays (read MCs, or rappers) describe as "strictly reality". Everything from local politics and crime to ghetto morality, from graphic depictions of murder to very explicit and pornographic details of the bedroom, gets put to rapid-fire boom-beats and is broadcast throughout the global community of Yardies. Lyrics, which in most cases are community property, belonging only to the moment of expression, range from the sublimely terrifying to the incredibly stupid.

Take for example the latest masterpiece in the "gun talk" genre, that subcategory of ragga chats which are devoted exclusively to the celebration of guns and the street credibility and power derived from them: "Shine and Criss" by the massive Shabba Ranks. Some of these tunes are explicitly metaphorical, celebrating the fierce competitions within sound culture; but these metaphors get strained due to that proximity between life and art, that closeness between a metaphorical "Sound Boy Killing" and, in the words of Terror Fabulous, "Literally Killing". I quote this track at length, not because it is definitive but because it is the latest and the most self-conscious of the genre. It is also a major hit:

> Oil up all a the gun dem, keep them shine and criss
> A copper shot, you fe carry inna you gun,
> mek a bwoy tum purple any time him get it, Lawd . . .
> Me say the A.K. whe you bury, me a beg you dig it up,
> here is a bottle of pepsi to cut off the rust
> Finger pon the trigger, machine ready fe bus,
> Boy fe lay down like the gun me dig up
> If me cock it inna your nose, you haffe sniff it up
> If me push it inna your mouth, hold your breath and no cough,
> and no mek me see your teeth like a laugh you want laugh:
> the gun inna me hand a no looking glass . . .
> I don't trust no shadow when me come after dark
> Me kill first and a me last pop off Tell them say that gunshot do all of the talk.

The opening sample ("Original Gangster") is of course the ultimate statement of ghetto-political authenticity in Afro-American "gangsta rap". And this is where the potential in a hip-hop/ragga cross-cultural discourse was first articulated on the street level. But what Shabba does in "Shine and Criss" is offer a view into the mind of a Yardie whose world is one of extreme violence, a world that has no time for what Bajan writer George Lamming called "the pleasures of exile". Guns are a sign of entirely different assumptions about cultural positioning; or as Mad Cobra has said in his massive "Shot No Talk": "Fe me gun shot / don't hold no argument." Some of these tracks are so vivid and violent that they are merely long, wrenching descriptions of slow torture and boasts about the most brutal ways to kill – not only one's enemy, but his family and friends (and one ridiculous line which pops up every now and then involves the murder of the family cat!). Indeed, some tunes are merely lists of the dead ("Roll Call" by Tenor Saw, or Super Cat's "Nuff Man a Dead") and celebrations of one's own homicidal history. As for the incredible stupidity – especially as it relates to sexual "slackness" – more on this later.

For those within this floating cultural context, Africa is less important – in fact it often gets in the way of – contemporary Third World ghetto life. As a British rudie once said to me, "Africa nah go mek me bullet-proof!"[2] More important, though, raggamuffin and dancehall narratives map out a sprawling Third World urban geography which stretches from the gun-loud poverty of Kingston to the bass-heavy housing estates of South London and over to that place that Raymond Williams located as the centre of modernist exile – New York City. This is a discourse that is obsessively local but well aware of the global network of Afro-Caribbean migration and the discontinuous histories of black diaspora. Inside the dense sound-sculpting of ragga mixology, the references begin and return to Yard, but in between the signifiers travel through the Jamaican communities in England ("London Massive, Brixton Crew"), New York ("Brooklyn Massive, Flatbush Posse") and Canada ("Nuff Respect Toronto Massive!"). This is the matrix of dancehall music and culture: creating a new sense of national belonging beyond the boundaries constructed by politics and geography. Community is narrated there in that very tense space between the local and the global: the space they call "the borderline".

Although Seaga's Jamaica, Thatcher's England and Reagan's America gave ragga the kind of painful birth necessary for their mythic function, they really were always there. They were overshadowed by the spectacle of Rasta and its pious moralisms, but they were there nonetheless, stalking Jamaica's neocolonial streets and consuming American cowboy and gangster films as well as the Old Testament and Pentecostalism. They existed within Rasta from the moment it defined itself as an urban phenomenon and as a place for those suppressed by the hierarchical and colour-stratified social structure of Jamaica. During the 1960s, before the hegemony of Rasta in the consciousness of ghetto sound, the earliest manifestation of the ragga could be located in the rude boy phenomenon which swept the tiny island. The rudies, like today's "gangbangers" in America, were young males who had little access to education and were victims of the incredible unemployment endemic to Third World urban centres. Their political consciousness was as developed as the Rastafari, but where the Rasta solution was one which often refused to engage directly with the harsh realities of ghetto and Third World life and frequently got lost in cloudy moments of rhetoric and myth ("roots and culture"), the rudies clung fiercely to "reality" – that trope central to today's ragga/dancehall culture. They terrorized the island, modelling themselves after their heroes from American films and glorying in their outlaw status. They killed, robbed and looted, celebrating their very stylish nihilism. And ska and reggae – especially deejay reggae,[3] the beginning of rap/hip-hop – were their musics.

Today the dreadlocks vision has been superseded – at least in the realm of sound and culture – by the rudie vision. The crucial differences between them can be seen quite vividly in their relationship to Babylon. Where in Rasta and other forms of popular Negritude there has always been some degree of nostalgia for a precolonial/preindustrial/precapitalist Africa, raggamuffin culture is very forward-looking and capitalist oriented – as are most black people, despite the fantasies of many self-appointed nationalist leaders. These rudies focus their gaze, instead, on America, absorbing commodity culture from the fringes of the global marketplace, responding to it positively. This means that in the context of a Third World ghetto where there are more guns per capita than anywhere else in the world, where legitimate employment is often a fantasy, where the drug trade and music provide the only available options for success, these young men find affirmation in the various messages that radiate out from America, an America that is not the "centre" but rather an imagined source of transmission. Messages like *The Godfather* get picked up and translated into island style. For example, one of the titles of utmost dancehall respect is "don".

The raggamuffin pantheon is full of deejays with names like Clint Eastwood, Johnny Ringo, Al Capone, Josey Wales and Dillinger; and today's dons boast names like Bounty Killer, Shabba Ranks (named after a famous Jamaican gunman) and John Wayne. Also, the Jamaican underworld has always been full of characters who inscribe themselves into ghetto myth by renaming themselves in much the same way. Male identity in this context is a necessary pastiche, and the allegorical representations of America's dreams of itself become rewritten with a pen soaked in the blood of colonialism, slavery and black ghetto style. The gunfighter/outlaw image has always been there in reggae; it is now, however, without overt references to the Western world as the "Sheriff", as in Bob Marley and the Wailers's classic "I Shot the Sheriff". For the ragga, this metaphor is no longer apt, for now they shoot each other in a lawless postcolonial terrain. Indeed, Ninjaman has described Jamaica as a "Cowboy Town".

These names – and the notion of crime as political/cultural resistance that they signify – were there during Rasta's moment, but where the more Afrocentric embraced the Marley vision, the ghetto youth, the "badbwoys", were smuggling in specialized weaponry like M16s, Glocks and Bushmasters, killing each other and following their favourite sound systems[4] around the island. And, of course, the cocaine and marijuana trade was booming. In fact, it was booming in such a way that in the 1980s a few of the more enterprising Yardies invested some of this money which came to the ghetto in – believe it or not – state-of-the-art digital computer technology. Thus began what Jah Fish (Murray Elias), an avid follower of Jamaican music, has called the "the modem era" (Fernando 1993) of Afro-Caribbean sound and culture.

This, then, should help describe the raggamuffin sound, what Dick Hebdige has called "an ultra-modern maisonette where all the surfaces are clean and shiny" (Hebdige 1990, 151): a highly produced digital and floppy-disc driven sound from a country which, ironically, has no significant computer technology to speak of. The ragga youth are immersed in this technology, fascinated with it in much the same way that early reggae mixers and producers were with multitrack technology. For them this technology and the highly experimental rhythms that they produce in it – as much akin to German and Eastern European avant-garde synthesizer music as to West African percussion and calypso – allow them to play with the signifiers and symbols of cultural history in the ontological space of sound. It also plugs them into an information network spread across the Atlantic, one focused on the potential for cultural and economic exchange in the New World instead of a fixation with their roots in the Old. This is all summed up, I think, in the words of the truly large Cutty Ranks:

> Me raggamuffin and me international, to kill a deeyjay me don't partial,
> right yah now, Jah man, me got me credential,
> and when me come a dance-hall man me well official . . .
> Me got the stopper,
> to every deejay them have fe talk to me proper,
> say galang Cutty Rankin', gwaan go kill them with the culture . . .
> London, Paris and even California, down a Japan or me gone down a
> Africa
> down a New Zealand or even inna Canada,
> yes, Cutty Rankin' a go kill you with the lingua.

Let me provide a practical example of how this specific network within diaspora operates. The legendary team of Steely and Cleevie in Jamaica, or maybe Bobby Digital in Kingston, may send a floppy disc with the basic rhythm track to Daddy Freddy, who is in London with the up-and-coming production team of Mafia or Fluxy (or maybe Fashion, today's dominant UK sound). This track may feature the latest craze in dancehall rhythms – sampled Indian tablas mixed with Jamaican mento[5] patterns from the 1950s.

After a brief vocal session, that same information could go to Massive B in the Bronx for hip-hop beats or to Sting International in Brooklyn where R&B touches are added. Again, all of this is by modem or by floppy disc. Within a few days this mix is booming down the fences at the weekly "sound-dash" between Metromedia Hi Fi and the mighty Stone Love Sound System somewhere in a crowded field in West Kingston, or in a community centre in Brixton. An "authentic" Jamaican product! And this trade goes both ways, circulating throughout diaspora. (Even in Lagos, Nigeria, I have sat listening to Igbo rude boys and Yoruba dreads rap in Jamaican Patwa about the virtues of Eddy Murphy.)

Here we can witness an attempt to connect the various points of black/Afro-Caribbean disembarkation into one transnational, commodity-based space. One postnationalist city of blackness – but with many, many suburbs. Maybe this is the only Zion possible: a place where the subversion and redefinition of First World technology and the loosening bands of racial/nationalist ideologies allow dancehall to create a new "Africa" within the postmodern networks of multinational capital; a virtual "black" community informed by the very arbitrariness of the racial signifier itself. And, like the Rastafari before them, they use sound to invent this space of black belonging. Sound which conveys cultural and historical meanings encoded in beats, grooves and samples: digitized culture production.

Tragically, violence and the drug trade follow this same route – these young men and women die in diaspora as quickly and as often as they enter into it. The bullets and gunshot sounds central to dancehall music, and the lyrical gun fetishization of the deejays, are not simply rhetorical figures; they reflect a certain reality. And the obsession with space, with controlling borders, is such that on the micropolitical level it leads to some of the fiercest territorial and aesthetic disputes in the world. Not only have reggae and dancehall been known for their deep intimacy with crime, but the very rituals of sound system culture celebrate a certain ruthless parochiality. Sound clashes often end in violence, with deejays and posses killing each other over lyrics, money and volume disputes. And the lyrics of many ragga-chats are about the celebration of one's belonging to and willingness to kill and die for one's sound. Also, one of the most heartfelt ways of showing appreciation for the selector (he who controls the psycho-acoustic space of the dancehall and spins the records) is by firing real guns into the floor or off into the Jamaican night sky. These days applause has been replaced in sound sessions by the verbal chants of "Bo! Bo! Bo!" or "Booyaka" – imitation gunfire. Here, borders are patrolled because there is ever the fear of having some other sound encroach upon yours.

But it is in language that the cultural barriers between blacknesses are more clearly visible. There have always been fast talkers in various West Indian musics, and the vernacular has been long accepted as the medium of truly popular discourses throughout the Caribbean. Rasta also featured its own language, one subtly independent of the Jamaican vernacular. Some called it "Iyaric" and thought of it as the first step to complete semantic freedom from the "politricks" of neocolonial structures of power. The ragga strategy, however, is not to escape the language but to use it to stress their specific "Yardness". They so stress their Jamaican Patwa, by exaggerating, stretching and speeding it up (almost to and sometimes beyond the point of parody) so it is incomprehensible and intimidating to those on the outside. This language is consciously as fast as the ragga beats, as garish as their style, replete with in-jokes, neologisms, specific island/cultural references, and full of more assertions concerning class and gender than racial authenticity.

Indeed, where Rasta and various Black Nationalisms and Negritudes tended to segregate women into a phallocentric ghetto – voices, identities and bodies covered in some kind of revolutionary propriety – the ragga moment is one which is dominated by explicit representations of the sexuality of black women. In addition to urban tales of survival, machismo and violent retributions, the body of the black woman is at the centre of ragga cultural discourse.[6] Not as metaphoric "Mama Africa", to quote Peter Tosh (or any of the poets of French Negritude), but as a threatening physical and economic presence. An aggressive and predatory figure to be guarded against in some cases, and catered to in others. This is important because in Rasta, women were a conspicuous absence in the rhetoric and in the rituals of culture. And except for women like the I-Threes, who sang back-up for Bob Marley and the Wailers, they were absent in the iconography. But not only do women function in the symbolic order of raggamuffin sound, they are very present in the culture itself. They consume more records than the men do, and they control the dance floor. Most deejays today – acknowledging the market – orient their lyrics toward these women. From a Western liberal-feminist perspective these lyrics, because they are boldly heterosexual and disdainful of bourgeois sentimentality, seem very sexist and objectifying of women. However, down there in the mire of postcolonial reality, where power is a rare but prized commodity, these women find both affirmation and power in the fear that their sexuality creates in the men. It allows them the freedom and security to navigate in and around a world of brutality, violence and economic privation.

And because this aesthetic is one of raw materialistic presence, where the pressures of history succumb to the intensity of the moment, the obsession with the body of woman – admiring it, celebrating it, possessing it, controlling it or fearing its power – seems to pick up where the obsession with "Africa" left off. But here it is without the gendered romance of Negritude or Rasta-nationalism. Here racial romance has given way to something much less pastoral and much more vicious. With titles ranging from "Want a Virgin" and "Love Punaany[7] Bad" ("Punaany it so nice / Punaany it so slick / Come put your lips on a 12-inch d**k") and with lyrics ranging from horrific celebrations of male sexual aggression ("Me ram it and a jam it till the gal start to vomit") to lyrics mapping out the rituals and morality of ghetto relationships, this music articulates a world completely devoid of sentimentality and intimacy – a world where one is, in the words of Don Gorgon Ninjaman, "Married to Mi Gun". And many of the women who pick up the mike today and attempt to "ram up session" demand not equality but that their dons "ride and provide".

It is also important to note that the particular uses of language in raggamuffin sound culture tend, as was my point earlier, to consciously separate them from blacks met in New York, Miami or London. They use language, as many Afro-Caribbean immigrants have, to signify and create cultural difference within the nationalist monolith of "blackness". Despite the fact that pan-Africanism is in many ways an invention of the West Indies, the specific racial dynamics of the ideology require that culture often be elided for the sake of "race", that the specifics of one African experience be lost in the Atlantic for the sake of an ahistorical, transcendental "ness". This has created certain hostilities which conveniently escape the annals of black historiography – nationalist or otherwise – because they would strip "racial" affiliations of their often merely rhetorical power. The longstanding tensions between Jamaicans and black Americans in Harlem – between Garvey and the Harlem "Niggerati", for example – attest to this crisis of affiliation. This use of language and culture, this particular intraracial silence, functions as a reaction to the shock of seeing each other; to being ambivalently placed between an assumption of racial affinity and the differential truths of black history. Once again, the "borderline" that figure so prominently in raggamuffin sound.

None of this, however, is to suggest that there is no ground of commonality – as with history, racism, slavery, exploitation. Not even the most nihilistic "dogheart" deejays would assert such a thing. By now it is clear to me that diaspora is a memory bank of signifiers and symbols of black authenticity constructed over the last century or so and is moored by an assumed racial/cultural commonality. Without this assumption there really is nothing to talk about; there really is no "we" or, in some cases, "them". But due to the assumption, there is now more exchange between and among blacknesses than there has been since the slave trade. The ragga response, however, is not to accept themselves as passive victims in an overwhelming Babylonian structure, not to represent themselves as "wailers", as victims of history belonging to a helplessly innocent race. This can be seen in the incredible boasting and self-assertions that are typical of dancehall and the "fearless" rude boys who "ride the riddim". Instead, they see themselves in many ways as being free within Babylon to destroy history and rebuild community – to, in T.S. Eliot's words, "murder and create".

Unfortunately this equation tilts too often to the "murder" side – as in two recent ragga hits, "Murder She Wrote" and "Murder Dem!" – due to the intense competition, violence and wanton bloodshed central to the crack/cocaine trade, the Jamaican record industry and the vagaries of ghetto living and grassroots capitalism. Nevertheless, the ragga are here, there, everywhere, stalking the ever-extending streets of diaspora with a lethal and dangerous style. Imagining freedom within the virtual networks of dissemination and consumption, they circulate, never achieving a fixed moment of landfall. They follow their sound and their sound follows them, defiantly asserting noisy difference in the centre of that dream space called diaspora.

> Now big up all massive, London massive, New York bad bwoy, Toronto massive-all crew! Rude bwoys a foreign and rudie's a Yard big up cause you know say all a we a Jamaicans. And we know that no dibby-dibby sound-bwoy can cross the border, cause if him test it, him a go dead-pure gun-shot inna him head! So come now, my selector, come with a next riddim cause we no skin teeth and fret fe the sound-bwoy dem. Come, raggamuffin, enter inside this ya sound. (Skyjuice, selector from Metromedia Sound System)

ACKNOWLEDGEMENTS

A slightly different version of this chapter was presented at a conference titled "Art, Aesthetics and Politics in Africa and the Caribbean", which was held at the University of California, San Diego, in 1994.

NOTES

1. Dancehall and raggamuffin ("ragga") are terms used often interchangeably to describe the new computer-driven musics coming primarily out of Jamaica in the wake of traditional reggae music and culture. Although some of it sounds merely like hi-tech reggae, most of it sounds nothing like its predecessor at all. These terms also describe the musics attendant cultural superstructure – attitudes, styles, language and sociopolitical orientation. Originally the dancehall was (and still is) the physical space – an open field, a rented auditorium – in which sound systems strung up and held public dances. It is in this context that the discourses of Jamaica's urban, working-class culture worked themselves out in sound and expressive culture.

   But I prefer to think of a difference between ragga and dancehall in much the way many see the distinction between hip-hop and rap: the latter is more commercial, dealing with the music that has got mass attention and become streamlined for popular tastes, whereas the former also connotes a culture and is more disdainful of popular acceptance.
2. Heartical respect to Welton Irie and all Ladbroke Grove massive.
3. Deejay-reggae is the form of reggae that dancehall and hip-hop descend from almost exclusively. It features the use of pre-recorded instrumental tracks ("versions") or strategic breaks in a tune as spaces for the deejay to improvise new, spoken lyrics. This form of reggae has only recently got the international attention it deserves but has ruled in Jamaica even from when Bob Marley was the global "Reggae Ambassador".
4. Sound systems are one of the black diaspora's most enduring and frequently unacknowledged cultural institutions. Although variations can be found throughout diaspora history, the

form they have today can be traced back to those mobile discotheques in Jamaica during the late 1950s/early 1960s which would set up in empty fields around the more economically depressed areas in Kingston. Cane cutters who were taken to Miami for brief stints of migrant labour would return to Jamaica with the latest R&B records and play them on homemade stereos customized to produce a level of volume that was nothing less than insane. Especially the bass frequencies. These rapidly became the only social and cultural space that catered to the ghetto dwellers. Shunning popular media – neocolonial radio and television which expressed the views of a culturally insecure elite – these systems became the primary space of cultural discourse in the vernacular. Indeed, it is this sort of discourse that reinvented Africa and celebrated Garvey where the national media evaded such issues; it is here that the fissures in the official narratives of race and nation were opened up for popular scrutiny, culminating in the development of ska, rocksteady, and then reggae and ragga.

With the migration of Jamaicans to London in the late 1950s, sound systems became a space of exile where for a loud bass-thick moment, "home" could be invented there in the midst of Babylon. With the success of West Indian music and style in England, the sound system structure was picked up by various youth subcultures who reaccentuated it, eventually creating the digital sound cultures we see throughout Europe today. And the technical and musical innovations developed in ghetto studios because of the need to circumvent the limitations of poor equipment have become standard in state-of-the-art dance music and production in the West. In New York, this alternate media structure was central to the formation of hip-hop music and the foundation of its attendant subculture.

5. Mento was the earliest music fully acknowledged as indigenously Jamaican. In the late 1950s its mixture of African and Latin percussion was the foundation upon which subsequent musical forms were built. Oddly enough, after years of bass dominated harmonies, mento has returned in Jamaican music via sampling technology which seems to inspire artists to dig into the past and reshuffle (remix) their roots.
6. A much better and more specific discussion of the sexual politics of dancehall can be found in Cooper (1989, 14).
7. "Punaany": crude slang term for the female genitalia. Usage very popular in ragga.

REFERENCES

Cooper, Carolyn. 1989/1990. "Erotic Play in the Dancehall". *Jamaica Journal* 22, no. 4: 12–20.

Fernando Jr, S.H. 1993. "Hip Hop Meets Reggae inna Soundclash". *Dub Catcher Magazine: The Soul Voice of Jamaican Roots*. Winter.

Hebdige, Dick. 1990. *Cut 'n' Mix: Culture, Identity and Caribbean Music*. London: Routledge.

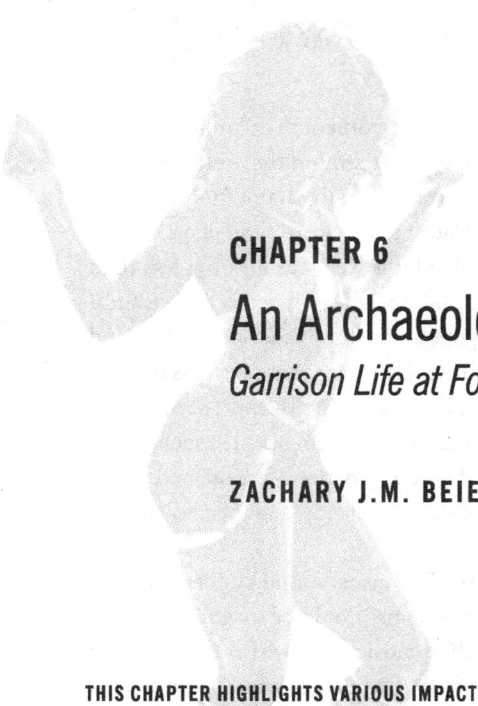

CHAPTER 6

An Archaeology of Dancehall

Garrison Life at Fort Rocky

ZACHARY J.M. BEIER

THIS CHAPTER HIGHLIGHTS VARIOUS IMPACTS OF POST-ABANDONMENT ACTIVITIES at Fort Rocky, which have transformed this site into a prominent place for the performance of contemporary Jamaican identities, especially dancehall culture, resulting in a range of material evidence. These activities, including graffiti and music video production, are potent acts of identification among segments of contemporary Jamaican society whose input is generally absent from scholarly approaches in archaeology and heritage studies. Unfortunately, these cultural formation processes (see Schiffer 2002) may be at risk of further degrading the built environment of this historical site. Heritage work at Fort Rocky should strike a balance between preserving historical contexts and recognizing the significance of contemporary popular culture appropriation practices to present a total living history of this Caribbean ruin.

When I first visited Fort Rocky in 2012 to begin archaeological investigations (see Lenik and Beier 2016), I had a defining moment of déjà vu. I had already seen this site; its intimidating entry of reinforced concrete, its crumbling foundations and scattered works of graffiti. I had seen these, not in tourist pamphlets or archaeological site reports, but in Jamaican dancehall music videos, more specifically, Mr Vegas's (2007) video for "We nuh Want no Fren/Tek Weh Yuself". During the 2012 to 2013 archaeological field seasons at Fort Rocky, this form of reclamation as well as others were palpable from awkward encounters between archaeologists and visitors hidden behind tinted automobile glass who pass through to a shady portion of the fort complex and then leave without exiting their vehicle, to the discovery of piles of reclaimed drugs burned by Jamaican authorities, and even worse, an encounter between the 2012 field crew and a recently dead body – an apparent casualty of the high crime rate characterizing urban life in Kingston. Additionally, as described in later sections, the variety of graffiti has increased over the years I have frequented the site (2012–2019).

What began strictly as an archaeological research project investigating the nature of the military community at Fort Rocky has detoured into something unexpected: an examination of the reclamation of a colonial place and its transformation into a Jamaican space through indigenous forms of cultural expression, including dancehall. This investigation imagines dancehall culture more broadly than individual vocalists and particular music style. Following the approach articulated by Sonjah Stanley Niaah (2010), dancehall culture emanates from a space created by poor Jamaicans that encompasses dance, fashion, gender politics and other cultural forms and symbols associated with inner city or garrison life. The next sections of this chapter summarize material evidence documented beginning in 2012 that illuminate patterns of cultural appropriation at Fort Rocky, in the form of graffiti and dancehall music videos.

FIGURES 6.1–6.6. Photos of Fort Rocky by the author.

AUTENTIK
L3L

18/5/2011
Skinny
&
Kartel
fuck HERE!

MORE MON

GRAFFITI

Examples of graffiti are scattered throughout the Fort Rocky complex. In general, these writings or drawings are located on the interior or exterior walls of buildings once serving the British army and local Jamaican forces. This above-ground data is largely concentrated in buildings located along the eastern and southern boundaries of the complex, including buildings listed on a 1912 "General Plan" (Jamaica – Rocky Point Record Plan, 1912, National Archives, London WO 78/4905), like the oil store, engine room, accumulator room, artillery store rooms and workshops.

Graffiti is most often associated with illicit behaviors that leave a material trace for public view. These modifications to the built environment also have an important historical and political dimension as modes of attaching meaning or affiliation to places outside the typical power structure of modern life; a form of bottom-up place-making. In the Jamaican context, murals and graffiti have previously been studied as aesthetics linked to criminal governance, political affiliations and social criticism among the urban poor (see Jaffe 2012; Jaffe, Rhiney and Francis 2012). At Fort Rocky, the earliest graffiti so far identified dates to the early-1960s, around a decade after the fort was abandoned, and extends all the way up to today. Most of the documented examples are textual forms of graffiti featuring names ("R. Kenward", "Ian Garbutt", "Rennie", "Dermont Thomas", "G. Grant", "Ivy and Blue", "Squingy and Kartel"), presumably of the author or someone familiar to them; dates ("1960", "27/3/61", "1/1/65", "11-12-77", "May 1982", "Oct 2 1982", "1992", "18/5/2011"); sometimes the author's region of origin ("Dermont Thomas, Petersfield" in Central Westmoreland; "Soltau", a region in Germany and a last name occurring in Jamaica; and "Detroit Rock"); and other associated messages and symbols, including those proclaiming love ("Ivy loves Blue"), sexual conquests ("Lacy's Playhouse was here", "Squingy and Kartel fuck here") and other coarse language ("eat pussy", "fuck standing"). This chronology of bottom-up place-making also demonstrates the presence of different styles of graffiti, with earlier versions often relying on physical etching, stencils or natural dyes like charcoal over spray paint. Perhaps this pattern of production reveals the casual and temporary nature of the encounter between author and canvas, as opposed to a consciously planned mural.

Amid the many examples of graffiti visible on the walls of Fort Rocky are materialized messages typical of dancehall culture. Participants in dancehall culture often strongly mirror sentiments tied to their communities of origins and the wider ideological networks of the urban poor (Stanley Niaah 2010). Messages like "power", "see more society" and "champion boy" communicate a desire to transform traditional perceptions of marginality into new and empowering social identities, while visual media illustrating Rasta figures or terms like "Jesus", "Yahweh", "Jehovah" and "Glory to Jah" reflect connections with Rastafarian postcolonial consciousness. Other examples of graffiti impart themes of conflict or "slackness" (see Cooper 2004 for analysis of this concept) that seep from dancehall lyrics and performance, including "Hothead", "Tek Sleep Mark Death", "Jungle Fever" and others.

Interestingly, through the course of documenting patterns of graffiti at Fort Rocky in conjunction with the analysis of dancehall music videos filmed in this space, it is apparent that certain forms of this visual media are created or used for these dancehall performances. The use of red and black paint on the interior of walls and roofs is visible in Tommy Lee Sparta's (2012) video for "Shook". I-Octane's (2012) video for "More Money" shows the painting of this slogan in bold white letters on the interior bastion walls of the complex. Romain Virgo's (2013) video for "Scary Movie" relies on a black painted star on the interior of a building. Most recently, Aidonia's (2016) video for "Trigger Work It" shows new graffiti bearing the name of the artist and his associated crew ("4th Generation"). Similarly, other artists strategically utilize preexisting graffiti from these earlier music videos. For instance, Chronixx's video for "Capture Land" (2014) at Fort Rocky uses some of these examples of graffiti created in prior video productions or performances, including "DJ firereds" on the exterior wall of the soldiers' barracks and the "More Money" slogans previously mentioned. The recently filmed video for "Ova Here" (2016) by Coco and Protoje also features slogans from the "More Money" performance. The next section more fully investigates the significance of dancehall video production at Fort Rocky.

MUSIC VIDEOS

Along with the rise of the music video in the 1980s as a popular performance and marketing device, increasing accessibility in the last twenty years to the World Wide Web and online video screening platforms like YouTube, along with video production technology (cameras and computer editing software), has resulted in the integration of Jamaica dancehall culture with this form of visual media. A successful artist is often labelled as such because of music, concert and merchandise sales, but also in terms of the number of views his or her track has received. The relative isolation of Fort Rocky from relevant authorities mixed with its relative proximity to Kingston, where many of these artists originate, and its picturesque ruinscape has lent to the use of this heritage site as a stage for many of these filmed performances.

Since beginning this research in 2012, I have identified a total of thirteen music videos filmed at this military complex by Jamaican dancehall artists, including Mr Vegas's video for "We nuh Want no Fren/Tek Weh Yuself" (uploaded in 2007), Vybz Kartel's video for "Yuh Love" (uploaded in 2009), I-Octane's video for "More Money" (uploaded in 2012), Tommy Lee Sparta's video for "Shook/Uncle Demon" (uploaded in 2012), Elephant Man's video for "Miley Cyrus Twerk" (uploaded in 2013), Romain Virgo's video for "Scary Movie" (uploaded in 2013), Chronixx's video for "Capture Land" (uploaded in 2014), Alkaline's video for "Fleek" (uploaded in 2015), Coco and Protoje's video for "Ova Here" (uploaded in 2016), Aidonia's video for "Trigger Work It" (uploaded in 2016), Gage's video for "Motivation" (uploaded in 2018), Popcaan's video for "Firm and Strong" (uploaded in 2019) and and Elephant Man's video for "Find It" (uploaded in 2019). Many of these music videos have well over one million views on YouTube, far outpacing visitor or scholarly interest in Fort Rocky. There are surely more video examples of various qualities and levels of distribution that must be added to this research project, along with interviews of artists and producers involved in performances at the site. But this sample of thirteen music videos demonstrates some interesting trends, such as the prevalence of male artists in the leading roles with women appearing as various secondary characters. Gendered identities common in contemporary Jamaican society no doubt impact the fabric of these video productions and this topic requires further investigation (see Cooper 2004; Hope 2004, 2010 for relevant discussions of gender identities in dancehall culture). Of importance to the scope of this study is the use of Fort Rocky as a symbolic stage for various filmed performances, which are popularly consumed by local, regional and international audiences.

A common use of the ruins at Fort Rocky by the sampled music videos is as a performative stage for the reinterpretation of the site's historical significance. This is a pattern where the fort is treated as a tangible blank slate, creating room for a variety of interpretations by contemporary Jamaican dancehall artists and videographers. Most of the music videos used in this analysis rely on this pattern, but it is perhaps most clearly demonstrated in examples by Mr Vegas and Elephant Man. In "We nuh Want no Fren/Tek Weh Yuself" (2007), Mr Vegas provides a "split video" featuring two opposing dancehall styles, including battle style versus ravers anthem. In the first portion of the music video titled "We nuh Want no Fren", Fort Rocky is turned into a dark, masculine scene filled with cowboy fashioned figures who could have been pulled out of the "American Old West". In the second portion of the music video, entitled "Tek Weh Yuself", Fort Rocky shifts from dark to light and features a series of dancers from different crews carrying out intricate choreographed dance moves, which are dominant features of affiliation and expression among dancehall participants. Similarly, Elephant Man's music video for "Miley Cyrus Twerk" (2013) reimagines this World War-era fort into a seat of power for a classic Egyptian ruler. In this transformation, King Elephant Man is surrounded by his masculine legions and scantily clad female attendants who showcase dance moves from dancehall culture, in this case in the form of crouched gyrating of the backside ("twerking").

In a similar fashion, other Jamaican dancehall artists use Fort Rocky as a performative stage to impart an ominous and foreboding social environment, perhaps reminiscent of the harsh realities of contemporary garrison life in Kingston and elsewhere in Jamaica. These portrayals are typically devoid of any real connection to a particular historical context but instead highlight the darkness and crude nature of this isolated ruin. This trend is best seen in videos by Tommy Lee, Romain Virgo and Alkaline. For instance, in both Tommy Lee Sparta's video for "Shook/Uncle Demon" (2012) and Romain Virgo's video for "Scary Movie" (2013), Fort Rocky is turned into a horror world filled with blood, gore and dancehall culture; a space that arouses fear and avoidance strategies.

Finally, the ruins at Fort Rocky are used as a performative stage for promoting social and historical consciousness. This is a trend rarely seen among the documented examples of music videos filmed at this site, but is apparent in I-Octane's video for "More Money" (2012), a song set in a post-apocalyptic environment where contemporary Jamaican "ghetto youth" are rioting using song and dance as their weapon for greater social and economic access. Chronixx's music video for "Capture Land" (2014) is the clearest example of the use of Fort Rocky in the promotion of social and historical consciousness. This video features Fort Rocky along with scenes from other sites of colonialism, including Port Royal (Fort Charles/Victoria Battery), Spanish Town and downtown Kingston. In this song, Chronixx proclaims that the powers that be "turn[ed] paradise into plantation", and as a result, "Rasta nah live on no capture land." The music video relies on these scenes of captured lands, like Fort Rocky, to provide a potent critique of colonialism in contemporary society, using the ruins of this unequal and invasive endeavor.

CONCLUSION: GARRISON CULTURAL HERITAGE

Investigations at the ruins at Fort Rocky have attempted to capture the movements in and out of this garrison during the colonial period and in the recent past. Historically, colonial governments abandoned military garrisons following the end of global hostilities and colonialism. A trend observed among Caribbean plantation archaeologists is the movement of descendants of enslaved Africans back into previous areas of authority, an activity interpreted as an overt response to that power (Armstrong 1990, 91). I believe this type of re-entrance and appropriation of former spaces of colonialism is a distinctive feature of African-Caribbean societal formation. Post-abandonment acts of identification at Fort Rocky contribute to the creation of "a new palimpsest of national identity" (Paul 2009, 176) outside formal government authorization. The layering and connectivity of history that this concept implies is a common theme in Caribbean history but has largely been considered as political manoeuvring by the ruling class to engineer a sense of unity in a highly fractious postcolonial state. The evidence of graffiti and music videos at Fort Rocky demonstrates attempts to revise the institutional qualities of colonialism with new signs, some with clear connections to dancehall culture originating among the urban poor in Kingston, which are more attune to contemporary modes of being in Jamaica. With the application of graffiti to a now crumbling wall or the coordination of choreography to the rhythm of dancehall on different built features of this military installation, these contemporary visitors to Fort Rocky seemingly make the colonial minority, the entity most responsible for the production of history, invisible, or at least the backdrop of more significant actions. But these transformations are not entirely free from the past. Certain elements remain, including this military site's long-standing association with hyper-masculine functions and the representation of women as ephemeral and highly sexualized objects.

In the eyes of many, especially heritage managers, historians and archaeologists, these contemporary movements into this historical site are associated with the behaviors of squatters, trespassers and the uninformed. While the ruins of Fort Rocky must be preserved for further research and public interpretation, this site's contribution to memories and narratives central to national and cultural identity should not be defined in strictly historiographical and archaeological terms (for example, documents, architecture and artefacts). The anthropological process of how contemporary Caribbean societies deal with their ruins must be included in heritage work at Fort Rocky, along with the multiple voices involved in its survival, to provide individuals and groups a space outside the mainstream where alternative histories can be made. This will involve creative conservation strategies linking historical sites like Fort Rocky to sectors of Jamaican popular culture through various public/private and local/international partnerships. Ideally, Fort Rocky can serve as both a reminder of the past and a stage for the present to perform their future.

In a region that has traditionally been written about, this chapter lets the history of the region write itself. In this way, the ruins of the Caribbean, primarily plantations and forts, can be imagined as more than fixed strategic points along a Eurocentric map and instead as places of becoming. History, archaeology and heritage studies must strive to make their messages accessible and relevant so this information can begin to be more effectively dispersed through channels of popular culture and consciousness.

REFERENCES

Armstrong, Douglas V. 1990. *The Old Village and the Great House: An Archaeological and Historical Examination of Drax Hall Plantation, St Ann's Bay, Jamaica*. Urbana: University of Illinois Press.

Cooper, Carolyn. 2004. *Sound Clash: Jamaican Dancehall Culture at Large*. New York: Palgrave Macmillan.

Hope, Donna P. 2004. "The British Link-Up Crew: Consumption Masquerading as Masculinity in the Dancehall". *International Journal of Postcolonial Studies* 6, no. 1: 101–17.

———. 2010. *Man Vibes: Masculinities in the Jamaican Dancehall*. Kingston: Ian Randle.

Jaffe, Rivke. 2012. "The Popular Culture of Illegality: Crime and the Politics of Aesthetics in Urban Jamaica". *Anthropological Quarterly* 85, no. 1: 79–102.

Jaffe, Rivke, Kevon Rhiney and Cavell Francis. 2012. "'Throw Word': Graffiti, Space and Power in Kingston, Jamaica". *Caribbean Quarterly* 58, no. 1: 1–20.

Lenik, Stephan, and Zachary J.M. Beier. 2016. "Military and Military Life in the British Caribbean: Historical Archaeology of Fort Rocky, Kingston Harbor, Jamaica (ca. 1880–1945)". In *Spaces in Between: Archaeologies of Freedom and Slavery in the Caribbean*, edited by Lynsey Bates, John M. Chenoweth and James Delle, 279–306. Gainesville: University Press of Florida.

Paul, Annie. 2009. "'Do You Remember the Days of Slav'ry?' Connecting the Present with the Past in Contemporary Jamaica". *Slavery and Abolition* 30, no. 2: 169–78.

Schiffer, Michael Brian. 2002. *Behavioral Archaeology*. New York: Percheron Press.

Stanley Niaah, Sonjah. 2010. *Dancehall: From Slave Ship to Ghetto*. Ottawa: University of Ottawa Press.

CHAPTER 7

Sampling City

Kingston in the Social Imaginary of Jamaican Popular Music

ANNA KASAFI PERKINS

JAMAICA'S CAPITAL CITY, KINGSTON (AND ITS INNER-CITY COMMUNITIES such as Trench Town and Tivoli Gardens, and the various neighbourhoods of the adjoining parish of St Andrew such as Waterhouse and Seaview Gardens), is the birthplace of dancehall and a centre of cultural creativity in the Caribbean (Howard 2012). Indeed, Kingston's seminal role in the creative industry in Jamaica was recognized in 2015, when it was named one of UNESCO's creative cities of music,[1] having given birth not just to dancehall but six other distinct popular musical genres in the twentieth century, including reggae, ska and rocksteady. Stanley Niaah (2010) and Howard (2015) provide three potent and interweaving images of Kingston as sacred drum, echo chamber and amphitheatre. All three highlight the geographical location of Kingston, with its mountain backdrop and natural harbour in which daily life is performed and transported across the globe via music. Physically and metaphorically, therefore, Kingston is a creative space in which postcolonial subjects script their life stories through music and transmit them to the world. Unsurprisingly, therefore, performing artistes, especially deejays, regularly "big up" "City Kingston"[2] in their performances and name check the capital and its environs in numerous tunes.

Even so, commentator Mel Cooke (2010) maintains, in his discussion of Josey Wales's "Kingston Hot", that not many songwriters make Kingston proper a topic of their creations. Indeed, he argues:

> Few song writers take on Kingston. While parts of Kingston – notably the "garrison" areas – and some of its more striking residents have consistently made their way into popular song, relatively few songwriters have taken on Jamaica's capital as a whole. Ironically, two such songs, the 1970 "Kingston Town" by Trinidadian-turned-Jamaican Lord Creator done over by British band UB40 in 1990 and Italy-born Albarosie's 2009 song of the same title but of different composition, were done by non-Jamaicans.

If "taking on" Kingston is to be judged simply by the number of compositions with "Kingston" in their titles that may appear to be the case. However, innumerable tracks directly reference Kingston even when titles give little indication that will be the case. One example: Duane Stephenson's version of "Think Twice" (2011). Stephenson croons, "Just think about it, life in Kingston Town." Cooke (2010) himself reminds us of Chalice's song "Heroes" (1985), which reflects on the dangerous underbelly of Kingston. Similarly, indirect references abound with mentions of "ghetto" and "ghetto people", who reflect the place from which they hail – for example Richie Spice's "Ghetto Girl" (2004), who is ambitious, a warrior and a champion; she just needs a chance. Or Baby Cham's very popular "Ghetto Story" (2006), which is a narrative of survival in the face of overwhelming odds in inner-city Kingston. Indeed, it is possible to argue that Kingston and its inner-city communities are dramatis personae in these musical offerings (much in the same way Jamaica is imaged as a woman being wooed in Chronixx's "Smile Jamaica" [2013]). At the same time, Kingston functions as an important part of the very social imaginary of the inhabitants of the capital itself. Stanley Niaah (2010) confirms this point when she notes that "dancehall displays an emphasis on space and locality in the movement and lyrics highlighting the city, the area, the ghetto, the street or other socio-political data" (31).

This chapter explores the nature of the city of Kingston, as it is present in the social imaginary of Jamaicans, particularly as it is expressed through popular music, notably dancehall. It argues that it may well be the case that the idea of Kingston in the urban social imaginary has changed over time, from a space of celebration (the 1970s) to be one of danger and violence post-1980, "the end of the decade that changed the city forever" (Cooke 2010). Yet, this proposed trajectory is complicated by the presence of contending images even in the presence of the identified dominant tropes. The discussion proceeds by "sampling" select iconic tracks from various genre in a more or less chronological fashion: Lord Creator's "Kingston Town" (1970), Toots and the Maytals' "Funky Kingston" (1973), Josey Wales's "Kingston Hot" (1982), Damian "Jr Gong" Marley's "Kingston 12" (featuring Stephen Marley, 1996), Alborosie's "Kingston Town" (2008), Busy Signal's "Kingston Town" (featuring Jr Gong, 2011), Proteje's "Kingston Be Wise" (2012), Toian's "Kingston Town" (2014) and Vybz Kartel's "Downtown Kingston" (2014). They will be woven together in the telling of the story of Kingston since independence. These sample tunes all feature the name "Kingston" in their titles and may themselves be sampling other songs.[3] Sampling in popular music can be seen as intertextuality at play through the deliberate referencing or alluding to other songs and melodies in a later piece. Unsurprisingly, this short list is composed of mainly dancehall songs, currently the most popular genre of Jamaican music. This may well be so also because the discussion focuses on Kingston and Kingston is the spatial centre of dancehall (Stanley Niaah 2010).

SOCIAL IMAGINARY

Social imaginary is an important concept in the socio-spatial experience of people; it refers to "the way ordinary people 'imagine' their social surroundings . . . carried in images, stories, and legends . . . it is shared by large groups of people, if not the whole society . . . the social imaginary is that common understanding that makes possible common practices and a widely shared sense of legitimacy" (Taylor 2002 in Jaffe 2012b, 676). Undoubtedly, popular music forms a part of the social imaginary of the inner-city dwellers in Kingston as it carries images and stories that make possible common ways of being for ghetto dwellers, in particular. Jamaican popular music also provides a sense of legitimacy about the ways that they respond as ghetto people. Essentially, dancehall, for example, functions as *text* that can be *read* to uncover the social imaginary that it expresses and shapes. It is an authorized mode of constructing shared meaning (Jaffe 2012b).[4] At the same time, real and diverse experiences and memories of the city are always multiple and can never be grasped fully in the present or past by any one person. Other cultural modes of expression have contributed to Kingston's social imaginary alongside popular music – art and sculpture, literature, poetry and media discourse. These modes of expressions are at the same time part of the social imaginary, as they "both reflect upon and contribute to the collective imaginings of Kingston" (Evans 2014, 87). Shara McCallum (2011) demonstrates this in "Psalm for Kingston":

> City that lives under a long-memoried sun
> where the gunmen of my childhood have been replaced
> by dons that rule the neighbourhood as fiefdoms, where violence
> and beauty still lie down together. City of my birth –
> if I forget thee, who will I be, singing the Lord's song in this strange land?

The common understanding of Kingston shared between McCallum's poem and other examples of popular music is telling. McCallum is a Jamaican in diaspora, who is remembering intertextually the changes in the life of a city in which beauty and violence are intertwined.

This exploration is meaningful as popular music shares in the social imaginary of the Jamaican people, especially those of inner-city Kingston, whose reality it gives expression to as well as shapes. Indeed, the social imaginary of the ordinary person shapes commonly held practices and conveys a sense of legitimacy as they negotiate quotidian activities. It can therefore be argued that dancehall conveys the social imaginary of its creators as well as being a part of the social imaginary itself. As will be argued, an important element in the social imaginary of Kingston is the city as a social space of marginalization and exclusion, usually captured in the idea of the ghetto. In particular, ghetto life for Kingston and its environs, several of which are garrison communities,[5] includes experiences of deprivation, violence and danger. This is in line with Jaffe (2012a), who argues that the ghetto is a discursive space that refers specifically to urban experiences of socio-spatial marginalization in black popular culture, including dancehall. In Jaffe's analysis, this idea of the ghetto as a space of social immobility, whether actual or real, is a mobile social imaginary and travels across various international, racial, ethnic and other borders. Jaffe (2012a) argues, however, that, dancehall, even more than any other Jamaican musical genre, embraces the imaginary of the ghetto.

This idea of social imaginary has much in common with Stanley Niaah's performance geography in which she argues that certain urban spaces like downtown Kingston,

Jamaica, and Laventille, Trinidad, have "produced particular 'brands' of performance, with unique citizenry and community-building strategies" (2010, 36). Such citizens suffer from the effects of a triple form of exile which impacts their core creative energies. They are exiled from their ancestral origins as descendants of formerly enslaved Africans; further, they are exiled physically, politically and economically, which is compounded by the second exile which "militates against progress toward personal and collective aspirations, visions of self, and advancement generally" (2010, 36). Yet, even in the face of such exiles, the inhabitants manage to draw upon reserves of creativity and innovation, which are demonstrated in the ghetto stories that abound in the popular music imaginary. Even so, Stanley Niaah makes the claim that dancehall maintains a tenuous space in the popular consciousness of Jamaica given that sentiments vary as to the life-giving nature of the space, with concomitant arguments for censorship of the space and the performances arising from the space. Indeed, she argues further that dancehall occupies ambivalent spaces in Jamaican consciousness – by occupying marginal spaces while at the same time being simultaneously central to national identity.

KING'S TOWN OR JAH JAH CITY

Lucy Evans warns that Kingston accommodates multiple realities such that it is futile trying to get to "the real Kingston" (2014, 114). "Given the division of the city into socially polarised micro-communities, and bearing in mind its complex social and political history, it would be impossible for any writer [or singer] to capture Kingston in its entirety; any account of the city is necessarily limited and partial" (114). As such, middle-class or even imperial perceptions of the city are critiqued while being accepted as part of the city's complex imaginary.

Kingston was founded in 1692, after the destruction of Port Royal by an earthquake. At that time, Jamaica was a plantation society under British rule and slavery was in full swing. The British had a way of naming places throughout their empire recalling the historic ownership of the land by the Crown. So, on one level, the name "Kingston" – "the King's town" – resonates with the echoes of empire. King William III was on the throne when Kingston was established, although it was not declared Jamaica's capital until 1872, during the reign of Queen Victoria. In that sense, the power of the British monarch was stamped on the very centre of Jamaican life. One another level, King's to(w)n is now to be recognized as the "Jah Jah City" of conscious Rastafarian artiste Capleton. Kingston is reclaimed for its "rightful ruler", His Imperial Majesty Emperor Haile Selassie I, King of Kings and Lord of Lords. Capleton[6] lashes out against happenings in Kingston that want to turn it into a "cowboy town", "a bloody town", instead of acknowledging its true identity as "Jah Jah Town". So, like the country of which it is the capital, Jahmekyah (Jamaica), Kingston embodies something of the sacred in relationship to Jah Jah (King of Kings and Lord of Lords). Even when it is not acknowledged or efforts are made to erase it, this sacred positioning may never be far off in the lyrical homage paid to the King's to(w)n.

1970S: WHEN I AM KING

Lord Creator's "Kingston Town", which was recorded in 1970 for producer Clancy Eccles, is the habitat of earthly kings or, as Rasta would call them, "kingman". A Trinidad-born soca and calypso artiste, Lord Creator (born Kentrick Patrick) is considered one of the influential outside forces in the development of Jamaican music. In 1962, he recorded "Independent Jamaica",[7] the tune that marked Jamaica's independence from Britain. Indeed, it was independence that freed King's town to be claimed by its true monarch. Lord Creator's first-recorded calypso classic, "Jamaica Farewell", is permeated with upbeat if nostalgic notions of the King's to(w)n: "Sad to say, I'm on my way / . . . had to leave a little girl [i.e., a girlfriend] in Kingston town." (Like "Kingston Town", "Jamaica Farewell" has been covered several time, by artistes like Harry Belafonte and Jimmy Buffett.). "Kingston Town" is iconic in setting the tone of Kingston as an idyllic space for romance. Kingston has a softer, lighter side. This is visible again in Toian's 2014 song "Kingston Town".

Lord Creator's "Kingston Town" represents a powerful part of the imaginary about Kingston that is also played out in the calypso-influenced tunes mentioned previously. These songs tell stories of magic and happiness that are also reflected in nights that fade while "moonlight lingers on", "wonders for everyone", "stars shine so bright" for "there is magic in Kingston town". Like "Jamaica Farewell", "Kingston Town" is a place that is longed for and valued more than the whole world ("If I had the whole world / I would give it away / just to see the girls at play"). A clear attraction of this magical town is the presence of the girls who play enticingly; one of these girls is the future "queen" to Lord Creator's "king". He is clear that he is a king in King's to(w)n. His queen will come at dawn (after the playing) and "she'll be waiting in Kingston town" – surely the place for true romance. One day when they are together he will have "a palace and everything" – all the trappings of royalty/divinity. This is a town caught between modernization and Westernization and shadowed by an inward turn to celebrate "blackness" and Jamaican culture (Witmer 1987).

This magical King's town is the same Kingston that three years later Toots Hibbert celebrates as "Funky", that good old African American word[8] that means having a strong dance rhythm. (Of course, a secondary meaning these days is around a bad or sour smell and could well be used to describe the inner city.) Toots, as one of the musicians who created Jamaica's indigenous popular styles, would be described by Witmer (1987, 19) as "bimusical", that is, "functioning in the American-based popular music culture of their capital city, . . . hav[ing] had some familiarity with various vernacular musical styles and practices, for example, Jamaican mento and Afro-Christian cult music, Trinidadian calypso, and various styles and genres of Latin American and Caribbean music". Toots's Kingston is suffused with music that makes the listener want to "shake it shake it, baby". The funk is in the guitar and the piano. In the reggae. From east to west(ern) Kingston, Toots, not girls, plays this funky music. The girls dance and shake in earnest. From north to south, Toots plays his funky rocksteady-cum-reggae beat and ushers in the reggae genre. (His 1968 single "Do the Reggay" was the first song to first use the word "reggae". It is credited with naming the genre and introducing it to a global audience.) The playfulness of Lord Creator and the playing of funky sounds are to be contrasted to the dire statement that "Kingston a no play thing, no keyboard nah guitar" that would arise twenty-plus years later in Busy Signal and Jr Gong's "Kingston Town". By then King's town had changed dramatically and the danger and menace lurking quietly in the wings were now characteristic of the royal city.

FUN(K)Y KINGSTON NO MORE

"Funky Kingston" is the third track on the album *Funky Kingston* (1973) by Toots and the Maytals. Ulibas (2016) describes the song as "laid back . . . paint[ing] a vivid soundscape of the happenings of Kingston, Jamaica. Toots' rough vocals and the backing harmonies and rocking backing track provided by the Maytals make this tune a funky trip." The musical offerings are celebrated as "funky", thereby bestowing funkiness on their place of origin: Kingston. At a live performance of the song for Winterland, San Francisco, California, in 1975, Toots can be heard in the intro ad libbing, "Music is one of God's gift / going to find some way to make it." And have fun(k) in the process. "Fun(k)y Kingston" is what is being offered to the listeners. Again, there is no hint in this track of any discord, although there was unease aplenty in the socio-political sphere with democratic socialism in full swing in the shadow of the Cold War. Political violence was on the rise and in 1976, for example, an attempt was made to assassinate Bob Marley after he was perceived as being in support of one political party. He fled into voluntary exile in the United Kingdom, only to return in 1978 for a peace concert aimed at uniting the warring political tribes. This is the kind of discord and violence that spilled over into the 1980s with full-scale political violence that saw the inhabitants of Kingston bitterly divided among themselves between the two major political parties. As Mel Cooke (2010) reminds readers, 1980 was a turning point in Jamaica's political history, with over eight hundred people killed in the run-up to the October 1980 general elections. But clearly, the totality of Kingstonians' reality in the 1970s was not the burgeoning political violence or the material deprivation of democratic socialism. Popular music opened the possibility of imagining a different reality. Kingston can indeed accommodate multiple realities, as Evans warned.

1980S: KINGSTON HOT

After the "magical" moments of the early 1970s, the stories give way to some common themes of death, poverty, violence and murder in the 1980s, 1990s[9] and 2000s, as the lyrical offerings from that period demonstrate. Indeed, such offerings record historical events in song "rather than primarily in the official annals or history books" (Jaffe 2012b, 688). The aural-historical-political records of reggae and dancehall are part of a longer tradition of Caribbean music documenting and circulating news of events, as well as offering incisive critique and celebrating achievements evident in forms like calypso.

"Kingston Hot" by "the Outlaw" Josey Wales provides an "aural-historical-political record" of life in downtown Kingston in the run up to the 1980 elections. In painting the scene, Wales describes youth hustling "selling kisko pops",[10] dreadlocks jogging in tracksuits (referencing the style started by Bob Marley and other prominent Rastas like footballer Alan "Skill" Cole); however, the unfolding spectre of violence in the shape of tribal war had already raised its head and Wales laments the presence of this war in the ghetto, which has led to his children and grandmother being killed (not a real event). Even the trek from King Street to North Parade in the heart of the commercial section of the city is a source of fear for those who know he continually walks that route. Wales had personal reasons to be afraid; he had been shot on two different occasions.[11] "Kingston Hot" clearly does not refer to the ambient temperature but rather the tense social environment. Indeed, ten years later, Josey Wales recounts his intent: "(I mean) politically hot. If a man inna him green[12] an go down so him get caught up. If a man inna him orange and him go up so him get caught up" (Cooke 2010). His was "a commentary on the actions and the state and the structure of Jamaica at the time" (Cooke 2010). The "especially hot areas at the time" were downtown Kingston, Kingston 11, 12 and 13, Tower Hill, Waterhouse, Cockburn Pen, Drewsland, Majesty Gardens, and Payne Land – all parts of City Kingston. "All those people were at each other's throats politically. . . . Is the system set it that way. Is not the brethren's desire. Is the 'politrickshan'."[13] I was pointing out how cruel it was" (Cooke 2010).

Even the famed peace treaty of 26 August 1988 did not end the aggression and violence. (A similar peace treaty had been called by the gang leaders in 1978. They persuaded Bob Marley to return to Jamaica to stage the One Love Peace Concert, at which he asked Michael Manley and Edward Seaga, then leaders of the warring political parties, to shake hands.) The peace treaty was an "agreement and declaration on political conduct" outlining limits to political actions and establishing a bipartisan committee to settle grievances (Kurlanksy 1988). Any action intended "to provoke, threaten or intimidate", along with personal attacks on candidates and their families, were prohibited. Peter Tosh mocks this 1978 peace treaty in a song of the same name (1983), and, in his usual artful way, deconstructs the meaning of King's town and treaty: "Do you remember the peace treaty? / You sign in a *kill some city* / Do you remember the peace treaty? / Them sign in a *kill some city*" (emphasis added). Tosh recalls the failed 1978 Treaty and the One Love Peace Concert at which he was the only one to raise concerns and denounce hypocrisy (Ehrengardt 2012/2013). By the 1980s, Kingston had indeed become "Kill-some City", a place marked by death where even peace treaties join bodies in the cemetery. Furthermore, the very essence of the city is that it is "kill some shitty".[14]

2010: KINGSTON NO WISE

So too, Proteje's "Kingston Be Wise" is part of the aural-historical-political record. YouTube describes the track as "a short story based on the events of 23 May 2010, when the Jamaican government deployed its military might into Tivoli Gardens in the Capital city of Kingston". Tivoli Gardens, often described as "the mother of all garrisons", was then the base of feared gang leader and area don Christopher "Dudus" Coke. When the smoke cleared after the incursion, more than seventy persons had been killed, including one member of the security forces, but only six guns were recovered. An entire community was traumatized and Christopher Coke, the gang leader whom the incursion was meant to capture for extradition to the United States, at that point, was not found. This leads Proteje to lament, "Nuff bodies unidentified and just a lie deh / then where the gun deh? Dead pon Saturday / Buried Sunday like Solomon O'Gundy." He raises the image of unclaimed bodies piled in the graveyard at May Pen Cemetery (Schwartz 2011). He questions the value of the lives of the residents of Tivoli, who were adjudged to be necessary sacrifices as bearers of collective guilt for the way Coke ran things in "the Garden", as Tivoli is often called (Schwartz 2011).[15]

Onomatopoeic sounds litter the lyrics of the post-1980 samples. All focused on guns and shooting: "ratatatatana" in Albarosie's "Kingston Town" (the bark of guns); click-clack-blow" in Proteje's "Kingston Be Wise" (sound of guns being cocked and fired?), "ratta-tatta-tatta when you pow-pow-pow" in Proteje's "Kingston Be Wise" (shots firing). Guns pervade the space: "machines", "things", "M-16 of the security forces". Perhaps there is reason for Italian-born deejay Alborosie to repeat over and over again "siblilidowndown",[16] which may well be an entreaty to "simmer things down, down". No one is pardoned in the murder spree, which, according to Alborosie, rivals 9/11's body count. Killings of the old and young are the results of the actions of both security forces ("Squaddy",[17] "Babylon",[18] "plain clothes",[19] "Ratty",[20] JDF,[21] "Soldier man in them lorry"[22]) and the shottas/rude bwoys/badmen. Both are a "set a monster" in Alborosie's eyes, as they

> dig more grave than rooms upa Hilton
> Small community get wash out by a blood storm
> every weekend same routine
> what you function
> push them cause more dead than 9/11 destruction.

The highest rates of homicide are found in Kingston's inner-city communities (Figueroa et al. 2008 in Jaffe 2012a). The response to these high homicide rates has included law enforcement strategies that are increasingly militarized, as the Tivoli incursion demonstrates. Tough policing has led to the high incidence of fatal shootings by police and communities filled with hatred and fear of "plain clothes [policemen]", "di ratty and di squaddy patrol a drive up" (see Ehrengardt 2012/2013).

Recurring images of death and dying are seen in contrasting descriptions of blood on the ground against the backdrop of white sand (Alborosie) or coffins and graves. Amid this is the smell of and sale of ganja (weed, marijuana; aili [oilie]).[23] Extortion is rife: "Extortion pressuring the shops 'pon di lane'" – according to Busy Signal and Jr Gong. The image of outlawry is flavoured by the beloved Westerns that influence the framing of the badman/rude boy ghetto persona.[24] The King's town is now a rude boy town (Albarosie), an outlaw town; it is "a Wile Wile West show down" (Busy Signal and

Jr Gong). The full moon no longer gives light to a beautiful night but is rather a sign of danger, as dogs howl a warning (as in Busy Signal and Jr Gong's "Kingston Town").

As things heated up in 1980s, the Outlaw called upon Almighty God and his belief in Jah Jah as his source of protection – "inna Jah Jah mi put mi trus(t)" (Josey Wales, "Kingston Hot"). The presence of a pastor "in him long black gown" intoning "ashes to ashes / dus(t) to dus(t)" alludes to a funeral for someone killed in the tribal warfare of the 1980s. Josey Wales himself escaped, narrowly "reach[ing] Dovecot [Cemetery] / in criss board box / with looking glass pon top".[25] The biblical story of Lot's wife turning into a pillar of salt (Genesis 19:26) is prominently referenced. "Just like how Lot wife tun a pilla a salt / yout can't fine food a no Jah Jah fault." Wales muses that "it dread [i.e., things are difficult] pon poor people an even [a]ristocrat"! This is a later realization as earlier in the track the suggestion was that the rich were at ease with "di rich man siddung and a smoke him cigar" while the youth have to be hustling. The cigar smoking contrasts with the ganja smoking of the inner city that is present in several of the tracks. The "squaddy a patrol a drive up" leads to the "man with wid weed run anna de hide" (Busy Signal and Jr Gong) because "JDF a move rough / dem buss di M-16 / . . . The smell of marijuana round the corner dem juggling [hustling]" (Proteje). Juggling connotes attempts at survival both legal and illegal. This is part of the informal economy which has burgeoned in inner-city Kingston due to a decline in the formal economy in the 1980s: "Whereas the informal economy has had the beneficial effects of helping the poor to make ends meet and frequently even smoothed operations in the formal sector, it also lent itself to illegal activities – drug deals, large scale fraud, money laundering and black market foreign exchange trading" (Johnson 2005, 583).

Lord Creator's "king" of King's town, by the early 2000s, has become a king / don fighting for turf and taking lives. "Every man a fight fi wear di king's crown" (Busy Signal). But in fact, Alborosie is clear that "there's no crown and no throne / it ago lick you down / wi di dancehall soun". Even dancehall has become a weapon of sorts. The men are now rudeboys and shottas,[26] who "show off girls and bling" (Alborosie). In these sampled tracks, these girls are no longer described as simply queens but as tricksters on the make/take (Alborosie):

> Di gal dem pants tight like rubber suit
> and dem blouse tight supn hide up perfect boobs
> dem always a smile if you go baby hi
> dem a go play you one trick if you a mama's boy.

A man is no more lover but a mark to be conned and ridiculed. Furthermore, there is no more "palace and everything". It is a "tough man town / there's no crown and no throne" (Alborosie). Lots of coffins, graves and wreaths are on offer, though. Capleton in "Jah Jah City" calls it a "cowboy town", a "badman town", which progresses to a "dead man town", "a bloody city, bloody town" where "dem promote too much death".

Money ("green" in Alborosie and "billfold" in Capleton) is key. The darkside of Kingston is seen where every man wears a frown or "a screw face", which denotes seriousness of purpose. "Fi a next man survive one haffi get throw down." The idea of a brutal dog eat dog world is deepened by further canine imagery: "hyena nyam yuh food or greyhound / . . . dogs a howl / . . . dem savage like animal". The idea of murder, displacement, coup d'état are all present in the idea of "throw down".[27]

The heights of poverty are the "mad man[28] [who] get him food straight outta di garbage bin" (Alborosie). Their imaginary is fuelled by shared emotions of fear, love, awe and trust in dons, on whom many depend for their daily livelihood. The irony of their existence is that most inner-city dwellers remain mired in poverty while the dons have amassed enormous personal wealth through their illegal activities. These dons maintain their political connections to Green (Jamaica Labour Party) and Orange (People's National Party) without the previous clientelistic dependence. In the past, gangs depended on political patronage to survive; however, this relationship has broken down with the reduced resources available to bestow political patronage and obtain loyalty, protection and votes. Gangs have now branched off into their own criminal enterprises, like drugs and extortion, although maintaining ties to politicians. "To this day, Jamaica is still waiting to recover from the wounds" inflicted by such politician-led and supported violence (Ehrengardt 2012/2013).

2014: PLAY BY THE KING(MAN)

Forty-seven years after Lord Creator does his "Kingston Town", up and coming female dancehall artiste Toian sings of her "Kingston Town" (2014). American-born MoBay-grown Toian Keisha Gichie was not born when Creator was creating, the Maytals were getting funky or even Wales was beating the heat. By 1991, when she was born, much had changed, as Josey Wales, Alborosie, and Busy Signal and Jr Gong demonstrate. Yet, she demonstrates that the romantic idea of Kingston town is not totally lost. Toian expresses a longing for Kingston, due to the presence of a lover ("king", "bwoi", "bae-ae-ae"), whom she has not seen in a while; this is central to her desire to get to town quickly: "It's been a while, mi nuh see yuh baby (ayyy) / Oh boy, me soon reach a Ochi." She leaves MoBay[29] early to take advantage of the modern highway, which will get her to Town and into his arms quickly. Her lover is not a dream to be sought after like Lord Creator's queen, but a real king(man) to play by. The idea of the king(man)[30] may be present in Toian's yearning: "Play by the king, cause love is all I bring / This dedicate to di ones in Constant Spring / Ooooh yeah-eah-eah." Echoes of Althea and Donna's popular 1978 reggae tune "Uptown Top Rankin" can be heard in these lyrics, which "sample" that hit. This is a clear case of intertexuality giving voice to Kingston in the imaginary. Given that she is going into Town to see him and not vice versa suggests that she may play by his rules. There may still be an element of playfulness and magic that gets expressed by "Mi lef' wid yuh heart / me a bring it back again". Kingston town can still be a place of romance and happiness.

DOWN A TOWN KINGSTON

Is there a lighter side in all of this? "Downtown Kingston" was also released in 2014 by Vybz Kartel's babymother Tanesha "Shorty" Williams, through her Short Boss Music Productions. It is one of the tunes released by Shorty while Kartel was incarcerated, hence the appellation given to the artiste: "Adi the Innocent". This was part of an attempt to rehabilitate Kartel in the eyes of the public. He has since been sentenced for murder and is awaiting his appeal. Interestingly, the tune celebrates Kingston as the commercial mecca of Jamaica, where just about everything is available for sale. No hint is given of any danger or disturbance. Kingston is the place that "mek tings happen". The lyrics are delivered in a fast paced upbeat fashion and the listener cannot help but smile at the litany.

Kartel names all the streets on which selling of all kind takes place:

> Orange Street and Princess Street
> Plus Fudge Street and Kings Street
> East Queen Street . . .
> Matches Lane,[31] Luke Lane.

These are the very streets that in "Kingston Hot" posed a danger to traverse. Some things have changed for the better but the city is still a dangerous place, as other artistes continue to lament. The tempo and lyrics of the chorus mimics the tone and pace of in-store hawkers who blazon their store's wares over microphones and pull window shoppers in with the "big soun" "string up" by the store owner:

> You waan get a sale
> come roun here
> you waan buy hair
> come roun here
> yo waan buy a chain
> come roun here.
>
> Downtown Kingston mek tings happen . . .
> waan buy a plane or a name
> . . . everything deya . . .
> everyting sell a town
> you can go de black and lef de brown.

Perhaps the references to changes in colour and name are direct wry reflections on his own circumstances with skin bleaching (see Brown-Glaude 2013) controversies and regular new self-bestowed epithets: "Adi di Daddi", "Teacha", "Voice of the Ghetto" and now "Adi di Innocent". Downtown Kingston is displayed as a place of energy and opportunity through commercial trade.

Not to be ignored are the garrisons like "Kingston 12" – Trench Town – an eponymous track from Jr Gong's 1996 album *Mr Marley*, in which he pays homage to his father's music. Jr Gong celebrates Trench Town (the locale that nourished his father's music and was the prototype of the garrison system) in this updating/sampling of Bob Marley's "Trench Town Rock". This is the community that Ehrengardt (2012/2013) introduces thus: "Welcome to Kingston 12, Trench Town – an urban ghetto with its small streets, its *maga* (meagre) dogs, its walls crumbling down, its filth and misery. Violence dwells here. Even when you can't see it, you can feel its almost unbearable pressure – like a deafening mute cry" (47). Ehrengardt opines that the little community of Trench Town has been through many tempests (some of it captured in the music of Bob Marley) and its drift downwards is a very symbol of the downward spiral of the Jamaican nation itself.

Still, Jr Gong reminds us of the less dominant but always lurking images of Kingston and emphasizes that all is not bad in Kingston 12: "a lot of goody goody [good people] in Kingston 12; no licky licky [greedy people], non-progressives or lazibodies [lazy people] wanted in Kingston 12". In keeping with the often-present religious flavour of Jamaican tunes, he encourages the reading of the scriptures: "A chapter a day keeps the devil away, so read your Bible and go down on your knees and pray . . . no waan yuh fi galang so / no waan yuh fi cole mi up." He, of course, is echoing his sire by intertextually referencing his music. At the same time, he calls for ghetto people to get a hearing: "Go down in the Ghetto and hear what the people say [about themselves and their experience]." His music is one way of unveiling the ways people outside of Kingston 12 view Kingston 12 and how this informs the ways they behave toward the community that nurtured his father's talent.

CONCLUSION

Popular culture narratives which give expression to the social imaginary of the people of the city of Kingston, Jamaica, play an important role in shaping the identities and repertoires of its citizens. In this chapter, a sampling of select popular music tracks that have Kingston in their title were subjected to interpretive textual analysis in order to tell a partial story of the changes in the way Kingston has been imagined since independence. Kingston is first an imperial creation named for and placing the British monarch in the centre of Jamaica's commercial, social and political life. Contemporary renderings of King's town, therefore, rightly reclaim it for its rightful ruler, His Imperial Highness. At the same time, this reclamation is threatened by a dominant element in the contemporary social imaginary of Kingston, the ghetto, a social space of marginalization and violence. In particular, ghetto life for Kingston and its environs, several of which are garrison communities, includes deprivation, violence and danger. This contemporary idea of Kingston in the dancehall imaginary represents a change for the worse. Gone is the wonderment of Lord Creator's "Kingston Town" and the funkiness of Toots's "Funky Kingston" from the 1970s. Kings no longer inhabit a fairy tale space searching for a "queen" who is certain to arrive. Palaces and the other trappings of royalty, which were then the preserve of the ordinary male, are no more. Since 1980, when there was the bloody October general elections in which politicized violence left eight hundred dead, the King's town is imagined, experienced and remembered as a dangerous place dominated by trigger-happy gangs fighting for "throne" and "crown". These gangs are often involved in shoot outs with other rudeboys in "di gun land" that King's town has now become. Members of the security forces are part of this "set a monster", who kill innocent youth and women and "wanted man" alike. Women are both victims and playthings who dress and pose for male pleasure and use. They are not averse to turning a trick or two on an unsuspecting male.

Yet this King's town is also a source of creativity and innovation, which is evident in the various musical genres it gave birth to, including reggae and dancehall, which it shapes and is shaped by. Popular music is responsive to and constitutive of city Kingston. King's town is also a source of mercantile possibilities wryly described as "everything sell a town / if yu go de look Black / yu can lef look brown". In the mix are journeying activities in search of true love, from MoBay cruising along the new highway, to Kingston town. The king(man) lover may well set the terms, so his woman comes to him. But she holds on to his heart. She returns his heart that she had previously taken away to the now notorious MoBay. Make no mistake, while "earthly kings continue to fight for crowns and thrones" (existent or otherwise), leading to Kingston being a "kill some city", it is still "Jah Jah City". And a king plays on by . . .

NOTES

1. UNESCO Headquarters, "47 Cities Join the UNESCO Creative Cities Network", 11 December 2015, https://en.unesco.org/creative-cities/events/47-cities-join-unesco-creative-cities-network. This is celebrated with banners all along the Palisadoes strip to the airport. It was also named as one of the New York Times' 52 Places to Go in 2017 (http://www.nytimes.com/interactive/2017/travel/places-to-visit.html?_r=0). Of course, the reasons for this designation also include music.
2. A popular way of referring to Kingston among urban Jamaicans is "City Kingston" or "Kingston City", perhaps an example of the reduplication which is a feature of the Jamaican language.
3. The criteria for selection of these tracks was the presence of Kingston in their title, the recommendation of a dancehall scholar and their being produced after 1962, the year of Jamaica's independence. The starting point of independence is important to the sense of ownership and belonging which one would expect to find at that point. Suggestions for several of these tracks were provided by dancehall scholars Dennis Howard and Sonjah Stanley Niaah. Howard suggested Josey Wales's "Kingston Hot", Albarosie's "Kingston Town" and Lord Creator's "Kingston Town". Sonjah Stanley Niaah suggested Capleton's "Jah Jah City" (2000) and Jr Gong's "Welcome to Jamrock" (2004). Stanley Niaah's suggestions, while not meeting the criterion of having "Kingston" in the title, are relevant for their referencing City Kingston and confirm the intuition about how notions of the city have changed over time. Zachary J.M. Beier, a panellist at the 2017 Global Reggae Conference, suggested "Kingston Town" by Toian and so identified a female voice for the conversation. To these, the author has added from her own listing: Toots and the Maytal's

"Funky Kingston", Busy Signal and Jr Gong's "Kingston Town", Proteje's "Kingston Be Wise", Damian Marley's "Kingston 12" and Vybz Kartel's "Downtown Kingston". For a contemporary discussion of sampling, see Planton (2016).

4. Jaffe does remind us of the necessity of moving beyond text to visual performance, but that is not the intent of this more narrow offering. Each of these songs is accompanied by a music video that presents vivid images of Kingston and the people that contribute to the unfolding of the social imaginary, which bears further investigation.
5. Garrison communities are politically homogenous spaces that have been carved out by political leaders to maintain power. Power and control are maintained by the violence of politically affiliated gang leaders known as dons and the political and personal patronage they dole out (less so now). The most famous of these is Tivoli Gardens, created by the bulldozing of the Dungle under Edward Seaga and the Jamaica Labour Party in 1963 (completed in 1965).
6. Capleton is among a cadre of Rastafarian artistes who have been deemed "conscious", having arisen to condemn and denounce the glorifying of violence and the slackness which epitomized the popular music of the 1990s. Such artistes portray themselves as prophets, chanting down the Babylon of slackness arising from the bowels of Kingston. At the same time, with the ascendancy of the Rastafari faith in Jamaica and the impact of members on Jamaican popular music, particularly reggae, dancehall and dub, it is unsurprising that their particular/unique/idiosyncratic world view has deeply influenced the Jamaican social imaginary, especially inner-city Kingston, arguably the birthplace of Rasta, and Rasta global icons like Bob Marley, who Ehrengardt (2012/2013) believes has taken the world for a walk through inner city Trench Town via his music.
7. This was the first record on Chris Blackwell's newly formed Island Records label. Blackwell later went on to produce Bob Marley and the Wailers.
8. Jaffe (2012b) makes the case that Jamaican popular music in the 1960s and 1970s was heavily oriented to US soul, R&B and funk, with Jamaican musicians covering many American hit songs. This is evident in the work of Toots and the Maytals, who, on their 1973 album Funky Kingston, covered several R&B songs. Indeed, Toots declares in the title single "Funky Kingston", "I love black America." Interestingly, he continues, "People keep asking me for / Funky Kingston / but I ain't got none / somebody take it away from me." There is a sense of cross fertilization and sharing of music in this statement. The flavouring of the language with words like "ain't got none" from African American speech cannot be missed. Indeed, it is in that period (1960s and 1970s) that Jaffe identifies the beginning of the idea of the ghetto as part of the mobile imaginary of black popular culture across the world. Gordon Roehler looks back at the 1960s and sees "the creative flowering of people's music in Kingston's dry desert of stone" (Evans 2014, 114). Witmer (1987, 7) demonstrates that popular music culture in Jamaica in the early twentieth century was indeed "firmly under the influence of US popular music culture".
9. Only one track from the 1990s was identified with the name Kingston in the title – Jr Gong's "Kingston 12".
10. Kisko was replaced by bag juice, which has largely been replaced by bottled beverages of all kinds.
11. See Thibault Ehrengardt (2012/2013) for a discussion of the involvement of popular music artistes in the gang warfare in Kingston.

12. These colours represented the two warring political parties: green, Jamaica Labour Party, and orange, People's National Party.
13. "Politrickshan" is Rasta talk for politicians using word play to point out the nature of politicians as corrupt and lying, ready to play a trick on the people for their own benefit.
14. The abduction, rape and murder of a school girl, who wore the wrong colour school uniform, was the nadir of such "kill some shitty"-ness (Ehrengardt 2012/2013).
15. Since that time there has been an official enquiry into the Tivoli incursion. No one was punished for the deaths or the destruction of property. The government has agreed to compensate some residents. The post-incursion drama continues.
16. The Internet is rife with questions asking the meaning of this particular phrase.
17. Member of a squad, usually of policemen; from Busy Signal and Jr Gong's "Kingston Town".
18. Rasta has introduced this term in reference to the police force, which is viewed, perhaps due to it habitual use of violence against the innocent, as the embodiment of the Whore of Babylon referred to the Book of Revelation. Babylon is the representation of the empire which is against Rasta.
19. Policemen in civilian garb; from Proteje's "Kingston Be Wise".
20. Ratty is a member of the "Rat Patrol", which is a popular way of referring to the Jamaica Defence Force and Jamaica Constabulary Forces' combined patrols, which are often feared by inhabitants of the inner city.
21. Jamaica Defence Force (the army).
22. Proteje, "Kingston Be Wise".
23. Tracks extolling marijuana are legion. See, for example, Richie Spice, "Marijuana pon di Corner".
24. See Gunst (1996). Also, Jamaica's iconic movie *The Harder They Come*, which tells the story of the outlaw Rhygin.
25. Dovecot is a privately owned cemetery in St Catherine, Jamaica. The cris(p) board box with a mirror on top refers to a nice coffin.
26. Young boys/men who are hardened criminals who are often recruited to shoot people.
27. In rap and hip hop, a "throw down" is a competition between rappers.
28. The public faces of the homeless or, as they are called in Jamaica, "street people" or "mad people" (street boys, street children, men, women), is a taken-for-granted part of the urban landscape. The 2012 Report of the Committee on Homelessness places the number of homeless at least 1,160, with men making up the majority of that number. See Muir (2017) and Perkins (2019).
29. Sadly, Jamaica's second city, Montego Bay, has now become a very violent place, leading to a state of emergency in January 2018 in an attempt to curb the criminality.
30. Kingman is a term from Rastafari, particularly the Bobo Shanti, which speaks to the superiority of the male. All men are really kings. See Lake (2014).
31. Matches Lane (more correctly Matthews Lane), for example, is the domain of jailed don Donald "Zekes/Zeeks" Phipps, who is known to be closely aligned to the People's National Party.

REFERENCES

Brown-Glaude, Winifred. 2013. "Don't Hate Me 'Cause I'm Pretty: Race, Gender and the Bleached Body in Jamaica". *Social and Economic Studies* 62, no. 1: 53–78.

Cooke, Mel. 2010. "Story of the Song: Kingston Still Hot 27 Years after Josey Wales' Hit". *Sunday Gleaner*, 19 December. http://jamaica-gleaner.com/gleaner/20101219/ent/ent6.html.

Ehrengardt, Thibault. 2012/2013. *Gangs of Jamaica: The Babylonian Wars*. Paris, France: Dread Editions/Jamaica Insula 05.

Evans, Lucy. 2014. *Communities in Contemporary Anglophone Caribbean Short Stories*. London: Oxford University Press.

Gunst, Laurie. 1996. *Born fi Dead: A Journey through the Jamaican Posse Underworld*. New York: Holt.

Howard, Dennis. 2012. *Rantin from Inside the Dancehall*. Kingston: Jahmento Publishing.

———. 2015. *Creative Echo Chamber: Contemporary Music Production in Kingston, Jamaica*. Kingston: Ian Randle.

Jaffe, Rivka. 2012a. "Criminal Dons and Extralegal Security Privatization in Downtown Kingston, Jamaica". *Singapore Journal of Tropical Geography* 33:184–97.

———. 2012b. "Talkin' 'bout the Ghetto: Popular Culture and Urban Imaginaries of Immobility". *International Journal of Urban and Regional Research* 36, no. 4 (July): 674–88.

Johnson, Hume. 2005. "Incivility: The Politics of 'People on the Margins' in Jamaica". *Political Studies* 53:579–97.

Kurlansky, Mark. 1988. "Showdown in Jamaica". *New York Times Magazine*, 28 November. http://www.nytimes.com/1988/11/27/magazine/showdown-in-jamaica.html?pagewanted=all.

Lake, Obiagele. 2014. "Cultural Ideology and Rastafari Women". In *Rastafari in the New Millennium: A Rastafari Reader*, edited by Michael Barnett, 222–38. New York: Syracuse University Press.

McCallum, Shara. 2011. *This Strange Land*. Farmington, ME: Alice James Books.

Muir, Sheryl. 2017. "Dealing with Homelessness in Jamaica". *Jamaica Observer*, 27 March. http://www.jamaicaobserver.com/columns/Dealing-with-homelessness-in-Jamaica_93757.

Perkins, Anna Kasafi. 2019. "Moving Again: Women, Catholic Social Teaching, and Disguised Homelessness in Jamaica". In *Street Homelessness and Catholic Theological Ethics*, edited by James F. Keenan and Mark McGreevy, 245–64. Maryknoll: Orbis.

Planton, Adelle. 2016. "Beenie Man Talks Drake's 'Controlla' Sample: Dancehall Is a Culture Everybody Wants to Be Part Of'". *Billboard*. http://www.billboard.com/articles/columns/hip-hop/7356849/drake-views-beenie-man-controlla.

Schwartz, Mattathias. 2011. "Massacre in Jamaica: After the United States Demanded the Extradition of a Drug Lord, a Bloodletting Ensued". *New Yorker*, 12 December. http://www.newyorker.com/reporting/2011/12/12/111212fa_fact_schwartz#ixzz1kQAOsqCF.

Stanley Niaah, Sonjah. 2010. *DanceHall: From Slave Ship to Ghetto*. Ottawa: University of Ottawa Press.

Ulibas, Joseph. 2016. "The Top 10 Best Toots & the Maytals Songs". *AXS*, 9 March. http://www.axs.com/the-top-10-best-toots-the-maytals-songs-78202.

Witmer, Robert. 1987. "'Local' and 'Foreign': The Popular Music Culture of Kingston, Jamaica, before Ska, Rock Steady, and Reggae". *Latin American Music Review/Revista de Musica* Latinoamericana 8, no. 1 (Spring–Summer): 1–25.

TRACKS

Alborosie, "Kingston Town" (*Soul Pirate*, 2008)
Baby Cham, "Ghetto Story" (*Ghetto Story*, 2006)
Busy Signal featuring Damian "Jr Gong" Marley, "Kingston Town" (*Reggae Music Again*, 2011)
Capleton, "Jah Jah City" (*More Fire*, 2000)
Chalice, "Heroes" (*Catch It*, 1985)
Chronnix, "Smile Jamaica" (*Smile Jamaica*, 2013)
Damian "Jr Gong" Marley, "Welcome to Jamrock" (*Welcome to Jamrock*, 2004)
Damian "Jr Gong" Marley, "Kingston 12" (*Mr Marley*, 1996)
Duane Stephenson, "Think Twice" (*Think Twice Riddim*, 2011)
Josey Wales, "Kingston Hot" (Vinyl, 1983, Riddim – Answer/Never Let Go)
Lord Creator, "Kingston Town" (Vinyl, 1973)
Peter Tosh, "Peace Treaty" (*Mama Africa*, 1983)
Proteje, "Kingston be Wise" (*8 Year Affair*, 2012)
Richie Spice, "Marijuana pon di Corner" (*Spice in Yu Life*, 2004)
Richie Spice, "Ghetto Girl" (*Spice in Yu Life*, 2004)
Toian, "Kingston Town" (*Strictly the Best 50*, 2014)
Toots and the Maytals, "Funky Kingston" (*Funky Kingston*, 1973)
Vybz Kartel, "Downtown Kingston" (*Reggae Love Songs*, 2014)

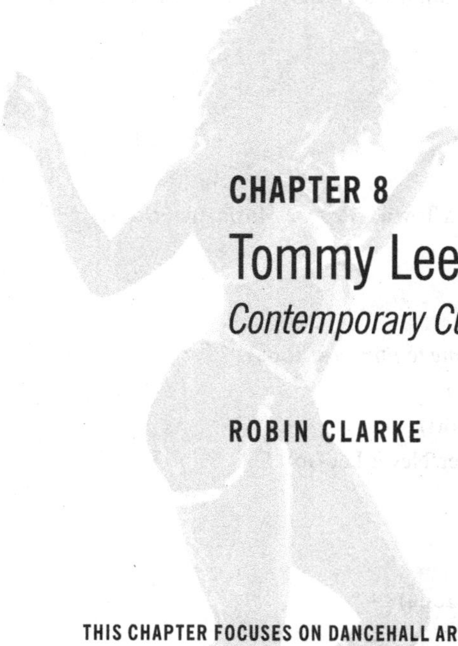

CHAPTER 8

Tommy Lee as "Uncle Demon"

*Contemporary Cultural Hybridity in Jamaican Dancehall**

ROBIN CLARKE

THIS CHAPTER FOCUSES ON DANCEHALL ARTISTE TOMMY LEE SPARTA and his representation as "Uncle Demon". It argues that Tommy Lee Sparta represents a move away from traditional discourses of Rastafari and fundamentalist Christianity in postcolonial Jamaica toward a new hybrid. This hybrid is conflates gothic aesthetics, Afro-Jamaican religious beliefs and North American "twilight" popular culture[1] with that of Jamaica popular music culture, that is, dancehall music and culture. The dark, anti-Christian, demonic stylistic cultural identity of Tommy Lee Sparta is rejected and negated in Christendom and other forms of hegemonic discourses of representations about what constitutes good and bad, right and wrong, moral and immoral. All forms of Jamaican popular music, including mento, ska, rocksteady, dub, reggae and dancehall have been negated in hegemonic discourses that wield the power of institutional authority in Jamaica. They were, and to some extent are still, considered a part of residual/low/inferior culture. The exported baggage of colonial culture – opera, classical music, jazz – was embraced by a neocolonial aristocracy. While many of the former maybe true about the criticisms of Jamaica popular music, Tommy Lee Sparta is criticized by dancehall artistes themselves (such as Bounty Killer and Ninja Man) who see him as transgressing the preferred culture of dancehall[2] and Jamaica by embracing an entity that was never embraced in Jamaica or in Jamaican popular music and culture, that is, the devil or demon. Tommy Lee Sparta's defiant stylistic expressions seemingly toe the line of the unforgivable as he, along with contemporary artistes such as Alkaline, discursively moves away from traditional aspects of dancehall music and culture that constitute components of the Jamaican identity as a Christian country. Here, Tommy Lee Sparta's persona disturbs the religious conscience of fundamentalist Jamaicans and tampers with the sacred narratives of Judeo-Christianity and its institutional discourses that are part of Jamaica's traditional hegemonic sphere.

* Previously published in *ReggaeStories: Jamaican Musical Legends and Cultural Legacies*, edited by Donna P. Hope (Kingston: University of the West Indies Press, 2018), 45–65.

For the purpose of this chapter, the manifestation of Tommy Lee as "Uncle Demon" is specifically examined through his live performances, dark videos, lyrical treatises, sartorial dress-code, (personal) interviews and his adoption of various tattoos and body markings. In attempting to unpack and unearth some of the metanarratives surrounding the entertainer, I argue that Tommy Lee formed an alliance with Vybz Kartel of the Portmore Empire by relocating to the new hub of dancehall gladiators and deliberately introduced a cultural hybrid that would generate controversy. He then used this controversy to propel himself to the upper echelons of dancehall music and culture. This rise to the top of dancehall was further facilitated by the physical absence of Vybz Kartel, king and ruler of the Portmore Empire, who remains incarcerated at the time of writing.

DANCEHALL'S GENESIS/GENEALOGY

The genesis of dancehall music and culture represents a watershed moment in the genealogy of Jamaican popular music. This distinct musical form and its accompanying culture came to the fore in the 1980s, a period described as Reaganism and Thatcherism by Stuart Hall (1978) and other cultural analysts (Stanley Niaah 2005) when the new world order moved to neo-liberalism, or free market capitalism. These shifts also impacted on Jamaica's cultural, technological, political and economic permutations – Jamaicans had lost hope in the *smadditization*[3] of the 1970s of the Michael Manley democratic socialist policies and the conservative movement of Rastafari, as well as in the conscious lyrics of reggae, dancehall's immediate precursor. Reggae, dancehall's predecessor, emerged in the 1970s at a time when the festive feeling of ska and the rude boy rocksteady are said to have failed to bring about revolutionary changes in the lives of Jamaica's poor in the post-independence era (Chang and Chen 1998). Arguably, a new set of revolutionaries (such as Burning Spear, Peter Tosh and Bob Marley) arrived in reggae music, particularly in its roots rock reggae form, significantly influenced by the world view and tenets of Rastafari. Thus, reggae's religious overtones brokered on Rastafari's interpretation, including the rebranding of a white Jesus with a black one, deification of His Imperial Majesty (HIM), the acknowledgment of a new ancestral heaven in Ethiopia and a new wave of black consciousness that gripped Jamaica in the 1970s (see Hope 2001, 2006a; Stanley Niaah 2010).

At the global level, there was much consternation by world powers, such as the United States and the United Kingdom and their allies, about the spread of communism or its diluted version of socialism. Socialism, embraced by Caribbean states such as Grenada and Jamaica, was supposed to have helped Jamaicans become "smaddy" (someone of worth), manifesting in socio-economic independence. Coupled with democratic socialism was an International Monetary Fund agreement that forced the government to adopt draconian measures, resulting in the state welfare policies being dramatically cut or stopped. This meant that socio-economic independence was not forthcoming and poor Jamaicans were left at the margins of an already impoverished state to fend for themselves. At the end of the 1970s into the early 1980s came reggae's successor, dancehall music and culture. The rise of dancehall music and culture is said to have signalled cultural, social and economic shifts from Michael Manley's democratic socialism to Edward Seaga's North American capitalism (Meeks 1996, 132). Dancehall is also identified by some as a deviant form of music and culture that moved away from the "reggae conscious" era that was wrapped up in African pride, black nationalism and a pan-Africanist ethos. To date, dancehall is described as the ultimate manifestation of Jamaica's move away from Christianity and the reggae "conscious" years.[4] The persona of Tommy Lee Sparta, the artiste, can be read as a rejection of the Rastafari/reggae ethos that is arguably more popular overseas than in Jamaica at this historical moment. His current popularity, especially among dancehall fans, attests to this fact.

TOMMY LEE SPARTA AND THE GAZA EMPIRE

Tommy Lee's point of entry onto the varying stages of dancehall music and culture took place first in Montego Bay in 2008 with the song "Spartan Soldier" and later in Portmore, St Catherine, as a part of Vybz Kartel's Gaza Empire. Tommy Lee, like dancehall artiste Popcaan, is a protégé or offspring[5] of Vybz Kartel and the Portmore Empire and therefore is part of a trajectory of controversial figures beginning, for this chapter, with Bounty Killer[6] who could be perceived as the grandfather, with his protégé Vybz Kartel[7] being the father, and Kartel's protégé, Tommy Lee Sparta, as the son. Another critical trajectory linked to geography also not to be missed in the lineage of these artistes is that Bounty Killer hails from Seaview Gardens in Kingston, Vybz Kartel originates from Portmore in St Catherine and Tommy Lee is from Montego Bay in St James. This geographical lineage is important to the larger conversations and debates that make the rounds of the popular media and within Jamaican popular music. Tommy Lee Sparta and Vybz Kartel operate outside the original nucleus from which dancehall music and culture derived, that is, the inner cities of Kingston.[8]

While Kingston remains the creative cluster of Jamaican popular music, Vybz Kartel and many of his offspring who are associated with Portmore and St James have made a permanent mark on dancehall historiography and geography in Jamaica. In this regard, Vybz Kartel repositioned the zone of authentic production and managed to propel Portmore into musical/lyrical prominence with labels such as Portmore Empire or Gaza Empire. This repositions space and place in the cultural production of Jamaican popular music and potentially signals a challenge to Kingston as the hub of creation of dancehall gladiators. In the words of Tommy Lee Sparta, "man psycho / Gaza run bout yah". (This man is crazy. Gaza runs the place.) Tommy Lee becomes the real-life version of Ivan (played by Jimmy Cliff) in the movie *The Harder They Come*, a poor youth from rural Jamaica who a look a "buss"[9] *inna de dancehall.*[10]

The repositioning of Portmore in St Catherine as the site for production of dancehall gladiators, and its branding by Kartel as Gaza, are both critical in the re/creating and re/claiming of musical turf. At the international level, Gaza is a plot of land that simultaneously joins and separates Palestine and Israel in decades of war/s. Each claims this plot of land as its own. At the local level, a section of Waterford Portmore originally called "Borderline" was rebranded "Gaza" when popular roots theatre actor Keith Shebada Ramsay[11] in the play "Bashment Granny" uttered the infamous line, "me deh pan de borderline" [I am on the borderline]. Gaza is symbolic of a space/place/turf that must be defended both lyrically and some would argue physically, because it has become an empire. It is this plot of land/empire that Tommy Lee must defend (especially in the physical absence but musical presence of the emperor Vybz Kartel), as he reminds listeners/onlookers:

> Me foot plant like a tree root.
> yet still Adijah a me father.
> me come fi rule and me nuh response.
> in case you never known me nah leff the Gaza.
>
> (My foot is planted like the root of a tree
> Yet Adijah [Vybz Kartel] is still my father
> I have come to rule and I do not care
> In case you did not know, I am not leaving the Gaza)

Thus, in adapting and adopting the name Sparta both for his own imaging and to reflect his connection to the name given to a section of the Flankers community in Montego Bay, St James, Tommy Lee becomes a Spartan, a warrior figure who must not only fight for and fight to maintain his place as heir to the Gaza throne but also to maintain and stay relevant *inna de dancehall.* Yet, Tommy Lee Sparta's gladiatorial move as a dancehall artiste is not new; his attempt to transcend his ordinary status and become a superhero/ warrior figure within the dancehall space is similar to what others have done and continue to do in this space. Indeed, warrior figures in dancehall include Bounty Killer (the Warlord), Super Cat (the Wild Apache), Merciless, Assasin, Mad Cobra, Ninja Man and Josey Wales (the Colonel) among others – all hardcore dancehall artistes who lyrically jousted to claim and maintain a presence at the upper echelons of the dancehall space. Tommy Lee Sparta makes this point:

> I am Uncle Demon and I am proud. . . . Everybody in dancehall play a character; everybody want to be different; you do not want to be nobody else. So you have Beenie Man is a doctor, everyone knows he is not a real doctor; you have Ninja Man who is not a real Ninja, he does not have sword and ah chop up people; you have Bounty Killer and he is no killer, he nah kill nobody; Vybz Kartel is Daddy Devil, but Kartel is not no real devil; Mad Cobra he is not a snake; Elephant Man is no elephant. So why when I say I am Uncle Demon me ah real demon? Me not no real demon. (*BVI Platinum News*, 2014)

CONCEPTUALIZING/THEORIZING GOTHIC DANCEHALL

Originally, nineteenth-century gothic literature was exclusively associated with white aristocratic and middle-class Anglo-European men and a few women. Similarly, the gothic scene that emerged in 1980s in the United Kingdom was started by Anglo-European male artists. This indicates that the gothic literary genre and its later manifestations in twentieth-century Euro-America is the province of white upper and middle class men and women. However, goth/ic aesthetics and tropes in the twenty-first century are a "multi-faceted, multi-dimensional force, . . . a style, an aesthetics experience and a mode of cultural expression that transverses genres, forms, media, discipline and national boundaries" (Byron and Townshend 2014, xxxviii). Thus, contemporary goth/ic culture moves across contemporary popular culture into new spaces and places, giving rise to new incarnations. Spooner (2006, 8) asserts, "The Gothic lurks in all sorts of unexpected corners."

Like dancehall, gothic aesthetics represent a watershed moment in popular music and cultural expressions of young Britons who rejected and rebelled against (white) elitist British nationalism. Being a cultural hybrid of the punk rock movement in the United Kingdom, goth/ic music is described as a subculture that came in response to the economic, social, cultural and nationalist fervor and upheavals in the United Kingdom during the Cold War era of the 1980s (Mueller 2008). However, goth has its point of origin in the popularity of eighteenth- and nineteenth-century gothic literary genre. Gothic literary themes included but were not limited to death and decay, evil, devil and Satan. Gothic aesthetics re-emerged and reinvented itself from a literary genre in the form of subcultural expressions in fashion and music in the 1970s into the 1980s. Since the 1980s, gothic literary thematics, aesthetics and kinaesthetics (appearance and performance) have been incorporated in global popular cultures, up to the time of writing, in hip-hop music and culture and Jamaica's own dancehall music and culture, in the form of Tommy Lee Sparta.

It must be emphasized here that the two cultural expressions – dancehall and gothicism – have never been in the same cultural space in Jamaica, although dancehall artistes and others, such as the late master dancer Gerald "Bogle" Levy, have always accessorized the physical body in spectacular and sartorial ways. This move toward what I label as gothic dancehall becomes a lyrical and metaphysical space and place where elements of dancehall music and culture are intermingled and cross-fertilized with Afro-Jamaican religious folk culture and North American Goth and "twilight" culture. Gothic dancehall becomes dancehall's latest invention and is one of the varying ways the genre is able to re/present and re/invent itself. Here, gothic dancehall therefore is a performative space and place where there is the cross fertilization of music, embodied acts, repulsive shock and awe, visual body rhetoric, profiling, masquerading, Afro-Jamaican magico-religious rituals (such as sorcery and obeah) and masking informed by dancehall body politics. As a hybrid, there is something sacred and profane about this new brand of dancehall having also its antecedents not only in popular gothic music and culture but also in African traditions of masquerading and Jonkonnu. Goth's shock and awe are similar and at the same time different from the cross-dressing masquerade and costume of Jonkonnu processions. Jamaican Jonkonnu was practised as early as 1725 and as late as 1951 (Lewin 2000; Torres 2011) and featured characters such as Belly Woman and the Devil. The current flamboyant aesthetics and kinaesthetics of male dress and dancing styles in dancehall music and culture arguably represent the repressed traditions of Jonkonnu re/presenting themselves in transatlantic black cultures such as dancehall and hip-hop (Torres 2011). In this way, Euro-American gothic aesthetics and "twilight" culture are similar to Afro-Jamaican rituals, beliefs and customs; for example, in their belief in magic, witchcraft, sorcery and exorcism. Thus, I posit that gothic dancehall at the time of writing is a space and place where historical and contemporary discourses overlap, intermingle and cross-fertilize. These webs of discourses include but are not limited to plantation entertainment and social dances, hybridization, transnationalism, globalization, free market capitalism and the contemporary global wave of cinematic twilight/gothic culture. It is a complex, overlapping disjuncture where gothic aesthetics waxes and wanes in a reflective cycle of aesthetic sampling.

TOMMY LEE SPARTA AS UNCLE DEMON

Tommy Lee emerged in 2008 in Montego Bay and performed at local shows in this section of Jamaica. However he exploded into popular imagination one year after the second release of *The Twilight Saga: New Moon* in 2009, which was followed by *The Twilight Saga: Eclipse in 2010*, *The Twilight Saga: Breaking Dawn, Part 1* in 2011, and *The Twilight Saga: Breaking Dawn, Part 2* in 2012. Checks with Palace Amusement Cinema in Jamaica revealed that the last three films had special premieres and were huge hits in the year of release. Where dark and gothic aesthetics are concerned, the rise of the Twilight Saga series in popular cinema culture globally presents dark and light images and presents new ways of being in the contemporary era – new forms of identity-making for those who seek new platforms. In this era, therefore, Tommy Lee Sparta represents a new wave of artistes (including Ryme Minista, Gramma Stamma Sparta and the very controversial Alkaline) whose aesthetic choices and self-presentations borrow from these gothic forms and are controversial in Jamaica's traditional sociocultural spaces.

Tommy Lee's explosion onto the stages of dancehall music and culture in 2010 with his first hit "Warn Dem" incarnates a new brand of dancehall signifying the kind of identity formation that transgresses traditional central themes of sex and sexuality, hyper-masculine heterosexuality, the lyrical/physical conquest of the pudenda, ghetto levity and survival to become the metaphorical "Uncle Demon".[12] "Uncle Demon" must be analysed in its appropriate cultural climate: the moniker came at a time when dark, gothic fixtures in movies such as *Twilight*, *300* and *Lord of the Rings*[13] had, arguably, normalized these figures, with some of the dark figures presented in these movies and series being transformed into having feelings and human emotion, and being loving and affectionate. It could be that fans of Tommy Lee Sparta no longer feel threatened (real or imagined) by his embrace of a demonic moniker. Additionally, he came to prominence at a time when there was, arguably, a void in dancehall with the incarceration of dancehall artiste Vybz Kartel and the perception that hardcore fans of dancehall were seeking something new, spectacular and controversial. While dancehall is used to controversy, one can argue that Tommy Lee Sparta rode a new wave of controversy that used deliberate

FIGURE 8.1. Clovis cartoon courtesy of the *Jamaica Observer*.

attempts (and successes in some instances) at inflaming hegemonic structures and social institutions, such as the monolithic Jamaican Christian orthodoxy. Yet, this new wave of intense controversy was not initiated by Tommy Lee, but with Vybz Kartel, an artiste considered one of dancehall's most controversial artistes. Hope (2014) catalogues Vybz Kartel's wave of controversies, beginning with his lyrical and physical clash with veteran dancehall artiste Ninja Man at Sting 2003 (an annual dancehall music festival where artistes clash one another lyrically), his subsequent Gully/Gaza feud with archrival dancehall artiste Mavado, his normalization of fellatio, and his constant lyrical stabs at media entities such as the Broadcasting Commission, among others. In this regard, Tommy Lee Sparta becomes Vybz Kartel's (who also dubbed himself Daddy Devil) protégé of controversy, a wave now being ridden by Alkaline, another of dancehall's controversial artistes.

Tommy Lee's controversial, highly charged and secular lyrics and his dabbling in "demonic" aesthetics were seen by institutional authority and Jamaica's strong religious arm as a manifestation of the end of days, the book of Revelation coming to fruition, and this perception travelled outwards into the wider Caribbean region. This is exemplified in the cartoon (figure 8.1) in the *Jamaica Observer* (5 March 2014) by popular cartoonist Clovis.

The Clovis cartoon reflects on responses to Tommy Lee's 2014 visit to Dominica,

FIGURE 8.2. Tommy Lee Sparta at Sting 2012. Courtesy of the *Jamaica Observer*.

where one pastor in Dominica describes Tommy Lee as a threat to the safety of his entire nation. Tommy Lee Sparta's inflammatory brand of gothic dancehall was then laced with the images of demons or Satan and signalled an ideological/musical transition from "dangerous" dancehall to one of "dark/er dancehall". The cartoon simultaneously reflects on Tommy Lee's gothic entrance and performance at Sting 2012, his first appearance on dancehall's annual gladiatorial event, where artistes are lyrically crowned or dethroned. His costume incorporated gothic/demonic tropes, including a "demon" face mask, a long black leather coat and his lyrical delivery of themes like imprisonment, madness, monstrosity and haunting (figure 8.2).

This radical move in dancehall aesthetics and performance at Sting 2012 generated intense controversy among aficionados of dancehall, religious groups and all across Jamaica and into many parts of the Caribbean. Many wondered if Tommy Lee Sparta was a part of the Illuminati, or some secret society, or if he was the devil reincarnated or a sign of biblical Revelations coming to pass. The explosion of debates in Jamaica's dailies (the *Jamaica Observer*, the *Gleaner* and the *Star*) and social media as well as discussions on the ground expressed concerns about whether dancehall was being pushed way too far and transgressing even some of its major tenets. Dancehall veterans also provided harsh criticism; for example, Ninja Man stated, "In the name of Jesus, yuh affi rebuke the devil" (In the name of Jesus, you have to rebuke the devil); veteran artiste Bounty Killer declared that "Christmas is fi Christ so nuh demon or devil cyaah win . . . dem a dead a Sting!!!" (Christmas is for Christ so no demon or devil can win . . . they are going to die at Sting) (Clarke 2012); and academics such as Michael Barnett, of the University of the West Indies' Mona campus, who presented a conference paper at the International Reggae Conference 2013 in Jamaica titled, "Has Dancehall Lost Its Way?" and used his presentation to argue that it had.

Yet, I argue that Tommy Lee Sparta's transgression was not only inflammatory but pointed to a new, cross-fertilized hybrid identity in the dancehall: a hardcore man who uses the dark, gothic twilight images associated with demons as cultural referents. This updated hybrid on the stages of Jamaican dancehall has clear historical antecedents in the trajectory of images found in North American popular culture, starting with the likes of Marilyn Manson to Manson's hip-hop contemporaries Lil' Wayne and Tyga, among others. While the persona of "Uncle Demon" is pulled from elements of American pop culture, Tommy Lee Sparta marries these with what Hope (2010) identifies as the don/shotta masculine identity[14] of dancehall music and culture. Thus, the persona of Tommy Lee Sparta as Uncle Demon was costumed with controversial and for some offensive imagery, including the four-leaf clover (which is believed to bring good luck), a fairy (one which has magical power and watches over subjects), the Ankh (connected to ancient Egypt which means eternal life), the moon, the sun (plays into the light/darkness dichotomy) and a swastika sign (originally associated with religions like Hinduism and Buddhism, but later German Nazism and its brutal regime that committed atrocities against humanity).

These body modifications and select costuming allowed Tommy Lee Sparta to brand his mundane self in hyper/visible and powerful ways that connect with Hollywood and North American moves in global cinema culture. Further, they helped to reposition and re/script him as part of the adopted persona of "Uncle Demon" and along with the swirling controversy surrounding him and "Daddy Devil" (Vybz Kartel) to "accrue significantly greater and cultural power" inna de dancehall. Using this artifice and self presentation, Tommy Lee Sparta became a "celebrity figure . . . an object of public attention because he was perceived to embody possibilities of individual achievement; conversely, he also represents deviation from religious and social norms" (Bhattacharya, 2012, para 4). His hyper/visible body was made in ways similar to those which Hollywood and hip-hop stars make of themselves via sensational and sartorial dressings and body markings, for example, Lil' Wayne, Tyga and Thomas Lee Bass of the metal band Mötley Crüe. Tommy Lee's lyrical treatises also converged with his adornment and costuming to project him as the deviant Uncle Demon.

TOMMY LEE'S LYRICAL DEVIANCE

A careful examination of Tommy Lee's lyrical repertoire up to 2014 suggests that it can be catalogued under several major themes (see Campbell 2013). First, there is the description, critique or endorsement of acts of violence; second, sexual encounters, prowess and taboos; third, harmonious and dissonant interpersonal relationships; fourth, socio-economic/socio-political struggles of Jamaica's marginalized groups; fifth, ghetto/inner-city strategies of day-to-day survival; sixth, the general ways of entertaining oneself; and seventh, the recognition of supreme entities (God/Satan) in daily life. This ties into Hope's (2011, 19–23) identification and description of the "six G's and others" as key themes in contemporary dancehall music and culture: gun, gyal, ghetto, gays, ganja, God and money/bling.

Following on the trajectory of many hardcore dancehall artistes like Ninja Man the "front teeth, gold teeth don gorgon", Super Cat, Bounty Killer and Vybz Kartel, Tommy Lee Sparta's inflammatory lyrics, his dark and anti-Christ music videos, coupled with Satan as a cultural referent as well as his overtly accessorized physical body positioned him as the cardinal incarnation of gothic dancehall. With his gothic aesthetic sampling, Tommy Lee Sparta gave a fresh energy and power to contemporary dancehall. He crossed the soundscape of Montego Bay to become a part of the Portmore Empire and burst into prominence upsetting some while becoming the object of attention of many others. His song "Warn Dem" (November 2010) was followed by "Some Bwoy: Link Pan Wi Chain" (October 2011), and then it was "Psycho" (June 2012), "Bus a Blank" (October 2012) and later "Shook (Uncle Demon)" (2013). Most of his songs, live performances and music videos rely heavily on gothic tropes to convey the intensity of terror and pain and a few are examined below.

"Uncle Demon", as is referenced in his songs, is a creation, an alter ego who appears and disappears at will. Staged identities are important variants within the dancehall space and form part of becoming a successful and relevant artiste. Unlike other members of the Gaza Empire who were/are unable to access the upper echelons of dancehall music and culture (for example, Gaza Slim, Lisa Hyper, Jah Vinci), Tommy Lee Sparta discovered a "winning formula" with his creation of gothic dancehall and its complementary lyrics. For example, in "Psycho", Tommy Lee Sparta inverts one dimension of being Uncle Demon, "man psycho":

Dem nuh bad, act dem a act
Talk dem a talk, dem a chat
A Tommy Lee me a talk from me heart
Wid bere badness back a dat
Hmmmmmm hmmmmmmm hmmmmmm
Man Psycho
Gaza run bout yaaa
Fool. . . .

(They are not bad, they are acting
They are talking, they are chatting
This is Tommy Lee, I am talking from my heart
With pure badness to back it up
Hmmmmmm hmmmmmmm hmmmmmm
I am psycho
Gaza controls here
Fool. . . .)

Tommy Lee Sparta announces his "madness" to the world and to his enemies and critics alike. This madness is as a result of being evil and about the violent and unfeeling ways that he would go about getting rid of an enemy "in front pastor, school pickney", meaning in front of a religious authority figure, or a child in school (who should be protected from such things). In other words, a person would have to be mad/insane to be this violent. Tommy Lee (or the lyric persona) reinvents himself as an extraordinarily violent and unfeeling type of being, one who is mad, loathsome, threatening and otherworldly. The lyric persona is more aggressive in lyrics, tempo and timbre. He tells his enemies in Lucifer/"Uncle Demon 2" about his destructive potential:

Scream and cry to yo self
Lord, call and run to yo God
Nothing in this world could save yo
Tonight you a dead like dog
Aches to aches, dust to dust
Like a wild pit bull mi bullet dem rush
Shot kick yo in a yo face till yo fucking skull crush
Any bwoy feel dem cyaa get touch

(Scream and cry to yourself
Lord, call and run to your God
Nothing in this world could save you
Tonight you are going to die like a dog
Ashes to ashes, dust to dust
Like a wild pit bull my bullets will rush
Shots will kick you in your face until your fucking skull is crushed
Any boy who feels they can't get touched)

This nihilistic projection and destructing potential becomes a haunting leitmotif for the lingering pain and terror that his enemies will endure as they are killed and buried. Here, Tommy Lee Sparta/lyric persona is the sorcerer/obeah man/obayifo who must be feared. Bastide (1972) describes the general purpose of the obayifo/obeahman: "Their business is to prepare objects that are meant to kill or cure . . . They can fly through the air, suck the blood of their victims, radiate light from their anus, and turn themselves into animals. They have a special connection to Satan" (77). The lyric persona has mystical and magical but deadly powers. Thus, the lyric persona is angst-stricken and his tone is predominantly sinister, mysterious, haunting and monstrous.

In "Shook (Uncle Demon)", he announces the persona "Uncle Demon" and uses it as a reference point to demonstrate how he parallels the epitome of evil or badness associated with the devil and his legions:

Intro
Uncle demon
Nephew demon
Legion is uncle demon legion

Chorus
Any boy put a foot a get shook
Mi no care weh yo come from shook
Somebody head affi go open like book
When mi walk a yo place an shot out yo face
Look in a yo marrow awe shook
God kill mi mi no have no heart
Mi evil than how mi blood cloth look
A mi first deh corrupt the war part
Legion

Intro
(Uncle Demon
Nephew Demon
Legion, it's uncle demon, legion

Any boy who puts a foot [out] is going to get shaken
I don't care where you are from, shook
Somebody's head is going to open like a book
When I walk over to your place and shoot out your face
[And] Look in your marrow, awe, shook
God strike me down, I don't have any heart
I am more evil than how I bloodcloth look
It was I who first corrupted the war path
Legion)

While mentioning the name "Uncle Demon" and using the word legion, in this song, Tommy Lee Sparta is more particularly playing into the broader trajectory of evil/warrior/violent masculinities that make the rounds in Jamaica popular music, especially dancehall. What is clear is that he uses the demon/ic references to identify and highlight his ultimate and excessive degree of badness (violence) on a metaphysical plane, as he reminds his foes and mocks the structures of power espoused by them: "Dem nuh bad, non a dem bwoy de nuh bad / Dem no bad like we, dem bwoy de no bad" (They are not bad, none of those boys are bad / They are not as bad as we, those boys are not bad). Here, the badness/violence of which Tommy Lee Sparta mentions is other-worldly, one that is metaphysical, far beyond the ordinary. In this instance, Tommy Lee endorses and plays into the gun/violence, don/shotta dichotomies that emanate within the dancehall specifically and within the wider Jamaican society. He suggests that other than mere guns and human foot soldiers, he is equipped with far more powerful and extremely violent entities as part of his brand of badness, in other words, legions, duppies and Satan – metaphysical entities beyond this realm that cannot be defeated by humans. Here Campbell (2013, 3) notes that "in fact, the demonic references seem to be directly related to this attempt at showing how psycho he is why 'dem nuh bad like a we'/they are not as bad as we are". Indeed, in a careful examination of Tommy Lee's lyrical output up to the point of writing, none of his songs mention Satan, demon or legions as entities to be worshipped or praised, but form part of his larger metanarrative about his legitimacy not only to the throne of the Gaza Empire (some argue it no longer exists) but a new cultural hybrid who is now a gladiator of dancehall music and culture. As the Gaza Empire is dethroned and thrown into non-existence, Tommy Lee Sparta brings Montego Bay into prominence by creating a new empire.

The point should be made clearly that the foregoing was Tommy Lee Sparta's attempt to advance to the highest ranks of lyrical gladiatorship in dancehall culture. His later retreat from same, as well as from the "Uncle Demon" moniker, came in response to the significant backlash he received from within and beyond the dancehall. Jamaica and the Caribbean remain locked within the strong fundamentalist Christian mores that view delving into spiritual other-worldliness as evil and of the devil. Therefore, Tommy Lee Sparta moved away from the "Uncle Demon" moniker and its related lyrical output because of the severe social and economic backlash he received from various agenda setters and authority figures in dancehall, Jamaica and the Caribbean region. For example, in a 2014 interview, he spoke about the pressures he was then facing from the security forces that represented the face of the hegemonic governing structures in Jamaica. His retreat should also be understood in light of the arrest and later conviction of Vybz Kartel. The conviction of Vybz Kartel for murder in 2014 was seen as a return to law and order for many in Jamaica. This was heavily policed around this time and dancehall artistes associated with Vybz Kartel were held firm under the panoptic gaze of the state. In one instance, Tommy Lee was blocked from performing at Sumfest 2015 because it was believed he posed a threat to the safety and stability of the event and its environs. He also does not have a US visa, a revered possession in Jamaica, and is currently unable to break into corporate Jamaica.

CONCLUSION

Dancehall espouses a loose and informal set of collective beliefs and articulates problems associated with Jamaica's poor, black majority. As a form of Jamaica popular culture, it continues to clash with the vanguards of morality and decency in Jamaica. The cultural dissolution or dissonance of the late 1970s into the 1980s (Meeks 1996) created a space and place where ordinary Jamaicans could become extraordinary, such as the very controversial Vybz Kartel. Tommy Lee Sparta's later alliance with Vybz Kartel, an artiste who continues to create and ride his own waves of controversy, aided his ultimate meteoric rise between 2010 and 2014, particularly since Vybz Kartel has been physically absent from the stages of dancehall since 2009.

The meteoric rise of Tommy Lee Sparta as a gothic dancehall artiste was a deliberately engineered activity that was developed and crafted around the marrying of cinematic gothic global popular culture and the controversial planks and themes that emanate in dancehall music and culture. His costuming or aestheticization ruptured conventional dancehall themes and challenged Jamaica's traditional moral and religious foundations. Like his mentor, Vybz Kartel, Tommy Lee Sparta became the object of public scrutiny within and beyond the shores of Jamaica and the Caribbean (up to 2014). His controversial popular cultural moments raised concerns especially among Jamaica's/Caribbean's Christian orthodoxy about his influence on the youth and the wider Jamaican public, even while the society's ethical and moral hegemonic structures continue to face significant challenges from rising rates of crime and violence, indiscipline among teenagers, among other things. Tommy Lee Sparta's aesthetic sampling is a revolt against Jamaica's religiosity, superficial philosophy and the traditional, Victorian moral tenets that form part of the mechanisms used in the policing of Jamaican popular music. Since 2014, Tommy Lee Sparta's later retreat from the public domain as Uncle Demon has had a serious impact on his career as the spectacle, shock and awe that he originally generated has waned. The cultural production of sartorially costumed images and shocking, inflammatory lyrics that are part and parcel of dancehall culture's celebrity-making processes continues to battle with the traditional moral and ethical structures of contemporary Jamaican society.

NOTES

1. *Twilight* is a book turned movie that shows images of vampires and other gothic creatures such as wolves. Vampires are usually portrayed as scary and evil but this movie trilogy romanticizes and sanitizes vampirism making it cute and sexy to Jamaican youth, and others. The word twilight itself is a hybrid of light and darkness meeting at an intersection.
2. Dancehall is the musical genre of Jamaican popular music that emerged in the late 1970s into the 1980s routed/rooted in the sound system culture of the 1950s and the early "toast" or "talk over" style originally done by U Roy, Big Youth and King Tubby among others. It evolved into a cultural phenomenon and has a subculture of its own, including its fashion, style, dance moves, lyrical treatises and live performances. It is a physical place as well as a socio-political space that speaks chiefly to debates about national development, social justice and reform.
3. The word "smaddy", the root/route word of "smadditization", is the Jamaican Creole for "somebody". The concept and process of "smadditization" is credited to cultural scholar and intellectual giant Rex Nettleford. It was, however, originally used by Tony Laing, popular arts consultant and talk-show host, who characterized the 1970s as the period of "smadditization". The 1970s constitutes a period when Jamaicans from "below" or lower classes got a sharper sense of personhood than ever before in Jamaica's twentieth-century history (see Nettleford 1998, 259). "Smadditization" should also be seen as a continuous process by dancehall artistes to re-engineer or re/create the ordinary self to the sensational and the spectacular, and in the case of Tommy Lee Sparta, the grotesque.
4. Jamaica's popular musical etymology is catalogued in the works of Hope 2001, 2006b; Stanley Niaah 2010; Cooper 1993; White 1984 and so on.
5. Arguably mimicking the persona of Ninja Man, another dancehall legend of the late 1980s into the early 1990s, Bounty Killer emerged during the golden era of dancehall music when many new artistes came onto the dancehall scene and mounted successful careers. Now

a dancehall legend, Bounty Killer is an artiste who emerged in the dancehall space in the 1990s as the "poor people govana" with hit songs such as "Anytime" (1999) and "Fed Up" (1996) that spoke to issues of social justice. He is a multifaceted and multidimensional artiste who belongs to the upper echelons of dancehall music and culture, and who is credited for bringing the newest dancehall artistes onto the musical landscape.

6. Vybz Kartel is considered a protégé of Bounty Killer. Bounty Killer is the person who is credited with introducing Vybz Kartel to the dancehall industry in 2001 at a dancehall event, Reloaded, in Portmore, St Catherine. Vybz Kartel is considered part of a new generation of artistes (including Wayne Marshall) who emerged at the turn of the twenty-first century with a distinct sound, lyrical prowess and vocalizing abilities. His controversial moments in and outside of dancehall include the Gully-Gaza feud with dancehall artiste Mavado; his banned song "Rampin Shop" (2009) featuring dancehall artist Spice; and his ultimate arrest and murder conviction (along with three co-accused) in 2014. He is currently serving a thirty-five-year sentence and eligible for parole.
7. In an interview with the author on 21 September 2014, Tommy Lee Sparta stated that he was very popular in Montego Bay but it was Vybz Kartel, having invited him to relocate to Kingston, who brought him to dancehall/musical consciousness in the imagination of dancehall fanatics.
8. Urbanization is the process by which large portions of a population migrate from rural to urban areas. Jamaica has seen its wave of urbanization as is captured in the movie *The Harder They Come* (1972) where Ivanhoe Martin, the protagonist played by Jimmy Cliff, leaves his rural home when his grandmother dies to live in the inner cities of Kingston with his mother. This was his attempt at getting meaningful employment. However, he faced economic deprivation in eking out a living and therefore turned to a life of crime. These waves of rural to urban migration continued into the 1980s, 1990s and 2000s to other parts of Jamaica, including St Catherine (especially Portmore), St James (Montego Bay especially) and St Andrew. This also resulted in the spread of inner cities in these areas as social and economic pressures presented survival challenges for the poor. Vybz Kartel from Portmore, St Catherine, and Tommy Lee Sparta from Montego Bay are the offsprings of migrants who migrated to the urban areas of these parishes and represent a new generation of lyrical griots who demand a space and place in dancehall music and culture.
9. The word "buss" in dancehall music and culture means burst or get a break in the musical space. This means that the individual artiste not only has a song, but a popular song that leads to real rewards such as bookings for popular dancehall events.
10. The phrase "inna de dancehall" when translated means "in the dancehall". This means all the activities that are taking place within the cultural and musical space and place of dancehall, for example, the latest trends in fashion and so on. The phrase was originally the title of a chapter in the book *Reggae Routes* (Chang and Chen 1998), written as *Inna the Dancehall*. The phrase was later adopted and adapted by dancehall scholar Donna Hope (2001) in her book *Inna di Dancehall: Popular Culture and the Politics of Identity in Jamaica*.
11. Keith Shebada Ramsay is a popular roots theatre actor who plays highly androgynous or feminized roles. In the dancehall, he is considered a homosexual, a masculine identity that is negated in this music and culture. Because of the use of the word "borderline" by

Keith Shebada Ramsay in his play *Bashment Granny*, suggesting that he was neither man nor woman, dancehall gladiator Vybz Kartel felt the need to change the name of his community to distance himself as well his community from a perceived homosexual.

12. In my informal interviews with Tommy Lee Sparta, he explained that the moniker "Uncle Demon" was the name of his then manager, Heavy D. He explained that one day when he was in the studio recording, someone came and asked for Uncle D, meaning Heavy D. The individual stated, "Weh Uncle D mon deh?" which translate to mean "Where is Uncle D?" Tommy Lee Sparta stated that since that incident, the moniker "Uncle Demon" got associated with him and decided to embrace it, even though the moniker was for his then manager and not himself.
13. The movies *300* and *Lord of the Rings* are not considered traditional gothic movies. However, they are relevant to discussions about gothic aesthetics emerging in Jamaica at the time of writing. Both movies "borrow" certain images from gothic fiction and are laden with gothic trappings (creepy and dark settings), the uncanny (strange and supernatural beings) and supernatural entities and forces (such as a ring having power to save and or doom Earth).
14. The don/shotta masculine identity is routed/rooted in a Machiavellian male figure who commands respect but also feared by his peers and others. This variant of masculinity is linked to violence and aggression and uses the gun in song lyrics and on stage as a powerful and explosive weapon. Donna Hope (2001, 2006a, 2010) argues that this variant is linked to Jamaica's sociocultural manifestations of hegemonic lower-class masculinity.

REFERENCES

Bastide, Roger. 1972. *African Civilizations in the New World*. New York: Harper and Row.

Bhattacharya, Saradindu. 2012. "Demons and Demos: Voldemart, Democracy and Celebrity Culture". *Looking Glass* 16, no. 1.

BVI Platinum News. 2014. "Tommy Lee Sparta Delivers' Says 'I Am No Real Demon, It's Just a Character'". *BVI Platinum News*, 31 January.

Byron, Glennis, and Dale Townshend. 2014. *The Gothic World*. New York: Routledge.

Campbell, Winston. 2013. "The Collective Opuses of Tommy Lee Sparta: A Theoretical Response". Paper presented at the International Reggae Conference, University of the West Indies, Mona, Jamaica, 15 February.

Chang, Kevin O'Brien, and Wayne Chen. 1998. *Reggae Routes: The Story of Jamaican Music*. Kingston: Ian Randle.

Clarke, Curtis. 2012. "Bounty Lashes Out at Tommy Lee: Others Also Voice Concern about Demonic Songs".*Star*, 11 September. http://old.jamaica-star.com/thestar/20120911/ent/ent1.html.

Cooper, Carolyn. 1993. *Noises in the Blood: Orality, Gender and the "Vulgar" Body of Jamaican Popular Culture*. London: Macmillan.

Hall, Stuart. 1978. The Great Moving Right Show. *Marxism Today* (January): 14–20. https://tendancecoatesy.wordpress.com/2013/06/21/stuart-hall-thatcherism-and-marxism-today/.

Hope, Donna P. 2001. "Inna di Dancehall Dis/Place: Sociocultural Politics of Identity in Jamaica". MPhil thesis, University of the West Indies.

———. 2006a. *Inna di Dancehall: Popular Culture and the Politics of Identity in Jamaica*. Kingston: University of the West Indies Press.

———. 2006b. "Passa Passa: Interrogating Cultural Hybridities in Jamaican Dancehalls". *Small Axe* 10, no. 3: 125–39.

———. 2010. *Man Vibes: Masculinities in the Jamaican Dancehall*. Kingston: Ian Randle.

———. 2011. "Dancehall: Origins, History, Future". *Groundings*, no. 26 (July 2011): 7–28.

———. 2014. "The Kartel Phenomenon: Popular Culture and the Culture of Celebrity in Jamaican Dancehall". Paper presented at the Institute of Cultural Studies seminar series, University of the West Indies, Mona, 11 April.

Lewin, Olive. 2000. *"Rock It Come Over": The Folk Music of Jamaica*. Kingston: University of the West Indies Press.

Meeks, Brian. 1996. "The Political Moment in Jamaica: The Dimensions of Hegemonic Dissolution". In *Dispatches from the Ebony Tower: Intellectuals Confront the African American Experience*, edited by Manning Marable, 52–74. New York: Columbia University Press.

Mueller, Charles Allen. 2008. *The Music of the Goth Subculture: Postmodernism and Aesthetics*. Florida: Florida State University.

Nettleford, Rex. 1998. *Mirror Mirror: Identity, Race and Protest in Jamaica*. LMH Publishing.

Spooner, Catherine. 2006. *Contemporary Gothic*. London: Reaktion Books.

Stanley Niaah, Sonjah. 2005. "'Dis Slackness Ting': A Dichotomizing Master Narrative in Jamaican Dancehall". *Caribbean Quarterly* 51, no. 3–4: 55–76.

———. 2010. *Dancehall: From Slave Ship to Ghetto*. Ottawa: University of Ottawa Press.

Torres, Lena Delgado de. 2011. "Swagga: Fashion, Kinaesthetics and Gender in Dancehall and Hip Hop". *Journal of Black Masculinity: The Philosophical Underpinnings of Gender Identity* 1, no. 3: 1–2.

White, Garth. 1984. "The Development of Jamaican Popular Music, Part 2. Urbanization of the Folk: The Merger of Traditional and Popular in Jamaican Music". *ACIJ Research Review* 1:3–15, 24–36.

CHAPTER 9

Dancehall Political Patronage and Gun Violence

Political Affiliations and the Glorification of Gun Culture[*]

DENNIS HOWARD

INTRODUCTION: A POLITICAL DANCEHALL?

Cultural theorist Donna Hope has asserted that dancehall and dancehall culture are squarely apolitical and anti-establishment in their focus and essence (Cooper 1993; Hope 2006; Stolzoff 2000). Scholars such as Carolyn Cooper have also argued that the violence in dancehall falls in the realm of metaphor and role play and that literal interpretations of these lyrics are inclinations to "criminalise the idiom and demonise the culture" (Cooper 2004).

Hope, when interviewed by Cliff Hughes on the Jamaican current affairs television programme *Impact*, responding to my assertion of an inadequate use of popular music in the People's National Party (PNP) presidential campaign and my suggestion that one of the candidates should have relied on the entertainment community which is very vibrant in his constituency, declared that this would not have been a viable option: "From my work in dancehall, I have found that the dancehall itself as space is very apolitical. There has not been any concerted move by any dancehall artist to support any candidate overtly. Dancehall criticizes the political structure very clearly. So you will not have any dancehall artist aligning with any political group or leader" ("PNP Riddims", CVM Television, 18 September 2005).

In her essay "Lyrical Gun: Metaphor and Role-Play in Dancehall Culture", Cooper states:

> Simpleminded evaluations of the verbal violence of Jamaican dancehall lyrics often fail to take into account the promiscuous genesis of these discourses, instead representing them as unambiguous signs of the congenital pathology of Jamaican popular culture and its creators. Conversely, I argue that *badmanism* is a theatrical pose that has been refined in the compli-

[*]Previously published in *Jamaica Journal* 32, no. 3 (2010): 8–15.

> cated socialisation process of Jamaican youths who learn to imitate and adapt the sartorial and ideological "style" of the heroes and villains of imported movies. (Cooper 2004, 146–47)

While recognizing and agreeing with many of the views of these two noted scholars and applauding their insights into postcolonial cultural patterns, I must assert that these analyses are not far-reaching enough and that further study would indicate additional variables to these very complex issues. I am of the opinion that dancehall has been a major political force with all its attending biases and partisan elements, and that the glorification of gun violence is not merely metaphorical or a theatrical pose.

CULTURAL IMPERIALISM AND ITS EFFECTS

As far back as the 1960s, when reggae music was in its infancy, the influence of American culture, especially American Westerns, spaghetti Westerns and gangster movies, was evident among the inner-city masses. The Skatalites, the seminal ska band, had songs with names such as "Guns of Navarone", "Dick Tracy", "Ball of Fire", "Cleopatra", "Ringo", "President Kennedy" and "Fidel Castro". These titles were influenced first by movies and second by news coming out of the United States and Britain via the Voice of America and BBC. "Guns of Navarone" and "Cleopatra" are titles taken from movies of the same name, while "Dick Tracy" comes from the comic strip about the famous crime fighter. "President Kennedy" and "Fidel Castro" show the influence of the political tensions of the Cold War and the Bay of Pigs incident that almost precipitated a third world war (Cooper 2004).

In the late 1960s and early 1970s, with the emergence of rocksteady and reggae, this fascination with political themes and American culture continued. Lee "Scratch" Perry, who named himself "The Upsetter" in the tradition of the spaghetti Westerns of Italy, made several tracks with names from many spaghetti Westerns and even adopted the spaghetti Western attire, which can be seen in the *Soul Revolution* album he produced for the Wailers. King Stitt became the "Ugly One" from the movie *The Good, the Bad and the Ugly,* while many artists adopted the names of American, Italian, Hong Kong Chinese[1] and British heroes and anti-heroes, including the Avengers, the Titans, Silver Fox, Josie Wales, Ninjaman, Jackie Chang, Clint Eastwood, Lone Ranger, Dirty Harry and Dillinger. This fascination was not limited to "rude bwoys" and entertainers, as many law enforcement officers adopted foreign monikers, for example "Trinity", "Django" and "Bigga" Ford ("Bigger" from the spaghetti Western *Trinity*). In fact, the phenomenon went so far as to influence the criminal gangs which had emerged.

This was a direct manifestation of a neocolonial, postcolonial Jamaican environment where a marginalized black population struggles with issues of identity and seeks to construct identities from the sources available to them. I concur with Cooper's (2004) analysis of the "indigenous tradition of heroic 'badness'" (147) in that such elements together form the basis of an affinity to these foreign cultural expressions of bravado and "star-bwoy" qualities.

FIRE BURNING WHILE JAH KINGDOM GONE TO WASTE

As much as the overriding political message of the 1960s and 1970s was anti-establishment and politically non-aligned, there was also at the same time a political message that was very parochial, partisan, localized and directly linked to gangsters and politicians of the inner cities. Gangsters played a prominent role from early on: Duke Reid, sound system owner and producer, was famous for using thugs to intimidate rivals at the early sound clashes between rivals such as Clement "Coxsone" Dodd and Vincent "King" Edwards (Barrow and Dalton 2004, 15). While the Wailers, Culture and Ras Michael and the Sons of Negus were chanting down Babylon, there were artists who were forging ahead with a thinly veiled partisan political message to influence the Jamaican masses to political activism. It was Prince Buster, the "voice of the people" and popular singer and producer, who introduced Edward Seaga to Western Kingston on the strength of his popularity as sound system owner and popular artist. Michael Manley, as leader of the PNP, more than anyone before him, understood the use of popular music in political campaigning and outmanoeuvred Hugh Shearer of the Jamaica Labour Party (JLP) in the use of popular music in the 1972 general elections. Manley used popular songs such as Delroy Wilson's "Better Must Come" and Max Romeo's "Let the Power Fall On I" to great effect, mobilizing the masses to deliver a massive landslide victory for the PNP (see Gray 2004).

In fact, according to Tony Laing (personal interview, January 2005, Kingston), many popular bands and performers were on the campaign trail with the PNP, including the Wailers, Inner Circle and Max Romeo. It must be noted that many of these performers came from PNP-dominated areas such as Trench Town and Mona. This connection heightened as the 1970s progressed, during the political fervour of socialism under the Manley-led government of the PNP. In the 1976 election Neville "Struggle" Martin recorded the political classic "The Message" extolling the achievements of the Manley government and stating, among other things, that "My Leader Born Ya" (my leader was born here), playing on the fact that Michael Manley's political rival Edward Seaga was born in the United States while Manley was born in Jamaica. The song was produced for the PNP by pioneer reggae producer Clancy Eccles, who was known for his open support of that political party. Pluto Shervington's "I Man Born Ya" and Lord Laro's "Foreign Press" were viewed as patriotic songs, but a deeper examination of these classics reveals that they were very political and partisan in many respects and had a direct relationship with the ruling party at the time, the PNP.

It is easy to understand the preference for these musicians to gravitate toward the Manley government when one looks back at the record of the JLP in the 1960s as it relates to creative expression. The Hugh Shearer–led government had been known for banning many popular Jamaican songs, including the Ethiopians' "Everything Crash". Songs were not the only artefacts the JLP censored; they had also banned many books they labelled subversive and had even deported Walter Rodney, a University of the West Indies lecturer. This had left a bitter taste in the mouths of many artists, who were inspired by the anti-colonial struggles in Africa and the civil rights movement in the

United States. Manley, on the other hand, openly respected the arts and had developed good relationships with many of the singers and musicians.

In contrast to this implied alliance between Manley and many musicians, songs like Ernie Smith's "Power and the Glory", Bob Andy's "Fire Burning" and Max Romeo's "No Joshua" were direct attacks on the PNP government of the 1970s. Andy would later state that he had been angered by the divine Moses persona that Manley had campaigned on with his "iron rod of Joshua" and lamented that nothing positive was happening for the people (personal interview, March 2005, Kingston). "We got caught up with the Hollywood style of the politicians, and missed the reality that nothing was really happening." Andy also admitted that he had had personal issues with the Manley-led government, hence he was inspired to write "Fire Burning" as an expression of his anti-PNP sentiments.[2]

From the 1970s, big dancehall sound systems like Socialist Roots from Arnett Gardens, a PNP stronghold, used the pulpit of the sound system to "big up" political bosses and political representatives, as I observed at a weekly street jam on Brentford Road. In the 1970s, all PNP sounds had to have "The Message" and Neville "Struggle" Martin's "Stand Firm"; all JLP sounds had to have "Turn Dem Back" (sung by Pearnel Charles) and "High Up". From the 1970s onwards (and in fact even up to the present), "Ring My Bell" by Anita Ward could not be played in many PNP areas; while in the 1980s and 1990s, in JLP areas the playing of "One Man Against the World" by Gregory Isaacs was the occasion for a gun salute in tribute to Jim Brown, then don of Tivoli Gardens, as I witnessed several times at several venues, including Backline, a weekly street jam in Tivoli Gardens, before Jim Brown's death.

POLITICAL DONSHIP AND DANCEHALL PATRONAGE

In the early days of dancehall music, circa 1979–1985, the dons were part of the driving force in the promotion of the music. In fact, in Arnett Gardens, Tony Welch, a PNP supporter and area don, was patron of Socialist Roots. Welch and his cohorts, including George "Peppa" Phang who in the 1980s ran one of the most successful dancehall labels, Powerhouse,[3] promoted many of the major dances in the area. Socialist Roots had one of the popular deejays of the time, Ranking Trevor, who was known for his PNP affiliations. Yellowman (Winston Foster), the first dancehall superstar, attributes his early success to the encouragement of well-known PNP affiliated gangster Starky (Anthony Tingle, who took his name from the American television police series *Starsky and Hutch*). Yellowman recalls that it was Starky who ensured that he got his chance on the "mike", so that he could show his skills, giving him the space to develop into the superstar he became (personal interview, September 2005).[4]

Another famous "Junglist" was the inimitable Peter Metro (Donovan Harris), who openly enjoyed the protection of the political machinery of Arnett Gardens. Metro was not shy about promoting his political allegiance on stage and in the dancehalls, as I observed many times while attending dances in western Kingston in the 1970s and 1980s.

As Norman Stolzoff (2000, 11) accurately states, "Integrating rivalries marked by political affiliation and control of the drug trade, the so called tribal wars, have also played themselves out in the dancehalls. Some of these gangsters are participants in the dancehall scene either on the business side of things as record producers, sound system owners, and entertainment promoters, or on the performance side as sound system selectors, DJ s, or dancers." Many young artists owed their early development to the patronage of these area dons and leaders who might not necessarily be gangsters but were always political. Stur Gav, "The Immortal", the dancehall sound system headed by the legendary U Roy (Ewart Beckford), was located in an area which was aligned to the JLP and so was seen implicitly as a JLP sound. In fact, some of the deejays on the sound have themselves been perceived to have been directly aligned to the JLP, namely Josie Wales (Joseph Sterling) and U Roy himself. In the 1980s, Sur Mars, the sound system of popular PNP supporter Kenneth "Skeng Don" Black, was not only a musical force but also a political one, which openly promoted the principles and philosophies of the PNP. Black was known for his patronage in his parish of birth, Clarendon, but also in Kingston and Manchester where he lived and had his base. Deejay Super Cat (William Maragh) never hid his affiliation with the PNP and with strongman Skeng Don.

Robert Livingstone, famed manager of Super Cat and Shaggy, credits his "buss" (break) in the business to Matthews Lane political strongmen Glenford "Early Bird" Phipps and Donald "Zekes" Phipps, who he said supported and encouraged any youth in the area who had ambition and persuaded Gregory Isaacs to take him on tour as his assistant (personal interview, June 1999).[5] In all music centres island-wide, there existed alliances of music and politics. Usually, each alliance was centred around a sound system, controlled by a political activist. Artists who were affiliated with these sound systems were supported and protected by the political dons. Most sound system owners transitioned into music production to support the artists in their camp. Hence, due to the affiliation, most artists had to mirror the political views of their boss. There developed a kind of music clientelism similar to the political clientelism discussed by Carl Stone in his brilliant work *Democracy and Clientelism in Jamaica* (1980). The patronage is reciprocal, and artists are expected to return the favours to the dons from whom they get protection and endorsement. This is done in a variety of ways. First, many dons are show and dance promoters (of events such as Spanglers Dance [PNP] or Champion in Action [JLP]) and an appearance by the artist at their show or dance is mandatory and must be at a concessionary fee or no fee at all. Second, money is always welcome, ostensibly for "community development" or as a contribution to the candidate for the constituency. Finally, the ubiquitous "big up" of the area leader is very important and is viewed by the area don as an important endorsement – an effective public relations tool that establishes the don's prestige, power and visibility. The "bigging up" of garrisons is not a voluntary act by the artists but is a demand by area leaders and dons. Entertainers who refuse to "big up" an area leader or don live or on records feel the don's wrath. With no other option, many artists have felt the need to protect themselves by "bigging up" leaders from both sides.

In most garrison communities, the artists who live in these areas invariably have no choice but to become the mouthpieces of the area dons and, by extension, their political representatives. While working on Eastfest 2003, I witnessed Buju Banton inviting Zeeks, who had been on his international tour, on stage.

A POLITICAL PASS FOR ENTERTAINERS

While many entertainers have had political affiliations, this has been concealed through a device I call "partisan immunity". In fact, in earlier days, artists moved freely between opposing areas without fear. This was due to the mutual respect that gangsters and artists shared. Bob Marley was a popular figure within political tribal circles. He was known to be a friend or associate of a number of well-known, alleged political dons, including Claudius Massop (JLP), Milton "Tony" Welch (PNP), Earl "Tek Life" Wadley (PNP) and Carl "Bya" Mitchell (JLP). All were notorious, reputed to be very dangerous and responsible for the political warfare of the time. They were highly connected politically, and routinely "buss" (beat) the cases which were brought before the courts against them.

King Jammy's Studio, owned by Lloyd "Jammys" James, is located in Waterhouse, a PNP enclave. King Tubby Studio, owned by Osbourne "King Tubby" Ruddock, was located in Tower Hill, a JLP area.[6] These two studios provided most of the dancehall music of the late 1970s and early 1980s; hence they were frequently visited by scores of entertainers. Recording artists were very aware of the political imperative of being sensitive to the partisan realities of recording at both studios. Veteran deejay Lady Anne in an interview in *West Indian Times* (http://www.westindiantimes.net/ent/entnws/92.html) recalled that to enter King Tubby Studio one had to pass gunmen who demanded to know whether the visitor was "PNP or JLP", and in order to get past one had to answer "Musician", using one's *partisan immunity*. She noted that it was very dangerous to be in the area and that artists and engineers confined themselves to the studio.

Tony Rebel's (Patrick Barrett) anthemic "Sweet Jamaica" (1993) is usually lauded for its patriotic overtones but is viewed in some circles as a blatant partisan song that is an apology for the failures of the PNP government of the 1990s. To ensure his partisan immunity, he inserts the line "What a nice place fi live, sweet Jamdown, / The only problem is, dollars nah run." Rebel is known for his affiliation to the PNP and was even rewarded, it has been suggested, with a national honour, the Order of Distinction (officer class) which many music insiders argued came too soon. Rebel performed at several campaign meetings for the then incumbent Arnold Bertram in St Ann in the general election of 2002.

Beenie Man (Moses Davis) also went on the road in support of the PNP; his manager at the time, Patrick Roberts, was also a PNP candidate. Nevertheless, artists such Beenie Man, Bounty Killer and Ninjaman (Desmond Ballentyne) are all affiliated with area dons on both sides, as evidenced by their endorsement of the stage shows and dances these dons promote and the constant visits to different garrisons to pay respects to these dons, an activity that I have witnessed many times.

Similarly, the simultaneous "bigging up" of Jungle (PNP), Rema (PNP), Tivoli (JLP) and "Matches" Lane (Matthews Lane, PNP)[7] is no accident, as illustrated by Elephant Man in "Bad Man Holiday" (2003):

No, Tivoli man nuh play (Pop it off now)
Jungle man dem nuh play (no say nothin')
Stush mouth man nuh play (no say nothin')
Matches Lane man nuh play (no say nothin')
So come out a di way when wi a spray (no say nothin')
Cau yuh know wi nuh have no head from morning (get mad now)

MINE YU MOUT BWOY

Despite the fact that most artists enjoy partisan immunity, any attempts to attack the political system or parties without backing are swiftly dealt with. This was the case for Gabriel (Levardes Fisher), Kip Rich (Marlon Plunkett) and Bounty Killer (Rodney Price). Gabriel, an up-and-coming deejay at the time, in 2001 recorded a song that "dissed" (disrespected) both PJ Patterson and Edward Seaga, then prime minister and leader of the opposition respectively. The selector of a visiting sound system made the mistake of playing the song at an area dance in the Matthews Lane area – a garrison community.[8] The sound was immediately turned off and the deejay "dealt with" for his disrespect.[9] That song was not subsequently played by any other sound system in the garrisons. Since that incident, Gabriel's career has not recovered. Similarly in 2000, when Kip Rich took the occasion at the music festival Reggae Sumfest to disrespect both PJ Patterson and then minister of finance Omar Davies, the leadership of Matthews Lane summoned him and he was "dealt with".[10] He subsequently made a public apology for his indiscretion. In 2002, Bounty Killer was reportedly unceremoniously chased out of Arnett Gardens after attempting to "diss" Patrick Roberts, Beenie Man's PNP-activist manager who ran against Andrew Holness in the Tower Hill area of St Andrew in the last general election.

LYRICALLY LOADED (FANTASY OR REALITY)

Carolyn Cooper, as I have discussed earlier, has attempted to sanitize the violence associated with reggae and dancehall in particular. Cooper further states:

> Indeed, one must immediately raise an admittedly controversial issue about the function of violent talk in predominantly oral cultures like Jamaica. Violent, daring talk such as that of the DJ and the rapper can function as a therapeutic substitute for even more dangerous violent action. Cathartic talk does not so much incite to violence as it controls violence in a socially accepted way. (Cooper 2004, 159)

While such analysis is on point in terms of the role of metaphors and role play, it shows an incomplete understanding of the nexus between the artist and the political/gangster underworld and "the way that dancehall is integrated into daily life and how the meanings of songs are contingent on historical, productive, and performative factors" (Stolzoff 2000, 19). It is important to include socio-political factors that can never be unearthed by content analysis of lyrics. The relationship between artist and don is a symbiotic one, which by its nature supports and promotes the criminal acts that are sometimes performed by these badmen/rude bwoys. Elephant Man's emphatic war cry of "Put yuh AK ova di wall" (in the song "Ova di Wall" [2004]) is certainly not metaphorical by any stretch of the imagination and has no place in the category of metaphor and role play:

Ova di wall, ova di wall
Blood a go run like Dunns River Fall . . .
If them mek we pop out we gun pan dem
All five magazine we would a dun pon dem . . .
If a me we would a drop a bomp pan dem
Kidnap them daughter or son from dem
Give them K bullet if magnum want dem
To all badman this a the gun anthem . . .
So we big up all the shottas and we gun man friend

Vybz Kartel's (Adijah Palmer) "Guns Like Mine" (2001) is instructive:

Dem nuh got no guns like mine, no KG 9
A coppershot a buss dem big head and bruck spine
Me sey one at a time bad bwoy form line
Then beat carbine who nuh dead get blind
Me have them life pan line like clothes pan line
Kartel buss one inna b-- bwoy spine

Ward 21's chilling "Blood Stain" (2002) leaves nothing to the imagination:

see dem run, see dem run, see dem run
when I bus my gun, my gun, my gun . . .
Da one yah name blood stain . . .
mi coppa fall like rain
cardiac arrest a lock di hardest to your brain
and rapidly wi tear some p-- face like cellophane

The deejays' motive in these examples is clear: it is a blatant glorification of badmanism and the gun culture. Beenie Man in "Any Mr Man" (1996) endorses inner-city gun manufacturing:

Di gun is here, laugh
Oh bad guys beware, laugh
Bad man is here . . .
Brand new gear . . .
A me name never happy
Me mek duppy

Dis badman like yuh tek man fi claffy
Copper shot a pick yuh like how crook pick ackee
Shouldn't dis di man from brook valley
[Emphasis mine.]

These are narratives of the harsh realities of life for some in inner-city areas, a life which is fuelled by the political gangsterism that is endemic in Jamaican society. The violence and dehumanization which are meted out to the poor in many inner-city areas by the state and the area dons have been normalized. In the above examples, analysis of the lyrics indicates no evidence that the artists are utilizing metaphors. While this graphic storytelling can have the effect of highlighting the realities of inner-city life and shocking the society to engage in fundamental changes in the body politic, it can also have a reinforcing effect.

I suggest that there are those in the criminal underground who use the glorification of violence in dancehall lyrics as inspiration and justification for their criminal behaviour. These songs also influence youngsters to enter the underworld due to its endorsement by their musical "heroes"; such youngsters in their search for identity see the example of the rude bwoy as the only way to gain recognition.

Stolzoff (2000, 11) observes: "The gangster lifestyle, based on a conspicuous display of masculine symbols of power (women, cars, money) and willingness to use violence to achieve desired ends, has become a model of the good life for thousands of male youths in the ghettos. The figure of the gangster has thus become a central theme in the dancehall performance."

In a study published in 2003 by the Department of Psychology at Iowa State University (Anderson, Carnagey and Eubanks 2003, cited in Gardener 2003), it was found that violent lyrics influenced young people in a negative way and influenced their thoughts and actions. In the study, violent lyrics clearly increased feelings of anger and hostility. These feelings were not an effect of differences in musical genres or of a specific artist; it was the lyrics that appeared to be responsible for increased aggression in feelings. Commenting on the study, psychologist Alan Hifer states: "At some level we have a fantasy that musicians and songwriters are the poets of our generation and that they have a unique insight. People decide this must have some validity to it and, if it has you sometimes follow it."[11] Psychologist Craig Anderson, author of the study, observes:

> Generally speaking, we don't worry about one exposure. It's the cumulative effect that worries people and should worry people. If you're increasing aggressive thinking every time you're exposed to violent lyrics, how many exposures does it take before that way of thinking becomes habitual, when it doesn't require a violent song or video game in order for the person to be thinking violent thoughts all the time? The problem is heightened because the lyrics effects are compounded by violent television, movies, video games, and hostile behaviour in the home or in the neighbourhood.[12]

It is becoming more and more difficult to decipher fantasy from reality. There are many instances of the same artists who are using the "metaphorical gun" themselves being involved in gun possession and crimes involving the gun. This issue goes as far back as veteran reggae crooner Gregory Isaacs, who in his heyday was charged with possession of an illegal firearm (in 1984) in addition to numerous cocaine possession charges. Others similarly charged included producers John Marshall and John Myrie, both arrested in 1996 for crimes ranging from murder to bank robbery. In that same period, Mickey Spice (in 1998), Abdel Wright (in 1996) and Jah Cure (Siccaturuie Alcocks, in 1999) were sent to prison having been convicted on charges of rape and possession of a firearm. Papa San (Tyrone Thompson) and Ghost (Carlton Hylton) were charged with gun possession in 1993 and 2000 respectively; Sizzla (Miguel Collins) was arrested in 2005 and questioned about a large stash of high-powered rifles found in Judgement Yard. In Sizzla's case, these charges give literal meaning to his lyrics: "Big long gun we a run out pon dem, extra magazine we done pon dem" (2005).

In 2005 Beenie Man was implicated in the murder of dance icon Bogle, prompting him to record the song "One Bag a Lie" (2005):

> Who dat a talk bout a mi? Well yuh know I a nuh mi
> A music mi study, mi nuh kill nobody
> Who dat a talk bout a mi? Mi nuh kill nobody
> Who dat a talk bout a mi? Well yuh know seh a nuh mi
> Yuh neva see mi wid nuh mac 10 nah nuh Uzi
> Cau if a mi, mi would a get rid of Bounty
> And if a mi Capleton Bobo couldn't box mi
> And if a mi, Carlene couldn't give di punny
> Cau dem deh bwoy deh would a dead and bury

Vybz Kartel was arrested for gun possession and questioned about several murders in 2003; Spragga Benz (Carlton Grant) was implicated in gang warfare in his community in 1995; Ninjaman has been repeatedly charged for gun possession, murder and drug-related crimes and is currently still awaiting trial for murder.

CONCLUSION

Several scholars have pointed to the anti-establishment lyrics of dancehall, but few have acknowledged the politically partisan messages of some of these lyrics and their artists. On the other hand, assertions such as those of Donna Hope on the apolitical nature of dancehall are based on a very limited analysis and contextualization of the inner workings of dancehall culture. The nexus of gangsters and musicians is not a new phenomenon; since the beginning of the sound system movement and the recording music industry, the connection of the music and gangsters has been firmly entrenched.

Many songs that are seemingly apolitical in their social commentary are in fact political. For example, dancehall hits such as Bounty Killer's "Poor People Fed Up" (1996) and "Anytime" (1998) are in some ways thinly veiled partisan messages. It is no coincidence that these are performed and produced by artists who are implicitly or explicitly associated with the JLP. This is not to undermine the serious work of the dancehall in positioning itself in the debate of disenfranchisement and lack of justice for Jamaica's poor. It is not also to deny the message of dancehall and reggae as a powerful force of empowerment. These are important contributions that we recognize and applaud. However, the nuances of the culture suggest that such analyses are just the beginnings of the project. Dancehall is a product of a very politically partisan, race- and class-conscious environment, and it is hard to imagine that the culture would divorce itself from the socio-political milieu that created it. Undoubtedly, there is strong non-alignment in dancehall and we cannot question the wonderful tradition of metaphors and symbolism in the lyrics of our popular music. However, to disregard or fail to identify the pervasive clientelism, political and partisan overtones which exist between political dons/criminals/area leaders/members of Parliament and musicians/deejays/producers, especially at the community level, is to ignore them at our own peril.

NOTES

1. The phenomenon of kung fu movies exploded in the 1970s and also brought with it heroes and anti-heroes such as Bruce Lee, Wang Yu, Jet Lee and the comedic Jackie Chang. Famous villains include Chang Seng and Bolo (of *Enter the Dragon* fame).
2. In the interest of fairness, it should be noted that Andy also stated that he was apolitical as none of the Jamaican political parties shared his world view.
3. The Powerhouse label produced dancehall classics such as "Greetings" and "One Big Family" by Half Pint (Lindon Roberts), "Lick Shot" by Michael Palmer, "Buy Out the Bar" by Sugar Minott and the classic tracing song "Face Look Good (Body Nuh Ready)" by Winston Hussey.
4. Yellowman, an albino, was scorned for his perceived abnormality and would not have been given much of a chance under normal circumstances. It was only through the intervention of Starky that he was able to "buss out" to evolve into the star he became.
5. Livingstone used this opportunity to become one of the most successful managers in the Jamaican music business. When Shaggy (Orville Burrell) had his platinum party at James Bond Beach some years ago, which I attended as an entertainment journalist for the *Jamaica Observer*, Zekes was one of the recipients of a platinum plaque.
6. King Tubby was killed in February 1989; the studio then closed.
7. These are all inner-city areas with strong political ties.
8. "Garrison" is the name given to political strongholds controlled by both political parties, but in recent times it has evolved in meaning and is used to describe any inner-city area.
9. Observed by James Howard, 2002. Howard, my father, is a businessman, sound system owner and former dance promoter who has a long history in western Kingston.
10. Observed by James Howard, 2000.
11. Hifer is a psychologist with the child and adolescent unit of Maimonides Medical Center, New York City. See Gardener (2003).
12. Anderson is a professor and chairman of the Department of Psychology, Iowa State University. See Gardener (2003).

REFERENCES

Anderson, C.A., N.L. Carnagey and J. Eubanks. 2003. "Exposure to Violent Media: The Effects of Songs with Violent Lyrics on Aggressive Thoughts and Feelings". *Journal of Personality and Social Psychology* 84: 960–71,

Barrow, Steve, and Peter Dalton. 2004. *Rough Guide to Reggae*. London: Rough Guides, 2004.

Cooper, Carolyn. 1993. *Noises in the Blood: Orality, Gender and the "Vulgar" Body of Jamaican Popular Culture*. London: Macmillan.

———. 2004. *Sound Clash: Jamaican Dancehall Culture at Large*. New York: Palgrave Macmillan.

Gardener, Amanda. 2003. "Violent Lyrics Beget Violent Thoughts and Feelings". *HealthScout News*, Yahoo News, 5 May, http://www.redorbit.com/news/science/5828/violent_lyrics_beget_violent_thoughts_and_feelings/index.html.

Gray, Obika. 2004. *Demeaned but Empowered: The Social Power of the Urban Poor in Jamaica*. Kingston: University of the West Indies Press.

Hope, Donna, 2006. *Inna di Dancehall: Popular Culture and the Politics of Identity in Jamaica*. Kingston: University of the West Indies Press.

Stolzoff, Norman C. 2000. *Wake the Town and Tell the People: Dancehall Culture in Jamaica*. Durham, NC: Duke University Press.

Stone, Carl. 1980. *Democracy and Clientelism in Jamaica*. New Brunswick, NJ: Transaction.

DISCOGRAPHY

Beenie Man. 1996. "Any Mr Man". VP Records, Shocking Vibes.

———. 2005. "One Bag a Lie". Shocking Vibes.

Elephant Man. 2003. "Bad Man Holiday". In the Street Records, Greensleeves.

———. 2004. "Ova di Wall". Q45 Production, Greensleeves.

Rebel, Tony. 1993. "Sweet Jamaica". Digital B, Crage Music/Rebellious Vibes Music.

Sizzla. 2005. "Run out Pon Dem". VP Records, Zabbogabbie Music/Xterminator.

Vybz Kartel. 2001. "Gun Like Mine". Carleon Records, Greensleeves.

Ward 21. 2002. "Bloodstain". Jammys Records, Jam One.

PART 3

ENGAGEMENT, SPECTACLE AND THE LANGUAGE OF PERFORMANCE

CHAPTER 10

Video Light

*Dancehall and the Aesthetics of Spectacular Un-visibility in Jamaica**

KRISTA THOMPSON

CAMERA, SCREEN AND THE EMANCIPATED SPECTATOR IN THE ERA OF VIDEO LIGHT

By the late 1990s and early 2000s, the videographers had gone from being visual recorders of the dancehalls to even more central instigators of their happenings. Indeed, the term "video light" came into currency to describe the video camera and its interaction with its subjects in these spaces. It is unclear who coined the term "video light", but the dancehall artiste Frisco Kid used it as the title of a popular song he performed in 1996.[1] The term did not gain currency in the local press, however, until around 2002.[2] It was used to characterize the video camera and the illumination from its mounted camera light and was associated with a desire, willingness and readiness to be seen.[3]

By the early twenty-first century, the ephemeral illumination of the video camera had reoriented the dancehalls. In this period it was common for dancing to take place only after the videographer turned on the light to his camera or after the proceedings seemed activated in the space delineated by the camera's light (figure 10.1). In the estimation of several dancers, there was "no point of dancing" without the video light.[4] They also thought that videographers had become more indispensable to the dancehalls than DJs. In some spaces, like Uptown Mondays, the video light would be the only source of illumination. While in the early 1990s dancehalls had commonly had a single videographer, a decade later they could contain as many of five, who divided the space into different electrified zones.[5] The videographers were typically from Jamaica's urban communities but by the 2000s could be from as far away as Japan.[6] Typically, videographers and still photographers (who continue to have a presence in the venues) would follow the videographer who had the brightest light, trailing after him like a mini paparazzi following.

The decade of the 2000s was a period marked by fierce competition for the cameraman's

*This chapter is an extract from *Shine: The Visual Economy of Light in African Diasporic Aesthetic Practice* (Durham, NC: Duke University Press, 2015), 126–44.

FIGURE 10.1. Video light at Passa Passa dancehall, Tivoli Gardens, Jamaica, 2009. Photo by author.

attention. Many dancers aimed to debut creative moves to lure the video light (figure 10.2). On occasion fights broke out between rivals who sought the camera's illumination. The local tabloid the *Star* ("Women Fight for Video Light", 12 August 2008) reported on one such incident, involving two women, that wound up before a judge. An informal payola system even existed through which some videographers received contributions (in dollars and pounds) from dancehall attendees seeking the touch of the camera's spotlight.[7] Jack Sowah, one of the earliest videographers to work in dancehalls, recalls one dancehall attendee who offered him US$20 every time his camera strayed from him, eventually spending US$200 to remain in the light.[8] Many people who crowded before the videographer's camera and before my videographer's lens often addressed or talked into the video light (figure 10.3). They offered a series of shout-outs to audiences far and wide, living and dead, in the present environment and in the future. The light seemed itself to represent and bring audiences into being. It also represented elsewhere, locations way beyond the island nation. This range of responses highlights how inhabiting the light of the video camera, the luminous moment of videographic capture, was intrinsic in the dancehalls.

The very term "video light" calls attention to the importance of the technology of light in the dancehalls. Sowah, when asked what accounted for his popularity as a videographer in the dancehalls, identified the intensity of his camera's light.[9] He powers his camera's light – a three-hundred-watt bulb – through electricity. Choosing not to rely on a battery, this veteran videographer plugs in to ensure the quality, consistency and longevity of his light. Often the cords from his video camera bifurcate the space,

FIGURE 10.2. Video light at Passa Passa dancehall, Tivoli Gardens, Jamaica, 2009. Photo by author.

FIGURE 10.3. Video light at Wedi Wedi dancehall, Kingston, Jamaica, June 2010. Photo by author.

making everyone navigate around his visual technology. The light from Sowah's video camera and that of many other dancehall videographers is an electrifying bright white light not tempered by a filter (figure 10.4). In commercial videography and still portrait photography, filtering equipment is typically attached to the front of video camera lights

FIGURE 10.4. A woman before the video light at Wedi Wedi dancehall, Kingston, Jamaica, June 2010. Photo by author.

or standing lights to soften and diffuse lightening and shadows.[10] Without such diffusion, video light is relentless in its intensity. One journalist aptly described the video light as "a lance of bright light . . . [that] cuts the darkness like a white knife" (Mills 2002, 8). The video light is especially harsh for persons immediately in front of the camera's lens; they can be momentarily blinded as they come into the spotlight. Emitted from a continuously moving camera, this light throws a stark white illumination across the mainly black bodies of dancehall attendees, creating an interplay of brightness and shadows across the often nocturnal environments of the dancehalls. The light unflinchingly saturates the scene, unfiltered, unmediated, unyielding and uncontrolled. It selectively makes parts of the dancehalls scopically open and available as it sweeps and scopes around the space. As Sowah put it, "The video light catches everything."[11]

Video light is often so intense that it cannot be directly looked at for very long. It demands visual attention, yet it can induce blindness. It creates a form of visual experience that is felt and experienced in the body, sometimes painfully so (as suggested in the description of the video light as a type of visual "knife" within the space of the dancehalls). If the still camera and video camera had previously played a role in recording the activities of the dancehall for the purpose of memory, video light functioned by burnishing images, after-images, in the body. Laura U. Marks (2000) uses the term "the skin of the film" to characterize the way film and video created by artists living in diasporic communities evoke the memory of their cultural experiences through an appeal to the senses or through a haptic visuality, a mode of visual perception that can exceed and extend sight alone to create a sense of touch.[12] She argues that certain transcultural videos and films can produce a form of contact with viewers through the materiality of film, its skin, which can be touched "with one's eyes" (xi). Such a description seems an apt characterization of the visual experience of video light, which creates a form of haptic visuality that seems to exceed the sensory limits of sight. Arguably, the blinding brightness of the light, especially when viewers directly encounter it, precisely highlights the limits of visual perception. The intense video light produces a felt or an "embodied experience", to use Marks's words – ephemeral after-images that live on in the memory of dancehall attendees (xiii).

The videos produced in the dancehalls have a particular material character because of the videographers' use of the bright video light, which adds further to the visual noise evident in some dancehall footage. In these videos, light blurs and streaks across their subjects as well as across the screen, affecting the subsequent viewing experience of the footage. This is in part the result of video technologies that are "optimized" to focus on Caucasian skin. Light-based cameras can flatten darker-skinned complexions because of a narrow chromatic range designed for white skin, a technological constraint whose effects seem to be exacerbated by video light. This is evident in a video still of the La Roose dancehall taken by Sowah in 2000, in which Bogle directly engages the video camera. A light from a second video camera appears in the lower left of the darkened frame, registering as an impressionistic stroke of light. Bogle's face reflects the bright lights. It is so saturated with illumination that only the slightest contours of his eyes, nose and mouth remain decipherable between pixelated planes of white and mauve that represent his skin. His jewellery is the most legible feature of his body. His upper body is captured in blurred movement in the still. The image is but one instance of the distortions, the blurriness, the visual disruptions effected by the video light and video technologies. In the image the skin of the subject and the surface of the video conveyed through light merge.

Another challenge the video light poses to the production of footage is that even more recent digital video technologies have not been calibrated to achieve colour balance promptly in conditions when black and white colours appear in close proximity.[13] Such ever-shifting contrasts in light and darkness are often produced through the use of video light. Resultantly, from the moment of production, the video cameras capture black subjects in the dancehalls at night in ways that produce visual distortions and image loss. The strains and the limits of the technology are visually evident in the footage. In the dancehall videos, often "detail is destroyed as realist representation fades into pulsating light", to quote Brian Larkin's (2008, 237) words describing pirated videos in Nigeria. Marks's characterization of "the skin of the film" seems literalized in some dancehall footage. The presence of undiffused bright light on black skin of varying hues and the reflection of light from some types of clothing and accessories all draw attention to the multiple surfaces in the dancehall. These shining elements appear across the material surface of the screen on which the footage is viewed.

Another component of video light – one innovated by Sowah – is the use of screens, or what he describes as "live video", to project the camera's view within the space of the dancehalls (figure 10.5). Sowah recollects that initially he "suffered many embarrassments"

FIGURE 10.5. A loose-fitting sheet forms a screen used by Sowah in the Wedi Wedi dancehall, Kingston, Jamaica, August 2011. Photo by author.

because people did not want to be recorded or were annoyed by his bright video light.[14] What was eventually key to the acceptance of and integration of his video's light in the dancehalls, he believes, was his introduction of televisions and later video screens into the venues. Sowah notes that he would put up two televisions, one near the entrance and another directly across from the selector. It was the combination of the video camera, its light, and the public display of the television screen that led to the popularity and proliferation of video light.

Video light was intrinsic not only in recording and projecting the various spectacular appearances and occurrences in the dancehalls but also, I would maintain, in the creation of a community formed around the experience of seeing, the visualization of the process of seeing and being seen. It allowed many people to experience themselves on television or projected on a larger-than-life screen. Persons before the video light went from feeling themselves being seen within the heat of the video light to almost instantaneously seeing themselves being seen on the screen. The trio of visual technologies offered a doubled sense of one's visual presence as well as a view of a broader network of representation of which dancehall attendees were at the centre. It brought a prestige, becoming "a paparazzi thing", as Prince Sowah (Jack Sowah's son and fellow videographer) describes it.[15] The selector, located directly across from the screen, at times offered further verbal affirmation of the person looming large within the screens, "bigging up" that person over the speakers. It made individuals in the dancehalls momentary celebrities and likely offered some people the first opportunity to see themselves represented on television or on a "big screen".

Sowah stresses that the video light did not solely focus on the queens of the dancehall but captured everybody: "It highlight a whole set of people."[16] The street woman

Medusa, who became famous in dancehall videotapes and would receive remittances from abroad from people who viewed her in the footage, highlights how video light was in many respects democratic in whom it featured in its frame.[17] The dancer Kendrick Brown (known as Sick in Head) noted too that through the screens, notions of centre and periphery were constantly destabilized.[18] The screens made people share the same visual space, often making those on the margins more visible and shifting those in the centre of the dance floor to the periphery.

But what is strikingly evident in the screens in the dancehalls is that in addition to providing dancehall-goers with technological confirmation of their visibility, the projected images call attention to the very process of seeing. On the night I met Sowah, for instance, at the dancehall Stone Love before the event reached its height, the videographer from his company scoped around the side of the dance floor's ill-defined perimeter, appraising dancehall attendees one by one. The cameraman literally scanned the woman next to me, who turned her face slightly to the side, simultaneously appearing to ignore and confidently invite the attention of the camera. The camera moved slowly up her body, taking in and showing everything from her stylish shoes to her pierced glossy lips, and then lingered on her face. It then turned to a young man next to her, moving from his alligator boots to the brim of his cowboy hat, which somewhat shielded his face. He did not physically acknowledge the camera, but the second it left him he glanced at the screen, seemingly hoping to catch a glimpse of himself. Just then the selector's voice started to boom over the loudspeakers and the videographer's attention seemed lost. The screen showed an erratic movement of the camera across people, parts of their bodies, the ground, the wall, blurred objects that appeared too close to be rendered legible on the screen. When Sowah arrived and took ownership of the camera, dancers seemed to gravitate toward him and his light and he and it toward them, in part because he is an

FIGURE 10.6. Sowah and his video camera, Wedi Wedi dancehall, Kingston, Jamaica, August 2011. Photo by author.

affable and recognized figure in the dancehalls (figure 10.6). In his hands the camera was even more mobile and projected a view that moved in response to the sonic experiences of the space.

While the video light often centres on individuals or groups of dancers, a part of what the video camera and screens do is to make the very process of viewing visible to the people in the dancehalls. It makes the process of looking, of scoping out, of selectively focusing in or cropping visible in the venues or in the transformed public streets. The bright light from the camera also enhances this awareness of the camera, of the technology of video, by calling attention to the process of seeing through its searing illumination. The makeshift screens, wrought sometimes out of loosely secured plastic, also draw attention to the surface of the projected image. In these ways, the video camera and screen unite dancehall attendees in this active process of looking, inscribing themselves into the simultaneous and constantly changing roles of videographic subject and communal spectator.[19] Rancière's description of the emancipated spectator, coined in his analysis of critical modes of engagement in contemporary art, may have bearing here. Video light produces a mode of "emancipation", which according to Rancière means "the blurring of the boundary between those who act and those who look; between individuals and members of a collective body" (Rancière 2009, 19).

SCREENS IN PUBLIC SPACE IN BRITISH COLONIAL AND INDEPENDENCE-ERA JAMAICA

Screens and projection were used in public spaces in Jamaica from 1947, when the British government's Central Film Organization projected educational films – sometimes in the open air – to facilitate "education by seeing" and to "elicit understanding and willing cooperation" (Correspondent 1952; on the Central Film Organization in Nigeria, see Larkin 2008, 73–122). As a correspondent for the *Times British Colonies Review* observed, for "unsophisticated" colonial subjects, the "screen has the prestige of being the first medium of mass communication to become a part of their lives. For them, consequently, literacy and book-learning, however practically useful they may be found, may never have the aura, symbolic of new freedoms, that they had in the West" (Correspondent 1952). The earliest of these mobile units (composed of cinema vans, speakers and silent projectors) in Jamaica showed primarily films from England and Canada.[20] The same journalist recognized, however, that the Colonial Film Unit aimed to encourage local production, to "show the people themselves", to increase the acceptance of the subject matter featured in the films: "The film medium is once and for all accepted as something which touches recognizable and real things" (Correspondent 1952). They set up a "training school for local talent" in Jamaica in 1950 to create local documentaries (Correspondent 1952). The Jamaica Film Unit expanded the public screenings across the country, bringing "the experience and spectacle of electric light" to communities that had no electricity (Francis 2011, 110). Many of the Film Unit films focused on adult education, as a school report prescribed, without "glamour", "radiant stars", "glittering cars" or "publicity stunts".[21] The Film Unit – through the use of the camera and screen in public space and the aura of electric light – sought to teach better agricultural skills or support public health campaigns all aimed at the cultivation of healthy and illustrious colonial citizens. In other words, the aura and electric charge of the camera and screen in public space predates those of video light, even though in the case of the Film Unit they were employed for the purpose of creating productive colonial subjects.

Another early example of the communal viewing of screens in public spaces in urban Jamaica came at independence in 1962. The *Daily Gleaner* and the Philips Corporation set up public televisions in Gordon House and television receivers and speakers in Victoria Park that allowed people to view live the first session of Jamaica's parliament, which was attended by Princess Margaret of England ("Thousands Enjoy TV in Park", *Daily Gleaner*, 9 August 1962, 1). These televisions offered many Jamaicans "their first acquaintance" with the medium. In addition, people's earliest impressions of the practice of representative democracy in an independent Jamaica came through these publicly displayed televisions.[22] These earliest uses of the spectacle of electric light and of the communally viewed projected films and televisions were very different from the uses of screens in public space in the dancehalls. The history of these technologies in the early and mid-twentieth century offers interesting points of comparison and contrast with video light. If the prestige and aura of visual technologies were associated variously with eliciting the cooperation of colonial subjects, symbolizing new Western freedoms (to cite the aforementioned *Times British Colonies Review*), as well as projecting the ideals of the productive citizen and of representative democracy, is video light in keeping with or does it stray – and how far – from those early uses of the screen in public space? If the early emphasis on local documentaries aimed at shoring up the "veracity of film" by showing local scenes, does video light do other work when it visualizes and highlights the work of the camera and light, which often disrupts faith in video's veracity?

MALE CREWS, SKIN BLEACHING AND THE BODY AS PHOTOGRAPHIC SURFACE

Several transformations happened in the space of the dancehalls precisely as video light reached its new ascendancy in the early 2000s. During that decade, male performers started to dominate the dancehalls. Also in this period, skin bleaching became newly prevalent among male dancehall participants. It was the era, too, when what was described locally as a "bling-bling" aesthetics became explicitly manifest, that is, was often performed for the cameras in the dancehalls. Each of these phenomena suggests how the dancehall participants came to be increasingly invested in and transformed by video light.

When videographers illuminated the dancehalls in the early twenty-first century, they cast a spotlight on venues that were increasingly dominated by numerous groups of male dancers (figure 10.7).[23] While Bogle had been immortalized in videos since the 1990s, it was not until late 2002 that a large number of crews of male dancers started to perform in the dancehalls. Male dancers whom I interviewed cited Bogle (who was killed by gunmen in 2005) as central in making dance a professional possibility for them as

FIGURE 10.7. Male performers at Wedi Wedi dancehall, Kingston, Jamaica, June 2010. Photo by author.

men, and they often touted a professional link to him as a dancer.[24] These men started to perform choreographed dance moves and often dressed in a coordinated fashion. As had been the case since the 1980s, sartorial displays of material excess among artistes, dancers, models and other attendees also dominated the more male-centred spaces of the dancehalls.[25]

That fashionably dressed male performers started to "shark" and "overcrowd" the video light drew criticism from DJs of an older generation and from female dancers. In 2007 the DJ Admiral Bailey, for one, maintained that in the past "men were seen as rude boys. Dem a stand up inna di darkest corner of the fete. Back then women tek centre stage, nowadays men a tek over the dance and video light" (Henry 2007, F1). Former dancehall queen Carlene also recognized in 2006 that men were "dominating the field" (Evans 2012). To her mind "it doesn't look right, so many men dancing and carrying on. They do not look masculine doing it, but I guess society is changing and we are accepting it." A female dancer I interviewed, Kisama McDeod, who was in the company of many male dancers, also reiterated that "video light was for women".[26] These remarks reflect a more widespread criticism of the dominance of male dancers and indeed suggest a society still unwilling to accept the changing demographics of the video light. Carlene's complaint that the male dancers did not look masculine and Admiral Bailey's assertion that a male presence – a rude boy presence – was performed in the dark parameters of the dancehalls suggest that these observers understood video light as a technology that often lingered on women, its ephemeral illumination reflecting a male videographer's gaze on a sexualized female body.

In addition, Bailey and other dancehall DJs accused some male performers of not dressing in masculine ways and of wearing "tight pants, pink shirts and with bleached out skin" (Henry 2007, F1). They associated such aesthetic and sartorial practices with women. Such public policing of appropriate male dress and concerns about men not looking masculine reflect in part an entrenched homophobia that animated dancehall music and performance practices, as well as a broader fear – as Donna Hope (2006a, 63–64; 2010, 20–25) suggests – of the "feminine". Rather than narrowly interpreting the video light as historically focused on women, as some critics did, however, one might understand the history of the visual technology as one in which societal norms and expectations of gender, race and class have long been reconfigured. The space of video light, too, is the site of the new and the now. It creates the possibility of alternate forms of embodiment. The male dancers spotlight another instance in which the video camera offered a site for the constitution of new subjectivities or the unsettling of signifiers historically attached to ideals of gender.

If baring skin had previously dominated the dancehalls, from the late 1990s to the contemporary period another skin-related phenomenon became foregrounded in the venues: skin bleaching. Some men and women used a variety of epidermis-transforming means to lighten their skin. Products ranged from manufactured ones, like Ambi, Nadinola and Neoprosone, to homemade recipes composed of toothpaste, bleach, cornmeal, curry powder or milk powder.[27] The practice of skin bleaching was so pervasive that Jamaica's Ministry of Health initiated public health campaigns against the practice in the late 1990s and again in 2007. They warned of "killing the skin" – the dangers of chemicals on the body's surface – and banned the sale of some skin-bleaching creams (Reynolds 2009). The medical dangers of lightening products ranged from severe acne, stretch marks, increased risk of cancer and lesions to the interference with skin cell growth (Kovaleski 1999).

Skin bleaching has a long and complex history across different geographic contexts where social status and the rights of citizenship and personhood have been bestowed or denied based on skin colour. In Jamaica and other parts of the West Indies during slavery, British colonialists, colonial officials and plantation owners institutionalized white hegemonic social hierarchies, which privileged fair skin (Austin-Broos 1994; Barnes 2006; Ulysse 2007). The very justification for plantation slavery rested on the ideology that race existed, was visually discernible and was readable on the body's surface. But skin bleaching cannot be reduced simply to a desire for a white appearance and the prestige it afforded historically. As Natasha Barnes persuasively maintains, in the context of Jamaica, many people who bleach often aspire to be "brown", or to become a "browning" – a racial designation associated with the upper classes and with the appearance of mixed-race Jamaicans (Barnes 2006). Brownings garnered many privileges not available to black people in the social structures in colonial Jamaica, and they continue to enjoy more access to jobs in the banking and retail sectors and more opportunities for social mobility.[28] Two persons quoted by Donna Hope who bleached and who aspired to browning status said they did so because brown skin brought social visibility: "Yuh get more attention", and "[It's a] way out of the ghetto, cause people see you more when you brown."[29] Or, as another young woman, who appeared in the video

"Skin Bleaching and the Dancehall", opined, "People no look pon black people again" (McDonald 2012). While being a browning may be a desired ideal related to colour and class aspirations, many persons who bleached their skin thought they achieved a state of racial mutability because the bleached epidermal surface temporarily unfixes the skin as a racial signifier (Brown-Glaude 2007).

In the 2000s, skin bleaching in dancehall gained renewed attention when a number of dancehall artistes, most notably Vybz Kartel (Adidja Palmer) and Lisa Hype (Felicia Gooden), publicly espoused the practice. Hype even offered recipes of sorts for transforming the skin's surface in her song "Proud ah Mi Bleaching", and Kartel eventually marketed his own line of bleaching products (figure 10.8). Kartel boasted in his song "Straight Jeans and Fitted" (featuring Russian) that "gyal dem a watch me like ah stage show", and he credited the fact that he "washed mi face wid di cake soap" for his permanent state of stage show-like visibility.[30] Cake soap is a product that lightens skin. Kartel's lyrics suggest that he constantly felt like a celebrity being watched onstage because of skin bleaching. This artiste credited skin bleaching for his sex appeal, at a time when critics took him to task for engaging in what had been associated with a female beauty rite. He sought to shield himself from such accusations of being feminine and homosexual by touting the ways bleaching indeed supported his hypervirile heterosexuality. Kartel's public stance on bleaching came at a time when more men, including some male dancers, engaged in it.

Skin bleaching was more than an aesthetic practice that could be seen on dancehall attendees; it was a mode of preparation for the events and for the video light in particular. A dancehall-goer, for instance, explained to a *Gleaner* reporter that she only bleached her skin for the big dances and stopped immediately afterward: "Mi do it only like when mi a go a one big dance and mi know she mi have three weeks fi bleach and then from the dance cut mi just stop bleach" (Reynolds 2009). Dancehall queen Stacie matter-of-factly explained, "Ah girl haffi look good, and if she not hot, she affi bleach and go all out, x-rated clothes, loud ting and all just to get attention" (Mills 2002, 8–9). In her description, bleached skin seems just another accessory to be worn to gain recognition in the dancehalls. Dance hall researcher Sonjah Stanley Niaah found that bleaching was a "technology of the body" focused specifically on being in the video light: "If you bleached your skin, it was thought that you would become more ready for the video light. That you come into the light, almost, with the clearing of whatever pigment that was . . . darker in tone or whenever – it was thought to be obscuring the image, in a sense."[31] Greenlee noted too how some people who bleached would concentrate on the face only (and not their necks), where they thought the video light was most likely to linger.[32] These observations suggest that skin bleaching might represent a desire not simply to become "lighter" but to be more legible as a subject for the video camera. Bleaching allows dark skin to be more fully visible in the unfiltered video light that searches through the dancehalls at night. It allows black skin to be read through videographic technologies calibrated to focus on and represent an ideal of white flesh.[33] Such strategies to be rendered legible under the intense illumination of the video light call attention to the broader un-visibility of darker-skinned subjects in contemporary Jamaican society. Sowah noted, though, that

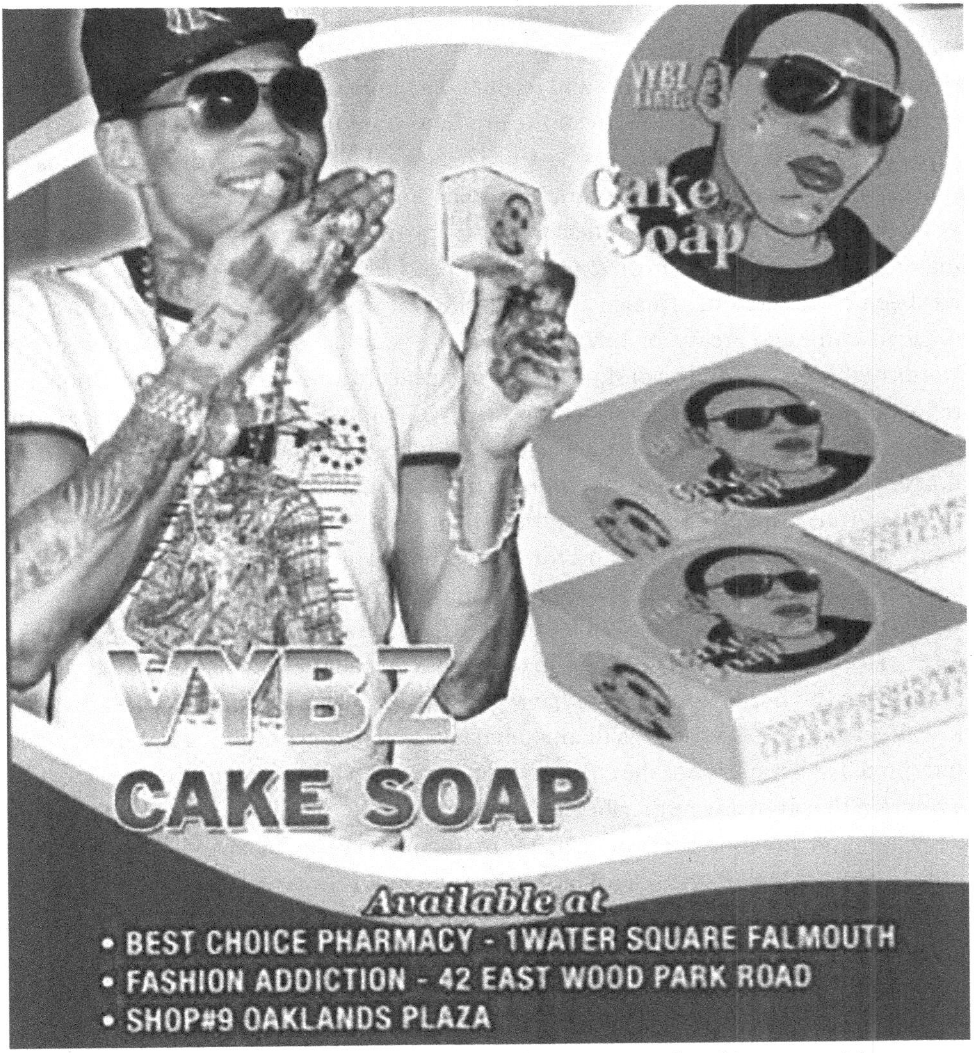

FIGURE 10.8. Advertisement for Vybz Kartel's Vybz Cake Soap. *Weekend Star*, 20–22 May 2011.

bleached black skin sometimes did not show up well on camera. Rather, the bleached faces (surrounded by darker hair and necks) and harsh video light resulted in a "white out", an illegible glare, on video.[34]

Might skin made "bright" by bleaching, as it is sometimes described, also enable dancehall-goers to carry the momentary visibility affected by the video light beyond the space of the dancehalls?[35] Does bleaching reproduce and inscribe the effect of light on the skin's surface? A member of the bleaching community, identified as Winston in a television interview, indeed explicitly described the effect of bleaching in the following terms: "It mek yuh look like yuh come inna di light."[36] Bleaching in his estimation reproduced the effect of being in the video light on the bodies of dancehall participants.

Taking Winston's words a step further, I would postulate that chemically treated skin not only reproduces the effect of light from the video camera but also indeed becomes like a photographic surface. The process of bleaching makes the body into a medium that absorbs, reflects, reproduces and records the impressions of light. Indeed, as health professionals have warned, many of the products used in bleaching literally make the skin light sensitive. Some bleachers have had to cover their skin in the daylight because of this heightened sensitivity to the sun (Reynolds 2009).[37] Different bleaching treatments also control the way the body reflects light. Hope intriguingly notes, in describing the material effects of cake soap on skin, that the product since at least the 1970s and 1980s has been considered in Jamaica a "dermatological wonder" capable of reducing "the dreaded 'shine and greasy' or 'tarry' look, leaving your face 'cool'" (Hope 2011, 183). Her words highlight this ability of skin-bleaching agents to affect the skin's absorption and reflection of light. In this way bleaching affects not only the physical appearance of the skin's colour but also its reflective capacities. Through these practices dancehall attendees not only readied themselves for the video camera but made their skin into photographic surfaces, into visual technologies, in their own right, that manipulated and recorded light. They made their bodies into a form of corporeal photograph. Bleached black skin became its own means and unit of photographic representation.

Much has been written on skin bleaching among Jamaica's urban communities as a form of self-hatred, as a manifestation of a racial inferiority complex or an expression of loathing the lived experience of having black skin (Charles 2003; Cooke 2006, A6; Kovaleski 1999; Jones 2011, F1; Williams 2012, H1). Lightening the body's surface has been interpreted as a response to the cultural memory of skin colour prejudice, or colourism, a reaction that arguably reinscribes racial hierarchies and ideals of beauty that privilege whiteness and brownness.[38] Some scholars maintain, however, that people who engage in different bleaching practices have high self-esteem and construct a range of non-white identities. They transform their skin rationally to attempt to secure and maintain power, and destabilize understandings of race as naturally manifest on the body.[39] I want to expand the frame in which one might understand these practices by suggesting that they engage and intersect with a history of visual technologies and commodities and their production of ideologies of race. Skin bleaching appears to embody and reconfigure the ways bodies have often been racialized and gendered through the flesh and through the technologies of light, like photography and video, and the techniques of lighting.

In Jamaica specifically, in the late nineteenth to mid-twentieth centuries, black subjects often inhabited the shiny surface of photographs, the grain of textured postcards and the luminous projections of lantern slides as ardent, disciplined agricultural and domestic labourers. A controversial and contested studio photograph taken around 1906 by Jamaican photographer J.W. Cleary that featured "a native washer-woman" next to a pail inscribed with the words "sunlight soap" offers one prescient example of such images (figure 10.9).[40] The postcard is part of a broader imperial economy that promoted new commodities, middle-class social values and British colonial ideals of civilization, cleanliness and whiteness.[41] In the island such early photographs taken by local, British and American photographers also pictured black Jamaican subjects in ways that recall Richard Dyer's observations regarding photographic depictions of non-

FIGURE 10.9. J.W. Cleary, *A Native Washerwoman, Jamaica*, c. 1906. Postcard. Inscription on pail (right): "sunlight soap". Collection of the author.

white and working-class women in American print media. These subjects appear with "light bouncing back off the surface of the skin", producing "the mirror effect of sweat" (Dyer 1997, 122). He contrasts such representations with the creation of a glowing and glamorous effect of light in photographs of white upper-class women from the early and middle twentieth century, as epitomized in advertisements for soap, which associated white women with notions of purity, cleanliness, beauty and civilized culture.[42] Video light produces quite a different visual effect from that of the soft haloed lighting of such soap advertisements. My synopsis here of the ways light historically was associated with particular notions of gender, class, race, labour and consumer culture is not meant to suggest that people who bleach aim to explicitly embrace or eschew the complex visual cultures that flesh out notions of race. These skin-bleaching practices surrounding video light represent "a redirection of what those technologies were supposed to be and the subjects they were supposed to produce", as Jamaican filmmaker Esther Figueroa (who worked with me as a videographer in Jamaica) has put it.[43]

In some respects, the dancehall participants who bleach seem to claim the light of the video camera so as to produce a modern black subject who is precisely not the laboring black body that sweats, who is depicted in a harsh light that emphasizes her or his "physicality, the emissions of the body and unladylike labour" (Dyer 1997, 122). It is revealing that one of the touted abilities of cake soap is that it reduces shine. It produces, as Kartel would assert, a "coolness".[44] Bleaching and video light may be read as efforts to use light in such a way that the black urban Jamaicans who do so may be seen as glamorous, beautiful and "clean" – to use another word often associated with bleaching. One woman who bleached her skin, Sheri Roth, explicitly expressed her desire to "walk into dance halls and feel like a movie star, a white one".[45] Her qualification that she wanted to feel like not just any movie star but a white one speaks perhaps to a sensitivity to the prestige associated with whiteness and white subjects and a desire to recreate that "feeling" of celebrity. Dancehall participants like Roth transform visual technologies of light as they relate to race and glamour – even materially so – but also firmly reinscribe and affirm them.

Skin bleaching, I am contending, may be viewed as a process of making the body into a visual technology, in which the skin functions as negative and print, source of and recorder of light, subject matter and material of the photograph. But what does it mean to achieve a photographic objecthood, to have skin marked by the light of visibility or a body functioning like a photographic surface? What kind of subject comes into being in the glare of the video light? What is the desired effect of such strategies in the broader public sphere? What, if any, political end might such strategies gesture toward?[46] Or do these expressions mark an end to or reformulation of the ideals of civic participation?

I maintain that the forms of visibility created by participants in the dancehalls – whether the visualization of being seen by means of the screens, the blinding light of the camera or the seeming merging of skin and photographic surface – contrast with and might respond to the "degrees of recognition, misrecognition, and nonrecognition" of dancehall culture within wider postcolonial Jamaican society and indeed reject a legibility within the political, social and cultural structures of its ruling class (Aching 2002, 5).

NOTES

1. The chorus of the song comments that "some gals not ready for the video light yet" because they lack an "upfront appearance". Frisco Kid, "Video Light" (single), Cell Block Studio Records, 1996.
2. The earliest reference I have found is Mills (2002, 8).
3. On occasion, videographers have a detached, handheld light.
4. MOB dancers, interview with author, Kingston, Jamaica, 27 June 2009, and Color Squad, interview with author, Kingston, Jamaica, 21 August 2009.
5. Jack Sowah, interview, 2011.
6. On dancehall in Japan, see Sterling (2010).
7. Richards, interview with author, Kingston, Jamaica, 6 June 2009, and Sowah, interview, 2013.
8. This seems an interesting reversal of the dynamics surrounding paparazzi or news scoops in the United States, in which people with cameras actively seek out and compete for subjects. Sowah, interview, 2013.
9. Sowah, interview, 2011.
10. The diffuser or scrim is a "translucent material attached to the front of a lighting fixture to disperse and soften the light quality, or to reduce its intensity. Spun-glass sheet and frosted plastic sheeting are widely used" (Millerson 1975, 148).
11. Sowah, interview, 2011.
12. Marks (2000, xi, 21–22) focuses on how filmmakers working between cultures use cinema, and video to translate a physical and multisensorial sense of place and culture.
13. Marc Ogden, a video engineer at CBS, quoted in Roth (2009, 129). See Roth (2009) too on the technological challenges of representing non-Caucasian skin because of racial bias.
14. Sowah, interview, 2011.
15. Sowah, interview, 2013.
16. Sowah's sense that everyone deserved to be in the video light made the technology democratic in the sense that it was all-inclusive, available and accessible to all. Sowah, interview, 2011.
17. Johann Dawes, interview with author, Kingston, Jamaica, 19 June 2009, and Radcliffe Roye, interview with author, Brooklyn, 12 October 2012. Sowah, interview, 2013.
18. Kenrick Brown ("Sick in Head"), interview with author, Kingston, Jamaica, 8 June 2009.
19. The dynamics of the dancehall recall Rancière's (2009, 13) description of emancipated spectatorship, which "challenges the opposition between viewing and acting".
20. In Jamaica the Central Film Organization showed films at first in Kingston "in schools, churches, colleges, the Poor House, the Verley Home, the Wortley Home, the Creche, Youth Clubs, to boy scouts and girl guides, Parent-Teachers Associations, Co-operative Societies and to numbers of other organisations" (Sutherland 1949, 8).
21. Martin Rennalls cites the report in "A Career Making a Difference: Autobiography by Martin Rennalls", unpublished manuscript, 1991, quoted in Francis (2011, 112).
22. Philips Corporation in 1962 "heralded the dawn of television in Jamaica with those free public shows in the Victoria Park" ("TV in Jamaica Began with Philips", *Daily Gleaner*, 19 July 1965, 9).
23. On the emergence of male dancers in the dancehall, see Stanley Niaah (2010, 125); Hope (2006a, 2006b); and Ellis (2001).

24. Dancers would indeed often look directly into the camera and offer a shout-out to Bogle, acknowledging him and other people who had been influential on them, as if the camera offered a portal to these figures. MOB dancers, interview; Ian Dice Charger, interview with author, Kingston, Jamaica, 19 August 2011; Davian A. Hodges, interview with author, Kingston, Jamaica, 19 August 2011.
25. As Donna Hope chronicles, fashions among men in dancehall went from "the 1980s/1990s dalliance with multiple and heavy gold necklaces, pendants and rings complemented by linen and lace costumes, to the platinum and 'ice' (diamond) craze of the late 1990s (a cross-fertilization with American hip-hop culture), to the current [2010] manifestation of dancehall male fashion [which] is the dancehall 'modeller' who complements his jewellery with expensive brand name clothing" (2010, 95).
26. Kisama McDeod, interview with author, Kingston, Jamaica, 21 August 2011.
27. Popular skin-bleaching ingredients include potent topical steroids, such as betamethasone and clobetasol. On skin-lightening products, see Hope (2011, 41), Wallace (2009, 27–28) and Reynolds (2009).
28. For a critique of contemporary colour privilege in Jamaica, see Cooke (2012).
29. Hope quotes participants in the panel discussion "Loving the Skin You're In", including final-year students at the Caribbean Institute of Media and Communication held at the basic school in the Mona Commons community, 1999 (2006a, 42).
30. In the tune "Look Pon Me", Kartel reiterated a similar sentiment: "Di girl dem love off mi brown cute face, di girl dem love off mi bleach-out face." See discussion of Kartel and skin bleaching in Hope (2011, 180–82).
31. Stanley Niaah has also noted: "One particular interviewee said, yeah, you bleach your skin on Thursday, there's a certain process, so that by the weekend you would be ready for the light" (interview with author, Kingston, Jamaica, 15 August 2011.
32. Greenlee, interview.
33. Winston (1985, 121), Dyer (1997, 90) and Roth (2009) note that film stocks, cameras and lighting were not developed to focus on black skin. Winston, discussing technologies developed by Kodak, makes the important point that these technologies represented an "optimum" culturally determined ideal of skin tones, preferring "a whiter shade of white".
34. Sowah, interview, 2013.
35. "It brights them up and makes them look pretty", one interviewee states in McDonald (2012). See too Kovaleski (1999).
36. "Winston", interview, *Our Voices*, CVM TV, Kingston, Jamaica, 7 April 2003, quoted in Stanley Niaah (2010, 135).
37. In McDonald (2012), one interviewee describes how sun "activates" the skin, and the video includes footage of people protecting their skin from the sun's rays by various means.
38. On skin bleaching (in Ghana) as "an expression of a cultural memory anchored in colorism and its antecedent colonialism", see Blay (2007). On its manifestation in Jamaica, see Wallace (2009) and Cooke (2006).
39. See elaborations of such arguments, in the order mentioned, in Charles (2003), Wallace (2009) and Brown-Glaude (2007, 35).
40. In 1910, the image drew the public ire of Garveyvite H.A.L. Simpson, who protested the libelous representation of the island's inhabitants in this image. For a description of the controversy surrounding this image, see Thompson (2006, 71–74, 98).

41. On this score, see McClintock (1995, 207–31).
42. The use of a three-point (or more) system of lighting techniques – consisting of a primary light, a second softer light and backlighting – created a glamorous haloed effect of light, one that he associates with Hollywood filmic iterations of whiteness. See Dyer (1997) and Stacey (1994).
43. Esther Figueroa, interview with author, Kingston, Jamaica, 15 August 2011.
44. On making one's skin cool, see Charles (2003, 711–28).
45. Kovaleski (1999) quotes Sheri Roth: "I know that they can do bad to your skin, but I have nothing to lose in wanting to be a brownin'."
46. Natasha Barnes (2006, 89), in considering the "skinless" practices of females in dancehalls, raises a question that bears re-posing here: "Is visibility enough of a liberatory strategy to convert the subversive act into an emancipatory politics?"

REFERENCES

Aching, Gerard. 2002. *Masking and Power: Carnival and Popular Culture in the Caribbean*. Minneapolis: University of Minnesota Press.

Austin-Broos, Diane J. 1994. "Race/Class: Jamaica's Discourse of Heritable Identity". *New West Indian Guide* 68, nos. 3–4: 213–33.

Barnes, Natasha. 2006. *Cultural Conundrums: Gender, Race, Nation, and the Making of Caribbean Cultural Politics*. Ann Arbor: University of Michigan Press.

Blay, Yaba Amgborale. 2007. "Yellow Fever: Skin Bleaching and the Politics of Skin Color in Ghana". PhD diss., Temple University.

Brown-Glaude, Winnifred. 2007. "The Fact of Blackness? The Bleached Body in Contemporary Jamaica". *Small Axe* 11, no. 3: 34–51.

Charles, Christopher A. D. 2003. "Skin Bleaching, Self-Hate and Black Identity in Jamaica". *Journal of Black Studies* 33, no. 6: 711–28.

Cooke, Melville. 2006. "Blaming the Bleacher". *Gleaner*, 26 January. http://jamaica-gleaner.com/gleaner/20060126/cleisure/cleisure4.html.

Correspondent. 1952. "Learning from Films: Keen Interest in Local 'Documentaries'". *Times British Colonies Review* (Winter): n.p.

Dyer, Richard. 1997. *White*. New York: Routledge.

Ellis, Nadia. 2001. "Out and Bad: Toward a Queer Performance Hermeneutic in Jamaican Dancehall". *Small Axe* 15, no. 2: 7–23.

Evans, Teino. 2006. "Female Dancers Beg a 'Bly' – Say Men Bombarding the Video Light". *Star*, 31 March. http://jamaica-star.com/thestar/20060331/ent/ent1.html.

Henry, Krista. 2007. "Dancehall Grows Away from Roots". *Sunday Gleaner*, 24 September, F1.

Hope, Donna P. 2006a. *Inna di Dancehall: Popular Culture and the Politics of Identity in Jamaica*. Kingston: University of the West Indies Press, 2006.

———. 2006b. "Passa Passa: Interrogating Cultural Hybridities in Jamaican Dancehall". *Small Axe* 10, no. 3: 125–39.

———. 2010. *Man Vibes: Masculinities in the Jamaican Dancehall*. Kingston: Ian Randle.

———. 2011. "From Browning to Cake Soap: Popular Debates on Skin Bleaching in the Jamaican Dancehall". *Journal of Pan-African Studies* 4, no. 4: 165–94.

Francis, Terri. 2011. "Sounding the Nation: Martin Rennalls and the Jamaica Film Unit, 1951–1961". *Film History* 23, no. 2: 110–28.

Jones, Ken. 2011. "Bleaching Is More Than Skin-Deep". *Gleaner*, 9 January, F1.

Kovaleski, Serge F. 1999. "In Jamaica, Shades of an Identity Crisis". *Washington Post*, 5 August, A15.

Larkin, Brian. 2008. *Signal and Noise: Media, Infrastructure, and Urban Culture in Nigeria*. Durham, NC: Duke University Press, 2008.

Marks, Laura U. 2000. *The Skin of the Film: Intercultural Cinema, Embodiment, and the Senses*. Durham, NC: Duke University Press.

McDonald, Kamila. 2012. "Skin Bleaching and the Dancehall". YouTube video. Posted by Kamila McDonald, 19 June. https://www.youtube.com/watch?v=Jb5aasZEBX4.

McClintock, Anne. 1995. *Imperial Leather: Race, Gender, and Sexuality in the Colonial Contest*. New York: Routledge.

Millerson, Gerald. [1975] 1991. *Lighting for Video*. Oxford: Focal Press.

Mills, Claude. 2002. "Heat in the City: The Layers of the Dancehall Queen". *Flair Magazine*, 22 April, 8–9.

Rancière, Jacques. 2009. *The Emancipated Spectator*. Translated by Gregory Elliott. New York: Verso.

Reynolds, Athaliah. 2009. "'Proud a Mi Bleaching': 'Skin-Bleachers' Defend Their Action Despite Health and Cultural Warnings". *Sunday Gleaner*, 15 November, A6.

Roth, Lorna. 2009. "Looking at Shirley, the Ultimate Norm: Colour Balance, Image Technologies, and Cognitive Equity". *Canadian Journal of Communication* 34: 111–36.

Stacey, Jackie. 1994. *Star Gazing: Hollywood Cinema and Female Spectatorship*. London: Routledge.

Stanley Niaah, Sonjah. 2010. *Dancehall: From Slave Ship to Ghetto*. Ottawa: University of Ottawa Press.

Sterling, Marvin. 2010. *Babylon East: Performing Dancehall, Roots Reggae, and Rastafari in Japan*. Durham, NC: Duke University Press.

Sutherland, L.K. 1949. "Visual Education: Work of Central Film Organization". *Daily Gleaner*, 27 April, 8.

Thompson, Krista A. 2006. *An Eye for the Tropics: Tourism, Photography, and Framing the Caribbean Picturesque*. Durham, NC: Duke University Press.

Ulysse, Gina A. 2007. *Downtown Ladies: Informal Commercial Importers, a Haitian Anthropologist, and Self-Making in Jamaica*. Chicago: University of Chicago Press.

Wallace, Derron. 2009. "Lighten Up Yu Self! The Politics of Lightness, Success and Color Consciousness in Urban Jamaica". *JENdA: A Journal of Culture and African Women Studies* 14: 27–50.

Williams, Paul H. 2012. "Bleach Boys". *Gleaner*, 26 February, H1.

Winston, Brian. 1985. "A Whole Technology of Dyeing: A Note on Ideology and the Apparatus of the Chromatic Moving Image". *Daedalus* 114, no. 4: 105–23.

CHAPTER 11

"Spar wid Me" and Other Stories of Civic Engagement in the Sound Clash Arena

JOSHUA CHAMBERLAIN

> In the world of carnival the awareness of the people's immortality is combined with the realization that established authority and truth are relative.
>
> —Mikhail Bakhtin, *Rabelais and His World* (1994, 256)

ON EASTER NIGHT 2004, BLACK KAT SOUND SYSTEM opened the Death before Dishonour sound system competition (part of Irish and Chin's World Clash series) in Montego Bay, Jamaica, with a fake news report recorded by the roots reggae artist Kandiman. To the delight of Black Kat fans, Kandiman assumed the identity of a newscaster and from the vantage point of the future proceeded to announce in great detail the "recent deaths" of Black Kat's rivals that night. The people in attendance who had come to see Black Kat "kill" the other sound systems, or perhaps had been swayed to Black Kat's side by the special recording, demonstrated their approval with celebratory curses, cheers, horns and lighters as well as the signature dancehall reggae response of putting a cigarette lighter to an aerosol can of bug spray in order to create a home-made flamethrower. Competitions like Death before Dishonour, called sound clashes, are a voyeuristic embodiment of dancehall practice and, to some, a disturbing symbol of dancehall's exuberant, and oftentimes dangerous, excess.

"How Dancehall Promotes Violence", the headline of a *Gleaner* column by Ian Boyne (2002), is an indictment of dancehall's excesses and captures the low social regard official Jamaican society projects onto sound clash practice. Inversion, subversion and social excess, inclusive of symbolic violence, are also key ingredients informing a politics of transgression in which subordinated groups upset established hierarchical norms. For example, where others saw sex, death and murder, Mikhail Bakhtin's (1984) critical theory of the *carnivalesque* maps alternative "dialogues" through which oppressed/low culture may claim social capital and political power from the grasp of official/high culture. In this chapter, the sound system arena becomes a civic space where competing claims of representation frame a politics of engagement that extends outside the soundclash arena. While to some it might be disturbing, according to civic engagement theory, it might be good for the community too.

Kandiman's was one of hundreds of special recordings played by five sound systems at Death before Dishonour that night. These "specials" (which is short for "dubplate special") are custom recordings, usually versions of existing songs, that are modified by the vocalist to raise the profile of, or "big up", a person (like a sound system selector) or group of people (like a sound system), or any other entity for that matter. The root of the word "dubplate" (one word) is "dub plate" (two words), which refers to a now defunct phonograph medium (originally acetate and later vinyl). The dub plate was so called as a reference to an audio recording being doubled, or "dubbed", onto the platter (plate). The dub plate format was popular during the second half of the twentieth century before ceding to recordable compact discs and now MP3 files. Further complicating the situation, the dubplate special is often shortened to "dubplate", or simply "a dub" in popular discourse.

"Dub" is also a universal term in music-making regardless of genre and, similar to the Jamaica etymology, refers to the "doubling" or copying of a track during the mastering process (Toop 2001, 115). In the 1960s, for example, a song recorded at one of Kingston's studios would be recorded to tape and then "dubbed" to an acetate disc. Acetate had a temporary lifespan and was not considered for public release. Sound systems, eager to offer patrons a brand new sound, welcomed "dubplates" and the labels took full advantage to gauge popular tastes. Ken Boothe explains the process of making a dub in the 1960s: "You make a dub of it and carry it to the [sound system] dance. When you see the reaction of the people, how they dance it, you know if the song going to hit or not, when to release or what" (personal communication, 17 March 2009). By the 1990s, in his book *Wake the Town and Tell the People,* Stolzoff (2000, 127) identifies the various players in modern dubplate practice – artists, sound systems, the middleman, studio personnel and the audience. Stolzoff says dubplate specials cannot be considered "separate from the dancehall event itself, but [are] themselves a crucial site of performance". He describes the modern dubplate as one performed in the studio but "as if in front of a live audience, and the crowd in the studio helps to generate the vibes of a dance because dubplates are used primarily in the heat of a sound system dance".

Stolzoff refers to the dubplate "big up" as a form of praising, or "paying homage" (175). Praising is a fundamental element of improvised, performed speech in Jamaican popular culture, particularly when performed for a live audience. The Jamaican vocalist as praise singer invokes the image of the West African griot and the social functions the position carries. Praise-singing in its West African context, according to Pellow (1997), is "a traditional form of oratory . . . actually proclaiming another's name to honour him/her" (583).

Barry G, aka the Boogieman, was the popular radio host on the most popular radio station, Jamaica Broadcasting Corporation (JBC), one of two radio stations in 1982 – the other being Radio Jamaica Rediffusion (RJR). In addition to radio duties, Barry G operated Wha Dat sound system. Ranking Toyan recorded a dub for Barry G that became a popular hit. As Barry G explains, "Toyan was paying tribute to me. He was meeting this guy who he heard on the radio. He did not know the commercial value [of "Spar Wid Me"]. He did it out of respect" (Cooke 2007).

> Jah me say come Barry Gordon, pack up di selection
> Day nah light til the morning
> Jah come pupa Toyan, nice up radio station
> Day nah light til the morning
> Cuz you fi spar wid me, me show you Barry G
> Bubble with me, me show you Barry G
> (Ranking Toyan, "Spar Wid Me" [Volcano 1982])

As Barry G says, he was more of a radio guy than a clash guy (although he did co-host two memorable radio clashes with fellow UK-based reggae radio selector David Rodigan). The sound system that made dubplates the de facto currency of dancehall in 1980s and 1990s and established a framework for clashing based on dubs that still exists today was Silverhawk Sound System, led by the famed production duo Steelie and Clevie. "We used to make specials without any inhibition", Cleveland "Clevie" Browne said. "Supercat used to come and talk the worst of the darkest words you want to hear and those we put on a special [recording]" (personal communication, 21 September 2011). At the time, Browne said he would do "[a]nything to annihilate the opponent" in a clash.

In addition to exclusive music, the sound system MC performing in a clash will make speeches, called "arguments", to punctuate the musical selections, adding meaning and force to the lyrical bullets. After playing the Kandiman special at Death before Dishonour, Black Kat sound system's selector, Pink Panta, dressed in camouflage pants and shirt, pointed to the camouflage backpack he was wearing and told the crowd, "Inside of this bag is pure explosive. After this round, clash done. Do you believe me?" While the crowd cheered, Panta directs his "selector" who operates the CD player to "throw one of the first *bloodclaat* [an expletive] grenade!"

Despite the lyrical "murderation" and other examples of deviant, antisocial behaviour, the sound clash is predicated on group participation. For sound system participants, voting is one of various overlapping ways that express autonomy of voice, in both its individual and community context. Here, audience members are active contributors to the confrontational discourse, employing a variety of symbolic noises, phrases and poses to respond to a particularly effective speech or dubplate selection. Shouts of "Bullet! Bullet!" or "Pram! Pram!" symbolize the noise a bullet makes when it leaves the gun, and represent a metaphorical example of the complimentary "gunshot salute". Selectors will also exhort their audience to "Put two gun hand inna di air!", which is done by substituting the thumb for a trigger and making the barrel of a gun out of one's middle and index finger. Although the occasional real gunshot is a real possibility, Cooper (2004, 159) says most "badmanism" is just a "pose: pure role play". And dancehall artiste Uton Green likens "soundboy killing" in the dancehall to the metaphorical masks and figures of the carnivalesque. "It's not a physical death", he says. "It's this sound playing a better song than the other so we now terms it as 'he kill you'. So mi say, [imitating the firing of a gun in the song "Can't Take"] *'Can't take di bloom bloom rata tata blam blam, fi me sound gonna kill another drumpan.'* 'Drumpan' meaning he don't play good like my sound. It's just lyrical killing, just musical" (personal communication, 30 December 2005). At Sting 2008 (an event known for the quality and intensity of lyrical clashing between artists), Ninjaman, a highly respected clash artist, warned rivals, "Me nah shoot you, but me murder you with lyrics."

In addition to the masquerade of gunplay, two roles that are politically and socially relevant to sound clash and carnivalesque politics are sex and sexuality. Cooper (2004, 17) argues that dancehall is "best understood as a potentially liberating space in which working class women and their more timid middle-class sisters assert the freedom to play out eroticized roles that may not ordinarily be available to them in the rigid social conventions of the everyday". Although not willing to accept gender liberation as the only function of sex and sexuality in dancehall culture, Donna Hope (2006, xix) does note both are critical "routes to identity creation" for male and female dancehall participants in Jamaica.

In the contemporary sound clash environment, sex and sexuality are foregrounded in speeches made by the selector who will either refer to personal sexual prowess, most often juxtaposed against a corresponding sexual inability of rivals. The argument being, rival sound systems do not have the sexual stamina, sexual charisma or sexual reputation to be a sound system champion. The sound clash also reifies pop culture sexual paradigms. For example, dubplate recordings and speeches accuse rivals of engaging in inappropriate sexual acts such as oral sex, which is often given lip service as an immoral and unhealthy activity. And the greatest insult in Jamaican society, "Suck yuh mada", meaning "suck your mother", is one regularly aired at sound clash competitions. Sexualized speech and behaviour not only challenge sexual convention and custom, they also draw attention to the primacy of homophobia and gender solidarity.

Sound clash discourse, much like dancehall culture at large, is a space where virulently homophobic themes, attitudes and behaviours are vocalized, primarily focused on male homosexual behavior. Homophobic performances are also a form of a carnivalesque body consciousness. In a clash situation, it is not uncommon for sound systems to indict each other for participating in various specific homosexual activities, from allowing homosexual touching to homosexual intercourse. Both roots and dancehall reggae artists tend to engage in this behaviour in their dubplate recordings. Tasha "Rozez" Bryan is a female selector based in Toronto and often faces gender attacks in and outside the clash by males and females: "If a male or female contender is using sexual tunes or comments to get ahead in a clash, I've turned it around and asked them if they'd like a taste. . . . Since that seems to be the topic of their tongue. That usually kills their arguments pretty quick" (personal communication, 3 November 2011).

Writing during the first half of the twentieth century, Bakhtin's (1984) close reading of European pop cultural texts revealed a dialogue in which low culture upset and redefined social as well as political values and practices. Formed around certain themes related to sex, death, profanity and blood sport, these threads of communication, or "chronotopes", reveal actual meaning, or in Bakhtin's words, "a measure of the world's weight and of its value for the individual" (171). This dialogue he followed backward in time, through medieval literature to a public square located in "the depths of folklore that pre-exists class structure" (159). There, within "the logic of realist folklore fantasy" (175) Bakhtin perceived a coherent culture of social inversion and subversion. According to Bakhtin, it is the folk figures of "ancient" oral traditions, or rather the ongoing recreation of them in modern day, who represent "a vital connection with the theatrical trappings of the public square, with the mask of the public spectacle, they are connected with that highly specific, extremely important area of the square where the common people congregate" (159). Bakhtin celebrated the "carnivalesque" cultural traditions of the public square for "bringing down the high and raising up the low" (177) and ultimately being "destructive of hierarchy" (187).

Words alone hold no substantive power but words dispense power in Bakhtin's carnivalesque tradition by and through descriptive body practices. Bakhtin was particularly keen on informal, everyday speech – the speech of the "common people" (177) – and their practice of creating "verbal series of objects that are in themselves reasonable, but become monstrous when linked together" (177). The verbal skills required of sound clash participants call attention to an important parallel between sound system tradition and the oral traditions that underpin Bakhtin's carnivalesque. Bakhtin, who believed in the "redemptive potential . . . of the modern verbal arts" (Hirschkop 1999, 4) would have been impressed with the public square of the clash where "word sound have power" is brought to life. Looking at the public square of the sound clash then, Bakhtin's grotesque, licentious and crude values correspond to the violent, misogynistic and sexualized values of slackness. Slackness, says Cooper (2004, 2), is "synonymous with licentiousness" within which "subversion is a quintessential feature" in the "contestation of conventional definitions of law and order" (4). In addition to revealing a moral conflict between traditional African Jamaican culture (the folk) and European culture (modernity), slackness "demarcates a space for alternative definitions of 'culture'" (4), and, I would add, alternative definitions, or imaginations, of identity and nation.

Profanity maintains a unique and special place for Bakhtin and sound system participants alike. For Bakhtin (1984, 177), obscene profanity employs a "special logic" based on a formula "whose ancient cultic importance has not yet been extinguished" (184). In the sound clash, profanity is the ultimate hyperbole, used to push a rival far beyond their comfort level, to a place from which they cannot recover or respond. Simply put, profanity and insults are both an offensive and defensive measure, used to manufacture tension in order to test and protect one's cool. Gary Exodus of Exodus Nuclear sound system says, in a clash when one "selector tells the other selector a bunch of things, some can hold it and another time can't hold it" (personal communication, 29 December 2005). A 2009 clinical study issued by the journal *NeuroReport* supports Gary Exodus's observation. The report found swearing increases tolerance to pain by triggering a "fight-or-flight" response (Stephens et al. 2009). The metaphorical dispensation and absorption of pain through profanity is not just a linguistic embodiment of the clash discourse, but it is also a physical embodiment of being human.

Profanity during the competition is just as much a feature of the clash as carnivalesque affirmations against its use at the beginning. Garfield "Chin" Bourne, promoter of the World Clash event said he tried to convince leading sound systems to refrain from using profanity in order to secure corporate partners but was unsuccessful. "I said, 'Hey [Ricky] Trooper', 'Hey Squingy' [from Bass Odyssey], we want to get sponsors and in order to get them you can't curse battyman. They say, 'Idiot thing you deal with!' With them telling me that, I looked at myself and I said they might be right and we [did World Clash] without sponsors which let me keep doing what we doing" (personal communication, 11 December 2011).

Sound clash MCs and promoters have difficulty extinguishing profanity in part because profanity is so closely entwined with the social structure of African Jamaican life where verbal clashing is a respected community skill. "Tracing" occurs when a woman scolds another person with a creative emphasis on similes. The poem "Cuss-Cuss", by Jamaican poet Louise Bennett (1983, 188), captures the sentiment in text when one of two quarrelling women tells the other, "Your lip hangs down like a mule who can't make up his mind." In African American culture, "playing the dozens" and "mama jokes" – "Your mother is so stupid she thought a quarterback was a refund" – are a similar diasporic form of competitive oratory employed in a number of hip-hop formats such as freestyle battles and cyphers. Freestyle battles are lyrics competitions in which hip-hop lyricists improvise, trying to beat their opponent, who is doing the same thing. Cyphers are breakdancing (or b-boying) battles – competitive dancing. Whether lyrically in a competitive situation or simply cussing out a neighbour, slackness implies an appreciation for argument and is considered an example of good citizenship.

Gary Exodus, whose family has been involved in Kingston's sound system community since the 1950s, equates the dialogue between two sound systems in a clash to a face-off between debate teams. "Just like when you are debating", he said. "When you are debating if you find that your opponent has a weakness, you try to prey upon that weakness, don't allow him to have a chance to come back, it's a similar thing" (personal communication, 29 December 2005).

Although not thinking of the sound clash, Richard Battistoni (2002, 33) has said, "speech, argument and persuasive communication are all important elements of democratic literacy". Sound system debate requires the same skills as part of a larger effort to mobilize people around symbolic boundaries. Obika Gray reaches a very similar conclusion in his study of the politics of the urban poor in Jamaica. In the book *Demeaned but Empowered*, Gray (2004, 1) describes a politics of the poor as being defined in part by carnivalesque notions of indirect "rebellion" such as "the ridiculing of power by gossip, character assassination and biting popular song". Responding to "low estimation of the significance" of these tactics by official society, Gray argues that while the poor have "not succeeded in toppling power holders and their radical claims on the society have often been integrated into the processes of the Jamaican political system . . . slighting the definite compulsion they exercise on relations of power, would be as unfortunate an error as overestimating the capacity of the poor to challenge power and unilaterally determine the terms and conditions of their lives" (4).

Within the everyday speech of carnival and the slackness of dancehall is a common respect for hyperbole – the bigger, the "badder" and the funnier the better. The standard format for dubplate special recordings calls for the sound system in question to be introduced as "the best", "the champion" or "the number one sound". In the clash, the question is not simply whether one sound can beat another but rather than how detailed can it be, how humiliating is the beating, how "deep" can the sound system be "buried", all of which puts emphasis on hyperbole. Accordingly, the excerpts Bakhtin presents in his essay "Forms of Time and of the Chronotope in the Novel" (1981) are, if anything, painstakingly thorough. Even Bakhtin acknowledges the prevalence of "varied" and "exaggerated" accounts of bodily functions, long lists and thick descriptions of food types and dishes. "The eating and drinking series are, like the body series", he says, "highly detailed and hyperbolized" (180). Bakhtin (1981) identifies three leading character roles in the "struggle against [social] conventions" and *for* the various facets of an authentic carnivalesque human being. They are the rogue, the clown and the fool. These figures are defined not by name but by the masks they wear. In their struggle against convention, the folk masks of the rogue, the clown and the fool "take on an extraordinary significance", Bakhtin writes.

> [Masks] grant the right not to understand, the right to confuse, to tease, to hyperbolize life, the right to parody others while talking, the right not to be taken literally . . . the right to act life as a comedy and to treat others as actors, the right to rip off masks, the right to rage at others with a primeval (almost cultic) rage – and finally, the right to betray to the public a personal life, down to its most private and prurient little secrets. (163)

Not only does Bakhtin's description capture the sound clash event but he also underlines Stanley Niaah's (2010, 132) argument that masking in dancehall culture facilitates the transition of participants to "their other selves and other roles". Reflecting dancehall's body politic, "masking (the body) in the dance" includes "dress, hairstyle (wigs, braids) and behaviors (language, 'profile')".

A form of masking in dancehall that would fall under language and profile and is also critical to carnivalesque transgression is comedic laughter – which Bakhtin praised as "the foremost devise" for destroying hierarchy (1981, 170). Laughter's democratizing force effectively destabilizes hierarchical structures. In "prosecuting their negative task", the rogue, the clown and the fool "are laughed at by others" – the community – "and themselves as well" (159–60). Accommodating self and community (anyone can laugh "with" the community or be individually laughed "at"), laughter enjoys special consideration and has been put forward as the source of social power behind the carnivalesque (Bell 1998, 106). Whereas profanity produces a "fight or flight" reaction in which individuals are defined by grotesque distances between each other (Stephens et al. 2009), laughter, on the other hand, is a unifying force based on a grotesque intersubjective truth. The fake news report recorded by Kandy Man that began this chapter, for example, drew as much laughter as it did "gunshot salutes".

The "negative task" of the rogue, the clown and the fool inevitably invite comparisons to that ubiquitous character of African-Caribbean folklore, Anancy. A trickster figure, usually portrayed as a spider, Anancy puts Bakhtin's rogue, the clown and the fool to work all at once, employing grotesque confusion, teasing, humour and the right not to be taken literally in order to weave webs of social tension around unsuspecting passersby. The Jamaican proverb of "play fool to catch wise" (performed ignorance can produce more knowledge than previously known) puts a similar carnivalesque spin on folk tradition by upending relations of power. Subjects of Anancy's attention eventually learn a lesson in responsibility or relationships – usually the hard way. Commanding both fear and respect, Anancy inhabits the spaces "where the common people congregate" in African Caribbean folklore, a contemporary crossroads where carnival and dancehall intersect.

Dancehall DJ Ninjaman is one such Anancy figure, an infamous rogue and a clash specialist rolled into one. Known as the Don Gorgon, a symbol of his stature in the dancehall community, he has also been called a fool, or versions of it, in clash situations. That said, it is difficult to find anyone who stood up to Ninjaman and earned the right to brag about it afterward. Ninjaman put Anancy and the carnivalesque on display at Death before Dishonour 2006, the year he MCed the sound system clash. Ninjaman introduced the event this way:

> It's not a policeman who is judging this thing. It's not a judge. It's a gunman and pure "bad-man" rule.
>
> I want tunes. I want positive tunes. I want tunes that say something to the nation. I want tune that kill people. I want tunes with reality. And when dub fi dub I want war.
>
> And remember I am a man of the part that says no profanity. I'm asking all you soundman to remember what happened to Bass Odyssey in England. Let your decency counteract your piggish mentality because no one should be disqualified tonight.

Ninjaman is referring to a clash in England where Bass Odyssey used profanity against David Rodigan and was therefore disqualified. Employing laughter, hyperbole, profanity and the grotesque, Ninjaman embodies a constellation of grotesque elements such that it is not possible to separate the laughter from profanity, grotesque from hyperbole, or hyperbole from reality. "All these series [profanity, food, sex, etc.] intersect one another", Bakhtin says. "By constructing and intersecting them [the rogue] is able to put together and take apart anything he finds necessary" (1981, 171). At Death before Dishonour, just a few minutes after his introduction and appeal for appropriate speech, Ninjaman was engaging the audience with magnificent profanity, all of which was met by laughter and approval from the audience. In this sense, Ninjaman's reality *is* hyperbole. He, like the folkloric characters of Bakhtin's carnivalesque, is one of "life's maskers", an Anancy figure whose "being coincides with their role and outside this role they simply do not exist" (1981, 159).

Despite being active in literary and philosophical circles as late as the 1920s and writing well into the 1950s, Bakhtin and the carnivalesque were relatively unknown in modern Russian academic circles until local scholars "rediscovered" him in the 1960s. A Western understanding of the carnivalesque was incomplete until 1981 at the earliest when the first English translation of Bakhtin's *The Dialogic Imagination* was published. Since then, renewed interest in the politics of transgression links a variety of disciplines, including gender politics, political science, cultural studies and more. In their rush to welcome Bakhtin, however, Renfrew (1997) questions what he alleges is an undifferentiated and unmediated reading of the carnivalesque. His criticism hinges on what he perceives to be a scholarly effort to *imagine* the "transfer of knowledge [and] power to 'ordinary people'" (192). However, Bakhtin himself was not unmindful of the possibility of the carnivalesque becoming a panacea for anyone inclined to apply it, for better or for worse. The temporary duration ascribed to carnivalesque agency is one poignant example of the extent to which Bakhtin "constantly stresses the extent to which the transgressive potential of the carnival is attenuated by the process of modernization" (Lane 1997, 330). The same could be said for sound clash.

Uniting the collective and upsetting hierarchical norms through a grotesque and confrontational sound clash discourse is an appealing theoretical framework, one that could provide sound system participants in Jamaica and around the world with access to social, cultural and political capital. However, extrapolating a politics or an ideology from carnivalesque theory is complex and contested. Stolzoff (2000, 267n17) sounds a warning note relative to a hyper-liberatory view of slackness, in regard to which he says, "Transgression does not automatically imply progress." Neither does transgression imply a rich source of social capital. For even though transgression is a political phenomenon, not all transgression is meaningful to the polity. In short, where does transgression end and social capital begin? Do sound systems reconcile the contradictory social forces in carnivalesque behaviour or is the basic, raw and uncut freedom of transgression the goal? And ultimately, is the carnivalesque "destructive of hierarchy" in Jamaican popular culture?

Social capital research provides a method with which to examine social and civic questions like these more thoroughly. According to Robert Putnam (2000, 19), social capital theory is based on the idea that "social networks have value . . . and [are] closely linked to civic virtue". Putnam also acknowledges the possibility that social capital can have far reaching antisocial effects. Referencing sociologist Xavier de Souza Briggs, Putnam cautions against a "'kumbaya' interpretation' of social capital" (21). The Klu Klux Klan, urban gangs and power elites, he says, are a few examples of those who have "exploited" social capital for "antisocial" ends. Mark Mattern (1998, 139), speaking of the communicative capacity of musical production and participation, also notes the unpredictable, and perhaps undesirable civic ends cultural participation may lead to: "Like other communicative vehicles, music lends itself to both integrative and disintegrative uses, either of which may have democratic outcomes."

SOUND CLASH IN A CIVIC CONTEXT

In the early days of sound systems, clashes were not formal events but impromptu affairs. Rules were secondary or left out altogether. Each sound was responsible for providing their own equipment – turntable, speaker boxes, amplifier – and ensuring that rivals did not sabotage it. The physical threat was real enough such that sound system and ska icon Prince Buster's first job in the music industry was as "muscle" for Duke Reid, a future rival.

The arrival of dubplate specials in the 1980s added a new variable to the clash format. To the extent that dubplates allowed sound systems to reproduce the aura of almost any vocalist, anywhere, an unwritten rule (nothing was written down) was added stipulating that once a particular song or dubplate was played it could not be played back by rival sound systems on that night. Opposing sound systems as well as patrons were responsible for oversight. In this way, fair play in the sound clash was self-regulated by the participating sound systems and the audience. Even with a single "playback" requirement, a sound clash could last well into the morning hours as long as the sound systems still had dubplates in their "box" that had not yet been played. Gary Exodus explains what a clash was like in the 1990s in Jamaica: "Just imagine, dubplate play from seven o'clock in the evening straight back to seven o'clock in the morning and nuttin can play back. That's what clash was" (personal communication, 18 October 2011).

In the event a song was "played back again" the audience would make their displeasure known using a chorus of vocal calls (such as booing) and body language (hand gestures, clapping, turning one's back to the deejay booth). The ultimate expression of crowd displeasure is to "clap off the sound", so named because it is literally the act of the audience clapping hands in unison, not in support rather than in opposition to the performance. In the clash, clapping enables the audience, or the collective, to indirectly "flip the script" on an official society where clapping signals support for the performer. Accordingly, to show their support, audience members will yell various sounds such as those mentioned earlier, use the gunshot salute, light a can of bug spray, whistle, bang pots and pans together or strike one's hand against a hard surface. In this way, the audience contributes to carnival excess in the sound clash by engaging in behaviour that is hierarchically distant from official, respectable expressions of approval and support. World Clash promoters Irish and Chin disrupted the traditional sound clash rules and in so doing created a pop culture juggernaut. An examination of World Clash changes to the clash format will help articulate the carnivalesque politics of sound clash culture.

The first Irish and Chin World Clash event was in 1998 at Amazura nightclub in the Jamaica neighbourhood of Queens, New York, featuring Downbeat (United States), Killamanjaro (Jamaica) and Sir Coxsone (London). In 2001, Irish and Chin brought World Clash to Pier One in Montego Bay for the first time, naming it Death before Dishonour. The franchise was also staged in Toronto (2004–7), London (2004–9) and Antigua (2005). At each event, World Clash was known for featuring at least four top-tier sound systems.

The most notable changes to the sound clash format were the introduction of self-contained "rounds", like boxing, and the management role of the "referee". At the beginning of every World Clash event a referee administers a public selection of numbers by each sound system to determine the order in which sound systems will perform. The referee outlines the format of the clash, including the length and purpose of each round, and reminds sound systems and the audience of the rules, including rules against "playing back" the same song and against profanity.

At the end of each elimination round the referee asks the crowd to choose which sound must "go home". At World Clash, Chin plays the role of referee. He calls each sound system by name and invites the crowd to show their hands in support. The sound system that receives the least amount of hands is sent home. One sound system is eliminated after each round until in the final round two sound systems are left standing. The last round is always the "tune-fi-tune" (tune for tune) round. During tune-fi-tune each sound system plays one dubplate special each. The crowd votes after each sound system has had a chance to play their selection. One point is issued to the sound the crowd determines to have played the best song and the process repeats itself in a best-of-ten situation. Both the introduction of the referee and implementation of rounds were specifically designed to increase expectations for fair play. Garfield "Chin" Bourne explains:

> Before Irish and Chin it was a free for all. You had sound systems that would do battle or clash and just play dubplates. There would be tune-for-tune until someone runs out [of dubplates], or someone drops dead, right? And then the crowd decides. We come in now and we say, ok, we doing the best of ten so if you win the most dubplate out of a ten-for-ten shoot off then you are actually the winner of tune-for-tune. There is no need for us to do dubplates for an hour. (Personal communication, 11 December 2011)

To some, for whom the "hotter the battle the sweeter the victory", World Clash cooled down the vibes. To them, Irish and Chin introduced an artificial imposition – why address fair play when, according to the carnivalesque, anything is fair game? Highlighting a familiar criticism, Gary "Exodus" Braithwaite compares World Clash to canned, or inauthentic, food: "Irish and Chin dem come mash up sound clash because them come deal with this microwave clash thing – meaning set rules and regulations. But music doesn't have no rules, nor borders nor boundaries. When you set rules and regulations like that the . . . only rule me feel you should have [is] in certain venues and thing, no slackness, or no indecent language. We can understand that" (personal communication, 18 October 2011). Boundaries were exactly what Chin thought the sound clash needed. A New Yorker of Jamaican heritage, Chin was a hip-hop fan as youngster and followed the development of the culture, including the DMC World DJ Championship competition. The DMC competition was launched by a corporate partnership of *Micmac* (a dance music magazine) and Disco Mix Club (a DJ remix service). DMC, says Chin, is "structured".

> There's a lot of people who respect what we did and a lot of diehearted clash fans who say we messed up the thing by interjecting referees. I put referee there to kinda control the biases so to speak to be able to present it to the audience the proper way. When I say civil competition I mean the word civil, as in civilized, a civilized competition, which means that it allows a more smooth playing field, a more even playing field. (Personal communication, 11 December 2011)

In the case of World Clash, Chin said he wanted a "civilized competition". While the carnivalesque, in both social and cultural theory, is rightly admired, or perhaps imagined, by the academy for its agency in creating autonomous spaces, I would be hard-pressed to suggest that the sound clash, in any form, can make hierarchical structures or hegemonic forces disappear. This is not Chin's fault, however. Laughter, for example, an integral aspect of the carnivalesque and the sound clash, is empowering only while in the act. The notion that hierarchies of power can be destroyed by laughter must be part of the joke. In sound system culture, champions are thrown down and new ones crowned on a nightly basis. Every victory then is tenuous and temporary. The carnivalesque can create space, change the direction of communication or even cause hierarchical structures to enter a state of instability or reorganization. In that specific, temporary moment of laughter or sound clash victory, when the "low" becomes the "high", hegemony is dissolved. Almost immediately though, new hierarchies form and a new struggle between high and low is engaged.

Stallybrass and White (1986, 14) underline Gray's assertion with regard to carnivalesque transgression. "It makes little sense", they write, "to fight out the issue of whether or not carnivals are intrinsically radical or conservative, for to do so automatically involves the false essentializing of carnivalesque transgression". Carnival, they argue, is not an either/or proposition. Indeed, carnival cannot be reduced to a day, an event or a single act of transgression. As Richard Schechner (2004, 6) explains relative to carnival in Trinidad, "Next year's carnival begins the day after this year's ends."

If there is nothing specifically essential worth "fighting out" with regard to carnivalesque transgression, I would argue there is clearly something experiential worth fighting *about*. It is not the length, the loudness or subtlety of the laughter that matter rather than the act itself. My point is not whether carnival is or is not liberatory but the extent to which it provides access to alternative ideology, practice and dialogue – some of which is liberatory, some of which is not, some of which promotes equality, some of which does not. In the soundclash, young people act out roles and test laughing with and against the rogue, the clown and the fool. Through carnivalesque participation, young people engage with hierarchies in and outside of their immediate social networks. The clash of social networks and the acting out of power relations that ensues is constitutive of the carnivalesque sound clash experience and the construction of political identity.

To better describe the politics of Bakhtin's carnivalesque, Hirschkop (1999, 3) begins by referencing Raymond Williams, who wrote, "Someone who writes about communication becomes in a sense without ever intending to have become, a social critic." Hirschkop references Williams to help make the point that Mikhael Bakhtin "stumbled" onto politics "via the side roads of language and culture" (3). Perhaps the same could be said of Cooper (2004) and other literary scholars with regard to carnivalesque language and culture as well as every person who listens to reggae or dancehall music. Cultural participation and commentary are departure points for participants, and young people in particular, to question, engage and perform "the terms and conditions" that influence their life and identity. The carnivalesque is an ongoing process – a means, so to speak, rather than an ends. Carnival may last as short as a good laugh or as long as a sleepless night of dancehall participation. Here, the experiential process does not "falsely essentialize" any particular act of transgression, however radical or conservative, or temporary, it may be.

Carnivalesque critiques centred on the temporary nature of transgression, specifically the theoretical elasticity some observers associate with carnivalesque-ness – such as determining when certain forms of the carnivalesque are more or less carnivalesque than others – are also examples of false essentializing. A good laugh at another sound system's expense, a full night of sound clash or a few days of carnival is really neither more nor less politically transgressive. They are all nominally "temporary". Rather than looking at the carnivalesque through a temporal lens, I argue a spatial lens is needed. In this way, every distinct laugh, clash and carnivalesque act is individual and temporary, yet also overlapping. As single points within a larger image, it is not the brightness or size of each point that is most important; rather the importance lies in their combined "social resolution". Social resolution is a term I use to acknowledge the temporary and sometimes tenuous nature of distinct carnivalesque dialogues as well as the long-term effect, or socialization, of experiencing or being exposed to the carnivalesque method. Obika Gray (2004, 12) alludes to this idea of social resolution in his discussion of "autonomous, small, persistent and cumulative acts of individual and group empowerment inside and outside the state apparatuses" by the urban poor. According to Gray, "these small acts of empowerment and the compulsion they exert on the society and on power holders" constitute "the social power of the urban poor" (12). Cumulatively, across time and space, the social resolution of the carnivalesque informs and projects a persistent, albeit unorthodox, politics.

In sound system culture, and particularly in the sound clash, the accumulation of carnivalesque moments create social resolution. Rather than engaging specific transgressive moments or trying to put a finger on the politically transgressive elasticity of the carnivalesque, social resolution speaks to the experiential learning and negotiation of the clash discourse, and of the socialization process for participants, most of whom are young people. The politics of fair play, negotiated through participation in the sound clash, provide one evolving image of that resolution.

REFERENCES

Bakhtin, M.M. 1981. *The Dialogic Imagination: Four Essays.* Translated by Caryl Emerson and Michael Holquist. Austin: University of Texas Press

———. 1984. *Rabelais and His World.* Indianapolis: Indiana University Press.

Battistoni, Richard. 2002. *Civic Engagement across the Curriculum.* Providence: Campus Compact.

Bell, Michael Mayerfield, and Michael Gardiner. 1998. *Bakhtin and the Human Sciences: No Last Words.* London: Sage.

Bennett, Louise.1983. "Cuss-Cuss". *Selected Poems.* Kingston: Sangster's.

Boyne, Ian. 2002. "How Dancehall Promotes Violence". *Gleaner,* 22 December.

Cooke, Mel. 2007. "Ranking Toyan Invites JA to Spar wid Me". *Gleaner,* 9 December.

Cooper, Carolyn. 2004. *Sound Clash: Jamaican Dancehall Culture at Large.* New York: Palgrave Macmillan.

Gray, Obika. 2004. *Demeaned but Empowered: The Social Power of the Urban Poor in Jamaica.* Kingston: University of the West Indies Press.

Hirschkop, Ken. 1999. *Mikhael Bakhtin: An Aesthetic for Democracy.* Oxford: Oxford University Press.

Hope, Donna P. 2006. *Inna di Dancehall: Popular Culture and the Politics of Identity in Jamaica.* Kingston: University of the West Indies Press.

Lane, Jeremy. 1997. "Sociology and Dialogics: Pierre Bordieu, Mikhail Bakhtin and the Critique of Formalist Aesthetics". In *Face to Face: Bakhtin in Russia and the West*, edited by Carol Adlam, Rachel Falconer, Vitalii Makhlin and Alistair Renfrew, 329–46. Sheffield: Sheffield Academic Press.

Mattern, Mark. 1998. *Acting in Concern: Music, Community and Political Action*. New Brunswick, NJ: Rutgers University Press, 1998.

Pellow, Deborah. 1997. "Male Praise-Singers in Accra: In the Company of Women". *Africa* 67, no. 4: 582–601.

Putnam, Robert B. 2000. *Bowling Alone: Collapse and Revival of American Community*. New York: Simon and Schuster, 2000.

Renfrew, Alistair. 1997. "The Carnival without Laughter". In *Face to Face: Bakhtin in Russia and the West*, edited by Carol Adlam, Rachel Falconer, Vitalii Makhlin and Alistair Renfrew, 185–95. Sheffield: Sheffield Academic Press.

Schechner, Richard. 2004. "Carnival (Theory) after Bakhtin". In *Carnival: Culture in Action: The Trinidad Experience*, edited by Milla Cozart Riggio, 3–12. New York: Routledge.

Stallybrass, Peter, and Allon White. 1986. *The Politics and Poetics of Transgression*. Ithaca: Cornell University Press.

Stanley Niaah, Sonjah. 2010. *Dancehall: From Slave Ship to Ghetto*. Ottawa: University of Ottawa Press.

Stephens, R., J. Atkins and A. Kingston. 2009. "Swearing as a Response to Pain". *Neuroreport* 20, no. 12: 1056–60.

Stolzoff, Norman C. 2000. *Wake the Town and Tell the People: Dancehall Culture in Jamaica*. Durham, NC: Duke University Press.

Toop, David. 2001. *Ocean of Sound*. London: Serpent's Tail.

CHAPTER 12

Death before Dishonour

Language and the Jamaican Sound System Clash

AUDENE S. HENRY

THIS CHAPTER BRINGS THE MODERN SOUND SYSTEM INTO focus by examining the discourse space of a "sound clash" and by concentrating specifically on the language employed by the sound system mic-man.[1] Jamaican sound systems are quite distinct from the generic sound systems used for the amplification of audio for large audiences. While sound projection is at their core, their role extends far beyond providing the technology to enable public address. Sound systems, instead, are what Stolzoff (2000, 1) describes as "sophisticated megawatt mobile discos". They have been at the centre of how recorded music, in general, has been enjoyed by Jamaicans and at the forefront of how indigenous music, specifically, has been both created and disseminated across the country. A sound clash is a musical battle that is fought between and among opposing sound systems in which the aim is to "fight" musically, until all of the sounds are "killed", excepting one, which is declared the Champion Sound. This chapter focuses on the language used by the sound system mic-man, explores how the outcome of a sound clash is affected by his discourse practices, and examines the key characteristics that successful mic-men possess that help to shape the discursive practices that dominate the sound clash.

DATA ANALYSIS FRAMEWORK

To examine these issues, I focus on mic-men who, in my own estimation, were prominent during the period ranging from the 1990s to the early 2000s. This allows me to concentrate on leading mic-men and sound systems in a more modern period of the existence of sound systems. The time range is also broad but allows for inclusion of several persons who dominated at different times during the period. I also concentrate on the sound systems that are described as being "clash sounds" as opposed to "juggling sounds"; that is, sound systems that have built their names on engaging in, and being victorious in, sound clashes and not those that are considered party sounds that are not competitive.[2] In supporting the discussion, I draw extensively on my own knowledge gained from

Table 12.1. Sound Clashes Examined

Data Sources	Sound Clash Featured	Sound System/Mic-Man Featured in the Clash	Length and Format
1	Death before Dishonour 5, World Clash 2005	Bass Odyssey ft. Squingy Mighty Crown ft. Sami T & Simon (Japan) One Love Sound (Italy) Freddy Kruegar Tony Matterhorn Black Kat ft. Pink Panther	2:01:42 hours video & audio
2	Bass Odyssey versus Killamanjaro 1996	Bass Odyssey ft. Squingy, Lenny & Glamour G Killamanjaro ft. Ricky Trooper	3:13:03 hours 4-part audio
3	Triple Loaded 2000 Matterhorn vs Adonai vs Jah Creation	Tony Matterhorn Jah Creation ft. Bad Rass	1:36:03 audio

attending sound clashes and listening to recordings of them for over twenty years. In addition, I focus on well-known clashes that have taken place for specific supporting data. I therefore gather data from the three sound clashes presented in table 12.1.

In relation to the first source, though sound clashes had always taken place in Jamaica, it was not until 2001 that there was an organized local event that pitted the biggest sound systems against each other. It was called "Death before Dishonour" and crowned the World Clash champion sound/mic-man for ten years from 2001 to 2010. The 2005 World Clash was chosen as a data source because six sound systems competed in it, four of the major clash sounds in Jamaica as well as two of the most well-known international ones. Also, over two hours of the clash, both audio and video were available online via YouTube, unlike the previous stagings of the event.

The second source used was a clash between Bass Odyssey and Killamanjaro held in 1996. I felt that it was important to include a sound clash that featured Killamanjaro, one of the biggest clash sounds in Jamaican history, and Ricky Trooper, a mic-man who is widely regarded by sound system enthusiasts as the best mic-man to have worked on Killamanjaro, and in general, one of the greatest of all time.[3] Ricky Trooper did not participate in "Death before Dishonour 5", but he was the winner of the World Clash in the following year (2006). Like the World Clash, the Killamanjaro versus Bass Odyssey clash is available online via YouTube. Over two hours of audio is available, which is ideal as it is difficult to easily access full-length video or audio of sound clashes online.

A sound clash featuring Tony Matterhorn, Adonai and Jah Creation sound called "Triple Loaded", held in Montego Bay in 2000, was also used. This clash was interesting because Jah Creation was a relatively new sound at the time. It was owned by a Rastafarian – Robroy "Spy" Williams – and featured Rastafarian selectors Bramganja and Fingers and Rastafarian mic-man Mad Ras. Jah Creation was a clash sound that differentiated itself by the insertion of a "conscious" approach to, and conscious music into, sound clashes. The sound became popular after defeating the mighty Stone Love sound and because it had one-of-a-kind dubs and specials[4] from sought-after artistes. They were subsequently "killed" however by both Bass Odessey and Killamanjaro. The dynamics in this clash therefore provided a good contrast to the two previous sources.

The naturalistic and observational data on which this chapter is based naturally support qualitative discourse analysis. Key principles which are characteristic of the ethnography of communication, one approach to discourse analysis, are incorporated into the methodology used. One such principle is that the method is largely anthropological, and the discourse practices are analysed in order to answer questions about the larger cultural constructs and social realities they fall within. The traditional participant observation was not carried out here since I relied on pre-existing data. However, the fact that the sound clashes were actual events that occurred and allowed for observation even after their completion lends support to their validity as data sources.

JAMAICAN CREOLE DOMINANCE

One fundamental observation in relation to the language used in the sound system clash is that it is dominated by Jamaican Creole. This point may at first seem like a statement of the obvious since not only is Jamaican Creole the mother tongue of the majority of Jamaicans but positive attitudes toward it have steadily been increasing (Jamaican Language Unit 2005), which has consequently led to progressive growth of the domains in which it is acceptable. However, this trend in the expansion of domains of Jamaican Creole use cannot be so automatically related to its dominance on sound systems.

The language of Jamaican popular music is, in general, English and not Jamaican Creole. This would become clear if an interrogation of the texts of the music of the most popular Jamaican artists were undertaken. From Alton Ellis, Jimmy Cliff, Burning Spear, Dennis Brown and Bob Marley and the Wailers, to Barrington Levy, Half Pint, Beres Hammond and Taurus Riley, it is predominantly in English in which the bulk of the music is delivered. In support of this, Cooper and Devonish (2004) highlight that in the 1960s the lyrics of the popular local music forms that developed (ska, rocksteady and reggae) "were predominantly in language varieties that would be regarded as English or a close approximation thereof" (298). In fact, Chang and Chen (1998, 4) suggest that it is this use of English that explains a lot of reggae's worldwide appeal since English is the de facto universal language of our age. It is only in dancehall music that Jamaican Creole is the principal language. Cooper and Devonish (2004, 301) conclude that Jamaican dancehall culture is a "megawattage sound system of [a] new globalized national identity". This identity is one in which the Jamaican Creole language, the traditionally "low" language within the diglossic community, is "challenging the authority of existing state structures" (301). But even as this change is underway, there is often a distinct shift toward more English types of delivery when the music is being done to target the international market or to have "cross-over" appeal. The language of the international "hits" of the most successful dancehall artists like Shaggy, Shabba Ranks, Sean Paul, Diana King, Lady Saw and Bounty Killa, for example, is extensively "Englishised".

It seems then that, historically, commercialization as well as the internationalization of Jamaica's music has correlated with English use within it. While as we have moved into the twenty-first century there has been a general trend toward intensification of Jamaican Creole use, sound systems, as a distinct part of our musical culture, are reflective of a very different development from what exists within popular music. There has been no wide-scale commercialization within the practice, and the language used within this sub-genre is unreservedly Jamaican Creole. I say this while acknowledging that the way in which language is used in music is not equivalent to the way in which it is used in speech. The language used in music is traditionally more conservative than that used in speech. Also, it is true that what mic-men do is not itself music, but there is a synergy between the music played and what mic-men say, which makes separating their linguistic behaviour from the music impossible.

While all of Jamaica's popular music is a product of the poor underclasses and was originally seen as low class, it is clear that it has experienced some rise in status (Cooper 2004; Hope 2006). This applies to reggae in particular, as dancehall music still struggles with perceptions that it is low-brow and ghetto. Sound system culture has also come to be most associated with the lower classes and the language of the sound system is reflective of this. The sound system clash in particular also represents a distinct community of practice, one in which (1) commonalities in language used by the mic-men, (2) rules of mutual engagement (Meyerhoff 2004, 527) in how clashes are conducted and negotiated and (3) a shared repertoire are all fundamental criteria for membership. In this setting Jamaican Creole wields considerable covert prestige. First, this is because the sound system dance is a male-dominated space. It is evident from the Death before Dishonour 5 clash that the audience was overwhelmingly male. In addition, at every sound system dance I have attended, women have been in the minority. The intersection of language use in this setting and the gender composition is in keeping with the generally more positive view of Jamaican Creole among men (Jamaican Language Unit 2005) as well as supporting linguistic findings relating to the correlation between sex and covert prestige established by Trudgill (1972) that is attached to the use of nonstandard varieties.

Second, Jamaican Creole use in the sound system clash has prestige because it is important for the mic-man to project an image of toughness. After all, he is fighting a lyrical battle that often has implications for his survival as a respected member within the fraternity. According to Henriques (2011, 182) for example, a "single night of a clash can literally make or break a Sound's entire career". The mic-man then is supposed to be the ultimate gangster and "badman" and this image cannot be sold to patrons if he speaks in English with its associated perception of refinement and "pretty-up" talk.[5] In Jamaican Creole, he can be "raw" and undiluted, qualities that are crucial for "kilin a soun bwai".[6] One of the most ubiquitous expressions in a sound clash, for example, is "mek mi si di gon fingga dem in a di ier"[7] or some other iteration of a similar sentiment. Devonish (1996, 225) explains that "within the culture of Dance Hall, shots are fired in the air by participants as a sign of appreciation". He explains further that this is a way of exciting the audience. This is certainly true in general, but in the context of the sound clash the simulation of gunshots does not only serve to acknowledge the potency of a "dubplate" that the mic-man is introducing but is also an affirmation of his "badman" image. At the sound clash "Triple Loaded", Tony Matterhorn, after playing a particularly effective Bounty Killer dubplate against his opponent Jah Creation Sound, said: "dem bwai de kyaahn kil mi kaa mi a badman. Mi hav di huol a di badman bakitiv mi niid in ier."[8]

Jah Creation, a Rastafarian sound system, despite their many dubplates and specials, did not embody the image of toughness in the way that Matterhorn did. In that, while "conscious" Reggae artistes and music are integral in a sound clash, Jah Creation seemed to draw too heavily on them. While they did incorporate some references to "gon fingga" and engaged in some "bigging up" of "badmen" and "dons", they did not heavily rely on these. Their mic-man did not project toughness in his linguistic choices, always seeming to be defending against Matterhorn's attacks and asserting their "righteousness". In one of Matterhorn's rounds, in introducing a song, he said, "unu a kom a war an unu no nuo di arts of war".[9] In introducing another song he said: "Big op aal chru Rastaman, bot unu pruuv ova de so se non a unu a no Rasta kaa unu se Rasta no miks op in a bangarang an ina Babylon. Wa di bloodklaat unu a du ina Babylon?"[10] In the end, Matterhorn had the crowd singing along with him so that Jah Creation needed to pack up their sound boxes and leave the dance. The very fact that they were Rastafarian and asserting this righteous identity within a clash seemed to disqualify them, at least in that clash, from being a part of the clash.

The use of Jamaican Creole, through its association with toughness and the symbolism of the reference to the "gon fingga", is also shown through the mic-man portraying himself as a "selecta" who is also a "badman". To an extent, he is also speaking and playing to an audience of "badmen", or in the very least, men who respect the "badman selecta". This association is also propagated in the way that the mic-man "bigs-up" known community dons or communities that have reputations for engaging in illegal activities. With Death before Dishonour 5, which was held in Montego Bay, this involved "bigging up" the communities of Flankers and Gully, garrison areas with a reputation of criminality. The link between the larger dancehall culture and violence and illegal activities is discussed by Hope (2006), who points to violence as not only being a part of dancehall lyrics and performance but to the performers' "allegedly close involvement with guns and violence in their real social relations". Further, she suggests that "mimicking violence in the dancehall [involves] making meanings of social and political practices that form a part of Jamaican inner-city reality and dancehall worldview" (86–87). An alternative perspective offered by Cooper (2004, 154) is that the violence portrayed in Jamaican dancehall is primarily verbal, is representative of a "lyrical gun", and signifies the "language of subversion and subterfuge" in the dancehall. She describes it as a metaphor, suggesting that "words fly at the speed of bullets and the lyrics of the DJ hit hard". In total however, as is the case with "badman" DJs such as Ninja Man, Bounty Killer and many others, the successful mic-man is one who pays homage to the power of the gun.

In the sound system clash, the linguistic choices of the mic-man are therefore central to his enactment of his role. These choices involve first the use of Jamaican Creole, as it is important to identity construction within the specific cultural context of a sound clash dance. This is in keeping with Bucholtz and Hall's (2003, 382) description of language as "a fundamental resource for cultural production [and] hence also a fundamental resource for identity production".

LYRICAL WEAPONS

In the subsections that follow, I will discuss the specific role that language plays in the progression of a sound clash. In discussing the strategies used, I incorporate specific focus on the mic-man's manipulation of his voice, interaction with the audience and rivalry with other competitors.

The Power of the "Voice"

In describing the power inherent in the voice of the mic-man, Henriques (2011, 200) explains that "very often, especially to the unfamiliar ear, the MC's voice completely dominates the sound of the session, drowning out the music". This is often achieved through his "hoarse, rapid-fire shouts, exclamations and comments". In addition, he describes what he believes to be at the core of the mic-man's voicing techniques. He suggests: "disembodied, the MC invisible in the darkness of the dancehall, this voicing is a paradigmatic expression of the *viva voce*, the living voice of the sounding of the word. Voicing mixes and mingles together meaning and feeling, intimacy and power, spirit and matter, and indeed speaker and listener, as no other kind of sounding can do." The mic-man who is able to achieve this level of dominance is described by Henriques as having the "touch" or as being "touched". This interpretation of voice is not purely linguistic, in the sense that it does not directly rest with the discursive features used. However, the "voice" cannot be overlooked or separated from the discourse because the impact of those discursive features on the audience is affected by the quality of the mic-man's voice. The issue of "voice" is therefore critical to the outcome of a sound system clash but may also be described as important within the wider dancehall culture, particularly in relation to the success of DJs.[11] In describing a mic-man it is quite possible that one may hear "im ful a mout, bot im no hav no vais".[12] The deriding of this limitation is also usually an indication and explanation of the limited success that he enjoys. A mic-man's voice is a key part of the weaponry he possesses due to its presence, distinctiveness and intensity. Based solely on hearing it, an audience should be able to not just identify its owner but be attentive to it. In the absence of this, then, it is all the more possible that what is said will not affect the audience in the ways that were intended.

An example that illustrates this point comes from Death before Dishonor 5, in which Freddy Krugar was one of the first mic-men to exit the sound clash in the elimination round. To be sure, his relative lack of experience when compared to the other sounds was a contributing factor, as was his limited cache of hard-hitting dubplates and specials. However, it was also very clear that, by comparison to the other mic-men, he did not measure up in terms of vocal "presence". This lack of command in his "voice" was put on display as the clash also featured giant mic-men like Squingy, Pink Panther and Tony Matterhorn, whose vocal presence muted his. He simply could not illicit crowd reaction at the level that he needed. At the end of his fifteen-minute set he announced, "Yu si tonait, mi jos kom ya fi shuo unu wa Freddy Krugar hav fi afa. An mek unu si se Freddy Krugar hav talent pan mi own tu."[13] Before the crowd was asked to select the sound systems that would be moving on to the next round, it was clear that he knew that he would not be one of them.

The "voice" is therefore significant as "its timbre, intonation, texture and auditory character" (Henriques 2011, 200) are the corporeal instruments of the mic-man's vocal apparatus (202). In addition, when a skilled mic-man delivers – through language – to the crowd, what he says will also be impacted by the auditory impact of his presentation. This will in turn impact on how meaning is derived from what the mic-man says.

Language Use in Crowd Interaction

Within the typical sound system dance, music and language are used purposefully in interacting with the crowd in order to generate crowd response, encourage crowd participation and ensure the general success of the dance. In a sound clash, however, the mic-man's role in relation to the audience is much more narrowly construed. It involves making music selections complemented by talking around the music that will (1) show off his skills in introducing the songs; (2) show off his knowledge and possession of music that will be impactful within that space; (3) cause the audience to respect him and his abilities and (4) champion as well as reinforce audience beliefs, prejudices, and positive and negative attitudes in a way that will increase the likelihood of his victory in the clash.

In his discourse with the audience, who is also his judge, the mic-man therefore embodies the art of persuasion and, to an extent, argumentation. Figure 12.1 offers a representation of the process.

Though the linguistic interaction in a sound clash may be described as a ritualistic performance,[14] the ultimate aim of the clash is persuasive since the audience is required to make a judgement in the end as to which sound system/mic-man is better. As such, the mic-man is required to present his audience with "claims" and "strong justification" for those claims in his quest to win the "argument" that is the sound clash. These persuasive tools are the critical components that he has at his disposal and that affect the nature of his performance. Here, I am relating *performance* to its usage in linguistic anthropology as described by Bucholtz and Hall (2003, 380), which involves a "highly deliberate and self-aware social display", and by Bauman (1977) as an aesthetic component that is available for evaluation by the audience. Bucholtz and Hall argue that performance involves *stylization*, "the highlighting and exaggeration of ideological associations". Stylization is unlike unconscious style of the sort described by Labov (1990), which includes making selections of linguistic variables based on other variables such as age, sex and social class. Stylization is highly conscious. It is described as exaggeration because it

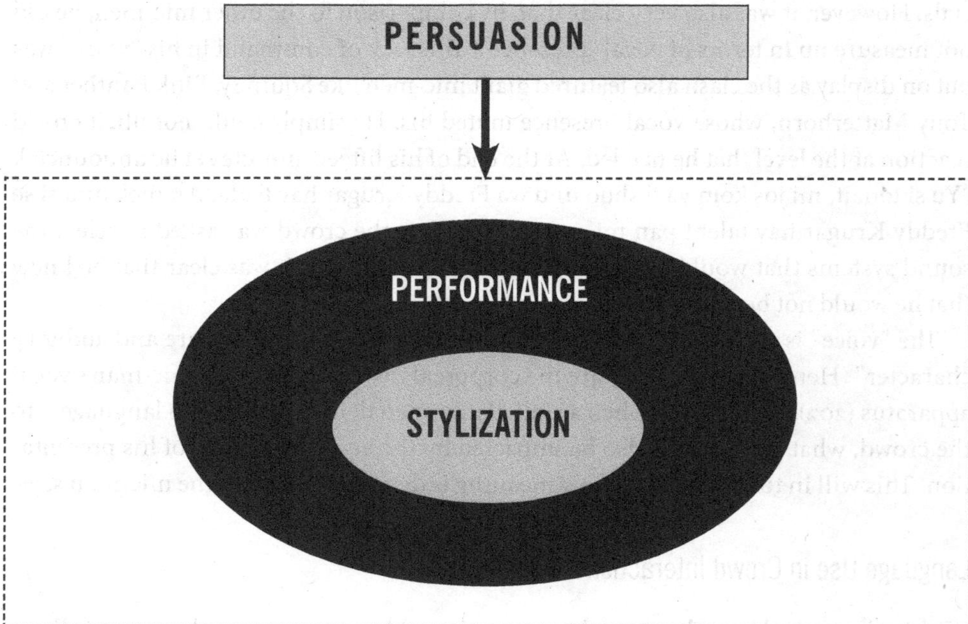

FIGURE 12.1: The process of interaction between mic-man and audience

"serves to emphasize ideological connections to particular social identities" (Eberhardt and Freeman 2015, 303–4). The discourse that the mic-man directs toward the crowd therefore falls within these parameters. He is performing a role that demands both recognition and action.

One of the persuasive strategies used is directing commands at and compelling requests from the crowd – all relating to those beliefs and prejudices which the mic-man believes he shares with them. For example, at Death before Dishonour 5 during the elimination round, Bass Odyssey's Squingy introduces a song in the following way: "Yu hav som man de ya, a batiman. Mi a go tel yu how yu si a batiman an spat dem out tonait. Enitaim yu si dem fool dem han, batibwai dat blodklaat. Frii op. All a di man dem wa lov pusi go so . . . tuu han."[15]

The song that followed was a Sanchez dupplate special: "Here I am, playing with some jrom pan sound again." The performance by Squingy here is not motivated by an actual intention for the crowd to identify homosexuals within their midst, and if a male among them did not put his hands in the air as instructed, he would not be viewed as a homosexual by the rest of the crowd. Squingy's performance is instead a reinforcement of a core shared belief within the space. In commenting on the prevalence of homosexual references in the larger dancehall culture, Hope (2006, 47) suggests that this is anoutput of culture in which there is a "heavily policed and tightly gendered order". This is intensified within the sound system culture which is a space that is primarily occupied by lower class Jamaican men. Hope goes on to argue in support of this that

> many of these men who fail to achieve the hegemonic goals of Jamaican manhood revert to ritualistic responses that are more accessible. Here, notions of sexuality become very important to many Jamaican men, especially those at the lower socioeconomic levels who have limited access to other symbols of real power that identify masculine status. A real man is one who can act as traditional hunter and provider. He is able to access the symbols of masculinity, that is, wealth and power – money. . . . For men who cannot access these symbols, the domination of women and issues of sex and sexuality attain primacy in laying the foundation for the definition of his identity.

In fact, in their response, the crowd is commenting[16] on the strength of the dub that was played in terms of the song choice, as well as how it was cut.[17] The crowd's response is also a strong indication of whether or not they believe that the mic-man deserves a forceful forward[18] based on the interconnectedness of the strength of his introduction and the song he introduces. In other words, the crowd is almost sure to share the mic-man's negative views on homosexuality, and both the mic-man and the crowd are aware of this as the dance is composed of people of like mind in that regard. However, the sound clash is about music and "chat", and if the "claim" presented in the mic-man's introduction is not followed by strong support, in the form of the song played, then the argument fails to be convincing. The argument here can be interpreted as the request for a strong reaction or "forward" from the crowd.

Another example of a request for a "forward" can be demonstrated by Freddy Krugar in the first round of Death before Dishonour. As an introduction to a Beenie Man dub, Krugar says: "Mi hier se waahn infaama in ya. If a no yu gi mi di gon fingga in a di ier . . . gon fingga . . . gon fingga."[19] Neither the introduction nor the song elicited very strong crowd feedback. As a follow up, Krugar therefore says to the crowd: "onli tree soun kyahn plie nyuu Beenie Man, Freddy Krugar, Matterhorn an Mighty Crown".[20]

The purpose of this statement is twofold. In the first instance, he wants to "talk-up" the artiste and the song. In other words, he wants to suggest that Beenie Man doesn't make many dubplates so the song is a treat for the audience. In the second, he wants them to favour him for having access to the artiste to be able to receive this dubplate. It is this line of reasoning combined with the strength of the song that is supposed to help persuade the crowd of Freddy Krugar's skill as a mic-man. In this instance, the audience was not persuaded, as Krugar did not make it beyond that round of the sound clash.

In his interaction with the crowd, and indeed, often with all major participants in the sound clash, the mic-man is also combative. The persona that he portrays has a stance and uses language that is angry, exceedingly insulting and often militant. He embodies the "badman" image that has been previously discussed. At the 2005 World Clash, for example, Pink Panther, the mic-man from the sound system Black Cat, was dressed in full army fatigue. He came to the dance ready for "war". Even in instances where there is laughter, it is usually scornful. This combative persona is in keeping with the lyrical warfare that is characteristic of a sound clash and explains the mic-man's attitude toward his competitors. But what of the anger he directs at the crowd? How is his goal of gaining approval from the crowd – his judges – achieved via this approach?

At Death before Dishonour, for example, Bass Odyssey played one line of a dub done by the artiste Perfect: "Hey officer take those cuffs off me, I can't take it anymore." In response, the crowd went wild. As the song stopped, Squingy angrily barked at them: "If yu a kuokhed kip yu han a yu blodklaat said."[21]

This was followed immediately by Capleton's "who do you think you are you're living in a small world". The crowd's response to this was even more frenzied than it was before. In the same sound clash, Sammy T of Mighty Crown played a special by Turbulance: "Panther tek di hier aaf a yu tiit an stap iit di gyal dem."[22] The song (or the line from the song) was immediately stopped and replayed and stopped again, at which point Sammy T said to the crowd: "Yu waahn hier da song ya agen? . . . Yu nuo wa, mi nat iivn a plie it agen, suck unu mada."[23]

In both of these instances, the mic-men are seemingly "dissing" the crowd. However, anger and combativeness are also a part of their performance, the persona they are enacting and their persuasive strategy. In both examples, the mic-men are in fact daring the crowd to *not* react positively to the songs. They both expect that as a result of the strength of the songs, the crowd will be compelled to "make noise", and so they have a licence to "diss" anyone in the crowd that does not comply. Of course, this is a gamble that the mic-men are making, because if the crowd is not impressed by the songs chosen, their collective anger would ensure that those sound systems lose points in the clash. In other instances too, mic-men hurl insults at their opponents' supporters who they feel are biased. Often, this comes about if the mic-men do not receive the "forward" that they think they deserve, or if they believe their opponents have "bought out the clash" – paid persons to come there to support them.

Crowd interaction is very revealing. The mic-man's stance toward the crowd, although seeming to be that of instructor and commander, is really more complex. He is much more beholden to the crowd than it would appear if one were to only consider the words he says on a very literal level. The topics he introduces are a part of the ritual of the clash; they form a part of the basis of his performance of the role he is enacting. It is also important to bear in mind that language use in the context of the sound clash is "transmitted and transformed via culturally patterned yet context-specific socializing interactions" (Riley 2012, 502). This means that the topics introduced are known and expected by his audience; it is therefore how successful he is at persuading them of his skill in navigating from topic to related song that is most important.

Language Use in Rivalry and Self-Exaltation

Arguably as important as the mic-man's interaction with the crowd is his rivalry with his opponents. A key factor in determining who wins a sound clash is the mic-man's use of his lyrical prowess to "diss", "kill", "murda" or "bury" opposing mic-men. Henriques (2011, 198) quotes Campbell (1997), who explains that the mic-man "is responsible for ridiculing his opponents . . . by taunting them . . . or telling embarrassing jokes which may be true or not true". In the context of a sound clash, nothing is off limits; everything is fair play for insult. The most popular insults relate to an opponent's sexual orientation; "degrading" sexual acts performed by an opponent on his girlfriend, mother or animals; information relating to the opponent's financial status, drug use, the status of his visa or how well travelled he is; and an opponent's overall character.

A related theme is the mic-man's exaltation of his own skill and lyrical prowess above those of his opponent. This accompanies the insults that are hurled at the opponent and is meant to disparage the opponent while simultaneously presenting himself to the crowd as a better person and mic-man. In doing this, he is trying to convince the crowd that he should be chosen as the winner of the clash. The examples of the use of this strategy within the sound clash are many. However, insults and exaltation relating to his sexual prowess and his opponent's lack thereof, and his opponent's engagement in oral sex, are some of the easiest to locate based of their pervasiveness. Hope (2006, 79–80) in referring to dancehall calls these "punaany lyrics", a Jamaican word for the vagina. She identifies these references as a part of the ritual of male identity negotiation in which there is a projection of masculinity, male sexuality and male dominance.

In the 1996 clash between Killamanjaro and Bass Odyssey, which was won by Killamanjaro, there were many insults traded between Lenny, Bass Odyssey's mic-man and Ricky Trooper, the mic-man from Killamanjaro. In one instance, as an introduction to Beenie Man's song "di gyal dem no waahn no iti biti tiini wiini likl bodi man",[24] Ricky Trooper said of Lenny: "No wuman no waahn no man huu kyaahn fuck dem gud ino. Di gyal dem waahn some man wid som big hood."[25] As a result of the crowd responding favourably to the song and his introduction of it, he followed up with this: "Wi a wiikn op di pusihuol dem an step ina dem nek laik chikin. Dem no ha no chune fi plie Jaro."[26]

Further in his set, Ricky Trooper again attacked Lenny's sexual choices. This was done right on the heels of him playing the opening lines of a Junior Cat special – "kilin pusi an wi kil dem fi fon"[27] – which caused an uproar in the crowd. As a follow-up he said: "Aal di bwai blodklaat Lenny we no stap bait op Suzi Q, yu tingk shi a no hat gyal? Suzi Q a no no hat gyal. All Ninja Man fuck dat, Ricky General fuck out dat tu . . . aal huu lov Jaro boo out Bass Odyssey out a di daans."[28]

Based on the response of thunderous shouting and simulation of firing gunshots, it was clear that this seemingly very personal insult combined with the impact of the Junior Cat song had found favour with the crowd.

Dell Hymes (1968) in "The Ethnography of Speaking" highlighted that the cultural contexts within which language is used are important; that all cultures have a variety of speech events; and that those events take place within a set of rules. This is applicable to discourse practices within a sound clash. Within this speech event, mic-men have a shared "linguistic repertoire" that is used in identity construction. From this "linguistic repertoire", they choose the lyrical weapons required for interaction with the crowd and their rivals. All the participants in this speech event have shared attitudes as well as shared norms of interaction (the specific behaviours and properties attached to speaking) and interpretation (the belief system of a community) (Hymes 1972, 63–64). A successful mic-man is therefore one who, through his performance, is able to skilfully and favourably manipulate the discourse practices of the sound clash.

CONCLUSION: AN ORAL TRADITION OF RITUALIZED LANGUAGE USE

At its core, a sound system clash is an oral tradition and, like performances in most oral traditions, it is characterized by ritualized language use. Henriques (2011, 182) describes the exchange between the mic-men of each sound as a "ritualized verbal form of combat, as found in numerous cultures across the globe". Vansina (1985, 27) defines oral tradition as requiring word of mouth transmission over at least a generation, as well as being specific to oral messages that are spoken, sung or called out on musical instruments only. A sound system clash is only loosely held to this definition. In the context of the clash, ritual language use involves a distinct set of linguistic forms, specific language behaviours from which the participants choose and rules governing the linguistic interactions. However, in this ritual context, the linguistic practices are not "blindly" repeated by all of the participants within the tradition. In addition, though there are some formulaic expressions used in the communication of shared ideas and convictions, there is great scope for individual variation in the performance of this ritual discourse. This is captured well by Ong's (1982, 41–42) description: "Oral cultures do not lack originality of their own kind. Narrative originality lodges not in making up new stories but in managing a particular interaction with this audience at this time – at every telling the story has to be introduced uniquely into a unique situation, for in oral cultures an audience must be brought to respond, often vigorously."

The sound system clash, like other oral cultures, is also characterized by what Ong (1982, 43) describes as an "agonistic" tone. In the same way that he describes proverbs and riddles as "not used simply to store knowledge but to engage in verbal and intellectual combat", so too are the discourse features of the mic-man used in verbal combat against his opponents. In addition, Ong suggests that it is standard across oral societies for there to be "reciprocal name-calling". Further, "bragging about one's own prowess and/or verbal tongue-lashings of an opponent figure regularly in encounters between characters in narratives" (44), from medieval Europe (such as *The Iliad* and *Beowulf*) to Africa (such as the Mwindo epic). These are all practices that are at the core of the mic-man's discursive practices.

While the linguistic expressions which form the bulk of the mic-man's repertoire suggest that he is combative, aggressive, homophobic, arrogant and sexist, one needs to look past the language in its literal usage to understand the role it plays within the sound clash. In the first instance, identity within the sound clash is an ongoing social and political process which is governed by the interactions within the space. In addition, as suggested by Bucholtz and Hall (2003, 382), language is "a fundamental resource for cultural production (and) hence also a fundamental resource for identity production". Within this social context, language use is indexical and therefore utilized by the mic-man to locate himself within the discursive identity of the sound clash.

NOTES

1. The mic-man is referred to by several different names both within the practice and in the literature. Henriques (2011, 125–26) refers to the "MC" as the person that chats and the "Selecta" as the one who plays the music. However, perhaps the two most popular references, in my experience, are "mic-man" and "selecta" (selector). I have chosen to use mic-man instead of "selecta" because the latter term also refers to the person who selects and plays the records on the sound system. I also refer to the mic-man using masculine pronouns because within sound system clashes in general, it is men who play this role.
2. It should be noted that "clash sounds" participate in dances that are just for juggling and partying, but a "juggling sound" does not readily participate in sound clashes.
3. Ricky Trooper left Killamanjaro in 2000 to start his own sound system "Sound Trooper" (Killamanjaro, the No. 1 Champion Sound) but his "Jaro" years are still regarded as the best.
4. A "dub" or "dubplate" refers to the recording of new music on the "rhythm" or instrumental of an existing track, while a "special" is a kind of dubplate that is "specially commissioned voicing of a particular tune by a leading artist who 'bigs up' the sound by name" (Henriques 2011, 296).
5. Unless the use of English is aimed at getting a specific effect at a specific point.
6. "Killing a sound boy."
7. "Let me see the gun fingers in the air."
8. "Those boys can't kill me because I am a badman. I have all of the support of the badmen that I need in here."
9. "You are coming to a war and you don't know the art of war."
10. "Big up all the true Rastamen, but you over there have proven that none of you are Rastas because you say Rasta is not involved in confusion and Babylon. What the (expletive) are you doing in Babylon?"
11. I am basing this claim on my general observation that DJs whose voice qualities are not distinctive in some way, and who do not have an identifiable vocal presence, are generally not as popular as those who do. This may partly explain why some novice DJs pattern their style and voice off the voices of popular DJs.
12. "He is full of mouth [meaning he has a lot of clever talk or talks a lot], but he has no voice."
13. "Tonight, I just came here to show you what Freddy Krugar has to offer, and let you see that Freddy Krugar has talent on his own too."
14. See the following section for a discussion of this.
15. "There are some men here that are gays. I am going to tell you how you can see a gay and recognize him tonight. Anytime you see them with their hands folded, that is a (expletive) gay. Free up. All of the men who love vagina, do this . . . two hands"
16. "Comment" here means response from the crowd in the form of ferocity of their shouts, whistling, and so on.
17. "Cut" here refers to how the original song was adapted or reworded for the purposes of the sound clash.
18. "Forward" is used to describe positive crowd response and endorsement of what a selector and mic-man are playing.

19. "I heard that an informer is here. If it's not you, then put your 'gun finger' in the air. Gun finger . . . gun finger."
20. "Only three sounds can play new Beenie Man songs, Freddy Krugar, Matterhorn and Mighty Crown."
21. "If you are a coke head [coke addict] keep your hands at your [expletive] side."
22. "Panther get that hair off your teeth and stop eating the girls."
23. "Do you want to hear the song again? . . . You know what, I'm not even going to play it again. Go suck your mother."
24. "The girls don't want a man with a very tiny penis."
25. "Women do not want men who can't fuck them properly. The girls want men with big penises."
26. "We are going weaken those (expletive) and step on their necks like chickens. They don't have any tunes to play against Jaro."
27. "Killing a pussy and we're killing them for fun."
28. "Even that boy (expletive) Lenny that keeps biting (a reference to oral sex) Suzi Q, do you think that she is a hot girl? She is not a hot girl. Even Ninja Man has fucked her. Ricky General has fucked her too. Everyone who loves Jaro boo Bass Odyssey out of the dance."

REFERENCES

Bauman, R. 1977. *Verbal Art as Performance.* Rowley, MA: Newbury House.

Bulcholtz, M., and K. Hall. 2003. "Language and Culture". In *A Companion to Linguistic Anthropology*, edited by A. Duranti, 369–94. Oxford: Basil Blackwell.

Chang, K.O., and W. Chen. 1998. *Reggae Routes: The Story of Jamaican Music.* Philadelphia: Temple University Press.

Cooper, C. 2004. *Sound Clash: Jamaican Dancehall Culture at Large.* New York: Palgrave Macmillan.

Cooper, C., and H. Devonish, 2004. "The Dancehall Transnation: Language, Lit/orature, and Global Jamaica". In *Sound Clash: Jamaican Dancehall Culture at Large*, edited by C. Cooper, 279–302. New York: Palgrave Macmillan.

Devonish, H. 1996. "Kom Groun Jamiekan Daans Haal Liricks: Memba Se a Plie Wi a Plie [Contextualizing Jamaican "Dance Hall" Music: Jamaican Language at Play in a Speech Event]". *English World-Wide*, 17, no. 2: 213–37.

Eberhardt, M., and K. Freeman. 2015. "'First Things First, I'm the Realest': Linguistic Appropriation, White Privilege, and the Hip-Hop Persona of Iggy Azelea". *Journal of Sociolinguistics*, 19, no. 3: 303–27.

Henriques, J. 2011. *Sonic Bodies: Reggae Sound Systems, Performance Techniques, and Ways of Knowing.* New York: The Continuum International Publishing Group.

Hope, D.P. 2006. *Inna di Dancehall: Popular Culture and the Politics of Identity in Jamaica.* Kingston: University of the West Indies Press.

Hymes, D. 1968. "The Ethnography of Speaking". In *Readings in the Sociology of Language*, edited by J.A. Fishman, 99–138. The Hague: Mouton.

———. 1972. "Models of the Interaction of Language and Social Life". In *Directions in Sociolinguistics*, edited by J.J. Gumperz and D. Hymes, 35–65. New York: Holt.

Jamaican Language Unit. 2005. *The Language Attitude Survey of Jamaica: Technical Report.* Kingston: Jamaican Language Unit.

Labov, W. 1990. "The Intersection of Sex and Social Class in the Course of Linguistic Change". *Language Variation and Change* 2:205–54.

Meyerhoff, M. 2002. "Communities of Practice". In *The Handbook of Language Variation and Change*, edited by J.K. Chambers, P. Trudgill and N. Schilling-Estes, 526–49. Oxford: Blackwell.

Ong, W. 1982. *Orality and Literacy.* London: Methuen.

Riley, C.K. 2012. "Language Socialization and Language Ideologies". In *The Handbook of Language Socialization*, edited by A. Duranti, E. Ochs and B.B. Schieffelin, 493–514. Malden, MA: Wiley-Blackwell.

Stolzoff, Norman C. 2000. *Wake the Town and Tell the People: Dancehall Culture in Jamaica.* Durham, NC: Duke University Press.

Trudgill, P. 1972. "Sex, Covert Prestige and Linguistic Change in the Urban British English of Norwich". *Language in Society* 1, no. 2: 179–95.

Vansina, J. 1985. *Oral Tradition as History.* London: James Currey.

PART 4

SEXUAL POLITICS AND AESTHETICS

CHAPTER 13

Out and Bad

*Toward a Queer Performance Hermeneutic in Jamaican Dancehall**

NADIA ELLIS

IN DECEMBER 2005 I ARRIVED IN A JAMAICA still in the throes of the dancehall dance craze. Dance, especially male dance, had been the most prominent trend in dancehall for a few years to that point. In retrospect, the arrival of Elephant Man on the scene in 2003 was perhaps one harbinger of this trend. Here was a deejay whose songs celebrated dancers, name-checked them, and who himself was an enthusiastic purveyor of new dances. Most famously (at least since Buju Banton [2001] had celebrated the giant of dancehall dancing, Bogle, in his eponymous hit of the same name), Elephant Man (2001, 2003) had crafted songs and performances that displayed the relay between dancehall deejays and dancers. Hits like "Pon de River, Pon de Bank" and "Log On" were songs in which lyrical content had movement analogues, producing a secular chorus of dancers who both prompted and responded to deejays' calls. It was the new millennium and time, apparently, to return dance to the dancehall. Elephant Man himself revelled in his status as the "Energy God": indefatigable performances and an exuberant sartorial style, which, even in a context of dancehall exuberance, stood out. (Elephant Man dyed his hair blonde, wore his plaits pointing directly upward and enjoyed leather.)

Elephant Man's rise was accompanied by several lesser gods, including the intriguing phenomenon of the dancehall boy bands Voicemail and T.O.K., the latter of which prophylactically produced the antigay "Chi Chi Man" as one of their first hits.[1] It was a moment in which the emphasis on dance seemed to liberate a certain form of Jamaican masculine high-spiritedness. In counterpoint to the jeremiads of Bounty Killer, "the poor people's governor", which dominated the 1990s, here was a set of songs and performances that allowed men to be unabashedly fun, to be relatively carefree about the social consequences of movement and to stretch even further the Jamaican investment in male grooming. Certainly Beenie Man, the other dancehall superstar of the

---

* Previously published in *Small Axe* 15, no. 2 (2011): 7–23.

1990s, exhibited a contrapuntal flair to Bounty's ghetto high-mindedness. His hetero performance tended toward playfulness and indulgence – as highly lacquered as his bright yellow Humvee. But even this exuberance was not the same as what I was experiencing in the street dances of the mid-2000s, if only because Beenie did not always ask us to dance.[2] Emphasizing the dance in dancehall enabled a loosening of the strictures around masculine expression. We had moved from Bounty Killer's incredulity, on the cusp of the new millennium, that "tight pants come in again", to five years later, tight pants being exactly the thing that badmen wore.[3]

Which tight pants bring me to the project at hand, namely, the development of a queer hermeneutic for popular performance in the Caribbean, especially in Jamaican dancehall. The tight pants, of course, are a metonomy, a metaphorical placeholder for a field of larger consequence and denser contradictions. But they are ready at hand and they are sturdy. For the pants are both the sign of masculine sartorial excess as well as the injunction against such excess. The meaning of the pants has not changed between Bounty's alarm about their proliferation and Bounty's *own* wearing of them, ten years later. In each case they are a sign of the perilous edges of Jamaican masculinity. What changed is that at a certain point in the 2000s it became just risqué enough, just bad enough, to live on the edges of the closely guarded rules around masculinity, and in doing so, to demonstrate a certain mastery over those rules. In his very eccentricity at the beginning of this trend, Elephant Man was flaunting a masculine supremacy over cultural rules about badness.

Which is how the phrase *out and bad* comes to mind as a summation of the intrigue and the possibilities of a queer dancehall hermeneutic. Within dancehall, "out and bad" implies a certain form of glamour and confidence – the phrase designates someone who is unabashed about his skills and looks, who enjoys prominence and spectacle, whose confidence is wed to an investment in being the centre of attention. Out and bad is also, felicitously, a yoking of two discrete discursive fields: US-style queer politics and Jamaican masculine imperatives. The result is a syncretic interpretative concept that sums up what it means to do queer analysis on Jamaican cultural texts in the globalized context. And to be clear, both text and interpretative method are now globalized. As has been amply demonstrated by critics such as Patricia Saunders, Donna Hope and Norman Stolzoff, dancehall exists in a critical, subversive and engaged relationship with Western markets, distribution methods and cultural lexicons (Saunders 2003; Hope 2006a, 2004; Stolzoff 2000). It gains much of its complexity by being at once unabashedly productive of and beholden to local practices and standards while simultaneously referential of and strategic toward American and European sociopolitical modes.[4] Similarly, cultural studies methodologies have become increasingly prominent in Caribbean studies, in part *because* of the vibrancy of dancehall criticism. The methods of analysis – including performance studies, anthropology, African diaspora studies and ethnomusicology – are of varied provenance and multiple application and operate within and between academic circles that intersect both "at home" and "abroad". (Indeed, publication practices make that distinction increasingly vague.) By offering queer studies here as yet another apt methodology for understanding dancehall culture, I hope to open a conversation about gender and sexuality in Jamaican popular culture that registers even as it exceeds the confines of discussions of homophobia that have so far dominated.[5]

So, as I say, "out and bad" becomes for me a phrase of possibility. *Out*, the US shorthand for queer public expression; *bad*, the Jamaican shorthand for masculine power. Both signal a relationship to public life. To be *out* in US discourse is to consider one's relationship to sexual identity as having a certain kind of meaning in relation to a social matrix that can read that identity. To be *out*, according to the logic of US-style gay politics, is in a classic performative way to have the declaration of sexual identity enact its outcome at the very moment of utterance. (I say I am gay and therefore I am gay.) Being *out* also suggests a network of social relations with the power to confirm or to disallow that identity – you have to have someone to be out to. *Badness* similarly relies on a social expectation of norms, the acceptance or rejection of which constitutes the identity of badness. In dancehall, deejays declare their badness lyrically; on the streets men claim to be *bad* at moments of disruption or threat. The necessity of declaration suggests an obligation to a social formation that legitimizes the declaration. Badness has long referred to male power and prowess in Jamaica, particularly in its gun-toting variety. But recently, precisely, it would seem, because of the resignification of "out and bad" in queer Jamaican communities, *badness* has become a signifier of queer.

On reflection, this development seems obvious. What could be badder – fiercer, braver, more unaccountably acting with impunity – than, say, male cross-dressing in Jamaica? A drag queen is one of the purest forms of masculine testing of limits, fiercer even in a context in which testing those limits can result in dire physical consequences, as has been reported in the Jamaican newspapers several times in the last half decade. This resignification of *bad* has seeped into the mainstream, with Queen Ifrica's "Keep It to Yourself", a popular song from her album *Montego Bay* (2009) that is an extended allegory on the incursion of flamboyant queer sexuality into the Jamaican mainstream:

> Yu feel like a badman
> Keep it to yourself
> Don't bring it to Jamaica
> Keep it to yourself
> We don't want dat a Jamrock
> Keep it to yourself
> We can't take no more slackness.

In subsequent verses Queen Ifrica plaintively discusses "the situation", which involves skirts of various kinds – men dressing in them, women allowing other women to look under them – and repeats Rasta and Christian invocations to "multiply and replenish the earth". She allusively refers to well-known tropes of homosexuality as pollution when she rhymes "me don't want no fish inna me ital dish".[6] Queen Ifrica's is an editorializing, proselytizing stance, a beleaguered rather than aggressive homophobia (she identifies herself as a "concerned citizen") that takes a different tack than the usual "bun battyman" rhetoric of hardcore dancehall. And in another sense, it registers a shift in the discourse around homosexuality in Jamaica because it acknowledges a new scenario in which nonnormatively masculine men, and indeed homosexual men, feel a greater sense of freedom, that is, *badness*, to publicly express their preferences, sartorial and otherwise.

If queer theory is to have a relationship to dancehall other than academic imposition, the *bad* has to modify the *out*. That is, there must be an equal relationship between the two terms and the two frames of reference. To this end, it may help to say what I mean when I say *queer*, since that term has an American critical theory provenance and cannot be invoked without bringing that tradition along with it. *Queer* is a useful term for me generally, and in relation to the project of studying Caribbean popular culture in particular, because of its fluidity.

Certainly, its use conjures up writing by white scholars in the American academy – Michael Warner, Eve Sedgwick, Diana Fuss, for example – whose work to destabilize the fixed terms of sexuality, hetero- and homo-, was pioneering but often ethnically unitary.[7] But *queer* also evokes African American sociologist Cathy Cohen's invocation to a queerer queer theory, one that would include subjects (for example, black urban mothers, black lesbians and gay men) whose relationships to normative social and political structures were just as, if not more, excluded and oppositional than those of the white, male gay activists who were most prominent in 1990s mainstream press (Cohen 1997). Indeed, at this point *queer* includes Juana María Rodríguez's (2003) nimble and provocative analyses of the homosexual and the homoerotic in Latin America and Latin *America*. Her queer *Latinidad* emphasizes identity formation in movement: slippery and mobile subjects wend their way across discursive platforms, and the queer is found *in* that movement rather than in a moment of rest. It extends to Omise'eke Natasha Tinsley's (2008) evocative and imaginative deployment of *queer Atlantic* to reimagine the archive of homosexual love and affiliation during the transatlantic crossing of the slave trade, affiliations that continued onto plantations of the Caribbean and beyond. It includes E. Patrick Johnson's (2005) creation of a US southern black "quare" poetics. And as I will show later, the theoretical frame surrounding my analysis of the relationship between the queer dancing body and dancehall lyrics' homophobia is indebted to José Esteban Muñoz's (1999) notion of disidentification, in which the subject works with and through the hegemonic to find something like the queer utopian. If *queer* began as critical term within a European American–oriented academic sphere, it has since expanded its limits, staying true to its roots as a term of unstable and shifting signification, and has been deployed by scholars of varied backgrounds, theoretical orientations and fields. By using it here I hope to generate a conversation about whether and how *queer* can be queered in relation to Caribbean studies. If Cathy Cohen asked for "punks, bulldaggers and welfare queens" to be considered queer at a moment when radical US politics could not imagine them to be so, then I am asking whether we can bring some Jamaican dance crews into queer consideration as well.

It should by now be clear, though it bears emphasis, that by *queer* I do not in any simple way mean *gay, lesbian, bisexual, homosexual* or any of the categorical terms we use to define people's sexuality. To be sure, I do not mean to exclude those categories from view. But I mean, perhaps, to supplement or modify them. *Queer* functions for me as a signifier of sexual and gender nonnormativity, a break in the line of gender.

This may include erotic exchanges between people of the same gender but is not limited to them. It is very often bound up with the homoerotic, though it need not be sexual. *Queer* emphasizes practice, action, not categorical state. *Queer* shifts, it moves, it does not rest. It names a practice, it names a moment, it names a person, sometimes all three simultaneously. It might name a different practice, a different person in another moment. Crucially, in my analysis *queer* does not depend on knowing in any assured way what a person feels about their sexual orientation. Indeed, it refuses the sense that "orientation" tells us anything concrete or stable about who we are and what we do. It *does* depend on there being a discursive field, a social matrix, that defines normative sexual and social practices against which the queer stands.

In what follows I offer readings of dancehall texts that I hope will open a conversation about dancehall interpretative practice more generally. The moments of greatest queer hermeneutical possibility have been, almost without fail, conglomerated dancehall texts in which multiple facets of the culture create a platform of meaning. There are the deejays' lyrics and performance. But there is also what the selector does with that performance in the context of a street dance. There is the intimate, dynamic and mutually constitutive relationship among song, selector and dancers. There is the crowd, and how its responses to songs and to dancers create a dancehall space and temporality. A street becomes a stage when bounded by the revelers' bodies.[8] The temporal rhythm of the dance is defined in conjunction with the selector and the dancers, often against the rigours of clock time. All of which is to say that a queer reading of dancehall encompasses the whole panoply of culture – the songs, dances, parties, sayings – that make up the experience of dancehall. In a sense there are multiple texts to be read, among them the third text that is created when the audience responds to the prompting of the dancehall, and something like a contract among deejay, selector, dancer and spectator that enables certain modes of masculine performance within the sphere of dancehall that may be disallowed elsewhere. The analytical hinge between *out* and *bad* is constituted by each of these interactions, as well as by the meeting of the critic and the dancehall moment.

Three dancehall events – a street dance, a comedy interlude at a dancehall club night and a music video – allow me to practise what I am calling a queer dancehall hermeneutic. In the first, I think about the dancehall street dance, Passa Passa in particular, as a space of perverse consecration of the queer.[9] In the second, I offer comedic parody as a queer commentary on the limits and absurdities of Jamaican heteronormativity. And in the last reading, I consider how the furthest extremes of dancehall's heterosexual tropes produce an excess that is queer.

BAD MAN WEAR TIGHT PANTS: DANCEHALL'S PERVERSE CONSECRATION

In a way, Ding Dong puts it best. His 2005 hit "Bad Man Forward, Bad Man Pull Up" announces the new regime of male dance with the following introductory claim: "You know how long the *real* badman want dance and cyaan dance? How comes? . . . Dancers! All out!" (Dong Ding 2007). Waiting in the wings all this time, apparently, had been Jamaican badmen who wanted nothing more than to put down arms and display a whole different set of skills. Ding Dong's song displays a certain kind of queer masculine syncretism. The lyrics and beat are ruthlessly simple – unadorned, pared down, serious. The song functions as a path-clearing for male dance and as such announces its Jamaican masculine bonafides. Ding Dong's vocal performance is strident and aggressive. There is no fooling around with any diversions or fancy lyrical twists. The refrain "badman forward, badman pull up" is repeated throughout the entire song, with only slight variations that name-check popular dancers and dance crews.

One of the dance crews Ding Dong mentions twice is Ravers Clavers – a group that gets me back to the dancehall scenes I witnessed in December of 2005. I drove with my friend to Tivoli Gardens, the downtown Kingston community that, early on Wednesday mornings, hosts the popular street dance Passa Passa. (Tivoli has been in the news recently for reasons not entirely unrelated to issues here, more on which later.) One is to arrive at Passa Passa at around 3:00 or 4:00 in the morning.[10] There will be people from all classes and all walks of life arriving too, in their finest dancehall gear. Cars of all makes and models will frame the street; they will have conveyed the middle class from off the hills and the more "recently wealthy" guys with their hot girls. There will be Japanese girls. There will be vendors selling drinks and snacks, Rastafarians selling herb. People will flank the street, facing speakers stacked two stories high from which an enormous wall of dancehall sound emanates. Eventually, some people will move from the sidelines to the middle of the street in order to dance.

There is a rhythm to how dancing happens. Some girls from the community will hold back at the edges until they hear the strains of a hot song, at which point they will rush to the middle with joyful squeals and begin to dance, often with a male partner. There is an overt sexuality to the dancing that happens in the middle of the street, the stage as it were, at Passa Passa. What is most immediately obvious is how the dancers form themselves into hetero pairs. The dances – what I saw then came to be known a year of so afterward as *daggering* – manage to be highly stylized and crudely representational at the same time. There is a commentary on sexual politics that happens in each coupling. Most often the woman is receiving the energetic thrusts of a man, generally from behind. Sometimes the woman mocks the man, as if he were too weak; sometimes she looks agonized by the intensity. Often, a boy child is encouraged to join in.

On the morning I was at Passa Passa something else caught my eye. A dance crew – one of the many community dance collectives who have the crucial role in dancehall culture of creating new moves to accompany riddims or songs – arrived early enough in the evening to do its own performances and to get the ordinary participants going. It was an all-male dance crew, dressed in matching black outfits. Many of them wore outfits that would not have looked out of place in a gay club in New York or London. That is to say, the jeans were tight, the shirts were closely fitted, the hairstyles were glamorous. The guys began doing choreographed dances together, one of which struck me immediately. Two men faced each other. One lifted his leg straight out, at a ninety-degree angle to his body. The other man grabbed his leg and fit it into the groove between his underarm and torso. Leg snug in groove, the dancers proceeded to rhythmically move the leg backward and forward, backward and forward. This was certainly more stylized and abstract than what I had seen men and women doing together, but it seemed to me an obvious representation of male-male sexuality: phallic, thrusting and queer. I was so shocked by how blatant it was that I looked around at the crowd to see if they noticed, to see if they would do anything. No one seemed perturbed; no one did anything.

The increased freedom of bodily movement has freed as well the limitations of certain male practices, meaning that the male dancing body has the freedom to tell different stories in the context of dancehall more than almost anywhere else in Jamaica.[11] Clips abound online that give a sense of what dance crews look like and that approximate what I saw that night. In one particularly rich video, Ravers Clavers and another popular dance crew, Sample Six, demonstrate various new dances at another outdoor dancehall event, Prendy's on the Beach.[12] The seven-minute clip shows about a dozen young men dominating the large, improvised stage on the sand made by the partiers clearing space for the professionals. The dancers are decked out in traditional crew wear – tight clothes; bold accessories of metal, gemstone and cloth; hair in relaxers and braids. One of the most striking moments in the video occurs toward the end when, as Elephant Man's "Nuh Linga" is mixed with Assassin's "Dem Nuh Want Nuh Gal" and the men's complete dominance of the dancing mise-en-scène is confirmed, the selector directs, "Get some girl involved inna di ting, yes." The camera pans and we see that a dance crew member is wining in extremely desultory fashion with a young woman at the edges of the stage. Despite the selector's entreaties, it is clear that she is uninspired to join the masculine fray, for she can sense in her bones that she does not belong there. In a few seconds it is all over. But the selector's comments have introduced some quality of anxiety amid the homosocial dance unity, and when the camera swings back to the centre of the stage, only one male dance member remains. He had been featured prominently in the video before – sleeveless T-shirt showing off sculpted arm muscles, he is pretty-faced and dimpled, with just a hint of skin-bleach, designer eyebrows, relaxed fade. Apprehending the unease in the selector's comment that "some girl a gwaan like dem cyaan bounce [the girls are pretending they can't dance]", the dancer performs a space-clearing passage across the sand. Balancing fluidity and power, with extreme eloquence in his limbs and blending modern dance lines with dancehall kinetics, he claims the space for himself and by extension his dance-brothers, reminding everyone that here is a space for the embodiment of the dancehall masculine queer. In his movements we see the freedom that the space of dancehall allows for precisely that which so many of its lyrics ostensibly disallow: curly hair, tight pants, bleached skin, funniness. (An aside: There are no still photographs here illustrating my descriptions – one of the difficulties of researching street dances is the relative ephemerality, by publishing standards, of their archive. But I find this absence productive, illustrative in the sense that it represents the impossibility of capturing movement in excerpt. Fixing the dancer in a single moment is precisely the opposite of what my argument here intends, in at least two ways. First, this dancer's movement across the sand, the swath he cuts across this immanent stage, is swift and protean as mercury. No one can pin him down. Second, and in apposition: I make absolutely no claims as to the sexual identity of this dancer.

To refer to his queer dancing body is to make a claim for the way his mobile physicality breaks out of certain Jamaican masculine norms. It is emphatically not to label him as gay or straight or anything else. Our inability finally to name him or fully represent his beautiful passage on the beach means that in a sense he has danced right off this page.)

The exclusion of women here is only one of the ironies of the dancehall masculine queer. There is also the irony, one that must be accommodated by a dancehall queer hermeneutic, that the freedom from heteronormative rigidities is often accomplished to the tune of hetero-normative hegemony. These are the lyrics that accompanied the Prendy's dancer's virtuosic space-clearing: "A coulda wah do dem guy deh? / How dem a live so dutty an dem a nuh Friday? / How yu have yu bed and mek annedda [another] man a lie deh?"[13]

This Sample Six–Ravers Clavers video was shot in 2008, and the selector's desire to create some heterosexual energy in the scene reflects the fact that by then, things were starting to shift. When I attended Prendy's on the Beach one night in the summer of 2009, I heard much more grumbling about male dancing and queer masculinity among the crowd. The selectors specifically disallowed male dance crews from getting any space or traction at the centre of the crowd. This was much different from the height of the male dancing trend in the mid-2000s – though even then the emphasis on the male body kinetic was not given universal approbation. One "Kartelyoung", on Dancehall/Reggae.com, had this to say in 2004:

> This dancin class ting has been going on forever. It's like all the selecta dem play in the dance [party/club] is dancing tunes. Too much fuckin dancin, go-go bullshit. When mi go a dance mi see man wah sey dem a badman [who say they are badman] a dance with each other and a wine up like gyal. Wah the fuck unno deh pon [What are all of you about]? Breddrin, big up the real dancers like Bogle and John Hype and Sadiki and all the rest of them. Real Badman come a dance and keep them back to the wall. Ah the gyal dem fi dance. (Kartelyoung 2004).

Fascinating ambivalences are threaded through Kartelyoung's post, perhaps the most striking of which is the distinction he makes between "real dancers" who deserve respect and badmen who don't dance at all but "keep them back to the wall". *Real* dancers are given leeway that mere pretenders don't have. They are aligned with women ("ah the gyal dem fi dance") but this association with femininity is not remarked. It appears that sheer skill distinguishes the dancing men who get respect from those who do not.

If Kartelyoung had a problem with all the male dancing being allowed (and he had ample company on that forum), then others wrote in registering their disapproval of those aforementioned tight pants – the tight pants which, in my observation, seem to associate themselves with the male dancer so closely as to be an analogue of his function. "Kingston_Badmon" (2004), on the DancehallReggae.com forum, had this to say in the same thread in which Kartelyoung weighed in: "Yeah I feel you. How the fuck tight pants come in style again? That is some bullshit that is farrin [foreign] to us. Niggas going around looking like straight fruits. It's a damn shame." *Straight fruits.* The queer readings going on at the level of dancehall participants requires almost no academic commentary.

But if the vibrant dissent over the wearing of tight pants and the dancing shows that flouting masculine norms was not an uncomplicated affair five years ago, then it also shows that this flouting was happening, good and strong. And let me be clear: I am not suggesting that tight male clothing always registers as queer. It is certainly true that at different moments in Jamaican popular culture tight male clothing has been perfectly acceptable – at the height of the 1970s, for instance, when Bob Marley's jeans were snug. And it is also true that there exists an attention to personal appearance in the Jamaican male context – indeed, arguably in black male culture globally – such that sartorial particularity need not register as queer in quite the same way it might in white US culture. However, there is the matter of Bounty Killer's injunction against tight pants. And there are several other reggae songs registering a suspicion of excessive male grooming. (I think, for instance, of Harry Toddler's "Bad Man Nuh Dress Like Girl" (1999): "We nuh bore nose and we nuh bleach face and / We nuh wear drop curl." Or Damian Marley's "It Was Written" (2001): "Did you know you cyaan go a heaven and a wear Jheri curls / Can't tell the boys from the girls." In spite of these injunctions however, and as I have come to think of it, *because* of the repetition of these injunctions, there was a distinct shift in what became allowable in masculine expression around dress and dance right at the midpoint of the new century in the newly revived space of the street dance. This shift allowed for queer masculine expression in specific contexts, with homophobic lyrics actually opening up a space for increasingly free expression.

At some point during the night I first attended Passa Passa, the selector played the Buju Banton song "Boom Bye Bye" (2001). The song acted as a homophobic disavowal of the space, ritualistically attempting to do away with "homosexuality" as such and creating a contract of disavowal such that nothing in the area was gay because nothing *could* be gay. This logic paradoxically enabled the kind of homoerotic display I saw that night. No one looked askance at the two boys dancing because they could not possibly be gay in the sense that had been abjected by the Buju Banton song. My argument is that the crowds and the performers enter into an unspoken arrangement that ritualizes and contains certain queer performances. This idea of the ritualistic function of homophobic lyrics makes sense of why a song like "Boom Bye Bye" would get played more than a decade after its initial release. Why would a culture that thrives on the new repeatedly go back to the old? The most obvious argument is that these songs emanate from the most homophobic aspect of Jamaican existence, securing and stamping it. But another way of seeing it is that the song has to be ritualistically returned to in order to absolve people from the allowances they make toward queer culture. The songs are played; no one is "gay"; everyone can turn a blind eye.

There are chilling consequences when queerness is enacted outside of the consecrated space of a street dance or club night where a homophobic song has been played, as increasingly queer Jamaicans are insisting that it must. For instance, there was a famous incident reported in the press in Kingston in February 2007, not in the supposedly fearsome space of the inner-city community but in a middle-class shopping centre. Three men were held hostage in a pharmacy by a mob for "being gay" – that is, for embodying queer masculinity in their tight clothes, hair extensions and, according to one eyewitness, their "brazen" display of "effeminate behaviour" (Walker 2007).

This eyewitness opined, "Jamaica has lost its way if men think they can openly flaunt being gay without any consequences. We don't want that kind of open gay life in this country." Fascinating, given that the men were wearing pants no tighter than many of the dancers at Passa Passa, certainly not any tighter or more colourful than Sample Six's tie-dyed tank tops and Ravers Clavers's skinny jeans. The difference seemed to be that these men were going about their daily business in broad daylight, not in the regulated and ritualized space of the dancehall. Understanding this difference requires a reading practice of dancehall that sees the homophobia of its lyrics as enabling rather than inhibiting queer performances, and this is a crucial if not singular aspect of a queer dancehall hermeneutic.

Which is why José Muñoz's notion of disidentification is apt here. For the queer dancer, working within a normative culture of homophobia requires a complex strategy of identifying with structures that radically exclude him. This identification is absolutely necessary if the exclusion is hegemonic, as homophobia is in most cultures. It is the only way to survive. However, the disidentifying performer tweaks that identification, parodying the culture's forms so that on closer inspection there is a powerful critique at the centre of the performance. The queer masculine dancehall dancer is a disidentifying performer. In appropriating the culture and working from within its very centre, he produces a bodily performance that gains him power. It is the power of mastery, of parody, and of getting away with it.

"FUCK ALL AH UNNU WOMAN": (DE)LIMITING THE TERMS OF HETERONORMATIVITY

The second scene I want to think about is even more subtle and confusing. During an average Dancehall Night at Asylum nightclub (R.I.P.), there was the usual mix of people dancing: many working class, some middle class, all dancing together on a packed dance floor. Nothing stood out as particularly noteworthy until again Buju Banton's song "Boom Bye Bye" was played. As I had been at Passa Passa, I was struck by what seemed to me its complete disjunction. I had been watching a scene of urban euphoria and this song seemed to rupture that. Dancing ceased and a certain seriousness descended on the crowd. Lighters were held aloft, people started singing along. The song was played for a long time, on a loop. It was so old, but its function seemed to be atemporal or beyond time. The line between the ritualistic and the mundane is a thin one. Ritual necessitates repetition, as does the mundane. But with ritual, repetition is infused with some other essence that produces several effects the mundane does not. Ritual focuses the attention. It gives a subject a sense of a community beyond him or herself, while the tyranny of boredom is experienced alone. Needless to say, I experienced an anxious boredom, though others around me seemed to merge ritualistically.

But then a little while later there was a performance that was a queer intervention, leaching some of the power from the "Boom Bye Bye" ritual – or at least drawing uncomfortable attention to its terms. A comedian came onto a tiny stage set up next to the selector's mixers. He was there to smooth the transitions between sets. I cannot remember any of the jokes he told except the last one, but it is important to note that the comedian embodied what in the United States would be called "camp". His routine was performed with a kind of excessive reference to body and gesture and expression. It is the kind of performance associated with Jamaican comic actors such as Oliver Samuels (and the theatre would seem to be another cultural space in which categories of gay or straight are not rigidly policed or even defined – witness the irresistible rise of Shebada). The comedian proceeded through his routine, mocking and joshing, and then suddenly became quite serious. I will paraphrase from memory: "And all a unnu ah sing 'Boom Bye Bye'; unnu 'bout yu a go bun out battyman. Unnu can gwaan go chase out all the battyman from here. Gwaan go bun dem out. Me will stay here and fuck all ah unnu woman."

It is hard to explain, but it was *precisely* in the moment of that last utterance, the camp comedian's claim that he would stay and have sex with all the women while the crusading heterosexual men went about hunting gays, that it occurred to me that the comedian *was* gay. Which is to say, his performance was queer by the terms I have outlined above, but this queerness seemed to align with some strong intuition that he was also homosexual.[14] His utterance was less boast than threat. It drew attention to the defining terms of traditional Jamaican masculinity and suggested that one of those terms, violent homophobia, apart from being an object of contemptuous mockery was in contradiction with another defining term, sexual prowess. The comedian was saying not only was it stupid and passé to get all hyped up about the idea of killing gays, it was also a misuse of time. In the meanwhile, gay men would have all the time in the world to demonstrate their sexual (ambi)dexterity.

I remember the crowd laughing. Certainly nothing bad happened to the comedian. But it did feel like a defining moment in my sense of the possibilities for a queer hermeneutic of Jamaican popular culture. I had to rethink my ideas about how to read queer sexuality in Jamaica as not just marginal and besieged but as expressive and resisting from the very centre.

This way of reading queer Jamaican culture and identity is shored up by two important things that I still need to test more deeply. One is the impact of the crowd, the assumption of being able to read a gathering as having a kind of independent will and affect. It is the idea of communal disavowal as a form of contract that, in specific ways and at specific times, enables what can be startlingly open performances of nonnormative sexual expression. The other thing that helps to underwrite my reading is what critics such as Carolyn Cooper (1995) point to as alternative Jamaican epistemologies: gossip, oral sources, the things that "everybody knows".[15] Earlier in the evening at Asylum, I had been having a conversation with one of my Jamaican friends who had told me that "everybody knows" there are certain spaces where gay men can express themselves in dancehall: as comedians, as dancers. Some of the most famous reggae dance innovators, the kind that get name-checked in dancehall songs, were supposedly gay. This mode of reading is also not without its complication, again around the issue of what we can know and how. There is a way in which Jamaican men confound certain queer epistemologies, ones I have been relying on, such as: extravagant affect is queer; tight clothing is queer. Jamaican men, arguably black men, have always had a certain access to dapperness and theatricality that other men do not. However, even if these categories become unfixed among men in Jamaican dancehall, they are also the very categories used *within* Jamaican dancehall to police masculinity and sexuality. I may be responding to stereotypical assumptions about gay male expression, but only because these very stereotypes are generated – and then, also, unhinged – in Jamaican popular culture itself.

"JAMAICAN PUM PUM, SWISS PUM PUM": EXCESS AND THE LEAP INTO THE QUEER

In my final reading I turn to a music video that, even a year and a half after I first viewed it, continues to arrest me and compel my attention – it is just that curious, outlandish and slippery. Jay Will's video for Lee "Scratch" Perry's "Pum Pum" (2008) is an excellent example of how transnational pop cultural circulation can in complicated ways finally confirm, rather than subvert, the imperatives of the local.[16] The video stages the incursion of global objects – clothing, jewellery, production values – in a way that reminds me of Eng-Beng Lim's (2005) term "glocalqueering". I would argue that at least two different things are happening to queer this dancehall text. The first is that the compression of objects that mark the acquisition of global capital – the masses of gold; the swathes of lamé; the Rolls Royces; the "pum pum", Swiss or otherwise – do much to sanction the *other* form of excess happening on Lee Perry's body, via the makeup and the dyed hair. In other words, there is a confluence of the signs of the transnational – the objects mentioned above and the production values of the video, which include MTV-style colour saturation, slow motion, focus-pulling and jump-cutting, as well as the beat of the song itself, which references dancehall but is outside of its traditional musical boundaries (the song was produced by American rocker Andrew WK). All these markers of Perry's transnational residence and acquisition enable him to produce a performance that is, on the one hand, queer – in the sense of gender nonconforming – and, on the other hand, beyond anything sexual at all. It is reggae pioneer as harbinger of doom, reggae's resident prophet madman showing dancehall the outer limits of its excesses.

The other queer thing that is happening is in a certain sense more obvious and requires more standard modes of literary and visual analysis: the song and the video are an extended double entendre – Perry is "looking for a pum pum for his kitty". Certainly, the sexually normative way to read this refrain would be that Perry himself is looking for woman to add to his stash of other women. However, given that the video director decided to emblazon the metonym "Kitty" across the chest of one of the video's dancers, it seems clear enough that a queer reading is also in play: Perry is looking for a woman for one of his *other* women. This interpretation reinforces what we see happening in the video – the enervated dancing of the women referencing the tiredness of the heterosexual imperatives of female video dancers; the overwhelmingly, almost claustrophobically, homosocial compression of women in the frame; the absolute lack of any sexual energy across gender; the gaudy decadence of the entire milieu. Here is the last gasp of the hetero empire of dancehall – its most active clichés pushed to the furthest extreme of their limits – and Lee Perry becomes a cross between a harem's eunuch and a procuress. The video reminds us of the maxim, theorized by the likes of Eve Kosofsky Sedgwick and accepted by conventional wisdom of all sorts, that where heterosexuality finds its most extreme expression – sports, let's say, or virulent homophobia – is where queerness begins to emerge. To protest too much, to insist too much – indeed, to do anything too much, to invoke excess – is to risk queering.

ENDINGS

It seems fitting to briefly update the story of Tivoli Gardens, home of Passa Passa and site recently of extraordinary events that tangentially relate to what I have been thinking about here. Tivoli has been in the news recently: the powerful don of the community, Christopher "Dudus" Coke, patron extraordinaire of Passa Passa, name-checked on many videos of the street dance as "President", was extradited to the United States on 24 June 2010 to face weapons- and drug-trafficking charges. This was not before several dancehall deejays' US visas were revoked in what many believed was an action related to the Jamaican government's initial refusal to comply with extradition orders, not before Tivoli became a fortress to guard against Dudus's arrest, with the Jamaican police and military descending in full force to try to infiltrate and the government declaring a state of emergency. Eighty people were killed in ensuing days of violence, and for weeks Dudus eluded the authorities.

He was finally arrested in June, and very soon after, photographs of his mug shot circulated in the local and international press. Dudus was wearing a curly wig – supposedly one of several lady accoutrements he used to remain incognito while on the run. The blogosphere erupted, reporting on cartoons, jokes and commentary being made by Jamaicans about Dudus's fall from grace (see Paul 2010; Mackey 2010). One particularly apposite post is by Kei Miller (2010), whose reflections on badmen wearing girls' clothes captures many of the ironies and ambivalences I have been reflecting on here:

> Dudus's place on the very top of Jamaica's Most Wanted List validates him as the ultimate Bad Man, and that he wasn't suitably decked out in Ultimate-Bad-Man-Gear (whatever that might be, we simply know it doesn't include a wig) gives many of us pause. . . . . [But] in a country where Dudus and the dear departed Natty [another famous don] could wear wigs and frocks whenever their minds took them to do it; and in a country where any tour of dancehall will feature a few male dance crews who always offer, on public display, the most profound and sometimes magical performances of Jamaican queerness; and in a country where badmen run across garrison communities – one hand holding onto their [U]zi guns, and the other lifting up the hem[s] of their frocks so as not to trip, then we know the real truth – that badman dress however de rass him want to dress.

Miller's comments suggest the term with which I began, *out and bad*. This phrase is of queer hermeneutical possibility in Jamaican dancehall because it registers a dialectic between *queer* and *gay* that is never resolved, that relays back and forth, producing an uncertainty about sexual identity and behavior that is usefully maintained in the Jamaican popular cultural context. Those men bad enough to ride the dangerous edges of masculinity can do so either in the service of hardcore machismo (backed up by Uzis) or to disrupt that machismo (with the dancer's graceful line), or both. That ambivalence is precisely the place in which the dancehall queer exists.

Ultimately, my project is to consider the possibilities of a queer hermeneutic across Caribbean and black diasporic popular culture, to learn how to read those moments when the culture itself produces or enables the queer.[17] I end, then, with a gesture toward another unbounded space of bodily performance: Trinidad Jouvert. I attended the pre-Carnival all-night street dance Jouvert in Trinidad last year specifically to look at comparisons with the Jamaican dancehall street. As the sun rose higher in the sky, bringing the night's festival to a close, the frenzy I had noticed toward the end of all the Carnival events heightened. As revelers became conscious of their limited time, there was a greater abandon, a keener adherence to the imperatives of pleasure and the body. I noticed two women: one white and one black, both Trinidadian, and both blurring traditional lines between femme and butch. Speculations on these women's sexuality seemed beside the point – as, I think, it was beside the point to decide on the sexuality of the men I observed at pretty mas' two days later, men who marched down the street in costumes made for women, blending soca with Beyonce's fiercest moves. Certainly, at least one of the men I saw marching – the one in a piercing, skin-tight blue costume, highlighting ornamental muscles and otherworldly facial beauty with striking blue eye makeup – did end up at the gay club at which I ended my Carnival night. The moves of the boys on the stage of that club were not altogether different from what I saw on the street earlier in the day. But the *meaning* was different, since there we were, in a gay club.

There is much to observe and far more work to be done to understand the workings of gay and lesbian community in the clubs of Port of Spain, at the hilltop parties of Kingston and in the Caribbean more generally. But there is less to say in a post-Carnival gay party about how carnival rituals specifically engender queer performance. On the streets of Port of Spain (or Kingston, for that matter), fixing people at a point on either side of a sexual binary, or even at a point along a sexual continuum, is not the purpose of a queer performance hermeneutic. Instead, what I want to say is that in those last frenzied moments of Jouvert, as the sun grew hotter and the newly visible sidewalks and hedges threatened to close down the revelry, a poetics of bodily pleasure superseded any perceived or remembered injunction against same-sex expressions of pleasure, producing in those moments a wholly Caribbean, wholly local queer aesthetic. A poetics that caused these women to dance with each other with a fluidity that it is impossible to describe here, their bodies equal in size and scale, welded together as if they were matching halves, spiritual twins – one light, one dark – creating a synthesis of race and gender through linked and coordinated body movements that seemed memorized in another time and invoked here by the music, the rum, the crowds, the sun. Evoked by the license provided by a centuries-old tradition that named the carnivalesque – the parodic, the subversive, the topsy-turvy inversion of all that is normative and status quo. These women were the most arresting images of Jouvert that morning because their pleasure instantiated a queer performance that was wholly of its place and time, consecrated by the popular traditions at the very heart of the nation.

NOTES

1. From dem a par [hang out] in a chi-chi man car
Blaze de fire mek we bun dem.
From dem a drink in a chi-chi man bar,
Blaze de fire mek we done dem.

T.O.K., "Chi Chi Man" (2001). Apart from the more obvious financial gains of releasing as one of their first singles an anti-"battyman" song (in the dancehall market, a sure-fire way to win sales), T.O.K. arguably had to protect themselves from questions about their own heterosexuality. They were, after all, a group of men arrayed together making melodies. Additionally, members of the group met at Campion College, an uptown high school in Kingston, and certain markers of middle-class masculine identity map onto perceived homosexual ones. Exploring the particularities of middle-class gay Jamaican identity is beyond the scope of the current essay, but deserves much closer attention.

2. "World Dance" notwithstanding (Beenie Man 1995).

3. Bounty Killer's "Can't Believe Mi Eyes" (1998) is an early example of the sort of beleaguered heterosexuality we would find expressed by many other artists in the years to come, a trend that bloomed not coincidentally alongside increased visibility of homosexuality in Jamaica. He sings,

Well I can't believe a how battyman get so bold,
Me can't believe seh Rasta man a tun [turn] pussyhole, . . .
Mi can't believe some name me a hear seh a men [gay],
Me can't believe seh tight pants come in again,
Me can't believe seh gun man and battyman a fren [friends].

In the next stanza, the tight pants are conceptually aligned with the "certain man and certain man" who are "guy" (that is, gay).

4. This can produce discursive fields of dazzling contradiction: again, witness Elephant Man's invocation of a sign of global capitalistic liberalism – the internet – as a sign of heteronormative national protectionism in "Log On" (2001):

Log on
And step pon chi chi man
Log on
Cause yu know seh we nuh dicky man
Log on
And step pon chi chi man
Dance we ah dance and a bun out de icky man.

5. For an in-depth analysis of the contours of Jamaican homophobia, as well as the most exhaustive accounting of homophobic dancehall songs I have yet encountered, see Gutzmore (2004). Chin (1997) describes the controversy over Buju Banton's "Boom Bye Bye". This controversy included a well-known intervention by Cooper (1994) on the politics of translation from Jamaican Creole to American English in response to US news coverage of Buju Banton and dancehall homophobia. More recent debates about dancehall and homophobia include the "Stop Murder Music" campaign organized by UK-based activist Peter Thatchell, which resulted in the cancellation of several international dancehall concerts in the mid-2000s.

6. *Fish* is slang for "gay man".

7. Groundbreaking work by these scholars in the early 1990s is generally invoked as the beginnings of queer theory. See Warner (1992, 1993, 1999). See also Sedgwick (1990, 1992) and Fuss (1995).
8. For astute reflections on the principle of shifting boundaries in dancehall, see Stanley Niaah (2010, 2004).
9. This evocative phrase – "perverse consecration" – was suggested by a conversation on this topic with anthropologist Charles Carnegie, June 2007, Miami.
10. For evocative descriptions of Passa Passa, see Stanley Niaah (2004) and Hope (2006b).
11. Writing about Passa Passa, Donna Hope has suggested that the emphasis on dance as theatre has enabled a certain leverage in masculine performance. See Hope (2006).
12. "Ketch di Dance – Sample 6 vs. Ravers Clavers", http://jamaicahtube.com/video/c46021aecab15fd/Ketch-Di-Dance--Sample-6-vs-Ravers-Clavers.
13. The second line is a pun on yet another popular dancehall event, Dutty Fridays.
14. See also Harper's (2000) account of the place of intuition in queer practice – his notion that so much (safety, sex) depends on minute readings of gestures, signs; that there is finally nothing at all between the queer subject, perhaps any subject, and sociality except acute readings of performances, daily performances, bodily performances.
15. On this point of the legitimacy of gossip in establishing sexual orientation in Jamaica, see also Gutzmore 2004.
16. "Pum Pum", Lee "Scratch" Perry, music video, dir. Jay Will (2008), http://vimeo.com/1738674, featuring Lee "Scratch" Perry.
17. Since beginning this research the possibilities have multiplied in exciting ways: from Carnivals across the Caribbean to early R&B and Blaxploitation to New Orleans Sissy Bounce.

REFERENCES

Chin, Timothy. 1997. "'Bullers' and 'Battymen': Contesting Homophobia in Black Popular Culture and Contemporary Caribbean Literature". *Callaloo* 20, no. 1: 127–41.

Cohen, Cathy. 1997. "Punks, Bulldaggers, and Welfare Queens: The Radical Potential of Queer Politics?" *GLQ: A Journal of Lesbian and Gay Studies* 3, no. 4: 437–65.

Cooper, Carolyn. 1994. "'Lyrical Gun': Metaphor and Role Play in Jamaican Dancehall Culture". *Massachusetts Review* 35, no. 3: 429–47.

———. 1995. *Noises in the Blood: Orality, Gender, and the "Vulgar" Body of Jamaican Popular Culture.* Durham, NC: Duke University Press.

Fuss, Diana. 1995. *Identification Papers.* New York: Routledge.

Gutzmore, Cecil. 2004. "Casting the First Stone!" *Interventions: The International Journal of Postcolonial Studies* 6, no. 1: 118–34.

Harper, Phillip Brian. 2000. "The Evidence of Felt Intuition: Minority Experience, Everyday Life, and Critical Speculative Knowledge". *GLQ: A Journal of Lesbian and Gay Studies* 6, no. 4: 641–57.

Hope, Donna P. 2004. "The British Link-Up Crew: Consumption Masquerading as Masculinity in the Dancehall". *Interventions: The International Journal of Postcolonial Studies* 6, no. 1: 101–17.

———. 2006a. *Inna di Dancehall: Popular Culture and the Politics of Identity in Jamaica.* Kingston: University of the West Indies Press.

———. 2006b. "Passa Passa: Interrogating Cultural Hybridities in Jamaican Dancehall". *Small Axe* 10, no. 3: 125–39.

Johnson, E. Patrick. 2005. "'Quare' Studies, or (Almost) Everything I Know about Queer Studies I Learned from My Grandmother". In *Black Queer Studies: A Critical Anthology*, edited by E. Patrick Johnson and Mae Henderson, 124–60. Durham, NC: Duke University Press.

Kartelyoung. 2004. "Me a Bad Man, Mi Nuh Go Go". *DancehallReggae.com*, 12 September. http://forum.dancehallreggae.com/showthread.php/38133-Me-a-Bad-Man-Mi-nuh-go-go?s=946bc1a874afd5e192108f8c6a79b322?s=946bc1a874afd5e192108f8c6a79b322.

Kingston_Badmon. 2004. "Me a Bad Man, Mi Nuh Go Go". *DancehallReggae.com*, 12 September. http://forum.dancehall reggae.com/showthread.php/38133-Me-a-Bad-Man-Mi-nuh-go-go?s=946bc1a874afd5e192108f8c6a79b322?s= 946bc1a874afd5e192108f8c6a79b322.

Lim, Eng-Beng. 2005. "Glocalqueering in New Asia: The Politics of Performing Gay in Singapore". *Theatre Journal* 57, no. 3: 383–405.

Mackey, Robert. 2010. "Jamaicans Ponder Cross-dressing Gangsters". *The Lede Blog*, NYTimes.com, 25 June. http:// thelede.blogs.nytimes.com/2010/06/25/jamaicans-ponder-cross-dressing-gangsters/.

Miller, Kei. 2010. "Bad Man Nuh Dress Like Girl". Facebook, Kei Miller's Notes, 24 June. http://www.facebook.com/note.php?note_id=471431418568&id=167074302410&ref=mf.

Muñoz, José. 1999. *Disidentifications: Queers of Color and the Performance of Politics*. Minneapolis: University of Minnesota Press.

Paul, Annie. 2010. "Crying Out for Peace in Jamaica: The Extradition of Christopher 'Dudus' Coke". *Active Voice*, 24 June. http://anniepaulactivevoice.blogspot.com/2010/06/crying-out-for-peace-in-jamaica.html.

Rodríguez, Juana María. 2003. *Queer Latinidad: Identity Practices, Discursive Spaces*. New York: New York University Press.

Saunders, Patricia J. 2003. "Is Not Everything Good to Eat, Good to Talk: Sexual Economy and Dancehall Music in the Global Marketplace". *Small Axe*, no. 13 (January): 95–115.

Sedgwick, Eve Kosofsky. 1990. *Epistemology of the Closet*. Berkeley: University of California Press.

———. 1992. *Between Men: English Literature and Male Homosocial Desire*. New York: Columbia University Press.

Stanley Niaah, Sonjah. 2004. "Making Space: Kingston's Dancehall Culture and Its Philosophy of 'Boundarylessness'". *African Identities* 2, no. 2 (October): 117–32.

———. 2010. *DanceHall: From Slave Ship to Ghetto*. Ottawa: University of Ottawa Press.

Stolzoff, Norman C. 2000. *Wake the Town and Tell the People: Dancehall Culture in Jamaica*. Durham, NC: Duke University Press.

Tinsley, Omise'eke Natasha. 2008. "Black Atlantic, Queer Atlantic: Queer Imaginings of the Middle Passage". *GLQ: A Journal of Lesbian and Gay Studies* 14, no. 2: 191–215.

Walker, Karyl. 2007. "Cops Save Three Alleged Homosexuals from Angry Crowd". *Jamaica Observer*, 15 February. https://www.jamaicaobserver.com/news/119155_Cops-save-three-alleged-homosexuals-from-angry-crowd.

Warner, Michael. 1991. "Introduction: Fear of a Queer Planet". *Social Text*, no. 29 (Winter): 3–17.

———. 1993. *Fear of a Queer Planet: Queer Politics and Social Theory*. Minneapolis: University of Minnesota Press.

———. 1999. *The Trouble with Normal: Sex, Politics, and the Ethics of Queer Life*. New York: Free Press.

DISCOGRAPHY

Assassin. 2009. "Dem Nuh Want No Gal". *Ragga Ragga Ragga 2009*. Greensleeves.
Beenie Man. 1995. *Blessed*. Island Jamaica.
Bounty Killer. 1998. "Can't Believe Mi Eyes". *Next Millennium* (TVT).
Buju Banton. 2001. *The Best of the Early Years: 1990–1995*. Penthouse Records.
Dong Ding. 2007. "Badman Forward, Badman Pull Up". *Reggae Gold 2006*. VP Music Group.
Elephant Man. 2001. *Log On*. Greensleeves.
———. 2003. *Good 2 Go*. VP Records.
Marley, Damian. 2001. *Halfway Tree*. Motown.
Perry, Lee "Scratch". 2008. *Repentance*. Narnack Records.
Queen Ifrica. 2009. *Montego Bay*. VP Records.
Toddler, Harry. 1999. "Bad Man Nuh Dress Like Girl". *Reggae Gold 1998*. VP Records.
T.O.K. 2001. *My Crew, My Dawgs*. VP Records.

CHAPTER 14

Fashion Ova Style

*Dancehall's Masculine Duality**

DONNA P. HOPE

Resistance is futile, you will be assimilated.
—The Borg, *Star Trek: The Next Generation*

THIS CHAPTER EXAMINES ONE OF THE MOST CONTEMPORARY and controversial expressions of masculinity in the Jamaican dancehall which I label "Fashion Ova Style". It is brokered on a range of feminized aesthetics, public presentation of the male body in dance performance and high levels of male homosociality in the public performance space. In this chapter, relevant examples are drawn from the costumes of men in the dancehall, dancehall performances, and the conspicuous attire and practices of male dancehall artistes like Elephant Man. The burgeoning appropriation and recasting of stylistic dancing by hardcore dancehall men is explored as a part of this refashioning and repositioning of dancehall masculinity as a newly constituted variant that incorporates facets of all four dancehall masculine exemplars explored in Hope (2010).[1]

MEN IN PINK DRESS (STYLES): ENGENDERING DANCEHALL FASHION AND STYLE

The Fashion Ova Style variant of dancehall masculinity is first highlighted in the transgressive aesthetic rituals and fashion choices of men in the dancehall, which marks a progressive move from the Bling Bling variant examined in chapter 5 of Hope (2010). Here, Fashion Ova Style reflects the cross-fertilization with high fashion and style from the developed capitalist metropoles, American hip-hop culture, and the historical imperatives for African flamboyance and ostentatious costumes. The result is a distinct preference for designer fashion as accepted high fashion and style for the hardcore dancehall male within the traditionally restrictive structures of Jamaican masculinity. At this juncture, external pressures heightened by the advent of globalization, and its attendant economic,

*This chapter is an extract from *Man Vibes: Masculinities in the Jamaican Dancehall* (Kingston: Ian Randle, 2010), 124–42.

social and cultural facets, have converged with the dancehall community's agenda for self-development and enhancement. Popular fashion magazines, mainstream cinema, electronic media and the internet project prescriptive (and often competing) images of the feminine and masculine ideal across the dancehall body. These and other factors feed into a creeping ideological acceptance and practice by hardcore dancehall men of feminized aesthetics and rituals that were once rigidly demarcated and branded as taboo. In Jamaica, practices and rituals of this variety include regular visits by even the most hardened ghetto youth to cosmetologists for facials, manicures and pedicures, and regular visits to salons for hair-care. This is complemented by a corresponding explosion in the numbers of hardcore men sporting conspicuous and intricate hair styles (for example, intricate cornrows), and plucked, trimmed and fashioned eyebrows. Men who cannot afford these costly rituals at formal establishments utilize the inexpensive route of over-the-counter skin care and skin bleaching (lightening) creams, visits to the community barbershop, and in-house hair-care and maintenance by female family members or friends. This excessive and highly narcissistic focus on the body, its care and public presentation, is complemented with an emphasis on stylized coordination of expensive brand name clothes (for example, Moschino, Versace, Dolce and Gabbana), jewellery (authentic or fake gold, diamond and platinum), shoes and other accessories. These aesthetic activities are accompanied by exaggerated public display and self-presentation both within and beyond the performative space of the dancehall.

These practices and behaviours are linked to the sartorial excess and conspicuous consumptive ethos of men like those of the British Link Up Crew (see Hope 2010, ch. 5; Hope 2004). However, a distinctive shift in the depth of narcissism displayed by these Fashion Ova Style men has simultaneously occurred, together with a radical dash toward a "softened" variant of dancehall masculinity which is in direct opposition to the historical imperatives toward the "tough", "rough" and "hard" variant of hardcore dancehallized masculinity. The tell-tale, glossy sheen of nail hardeners or natural overcoats on manicured and pedicured fingers and toes that was once used as "incriminating evidence" in Jamaica to identify a *maama man* or a *chi chi man* is now openly flaunted by "hardcore" dancehall men who proudly display this evidence of their appropriation of a ritual of bodily care that purportedly signals wealth, luxury and high status.

Dancehall's fashion culture operates in a cosmopolitan and transnational space that continuously engages the global codes of fashion and style in a constant stream of cross-fertilization. The new millennium's global codes of fashion and style include international fashion culture's retro impulse and its return to the 1970s asexual style of tighter-fitting clothes for both men and women, as well as the revolutionary efforts to un-gender the colour pink, heralded by the global entertainment industry, and the visibility of prominent men in popular music cultures wearing pink (for example, American hip-hop culture). Consequently, colours originally denoted as feminine or feminized in an earlier era in popular Jamaican culture, including light pastels like peach and the highly feminized pink (once taboo and therefore shunned by most men), is a displayed favourite among many dancehall adherents. For many years, the preferred colour of dress for a real, hardcore, dancehall badman has been the powerful black, with pink its antithesis. For example, dancehall artiste Bounty Killer chose black as his signature colour for many years to cement his warlord, gladiator, badman identity in dancehall. The transformation in colour preferences is matched with a displayed fondness for donning close-fitting or skintight pants – an aesthetic choice that also purportedly identified the antithesis of the dancehall's heterosexual masculinity when men wearing tights or tight pants were often identified as homosexual. In contemporary dancehall, men who favour these aesthetic and fashion choices and are identified as gangster and hardcore create a truly contradictory and paradoxical variant of masculinity. This is so because their refashioned bodies simultaneously articulate a gangsterized, hardcore and feminized masculinity that, based on the traditional codes of accepted male identity, is highly transgressive and revolutionary. The sculpted, costumed and softened Fashion Ova Style men in dancehall simultaneously project a highly feminized aesthetics alongside the behaviours that define a badman, including the rough, coarse voice, the use of expletives and regular references to violence, as well as the signature badman slouch and "screw face". One can only speculate on whether the only key factor is that fashion and style cues in the international arena may have contributed to the ascendancy and creeping acceptance of these feminized styles and colours within the rigidly guarded spaces of dancehall and inner-city masculinities as, in the fashion-conscious space of dancehall culture, fashion and style take precedence over and direct the cues of masculine being and identity in Jamaica. Yet, the primping, preening, styling and sculpting which these men undergo create a contradictory version of dancehallized masculinity that moves away from the early reliance on the traditional, hegemonic standards of Jamaican masculinity constituted at the historical moment of dancehall's ascendancy in the 1980s.

In a late 1990s backlash against the first wave of this propensity to refashion the dancehall male body using feminized and therefore transgressive, codes, dancehall artiste Elephant Man noted in a popular song, "Dress Like Girl": "Badman nuh dress like girl / Wi nuh bore nose and wi nuh bleach face and wi nuh wear drops curls / And some freaky freaky bwoy nuh stop dress like girl." (Badmen don't dress like women / We don't pierce our noses and we don't chemically lighten our facial skin and we don't wear our hair in [drop] curls / [And] some freaky freaky boys won't stop dressing like women.) In this song, Elephant Man lyrically distances the Badman from the early re-imaging of dancehall's hardcore male identity and, in so doing, documents several practices that are considered to be precipitously close to the gendered borderline, including several aesthetic choices such as the piercing of nose, bleaching (lightening) of the face, wearing "drops curls" or elaborate hairstyles and dressing in styles that closely resemble those chosen by women.

However, as one of dancehall culture's international stars of the twenty-first century, Elephant Man's excesses of feminized fashion and style incorporate his signature hair colours, multiple, large earrings and body art. His expensive, brand name costumes and penchant for high fashion pinks and pastels and brilliant neon colours broker on his early status-hungry admonitions for visibility in his signature phrase at dancehall events, "Shine di light inna mi cute and dainty face." (Shine the videolight in my cute and dainty face.) In addition, Elephant Man, dancehall's Energy God and Chief Jester, has parlayed Bogle's dancing and edgy style of dress into a dancehall character that incorporates the radical aspects of today's Bling Bling costumes for dancehall men. His success underscores the space that exists for this variant of identity as it flits across dancehall's stages. Indeed, while the late dance icon Bogle is credited for the development of flashy dance styles, Elephant Man must be credited for the upgrade and transformation of what I refer to as "Bogle's Progeny" into a variant of dancehall male artistes that has spawned its own successors and carved out is own identity-space.

Since the turn of the new millennium, Elephant Man's signature hair colours, up-to-the-minute colourful costumes, energetic, impish behaviours and promotion of nouveau dance styles underwritten by popular songs have driven a new wave of dance in dancehall culture. Dancehall groups like Voice Mail and, more particularly, the dancehall duo RDX (Renegade X and Delomar X), broker on Elephant Man's portrayal of this variant of a successful dancehall artiste/male to expand the repertoire of music, dance and identities that now coalesce in the dancehall. RDX's colourful hair styles, their cheerful, humorous personalities and their development of a cadre of songs that are brokered on or drive new dance styles in the dancehall speak particularly to this line of succession.

This transition in the presentation of the male body in dancehall has not been without its detractors. For example, the lyrical treatise released in late 2005 by female dancehall artiste Cecile underscored the hesitation of many dancehall adherents to legitimize the new wave of feminized male Fashion Ova Style as dancehallized masculinity. In her song "Woman Tings", Cecile defines and condemns what she perceived as a disturbing trend in men's fashion in Jamaica. In the intro, she insists that some unidentified entity must leave "women's things alone": "Let me tell u something / Low woman things, low woman things let me tell u something." (Let me tell you something / Leave women's things alone, leave women's things alone, let me tell you something.) In the chorus of this song, Cecile identifies men as the perpetrators of this problematic behaviour:

We cant hot again cause a di man dem
Dem a buy off we blouse and we pants dem
Them thief we pink colour my God then
Dem nu soon start want wear wi thong then

(We [i.e., women] cannot be hot/fashionable anymore because of the men
They are buying out our blouses and pants
They have stolen our colour pink, my God
Then won't they soon begin to want to wear our thong [panties] too)

In each subsequent verse she makes particular references to different behaviours and aesthetic choices that are deemed problematic in their borderline leanings. For example, in verse 1 she asks youth (that is, young men) why their clothing styles must rival those of women and highlights the scandalous nature of male appropriation of female clothing styles with a reference to the *XNews*, one of Jamaica's then popular tabloids.

My youth why u pants fi tighter than mine
And why u pants no de a you waistline?

Hipsters a fi gyal dem design
Me and u nuffi ina di same kind
Go GO WEST cant find no gyal clothes
Whe dem gone only God he knows
U want know read *XNews* page four
A group a man a buy dem off fi go a dancehall go pose

(My youth, why should your pants be tighter than mine?
And why is your pants not at your waistline?
Hipsters is designed for girls/women
You and I should not be in the same kind [of design]
[I] went to Go West [clothing store] and could not find any girls'/women's clothing
Where have they gone only God knows
If you want to know read page four of the *XNews* newspaper
A group of men purchased them all so they could go to the dancehall and pose)

In verse 2, Cecile highlights the paradox of "gangsters" who are feminine thus:

Gangster youth u nuffi look like Sally
And u nuffi pretty pretty and favour dolly
U fi be Ken u nuffi be di Barbie
From u look feminine boy you can't chat to me
Man all a make mistake call u Shorty
Cause di style a u clothes make u favour Shari
Stop buy di gyal dem clothes nuh Marky
And gi u hipsters dem to u sister Sani

(Gangster youth, you should not look like Sally [a woman]
And you should not be pretty and resemble a doll
You should be Ken, you should not be the Barbie [doll]
Once you look feminine boy, you cannot speak to me
Men are even making the mistake of calling you Shorty[2]
Because the style of your clothing causes you to resemble Shari [a woman]
Marky, stop buying the girls'/woman clothing
And give your hipsters [jeans] to your sister Shari)

Cecile pinpoints what she sees as inconsistencies in the presentation of hardcore masculinity as it has been historically defined in popular culture and in dancehall. In verse 3 of her song she notes that for her (and others), women's clothing, the colour pink, tight pants and "di wining and di bruk out bruk out" (the gyrating and explicitly sexual gymnastics) dance styles all constitute markers of femininity which have been selectively appropriated by men in a highly transgressive move. Using select verbal play, Cecile ridicules men who engage in these practices, comparing them to women and denouncing their slippage into femininity as regressive:

Lollypop and tight pants a fi di gyal dem
Pink clothes, bore u nose boy u wrong den

A shave u eyebrow like Sharon dem
And nu see say something wrong boy u condemn
Left di wining to Keiva and Michelle dem
And di crawl up pan di box to Stacey dem
And di bruk out bruk out to Junkoo dem
Who nu like when mi talk try something then

(Lollypop and tight pants belong to the girls/women
Pink clothing, pierced nose, boy you are very wrong
Shaved eyebrows like Sharon and the others
And you don't see that something is wrong, boy you are condemned
Leave the "wining up" [erotic dancing] Keiva and Michelle[3]
And the crawl up onto sound boxes to Stacey[4] and others
And the frenzied dance styles to Junko[5] and others
Anyone who does not like what I am saying should try to do something about it)

In this final verse she identifies what are perceived as markers of femininity, such as pierced noses and shaved eyebrows. In the dancehall, these facial enhancements are often accompanied by another popular practice, that of skin bleaching or skin lightening.

Skin bleaching has historically been coded as feminine in the dancehall and in the wider Jamaican society. The clarion call of Bembe Thursdays, Kingston's then popular Thursday night dancehall gathering, was "No tight pants bwoy! No bleach out face bwoy!" In an era where male dancers predominate and male posers colonize the centre of dancehall's spaces, Bembe Thursdays valiantly attempted to re-centre women in dancehall culture and, thus, was ostensibly demarcated as "fi di girls dem". The correlation of bleaching with tight pants suggests a marked transformation in the range of aesthetic rituals that are practised by men in dancehall. Hardcore dancehall discourses of the twenty-first century project cantankerous debates about the trend toward male bleaching in Jamaica. For example, dancehall sensation and protégé of Bounty Killer, the Gully God, Mavado, in his 2008 treatise "Nuh Bleach Wid Cream", documents the realities of shottas[6] whose slippery grasp on hardcore heterosexual masculinity is identified by their propensity to bleach. Moving beyond the tracing match with arch-rival Vybz Kartel in which he constantly railed at Kartel's lack of male power because of his obvious altering of his epidermis,[7] Mavado documents his concern with the crossing over of hardcore masculinity into the feminized arena of bleaching in violent and derogatory terms:

Mi nuh bleach wid cream, mi bleach wid mi M-16
Wid extra magazine, mi alone create mi crime scene

You a disgrace, bleaching yuh face
Tru yuh fuckin face yuh marrow drop

Yuh bleach wid cream, but mi bleach wid mi M-16
An mi nuh bleach wid team, mi alone step pon mi crime scene aaaay
Shotta nuh bleach wid cream, Wi bleach wid wi M-16

(I don't use bleaching creams I use my M-16
With extra magazines, I create my crime scenes all by myself

You are a disgrace, bleaching your face
Through your fucking face your marrow falls

You use creams to bleach but I bleach with my M-16
And I do not bleach in a team, I step on my crime scene all alone aaaaay
Shottas do not use bleaching creams, we bleach with our M-16s)

Mavado's double-talk employs the Jamaican Creole meaning of the verb "to bleach".[8] He suggests that real hardcore badmen, the shottas, endure the long hours of dark(ness) into (day)light with their weapons – without any visible physical deterioration.[9] The response of Rastafari artistes to skin lightening/bleaching (for example, Queen Ifrica in "Mi Nah Rub" and I-Wayne in "Bleacher") parallels that of the dancehall artistes, while simultaneously encoding the socially accepted definitions of bleachers as mentally unstable, traitors to their race and colour, and social deviants and outcasts. Nonetheless, the trends that propel the Fashion Ova Style aesthetic in dancehall continue to gain a foothold, and consequently skin bleaching is simultaneously derogated and uplifted. For example, Captain Barkey's "Bleach On" uses an understated variation of humor to treat with the aesthetic rituals of women. He encourages women to engage in a range of image-altering practices, if they result in enhanced and accepted modes of beauty. His focus on skin bleaching parallels the explosion of bleaching that swept Jamaica at the turn of the millennium and encodes the growing ambivalence to the pervasive practice:

Settle yah mi gyal because you come fi mash it up
Han inna di air cause yuh nuh chop up chop up
Rail up mi gyal you nuh ole an mash up
Wooooeee!
Mi dainty gyal dem!

(Take it easy my girl/s as you have come to
Wave your hands in the air because/if your skin is free of marks and scars
Jump up and prance around my girl/s because you are not old and broken down
Woeeeeee!
My dainty girls!)

Chorus
If you a bleach an bleaching fit you
Bleach on Bleach on
Yuh have you false hair and false hair fit you
Weave on Weave on
If you a lead and leading fit you
Lead on Lead on
You tek di pace an speeding fit you
Speed on Speed on

(If you are bleaching/lightening your skin and it suits you
Continue to bleach/lighten, continue to bleach/lighten
If you are wearing false hair [weaves] and it suits you
Continue to weave, continue to weave
If you have taken the lead and being in the lead suits you
Continue to lead, continue to lead
You have set the pace and it suits you
Continue to speed ahead, continue to speed ahead]

Fi all di gyal dem whe a bleach an know say bleaching fit you
Nuh badda go falla nobaddy because you know say Barkey with you
Ah you go buy you tings so none ah dem cyan come box an kick you
An when yuh a bleach it never burn yuh up it never sick you
Dem say you nuh look good but a trick dem a try fi trick you trick you
Dat nah go stop you man from hug you up and kiss you
Dem better get it inna dem head that you ahead Alicia

(For all the women who are bleaching/lightening and know that it suits you
Do not listen to anyone as you know that Captain Barkey is in support of you
You bought your things/products so no one can box and kick [abuse] you
And when you are bleaching/lightening your skin it has not damaged your epidermis or made you ill
They say that you do not look pretty, but they are only trying to trick you
That will not stop your boyfriend/partner from hugging and kissing you
They had best understand that you have moved ahead [up] Alicia)

Barkey, like many dancehall adherents, projects bleaching as positive, especially when it "fit you". This is related to the use of hair extensions ("false hair") where he entreats his girls to "weave on, weave on" if the use of these cosmetic props results in aesthetic enhancement. In addition, the idea of capitalist property and ownership is intertwined with these contemporary debates. Your personal expenditure ("Ah you go buy yuh tings") suggest ownership and control over their utilization of these aesthetic artifices, regardless of public condemnation of the practice ("so nobaddy cyan come box and kick you"). This is one popular rebuttal to admonitions about skin bleaching and many bleachers claim that since they purchased their skin products, they are at liberty to use them. In addition, since the epidermis in question is their personal property, they are also at liberty to alter its shade at will, regardless of any dangers, real or imagined. Affirmation by partners, male or female, is also essential, and Barkey underscores not just his support for female bleachers but also the fact that the partner in the mix "nah go stop hug up and kiss" the woman who bleaches.

The common thread running throughout these debates in dancehall is that skin lightening/bleaching is a feminine activity. In concert with other modes of cosmetic artifice, the superficial application of skin products, whether demonized or reified, remained the purview of the female throughout most of the 1990s until its stealthy appropriation by men exploded in working class and dancehall culture. Both I Wayne and Ifrica capture the contemporary modes of bleaching as feminine and masculine and, as Mavado highlights in "Shotta Nuh Bleach wid Cream", both also signify the paradoxical presentation of shottas (or hardcore men) as bleachers. In his song "Bleacher", I Wayne speaks to this thus: "Still wid di guns and bling bling, / Nuh love demselves so dem bleach dem skin." (And even while they continue to consort with guns and bling bling/flamboyant aesthetics / They do not love themselves so they have bleached/lightened their skin.) Queen Ifrica poetically reflects in "Mi Nah Rub" thus: "See you pon di corner with you thuggy thuggy ways / But mi can't understand mek you go bleach out you face." (I see you on the corner with your thuggish/badman behaviours / But I cannot understand why you have lightened your face/skin.) Yet, while questions continue to be raised, this appropriation of feminine aesthetics and dress styles by men is also accompanied by behaviours that overturn accepted male practice. Elephant Man's projection of a refashioned dancehallized self is underscored by his affirmation of the need for dancehall adherents to be "bling and clean" and his lyrical contributions to the burgeoning wave of male dancing in dancehall culture. This explosive new trend in dancehall dancing is highlighted in the final verse of Cecile's foregoing song, where she entreats dancehall men to leave the erotic, gymnastic and frenzied dance styles to the female dancehall queens and divas. For Cecile, and many other adherents in the dancehall, recasting energetic and erotic dance as masculine in dancehall culture signifies a radical transgression in the embodied codes of hardcore masculinity in the dancehall. This is examined in some detail in the following section.

RE-CASTING MASCULINE DANCE IN DANCEHALL

> Real badman nuh wear people pants
> We tek dancing to a higher ranks . . .[10]
> Elephant Man, "Pon di River" (2003)

The rise of popularized male dancers in the dancehall is a critical masculine spectacle that points to the refashioning and repositioning of the male dancehall body within the spaces of Jamaican dancehall culture. Untamed, ritualistic, stylized and spiritual dance rites form part of the broader practice of dance that has characterized the dancehall since its development in the early 1980s. The drama that infuses any dancehall event is also characteristic of the wider cultural and political anthropology of Jamaica, for example as it unfolds in the African-based religious rites of Kumina and Revival groups or the celebratory ethos of Jonkonno groups. In the dancehall, a popular dancer is celebrated and lauded to the extent that she (and now he) assumes a god-like aura.[11] Dancehall queens, modellers and dancers (for example, the original dancehall queen Carlene and others like Stacey, Keiva, Mad Michelle and Junko) have used erotic posing and gymnastic and erotic dancing to claim the status of queens in the dancehall, based on its earlier propensity to elevate the feminine in the public space of (erotic) display, style and fashion. While the titular "queen" implies the existence of a male as the counterpart "king", the corresponding masculine ethos most popularized in the persona of dancehall's first magnificent male dancer, performer and creator, the late Gerald "Bogle" Levy, met no such royal appeal. Indeed, dancehall artistes King Yellowman and Beenie Man have both been crowned kings of the dancehall. This reflects the dichotomous split between the word and its use and control as masculine and powerful and the display and eroticization of the female body as a subsidiary and powerless binary. This is perhaps underscored by a patriarchal reluctance to frame the male as a desirable object. Other longstanding, popular dancehall male dancers, like the elder Labba Labba, have been immortalized in dancehall song and myth but receive little public accolades beyond the boundaries of local dancehall events in Jamaica.

One must note that dancehall culture coalesced in a society where the historical spaces for men who dance have been cast as middle or upper class (for example, dance groups like the National Dance Theatre Company), or deeply religious (for example, Kumina and Revivalism and the spiritual healing profession) or as feminized and homosexual, and therefore taboo. The patriarchal hesitance to pin the male body as desirable object contributed to the reluctance of many Jamaican men to engage in public dance spectacles. All together, these factors negated and ideologically exiled public dancing as routes for masculine expression and ascendancy by hardcore dancehall men in dancehall culture's lower class, secularized and deeply patriarchal space. Over time, it has been common practice for boys and men (particularly those from the inner cities) to avoid formalized careers in dance because of the social and gendered stigma that it carries. Men and boys who "wear tights" (that is, dancers) have been ritually denounced in Jamaican life and culture and often demonized as feminized, "maama man" and "battyman". This convergence of ideas about masculinity with class of origin has meant that many men avoid all forms of contact with "middle-class" dance groups like the National Dance Theatre Company[12] because of the perception that any such contact will have negative repercussions on their masculine identities. Yet, men and boys often participate in less sensual dances, with their bodies clothed in loose and patently masculine clothing, as opposed to the asexual tights and clinging bodysuits that purportedly project the male body as erotic and sexually desirable.

The spectacle of dancing men in dancehall was also more critically negated in dancehall's heavy focus on sex and sexuality and its propensity to engage with the female body as a source of male empowerment. This masculinist predisposition has been reflected in dancehall's strident anti-male homosexual discourse which has been taken to task by gay lobbyists like GLAAD and Outrage in 1993 and 2004 respectively, and which has continued into the current era with Buju Banton's *Rasta Got Soul* album tour facing protests and cancellations.[13] Consequently, dance, as celebratory performance and spectacle in dancehall, remained historically coded as feminine and women gained ascendancy as dancehall queens and dancers while men did as deejays and posers, replicating the dichotomous power split between the feminized and often disempowered erotic display of the body and the masculinized and power-making control over of language that was ratified in dancehall. Since the turn of the millennium, however, the phenomenon of male dancers has progressively become accepted practice in the spaces of the dancehall and is complemented by escalating male activity, particularly in groups, in the wider sphere of professional, staged dance by groups of young men.[14] Here, men are positioned as objects of desire in a radical challenge to dancehall's propensity to allocate discourses of homosexuality and effeminacy to men who dance.

This explosion of male dancers has created intense competition for space on the dancehall stage, as female dancers and modellers battle to share the centre of the dance and the dancing stage with their male counterparts. Dancehall events provide central spaces for the presentation of self and status for individuals from the marginalized spaces of Jamaica with the omnipresent videocameras and other forms of electronic media that result in visibility, recognition, status and the promise of resources to those whose images are captured in action at these events. In this regard, dancehall stage shows and popular events create a multifaceted, theatrical stage for marginalized men. The feminized centre of the dance, which is simultaneously the space circumscribed by video cameras at a dancehall event and once sparsely visited by a few enterprising dancehall men during dancehall's early development, has now been colonized by male dancers, many of whom have brokered their dancing prowess into spaces of social empowerment and wealth creation.[15]

In addition, there is now a distinct separation between male and female dancers on the dance floor and contemporary dancers and dance groups often dance in all-male or all-female groups at most dancehall events, except when there is convergence of space created by the usual intense competition for the space circumscribed by the light of the video cameras. This male/female separation of the centre space at the dancehall event is a significant departure from accepted dance practices and gendered rituals in dancehall culture. Since the early era of dancehall in the 1980s, the normative practice has been for women to take the stage and publicly perform their dances in the space selected as the centre of the dance, while men remain on the fringes individually or in groups to "profile" or "hang out". The historically accepted practice is for male dancing in the centre of the dancehall to be tolerated only when the man in question is dancing erotically with a female or when the man is particularly skilful and is consequently allowed a moment in time to signify his dance prowess, preferably using a dance coded as hardcore and masculine like the "Cool and Deadly". Any man who dared to breach this gendered divide and display any prowess in the erotic, sexual and feminized butterfly dance would find his masculinity questioned and be verbally chastised, booed and even chased from the dance. These gendered boundaries effectively stifled the rise of male dancers and the late Gerald "Bogle" Levy[16] remained the only highly publicized and popular male dancer in the dancehall for nearly two decades. Bogle's own membership in the popular Black Roses Crew helped to dispel any aspersions that could have been levelled against his claim to hardcore masculinity as the Black Roses Crew was simultaneously a dancehall sect/crew similar in constitution to the British Link Up Crew (see Hope 2010, ch. 5; Hope 2004) but even more importantly, a ghetto gang, hailing from the inner-city community of Arnett Gardens and reputed to be involved in illegal gun, drugs and money-laundering activities. Thus, Bogle's masculinity enjoyed multiple representations in dancehall's preferred hardcore spaces and could subtly transgress the boundaries of dance without fear of gendered sanctions. Consequently, the phenomenon of myriad young men claiming this once feminized, public space in the centre of the dance as individual dancers or in groups without the intervention of a female or in direct competition with a female dancer signifies an alternative rendering of masculine roles in the dancehall. This phenomenon also highlights dancehall culture's propensity toward duality, with increasing levels of homosociality publicly displayed in the choreographed dances and close male-on-male physical contact in the centre of the dancehall, even as dancehall continues its lyrical dis/engagement with male homosexuality.

As one component of this development, male dancers accompany artistes on their tours abroad and often organize their own tours to perform at clubs and other popular cultural sites in the Jamaican diaspora and, as such, creative displays of dance prowess and acrobatic style by men is increasingly being viewed as another useful way to access resources and as a viable route to economic mobility and social visibility. Dancehall's hardcore male dancers use the dancehall stage to parade their popular dance moves and signify their elevated status as they transcend their rigidly bound socio-political spaces by playing to the amorous advances of the ubiquitous high-technology video and camera equipment. Male dancers and dancing crews are now essential components of the rituals and competition for space that characterize dancehall street dance events like Passa Passa and operate as organic components of the rituals and competition for space, as well as the onstage performance and video productions of many dancehall artistes.[17]

The rise of Fashion Ova Style masculinity is also denoted by the un-gendering of dance styles and movements in the dancehall. Dancehall's dance moves have historically been branded with names that encode narratives of cross-fertilization with international media and film, identification with local or global characters or activities, and even body parts. In addition, most dance styles and moves have also been rigidly gendered, with many historically coded as either masculine or feminine and a few as asexual. The Cool and Deadly dance style of the early dancehall era was an obviously masculine dance, while the erotic and sexual Butterfly of the early 1990s was a patently feminine one and, as Stanley Niaah (2004, 112) notes, the popular Bogle dance was created specifically for men by the late master dancer Bogle. Since the late 1990s into the new millennium, however, there has been an explosion of aptly named and genderless dance styles that reflect what I perceive as a creeping "genderlessness" in the dancehall, or a loosening of the rigid strictures that bound dancehall's masculine stereotypes to the traditional and dated tropes of Jamaican masculinity. These ungendered dance styles include the Blasé, Pon di River, Tall Up Tall Up, Higher Level, Signal Di Plane, Parachute, Zip It Up, Internet and Sweep. This proliferation of new and un-gendered dance styles in the dancehall converges with Elephant Man's rise to stardom and his dissemination of lyrics which are organically driven by (and which drive) the creation of new dances. For example, his songs "Log On", "Pon di River Pon di Bank", "Signal di Plane" and "Blasé" are also the names of some popular dances.[18] Other popular songs by Elephant Man in this genre include "Dance di Chaka", "Sweep", "Dancing Demention", "Do the Sponge Bob", "Willie Bounce", "Gangsta Rock", "Fan dem Off", "Nuh Linga" and "Gully Creepa(er)" which are also the names of popular dance styles. The rise to stardom of the duo RDX in 2008 has expanded the proliferation of songs driven by, or which drive, popular dances. RDX's popular songs include "Everybody Dance", "Bend Over", "Daggering", "Nuh Linga", "Dancers Anthem", "Wibble Wabble" and "Dagga Train". Other dancehall artistes have contributed to the expansion of these dance/songs, including Tony Matterhorn with his controversial "Dutty Wine", Beenie Man's "Row Like ah Boat" and "Swing It Weh", Ding Dong's "Bad Man Forward Bad Man Pullup" and Mr Vegas featuring Overmars with "Raging Bull/Tek Weh Yuhself".

Yet, the propensity to create songs which name, describe or are interrelated with popular dance moves is not new in dancehall culture. In the early 1980s several dancehall deejays recorded full songs with dance instructions, including "Heel and Toe" by General Trees, "Jump Up", "Della Move" and "Butterfly" by Admiral Bailey and "Water Pumpee" by Johnny Osbourne. In the early 1990s "Bogle" by Buju Banton (named after master dancer Bogle) and "World Dance" by Beenie Man were popular dancehall hits and dance tunes. However, the proliferation of dance songs in the new millennium has far outstripped the intermittent forays in this area by early dancehall artistes and points to the opening up of spaces for male energy in dance discourse and activity as a component of the transitions in male activity and identity in dancehall culture. The overlapping of the careers and identities of dancer and artiste also points to the fluidity of boundaries that exist in dancehall which make way for these transformations.

CONCLUSION

Fashion Ova Style masculinity is brokered on feminine aesthetics, homosociality and the presentation of men as objects of desire in dancehall culture. This arguably reflects the society's responses to challenges and contestations from the underclasses internally, and powerbrokers externally. In dancehall's culturally exalted renderings of masculinity, its ultimately hegemonic exemplars, the badman and the Ole Dawg, have historically been positioned antithetically against the gay male where the badman and Ole Dawg is everything the gay male is not. However, this paradoxical Fashion Ova Style masculinity tampers with this dichotomy. The Fashion Ova Style male body is clothed in feminized fashions and displays his prowess from a feminized stage, while simultaneously donning the facial expression of the hardcore badman and disseminating his speech in the harsh, staccato and often coarse language of the badman. Thus, this variant of dancehallized masculinity is projected as aggressively heterosexual while promoting feminized aesthetics and behaviours – a truly borderline version of dancehall masculinity.

This use of feminized aesthetic rituals, styles of dress and dance styles to create a new variant of masculinity in dancehall transgresses the strong hegemonic impulses that have directed dancehall culture's conceptualization of masculinities as hardcore and rigidly heterosexual since its evolution in the early 1980s. It also transgresses dancehall culture's revolt against Jamaica's middle-class hegemony by its acceptance of what has historically been defined as a "middle-class" propensity toward energetic, erotic, spectacular and public dance as an accepted behaviour and practice for lower-class, inner-city and dancehall men. Fashion Ova Style masculinity is a dynamic and momentary articulation that bears conceptualization herein because of its radical opposition to the core masculine values that energized the dancehall since its evolution. These core masculine values drew selectively on the constituent facets of Jamaica's hegemonic masculinity by orienting its images around the twin towers of pro-heterosexuality and anti-homosexuality. Yet, with the presentation of Fashion Ova Style, the male homosexual is again rendered invisible, this time by the projection of a masculine exemplar that utilizes a gay aesthetic to hide the male homosexual in full view. This radically transgressive variant of dancehall masculinity expresses dancehall's dualities and inversions, and simultaneously raises questions about the current constitution of Jamaica's hegemonic masculinity from which dancehall culture ultimately draws its strength.

NOTES

1. See chapters 2 to 5 in Hope (2010), where I explore and theorize on four variants of dancehall's masculine exemplars.
2. Here, "Shorty" reflects the cross-fertilization with American hip-hop culture in its affectionate and diminutive reference to a woman.
3. Keiva and Mad Michelle are both popular female dancers in the dancehall. Mad Michelle was crowned dancehall queen 2003 at the annual Dancehall Queen contest held in Montego Bay, Jamaica.
4. Stacey is another popular female dancer in the dancehall who was crowned dancehall queen 1999 at the annual Dancehall Queen contest held in Montego Bay. Stacey is popularized for her gymnast-like feats, including the propensity to jump up onto the top of sound system boxes at dancehall events and use this vantage point to display her dance prowess to the dancehall audience.
5. Junko "Bashment" Kudo is a Japanese woman who was the first non-Jamaican to be crowned dancehall queen 2002 at the annual Dancehall Queen contest held in Montego Bay. Junko subsequently became a popular staple at dancehall events in Jamaica and was featured in several dancehall events. She opened a school to teach Jamaican dance in Tokyo, Japan.
6. The literal translation of "shottas" is shooters. The term refers to gunmen or "real badmen" who epitomize the type of violent heterosexual masculinity that is lauded in dancehall.
7. For example in Mavado's song "Mr Palmer (New Name fi Informa)", 2008.
8. "To bleach" in Jamaican Creole also means to stay awake all night without sleep until day lights, that is, from darkness to light. It is often associated with staying out at parties, dances, wakes or similar events. Thus, people who work night shifts will not usually say that they "bleach", but someone who attended a party or a wake will claim to have "bleached" all night. A good "bleacher" is someone who can stay up all night and then conduct their regular daylight duties at work or school without any visible effects of having missed a night's sleep.
9. Dancehall's daily calendar incorporates ample opportunities for this alternative notion of "bleaching", as regular dancehall activities usually get underway close to midnight and taper off after daybreak, oftentimes close to 8:00 a.m.

10. "Really bad men do not wear pants that belong to other people. / We take dancing to a higher level."
11. See Stanley Niaah (2004) for a discussion on this, in particular pages 112–13.
12. The National Dance Theatre Company was pioneered over forty years ago by university intellectual, dancer and choreographer Professor Rex Nettleford. It remains one of Jamaica's most prominent dance groups. Others include L'Acadco, the Company and the University Dancers.
13. See chapter 4 of Hope (2010) for a discussion of the role of extreme and often violent anti-male homosexual discourses in creating alternative discourses of dancehall masculinity.
14. In her *Sunday Gleaner* article of 3 July 2005, Tanya Batson-Savage discusses the increase in male dancers in professional dance ensembles like the National Dance Theatre Company (NDTC) which seemingly indicates an erasure of the homosexual and feminized stigma that haunted this activity.
15. Popular male dancers include Bogle (R.I.P.), Willie Haggart (R.I.P.), Labba Labba, Bruk Up, Shelley Belly, Overmars, Ding Dong, Bwoysie, John Hype, Ice (R.I.P.), Craigy Dread, Tippa (R.I.P.), Sick in Head and Sadiki. Popular male dance crews include Black Roses, Ravers Clavers, M.O.B., Black Blingers, Timeless Dancers, Kadillac Dancers, Sample Six and Chef Squad.
16. Popular dancer and dancehall icon Gerald "Bogle" Levy was murdered in January 2005.
17. Notably, this phenomenon does not highlight a new wave of dancing among Jamaican men but represents the resurgence of a persistent ethos of male dancing in Jamaican culture that was suppressed and forced underground beneath the pressures of dancehall cultures extreme discourses of anti-male homosexuality and effeminacy, and its projections of male dancehall male as hardcore, violent and unfeminine.
18. Elephant Man's 2003 album *Good 2 Go* features a significant number of tracks which have driven the creation and naming of popular dance styles from 2002 onwards.

REFERENCES

Batson-Savage, Tanya. 2005. "Boys Take to Dance". *Sunday Gleaner*, 3 July, E1–E2.

Hope, Donna P. 2004. "The British Link Up Crew: Consumption Masquerading as Masculinity in the Dancehall". *Interventions: International Journal of Postcolonial Studies* (Special issue on Jamaican popular culture) 6, no. 1 (April): 101–17.

———. 2010. *Man Vibes: Masculinities in the Jamaican Dancehall*. Kingston: Ian Randle.

Stanley Niaah, Sonjah. 2004. "Kingston's Dancehall: A Story of Space and Celebration". *Space and Culture* 7, no. 1 (February): 102–18.

CHAPTER 15

Ghetto Girls/Urban Music

*Jamaican Ragga Music and Female Performance**

TRACEY SKELTON

> I've been on my own since I was 14. I'm ragamuffin sexy, taking it to a different level. I'm still single. I'm setting an example to the ghetto girls. And I'm doing it because it's real.
> —Patra interviewed by O'Brien (1995, 12)

PATRA IS A FEMALE DANCEHALL/RAGGA STAR FROM JAMAICA, now residing in New York and being interviewed by Lucy O'Brien for the *Guardian* in London. Whenever she appears on television or is interviewed in print she firmly locates herself within the urban space of Jamaica. Patra aligns herself with the ghetto – its culture, its music and its people. Patra is a ghetto girl, a performer of urban music. She is a Jamaican dancehall star – she reflects the struggle that women in urban Jamaica face on a daily basis and at the same time she is a success story. For Patra, along with other women within dancehall music, dance or fashion, has created a space for herself within a musical genre which has been strongly associated with male performance, prowess and heterosexual patriarchy (Skelton 1995a).

In this chapter I wish to discuss the ways in which contemporary Jamaican[1] female dancehall performers are creating and establishing spaces for themselves in which they debate, contest and subvert the socially constructed gender roles and relations of Jamaican society; to consider the ways in which the women are playing around with gender and constructions of space. First, though, it is necessary to discuss what I mean by the term "dancehall", a very interesting one in cultural geography. It means the actual place/space where ragga music is played and at the same time is also the name for a specific Jamaican cultural production. Dancehall then has a physical entity. In Jamaica the dancehall is invariably an open-air space where a stage is constructed and sound systems set up – it can be any open space where ragga performance takes place. However, the term also defines a musical genre which is called ragga and encompasses a style of dance and fashion which are both firmly associated with the musical form.

---

*Previously published in *New Frontiers of Space, Bodies, and Gender*, edited by Rosa Ainely (London: Routledge, 1998), 142–54.

Throughout the chapter I refer to ragga when I explicitly discuss the music, and dancehall/ragga when I refer to the wider context of this cultural production, namely dance, fashion and the actual space of the dancehall.

To date there is relatively little written about women, Jamaican dancehall and ragga music apart from media commentaries. There are notable exceptions, such as the work by Carolyn Cooper (1993, 1994, 1995) and also the film *The Darker Side of Black*, directed by Isaac Julien (1994), which had a specific section devoted to the issues of gender and sexuality within ragga music. There are also useful comparisons to be made between women and ragga music, and women and rap music; to this end I will be drawing upon the work of Tricia Rose (1994) and Beverley Skeggs (1993). Such comparisons can be justified for two reasons: first, because of the analysis based on women's experiences within these new urban musical forms; second, because there already exists a debate on the interconnections between Jamaican ragga music and US hip-hop and rap:

> [T]he most obvious influence on Jamaican music in recent years has been from hip-hop. . . . More recently, following the success of cross-over artists such as Shabba Ranks, collaborations between US singers and Jamaican deejays have been promoted by record companies in a calculated manner. . . . [B]ut dancehall/*ragga* has had a remarkable impact on African-American hip-hop artists as well, and the Jamaican presence is now firmly established . . . on black-oriented radio in cities like New York and Washington, D.C. (Bilby 1995, 179; original emphasis)

Such intersections between the musics mean that some of the academic analysis of the role of women in the US musics of hip-hop and rap can be useful as a context for establishing discussion on the role of women in Jamaican dancehall/ragga.

DANCEHALL/RAGGA MUSIC IN THE SOCIAL, POLITICAL AND ECONOMIC CONTEXT

Dancehall/ragga music, dance and fashion are very firmly located within the urban setting of Kingston's "downtown" areas, or, as they are often referred to, both pejoratively and with a sense of fierce pride and identity, "the ghetto". These areas are spaces of extreme urban poverty with very high rates of unemployment and also of street violence. If a person has a "downtown" address then opportunities for secure employment are non-existent. The physical appearance of the ghetto areas is striking in its complexity and density. Narrow, bare-earthen alleyways are defined by boundaries of corrugated metal sheeting (usually referred to as "zinc" or "galvanize") and wood. The ghetto areas can be likened to a labyrinth or maze, each corner resembling the last. Behind the "walls" are mostly small wooden shacks and yard space. Where there is electricity it will feed just one light bulb and possibly a single socket; cooking is commonly done in the yard outside on a coal-pot burning charcoal or on pieces of galvanized sheeting over a small open fire.[2]

The neighbourhoods are dense, and, as individuals and television directors (Zabihyan 1995) testify, tensions and animosity between people can often explode fatally. Guns are commonly used, but for the very poor, acid throwing is a vicious and painful weapon. If a victim survives an acid attack it is usually with appalling scars burned deep into the skin. Gang cultures exist and innocents are often caught in the "crossfire", frequently all too literally. The policing of the "downtown" areas is brutal, heavy-handed and brings with it its own abuse of power and authority (Zabihyan 1995).

Out of such deprived economic environments, out of places with little political voice or representation, comes a music, dance and fashion form which is part and parcel of the ghetto, which reflects ghetto experiences and life qualities. Just as its forerunner reggae was, ragga music is formed out of "downtown" life and reflects the experience back to its audience. Ragga music is the culture of the ghetto, it speaks from the ghetto and it tells of ghetto experiences. Further, the rhythm and performance of the music mean that it can also transcend cultural and geographical boundaries and scales. So it can speak to people who have no specific memory or experience of the Jamaican ghetto, but who at the same time can identify with the message of the music – either its call for black self-esteem or rebellion and its admiration for male feats of sexual exploitation or, for the female audience, a woman's voice challenging sexism and patriarchal forces which hold women back. The experience of ragga and dancehall then has several layers of resonance for Jamaican and Caribbean diasporic communities, many members of which may never have seen the specific place of the Jamaican "downtown" ghetto.[3]

Returning to Jamaica, the experience of the grind of everyday life in Kingston "downtown" means that the space of pleasure which the dancehall provides on Friday and Saturday nights is central. The opportunity the dancehall provides to wear "fake" glamour, one's best clothes (many of them designed and worked on by the wearer him- or herself), to dance and perform showing the skill and beauty of one's own body, means that ragga music offers a cultural space away from the deprivation of the everyday life of the ghetto. The dancehall does not offer an escape from reality, since the music is formed out of and reflects ghetto experience and identity; it is, in the words of Patra above, *real*. Performers sing of the "dirty reality" that is ghetto life. Nor is the dancehall always a safe space – gang feuds often spill over into the space of the dance and the police may "invade" at any given time and carry out random body searches and arrests (Skelton 1995b). Nevertheless, dancehall/ragga speaks to people and it is a popular cultural form in which they invest heavily: "[H]undreds of hopeful young *ragamuffins* congregate day after day in front of Kingston's dozens of recording studios, patiently waiting for auditions. . . . Jamaica, after all, is reputed to have the highest per capita output of records of any country in the world" (Bilby 1995, 180). Despite the fact that the genre of ragga is male-dominated, as all musical forms of Jamaican music have been – and indeed as most musical forms are – there are notable numbers of women rising to the fore. For the purpose of this chapter I will focus on Patra and Lady Saw, both of whom have gained some recognition from the UK national press and beyond. In the cultural form of dancehall women have always been central through their dance (much of which is highly acrobatic) and the dancehall fashions which they have developed. So women play an important role in the ensemble which is dancehall performance in Jamaica and throughout Jamaican diasporic communities. Indeed the appropriateness of such roles and performances has been the subject of several levels of debate both in Jamaica and the United Kingdom concerning whether women should be party to "slackness" (Brinkworth 1992) or whether "slackness" is a celebration of women's sexuality and at the same time a defiance against the dominant standards of what is decent (Cooper 1993, 1994).

This is an ongoing debate. What I now want to address are the ways in which Patra and Lady Saw have both created a space for women within dancehall/ragga and been part of a disruptive discourse about women's sexuality, gender relations and male power. These female performers of ragga music are both interrupting and creating this vibrant, dynamic and controversial urban music. Rather than presenting this analysis directly through the music and lyrics of Lady Saw and Patra, I am going to work through their self-representations in mainstream media, such as the *Observer* (Sawyer 1995) and the *Guardian* (O'Brien 1995). I will also draw upon the voices of Jamaican women represented in Isaac Julien's film *The Darker Side of Black* (1994), threading through comparisons with the work of Beverley Skeggs (1993) and Tricia Rose (1994), who both analyse black women and rap music.

GHETTO GIRLS MAKING SPACE FOR WOMEN: LADY SAW AND PATRA

Lady Saw is a Jamaican dancehall star who has remained in Jamaica, a performer of the Kingston ghetto. For the article in the *Observer* (19 February 1995) by Miranda Sawyer, Lady Saw is interviewed in Kingston. The preamble of the article discusses Lady Saw's recent performances, the furore she often stirs up in Jamaican press and the role of musical production in urban Jamaican culture. Consequently, Lady Saw is firmly placed in Jamaican urban space. The front cover of the "Life" section of this particular *Observer* named Lady Saw as Jamaica's answer to Madonna. It is interesting that a black woman from "downtown" Kingston, who sings a particular musical form firmly located in the place and space of Jamaica, should be compared with US-born, white pop star Madonna. Indeed this comparison is used regularly for female ragga stars: the interview with Patra in the *Guardian* (O'Brien 1995) is headed "The Making of a Black Madonna". Clearly it might be a play on the symbolism of the Black Madonna in the monastery in Montserrat, Catalonia, as well as directly alluding to the pop star Madonna. But in terms of the comparison between Lady Saw and Madonna the only apparent similarity is the way they perform sexuality on stage: "Lady Saw shakes everybody's hands, smiles demurely for photographs and launches herself bodily into a routine now familiar to the whistling multitudes of skunked-up skankers. Stepping, stomping, grinding, bumping with plenty of dramatic pauses for hip-height boot ballet and a quick burst of below the belt banter. A performance of Amazonian uninhibitedness" (Sawyer 1995, 34). Lady Saw had just been given the Jamaican "Lady DJ of the Year" award (1995), which was highly significant as she was not even nominated in 1994 (Cooper 1995). She is raw, nasty, sexy and vulgar. Her Jamaican Patwa has to be translated for the interviewer. She repeatedly fails to make arranged meetings for the interview. Lady Saw becomes firmly defined as a Jamaican, of the ghetto, of the city – she is behaving in an unprofessional way, she is on "Caribbean time".

Lady Saw is interviewed in the presence of the man who is her manager, producer and boyfriend – although in his boyfriend role she has to share him with another woman. Lady Saw is therefore in reality one of the women she sings about in "I Want a Man of My Own":

> Oh Lord, please work a miracle for me to fin' a man of my own,
> Because dear Lord I am tired of sleeping all alone,
> Dear Lord I know that good man is very hard to find
> Dear Lord please find me someone who will come home at night
> Me no want no badman to steal me DJ money
> Me no want no married man lef wife fe take a liberty
> Dey have an odd love affair, but dey not guan get me
> Release me now, oh let me be free
> Oh Lord, please work a miracle for me to find a man of my own.

She has to share her man and does not know why he cannot be faithful to her. This is a common lament among Jamaican women and women of the Caribbean generally. African Caribbean men invariably have more than one sexual partner and often have long-lasting relationships with both or all of the women (Ellis 1986; Skelton 1989). The knowledge that this is a reality for many women of the region does not prevent their individually longing for loyalty and someone to depend upon; nor does it liberate the women in terms of their own sexual behaviour. Women who are not faithful, quiet and patient may find violence becomes part of their relationship, and social censure a severe comment on their morality. The interview with Lady Saw shows her authentic experience: even this nationally famous dancehall DJ cannot be sure of her man's fidelity. When Lady Saw speaks, she reiterates her connection with the ordinary people and her commitment to sing for the "ladies": "I do speak for other people, on behalf of the ladies . . . .You watch the way people live and what's going on and then you don't do it yourself alone. The talk in the dancehall, that's the talk I use" (Lady Saw interviewed by Sawyer 1995, 34). When interviewed by Isaac Julien, Lady Saw makes a similar comment about the ways in which she can use her own musical abilities to speak up for Jamaican women, and also the ways in which her work combines with that of the other Jamaican women, the dancehall models, to create a central stage for women:

> Men DJ, right, you get some men and they will go diss [disrespect] the Ladies, but then I am not for that, right, I'm for the ladies, so I go there and defend it and cool it down, right. . . . The ladies are more up front now, you know, they want to be in the limelight – like dancehall models for instance in Kingston here, they are very X-rated on stage and the man go wild for them. So from the body is clean and thing, I think you can show it off. (Lady Saw interviewed by Julien 1994).

The closing comments made by Miranda Sawyer ensure that Lady Saw's performance and identity remain embedded within Jamaican dancehall culture – she is almost too Caribbean, too Jamaican, too "downtown" Kingston, too sexy, too hardcore to be able to change cities and spaces to come into "civilization". "It is doubtful whether Lady Saw's industrial strength will ever be welcome in Britain, where the preferred area of anatomical stiffness is the upper lip. Whether she will be able to shake off the dust from the ghetto sex wars is equally in doubt. The lady herself is keen to spread her wings: 'Send for me, please! I can work for the British people. I know they would love me'" (Sawyer 1995, 34).

Miranda Sawyer's "Britain" clearly fails to recognize the presence of a Caribbean, and in particular a Jamaican, diaspora who not only do not hold with the stiff upper lip culture but who also create music from their urban experiences. The British Caribbean communities would and do welcome Lady Saw – her lyrics can hold a reality for them too.

The ways in which Jamaican women are creating spaces for themselves in the urban context of Jamaica also has a resonance for those of Caribbean descent in other urban settings. Indeed these created spaces can transgress not only the expected gender roles and relations but also expected sexual behaviours. Ragga music has an image of intense heterosexuality and elements of the music and some of its performers are very homophobic (Bilby 1995, 240; Skelton 1995a). However, just as ragga music itself is diverse and multi-layered in its rhythmic origins, then so too are the social-relational contexts in which the music is heard. Paul Burston, writing in the *Independent* (1995), talks of gay club nights where black lesbians and gays can enjoy ragga: "Black gays and lesbians, spurred by the rhythms of ragga, are changing the face of London clubland" (1995, 22). Inge Blackman is a film director interviewed by Isaac Julien. She, like some of the people Burston talked to, felt it was important to emphasize that not all of ragga is homophobic, and that not all ragga performers were anti-gay. In fact Blackman discusses the ways in which ragga and dancehall in the United Kingdom have given black lesbians a specific space:

> Black lesbians actually do participate in dancehall culture. Dancehall culture, particularly in England, acts as a celebration of black women's sexuality and it's a way in which black women can bond with each other on the dance floor, this is very, very strong. Black women can dance with each other in a very sexual, in a very lustful way on the dance floor in ragga culture. It's not really allowed in any other black popular culture. (Blackman interviewed by Julien 1994)

What the interview with Lady Saw in the *Observer* clearly establishes and echoes are the ways in which Lady Saw herself feels strongly that she has a role to speak for women and make a space for women in which they can articulate what matters to them in their ghetto lives: whether this is demanding athletic sexual satisfaction, singing about her own sexual abilities, or calling for a change in men's sexual and relationship behaviour.

Patra in the *Guardian*

In the interview with Lucy O'Brien for the *Guardian* Patra is represented, and self-represents, in a context of "improvement", of "civilization". What is made repetitively clear is that she is "toned down", she has "undergone a transition" (O'Brien 1995, 12) and is the "acceptable" side of urban Jamaican ragga. We are then left with a cultural dichotomy

– Patra claims a raw, nasty and ragamuffin style for herself, while the media wishes to show a woman who had matured through her experiences and who has relocated herself away from the ghetto. The reason for Patra being in the media is because of her explicit, raunchy sexual performances, but when we meet her face to face she is represented as a sure-minded performer with business sense: "This is a serious business. When I first met Patra two years ago she was a slightly shy 20-year old with a strong Jamaican accent. Now, she sports a slimmed-down-worked-out body, discrete, New York black lycra, killer braids and shiny red talons" (O'Brien 1995, 12). The body is controlled, kept in shape, the accent which firmly places Patra as a Jamaican is softening, she is serious – but there is still danger held within this sanitized version of the former raunchy girl of Jamaica, in her killer braids and dangerous talons. Patra builds on this apparent contradiction to present an image which is positive (and acceptable in the non-Jamaican context) and yet still grounded in a disruptive and resistant (ragamuffin) identity: "The way I dress is more elegant and classy, whereas in the back of my mind I'm still ragamuffin and hardcore" (Patra interviewed by O'Brien 1995, 12).

When discussing ragga and where she began, Patra admits to the difficulty of the battle – the battle to get a space for women performers – and that in some cases that battle was with other women DJs, but mostly the fight was with men, who also often demanded that women be as "x-plicit" as men: "It was very tough, a male-dominated field. Getting into the business was like getting through firestones because people fight you left, right and centre. [Commenting on her earlier, often very lewd songs] Back in those days, it was reality, I don't regret it. You call it a start, y'know. It was a gimmick" (Patra interviewed by O'Brien 1995, 12). What is clear in this newspaper interview, and in other interviews for mainstream media such as the Channel 4 *Passenger* (1994) programme (see Skelton 1995b for a detailed analysis), is that Patra represents herself as a role model, someone women, including teenage women, can look up to and draw strength from. Responding to a question about her highly sexual performances and the fact that Jamaica has a high teenage pregnancy rate, Patra describes her own reality and experience:

> I've been on my own since I was 14 years old. My father died when I was three, I had opportunities to mess up. I could have had 10 kids if I wanted. But once you have a goal in mind, you won't think of pregnancy. You have to keep an independent space: a lot of women don't do that. The most I can do for teenagers is guide them the right way. (Patra interviewed by O'Brien 1995, 13)

The importance of a space for women is therefore central in Patra's definition of how women can succeed and make something of their lives. Elsewhere (as well as in the *Guardian* interview), Patra has admitted that she is not doing anything very differently from what other women in Jamaica are doing but she has the drive and determination to achieve the goal of being a music star, and currently that means moving to the United States and specifically New York. However, her self-naming as "ragamuffin" means that she resists selling out completely and that she still locates her identity within, and as part of, Jamaica.

CREATING THROUGH RESISTING: MAKING THE CONNECTIONS

What women performers within dancehall/ragga music are doing through their very presence is creating space for women: through the pathways they have made for other women performers; through making a lyrical and musical space which reflects women's lives, experiences, desires and demands; and through being there, on the stage, in the sound, speaking directly to women in the audience. This connects with Tricia Rose's analysis of black women in rap:

> Black women rappers interpret and articulate the fears, pleasures, and promises of young black women whose voices have been relegated to the margins of public discourse. They are integral and resistant voices in rap music and popular music in general who sustain an ongoing dialogue with their audiences and with male rappers about sexual promiscuity, emotional commitment, infidelity, the drug trade, racial politics, and black cultural history. (Rose 1994, 146)

Women in dancehall/ragga in Jamaica and throughout the diaspora are doing very similar things within their own social, political, sexual and cultural milieux. Rose offers an analysis that contradicts popular media conceptions of the role of women in rap, conceptions that have served to establish a binary division of male/female. This, she argues, delimits the work women in the music have done to simply being "anti-sexist" or even anti-male. In fact, Rose argues, black women rappers, alongside many male rappers, are "struggling to define themselves against a confining and treacherous social environment", that is, a white dominant US culture (1994, 148). That is not to deny that female rappers have a central focus on sexual politics and demand some renegotiation of gender relations. Patra is especially sensitive to the latter and clearly feels that showing young women the "right way" will lead them through exploitative sexual relations (which leave them pregnant at an early age) and help them assert their autonomy and independence.

Lady Saw's self-presentation, combined with descriptions of her musical performance, finds an echo in Skegg's work (1993), where she investigates black women rappers and the way in which they assert their sexual power and independence by speaking what they should not, and how they refuse to be contained within a particular form of femininity. She discusses the ways in which black women rappers are challenging both the silencing of black women's cultural responses and the silencing of black women's sexuality, and how they will not play the game of the discourses of shame and honour (1993, 106). In Skeggs's eyes black women rappers are talking back and their target is the "White-Western civilising system which attempts to contain the expression of women's sexuality through the moralising discourses of conduct: politeness, respectability, caring, duty and responsibility . . . they speak against the power of masculinity [and its attempts to fit femininity to its fantasies" (Skeggs 1993, 108).

For women in Jamaican dancehall/ragga there is a slight variation on this in that they are less confrontational against masculine definitions of women, but they do call for a change in masculine behaviour. Through dance movements and fashion design the women involved in ragga also show, through the ways they inscribe their bodies on the public place of the dancehall, that they are *not* sexually submissive, sexually available as and when men want them, that they *are* in control of their bodies and that they, as women, *will* celebrate their own bodies and their own sexual identity. Consequently they refuse male definitions of themselves – they create a resistive space.

Alongside the resistance against male definitions, women in ragga disrupt and resist notions of "respectable" female behaviour within the socially and culturally dominant definitions of the Christian church and "uptown" Jamaican society. Women in dancehall/ragga are out in the public arena demanding sex, singing of women's sexual desires and pleasures. The women present themselves as confident, aggressive and resistant, they articulate the "demand discourse" (Skeggs 1993). The following selected quotes from Skeggs's and Rose's work demonstrate the close connections between such a discourse among women in Jamaican dancehall/ragga and women in US (and, to a lesser extent, UK) rap music: "When female rappers explicitly address sexual practices as direct pleasure and fun they locate themselves against good taste, polite conduct and civilisation. In the sense they are dangerous. They embody a threat to the moral and social order" (Skeggs 1993, 113). In the British media's representation of Patra, her danger is made explicit because although she has "changed" she still maintains "killer braids and shiny red talons" (O'Brien 1995, 12). Patra remains predatory and dangerous. Lady Saw is described as too "raunchy" to be able to come to Britain or to be welcomed if she did (Sawyer 1995, 34). While the media exploits the sexiness of both women there is the constant reminder that it should be held at arm's length: perhaps, in a rather unpleasant echo of the racist discourse of empire, colonies and slavery in the Caribbean (Cooper 1993), because it might "contaminate" other women?

Rose offers a detailed analysis of Salt 'n' Pepa's video for their duet with E.U., "Shake Your Thang", and many of her comments could be ascribed to a performance by either Patra or Lady Saw: "A primary source of the video's power is Salt 'N' Pepa's irreverence toward the morally based sexual constrictions placed on them as women. They mock moral claims about the proper modes of women's expression and enjoy every minute of it . . . . [The video] focuses directly on the sexual desirability and beauty of black women's bodies" (Rose 1994, 167). Hence for black women in rap and, to a probably lesser extent, for women in dancehall/ragga performance, the challenging of perceived and constructed notions of black women's sexuality, both by men and by the established dominant power structures in society, is a central part of the ways in which they resist negative, damaging representation of themselves, and, simultaneously, create positive and strong spaces for women.

This chapter draws upon specific moments and sites of representations of two women in Jamaican dancehall/ragga music and demonstrates the ways in which both envision themselves as "making space for women". However, it has to be remembered that these are moments in what is a highly dynamic and fluid musical and spatial expression. Through their very presence both on stage and through their music Patra and Lady Saw actively disrupt established notions of women's "place" and create images for other ghetto girls to identify with. For them, the placing of their music and the gendered experiences which are constructed in those particular places are an integral part of their performance. They sing "dirty reality" and through their music they talk about their lives, their dreams and their fantasies. It is this element of the gendered perspectives that the ragga women constitute as part of their music which creates the striking connections with black women rap performers in what they demand and display.

As with all discourses of race, gender and sexuality, the struggle for change and transformation within these social and cultural constructions is perpetual, is ongoing and can never be fully achieved. Nonetheless, through dancehall/ragga Jamaican women are offering a culturally inspired public space in which women can resist and engage in dialogic challenges and potential transformations. At the same time women in dancehall spaces have a really great time as they sing, dance and dress in such a way that they are able to leave behind for a while the problems of everyday life in poor black neighbourhoods – in Jamaica or anywhere.

NOTES

1. Throughout the chapter I use the term *Jamaican* and this mostly locates the subject within Jamaica. The term is also used to imply the wider Jamaican diaspora based mostly in the United Kingdom and the United States. A Jamaican is not just someone who currently resides in Jamaica, or has ever been resident there, but can also encompass those who define themselves as Jamaican. This is especially important in a discussion of a cultural form that transcends national boundaries and geographical scales of identity.
2. It is important to remind readers that this chapter was written in 1997 and published in 1998. As we are now in the 2020s then obviously "ghetto" areas have changed in many ways. These descriptions are therefore very much an element of earlier times.
3. For a more detailed analysis of the origins and connections between ragga music and other Jamaican music forms see Kenneth Bilby's chapter on Jamaica in Manuel's *Caribbean Currents* (Bilby 1995).

REFERENCES

Bilby, Kenneth. 1995. "Jamaica". In *Caribbean Currents: Caribbean Music from Rumba to Reggae*, edited by P. Manuel (with Kenneth Bilby and Michael Largey), 177–215. London: Latin American Bureau.

Brinkworth, L. 1992. "Why Are the Sisters Taking up the Slack?" *Guardian*, 25 June, 21.

Burston, Paul. 1995. "Faggamuffins' Night Out". *Independent*, 1 February, 22.

Cooper, Carolyn. 1993. *Noises in the Blood: Orality, Gender and the "Vulgar" Body of Jamaican Popular Culture*. London: Macmillan.

———. 1994. "'Lyrical Gun': Metaphor and Role Play in Jamaican Dancehall Culture". *Massachusetts Review* 35, nos. 3–4: 427–29.

———. 1995. "Lady Saw's Reward: Slackness Upfront". *Jamaica Observer*, n.d.

Ellis, Pat, ed. 1986. *Women of the Caribbean*. London: Zed Books.

Julien, Isaac, dir. 1994. *The Darker Side of Black*. Black Audio/ Normal Production for BBC TV, April, BBC2 (UK).

O'Brien, Lucy. 1995. "The Making of a Black Madonna". *Guardian*, 13 October, 12–13.

Rose, Tricia. 1994. *Black Noise: Rap Music and Black Culture in Contemporary America*. Hanover, NH: University Press of New England.

Sawyer, Miranda. 1995. "Lady Sings It Blue". *Observer*, 19 February, 32–34.

Skeggs, Beverly. 1993. "Refusing to Be Civilised: 'Race', Sexuality and Power". In *The Dynamics of "Race" and Gender*, edited by Haleh Afshar and Mary Maynard, 106–26. London: Taylor and Francis.

Skelton, Tracey L. 1989. "Women Men and Power: Gender Relations in Montserrat". PhD dissertation, Newcastle University, Newcastle upon Tyne.

———.1995a. "'Boom, Bye, Bye': Jamaican Ragga and Gay Resistance". In *Mapping Desire: Geographies of Sexualities*, edited by David Bell and Gill Valentine, 264–83. London: Routledge.

———. 1995b. "'I Sing Dirty Reality, I Am Out There for the Ladies', Lady Saw: Women and Jamaican Ragga Music, Resisting Patriarchy". *Phoebe: Journal of Feminist Scholarship, Theory and Aesthetics* 7:86–104.

Zabihyan, Kimi, dir./prod. 1995. *Yardies*. Observer Films, broadcast 21 February, ITV (UK).

CHAPTER 16

"A Uman Wi Niem!"

Sexual Desire and the Poetics of "Badness" in the Works of Lady Saw and Tanya Stephens

AGOSTINHO PINNOCK

BY EXAMINING SOME OF THE PERFORMANCE GUISES WHICH are routinely inhabited and deployed by dancehall women, this chapter considers "badness" as a distinctly female poetics in Jamaican popular culture. "Badness" is read as being performed for various reasons by women in the Jamaican dancehall, specifically female artistes, with a view to create and recreate their realities. The aim is to revise their place in the culture and with it actively contest projects of male entrapment (Pinnock 2017), both in the dancehall and wider society. Performing badness is, therefore, a means by which dancehall women revise and redirect overwhelming patriarchal effects in the wider society and the dancehall itself. As a result, they are able to fully occupy the "natural" and expected roles created for them in society as mothers, sex objects and the personal accoutrements of men, while still being able to sabotage patriarchal ideologies from within.

Dancehall women embody multiple performative guises with which they perform, while simultaneously deconstructing and reconsidering their roles in society. These strategies afford them needed space to critique the importance which is attached to their work and presence in the dancehall (Pinnock 2017). As such, these women deploy the poetics of badness to creatively underwrite their renegade mission to remake the world in their images and likenesses. Their deployment of this strategy does not afford them the luxury of being just mere entertainers for their own sakes (Pinnock 2017). Rather, through their confrontations with officialdom, dancehall women actively subvert the racialized class politics of Jamaican society, especially in its various efforts to define nationhood in exclusivist terms (Cooper 2004b).

Strategically, badness allows dancehall women the wherewithal to "cut and clear" space in the dancehall and the wider society. By so doing, they contest ideas about the invisibility and insignificance of black, lower-class women in Jamaican society (Pinnock 2017). This is especially in the context of a racialized, patriarchal culture which often sees women as less than viable (Pinnock 2007). Dancehall women's work is solidly focused, therefore, on resolving the conundrum of black Jamaican womanhood (Cooper 1995), which, while highly sought after for its presumably mythical sexual prowess, as articulated in the idea of a ghetto girl being able to give the "wickedest slam",[1] is nonetheless culturally expendable. Nadia Ellis's (2011) discussion of the idea of being "out and bad" in dancehall culture is important here. This is, in part, because so much of her argument discusses issues of embodiment and queerness[2] as alternate ways in which dancehall masculinities are constructed and performed in the context of badness.

Badness in this instance locates the question of masculinity and dancehall in the context of "femaleness", as Cooper (1995) calls it. Women and, specifically, dancehall women, are very central to the construction and performance of masculinity (Pinnock 2017), both in the dancehall as well as in wider Jamaican society. This is especially true regarding the deployment of the technology of badness as a creative device used to perform identity. The female persona which is often commodified and mobilized by men in the dancehall (Ellis 2011) is, thus, mobilized as a tool of social, cultural or even political capital to construct influence. It is a highly prized part of the projects of masculinity which it conducts. These are regarded as inherently "bad" (Pinnock 2007). To the extent that women form a central part of the narrative of constructing and performing badness in the dancehall also means that in its context dancehall culture is slippery and potentially problematic.

Dancehall women are not only bad, therefore, in the sense in which they enable the promotion of some types of violence in their work, they are potentially also at risk of being consumed by it. This is especially true with respect to the representations of themselves as sexual objects that fulfil the desires of men.[3] Susan Harewood (2006) notes, accordingly, that sexuality has its limits as a tool for women's liberation in the performance of popular culture. The slipperiness of sex as a space for political subterfuge and liberation proves problematic for women in the wider projects of badness which they use in popular culture to creatively undermine patriarchy. Harewood (2006) contends that, given the already contested and sexualized nature of their bodies, women are essentially constructed in the dominant patriarchal culture as sex symbols. Their sole purpose is to please men, which makes them already compromised.[4] By necessity, then, any efforts to read embodied acts of self-liberation in the context of badness as a political project which women can use to emancipate themselves potentially places them in greater danger of being further objectified.

The trajectories of female dancehall artistes like Lady Saw and Tanya Stephens, in particular how they navigate and negotiate dancehall culture, are fundamentally fraught. Their efforts to create space and right imbalanced power relations through the use of badness are key parts of their oeuvre. This potentially threatens the viability of badness as creative politics. This chapter probes the use of "badness" as a strategic literary and performative device in specific songs by these women. It explores elements of this strategy, how it works, as well as its historical currency and political import in contemporary dancehall culture, especially regarding dancehall women's creative work. In doing this, the chapter highlights how these artistes' works are connected by their articulation of the "bad gyal"[5] (bad girl) persona in dancehall culture. This chapter reads "badness" as part of a logic of black, lower-class, female emancipatory politics in Jamaica. It corroborates Alice Walker's vision of a distinctly black (read African-descended), "womanist" agenda founded in the works of marginalized black female artists (Walker in Christian 1985). Womanism rises from the ground up (Christian 1985). It fuels social justice movements with a view to righting lopsided power relations in society (Walker in Christian 1985). As such, the title of the paper, which is also written in Jamaican,[6] enunciates much of these concerns. It encapsulates the meanings of a black Jamaican female performativity as articulated through a poetics of "badness" in dancehall culture. This self-announcement calls attention to the works of dancehall women, like Lady Saw, after whose song of the same name the chapter is titled

Thus, the line "[a] uman wi niem" (a woman we name) embodies within it the compressed ideologies of Jamaican womanhood and their qualitative difference from the generally canonized tomes of "good" literary and other scholarship, often deemed appropriate for legitimate feminist critique. As a man, therefore, I wish to acknowledge that I share in the political agenda and activism of womanist scholars and artists who believe, like Frantz Fanon (1967), that culture is an important site of reassertion and contestation of colonial projects of erasure. I read "a uman wi niem" as a statement of a feminist logic, which bell hooks (1981; 1985) argues is for everyone. According to hooks, feminism not only counters the troubling supremacist ideologies of patriarchy, it is also a space of inclusion for both men and non-feminine others.

My aim, then, is not to appropriate the logic of female power and, by so doing, arrogate its potency as my own. Rather, I read Lady Saw's declaration, especially regarding its application to this chapter and my own relationship to female dancehall artistes, as simply acknowledgement. It indicates how Jamaican, grassroots, female sensibilities represent cross-cutting as well as declarative emancipatory politics. The line is not only a statement of womanist inclusivity, into which women of all classes, colours and creeds are welcome, but it is also an act of embodied resistance. This is, in many ways, part of the lived reality in which ideas about the state as well as the nation – as an outgrowth of colonial projects of nation-making (Forrest 2006) are contested. Women, in this case, literally use their bodies to dismantle the projects of erasure and hierarchical notions of gender imposed on them by patriarchy. Female artistes use their bodies – both in the pomp and pageantry of the dancehall as well as in their various states of un/dress – to debunk conflicting ideas about their place in society.

In this way, black, grassroots, Jamaican women are able to reveal the cracks in the fiction of nation-ness used to weld the various parts of the state together under the myth of racial homogeneity (Cooper 2004b). Both Saw's and Stephens's works, in particular, are discussed here, with a view to give voice to some of these concerns vis-à-vis the performance of "badness" in dancehall culture as a tool to destabilize and question "accepted" realities. This is part of a deliberate effort to subvert patriarchy. Through their creative performances, these women are able to realize a sense of their agency in the dancehall and wider society. The "poetics of badness" is the means by which they do so. This is especially in a context that routinely commodifies and reduces them (only) to their bodies; that is, in conventional readings of Jamaican popular culture (Cooper 2004a).

While not exclusively performed/used by women, badness as a literary trope uniquely gives dancehall women the wherewithal to operate as creative and cultural assassins in their various domains. Through its use, they are able to entertain while destroying their enemies and, often, without their targets' knowledge. Through an act of accommodation and compromise[7] (Nettleford 2003), dancehall women actively sabotage patriarchy from within. This suggests that their appearance of acceptance of their status as "other" is but a temporary, if not necessary, part of coming to consciousness. Effectively, dancehall women's sense of agency is effectively reflected in the realization, if not tense acceptance, of the apparent need to barter aspects of their embodied resources in exchange for power and other forms of materiality (Pinnock 2017).

Lady Saw's powerful declaration: "a uman wi niem", in the song of the same name, is a clear indication of this. It highlights much of the slipperiness of women's experiences under patriarchy, specifically in the Jamaican context where race, class and gender are often intersecting triads (Pinnock 2007). It also testifies to the strength of the grassroots womanist traditions (Walker in Christian 1985) in Jamaican society. Saw's exhortation treads the boundaries of victimhood and the possibilities of conquest. She is situated in the very heart of the issues that bleed into black women's lives (Walker in Christian 1984). Therefore, dancehall women's womanist realities do not always conform to standard and accepted feminist agendas, therefore, which traditionally centre a certain kind of woman while marginalizing others (hooks 1981).

Thus, Saw's assertation is a rallying cry for all women already pushed to the periphery by patriarchy in its contestation of their right to lay claim to their sexualities and bodies. Note, too, that black women, historically, have never had total control over their bodies in so-called New World societies (Beckles, 2003, 1995). Their subjection to forces outside of themselves, whether by white men or women, as well as by other men of African descent is well documented and in various ways (Beckles, 2003, 1995). Saw's claim that "A woman wi name, so we born lucky / All airplane we get just chru wi mucky" revises the sense in which black female sexuality is, traditionally, seen as permissive and therefore devalued (hooks 1981). Saw invests new meaning in a woman's right to use her body however she desires. She does not need or want external approval.

This almost auto-erotic reading of Saw's conceptualization of herself bears elements of what Cooper (1995) calls "women's resources". It is a means of self-empowerment (and pleasure). This capacity to receive material benefits in exchange for sexual resources is a practical decision that Saw and other women make. This is consistent with two very necessary realities which they experience as women, as articulated in the song. Sexual activities bring down dancehall/women's overall values, if there is no active maintenance. Saw is thus keen to advise that she gets "five thousand dollars" every week to attend to her hair, nails and make-up. This is a necessary part of her upkeep of her beauty and is essential to her capacity to attract and keep a man's interest.

Ironically, men also place Saw and women like her under pressure, sexually and otherwise. Thus, Saw's claim that "a uman wi niem" clearly inverts those power dynamics. She uses men's attraction to her as a screening process. This is a political economy (Thomas 2004) of competitive desires and is a key dynamic in the constructs of Jamaican womanhood as articulated in Saw's music. It is part of the embodied resources which she trades in order to navigate her way through the world. This is an effort to reverse the logic of male desire to eke out a sense of her own existence. Saw is the literal sign of her own power which, though men routinely abstract it for their own purposes, nonetheless makes her proud and powerful. She has what men want and desire from her. Saw recognizes this as a source of power. She proudly declares that her name is woman – a collectivized rejection of the cultural sense of powerlessness often imposed on her and the rest of her gender in relation to men because of it. Saw turns the role of sex object, and with it the desires which men direct toward women, into a means of empowerment.

Sex is, therefore, not a means of entrapment. If harnessed properly, it is a passport out of poverty and silence . Saw is not shy about stating as much. In some ways, this parallels Tanya Stephens's "I Am Woman", a cover of the Helen Reddy original in which the powerful sorority of sisters is likened to "lions" in the jungle of life. They have learned many lessons and are able to do anything. They wear their womanhood as a shield of invincibility.

Importantly, neither Stephens nor Reddy says lionesses. The clear appropriation of masculinity in their cross-species, biological metaphor is also a sign. Lions are powerful creatures regardless of gender. The concept requires no further context for its meanings to be understood. Stephens says:

> I am woman hear me roar.
> And I'm much too big to ignore.
> And I know too much to go back every day.
> Cause I heard it all before.
> And I've been down there on the floor.
> No one's ever gonna keep me down again (oh ohh).
> Yes I am wise but it is wisdom for the pain.
> Yes I paid the price, but look, how much I gained.
> If I have to I can do anything.
> I am strong. I am invincible. I am woman . . .

In this case, power comes from women's associations with men and is part of their badness. Dancehall women calculate that it is more useful to soak up men's attention, rather than shy away from it, in order to achieve their own ends.

Dancehall women negotiate a slippery divide between traditional perceptions of themselves as victims of patriarchy and the more renegade conceptions of themselves as conquerors. Both scenarios happen simultaneously and are bridging events in the political worlds of their badness as they reveal the complexities inherent in the lives they lead, both as women and proponents of dancehall culture in Jamaica.

Lady Saw trades sex for power, even while engaging in serious public commentary in the process. Richie Feelings's acknowledgement of Lady Saw as the "woman of rage" and the "muma of the dancehall" in the introduction of her 2004 *Strip Tease* album is the ultimate definition of this reality. Feelings, who is, in effect, Lady Saw in drag, is a very necessary part of the performance of her badness. His voice and personality not only afford her space to embody two different personae at the same time, they also allow her to be both the bad and "good" girl on the album. Saw plumbs the depths of sexual knowledge while also performing a celestial ode of celebration of womanhood. In the anthemic "Dedicated to Mama", Saw praises the fallen women in her life and it stands as a radical, if not ideal, contrast to the several other songs on the compilation (many of which detail various sex acts and the singer's insistence of her mastery over them).

"Dedicated to Mama" recounts the experiences of growing up female, black and Jamaican. It is Saw's contemplation of the roles played by her mother and grandmother in raising her into the woman she has become. The song reflects a loosening of her otherwise tight grip on the reins of power over her embodied badness. It reveals another layer of texture to her disposition. The badness used to describe such a move becomes, in the urban lingua franca, used to refer to its opposite – ultimate goodness, meaning the superlative best.[8] Listening closely to Saw's reflection on the importance of the women who shaped her path, both of whom are connected to the dancehall through her, one cannot help but hear a distinct prefiguration of her later transformation into a born-again Christian of the current era.

This movement from "woman of rage" and "Mumma of the Dancehall" as enunciated in Feelings's rhetoric at the start of the *Strip Tease* album to the saved and sanctified Minister Marion Hall, as she now refers to herself, extends the image of slipperiness and power that "badness" affords its users. It is instructive that Saw refers to "heaven" both as ultimate destination and salvation in this song, and the place from which both her relatives watch with their protective maternal hands, albeit spiritually. Not only does it show Saw's range and dexterity with respect to changing the tone and register of her badness, the potency of her reflection also marks her as the consummate woman. Reflected in the quiet intimacy of her ode to her mother is the subtle awareness of the power of raw and honest emotions in evoking similar responses in her audience. Unafraid to expose her vulnerabilities, Saw says:

> I know you are in heaven, somewhere, looking down.
> Even when mi sad, you teach mi not to wear a frown.
> This song is dedicated to my Mom [spoken].
> Mama, I love you even though you are not here with me.
> I miss you so much, I think of you constantly.
> God must have a reason why, He took you from me.
> Maybe that reason was to set your spirit free.
> Cause now I know, what it's like raising a family and being a wife.
> Struggling everyday, all when things tight.
> Trying to please everyone and never giving up a fight . . .

Saw ultimately reveals that hers is the kind of femininity which breaks down barriers in its multifaceted nature and popular appeal. She speaks not only to "rebel women" (Bush 1990), or even men desiring sex with her, but to all people who have experienced loss, in particular the loss of a mother. Her thematic range, in this regard, marks her as completely versatile and musically creative. Saw is equivalent, in many ways, to male artistes who speak to a range of issues unencumbered by their gender. She is the ultimate performer.

Saw's focus on motherhood evokes much of her own feelings about the role of Christianity in her early upbringing. It embodies her struggles with childbearing, a topic she also tackles in her follow-up album, *No Less a Woman (Infertility)*. Says Saw in that song of the same name:

> *Intro*:
> Infertility is a word that a lot of people are ashamed to mention
> A lot of people are so illiterate when it come to that word
> They act as if it's a crime if you can't have a child
> But I don't think so, I don't have a child, I may one day
> But in the mean time I am going to share all my love.
>
> *Chorus*
> Not having a child don't make me less than a woman,
> You see I got so much love to give, to so much unwanted kids,
> You can say all you want about me trying to ruin my reputation,
> But I have so much love to give to so much unwanted kids,
> Listen to my song

Saw's politics span a wide range of issues, showing her skilfulness and uncompromising stance as "bad gyal". She reprimands, without apology, all "illiterate[s]" who denigrate infertile women; in the process, she counterpoints biological motherhood with the larger, much more important concept to which she subscribes. Saw is the ultimate mother and, with it, the ultimate woman. From the spiritual mothering of her forebears – mother and grandmother – to the issues surrounding biology and infertility, to the love of a mother, Saw is fearlessly vulnerable. She is a fully developed woman and has both range and possibilities.

Saw is not perfect, however. Rather, it is the imperfections, some of which mark her as being bad (a word she contorts and twists to suit her purposes), that are foregrounded. The very focus on motherhood and the trajectory of her own "bad" experiences with it – a fact which she attributes in a 2017 Facebook post[9] to having been a victim of rape (when the issues of violence toward women once again became a serious concern in Jamaica) – points to her chameleon-like abilities. Saw moves between "bad" girl, "good" girl, vulnerable girl, yearning for motherhood, rape survivor and, now, born-again Christian with ease.

Indeed, Saw's transformation back to Marion Hall, this time as minister, is not at all accidental, though ironic. After all, she was Marion Hall – her real name – even while operating in the stage(d) persona of Lady Saw. Thus, her notation in an interview with popular Jamaican television music journalist Winford Williams that the Lady Saw character is now "lost in the wind" is another part of her enigma and charm. This is how the really good, "bad" artistes are able to transform and remake themselves at various points throughout their careers. Saw is, in this sense, a range of different things, simultaneously. Her claim that "I used to go to Church . . . get in spirit and all these things!"[10] is telling. In it one hears echoed ideas of the Derridian (1976) palimpsest holding the written impressions of the past.[11] She is the quintessential artiste and mistress of her various domains. She will not be dictated to by anyone and her lyrics reflect this awareness.

Saw's femininity remains intact even as she delivers important messages about the "coming of God" rather than the verbal and seminal ejaculations of man/men in songs such as "Man ah di Lease" and others. Here, she compares the importance of romantic/sexual love and desire and the desire for filial graces from the divine. Says Saw in the song:

> Mi nuh worry bout di coming of man, worry bout di coming of God.
> Worry how to make mi self one ah di Chosen Ones.
> Who me? Worry over man? You wrong!
> Excess baggage wi nuh carry.
> So tell ah gal bout we she affi worry.
> If ah me fi take ar man, my name go mention,
> dat deh day nah go come gal mi sorry!

Her declaration of her intent to focus on God, again, raises the matter of merging both the worlds of the sacred and profane and points to the liminal possibilities of "badness" in dancehall female culture. Contextualized by grassroots Jamaican culture, sexual knowledge parallels other knowledges and her subsequent focus on "higher-order" things. This is, effectively, what makes Saw a true "bad gyal". Her facile movement between the two spaces continues the earlier announcement by Feelings in the introduction to the album *Strip Tease*.[12] Thus, it is her commitment to badness which affords Lady Saw this critical platform on which to stand and the attendant opportunities it presents to influence and affect audience. In this sense, Lady Saw's dancehall persona symbolically and ideologically connects, therefore, to another kind of historical, Jamaican "Mumma". She is the contemporary, dancehall progeny of national hero (the only woman so honoured) Nanny of the Maroons.[13]

Tanya Stephens's *Gangsta Blues* album, released during the same period as *Strip Tease*, ideologically and creatively roots both herself and Saw firmly into the poetics of badness. Like Saw, Stephens embodies in her work much of the effort to undermine the taboos of Jamaican society. *Gangsta Blues* fiercely challenges male power in a head-on collision signified both in the titles of some of the songs on the album and its thematic content. Stephens's rebellion is part of the ethos of "bad" women who contest male authority. It repudiates the commodification of women under patriarchy. Stephens openly questions patriarchal authority in her ridiculing of the "big ninja bike" in the song of the same name. She points out the inadequacy of the bike and its rider, who "bruk dung outta Treasure Beach" long before arriving at their intended destination (in Negril). Stephens cautions the rider that it is "not a pain ting". The image of the bike is, obviously, code for the rider's penis as well as its size.

Stephens further highlights in the process that men's proclivities for communal sexual participation at the level of trading stories about women is also not okay. In Stephens's words: "dis is not a boast to yuh fren dem dung di lane ting". She lays the foundations of the intent. It is a "sermon" on the virtues of female pleasure and what it is that men need to know, in particular those who apparently derive more joy in telling stories than in starring in them. (Or, perhaps more appropriately in the case of the rider of the big ninja bike, riding, in them.) In Stephens's estimation, it is "just the works" – a reality which she readily supports in her declaration that she also desires to ride on a "big ninja bike".

Stephens is not necessarily vested in efforts to deny men their agency or even the power conventionally ascribed to them through the cultural glorification of their bodies as presumed storehouses of sexual pleasure. This is especially regarding the much-prized "big ninja bike" as the traditional signifier of larger-than-life male sexual endowments and presumed omnipotence. Rather, Stephens is keen on making full use of said competencies, but only if it is the "right one". She does not simply desire having sex for its own sake. Rather, Stephens highlights the importance of women taking control of their right to sexual pleasure in how they negotiate sex with men. She is not only interested in a sexual democracy; Stephens is equally eager to map the boundaries of that state as articulated in her "gangsta girl" poetics. This is another version of the "badness" used by dancehall women to articulate the womanist politics of of their situation.

Stephens is vested with concerns that extend beyond her own material body. She enlarges those concerns to extend the metaphor of the body to include both geographic borders and imagined spaces. In "Do You Still Care", for example, her angst turns to rage and the international agenda of a womanist scholar and activist. Stephens breaks political and geographical barriers in her poetic narrowing of time and space in the song. Jamaica and the United States become twinned in a cross-border narrative about gender and sexual politics, identity and race.

Stephens's supple movements between the US frontiers and the Jamaican homeland show both her versatility and the slippery continuum of issues about which dancehall women concern themselves and just how connected these are. Bubba from the Deep South is equally as bigoted as Bigga from hardcore, inner-city Jamaica – at least, that is what Stephens's persona wishes the audience to see. They are similar in their perceptions that people unlike themselves are to suppose die for no other reason than their obvious and not-so-obvious differences. Says Stephens in the activist anthem:

> Tell me why, can't you accept me as I am?
> Just the way I am, now.
> And that's the reason why, wars can't cease.
> If you no look like mi, mi ah go pop mi piece.
> And that's the reason why, we can't get along.
> If you not doing it my way, we can't get along.

She is clear. The similarity between the two men is a key ingredient in the hate that fuels them. Ironically, however, Stephens creatively contextualizes both Bubba's and Bigga's implied apotheosis, when they are saved by the targets of their disaffection: Bubba by a black organ donor and Bigga by men (and likely also women) celebrating "gay pride". This, after he is attacked by white racists in the United States. For Stephens, this international comparison is instructive in that it positions race and sexuality as key concerns in her identity politics. The two men are drawn together in one creative universe in which the spatialities of time and place are collapsed. This is further suggested in the aural similarities in the names they are given in the song: Bubba/Bigga.

Thus, Stephens enlarges the "body" of her concerns to include more than just the corporeal. She is not just preoccupied with sex, either. Rather, sexuality and political identities are also subsumed into her politics which is itself embodied. Stephens's agenda, in this instance, aims to disrupt the neatly bordered realities of life in Jamaica and the United States. Her concerns are much larger than a simple question of embodied pleasure and the vagaries of a "man and woman story", though she is also very interested in that. Instead, Stephens's joy and happiness come from another place on that very subject – a politics of identity, rooted in her own awareness of herself as a black (Jamaican) woman. Stephens's review of race, therefore, merges into a larger narrative about the role of skin colour and the related politics of identity in marking belonging to national organizations and bodies.

This enlarged border crossing, as it were, is registered in Stephens's unflinching refusal to shy away from the unpleasantness of words like "nigger" and "chi-chi", the latter being a Jamaican derogation of gay men. These words and actions are counterpointed with the violence and brutality of the guns used to shoot Bigga, who is rescued by a carload of people celebrating "gay pride", and the self-induced violence of alcohol abuse which destroys Bubba's liver. That the organ donor is black is both incidental and significant, at the same time, to Stephens's agenda concerning the politics of compassion. It signifies the sense in which collective apathy fuels much of the actions of those who consume – in this case, the liver of the likely dead "nigger", whose life and whole body are the necessary substances that save white lives. This is so, even while blackness and black bodies are denigrated and, in this case dismembered to accommodate the sustainability of a normative white politics. For Stephens, there is no doubt that "black lives [do] matter" and matter significantly.

Conversely, Bigga, which in this case rhymes with "nigger", is no less convinced that gay men's deaths are a necessary evil to, and in his own project of, enforced heteronormativity (Sheller 2012). This is so until he faces down death himself and is, ultimately, rescued by the very people he has been trained and has trained himself to hate. The aural rhyme scheme between "Bigga" and "nigger" is not accidental, either, as noted above. Here, the very "bad" Tanya Stephens clearly counterpoints ideas about race with concerns about homophobia in Jamaica and the United States, forcing a needed discussion as a result of this clever but necessary juxtaposition. This is especially so regarding the geographic and diasporic borders of the Jamaican society – a space routinely criticized for its homophobia (Chin 1999) even while championing racial equality.

Stephens's agenda is clear: all forms of equality are just that – equal. There is no separating out justice for one group while denying it to another. She cannot abide the convenience of the morality which advocates racial equality without an equivalent concern about sexual rights and freedoms. Stephens, therefore, does not shy away from the debate and marches headlong into the proverbial "eye of the storm". Like Saw, she is a modern-day Anancy, the trickster-hero. Stephens's method of delivery, with its range of thematic concerns (on the *Gangsta Blues* album), belies a seriousness which may be lost in the entertainment value of her music. As the contemporary version of the West African trickster-hero smuggled into the "Atlantic world" (Gilroy 1993) centuries earlier, therefore, Stephens sets herself up as her own hero in her various narratives of resistance. The poignancy of her critique in "Do You Still Care" draws needed attention to the injustices of systems of belief which model themselves off a strong sense of rightness even while causing harm to others.

Like Saw, Stephens as activist/poet and advocate happily moves between the worlds of the expected and the surprising. In one sense, Stephens's focus on the grim realities of bigotry gone global directly comments on the politics of fear which they engender (especially in the global "age of terror", in which ideas of peace are, at best, impermanent if not altogether unrealizable). Stephens's demeanour echoes some of the spirituality of a Lady Saw, as noted earlier. Except here, hers is not a call is not on a God (who lives in a distant universe), waiting to award salvation as glorious hallelujahs echo from the heavens. Rather, hers is a plaintive and insistent demand for human rights and justice as well as a simultaneous call to action.

Spirituality for Stephens, therefore, has a new if altogether different meaning. Little wonder she goes "gangsta" even as she preaches social justice. There is no separation of powers. The unapologetically carnal and spiritual are inextrocably linked in Stephens's repertoire. For instance, in "Little White Lie", Stephens is at once the powerful dragon-slayer and vulnerable lover. She narrates her fear that her lie may be discovered. She has misrepresented herself to the man with whom her persona now cohabits. The lie concerns the child she has "borne" him. In Jamaican terms, Stephens has given the man "a jacket", by which is meant she has awarded him someone else's child, even while claiming it is the biological product of their union, in which she also claims to have found happiness.

While on the face of it Stephens's reasons are clearly nefarious, her motivation appears to run a little deeper. Though she gives no stated reasons for the deception, it is implied that there are problems with the man, likely linked to his reproductive abilities. Either way, he is unaware of any such shortcomings and has even gone to the extent of tattooing the child's image on his arm. He also brags to his friends about his "firstborn". Conflicted, Stephens sings about a woman who dies daily on the inside in an effort to keep the peace and secure her child's future as well as her own heart. Says Stephens:

Now I can't sleep at night.
I've lost my appetite.
Everybody keeps saying
the baby looks kind of light
and I tell them that
every newborn baby looks the same.
While, I'm praying to God,
please make your colour change.
The emotions on his face
when he's looking at you.
I couldn't tell he ain't your papa even if I wanted to.
He's got your picture tattooed on his arm.
Now he's bragging to his friends about his firstborn.
Oh God, and I love him, really I do,

> if he ever found out it would kill me too,
> now I'm caught between a rock and a really hard place.
> I'd give anything to keep that smile on his face.

Stephens is clear: the sacrifice of deception is worth the joy and happiness of both the child and the "father". It is the mother, though, who bears the consequences of these weighty and, clearly, debilitating decisions. Hers, ironically, is the proverbial cross to carry to Calvary, almost as penance for her badness. Similarly, as womanist activist, poet and songwriter, Stephens transmogrifies into another version of her bad self in the almost eponymous track on the album. She is the heteronormative, bad girl for hire in "Gangsta Gal" – a riff on the name of the album. As the girlfriend of the gunman, it is Stephens who hides his weapon and washes out the blood from his shirt when he comes back from "work"; she is a real, "thugged-out" gangster herself.

As "gangsta gal", she articulates the deliberate awareness and complicity of a woman who aids and abets her man's criminality. She is defiant, refusing to be penned in by expectations of shame or even propriety concerning her support of her criminal lover. According to Stephens: "Every thug needs a gangsta gal to hug. You done know ah me dat, got your back baby!" She is unapologetic and is acknowledged by Spragga Benz, who is also featured on the single, as his "second". Stephens later advises that she is on her way to the (police) station with the "bail money". She declares that "Since you are my man you don't have to ask. I will lie pan di stan', even cry pan di stan'!" Stephens further advises:

> Mi a bag up di chronic till mi finger dem stuck together wit all a di gum.
> Mi a wipe down the bullet and a load the clip while you a gwan, oil up the gun.
> Mi a smile and hide the piece everytime we a pass the police.
> Everything a run smooth but, if you ever get hold by the beast trust mi.
> You doh ha fi worry honey mi a come down wit the bail money.
> Mi alone have the combination to d safe and mi a go get Johnny Cochrane pon the case.

Stephens is clear. She is prepared to lie and commit crimes in the interests of the love she shares with Benz's persona.[14]

The use of female bodies to enable and, in this case, facilitate the badness of decidedly criminal elements is also part of what is conveyed in the deployment of the poetics of badness by Stephens. Notably, the concept of an archetypal badman hero-figure has, over time, lost much of its early appeal in the earliest incarnations of Jamaican popular culture.[15] This is especially true given the realities of violence and criminal activities within the state which increasingly focused on the actions of men in certain sections of the community (Johnson 2005). Many of these men also had real and organic links to the music (Howard 2010). The lines between metaphoric and lived realities became so badly blurred as to influence shifts in the tolerance of musical claims of masculine badness as being anything but harmless.[16]

Given the heightened sense of patriarchal control of women in the society, therefore, female bodies came to fill this vacancy as an almost natural and logical development.

The increasing presence of such women in the music, not just at the level of patrons and consumers but also producers of culture,[17] ensured this. It would be a tremendous oversight, therefore, to reduce acts of female badness in dancehall culture to just one simple event or sets of events,[18] without also realizing this complexity. Thus, it might be recalled that the influence of the celluloid technology of the silver screen, as noted by Cooper (1995), was instructive in promulgating and making "normal" the image of the rude boy in the popular culture of the day.[19] The video light technology of the late 1990s and early to mid-2000s (Hope 2006a) is a further development of this, as is the current wave of social media (YouTube, Facebook, Instagram and others), which further extend the physical reach of "badness" in dancehall culture. Given its ubiquity, it is not entirely unexpected that women would ultimately perform badness in similar ways.

To momentarily return to the Richie Feelings character discussed earlier, his actions are an instructive critique of the poetics of badness in dancehall culture. He inadvertently gestures to the dancehall mythology of recasting ordinary people into the roles of superheroes[20] and, in this case, fairy tale princesses.[21] Dancehall women are, in effect, the grassroots versions of the state's conferment of the title of National Hero status on Nanny of the Maroons, a black, Jamaican woman with a strong sense of lower-class currency. Dancehall women collude with each other, therefore, to actively contest the boundaries of patriarchy[22] through the use of the poetics of badness. It is an effort in which many are engaged, though perhaps not always intentionally, and which is necessary for creating space both for themselves and others. Anything and everything at their disposal will be used as a result, including the power of their womanist and womanly desires as ways to ensnare men in their projects of embodied emancipation.

NOTES

1. This notion of a "ghetto girl" having the capacity to give the "wickedest slam" (meaning, very good sex) is immortalized in song by Moses "Beenie Man" Davis, in the song of the same name, "Wickedest Slam". It popularized the idea that women of certain socio-economic backgrounds are the best at sex, enshrining a view of lower-class, black women as being only able to engage in sex and nothing else. This idea builds on many of the mythologies of enslavement promoted by white male planters and others who routinely helped themselves to black women's sexualities (Pinnock, unpublished). In this way, lower-class women, the majority of whom are descended from the enslaved, continue to bear the weight of being "sexual champions" and hardly much else. This is not necessarily praiseworthy.
2. By queer here, Ellis (2010) does not so much refer to gay sexualities (though some of those resonances are implied in her use of the term) as much as a blurring of heteronormative (Sheller 2012) boundaries, as a way of suggesting this possibility. This implies the necessary ways in which "female-ness" (Cooper 1995) is also part of the how badness and masculinity are constructed and intertwined in the dancehall.
3. Susan Harewood (2006) is keen to highlight that, notwithstanding the potential benefit of a sexual emancipatory goal, as demonstrated in the works of popular female artistes across a range of Caribbean popular cultures, there are nonetheless key dangers involved.

4. Sex and and its related concerns are fundamentally complicit with patriarchal constructions of women as objects of male desire. Men effectively hijack the emancipatory ambitions of potential feminist readings of sex/uality, in much the same way middle-class discourses betray nativist struggles according to Fanon (1967).
5. This is a common feature of contemporary dancehall music, which various female artistes, including Lady Saw, Tanya Stephens, Ishawna, Cecille and others, constantly project as part of their performative identities. These women are not push-overs.
6. I specifically elected to use the Jamaican orthography system developed by linguists Frederick Cassidy and Robert Le Page. It is part of an attempt to underline the importance of using the "heart-language" to the agendas of the women in question. While not all of the song texts are written in this way, the title is. The aim of this is to foreground the abiding power of Jamaican language and culture to the role of being "bad" in the context of this argument. Focus is placed on grassroots Jamaican culture. The use of Jamaican to reference that is signified in the spelling used in the title of the chapter.
7. This concept refers to how accommodating an activity, or set of realities, also builds within it an opportunity to negotiate and arrive at compromise. It builds on the notion that the process of living in the "New World" was one in which the enslaved had to adapt in their environments, even while they sought to take control.
8. One could even say that, by showing such dexterity and range in her work, Lady Saw exemplifies the Jamaican expression "bad like yaws" as a statement of her power. Yaws is a tropical disease which affects the skin, bone and cartilage and was, likely, a common feature of life among enslaved Jamaicans. The expression "bad like yaws" historically acknowledges the stubbornness of the disease, given the often rudimentary or absent state of medical care in the community. It is also an acknowledgement of something or someone who holds power and is not readily or easily conquered.
9. Marion Hall suggested in a Facebook post, which appeared in my Facebook timeline early in 2017, that she is a rape survivor. Her admission and her subsequent declaration that the women in political office should rise up and stand with regular women who face the horrors of intimate partner and other forms of violence is part of the boldness and courage which marks her as "bad". She uses shards of her splintered life occasioned by the violence of rape to renew and remake herself in the dancehall as well as beyond it. It is a testament not only of a capacity to overcome but to also wrest control of the narrative about herself from others, especially men.
10. See interview with Jamaican journalist Winford Williams about her conversion to Christianity at https://www.youtube.com/watch?v=GRKW-st51oM&t=351s.
11. Derrida (1976) uses the idea of the palimpsest as a metaphor of writing. Like the palimpsest used by the preschool child who is learning to write, it retains all the markings of previous efforts. The palimpsest embodies a genealogy of knowledge retained many of the previous inscriptions by culture. The final outcome is never without the influences and impressions of the past.
12. Saw is not only a man in drag but, in the context of conventional Christianity, she is also the clear picture of the sinner before being converted. The *Strip Tease* album is, in many ways, a kind of apotheosis – an emergence out of what Erna Brodber calls the "kumbla" (a literary chrysalis) into which women of Jamaican grassroots origins go in order to

reemerge stronger and more self-aware (Boyce-Davies and Savory-Fido 1990). As queen of the dancehall, Saw is also heavenward-bound, at least reading from her easy movements between the two spaces – the worlds of the sacred and the profane. However, she has to be transformed and, subsequently, have her more daring persona "lost in the wind" of transformation, years later, for that to be fully realized. *Strip Tease* is, in many ways, a cardinal point in her evolution as artiste and grassroots Jamaican womanist. It reflects a yearning for something outside of herself but for which she is also in immediate need – salvation, and the obvious awareness of her current place as queen of dancehall culture.

13. Like her Maroon foremother, leader, strategist and, likely, "Mother Woman" – a term used to refer to heightened powers over the magical arts – Nanny is literally and figuratively evoked in Saw's imagination of herself as the ultimate bad woman. Nanny is, after all, for the purposes of Jamaican national history, the first and most popular of such characters. She is bad, without apology.
14. Benz later, laughingly, makes the point that she will also hide the gun in her "panty waist" at the first sign of the police, suggesting his own awareness of how easy it is for women to escape police detection and barricades in Jamaican inner-city communities which are routinely searched in these ways. Benz is also speaking to the clear, if not unfortunate, reality that women are often complicit in helping male criminal elements in certain communities in Jamaica to escape the law.
15. As Dennis Howard (2010) points out, this image of the male "rudey" lost much of its resonance as a purely literary device with the advent of urban gang warfare and other forms of violence. It blurred the lines between reality and art, which he attributes to an organic and very real link between the Jamaican criminal underworld and the dancehall entertainer. Badness as a cultural response took centre stage in the musical narratives which emanated from the Jamaican urban landscape (Cooper 1995), giving character to popular culture of the day. Much of that logic continued in the modern day in which dancehall culture took pride of place as the primary popular music created in Jamaica in the last half century.
16. Columnists, such as the late Ian Boyne and others, are among the key critics (Cooper 2004a). Cooper's concept of the "lyrical gun", in the estimation of scholars like Howard, increasingly sounded less resonant and likely not as plausible in the overall context of current Jamaican society. This is the general assessment of the role of the male dancehall deejay and his relationship to the realities of violence in the Jamaican state (Howard 2010).
17. Donna Hope (2006a), for instance, references such events as dancehall queen competitions in which women proliferated. These, it could be argued, enabled them greater spaces in which to create and transmit culture in a way that was often independent of men. It is generally male dancehall deejays, producers and likely also patrons who are often the visibly obvious parts of the space and culture and whose creative works are often analysed in the scholarship. Stephens's "Gangsta Gal" not only articulates in clear and unequivocal terms how female bodies are key to the performance and use of dancehall's poetics of badness but also suggests how their co-optation at this level was a seamless transition in the culture.
18. Women were, after all, already implicated in the performance of the fantasy of dancehall culture. The video-light technology, which in Hope's (2006b) view operates as another form of "eye", has the additional ability to stage an event. It transports the power of the performance across multiple borders, as well as creates the idea of dancehall culture as a

space of star-making. The star-making power of the technology of the video camera is, in many ways, part of Cooper's (2004a) reading of the phenomenon of the dancehall queen. Her analysis of the filmed version of this phenomenon makes the point and speaks also of the power of dancehall's poetics of badness in the enablement of dancehall women's fantastical reimaginings of themselves as superstars. Badness relies heavily on the need to have itself broadcast to wider versions of its immediate audience in the physical space of the dancehall.

19. This influenced the music and, in turn, created room to navigate badness outside even just the cultural projects of outsmarting and beating powerful opponents at their own game(s), as represented in the Anancy trickster figure. Instead, I am suggesting Anancy is a "bad-man" in the sense of a gun-toting, violent character. No. I am, instead, arguing that the resonance of the image of trickery and the need to outsmart opponents could well have been merged with the cowboy folk hero of those early Western movies, which, because of image moving technology, were transmitted to other parts of the culture and, in turn, helped enshrine the love of "badness" in the popular culture.

20. Or, perhaps it is more appropriate to say super-heroines in the postcolonial, digitized, up-tempo narrative. Dancehall is aimed at rereading official state culture(s) (Pinnock 2007). Encapsulated in the announcement by Feelings, who acts both as one who introduces Saw and is Saw herself (in drag, as noted earlier), are the passions and dimensions of the poetics of badness. It is a graphic, hard-edged performance that unapologetically traffics in sex and, if necessary, violence – though not usually for its own sake.

21. Writing about how Marcia transfigured into the omnipotent dancehall queen, Cooper (2004a, 125–26) points out how dancehall culture endows otherwise ordinary women with near superhero-like abilities. The persona of the various dancehall women who engage in badness assumes an archetypal heroine-like characteristic. Badness emblematizes a "Nanny of the Maroons" ethos, as noted earlier.

22. This is clearly articulated by Lady Saw and Tanya Stephens in their transformation into sexual high priestesses to control the lives of men and women around them. This indicates their gendered power. As a result of dancehall, women are able to realign the power imbalances between themselves and men and use badness as a performative device in their work. They are also able to affect the lives of other women as well. Dancehall women as Anancy figures, as noted earlier, mobilize multiple strategies in their lofty feminist/womanist ideologies and activism in the Jamaican dancehalll.

REFERENCES

Beckles, H. 2003. "Perfect Property: Enslaved Black Women in the Caribbean". In *Confronting Power, Theorizing Gender: Interdisciplinary Perspectives in the Caribbean*, edited by E. Barriteau, 142–58. Kingston: University of the West Indies Press.

Beckles, H. 1995. "Sex and Gender in the Historiography of Caribbean Slavery: Engendering History". In *Caribbean Women in Historical Perspective*, edited by V. Shepherd, B. Bailey and B. Brereton, 125–40. Kingston: Ian Randle.

Boyce Davies, C., and E. Savory Fido, eds. 1990. *Out of the Kumbla: Caribbean Women and Literature*. Trenton, NJ: Africa World Press.

Bush, B. 1990. *Slave Women in Caribbean Society 1650–1838*. Kingston: Heinemann Caribbean.

Chin, T.S. 1999. "Jamaican Popular Culture, Caribbean Literature, the Representation of Gay and Lesbian Sexuality in the Discourses of Race and Nation". *Small Axe* 5:14–33.

Christian, B. 1985. *Black Feminist Criticism: Perspectives on Black Women Writers*. New York: Pergamon Press.

Cooper, C. 1995. *Noises in the Blood: Orality, Gender, and the "Vulgar" Body of Jamaican Popular Culture*. Durham, NC: Duke University Press.

———. 2004a. *Sound Clash, Jamaican Dance Hall Culture at Large*. London: Palgrave Macmillan.

———. 2004b. "Enslaved in Stereotype: Race and Representation in Post-Independence Jamaica". *Interventions* 6, no. 1: 1–17.

Derrida, J. 1978. *Writing and Difference. Translated with an Introduction and Additional Notes by Alan Bass*. Chicago: Chicago University Press.

Ellis, N. 2011. "Out and Bad: Toward a Queer Performance Hermeneutic in Jamaican Dancehall". *Small Axe* 15, no. 2: 7–23.

Fanon, F. 1967. *The Wretched of the Earth*. Harmondsworth: Penguin.

Forrest, J.B. 2006. "Nationalism in Postcolonial States". In *After Independence: Making and Protecting the Nation in Postcolonial and Postcommunist States*, edited by L.W. Barrington, 33–44. Ann Arbour: University of Michigan Press.

Gilroy, P. 1993. *Black Atlantic: Modernity and Double Consciousness*. Cambridge, MA: Harvard University Press.

Harewood, S. 2006. "Transnational Soca Performances, Gendered Re-Narrations of Caribbean Nationalism". *Social and Economic Studies*, 55, nos. 1–2 (March–June): 25–48.

hooks, bell. 1981. *Ain't I a Woman, Too?* Boston: South End Press.

———. 1985. *Feminist Theory: From Margin to Centre*. Boston: Southend.

Hope, D.P. 2006a. *Inna di Dancehall: Popular Culture and the Politics of Identity in Jamaica*. Kingston: University of the West Indies Press.

———. 2006b. "Passa Passa: Interrogating Cultural Hybridities in Jamaican Dancehall". *Small Axe* 10, no. 3: 125–39.

Howard, D. 2010. "Dancehall Political Patronage and Gun Violence: Political Affiliations and the Glorification of Gun Culture". *Jamaica Journal* 32, no. 3: 8–15.

Johnson, H.N. 2005. "Incivility: The Politics of 'People on the Margins in Jamaica". *Political Studies* 53:579–97.

Nettleford, R.M. 2003. *Caribbean Cultural Identity: The Case of Jamaica, an Essay in Cultural Dynamics*. 2nd ed. Princeton: Markus Weiner.

Pinnock, A. 2007. "A Ghetto Education Is Basic: (Jamaican) Dancehall Masculinities as Counter Culture". *Journal of Pan African Studies* 1, no. 9: 47–84.

———. 2017. "Performing Subjectivities: Race, Nation and Gender Identity in Jamaican Popular Culture". Thesis, University of the West Indies, Mona, Jamaica.

Sheller, M. 2012. *Citizenship from Below: Erotic Agency and Caribbean Freedom*. Durham: Duke University Press.

Thomas, D. 2004. *Modern Blackness: Nationalism, Globalization, and the Politics of Culture in Jamaica*. Durham: Duke University Press.

PART 5

SOUND SYSTEM, RIDDIM AND PRACTICE

CHAPTER 17

A Caribbean Taste of Technology

*Creolization and the Ways of Making of the Dancehall Sound System**

JULIAN HENRIQUES

THIS CHAPTER TAKES ITS NAME AND INSPIRATION FROM Mad Professor's album *A Caribbean Taste of Technology*.[1] This makes a good place to start a discussion of creolization and technology – the dub reggae tracks of this album produced by British producer Mad Professor and released in 1985. So what I present here is a text and ideas *version* of the album, as it were. The album cover artwork sets the tone. The Mad Professor himself lays back in a hammock enjoying the drink in his hand (the glass containing the entire Caribbean archipelago), the sun-soaked beach and an array of the latest technological accoutrements of the era together with a selection of tropical fruits.[2] The technology is evidently not a threat, but a source of pleasure; he is relaxed about it. This is the key message: in the Caribbean context new technologies are an invitation to be creative, an impulse that leads to Afrofuturism.[3] This creativity is nowhere better expressed than in Jamaican music and the global influence this has in terms of sound, rhythm and phonographic performance techniques.

Jamaican music technology – the stage show, the sound system dance and the recording studio – provide examples of positive spin on the idea of creolization. The concept of creolization describes the mixing of cultural forms, specifically in the New World setting of the disruption of slavery and forced migration. It has a long and contested history. In postcolonial theory creolization has been criticized for its lack of account of the power relations in which cultures are constituted (Knepper 2006; Vergès 2003). Stuart Hall (2010, 29) counsels that with creolization "questions of power, as well as issues of entanglement, are always at stake". This limitation might have less of a grip on the ways of making of the street culture and technology of the sound system than on other cultural forms.

While there are often skirmishes with the police and the open-air dancehall venues are invariably shifting, the dancehall scene is comparatively autonomous and self-generating. This is because it is a street technology and culture of the ghetto, whose creolizing mixes

* Previously published in *Technosphere*, 15 April 2017.

FIGURE 17.1. *A Caribbean Taste of Technology* album cover, Ariwa, 1985, artist unaccredited.

FIGURE 17.2. *Youth Ghetto Ology*, Sizzla Kalongi, Greensleeves, 2009, artist Tony Dermott.

take place largely "under the radar" of the authorities. This is what makes the practices of the scene such an exciting prospect for investigation in terms of processes of creolization. Seven key features of creolization are picked out in what follows.

CREOLIZATION AS BRICOLAGE: MOBILE SOUND SYSTEMS

One important aspect of creolization is *bricolage*, the activity of bringing together disparate components into a new assemblage. The components themselves are not new; in fact they are often recycled or repurposed, far from the factory setting. Their novel functionality lies in the assemblage as a whole. As a type of bricolage, creolization involves working practices of experimentation, trial and error and ways of knowing through an *in situ* process of making. This contrasts with the architect or engineer's executing a pre-organized plan. Bricolage is a quotidian, one-off personalized do-it-yourself practice that makes use of whatever materials or components are readily at hand, as is commonplace in a huge range of settings across the globe.[4] On the street it is seldom the standard issue factory settings – instead it is re-engineered, often subverting the manufacturers' specifications and intensions.

The technique of bricolage often involves a repurposing of components. A good example of this would be Hedley Jones repurposing a telephone handset microphone as the pickup for his invention of the electric guitar (Henriques 2011). Street technology is the street art to the high art of the technology corporations. This is vividly expressed with Charlie Ace's Swing-a-Ling mobile record and recording shop and studio. Creolization provides local practical local solutions; note the vehicle is not only a shop but also claims to be a recording studio. The contingencies of the street culture exercise a

FIGURE 17.3. DJ Squeeze with his sound truck Thunder with Lightning generator in tow, circa 2002. Photo by author.

considerable influence on the technology. Without the resources that permanent venues require, mobility is most important.

A more contemporary version of this same mobile technology is provided by DJ Squeeze and his sound system on wheels; though more polished, it is essentially the same creolized solution of assembling together the two technologies of transportation and sound system. This is of course far from unique, with the sound floats of the Trinidad and Tobago carnival as an outstanding example (Henriques and Ferrara 2014). Both creolization and bricolage are sources of creativity and originality of the kind found with musical improvisation, as distinct from the interpretation of a musical score. Bricolage has also proved a valuable conceptual resource for the cultural studies approach to subcultures, as with Dick Hebdige's pioneering studies (Hebdige 1979). The critical edge of the term comes from the heterogeneity of the components it assembles together, as distinct from the operation media theorists would now describe as "cultural techniques" (Bernard 2014).

CREOLIZATION AS MIXING: REGGAE DUB MUSIC

It is widely recognized that Jamaican Patwa and other Creole languages mix cultures together to produce a distinctive new one. Similarly, the standard music studio post-production mixing technique brings together the separate tracks on which the individual musical instruments were recorded. So mixing makes the assembled bricolage of components more intense by actually merging them together – as chemical elements combine to form a new compound.

The technique of the dub mix has to be located in a New World geography specifically, that is, the recording studios in Jamaica in the 1960s and early 1970s. Its famous originators include Duke Reid, Coxonne Dodd, Lee "Scratch" Perry and many others. Unlike a normal mix or remix, a dub mix, like "Buccaneer's Cove" on the *Taste* album, removes all but a trace of lyrics, harmonies and instruments of the original track to let the drum and bass predominate. To this it adds in echo, reverb and sound effects, copying (that's what dub means) and doubling and re-doubling back (Henriques and Hillegonda 2019; Veal 2007; Hitchins 2014, 133–54). This idea of enfolding and repeating is also found Antonio Benítez-Rojo's (1996) concept of the repeating island in his book of that name.

Dub creolization can be heard as unmixing as much as mixing, taking elements out in what has been described as a *subtractive* aesthetic, by contrast to the *additive* technique of toasting, or the break beat sample of the catchy bars (Henriques and Hillegonda 2019). Instead, the more taken out of the music track the more room it opens up for the listener to enter into the vacated space – filling it with their own associations, pleasures and remembering of the vocal version.

The dub mix itself is then subject to the creolization of bricolage assemblage in that it is a recycling of the music track on the A-side of the 45, finding within it additional value to make the B-side dub mix. These tracks are then put together as dub albums, further adding value. As a street culture technique, invariably in a context of scarce resources,

FIGURE 17.4. King Tubby *Majestic Dub*, 1976, reissue Culture Press, 2000.

creolization is often about making more with less, or indeed something out of nothing. Like jazz music, dub music is energized by distinctly Old World musical traditions that are often rhythmic in character, specifically Nyabinghi in respect to reggae. These ancient elements are then "reimagined", as would now be said, with New World technologies of the recording studio, itself reinvented as a musical instrument in its own right. Thus one of the elements of creolization is that it is about the mix, literally so with dub music mix.

The geopolitical forces of colonization meant it was the New World where this technological mixing took place, just as it was for cultural and racial mixing, hybridity and Latin American *mestiça* societies. Creolization might be contrasted with that other New World phenomenon of *syncretism,* where one cultural form is superimposed on another, as for example Yorùbá Orishas are with Catholic saints in Haitian Voodoo. The mixture of creolization can be said to run deeper than two elements that blend to make a third. On the sound system scene this creolization also runs in parallel with syncretic conjunctures, as with the practice of washing inside the speaker cabinet or dusting off

FIGURE 17.5A. A Stone Love engineer with a dry paintbrush brushes down the controls before a dance. Photo by author.

FIGURE 17.5B. A Venus sound system engineer washes the inside of the bass bins, both suggesting a ritual purpose. Photo by author.

the mixer controls. It is a spiritual cleansing that is going on here, expressing the value system of *scyence* or obeah (Voodoo in Haiti) rather than technological science.

CREOLIZATION AS REPEATING: VERSIONING

A third musical example of creolization is the uniquely Jamaican musical practice of *versioning*, whereby a single riddim (rhythm) track is used as the musical backing by a number of singers and DJs. There are innumerable examples of this practice, possibly the most widely known being King Jammy's "Sleng Teng" riddim which has been subject of literally hundreds of versions.[5] Thus the Creole cooking pot never empties however many meals it serves. Greensleeves is one of the labels specializing in these single riddim albums. In terms of creolization this is another example of recycling a resource or component. In this instance, reiteration creates a multiplication of value. As well as maximizing the use of a resource, it also illustrates something of the distinctiveness of the Jamaican music scene where the riddim track has its own autonomy and particular importance.

CREOLIZATION AS SOCIALIZATION: STAGING THE SESSION

Another distinctive feature of the Jamaican music scene is the fact that the primary instrument for the enjoyment of Jamaican music is the sound system session, rather than radio, streaming, downloading, compact disc or indeed even the concert or stage show.

FIGURE 17.6. Greensleeves single riddim albums, a selection.

This provides an example of a fourth characteristic of creolization, that is, a *repurposing* not only of different technological components and devices but also the function for which the new assemblage is deployed. Very often creolization consists of *socializing* a technology; to share what was originally designed as domestic technological appliance with a much wider community of users. Thus creolization can encourage a resistence to individual consumerist accumulation. The sound system exemplifies this reverse social repurposing for the phonographic instrument of the gramophone. This is what the sound system remains, but at a size and scale that an entire community can enjoy.

The sound system session draws attention to the contrast between social and individually orientated usage of technologies. This has the important effect of changing the nature of the experience of listening itself. The mobile personal listening experience first afforded by the Walkman and subsequently by MP3 devices *inserts the music into the*

FIGURE 17.7. The dancehall crowd. Photo by Varun Baker, with permission.

FIGURE 17.8. Unloading speakers. Photo by author.

FIGURE 17.9. Stringing up the speakers. Photo by author.

FIGURE 17.10. Building speaker stacks. Photo by author.

listener by means of in- or on-ear headphones. This contrasts with the sound system listening experience in the session. As a travelled-to destination, this is where, in the company of others, *listeners insert their whole bodies into the music.*

In order to achieve this each dancehall session each evening has to be transported to the open-air venue, configured in the most advantageous manner for that venue, assembled together (called "stringing-up"), tested and sound checked. This nightly practice of assembly and disassembly for every session mimics the mixing and unmixing of creolization.

CREOLIZATION AS INTENSIFICATION: THE SET OF EQUIPMENT

The fifth characteristic of creolization is *intensification,* where mixing produces a release of energy in a chemical reaction. But this is an affective energy that could be thought of as being necessitated by the extremes of the New World environment with its histories of enslavement and indentureship. In short, a creolized culture has a substantial amount of work to do reconstituting shattered identities and remembering buried histories.

In the dancehall session this intensification takes place in the bowl of sound between the three speaker stacks or columns. This is a special kind of place of pleasure that could be described in terms of Homi Bhabha's (1994, 36–39) concept of a third space, or Hannah Arendt's (1958, 199) space of appearance. One of the ways these bass-heavy intensities are created is by what has been described as sonic *dominance* (Henriques

FIGURE 17.11. Passa Passa, Spanish Town Road, Tivoli Gardens, Kingston, circa 2005.

2003). This achieves an immersive, visceral, full body intensive listening, as distinct from ordinary audition via the outer ear. The physical scale and shared sociality of the sound system encourage such intensities, but again the repurposing techniques come into play. These auditory levels are furnished by the historically ever-increasing size of the amplification equipment.

The other way these intensities are created is with the inward orientation of the speakers onto the crowd (audience) in the centre, as distinct from the conventional PA where the speakers are on either side of the artist on stage. This simple reorientation from outward-facing to inward-facing can be described as the crucial twist of creolization. Phonographic technologies are thus used to place the audience rather than an artist as the focus of attention.

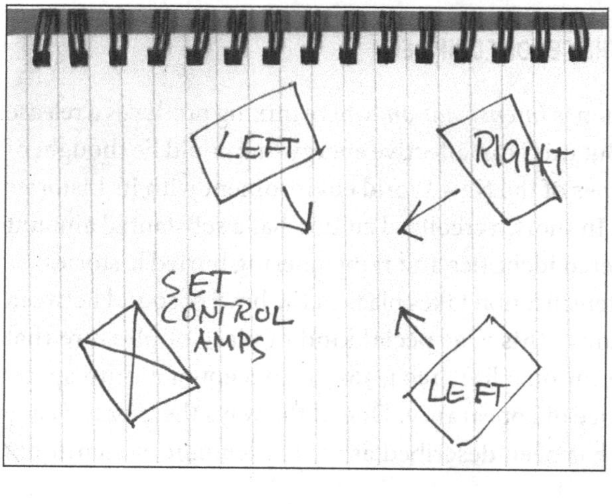

FIGURE 17.12. Notebook sketch of triangulation. Drawing by author.

CREOLIZATION AS SEPARATION: FREQUENCY SPECIALIZATION

The sixth characteristic of creolization can be described as *separation*, that is, the kind of unmixing by which dub reggae was described. This is the case with the separation of frequencies that is achieved by the sound system set, specifically by the crossover component. This assigns each of five frequency bands to a separate amplifier connected to its own separate specialist speaker – from tweeters at the top to sub-bass at the bottom end. This is done for each of the three speaker stacks.

The sound system engineers who have been responsible for these innovations have taken the phonographic instrument of the sound system to new levels of sophistication. They have a fine-grained understanding of how sound works on human bodies as much as in electronic circuits. This returns us to the starting point of the mix as the first creolization in the way of making of the street technology, but transduced into the medium of auditory propagation itself.

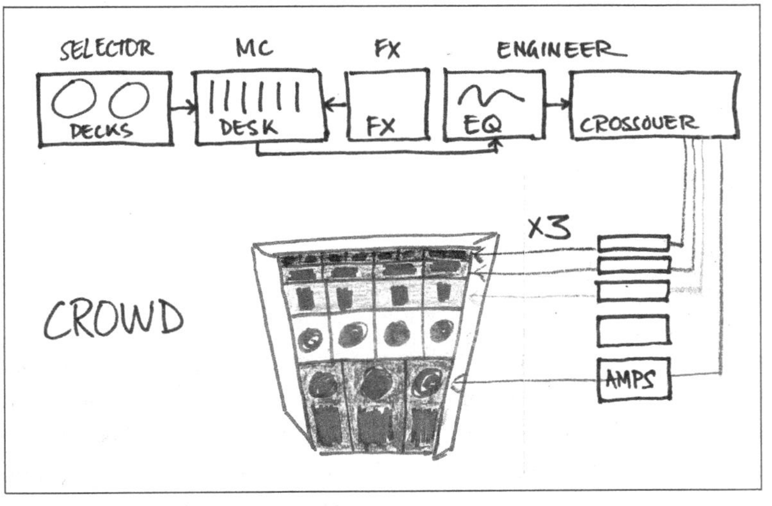

FIGURE 17.13. Crossover separation the frequency bands before amplification. Drawing by author.

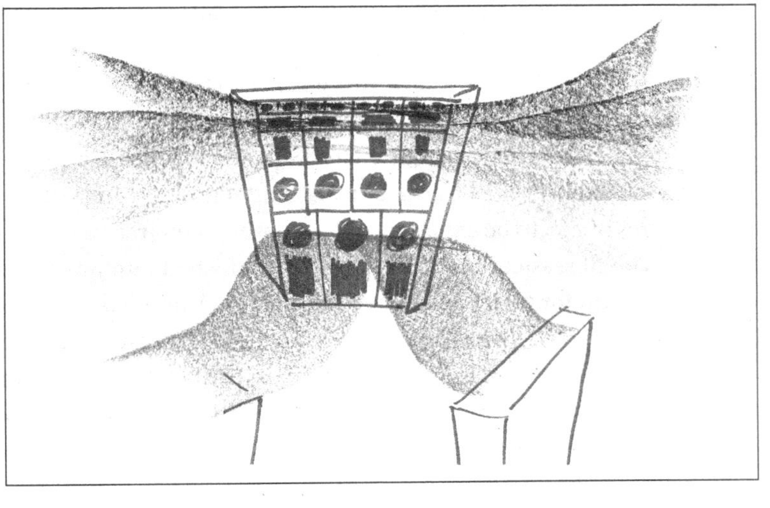

FIGURE 17.14. Frequency rainbow from one of the three speaker stacks. Drawing by author.

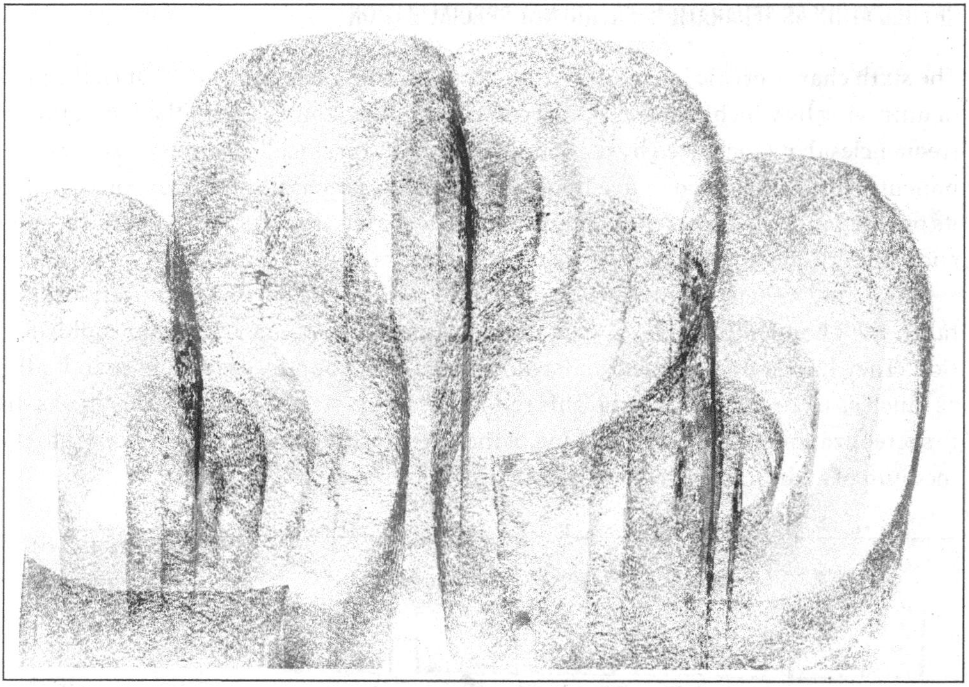

FIGURE 17.15. Frequency rainbow from three speaker stacks. Drawing by author.

CREOLIZATION AS REMIXING

The idea of creolization has informed this brief account of sound system technology – but at the same time the ways of making of technology itself has also informed what the process of creolization might be understood to be. *Remixing* can be considered as the final, seventh characteristic of creolization. Thus in addition to mixing, creolization creates value with both unmixing as well as remixing. It is not only a music track that is remixed but also the entire instrument of the sound system set, balanced and fine-tuned by the hands and ears of the engineers.

These thoughts on the aesthetic value of the mix take us back to the use of the word *taste*: Mad Professor's album title. The idea of taste resonates in various modalities, not least the style and fashion of the Jamaican music scene. Taste is of course a social, political and cultural achievement as Pierre Bourdieu (1984) taught us. Most important, taste foregrounds the pleasures of life, to be experienced, whatever your circumstances, in the intensities of the dancehall session. It is also what distinguished humans from animals – homo sapiens (the Latin for taste), as Michel Serres maintains, is the sensory source of wisdom (Serres 1984, 153–54). A sound system session gives a pleasurable taste of the experience of a creolized technology. For me it also recalls the tingling sensation of electricity, as a schoolboy experimenter, testing the charge of a little nine-volt battery by touching the two terminals on the tip of my tongue.

NOTES

1. The ideas for this image-essay are largely taken from chapters 1 and 3 of Henriques (in press) and from Henriques (2011). See also Henriques (2014).
2. Please see Louis Chude-Sokei's (2015) excellent account of this album.
3. See Henriques and Offeh (2017).
4. In India it goes by the name of *jugaad*, see Radjou, Prabhu and Ahuja (2012).
5. For a list of versions see http://www.jamrid.com/Riddims.php.

REFERENCES

Arendt, Hannah. 1958. *The Human Condition*. Chicago: Chicago University Press.

Benítez-Rojo, Antonio. 1996. *The Repeating Island: The Caribbean and the Postmodern Perspective*. Translated by James Maraniss. Durham: Duke University Press.

Bhabha, Homi K. 1994. *The Location of Culture*. London: Routledge.

Bourdieu, Pierre. 1984. *Distinction: A Social Critique of the Judgment of Taste*. Translated by Richard Nice. Boston: Harvard University Press.

Chude-Sokei, Louis. 2015. *The Sound of Culture: Diaspora and Black Technopoetics*. Middletown: Wesleyan University Press.

Hall, Stuart. 2010. "Créolite and the Process of Creolization". In *The Creolization Reader: Studies in Mixed Identities and Cultures*, edited by Robin Cohen and Paola Toninato, 26–38. London: Routledge.

Hebdige, Dick.1979. *Subculture: The Meaning of Style*. London: Methuen.

Henriques, J.F. 2003. "Sonic Dominance and Reggae Sound System Sessions". In *The Auditory Culture Reader*, edited by Michael Bull and Les Back, 451–80. Oxford: Berg.

———. 2011. *Sonic Bodies: Reggae Sound Systems, Performance Techniques and Ways of Knowing*. London: Continuum.

———. 2014. "Rhythmic Bodies: Amplification, Inflection and Transduction in the Dance Performance Techniques of the 'Bashment Gal'". *Body and Society* 20, nos. 3-4: 79-112.

———. In press. *Sonic Media: The Street Technology and Culture of the Jamaican Sound System*. Durham, NC: Duke University Press.

Henriques, J.F., and Beatrice Ferrara. 2014. "The Sounding of the Notting Hill Carnival: Music as Space, Place and Territory". In *Black Popular Music in Britain Since 1945*, edited by Jon Stratton and Nabeel Zuberi, 131–51. London: Routledge.

Henriques, J.F., and Rietveld Hillegonda. 2019. "Echo". In *Sound Handbook*, edited by Michael Bull, 275–82. London: Routledge.

Henriques, Julian, and Harold Offeh. "Afrofuturism, Technology and Fiction". In *Futures and Fictions*, edited by Simon O'Sullivan, Ayesha Hameed and Henriette Gunkel, 97–121. London: Repeater Books.

Hitchins, Ray. 2014. *Vibes Merchants: The Sound Creators of Jamaican Popular Music*. London: Routledge.

Knepper, Wendy. 2006. "Colonization, Creolization, and Globalization: The Art and Ruses of Bricolage". *Small Axe: A Caribbean Journal of Criticism* 10, no. 3: 70–86.

Radjou, Navi, Jaideep Prabhu and Simone Ahuja. 2012. *Jugaad Innovation: Think Frugal, Be Flexible, Generate Breakthough Growth*. New York: Wiley.

Serres, Michel. 1984/2008. *The Five Senses: A Philosophy of Mingled Bodies*. London: Continuum.

Siegert, Bernhard. 2014. *Cultural Techniques: Grids, Filters, Doors, and Other Articulations of the Real*. Translated by Geoffrey Winthrop-Young. New York: Fordham University Press.

Veal, Michael. 2007. *Dub: Songscapes and Shattered Songs in Jamaican Reggae*. Middletown: Wesleyan University Press.

Vergès, Françoise. 2003. "Kiltir Kreol: Processes and Practices of Créolité and Creolization". In *Créolité and Creolization*, edited by Okwui Enwezor, Carlos Basualdo, Ute Meta Bauer, Susanne Ghez, Sarat Maharaj, Mark Nash and Octavio Zaya, 179–84. Kassel: Fridericanum-Veranstaltungs GmbH.

CHAPTER 18

The Riddim Method

*Aesthetics, Practice and Ownership in Jamaican Dancehall**

PETER MANUEL AND WAYNE MARSHALL

THE DEVELOPMENT OF THE RIDDIM/VOICING SYSTEM

From the early 1970s reggae music – whose most popular form since around 1980 has been called "dancehall"[1] – has relied upon the phenomenon of the "riddim", that is, an autonomous accompanimental track, typically based on an ostinato (which often includes melodic instrumentation as well as percussion). While a dancehall song consists of a deejay singing (or "voicing") over a riddim, the riddim is not exclusive to that song but is typically used in many other songs – a practice which is, for example, uncharacteristic of rap, which also uses sampled accompanimental ostinatos.[2] On occasion, the same voicing may be rereleased with different riddims. Accordingly, the riddim has its own name, its own producer and owner and its own musical life independent of particular voicings by deejays.

This system of what we may call "riddim-plus-voicing", in which songs are built from separable component parts, is familiar to and largely taken for granted by those immersed in dancehall culture, whether as fans, producers or music journalists. Nevertheless, the system is so unique that it well merits focused scholarly attention. In this chapter we present a general description of the system and a cursory outline of its evolution and comment upon its distinctive compositional norms, aesthetic attitudes, historical considerations, relations to live performance practices and patterns of ownership as reflected in copyright and common practice.

A standard explanation for the practice of recycling riddims is that Jamaica is a poor country, and it has been natural to minimize the expense of record production by reusing accompaniment tracks rather than paying for studio time and live musicians. While there may be an element of truth in this explanation, the reality is certainly more complex, especially since counterparts to riddims have not come to be used in

* Previously published in *Popular Music* 25, no. 3 (2006): 448–62, 466–70.

the numerous societies that are even more impoverished than Jamaica. The reliance on riddims is better seen as being conditioned by and constituting part of the entire evolution of modern Jamaican music culture, including such features as its special emphasis on sound systems and studio production rather than live bands. In general, it is easier to trace and describe the evolution of the riddim system than it is to explain it.

Although the riddim-plus-voicing system did not become the mainstream norm in Jamaican popular music production until the latter 1970s, its roots lie in the early formation of Jamaican commercial music culture in the 1950s. One precondition was the convention, which still predominates, of dance music being provided by sound systems, playing records, rather than live bands. This orientation stands in contrast with other nearby countries, especially of the Hispanic Caribbean. Thus, for example, on a Saturday night in the mid-1950s in the city of Santiago in the Dominican Republic, dancers could gravitate toward any number of sites where accordion-based merengue groups would be playing; in Kingston, by contrast, music at lower-class dances would overwhelmingly be provided by sound systems, with their own equipment, personnel, dedicated followers and exclusive record collections. In the 1950s these records would consist primarily of R&B singles acquired from the US; distinctively Jamaican commercial popular music did not really flourish until the early 1960s, with the advent of ska. Subsequently, the primary locus of creativity and production became the recording studio, again in contrast, for example, to the Dominican Republic, whose recording industry stagnated until the 1970s. A distinctive feature of the record industry in Jamaica, since its effective emergence in the 1960s, is that many records have been produced less for mass public purchase than for use by sound systems; this distinction would apply in particular to various sorts of custom-made "specials", often recorded on acetate which wears out after repeated playing.

Related to the orientation toward studio production, and to the relatively late emergence of a local sound, was the vogue of cover versions. Many early ska recordings, including the 1964 hit "My Boy Lollipop", were cover versions of obscure R&B songs, enlivened by the bouncy ska off-beat syncopation. Given the effective absence of copyright restrictions on such local releases, and the fondness for hearing local versions of foreign tunes, the covers elicited neither legal restrictions nor aesthetic disapproval. The trend has continued, with many 1980s "lovers' rock" releases consisting of cover versions of contemporary African American R&B songs, and many modern dancehall songs freely borrowing tunes from various sources.

A step toward the actual use of riddims began in the early 1960s, when producer Clement (Coxson/Coxsone) Dodd of Studio One would record a vocalist like Larry Marshall singing over an existing imported record (Barrow and Dalton 2001, 100). But the most important development was the division of DJ labour between selectors, or the disc jockeys, who played the records and the microphone-wielding deejays who became artists in their own right. From the early sound system days, the deejay might shout at various points into the mic while the selector cued up records, encouraging dancers and "bigging up" himself and the system; in the 1960s, as these interjections – especially as rendered over instrumental recordings – became stylized and valued in themselves, the art of the deejay, and the practice of voicing over riddims, became established. The next step was to make studio recordings of deejays' vocalizations, as was allegedly done first in the late 1960s by King Stitt. More prominently associated with this development, however, was U-Roy (primarily as produced by King Tubby), whose recorded voicings over instrumental tracks of earlier rocksteady hits topped charts in Jamaica in the late 1960s and established the vogue of deejay recordings. The trend was further consolidated in the early 1970s by Big Youth and Dennis Alcapone, and later in the decade by Lone Ranger and Dillinger.

Related to this development was the convention, from around 1970, of having the B-side of a 45 rpm single contain not another song but an instrumental "version" of the song on the A-side; this version might simply consist of the instrumental accompaniment, or it might consist of a "mild" remix in which certain instruments, and sometimes vocal fragments, would drop in and out.[3] One offshoot of this development was the advent of dub (not to be confused with dubplates or dub poetry), comprising radically original remix recordings in which an engineer like King Tubby, Lee "Scratch" Perry or Scientist would dramatically manipulate the sound with faders, reverb and delay. More relevant to this chapter were the more straightforward instrumental B-sides and the uses to which they were put. As sound system selectors discovered from the 1960s or earlier, audiences at dances enjoyed singing along with the B-sides, but more importantly, the sides soon came to be used primarily as back-up tracks for deejays like U-Roy to voice over, offering audiences the pleasure of hearing familiar songs presented in a new manner (see, for example, Katz 2003, 166–67). As Barrow and Dalton (2001) note, "Throughout the 1970s, producers had often followed their big vocal hits with deejays or musicians giving their variations on a theme, employing the same rhythm track. They also sometimes looked further back to the music's past, particularly the rocksteady era, issuing their own cuts of earlier producers' rhythms" (275).

By 1980 the deejay-based riddim-plus-voicing format – whether in the form of a recording or a live deejay "toasting" over a riddim at a dance – had become the dominant idiom of popular music in Jamaica. The "roots" or "classic" reggae of Bob Marley, Jimmy Cliff and others – with its more conventional "song" format of melodies sung over extended chord progressions, often with bridge sections – was certainly familiar to and cherished by most Jamaicans, but since the latter 1970s it had come to constitute an internationally oriented music quite distinct from what the younger generation of Jamaicans favoured and were likely to hear at a Saturday night dance. Instead, the norm was dancehall – an older term now applied to the performance-oriented deejay art – in which a vocalist like Yellowman would voice, in a text-driven style with a simple, often one- or two-note melody, over a familiar riddim. The system prevailed both in record releases and in live shows, where aspiring deejays would line up to voice "pon de mic" while the selector played a vintage riddim over and over. In the early 1980s the competitive spirit of the sound system rivalry extended to record production, and producers rushed to release new deejay voicings over popular riddims. As Barrow and Dalton (2001, 275) note, "By 1983, indeed, it was unusual for anyone to have a Jamaican hit employing a completely original rhythm track."

FIGURE 18.1. The Real Rock riddim.

In the first half of the 1980s these riddims generally consisted of vintage B-side tracks from Coxsone Dodd's Studio One or, to a lesser extent, Duke Reid's Treasure Isle studio. Riddims of some songs, like "Real Rock", "Nanny Goat", "Mad Mad" and "General" (all from 1967) and "Heavenless", "African Beat", and "Full Up" (from 1968), were used this way on innumerable deejay records. (The incomplete listing on reggae-riddims.com, which was a vast and useful resource, cited 269 recordings using Real Rock and 249 using the Answer riddim.) Alternatively, deejay songs used updated re-licks of these classic tracks made by, say, Channel One studio's house band, the Roots Radics, whose renditions of these riddims, influenced by American funk, tended to be more stripped down in texture and often reduced the songs' chord progressions to simple ostinatos. Songs like "Real Rock" that were originally instrumentals lent themselves particularly well to being used by deejays. Invariably, the classic riddims used the familiar beat associated with the roots/classic reggae of Bob Marley, Jimmy Cliff and others, with its distinctive "skank" guitar or keyboard chord on the off-beat of each beat, and the "one drop" drum rhythm with kicks on beats two and four.[4]

In voicing over pre-recorded instrumental riddims, deejays like U-Roy established the basic format of what subsequently became known as dancehall. However, 1970s-style deejaying tended to differ in several respects from the modern dancehall style that more properly emerged in the mid-1980s. A primary distinction, pertaining to the use of classic riddims, involved the typical 1970s practice of deejaying over tracks to whole songs, rather than two- or four-bar ostinatos. In the late 1960s, before instrumental B-sides came into vogue, these songs might either be instrumentals like "Real Rock" or vocal songs. Often a deejay like U-Roy, Dennis Alcapone or Lone Ranger would retain the entire original recording, including, in the case of vocal songs, its sung tracks, inserting his own lines in the gaps between the verses of the original.[5] In other cases, the sung verses of the original might be cut out, but the track would retain the original's choral refrains, with which the deejay might sing in a call-and-response fashion.[6] The lyrics in such deejay versions (as well as the titles) would often relate thematically to those of the original. In some cases, the deejay might be regarded not so much as carrying the whole song, as in modern dancehall, but as following it, interjecting short verses and shouts here and there and interweaving his vocalizations around the original's verses or refrains.

Even when the original vocals were entirely removed, or were absent to begin with, the use of accompaniment tracks to entire songs could oblige the deejay to voice over extended harmonic progressions. Thus, while commonly used songs like "Throw Me Corn", "Real Rock" or "Never Let Go" contain only simple repeated chordal ostinatos, others like the popular "Satta Massagana" have more varied chord progressions and even bridge sections.[7] Dancehall deejays, to be sure, "sing" in the sense that they intone their verses using specific pitches (even if often only one or two notes); in this sense dancehall contrasts with hip-hop, where vocals more commonly resemble speaking than singing. At the same time, dancehall deejays do not necessarily cultivate the art of singing per se, and they are generally distinguished in emic discourse from "singers" like, for example, Barrington Levy (or, for that matter, Bob Marley), or from "singjays", who do both. (Hence our preference in this chapter for the standard emic terms "toast", "voice" and "chant" to describe the deejays' technique.)

Accordingly, deejays from the late 1970s to the early 1990s tended to voice in simple two- or three-note melodies or even virtual "reciting tones", such as are shown in figures 18.2a, 18.2b, 18.2c and the slightly wider-ranged 18.2d. These tunes easily cohere with the sorts of chordal ostinatos common in most reggae riddims, which typically alternate a major tonic chord with ii, IV, V or bVII. As dancehall matured, the practice – first appearing in the late 1960s – of using riddims made especially for deejaying gradually became the norm. Many of these riddims, as mentioned, were crisper, minimalist re-licks of vintage riddims – or of their fundamental chordal ostinatos – especially as produced by Channel One and the house bands the Revolutionaries and the Roots Radics. In the years around 1980, Coxsone Dodd produced many re-licks of his own vintage Studio One riddims. Paralleling this development was the change in deejay style from the loose, fragmentary phrasings of U-Roy and his contemporaries to the sort of more rhythmic, steady, "on-the-beat" chanting, using melodies such as those shown in figure 18.2; this

FIGURES 18.2A–18.2D. Four conventional dancehall melodies, typical of the 1980s and early 1990s; 18.2a and 18.2b are typical of verses, and 18.2c and 18.2d of refrains.

sort of phrasing, which appeared in the 1970s voicings of Lone Ranger, became standard in the early-1980s deejaying of Yellowman, Toyan and Eek-a-Mouse. The influence of rap is not to be discounted in this regard, especially as a Jamaican cover of the seminal "Rapper's Delight" of 1979 appeared only a few months later, in Welton Irie's "Hotter Reggae Music" (1980).

An oft-noted landmark in the production of riddims occurred in 1985 with the release of Prince/King Jammy's and Wayne Smith's "Under Mi Sleng Teng", whose riddim was generated entirely on digital keyboards, including, according to some accounts, an adaptation of a pre-packaged rhythm on a Casio. The rendering of this riddim as figure 18.3 does not attempt to do justice to its synthetic-sounding timbres (especially the overtone-rich bass). Sleng Teng was seminal in various ways, aside from coming to be used as a riddim itself in a few hundred songs. Sleng Teng further consolidated the trend toward the new production of riddims based on short ostinatos rather than reliance on vintage B-side tracks, with their occasionally problematic chord progressions. Further, with its catchy and thoroughly novel-sounding timbres, Sleng Teng promoted a departure from the overused Studio One classics, whose dominance in the earlier years has been cited as a sign of conservatism, or less charitably, lack of imagination (see, for example, Barrow and Dalton 2001, 261, 275). Third, in popularizing the digital production of riddims (the trademark of what in the United Kingdom is called "ragga"), Sleng Teng showed how any aspiring producer with a keyboard synthesizer, sequencer and drum machine, or access to these, could generate a new riddim, without having to spend money on studio time or studio musicians. Although sampling per se only became common in dancehall in the 1990s, the use of digital techniques has greatly increased with the rise of personal computers, music software and more sophisticated synthesizers. While posing a challenge to larger studios like Channel One, the digital era has also led to an exponential rise in the number of studios, large and small, and increased demand for keyboardists. (Meanwhile, as for Wayne Smith's voicing on Jammy's riddim, the song also perpetuated the dancehall tradition of adapting earlier tunes and phrases, with the catch phrase "Under me sleng teng" reworking both Yellowman's earlier "Under me fat ting" as well as Barrington Levy's "Under mi sensi".)

FIGURE 18.3: The Sleng Teng riddim.

RIDDIMS AND VOICINGS IN MODERN DANCEHALL

Since the latter 1980s, the dancehall scene has not undergone revolutionary changes, whether in styles, performance and production practices, or other parameters, such that one can speak of a relatively cohesive "modern" period commencing around those years. As before, roots reggae songs – whether classics of Marley et al. or newer releases by artists like Beres Hammond – continue to occupy a niche in the music scene, being cherished as evergreens and still played on radio and by sound systems at clubs and "oldies" sessions. Moreover, roots riddims (as in figure 18.1) and "culture" tunes periodically crest in popularity, captivating even the "hardcore" dancehall massive for a season or two. However, youth tastes, concerts, clubs and record production are overwhelmingly oriented toward contemporary dancehall (and hip-hop from the United States).

The riddim-plus-voicing system continues to prevail in dancehall, whether in concerts, dances or on recordings. "Live" events occur in a variety of formats, with their own conventional uses of riddims. At neighbourhood sound-system dances in Jamaica, deejays, whether aspiring or established, may still take their turn "pon de mic", voicing over pre-recorded riddims, although there is considerably less of this sort of live toasting than in the 1970s and 1980s, when a deejay might also be closely associated with a particular sound system, as was Ninjaman with the Killamanjaro system.[8] In such live contexts a deejay might be obliged to toast over whatever riddim is being played by the selector, rather than requesting a particular riddim or providing his own. For their part, established deejays who perform stage shows are generally accompanied by live musicians – typically trap drummer, bassist and keyboardist – who will endeavour to reproduce the riddims used in the recordings of the songs performed. While recordings in other music genres may aim to present the ambience of a live performance, the opposite aesthetic can be seen in dancehall stage shows, where the band may attempt to imitate studio or record-selector effects like the sound of a record being rewound (or "wheeled-back"/"pulled-up"). Most typically at a dance club or street dance, music is provided by a sound system, whose selector may play a potpourri of roots-reggae classics, contemporary dancehall hits and custom-made remixes of these (often alongside hip-hop, R&B and even disco). Often, in a practice called "juggling", the selector may play a medley of several songs which use the same riddim. Another "live" format is the unique institution of the sound clash, in which rival sound systems compete, primarily by playing "dubplates"; these are short custom-made recordings (traditionally acetates) in which, typically, a deejay will sing part of a known song of his or hers, to the same melody and riddim but with new lyrics which "big up" the sound system paying for the plate.[9]

Recordings themselves come in a variety of formats. The "classic" mode of vinyl 7-inch singles, with an instrumental B-side, is still marketed in Jamaica today, to some extent as before, mostly for use by sound systems and also for international disc jockeys and reggae connoisseurs. Cassettes, whether legitimate or pirate, were popular in the 1980s and 1990s but are less encountered today.[10] Most common in the 1990s and early 2000s, both in Jamaica and elsewhere, were compact discs, as variously released by foreign-based labels – especially Greensleeves (UK) and VP (New York) – by small- and middle-scale

Jamaican producers like Penthouse, by sound systems and mixtape disc jockeys and, last but not least, by unauthorized "pirate" producers. Most pirate CDs were compilations of songs by various artists, including many songs legitimately released only on 7-inch Jamaican singles and thus often difficult to acquire in other formats. Pirate CDs, often put out by local sound systems or disc jockeys providing music at parties, also sometimes have the most informative liner notes, in the sense that they often specify the riddim in parentheses after the song title; often the songs are grouped by riddims, evoking the "juggling" effect popular in live performance. Such CDs typically contain only a minute or so of each song, such that sixty or seventy songs can be included. Greensleeves, VP and smaller labels also released many single-riddim CDs, featuring up to twenty different vocalists on the same riddim. Individual-artist CDs or albums, although the norm in most popular music cultures, have been the exception in dancehall. Thus, top artists like Beenie Man and Bounty Killer might record thirty or forty songs a year but produce a full CD of their own only every two or three years, the remainder of their output instead appearing on various compilations.

As in the 1980s, the vast majority of songs are set to established riddims – typically one of the dozen or so riddims that are popular at any given time.[11] Generally, it is only individual-artist CDs – especially of top-rankers like Buju Banton – that feature songs that do not use established riddims. Classic riddims like Real Rock and Sleng Teng retain the names of the original songs they accompanied, though occasionally a re-lick can prove popular enough to lend its name to the riddim as well. The Mad Mad riddim, for instance, is also known as the Diseases, Johnny Dollar and Golden Hen after three popular songs recorded on subsequent versions of it. Most modern riddims, however, are composed independently of any given song or voicing and are given original names by their creators.[12]

The riddims themselves may vary in origin. Vintage classics like Real Rock still occasionally surface, whether in their original form, or in re-licks by Coxsone Dodd, King Jammy or subsequent producers. However, since the early 1990s the classic roots-reggae rhythm, with its moderate tempo skank (ca. 60 bpm), has become less common than a faster 3+3+2 beat, as popularized by a new generation of producers. Prominent among these are such figures as Gussie Clark, whose hi-tech Anchor Studio products have been known for their glossy, to some extent internationally oriented sound; the veteran duo of Sly and Robbie, who have long moved from being top studio musicians to producing their own riddims on drum machines and computers; and Bobby Digital, who graduated from working as an engineer at Jammy's to producing digital roots riddims and slick re-licks for Jamaica's most popular vocalists. The late 1990s saw the ascent of crossover-sensitive and computer-savvy producers such as Dave Kelly and Jeremy Harding. The ranks of producers have swelled in recent years with the advent of small, computer-based studios. The Greensleeves and VP riddim compilation series came to be dominated by young producers such as Stephen "Lenky" Marsden, Donovan "Vendetta/Don Corleone" Bennett and Cordel "Scatta" Burrell.

The most popular digital studio staple is the Korg Triton keyboard; the Akai MPC is also common, especially for composing drum patterns. Software programs, especially synthesizers and sequencers, such as FL Studio, have increasingly come into use, and digital multitracking software such as Pro Tools has, for practical and financial reasons, superseded analogue tape, despite the opinion of many Jamaican engineers, producers and artists that digital sound is cold and harsh compared to the warm, round sound that tape takes on, especially when performances are recorded "hot" or "in the red". Acoustic instruments are still used, however, and a percussionist/producer like Sly Dunbar takes pride in using drums or drum pads instead of or in addition to relying on programmed sequences and effects (see Bradley 2001, 513).

Compositionally, the riddim generally precedes the voicing, especially in the modern period. Most typically, a producer – more specifically, a "beat-maker" (who "builds" riddims, as opposed to the person who pays for the studio time or recording media) – generates a riddim and then contracts a given deejay to voice over it. The deejay, presumably after hearing the riddim, must come up with a song, that is, lyrics and a tune. Deejays are closely identified with their lyrics, even though some verses, especially in the case of prolific vocalists like Bounty Killer, are sometimes ghost written, or perhaps openly authored by a producer/songwriter like Dave Kelly. Alternately, in the case of a particularly popular and "hot" riddim, a deejay might contract the producer to voice on the song, perhaps offering terms more favourable to the latter.

The riddim-plus-voicing system engenders its own idiosyncratic marketing conventions. As mentioned, most songs appear – initially, at least – on 7-inch singles in Jamaica (which are shipped abroad to the selector and connoisseur market) and/or on compilation CDs, including Greensleeves and VP single-riddim CDs. Although the singles sell primarily to sound systems rather than individual consumers, sound-system sales can easily exceed two thousand, constituting a decent profit for an inexpensively produced record. Various factors and strategies may condition marketing procedures. A label like Greensleeves might limit the number of songs it would release on a given riddim in order to promote a given song and CD using it. Such restrictions seem to have been enacted, initially, at least, with some of Elephant Man's songs, such as "Pon de River", whose riddims are effectively exclusive to him. Similarly, "Selecta" of jamrid.com observed that the Penthouse label seldom releases more than five songs on a given riddim:

> I would think this is a planned strategy. If you have a stable of artists that you are building, as Germain has done with Buju for example, it is probably wise not to have too many artists on one riddim, because when the riddim is played [that is, at a dance] the time will be shared between the different cuts and if there is 12–15 cuts very little will be played from each cut, especially when played on radio. People won't be able to discover artist if he just appears a few seconds in some sort of megamix styled playing.[13]

Bounty Killer has voiced the same reservation about the desirability, from a marketing perspective, of having too many songs on a riddim: "Having ten man on the rhythm shorten the lifespan of your song, cause they have to shorten the play of your song to give a next man a play [i.e., in juggling at a club]. If you alone on the rhythm, they have to play your song till they tired of it. If they want that rhythm again, they come back to it."[14] The vogue of single-riddim CDs is also a controversial strategy, with some critics arguing that they debase the market by undercutting the more significant individual-artist CDs, while others applaud the sense of creative competition that they can engender.

STYLE AND STRUCTURE

Just as the timbres used in riddims vary, the composite rhythmic structures of dancehall riddims are similarly less standardized than are, for example, the rhythms of mainstream merengue, salsa or roots reggae. Thus, for example, Clappas (2003) has a distinctive swing-style triplet feel, Military resembles a march and Joyride is like a medium-tempo polka. Nevertheless, in the period of 1990–2003, most riddims feature a basic 3+3+2 pulse, at a tempo of around 90–110 bpm (although several songs in recent years have been faster). This pulse is far less prominent in the standard roots reggae rhythm, although it can be found in mid-century mento. In fact, in some cases, it is much closer to the rhythm of contemporary Trinidadian soca, which is, however, usually faster (ca. 130–60 bpm). The quintessential dancehall riddim, as boiled down in a minimalist fashion characteristic of the 1990s, can be skeletally represented as shown in figure 18.4. The chart shown in figure 18.5 schematizes the default dancehall drum pattern of the late 1980s and early 1990s (as in the Bam Bam riddim), which also has become the basic beat of reggaeton, as it was during this period that dancehall gained massive popularity in Panama, New York and Puerto Rico.

Many riddims, rather than being indefinitely repeating ostinatos, have two or three different sections, in which instrumental sounds appear or drop out.[15] These sections may be varied and looped in different ways for particular voicings; typically, some "instruments" might drop out during verses and return in refrains, but arrangements are often irregular. In general, in a practice growing out of the dub tradition, form is enhanced or even created by bringing various layers in and out over the course of the track. Nowadays, producers like Lenky Marsden may make customized versions of his riddims (as with Diwali) to match individual songs, adding melodic lines that mirror the melodies the vocalists sing and punctuating particular passages with "stop-time"-like interjections of silence and other effects. A few riddims foreground acoustic instruments, like Drum Song, with its "nyabinghi style" drumming, or Equinoxx, with its (squeaky) nylon-stringed guitar. More common, however, since the Sleng Teng revolution, are futuristic-sounding digital timbres.

Many riddims since the early 1990s (like Punnany, Pepper Seed and Mud Up) have been minimalist and spare, often consisting only or predominantly of percussion, but

	1				2				3				4			
kick drum:	x			x					x			x				
snare:							x								x	
hi-hat:	x		x		x		x		x		x		x		x	

FIGURE 18.4. The quintessential dancehall riddim.

	1				2				3				4			
kick drum:	X				X				X				X			
snare:				X			X					X			X	
hi-hat:	X		X		X		X		X		X		X		X	

FIGURE 18.5. The default dancehall drum pattern of the late 1980s and early 1990s.

FIGURE 18.6. The Diwali riddim.

many others, especially in recent years, have tended to be more elaborate and densely layered in their textures. As such, they are quite resistant to staff notation, although figure 18.6's schematic representation of the popular Diwali may give some idea of the sorts of sonorities that can be involved. As with the notation of Sleng Teng in figure 18.3, this transcription is unable to do justice to the synthesized timbres of the various parts. Other riddims have simpler textures and more clearly recognizable hooks, as in the case of Bam Bam (most popularized in the Chaka Demus/Pliers song "Murder She Wrote"), with its guitar riff: //:FF-C Eb C Eb - ://.

While the structure of dancehall songs merits more expansive analysis than can be provided here, a few general observations can be made. Most songs alternate verses and refrains. Before the 1990s, when a small set of relatively simple stock melodies were in vogue (like those in figure 18.2), there might not be a dramatic melodic contrast between the verse and the refrain, which would thus be distinguished primarily by the recurring and catchy text phrase (for example, as in the case of "Under Mi Sleng Teng"). More modern productions, particularly as emerging in the 1990s, generally present a greater contrast and thus have a more clearly defined structure. Typically, the verses are voiced using a simple, static melody, often based around one or two pitches, while the refrain is more melodic and is sometimes sung by the deejay and a backup chorus and frequently "doubled" by a synthesizer of some sort in order to provide further contrast.

In the 1970s and 1980s, deejay songs might be highly irregular in their phrase lengths, reflecting the spontaneity and informality of live toasting at a dance. By the late 1980s, however, song forms became much more regular, typically with eight- or sixteen-bar verses and choruses. This trend may reflect a shift in the dancehall industry toward an emphasis on recordings, which at this point were proving increasingly viable in metropolitan centres of the Jamaican diaspora and elsewhere. As the recording-as-commodity became a priority for producers, deejays receded from the sound-system scene and increasingly spent their time in studios. Today, selectors man the mics, while deejays, who are now full-time recording artists, put on concerts alongside singers and accompanied by bands.

Different songs using a given riddim can vary dramatically not only in their thematic content, but in their style and general character, as can be verified by listening to any single-riddim compilation or a "juggling" medley on a pirate CD. Thus, for example, songs on the Diwali riddim include Bounty Killer's hard-driving, empathic "Sufferer", Sean Paul's bouncy party anthem "Get Busy" and Wayne Wonder's tuneful, romantic pop crossover hit "No Letting Go" (with the riddim mixed in at a low volume below other instruments).[16] Similarly, the venerable Real Rock undergirds songs as different as the Clash's punk-style "Armagideon Time" and Sanchez's version of the ballad "If I Ever Fall in Love" (discussed below), not to mention a few hundred other settings.

"OUT-OF-TUNE" SONGS AND THE INDEPENDENCE OF RIDDIM AND VOICING

As we have suggested, one of the most distinctive and unique features of the riddim-plus-voicing system is the relative independence of the two entities. A given riddim may be set to dozens of different voicings, and conversely, a given voicing might, in various contexts, be set to different riddims. Thus, for example, Elephant Man's "Jook Gal", which originally appeared on a nameless hip-hop beat produced by Lil Jon, was popularly remixed and reissued over the Coolie Dance riddim. Similarly, as mentioned above, deejays at a live stage show might be obliged to voice their songs over whatever current popular riddims the selector is playing. Further, CDs of remixes – especially "underground" ones – circulate widely, often combining voicings with riddims other than their original ones. Such remixes often take advantage of a capella voicings which might be recorded as vocal tracks over riddims or as dubplates but then come to circulate on their own, often without the deejay's control.

One particularly conspicuous indicator of the independence of riddim and voicing is the way the two entities may occasionally be more or less "out-of-tune" with each other. Most commonly, this phenomenon occurs as a result of the deejay relying on variants of the same simple melodies, such as are shown in figure 18.2, which may or may not fit perfectly with the chords or tonality of the riddim. As we have seen, 1980s deejays often essentially ignored the extended chord progressions of riddims deriving from songs like "Satta Massagana". Even when newer riddims with simple chordal ostinatos came to predominate, tonal irregularities still occurred. Thus, for example, Papa San, in voicing his "Dancehall Good to We" (1991),[17] uses a simple tune akin to that shown in figure 18.2c, with a prominent major third degree; however, the riddim (Just Be Good to Me) is in a minor rather than a major key, oscillating clearly between minor tonic and subdominant chords.

A common and somewhat different sort of incongruity can be heard on Buju Banton's popular album *Mr Mention* (1993), some of whose songs use variants of the melody shown in figure 18.2d. This melody strongly suggests a C major tonality and is sung accordingly (in appropriate transpositions) on a few other songs from that album. However, in "Woman No Fret", while he sings the melody from the starting and central pitch of C, the riddim (the vintage Nanny Goat) consists of a I-I-IV-V ostinato in its original key of F major. The melody's central pitch of C is, of course, the fifth scalar degree of F major and was presumably chosen by Banton (who is a more "musical" singer than many deejays) because it fit his range and was sufficiently consonant. To an outsider's ear, however, the effect may seem odd, as can be appreciated by playing figure 18.2d on the piano while adding the chordal accompaniment: / F / Bb C7 F- /. In this case, as in many others, Banton has simply applied his stock melody to a pitch level that sounded roughly, and sufficiently, harmonious to him.[18] A third, and similar kind of irregularity can be heard in several songs of Shabba Ranks, who, with all due respect, might be regarded as particularly casual in terms of matching pitch to accompaniment. Thus, for example, in his "Fist-a-Ris",[19] he commences his simple tune – resembling the one shown in figure 18.2a – in consonance with the riddim's clear A major bass and keyboard ostinato but subsequently drifts upwards, through B-flat, then B-natural, such that by the end of the song he is singing the tune in C major, while the riddim resolutely reiterates its clear A major ostinato. In some cases, the incongruity is not a simple question of an individual DJ's voicing but involves more elaborate singing, as in a chorus rendered in two- or three-part harmony which, when heard against the riddim, may sound dissonant to observers accustomed to mainstream Western tonality.[20] In some cases, these irregularities can occur when a producer making a (typically underground) remix (mis) matches an a capella voicing with a riddim in a different key. In other cases, where the recording appears to be legitimate, the combination is enigmatic.

Incompatibilities may also occur in the case of cover versions of songs. Thus, for example, Sanchez recorded a cover version of Shai's song "If I Ever Fall in Love", which, in its original a capella vocal version, clearly outlines an extended chordal progression (for example, the harmonies of its refrain proceed, in Bb minor: Gb-F-Gb-F-Gb-F-Bbsus4-B7). However, while Sanchez sings the original melody faithfully enough, he sets it to the simple chordal vamp of the Real Rock riddim, with its simple and tonally incongruous Bb(major)-Ab-Bb-Ab ostinato (as shown in figure 18.1).[21]

In this chapter, the purpose of the discussion is not to make a digressive point about dancehall aesthetics but to show how a tolerance for "dissonance" both reflects and enables a relative autonomy of riddim and voicing. In order to be effective, the two must match in tempo, aspects of phrase structure and, perhaps *ideally*, tonality. But the very tolerance of tonal "incompatibilities" both enables and is a product of the practice of coupling riddims and voicings that have their own independent origins, uses and sometimes tonalities.

RIDDIM AESTHETICS

The "riddim system", with its distinctive form of song construction, has engendered its own aesthetic norms and arguments, as reflected in various forms of emic discourse voiced by assorted fans, critics, journalists and bloggers. One category of discourse comprises commentary on riddims and voicings themselves. Discussions of DJs and voicings tend to be circumscribed by the difficulty of describing – whether in words or via notation – the expressive nuances that are crucial to the art; hence, in some contexts, the lyrics may receive more critical attention than they might merit, insofar as they may be valued by dancers primarily for their rhythmic flow rather than semantic message. For their part, riddims may certainly be praised or disparaged by hardcore fans and bloggers. A few fanzine excerpts may give some flavour of the kind of discourse encountered:

> [The Ching Chong riddim] jumps right into a seriously bubbling mix of up tempo drum tracks and orchestral string punches. Ching Chong is a perfect crossover riddim in the Dave Kelly vein: Clean, up-tempo with just enough rude bwoy flavor to remind you of some dirty Kingston shit. This first time I played this riddim out, I brought it in from the "Fiesta" riddim and everything flowed lovely – All the Yardies will love the hardcore tunes on this riddim and the crossover crowds won't blink an eye when you mix it in from Diwali.[22]
>
> The remaining tracks are efforts for the brand new "Boasy Gal" riddim, presently one of the hottest and most anticipated riddims in Jamaica. The riddim caused such excitement on the dance floors that it led to the introduction of the new "Boasy Gal" dance. There's even an island-wide competition to find the best "Boasy Gal" dancer.[23]

A different level of aesthetic discourse comprises commentary on the riddim-plus-voicing system as a whole. Such commentary could be seen as a subset of general assessments of dancehall, which, while naturally cherished by fans, is criticized by many (especially older Jamaicans) for its frequent vulgarity, sexism, obsessive homophobia and glorification of violence. Disparaging perspectives on the riddim system focus on a number of issues, several of which are presented in Lloyd Bradley's informative, if aesthetically conservative, book, *This Is Reggae Music* (2001). Bradley quotes vocalist Dennis Harris, who deprecates dancehall as the "karaoke phase" of reggae:

> The whole thing about groups fell apart, the whole thing about learning your craft fell apart . . . just buy a Casio, plug it in in the studio and chat what you wanted to chat . . . Everybody used the same programs, you had no group input any more . . . And they don't even rework [a riddim] like it used to be, building a new track on an existing riddim, because it's so

> minimalist it's exactly the same . . . [All you need is] just a playback, and one microphone, and one man to chat some rubbish on it. (501–2)

Bradley quotes at length Gussie Clarke, who despite being a leading dancehall producer himself, articulates familiar criticisms of the riddim dominance. The system of having dozens of deejays sing on the same riddim, he argues, breeds a lack of creativity, a situation of more followers than leaders, more reproducers than producers and more versions than originals. It also promotes, he asserts, a spirit of rivalry that generates not originality but decadence: "With all this sort of competitiveness, the only way people could get the better of each other is by being more extreme. They can't do this by writing better songs, because this isn't about good songs. The riddims start to get more and more raw, and the lyrics of so many of the new records is just about slackness and gun and that" (510–11). Bradley goes on to quote Sly Dunbar, who laments how the availability of synthesizers and digital production techniques has generated a torrent of amateurish producers who lack musical training, talent or imagination (512–13). Kingston-based producer Mikey Irving, as observed in a recording session by Marshall, seems to agree with Dunbar – at least about the lack of musical training – but also recognizes that dancehall aesthetics have come to revolve around these less conventional approaches to rhythm, harmony and form. "The difficult thing about this kind of music", he said, referring to contemporary dancehall as well as hip-hop, "is that you have to fake illiteracy".

As might be imagined, there are many (including Bradley) who are quick to counter by pointing out the distinctive merits of the riddim/voicing system. While some might disparage deejays as uncreative for singing over stock riddims, it should be remembered that most of the top deejays are remarkably prolific, often recording thirty or forty songs a year (not to mention dozens of dubplates). Audiences also derive a particular pleasure from hearing several radically different voicings on a given riddim, especially on the dance floor, where the riddim generates an ongoing groove. Singing over different riddims can also offer its own pleasures to the deejay, as in the case of "Nathan", who opined on the versionist.com forum, "Personally, I get my kicks from the fact that I can step on a stage and put my songs over any riddim. That's where I'm good at, that's my music."

Another merit frequently voiced by fans is the profoundly democratic nature of the system, in which obscure, amateur, up-and-coming deejays compete, as it were, on a level playing field with established stars. No one can hide behind the skill of the producer, or rely on their good looks or on music-industry promotion. As one fan wrote on the futureproducers.com forum, "All the artists being able to lay down vocals behind any given riddim is what makes dancehall what it is. And sometimes the smaller artist may have the big tune on the riddim even if Beenie [Man] or Bounty [Killer] is on the same riddim. That is what makes dancehall more of a fair competition than hip hop."

Bradley describes how this populist character pervades the sound system dance scene:

> The beauty of deejaying has always been the lack of investment needed for talent to show up: even the smallest sound systems will attract their share of outgoing types who'll beg the operator to let them *hol' the mic, nuh*, and all that is needed is lyrics, an ability to ride a riddim, verbal dexterity, and a quick mind. No cash up front for studio time or for backing

> musicians; or, as would be likely, no need for a producer's patronage. And as for auditioning, the crowd would soon let you know if you were rubbish. Practically anybody could get up and have a go, and if a newcomer started seriously rocking the set down there on the corner, the bigger operations would soon snap him up. From which, the recording studio was just one (small) step beyond. (2001, 504)

The recycling of a riddim, while in itself arguably "uncreative", serves at the same time to foreground the very uniqueness and creativity of an individual voicing, which is so readily differentiated from other artists' voicings. Thus, intrinsic to the riddim/voicing system is the pleasure of hearing how different deejays will perform over the same raw material. In that sense the reuse of riddims, far from being an unfortunate drawback of the system, is an essential aspect of it. To quote another futureproducers.com fan: "I like to hear diff artist on the same riddim. IMHO [in my humble opinion], this is part of dancehall and it should remain so. I want to hear capleton, ele, assasin, mega banton, cecile, wayne marshall, and the others on the same riddim. After that, I want to say, 'PULL IT UP SELECTA'."

CONCLUSIONS: RIDDIMS AS A CREATIVE COMMONS?

From one perspective, the riddim/voicing system is not entirely new. Virtually all established music genres, whether folk, classical or popular, operate by drawing from and building upon an extant body of raw materials, synthesizing original creations from extant sources of inspiration. Many folk music genres worldwide rely on stock melodies and rhythms, with which audiences are expected to be generally familiar. The riddim/voicing system, in this respect, can be seen as one particular instance – albeit an especially distinctive one – of a worldwide practice of using stock accompaniment patterns. These are the ways that music and culture work, and the borrowing/signifying practices in dancehall simply signal a more explicit acknowledgment and embrace of the underlying processes of artistic creation and cultural production.

At the same time, however, dancehall is quite unique in the relative autonomy of the backing track from the "song", and the way that the riddim can take on an independent life of its own, both through being used with different melodies and, in many cases, being rearticulated in the form of fresh studio re-licks. The instances in which a given voicing may itself be set to different riddims even more dramatically illustrate a remarkable detachability of components which, in most world popular music, are generally more linked as integral elements of a given song.

As we have seen, the riddim system evolved in a very specific set of conditioning circumstances, characterized by the relative absence of copyright laws, a lively small-scale record production industry and a distinctive performance scene which combined live vocalizing with use of vinyl records. By the time that certain copyright norms eventually came into effect, and aspects of both the live and recording scene had changed, the riddim/voicing system had developed its own aesthetic logic, integrity and sophistication. Such, indeed, was the creative vitality of the evolving system that some of its innovations predated – and to some extent influenced – developments in the equally dynamic and demographically far larger African American music culture. Thus, for example, while Jamaican musicians have long found inspiration in black American music, Jamaican DJs were voicing over records and using turntables as musical instruments at least a decade before their counterparts in the Bronx. More dramatically, the way that riddims and voicings are detached and recombined in dancehall has been an important precursor to and a direct influence on the vogue of remixes and "mash-ups", especially as they now abound in hip-hop and R&B. The socio-musical circumstances of the Jamaican crucible have been unique, but they also can be seen as one efflorescence of the kind of musical creativity accompanying a broader condition of postmodern, secondary orality embracing new technologies.

A concomitant of this secondary orality, as intensified by globalization and mass access to tools like computers and the internet, has been the postulation and, to some extent, genuine growth of a "creative commons" of artistic materials which defy conventional copyright practices. The multiple recycling of riddims, with some qualifications, constitutes a remarkable instance of this sort of phenomenon. Insofar as the notion of the creative commons implies a set of raw materials which are accessible to all artists, without the confines of copyright, dancehall is only exemplary to a limited degree. It is true that especially in the relative free-for-all of the 1970s and early 1980s, many riddims were effectively treated by musicians and producers as if they were in the public domain. Even today, riddims widely circulate via dubplates and unauthorized "underground" remixes and mash-ups which are, in their own way, dynamic rather than destructive parts of the reggae scene. However, since the 1980s the use of riddims, especially on internationally marketed commercial recordings, has come to be incorporated into a broader system of international music copyright. There are those, of course, who decry this system, and who might argue that riddims are precisely the sort of resource that should be in the public domain. Others might not necessarily denounce the notion of copyright itself but would criticize the way that ownership of Jamaican music, including riddims, has so often tended to rest with financiers (if not outright thugs) rather than the creative musicians themselves. Still others might argue that, at the very least, a system of compulsory licensing should be established for riddims – and for samples in hip-hop – such that a musician would not need formal permission to use a riddim (or sample) but would simply have to pay the owner at a fixed statutory rate, as is the case with cover versions of songs.

Aside from the complexities of ownership, there is another, broader sense in which the riddim system already constitutes a remarkable instance of a creative commons. The notion of such a commons could imply an aesthetic sensibility, in which listeners not only tolerate but relish the particular sorts of recycling and repetition that might in other contexts be seen as uncreative or plagiaristic. Such recycling can be enjoyed precisely because of the way it can serve to highlight the individuality and distinctive creativity of the "original" aspect of the song, that is, the voicing. Similarly, working with the raw material of the voicing provides the artist with particular rewards and challenges.

The riddim system in this sense prefigures the entire aesthetic of the remix, less in the quirky and often simplistic combination of two pre-existing entities (for example, the mashup) than in the artful creation of a new entity to accompany a given raw material. Hip-hop and other offshoots (including jungle, drum'n'bass, UK garage and grime, modern bhangra and reggaeton) have maintained and, with digital sampling, even intensified these practices. These genres show that, as unique as the Jamaican system is, it is also simply a more explicit and dramatic example of what is increasingly becoming a generalized form of popular music production in the age of mechanical, and now digital, reproduction.

ACKNOWLEDGEMENTS

While assuming full responsibility for the contents of this chapter, the authors wish to thank Derrick Ashong, Mikey Irving, Dave Hucker, "Mr Marlowe", Ramsey Foster, Hopeton Browne and other informants too numerous to mention.

NOTES

1. The term *dancehall* in Jamaican parlance has a broad set of significations. In this chapter, we focus on the music that has been played in the Jamaican dancehall over the last several decades. Unfortunately, given space constraints, we do not address aspects of dance, space, fashion, phenomenology or other "extra-musical", but crucial, features of dancehall. See Stolzoff (2000) for an ethnography and social history of the Jamaican dancehall; see also Stanley Niaah (2004) for an article which explicitly focuses on the role of dance, space and bodily performance in the dancehall, as well as White (1984).
2. A few recent hip-hop songs have featured versions or remixes of Jamaican riddims, including uses of the Diwali riddim by Lumidee, Busta Rhymes, 50 Cent and Fabolous and of the Coolie Dance riddim by Nina Sky and Pitbull. Usher and Jennifer Lopez have both sung on the same Rich Harrison beat (released as Lopez's "Get Right" [2005]), but the Usher recording was not released.
3. The term "version" is used inconsistently in Jamaican music discourse to mean: (1) an instrumental side of a record, that is, what we refer to in this chapter as the "riddim"; (2) the different, fresh recordings or "re-licks" of particular riddims (for example, the Studio One and Channel One "versions" of the Mad Mad riddim); (3) a song (that is, an original voicing) recorded on a given riddim (for example, Bounty Killer's "Sufferer", recorded on the Diwali riddim). Barrow and Dalton (2001), for example, use "version" in this latter sense repeatedly (for example, 275). In this chapter we avoid this ambiguous usage, referring to these latter entities as "songs".
4. Funk influence may also account for the tendency for these early 1980s re-licks to shift to a kick-on-one/three, snare-on-two/four drum pattern.
5. See, for example, Dennis Alcapone's "Nanny Version", sung over "Nanny Goat" (on *Forever Version* [Heartbeat CD 3505]) or his "Ba-Ba-Ri-Ba Skank", over "I Can't Hide" (on Dennis Alcapone, *Ba-Ba-Ri-Ba Skank* [Lagoon LG2-1048]).

6. See, for example, U-Roy's "Natty Rebel", sung over "Soul Rebel" (both 1976), on Frontline Records.
7. See recordings of this song on the Abyssinians and Friends, *Tree of Satta: Volume 1*. Blood and Fire BAFCD 045.
8. Aside from "stage shows", which are events specifically intended for live DJ performance, the DJ as a soundman has largely been phased out of the sound system scene. Interestingly enough, the void has to some extent been filled by the selector, who no longer is necessarily the same person who cues and pulls-up (repeats) the records. Popular contemporary selectors, such as Tony Matterhorn or Fire Links, are major attractions in their own right, drawing thousands to the dances they headline. They tend to scream over the riddims, announcing the tune, calling for pull-ups and exhorting the crowd. Typically, while shouting at the audience, the selector – with one hand on the mic and the other on the volume knob – turns down the underlying track to make himself heard, often doing so at odd and unexpected moments.
9. Dubplates are generally recorded at small, inexpensive studios dedicated to that function; they use pre-recorded versions of well-known riddims and increasingly employ digital sampling to provide the desired accompaniment. Seen as an integral part of the reggae industry locally and internationally, the dubplate business coexists peacefully with more "authorized" industry niches.
10. Note, the "today" used in this chapter reflects the time of writing: circa 2005. Media formats have largely shifted toward the digital in Jamaica since.
11. See Pacey Foster's website, libraryofvinyl.blogspot.com/2005/06/six-degrees-of-reggae-riddims.html, for a computer-graphic representation of patterns of riddim use by different artists. All websites cited in this chapter were accessed in July 2005.
12. Whether or not the names are printed on CD covers, dancehall fans generally know the names of the popular riddims at any given time.
13. See his text for Heads Roll. In the text for the Splash riddim, he speculates that Greensleeves has limited the number of songs on that riddim in order to promote Mr Vegas's song using it (see text regarding Splash).
14. From an interview in www.reggaematic.com, as cited in jamrid.com.
15. "Selecta", on jamrid.com, observes that several riddims seem to have three sections; see his text on Grass Cyat
16. Two of these are on *Diwali* (Greensleeves GRLCD 727).
17. On *Dancehall Superhits* (Powwow 1952-77425-4).
18. A more familiar, if indistinct, example of this phenomenon is the voicing of Chaka Demus on the hit "Murder She Wrote". Insofar as his tune resembles figure 18.2c, but sung from the fifth rather than tonic degree, the major third (or is it a fourth here?) is dissonant with the flat seventh of the Bam Bam riddim (shown in example 5).
19. On *As Raw as Ever* (Sony ET47310).
20. For example, the song "Mama", by Ghost, on the *Mad Instruments* riddim (on Fire Island 7-inch single, flip side of Elephant Man's "Mad Instruments Dance").
21. "Fall in Love", on Sanchez, *One in a Million* (VP Records).
22. From a review by the Deadly Dragon sound system, on http://deadlydragonsound.com/v3_writing.php.
23. On http://reggae-vibes.com/rev_var/latino.htm.

REFERENCES

Barrow, S., and P. Dalton. 2001. *Reggae: The Rough Guide*. London: Penguin.

Bradley, L. 2001. *This is Reggae Music: The Story of Jamaica's Music*. New York: Grove Press.

Katz, D. 2003. *Solid Foundation: An Oral History of Reggae*. New York: Bloomsbury.

Stanley Niaah, S. 2004. "Kingston's Dancehall: A Story of Space and Celebration". *Space and Culture* 7, no. 1: 102–18.

Stolzoff, N.C. 2000. *Wake the Town and Tell the People: Dancehall Culture in Jamaica*. Durham: Duke University Press.

White, G. 1984. "The Development of Jamaican Popular Music, Part 2. Urbanization of the Folk: The Merger of Traditional and the Popular in Jamaican Music". *ACIJ Research Review* 1:3–15, 24–36.

CHAPTER 19

"'Sleng Teng' Dominate Bad, Bad"

Understanding Jamaica's "Computerized" Riddim Craze

ERIN C. MacLEOD

> What was it about a chance combination on a tiny Casio keyboard that could mesmerize an entire nation and change forever the course of reggae music?
> —Beth Lesser, *King Jammy's* (2002, 38)

A GREAT DEAL OF JAMAICAN MUSIC IS BASED on a foundation of recycled rhythms. Arguably, as with many musical innovations in Jamaica, this system has developed as a result of practical economic reasons. Instead of original singer-songwriter compositions performed as unique songs, a rhythm, or in Jamaican, *riddim*, is created by a specific producer. This is an instrumental track with no vocals. The instrumental riddim is then voiced by various singers or deejays (what, in other parts of the world, people might refer to as MCs or rappers). Each of these individually voiced tracks is referred to as a "version" of the original. The riddim is given a name – often the name of the first or most popular song on the riddim (Freedom Blues, Peanut Vendor or Queen of the Minstrels are a few examples). For decades, these riddims were created by bands, where a producer would gather together a group of studio musicians and record the riddim.[1] However, in 1985, this system was turned on its head by a scant three notes: the "Sleng Teng" riddim.

In this chapter I will discuss the birth and public reception of the Sleng Teng, considered the first "digital" riddim. A slowed-down rock rhythm from a tinny (and tiny) Casio keyboard, the Sleng Teng is extraordinarily simple but has been versioned countless times since its introduction to an audience on 23 February 1985 – an amazing 239 versions were recorded by October 1985 alone (Hebdige 1987, 12), not to mention a seemingly endless list of examples from that point until today. Clearly an immediate smash hit, the success of the Sleng Teng riddim and the subsequent interest in the "computerized" or "digital" riddims of "dancehall", as they and the genre have come to be labelled, have been long derided by Jamaican music historians as a decline from the 1970s "golden era" of reggae music.

I wish to suggest that the Sleng Teng is misunderstood as emblematic of a degenerative trend in Jamaican music and I want to present an argument that attempts to explain this misunderstanding as derived from a purist privileging of analogue/organic/authentic reggae over the digital/inorganic/inauthentic dancehall. Rather than fall on either side of the debate, the very nature of Jamaican music wholly resists such binaries in exchange for a consistently evolving and innovative conception of musical sound.

THE DIGITAL DIVIDE: RESISTING THE SLENG TENG EXTRAVAGANZA

Though "dancehall" has been used to describe a lot of popular Jamaican music since the early 1980s, most historians and critics view Wayne Smith's "Under Mi Sleng Teng" as the watershed moment dividing reggae from its degenerate dancehall offspring.[2] Reggae historian Lloyd Bradley (2001, 517) is quite plain: "If ever there was a point of no return for Reggae As We Know It, it was . . . 'Under Mi Sleng Teng".' In terms of sound, the tell-tale difference between what historian Bradley refers to as the pre- and post-Sleng Teng eras has to do with the issue of digitization; the move from live musicians to synthesized instrumentation. The extreme popularity of new "computerized" or "robotic" riddims, often created with the use of synthesizers, led to a reduction in the use of session musicians. Beth Lesser (2002, 38), a writer who witnessed the triumphant unveiling of the Sleng Teng first hand, reported that King Jammy, the producer behind the riddim, "had to reluctantly shelve over fifty 'human rhythms' he had made with his High Times band" in exchange for digital productions, "because no one wanted to hear them". Lesser's choice of words is apt. The digital riddims were and are placed in direct conflict with "human" riddims. The "powerful and pounding" riddim that had "all come out of a 'music box'" as opposed to real, live, "authentic" musicians mark a divide, referred to by Bradley (2001, 517) as a "line in the sand" between analogue/organic/authentic and digital/inorganic/inauthentic.

But this divide is not unique to 1980s Jamaica. Critics of the *Sleng Teng Extravaganza* (as one of the many bestselling compilations of Sleng Teng versions was titled) have suggested that this new way of making music "made it easier for producers without 'real' musical knowledge to enter the business, thereby lowering the creativity and quality of the music" (Stolzoff 2000, 106). Though Bradley (2001, 518) is quick to state that the lack of real bass line did not really provide a reason "why modern reggae . . . shouldn't have continued to do the job it had done", he ends a chapter bemoaning the post–Bob Marley era by suggesting "maybe it was losing the bass line" (530).

These comments, however, seem to echo Theodor Adorno's 1927 comment that the birth of the gramaphone transformed "the piano from a musical instrument into a piece of bourgeois furniture" (2002, 273), thereby suggesting that the introduction of technology tends to distance people from the act of creating music. Because it was recorded, in Adorno's case, people were no longer connected with the authentic act of creating music. In the case of digital riddims, a similar critique is levelled: technology moved Jamaican music away from instrumentation and therefore became less valuable – or "not even music" (Stolzoff 2000, 107). According to Bradley (2001, 518), with the new digital riddims came an era different from what had come before: "In the past, statues had been moved to one side and the new ones put up next to them; this time around those same statues were being determinedly kicked over. With big hobnailed boots." Michael Veal (2007) also underlines this fact, though with less force in that he establishes the notion of musical construction by engineers, not musicians. The new digital riddims are seen as not just disconnected from the 1970s analogue sound but disconnected from the very roots of reggae culture. This separation is extended to suggest that something intrinsic to reggae – something "human" perhaps – was lost in the 1980s.

Beyond the dislike of the act of digital creation, this new type of music is viewed as a lesser form of cultural expression, full of *slackness* (explicit sexual content), violence and nonsense. The problem is that setting up a connection between digital and dancehall denies the history of pre–Sleng Teng slack dancehall. It seems that this discussion lacks an ability to separate the issue of sound and technology used to create music and the lyrical content or attitude of performers.

General Echo became famous in the late 1970s by performing slack tunes such as the hit "Bathroom Sex" and "She Have a Pair of Headlamp Breasts" – all of his tunes on analogue riddims. One of his two albums was recorded under the apt monicker "Ranking Slackness" – no Sleng Teng on the record, but strictly slackness. Other artists like Lone Ranger and Yellowman cut slack or nonsensical tunes on the very same analogue riddims used by conscious deejays. For examples, one need only take a listen to Yellowman's gibberish hit "Zungguzzuzeng" on the Mad Mad riddim, a riddim famous for conscious tunes like Michigan and Smiley's "Diseases". Lone Ranger's "Barnabas Collins", a tribute to a vampire story that blurs the line between the thirst for blood and a strong sexual appetite, is performed on the Conversation riddim, a foundation riddim produced in the late 1960s by Bunny Lee.

However, Paul Gilroy (1987, 193) writes of post–Sleng Teng music that "the politically engaged content . . . evaporated from reggae as slackness [took] over". In Bradley (2001, 525), his sentiments regarding the Sleng Teng are far more disparaging: "During the decade or so since 'Sleng Teng' dancehall reggae – or digital, or ragga, or what ever you want to call it . . . [pushed] itself into new areas of musical bleakness and lyrical unpleasantness."

Though I am focusing here on the digital sound – the "musical bleakness" as opposed to "lyrical unpleasantness" – it is important to note that the Sleng Teng was born in the midst of a political climate that was profoundly different from the 1970s. Jamaica, in the 1970s, was governed by the progressive, socialist People's National Party (PNP) under Michael Manley. In 1980, after a violent election that claimed over eight hundred lives, Edward Seaga's more conservative, open market–friendly Jamaican Labour Party (JLP) came into power. Seaga liberalized the Jamaican economy such that it was more aligned with American interests in the Caribbean. Some argue that Seaga's policies, and/or the violent factionalism between Jamaica's two political parties, increased and exacerbated the already dire poverty and problems that existed in urban Jamaica and, as a result, the illegal and politically affiliated economy of drugs grew.[3] Under these circumstances, it might be argued that lyrical content simply reflected both the growing violence in Kingston as well as a desire to, as Bob Marley once sang, "forget your problems and dance" – hence the appeal of slackness and celebration of lighter, less grave matters.

Jamaican music historian Roger Steffens (who was the chairman of the reggae committee of the Grammy awards from 1984 to 2011) tends to use the very same differentiation as Bradley (2001), allowing him to also derisively judge and separate dancehall from "reggae". He does so by making reference to the actual sound of the music, describing dancehall as "hip hop style" – a term that connects dancehall to the American musical form of hip-hop, disconnecting it from reggae, the legitimate Jamaican musical form for Steffens. "[Dancehall] certainly isn't reggae except in the most far-stretched definition", he states. "These days, I don't know what the heck reggae is anymore. Dancehall has basically taken over, and . . . in Jamaica . . . the radio [is] filled with hip-hop style Jamaican music which is a far cry from the Melodians and the Techniques . . . and Bob Marley" (quoted in Locilento 2002, 114). As Carolyn Cooper (2005, 79) comments in reference to Beres Hammond's hit "Rockaway", a song that laments the rise of contemporary dancehall, "'music from the heart' versus *riddims* from the gut and pelvis, it would seem".

The recent commercial – and crossover to the American mainstream – success of "dancehall" reggae stars Sean Paul, Vybz Kartel and Popcaan, what with their songs about parties and *punaany*, have reaffirmed the popular sense of the term, that is that "dancehall" connotes a type of music less concerned with (and therefore less "real" than) the roots and culture themes popular in the 1970s.

This desire for music to contain some sense of authenticity and/or organicism crops up in arguments for analogue recording: "It retains the otherness of past time; digital recording fixes it in code. . . . With analog we keep discovering buried treasures; with digital we keep improving on a flawed but convenient medium" (Rothenbuhler and Peters 1997, 254). Though Eric W. Rothenbuhler and John Durham Peters are here discussing the value of vinyl over compact discs, the sense of digital as bereft of history is clear: whereas digital recording is the recording of data, analogue recording "contains physical traces of the music" (246).[4] The very language itself is suggestive of the historicity and authenticity of analogue; there's a reason why the music of 1970s Jamaica is called "roots" reggae. It is important to note that in Bradley's (2001) *Bass Culture*, which is described by Penguin books as a "complete history", he goes so far as to say that the Sleng Teng led to a larger commodification of music in Jamaica, distancing the very reasons for production from the supposed Rasta-inspired music of the 1970s, resulting in "the spirit of one of the world's most powerful folk musics [being] diluted" (518). Over three hundred versions of Sleng Teng later, perhaps the only plus Rothenbuhler and Peters (1997) might grant to this digital revolution would be the factor of "convenience".

Mike Alleyne, in his article "The Digital Imprint on Caribbean Music" (2001), takes this argument for authenticity a step further: digital riddims are not only transporting Jamaican music away from human musicians but also away from the African origins of Jamaican people. Contrasting technologically synthesized drums with African drumming, Alleyne suggests that "the core text [of African drumming] is reduced to a skeletal facsimile that characteristically lacks rhythmic malleability and fluidity. In addition, it is highly questionable whether such digital application complements with the communicative value or social cohesion of African drumming' (132). Interestingly, Stolzoff (2000, 107) argues the opposite: that the new digital riddims "drew on the rhythms of Pocomania and Kumina, two Afro-Jamaican musical forms" (107). King Jammy's Pocoman Jam riddim could be viewed as an example of what Stolzoff is talking about.

Either of these arguments – and any arguments that attempt to place some essential value on either analogue/organic/authentic or digital/inorganic/inauthentic – adhere to a "you're with us or you're against us" paradigm. Sleng Teng becomes associated with the degeneration of Jamaican music, the moment when it becomes essential to "talk about reggae's latter period in terms of only contrast, not continuation" for it would be "confusing" to not make this distinction (Bradley 2001, 520).

But the Sleng Teng does not just exist as a piece of music that can be analysed within such a paradigm. The paradigm is, in fact, more "confusing" than this. It exists outside of convenient binaries and classification systems, and instead lies within the dancehall. Perhaps Alleyne's (2001) statement could be helpful. Do digital riddims have "communicative value" that are able to create "social cohesion"? As Jamaican music entered the 1980s, had it lost communicative value? Was there anything specific about digital production that caused a shift? In order to answer either of these questions (which might just get us out of this debate) we can turn to the space where Jamaican music gains both its communicative value *and* its ability to create social cohesion – the dancehall.

DANCEHALL CULTURE VERSUS "DANCEHALL" MUSIC

To escape the binary we must think *inna dancehall stylee*; we must consider the importance of "dancehall culture" as opposed to "dancehall" music – this is not an argument solely about music production. As Norman Stolzoff (2000, 4) has illustrated in his landmark study *Wake the Town and Tell the People: Dancehall Culture in Jamaica*, "the Jamaican masses have been creating cultural counter worlds through secular music and dance performances in the 'cultural spaces' known as dancehalls for more than two centuries".

Though dances have always been intrinsic to Jamaican culture, since the 1940s public music listening in Jamaica has primarily been the domain of sound systems. Essentially a mobile disco that can set up anywhere, the sound system is considered by many to be the cornerstone of the Jamaican music industry. Says famed singer Sanchez, "Any time the sound systems from Jamaica die out, I think the music will be no more" (quoted in MacLeod 2005b). They may have started out as a more convenient, affordable form of entertainment than a traditional live band, but they've developed over time to not only set the template for hip-hop but also to create a vibrant cultural form that simultaneously creates and contradicts opinions and ideas.

A couple of factors lead to this rise: post–World War II immigration to aid with England's reconstruction attracted a large portion of Jamaicans and many members of the music industry; other musicians headed to work in resorts and hotels as part of the growing tourist industry (Stolzoff 2000, 41). As mentioned above, it is simple economics that led to the sound system innovation. The obvious choice for cost-sensitive local dance promoters was to string up speakers and a turntable, or hire someone to do so. "[Bands] did prove too expensive", explains producer Bunny Lee, "dem stop fi a break

. . . dem alone eat a pot of goat! So when sound come now, the sound no tek no break" (quoted in Barrow and Dalton 2001, 11).

Sound systems are able to not only function in a physical dancehall space, but their enormous speakers (there are members of sound system crews whose sole purpose is to move the huge speaker boxes) can be set up anywhere. Sonjah Stanley Niaah (2004, 109) has outlined numerous potential dance venues from clubs and halls to street corners and gully banks. Rather than a physical space, sound systems delineate sound spaces themselves. As Carolyn Cooper says, "When a sound system is set up on a corner, it creates a public space for the consumption of popular music. If you don't have these public spaces, then the music will become entirely domesticated" (quoted in MacLeod 2005a). The dance is where the music is, where the people gather; its boundaries are fluid, existing as long as the tunes are nice and therefore the "dance fi ram". This is the key – what Stanley Niaah (2004, 109) refers to as a "ram dance" philosophy: "the more persons busting the seams of the venue, the more successful the event".

Given this positioning of the dancehall space, it becomes apparent that the role of the dancehall is central to the creation of popular musical culture in Jamaica. Most popular music gains its fame through its acceptance by dancehall patrons and, therefore, all Jamaican music might properly be referred to as "dancehall". The current use of the word, however, tends to denote a specific genre of Jamaican music. In order to draw the dancehall "massive", the sound system must respond to the needs of the crowd. The first time the Sleng Teng was played, "the crowd went wild! People were cheering and throwing their hands in the air, blowing noise-makers and whistles" (Lesser 2002, 38). Following this debut in 1985, the crowd demanded the Sleng Teng. "Album after album of pure 'Sleng Teng' versions were released and every one sold", reports Lesser (2002, 38). As is evident, it is the crowd who drive the workings in the dancehall – they provided the much-needed screams, affirmative cries and rousing encouragement referred to as a "forward".

The problem with the critiques of Gilroy (1987), Bradley (2001), Alleyne (2001) and Steffens is that they all seem to take the music out of the context of the dancehall. Certainly, slackness and digital riddims can be heard anywhere one travels in Jamaica – blasting out of storefronts, portable stereos, busses, cars and at dances held by any of the hundreds of sound systems active throughout the island[5] – but the dancehall has always been a space where multiple types of music have been played. In order to keep the massive happy and encourage the dolling out of forwards, the sound system operators have to play for everyone in the crowd. "All the rude boys, take it easy", Ricky Trooper, operator of Killamanjaro sound, assured the crowd at a dance in August 1994, "because your tunes will come shortly" (quoted in Stolzoff 2000, 213). Legendary dancehall producer Sugar Minott also describes this need to please everyone: "I need to try to please different kind of people . . . dancehall style, Studio One, that's a must and a couple of roots and culture to keep a variety and there'll be a coupla Rasta man so I give them something" (quoted in MacLeod 2004). Selectors at dances such as Uptown Mondays, Boasy Tuesdays, Weddi Wednesdays and Rae Town Old Hits consistently announce different types of music – for the ladies, for the rude boys, for the dancers and so on.

Instead of being disconnected from history (or organicism or authenticity), the sound space of the dancehall requires that all types of music – from oldies to the latest pre-released tunes – be played. In addition, the dancehall space also suggests a fulfilment of Gilroy's characteristics of "all new world black musics [which provide] a living bridge between them and African traditions of music-making": "improvisation, spontaneity, and intimacy" (1987, 164). Far from being indicative of degeneration, the Sleng Teng and subsequent digital productions continued to open up possibilities for each of these characteristics – just as reggae had always done and continues to do.

First, although deejays were chatting over riddims before the introduction of the Sleng Teng, the speed at which new riddims could be produced increased exponentially – here lies the convenience Rothenbuhler and Peters (1997) mention. As Stolzoff (2000, 107) writes, the new technology allowed for a "chang[e] from a strict reliance on recycling classic reggae instrumental tracks", the tracks still today referred to as "foundation" riddims. Over the course of a very short time, a whole new foundation of digital riddims was created in the wake of the Sleng Teng: Tempo, Agony, Get a Lick, Punaany and Run Down the World to name but a few others. Since sound systems are always looking for the newest tune, deejays and singers had to rise to the task of meeting the demand. Barrow and Dalton (2001, 305) note that "the lower production costs of digital tracks meant that producers could again afford to take chances on untried rhythms". The staggering increase in production of tracks and versions that occurred during the 1980s and onward into the 1990s through to today is testament to the role of new technologies and production techniques.[6] To ride (meaning to talk or sing over) a whole new set of riddims necessitated levels of improvisation and spontaneity heretofore unheard of in Jamaican music. When there are dozens – if not hundreds – of competing tunes on the same riddim, the artists must be innovative enough to stand out.

In addition, dancehall music is nothing if not intimate – and this intimacy increased as the digital riddims took hold. Since dancehall patrons have always driven the dance (clashes between rival sound systems are solely decided by crowd response), there's an intimate relationship between the sound system selector and his (or, though very rarely, her) massive. The Sleng Teng and subsequent digital productions resulted from being a form of music that was demanded by the public. As Lesser (2002, 38) writes of the fans of dancehall in the mid-1980s, "all they wanted was 'Sleng Teng'". Also, this new music was not oriented toward international fans of Jamaican music, unlike roots reggae in the 1970s – especially, and specifically, Bob Marley. The "'Discourse of Dread' gives way to Rema, Tivoli Gardens and Jungle [all communities in West Kingston], particular 'Yard' (Jamaican) realities which do not function as global signifiers of black exile because they are so rooted in the urban myths of Jamaica's post-colonial history" (Chude-Sokei, quoted in Stolzoff 2000, 103).

Whereas the international sense of the Jamaican experience is either dreadlocked and clouded in marijuana smoke or the image of paradisal tourist resorts (with names like Hedonism II), dancehall brings Jamaican music back to the immediate and the local. This is a music that is intimate with the downtown ghetto sufferers rather than North American or British roots reggae fans. The ability of digital riddims, as with all

Jamaican music prior to them, to respond to Jamaican people problematizes Bradley's (2001, 520) insistence that the digital period is possible to be spoken of "in terms only of contrast, not of continuation" of "history, musical and cultur[e]". As Barrow and Dalton (2001, 305) write, "[digital is] the most populist form of all forms of Jamaican music[,] drawing freely from practically every aspect of Jamaican culture, including spirituals and hymns". Certainly, I would expand this statement to insist that it is in fact a very obvious step in a neverending evolutionary process in which artists are consistently interpreting and reinterpreting sounds and statements.

VP Records, in the summer of 2005, not only reissued a remastered *Sleng Teng Extravaganza* but also released *Sleng Teng Resurrection*, a collection of both contemporary and older artists versioning the tried-and-true Sleng Teng on the riddim's twentieth anniversary. A range of artists such as Sizzla, Anthony B, Luciano, Junior Kelly and others give the famed riddim a try, discussing a whole range of topics in their lyrics. Performers from the 1980s also make an appearance: Admiral Bailey and Ninja Man are here, and Junior Reid shines on the particularly apt "Don't Dis Foundation". Reid's tune reminds both listeners and performers that "respect [is] due to all foundation" and "if you dis the foundation, yes you're going to regret". This statement, on the riddim that supposedly exemplifies a lack of respect for tradition, is a powerful demonstration of the arbitrary division between supposedly reverent 1970s roots reggae and independent, disrespectful dancehall.

CONCLUSION

Certainly, the Sleng Teng did herald a change in the sound of Jamaican music, but it was not a death knell. There's no need to pick a side of the analogue/organic/authentic "reggae" over the digital/inorganic/inauthentic "dancehall". All Jamaican music, regardless of technological innovation, provides ways to express the multiplicity of both individual and Jamaican experience in a way that can be communicated to the massive.

Steve Barrow, reggae historian and co-founder of Blood and Fire records, a reggae reissue label, doesn't see the need to disparage dancehall:

> I was watching a documentary on Egypt. On the Nile on TV. And a guy went across a river and another guy got on with him and started playing the kora. And when the guy got off, the music stopped. But he had that music for the journey, and the music fitted the journey. The music expressed certain things about the river. . . . And that's what dancehall is in a way. That's what it is. The consumerism and the commercialism and the ebay-ism? That's something that comes after. It's added on. Music gives us a way of overcoming alienation and saying "I *do* mean something". I am somebody. If only for two-and-a-half minutes. I don't feel inclined to slag people off for jumping on a digi-riddim track and saying some half-remembered Buju pattern or some Ninjaman business or whatever. If it gives them a reason to live, makes them be somebody, that's what we need. We all need to be somebody. (Personal communication, 2 April 2004)

ACKNOWLEDGEMENTS

The research for this chapter was aided by the Social Sciences Research Council of Canada.

NOTES

1. A full discussion of the form and structure of the riddim system throughout the history of the Jamaican music industry is found in Manuel and Marshall (2006). The development of what Manuel and Marshall call the "riddim method" is described without the judgement so evident in many of the critics I discuss in this chapter. Their work is more descriptive than evaluative of the "quality" of a particular sound or riddim.
2. Interestingly, in the United Kingdom, where Jamaican music has consistently received more press and attention, the term for the new type of music that followed in the footsteps of "Under Mi Sleng Teng" is "ragga". The term "dancehall" is more often used by North American critics.
3. For an account of the history of Jamaican politics and its influence on the urban areas of Kingston from independence in 1962 to the turn of the millennium, see Gray (2004).
4. It might be valuable to look at the arguments for authenticity in hip-hop – arguably a musical descendant of Jamaican music. In Joseph G. Schloss's *Making Beats* (2004, 68) he quotes producer Jake One who "expresses his preference for 'vintage timbres', referring presumably to an analog production aesthetic, which he specifically opposes to a digital 'Casio' sound". In addition, Schloss presents hip-hop as resisting live musicians in exchange for samples of pre-recorded music: "a beat created with live instrumentation alone can lack a sense of purpose, urgency, and direction; it has no center" (69).
5. The Sound System Association of Jamaica, a now-defunct organization, had a website active until 2010 (www.cyberjam.net/ssaj), listing 128 registered sounds. Though the Sound System Federation of Jamaica has been established since 2015, it is now impossible to know the number of sound systems active throughout the island, but it is safe to estimate that dozens of sound systems draw crowds to dances held every day of the week across Jamaica.
6. Barrow and Dalton (2001, 305) claim an "unprecedented proliferation of producers and labels" in the 1980s, leading to the "staggering five thousand titles" released each year of the 1990s.

REFERENCES

Adorno, T.W. 2002. "The Curves of the Needle". In *Essays on Music*, edited by R. Leppert, 271–82. Berkeley: University of California Press.

Alleyne, M. 2001. "The Digital Imprint on Caribbean Music". In *Culture and Mass Communication in the Caribbean*, edited by H. Regis, 125–38. Gainesville: University of Florida Press.

Barrow, S., and P. Dalton. 2001. *Rough Guide to Reggae*. London: Penguin.

Bradley, L. 2001. *Bass Culture: When Reggae Was King*. London: Penguin.

Cooper, C. 2005. *Sound Clash: Jamaican Dancehall Culture at Large*. London: Palgrave.

Gilroy, P. 1987. *There Ain't No Black in the Union Jack: The Cultural Politics of Race and Nation*. Chicago: University of Chicago Press.

Gray, O. 2004. *Demeaned but Empowered: The Social Power of the Urban Poor in Jamaica*. Kingston: University of the West Indies Press.

Hebdige, D. 1987. *Cut 'n' Mix: Culture, Identity, and Caribbean Popular Music*. London: Methuen.

Lesser, B. 2002. *King Jammy's*. Toronto: ECW Press.

Locilento, M. 2002. *Shaggy: Doggamuffin Style*. Toronto: ECW Press.

MacLeod, E. 2004. "The Sweeter They Come". *Montreal Mirror* 20: 15.

———. 2005a. "Ring the Alarm: Montreal Sound Systems Come Fi Mash It". *Montreal Mirror* 20: 43.

———. 2005b. "The Suit Makes the Man". *Montreal Mirror* 20: 39.

Manuel, P., and W. Marshall. 2006. "The Riddim Method: Aesthetics, Practice, and Ownership in Jamaican Dancehall". *Popular Music* 25, no. 3: 447–70.

Rothenbuhler, E.W. and J. Durham Peters. 1997. "Defining Phonography: An Experiment in Theory". *Musical Quarterly* 81, no. 2: 242–64.

Schloss, J.G. 2004. *Making Beats: The Art of Sample-Based Hip-Hop*. Middletown, CT: Wesleyan University Press.

Stanley Niaah, S. 2004. "Kingston's Dancehall: A Story of Space and Celebration". *Space and Culture* 7, no. 1: 102–18.

Stolzoff, N.C. 2000. *Wake the Town and Tell the People: Dancehall Culture in Jamaica*. Durham, NC: Duke University Press.

Veal, Michael E. 2007. *Dub: Soundscapes and Shattered Songs in Jamaican Reggae*. Middletown, CT: Wesleyan University Press.

DISCOGRAPHY

I have attempted to provide as much information about the original release of the singles discussed in the chapter. Many record labels in Jamaica did not number their releases in the 1980s, so there are some singles that do not have release numbers. Also, the titles written on singles can often vary based on when and where they were printed.

General Echo. 1980a. "Bathroom Sex". Single. GRED 30. Greensleeves.

———. 1980b. "She Have a Pair of Headlamp Breasts". *12" of Pleasure*. GREL 15. Greensleeves.

Hammond, Beres. 2000. "Rockaway". Single. Harmony House.

Lone Ranger. 1979. "Barnabas Collins". Single. GG's Records.

Michigan and Smiley. 1983 "Diseases". Single. GRED 72. Greensleeves.

Smith, Wayne. 1985. "Under Me Sleng Teng". Single. Jammys.

Various. 2005. *Sleng Teng Extravaganza*. VPCD 2284. VP Records.

———. 2006. *Sleng Teng Resurrection*. VPRL 2285. VP Records.

Yellowman. 1982. "Zungguzzuzeng". Single. Volcano.

CHAPTER 20

Sleng Teng

Redefining Jamaica's Digital Riddims

RAY HITCHINS

BETWEEN 1960 AND 2000, A NUMBER OF NEW popular music genres and sounds emerged from Jamaica which had a profound impact, not only on the commercial music centres of North America, Europe and Japan but on academic communities around the world. From a local perspective, dancehall music might be considered the most successful genre to emerge from the island, rising to prominence at the start of the 1980s and continuing to represent the preferred music of Jamaican youth in the twenty-first century.[1] Despite the longevity of this success, dancehall music has not achieved reggae's synonymous association with a worldwide brand such as Marley, but it has earned international recognition through artists such as Shabba Ranks, Shaggy and Sean Paul. Moreover, the dancehall space has provided a creative well for the wider music industry and its practitioners regularly adopt and adapt the inherent richness of the sounds, movement, language and fashion associated with dancehall culture.[2]

Despite this international success, dancehall music is often perceived locally in a negative light. Reports such as Tyrone Thompson's *Gleaner* article of 4 June 2015, entitled "Devil in the Music: Dancehall Music Is the Source of Evil", reflects a stereotypical perspective that is widely accepted. This negative public image is reinforced with prominent practitioners of the genre being jailed for crimes ranging from murder to drug trafficking, resulting in a level of local derision that is unprecedented for a home-grown music. Much of the narrative that surrounds dancehall music therefore becomes a self-fulfilling prophecy fed by a complex range of social, political and economic forces, which I contend are compounded by a misunderstanding and misinterpretation of the creative and production process on which the music is based. While the precise origin of this negative perception is hard to identify, evidence of its existence can be found in the academic and enthusiast literature of the 1980s, which found resonance with the reggae establishment and conservative religious groups.[3] The cumulative effect was the creation of a voice that was loud and consistent in its direct or implied criticism of dancehall music, although it often lacked understanding of how the new music functioned. Notable exceptions include Peter Manuel and Wayne Marshall's 2006 paper on the use of riddims and Curwen Best's broader discussion on the use of technology in the Caribbean. These and other authors provide an important counter-narrative and reasoned appraisal of musical practice, including the way in which dancehall music and other forms of Caribbean musical expression embraced new technologies and the creative openings they offered. My research is in line with much of their thinking, but also the work of Timothy Warner (2003), Rene Lysloff and Leslie Gaye (2003), and Paul Greene and Thomas Porcello (2005), who probe recording context, production methodology and the timelines of technology's introduction with consideration for how and why music is made and the forces that inspire new forms of creativity.

My research on Jamaican popular music (JPM) is underpinned by two assumptions that I believe are critical in its study and represent consistent forces that influence musical development. The first is that popular music is by definition a commercial product and as such flows along predictable economic pathways. The consumer represents the gravity that continually pulls creative, technical and business interests in a single direction. The second is that recorded commercial music, particularly since 1960, represents a series of transitions that have led from the capture of the live to the programmed performance, where recorded sound has increasingly displaced performance as the central aesthetic. While these elements are often in a state of flux they remain critical in the understanding of JPM and its dominant modes of production.

Prior to the introduction of the drum machine at the start of the 1980s, the process of composing, performing and capturing the sounds of JPM were often intertwined as a single event that occurred in the recording space. The drum machine revolutionized recording practice by demanding a transition from what I term "parallel recording", where multiple musicians record the backing track as a single synchronized performance, to "serial recording", where the drum machine program is recorded and the musical arrangement is built by recording one instrument at a time. These distinct recording processes offer a range of quantifiable data and a much-needed measure in the discussion of Jamaican music production. When triangulated with other forms of qualitative data gathering, they potentially add clarity and rigour to research (see Veal 2007; Hitchins 2014).

In the discussion of popular music, an understanding of the production mechanism is by no means a necessity, but it does provide a factual framework to test hypotheses and speculation or even the claims of informants. I therefore contend that if the specific mechanisms of music making and sound capture are being discussed, there is a fundamental need for the researcher to understand the details of their operation and the value systems that drive them. This is particularly important in the case of JPM, where the process of writing, arranging, production and sound capture does not conform to music producton practices established in the United States and Europe. My discussion of dancehall music is premised on these ideas and I contend that a reappraisal of the narrative surrounding this music and the "digital" designation that is commonly attached to it is not only necessary but long overdue.

The sound recording titled "Under Mi Sleng Teng" (Jammy's, 1985) makes an appropriate case study for this reappraisal because it is undoubtedly one of the most discussed and, as I will argue, misrepresented sound recordings in the JPM canon. Dick Hebdige (1987, 12) was one of the first scholars to highlight this musical work in his seminal book *Cut 'n' Mix,* where he claims, "Wayne Smith made a record called 'Under Mi Sleng Teng'. It has been estimated that by October 1985, no less than 239 versions of this tune had been made."[4] Hebdige goes on to describe how the multiple interpretations of Smith's "tune" represents a process that he describes as "versioning", which he aligns with the emergence of a musical character that is forged through the mimicking of different vocal styles. The claims made by Hebdige are consistent with the concept of the traditional "evergreen" and "standard" composition, which is replicated by musicians and singers who develop their own style through mimicry. However, closer analysis of Smith's "tune" reveals that it was captured and reproduced only once. It was in fact the backing track or "riddim" of the sound recording which was employed 239 times. As such, this type of reusable backing track and its ability to be used with hundreds of different vocalists and their unique tunes ironically represents the antithesis of the mimicking of style and use of a single "tune" or melody as Hebdige suggests.

The Sleng Teng riddim not only undermines the initial framework on which *Cut 'n' Mix* is premised, but it more importantly signifies a revolutionary transition in the production of popular music. As such, at the start of the 1980s, dancehall music began to reject the tune, lyric and style of the vocalist as the primary text, replacing it with the riddim or backing track.[5] In this radically new approach the riddim becomes a single template employed underneath the performance of hundreds of different tunes, lyrics and stylizations; turning upside down a tradition that had dominated popular music since the invention of the gramophone.

This seismic change in the production of JPM represented a vibrant new approach that had an impact on many other genres and particularly urban forms of popular music where the riddim, or what is now widely referred to as the "beat", achieved new relevance. Evidence of this can be found in the fact that in 2017, many forms of popular music no longer use the traditional division of the songwriter's royalty, which was limited to the melody and lyric. It is now common for the writing royalty to be divided between the creators of the beat (backing track/riddim) and the melody/lyric. This represents a significant shift in the global publishing and music related industries, which is rooted in dancehall music, yet Hebdige unwittingly buries this significance through a misinterpretation of how the music functions.

In *Cut 'n' Mix* Hebdige further mischaracterizes dancehall music by portraying it as the creature of a capitalist political ideology, lacking creative substance, but does so without consideration for how the new music functioned or the economic system it served. He describes how "in Seaga's Jamaica Inc, sex, money, flash and nonsense have tended to become the new religion of the airwaves" (1987, 125), implying that dancehall music and its themes were limited to decadent behaviour, materialism and trite values.[6] This lays the groundwork for Paul Gilroy (1987), who also promotes this theme, claiming that "the largely Rasta-inspired singers, songwriters and dub poets who had guided the music to its place as a vibrant populist force in the society were brushed aside. . . . Under

Seaga, the singers' and songwriters' influence faded and they retreated from the revolution which their Rasta language had demanded" (188). The underlying message is not difficult to decipher and these influential scholars clearly see reggae as the pinnacle of Jamaica's musical creativity, representing the "good" and "wholesome", while dancehall music is framed as immoral, lacking musical value or creative substance.

This narrative has sadly been widely accepted despite the fact that these authors fail to explain what part Seaga played in the writing of Max Romeo's seminal 1968 hit "Wet Dreams", with lines such as "Lie down gal make mi push it up, push it up", or to explain how and why clean-cut rocksteady tunesmiths such as Alton Ellis were brushed aside by the new "Rasta-inspired" revolution of the late 1960s. Moreover, I argue that "sex, money, flash and nonsense" represent the staple diet of the music industry, evidence of which can be located in the popular music canon and iconic compositions such as The Beatles' "I Am the Walrus" (Parlophone, 1968), Led Zepplin's "The Lemon Song" (Atlantic, 1969), ABBA's "Money, Money, Money" (Epic, 1976) and Queen's "We Are the Champions" (Elektra, 1977).

Jamaica in fact has a long tradition of bawdy lyrics, which Richard Cullen Rath (1993, 712) notes in the observations of Dr Hans Sloane, who in 1688 writes: "The Negros are much given to Venery, and also hard wrought, will at nights, or on feast days Dance and Sing; their Songs are all bawdy and, leading that way." The connection between these African origins and dancehall music is also noted by Carolyn Cooper (1993, 2004), Sonjah Stanley Niaah (2006, 2010), Donna P. Hope (2006), Norman Stolzoff (2000) and other scholars from a wide range of academic perspectives, and yet dancehall music continues to be predominantly defined through the headlines that are attached to the misdemeanors or lifestyles of its artists as opposed to serious consideration for the music, its development or its production process.

An assessment of the narratives set in motion by Hebdige (1987) and Gilroy (1987) is important, not only because they misrepresent and misunderstand the function of dancehall music but because they apply an unrealistic value system to this genre that is at odds with the principal tenets of commercial popular music (see Hitchins 2014). This dogmatic approach to dancehall music seems to set the stage for a tirade against the genre during the latter part of the 1980s and 1990s. The themes set in motion by Hebdige and Gilroy, denoting reggae as a wholesome and righteous music ousted by the decadent and unruly musical bastard of American-led capitalism and soulless music technology, became popular. For example, Dennis Bovell in Lloyd Bradley's *This Is Reggae Music* (2000, 501) claims that "When computers came in, that's when the amateurs took over" and goes on to say, "You didn't have to take a group into the studio, or get yourself a riddim track or anything, just buy a Casio, plug it in the studio and chat what you wanted to chat."

Bovell not only offers a perspective that is repeated in much of the literature but notably also targets the Sleng Teng riddim and its unique use of the Casio MT-40 electronic keyboard.[7] However, Bovell fails to point out that the use of "computers" and instruments such as the drum machine, synthesizer and transition to the serial recording process were pioneered locally in the production of reggae and not dancehall music.[8]

Bovell's comments seem to reflect the attitude of many pre-1980 music industry participants who saw their livelihood being threatened by the public's increasing rejection of reggae and their own inability to compete commercially or assimilate with the new music technology and production methods of the 1980s. These anti-dancehall music commentaries not only ignore the inconvenience of indisputable fact regarding when and how technology was employed, but they are loaded with dog-whistle terms such as "digital", "synthesizer" or "computerized", used as derogatory and prejudicial terms that imply a lack of creative value and musicianship, representing the work of musical imposters. However, the instruments, technologies and resulting changes in recording practice were indisputably initiated in the production of reggae and not dancehall music.

During an interview with Cleveland Browne in 2008, he confirmed that in 1974 he played on Bob Marley's "So Jah Say", where a clearly discernable drum machine provides the primary rhythmic texture.[9] In addition, Willie Stewart in a 2017 interview confirmed that Third World's "Try Jah Love" (1981) employed live drums recorded to the "computerized" timing of a LinnDrum machine at the insistence of Stevie Wonder. Moreover, Robbie Lyn in a 2006 interview confirmed that synthesizers were being widely used in the performance and production of reggae by the close of the 1970s.[10] Despite this, terms such as synthesized, digital or computerized are rarely applied to the description of the music made by the above artists or indeed the many other reggae performers who readily embraced the new music technologies at the close of the 1970s. In addition, it is worth noting that well-established Jamaican performers such as Pluto Shervington, Ernie Smith and Paul Hurlock were prominently working during the 1970s using drum machines and synthesizer bass pedals to perform repertoires of rocksteady and reggae across the island, yet their pioneering use of new music technology is conveniently ignored.[11]

Based on the measurable assessment of recording practice at the start of the 1980s, it is therefore accurate to say that dancehall music assumed the instrumentation and recording practices associated with reggae, which included the drum machine, synthesizer, serial-recording process and eventually computers. What made dancehall music distinct was that its creators quickly discovered that the absence of microphone leakage, which the drum machine offered, opened a range of new technical, creative and economic opportunities that included what I term the "riddim-production method" and led to the repositioning of the riddim as the primary musical work (see Hitchins 2014).[12] This uniquely Jamaican interpretation of popular music production also required that the audio engineer assume responsibility for the musical arrangement. This was achieved by borrowing mixing concepts pioneered in the production of dub, using the mixing console's mute controls and faders, as noted by Michael Veal and others. Dancehall music was in fact positioned at the intersection of new and existing technology and discovered imaginative ways of integrating both to create a dynamic musical product.

In this unique Jamaican music production system, the audio engineer was elevated to a preeminent creative role through what I term "performance mixing".[13] As a result, the musician was increasingly limited to the role of writer and performer or programmer of catchy ostinato musical figures, dramatically changing the creative musical process and mechanisms for monetizing music.[14] This revolutionary transition, based on the application of new technology, was largely explored and pioneered in the production of dancehall music and resulted in the roles of recording participants and the sound of their musical products undergoing dramatic change throughout the 1980s. This shift in music production methodology was gradual but consistent throughout that decade, generating numerous shock waves that were felt in the main music production centres of North America and Europe. While aspects of these new production processes are discussed in the literature, we also see the term "digital" being widely employed as a derogatory adjective to describe dancehall music, despite the fact that most popular music production of the period shared the same technology, including reggae.

As a result, "Under Mi Sleng Teng" is inaccurately positioned in much of the literature as the harbinger of the synthesizer, drum machine and Jamaica's so called "digital revolution". Norman Stolzoff (2000, 106) asserts that "what was new about Smith's song is that it used a drum machine and synthesized instruments as the backing track", while Michael Veal (2007, 12) contends that "Jamaica would change dramatically in 1985, when seemingly out of nowhere the music suddenly went digital", echoing the claim of Kenneth Bilby (1995, 173), who states that "Prince Jammy (now known as King Jammy) released a song by Wayne Smith called 'Under Mi Sleng Teng'", and goes onto say he "ushered in the 'digital revolution'" (175).

I argue that the above assessments, which represent a dominant and widely accepted narrative, are not only inaccurate in their specific claims but their use of the term "digital" as a characteristic of dancehall music is misleading given that the same instruments and recording technologies of the 1980s were common to the production of reggae and many other forms of popular music. The claim that "Under Mi Sleng Teng" initiated a "digital revolution" is therefore in conflict with fact and elevates this sound recording to a key position in the JPM canon that is unwarranted.

While "Under Mi Sleng Teng" was one of the most popular Jamaican music products of the 1980s, in the context of its performance, use of technology and production process it was atypical. The Sleng Teng riddim was not a Jamaican creation but a sequenced pre-set stored in the memory of the MT-40 keyboard, created by Hiroko Okuda, as an employee of the Casio Company. The unique feature of this riddim was not that it was "digital" but that it was an open source riddim, made up from low-fidelity analogue sounds which, when recorded, were tied together on a single track. This significantly restricted the use of performance mixing, which by 1985 was the hallmark of mainstream dancehall music. "Under Mi Sleng Teng" was also recorded on a four-track recorder whereas mainstream dancehall music production in 1985 was commonly produced on sixteen and twenty-four tracks, specifically to facilitate serial recording, performance mixing and the riddim production method.

It is important to stress that the open source nature of the riddim meant that the producer did not control its dissemination and the riddim was therefore readily available to the general public, contrary to established dancehall music production practice. Although the analog bass sound of the Casio MT-40 was considered a fashionable production element for a period in local music production, this remained the extent of the Casio's sonic influence. It is therefore accurate to say that the MT-40s low-fi, analog sound textures and rhythmic pre-sets were widely rejected by the Jamaican recording industry, although the riddim was immensely popular, no doubt influenced by its open source nature and free dissemination.[15]

A more reasoned assessment of the Sleng Teng riddim therefore finds that it uniquely provided a free and open-source backing track with no copyright restrictions and, as such, anyone with access to the MT-40 keyboard or ability to copy the drum and bass parts could assume full and unrestricted usage of the riddim for monetary gain.[16] The extent to which the riddim was produced and reproduced by multiple industry players and entrepreneurs is yet to be assessed, but it would seem reasonable to assert that these unique circumstances played a significant role in the riddim's ultimate popularity.

These comments are not intended to detract from the achievements of Noel Davey, Wayne Smith and King Jammy, who crucially recognized the commercial potential of the MT-40 pre-set. However, the production method used for the resulting sound recording, by the very nature of the keyboard's physical and sonic limitations, its open source nature and restrictions as a four-track analogue recording, made it atypical in 1985. It was a unique recording event that did not represent established music production methodologies employed prior to or after this date and, as such, the riddim is an outlier in the JPM canon. The Casio MT-40, like David Bowie's use of the Stylophone in "Space Oddity" (RCA, 1969) did not represent a revolution in the use of technology, instrumentation or production practice. These entry-level domestic instruments, designed to be used by children, were nevertheless employed on massive commercial hits but, outside of this anecdotal fact, the instruments and their respective sounds left no long-term impression on the music industry.[17]

Despite the atypical nature of the Sleng Teng riddim production, it was important in the sense that its massive popularity acted as an unequivocal statement by Jamaican music consumers that dancehall music and the deejay could no longer be considered a temporary fad.[18] The Sleng Teng riddim signalled the imminent decline of reggae and the traditional singer, and the dominance of the deejay in local music performance. As a result, the riddim became a focal point of dissent for many established reggae musicians, who in 1985 were still trying to come to terms with the serial recording process, new music technologies and the emergence of reusable riddims based on simple ostinato figures. For the cynics of dancehall music, the open source, pre-packaged nature of the Sleng Teng riddim, produced on a child's instrument by an unknown musician, simply added insult to injury. It came to epitomize what was interpreted as Jamaican musical decline and the demise of "real music" and "musicianship". However, the Sleng Teng riddim and its use of the Casio MT-40 keyboard did not reflect how mainstream dancehall music was created, performed or produced. I therefore contend that the real significance of the Sleng Teng riddim is that it represented what Malcolm Gladwell describes as the tipping point in his 2000 book of the same name, where the primary popular music of Jamaicans transitioned from reggae to dancehall music. Ironically, the Sleng Teng riddim was an anomaly in the context of JPM and, put simply, the Casio pre-set just happened to have the right sound, in the right place, at the right time.

While the Sleng Teng riddim certainly deserves mention in the historical development of dancehall music, I contend that the attention it has received is not only disproportionate to its true significance, but the resulting discussions have diverted our attention from important questions that surround the genre and remain unanswered. There is a need to plot the influence of instrument textures such as the syn drum, Simmons drum and analogue synthesizer evident in Michigan and Smiley's "Diseases" (Greensleeves, 1982), the use of tuned drums to provide melodic content in Tiger's "When" (Steely and Clevie, 1990) and the revolutionary reinterpretation of Western diatonic harmony evident in Wayne Wonder's "Fast Car" (Penthouse, 1992). These sound recordings, the instruments they employed and their respective sounds had a significant influence on the development of dancehall music and potentially other music forms, but remain under-researched and form a significant gap in the literature.

Moreover, there are fundamental questions regarding the relationship between reggae and dancehall music, which shared many production processes throughout the 1980s. Both genres participated in an ongoing exchange of creativity that is simply undermined by the fallacy of one genre suddenly becoming "digital" in 1985. If we begin to consider the recorded works of this period in the context of their production practice, then terms such as "digital" simply become redundant outside of its meaning as a specific technology that began to emerge in Jamaican recording studios in the late 1970s. There are also questions regarding why some new music technologies were rejected in Jamaica while others were embraced. Despite the wide acceptance of sequencing at the start of the 1980s, dancehall music producers largely rejected this technology and use of quatization with the exception of the drum machine. The resulting live performance of ostinato figures in the dancehall music repertoire and nuanced variations in timing and dynamic represent a hybrid performance style that lies somewhere between the regimented sounds of electronic dance music and the concept of "participatory discrepancies" as noted by Charles Keil and Steven Feld (1994). What does the synthesis of live performance and drum programming tell us about the way in which JPM was created and the forces that directed production practice?

In conclusion, I argue that it is time for a reappraisal of the dancehall music genre and a need for popular music scholars to build on existing research, which includes challenging and discarding discussions that fail to factually represent music production methods and practice. The established narrative surrounding "Under Mi Sleng Teng" and the concept of dancehall music as "digital" is in desperate need of reassessment. The inaccurate use of this term not only misdirects our understanding of the music creation and production process but it also creates a shadow across areas of potentially rich research and new knowledge. I contend that the dancehall music genre, despite appearing on the surface to project a simplification of preceding musical forms and performance practice, in fact represents a complex expansion, including new and inventive approaches to music production. It challenges not only the concept of how popular music can be made but how it is defined.

From my perspective, the dancehall music genre represents a rich seam of musical creativity that shares many common elements with other forms of JPM; however, the mechanisms of teasing out and measuring these details cannot be based solely on traditional notions of performance or musicality. There is a need to consider the way in which dancehall music has pioneered the intersection of sound as a substitute for and enhancement of traditional forms of music making. Local concepts of groove and vibe, which are embedded in the Jamaican human experience, in conjunction with spontaneous approaches to musical performance in the recording arts, have the potential to dramatically contest traditional concepts of Western diatonic melody, harmony, rhythm and the form of the popular song. This challenge to the status quo by dancehall music represents a seismic event in Jamaica's musical development with a rich seam of potential discovery for a new generation of music scholars. As we look back at the emrgence and development of the dancehall music genre, it is my hope that it will begin to receive renewed attention with a focus on the music production process and rejection of terms such as "digital" that were coined not as a reasoned description of technology but as a derogatory term loaded with prejudice and bias. It is therefore time to provide this important Jamaican musical genre with the respect and attention it deserves.

NOTES

1. For the purpose of this document the term "dancehall music" refers to a range of popular music that was prominent in Jamaica from the early 1980s and the term "reggae" was prominent between 1968 and 1982.
2. Recording artists influenced by dancehall culture include Major Lazer, Drake, Snoop Lion and Justin Bieber.
3. The term "reggae establishment" refers to a group of commentators who see the golden age of JPM ending with the introduction of dancehall music. They act as gatekeepers dismissing much of post-1980s JPM on the basis that it does not comply to a musical form and concepts of musicianship that were established during the 1960s and 1970s.
4. Wayne Smith was the vocal performer and writer of the lyric and melody for the composition titled "Under Mi Sleng Teng".
5. Note that from a Jamaican perspective the song titled "Under Mi Sleng Teng" is distinct from the Sleng Teng riddim over which it was recorded.
6. Edward Seaga led the Jamaica Labour Party during the 1970s and 1980s and was prime minister of Jamaica from 1980 to 1989. The policies of "self-reliance" of Michael Manley's pro-communist PNP government were contested by the anti-communist, pro-American and capitalist policies of Seaga.
7. Outside of "Under Mi Sleng Teng", the Casio MT-40 was employed on a limited basis in the production of JPM because of the keyboard's physical and sonic limitations as a novelty instrument.
8. Based on my research and work as a music practitioner and production company owner during the 1980s and 1990s, computers were being employed in the production of some JPM but were limited to sequencing and synthesizer patch storing/editing during the 1980s. My research suggests that the first commercially successful digital recording to be made on a computer-based digital audio (DAW) recorder was Beenie Man's "Who Am I", produced by Jeremy Harding in 1996, more than a decade after the release of "Under Mi Sleng Teng". See Hitchins 2014.

9. Cleveland Browne is best known for his dancehall music production partnership with Wycliffe Johnson as "Steely and Clevie"; however, Browne worked as a prominent reggae drummer in the 1970s and purchased an Oberheim DMX drum machine at the start of the 1980s to produce reggae as well as other forms of JPM.
10. Robbie Lyn is a stalwart of the Jamaican music industry, starting with rocksteady playing in the Studio One recording group, and he has worked with a wide range of recording artists, including Peter Tosh.
11. This information is based on my attendance of performances by Pluto Shervington during the early 1970s where his work as a one-man-band was noted, but also on discussions with Hurloch and Smith during my work with them in my professional capacity as a musician during the 1980s and beyond.
12. The riddim production method is described, and how it differs to the local recording process as defined, by Peter Manuel and Wayne Marshall (2006).
13. Performance mixing is discussed at length in Hitchins (2014) and refers to the way in musical arrangements were created through a spontaneous mixing process.
14. I use the term "performance mixing" to describe the process of a spontaneous musical arrangement created by the audio engineer as the multitrack recording is being captured in the form of a two-track master. This unique approach is in stark contrast to the music industry norms of the period, where mixing was the responsibility of the producer, often crafted over the course of many days making incremental nuanced sonic adjustments to the captured musical performances, with the assistance of computers by the 1980s.
15. The only claim for the use of digital technology that is evident in this riddim is the fact that the sequenced sounds, which are analogue, were stored on a low resolution ROM chip. The sound recording otherwise depended on an analog recording process using a microphone, tape machine and mixing console.
16. In a 2006 interview with Noel Davey he confirmed that he had been paid a small performance fee for providing the Casio MT-40 keyboard from which the Sleng Teng riddim was recorded and some years later a local music publisher offered the producer, singer and Davey a publishing contract as the owners of the riddim. It is not clear to what extent the publisher was able to substantiate the ownership claim, but Davey confirmed that he had not received any further royalty payments after the initial signing advance. On some of its more recent electronic keyboards, Casio continues to issue copies of the pre-set now named the "MT-40 Riddim", which suggests that their ownership of the riddim is not contested.
17. The Stylophone was a hand-held electronic musical device intended for domestic use that allowed the user to employ a pen-shaped stylus to play monophonic melodies with a synthesized sound.
18. In the context of this document, the term "deejay" describes a style of vocal performance based on spoken and rhyming lyrics, which often employs a melodic structure.

REFERENCES

Best, Curwen. 2004. *Culture @ the Cutting Edge: Tracking Caribbean Popular Music*. Kingston: University of the West Indies Press.

Bilby, Kenneth. 1995. "Jamaica". In *Caribbean Currents: Caribbean Music from Rumba to Reggae*, edited by Peter Manuel, 143–82. Philadelphia: Temple University Press.

Bradley, Lloyd. 2000. *This Is Reggae Music: The Story of Jamaican Music*. New York: Grove.

Cooper, Carolyn. 1993. *Noises in the Blood: Orality, Gender and the "Vulgar" Body of Jamaican Popular Culture*. Durham, NC: Duke University Press.

———. 2004. *Sound Clash: Jamaican Dancehall Culture at Large*. New York: Palgrave Macmillan.

Gilroy, Paul. 1987. *There Ain't No Black in the Union Jack: The Cultural Politics of Race and Nation*. Chicago: University of Chicago Press.

Gladwell, Malcom. 2000. *The Tipping Point: How Little Things Can Make a Big Difference*. Boston: Little Brown and Company.

Greene, Paul, and Thomas Porcello, eds. 2005. *Wired for Sound: Engineering and Technologies in Sonic Cultures*. Middletown, CT: Wesleyan University Press.

Hebdige, Dick. 1987. *Cut 'n' Mix*. London: Routledge.

Hitchins, Ray. 2014. *Vibe Merchants: The Sound Creators of Jamaican Popular Music*. Farnham, UK: Ashgate.

Hope, Donna. 2006. *Inna di Danchall: Popular Culture and the Politics of Identity in Jamaica*. Kingston: University of West Indies Press.

Keil, Charles, and Steven Feld. 1994. *Music Grooves*. Chicago: University of Chicago Press.

Lysloff, Rene, and Leslie Gay. 2003. *Music and Technoculture*. Middletown, CT: Wesleyan University Press.

Manuel, Peter, and Wayne Marshall. 2006. "The Riddim Method: Aesthetics, Practice and Ownership in Jamaican Dancehall". *Journal of Popular Music* 25, no. 3: 447–70.

Rath, Richard Cullen. 1993. "African Music in Seventeenth-Century Jamaica: Cultural Transit and Transition". *William and Mary Quarterly* 50, no. 4: 700–726.

Stanley Niaah, Sonjah. 2006. "Kingston's Dancehall Spaces". *Jamaica Journal* 29, no. 3: 14–21.

———. 2010. *Dancehall: From Slaveship to Ghetto*. Ottawa: University of Ottawa Press.

Stolzoff, Norman C. 2000. *Wake the Town and Tell the People: Dancehall Culture in Jamaica*. Durham, NC: Duke University Press.

Thompson. Tyrone. 2015. "Devil in the Music: Dancehall Music Is the Source of Evil". *Gleaner*, 4 June.

Veal, Michael. 2007. *Dub: Soundscapes and Shattered Songs in Jamaican Reggae*. Middletown, CT: Wesleyan University Press.

Warner, Timothy. 2003. *Pop Music Technology and Creativity: Trevor Horn and the Digital Revolution*. Farnham, UK: Ashgate.

PART 6

RITUAL, CELEBRATION, SPACE

CHAPTER 21

Ritual and Community in Dancehall Performance

SONJAH STANLEY NIAAH

Jamaicans, especially rural Jamaicans, tend toward a collectivist or communalist view of society – here too they follow Africa.
—Mervyn Alleyne, *Roots of Jamaican Culture* (1988, 158)

A SORT OF URBAN DRAMA, A MATURE SOCIAL movement of some fifty years, dancehall is Jamaica's premiere "theatre", not in the sense of the privileged official mainstream stage or mega stage show event but more a power from the street, the cracks and the margins. It is the poor of Kingston who are its producers and perpetuators and though dancehall has gained international recognition, its creative home remains Kingston's ghettos.

Dancehall space – physical and political – is central to urban and national identity. It is as contradictory, nomadic, communal, hierarchical and competitive as it is celebratory and sacred. With dancehall events as everyday life for its innovators and perpetuators, and with no central organizing body, they are celebrations that are spontaneous, symbolic, ritualistic, private, public, seasonal, formal or informal, spatially processualized, urban as well as rural. What do such celebrations entail? What is their import? What do they celebrate? Is celebration an adjective, an aspect of dancehall or is it a corollary of it? Specifically, events celebrate the spectrum of life from birth to death, including birthday bashes, clashes, anniversary dances, events that celebrate oldies music, gangs, girls and queens, the return to school, the memory of an individual, and the more recent "link-up" events that celebrate Caribbean diasporic or community networks and wealth consumption. In these events are observable ritual elements closely tied to the power of the corner, the area or the local community, and by extension, to the revision of these definitions (see Stanley Niaah 2004a, 2004b).

Through over twelve years' participation in and observation of dancehall events and their character, I want to highlight that the nature of these celebrations speaks to something ancient and new in the meanings attached to everyday life. There is a sense in which performance through dance in dancehall events constitutes a street drama of total aesthetic and psychic transformation. The dancehall event celebrates birth, victory, anniversary, death, relationships and memory, and its accompanying norms around music, food, drink, dance and spontaneity constitute the rituals with which Afro-Jamaicans replaced lost African rituals (White 1984, 73). Even as we recognize the research by Hazzard-Gordon (1996)[1] and others that point to sacred practices being reinterpreted on their arrival in the New World, in this case the Caribbean, I want to emphasize even more than Garth White (1984) does that an understanding of dancehall within a ritual schema creates space for reinterpreting its role.

A READING OF RITUAL

My aim is not to argue that ritual understood in the traditional sense, such as that which is practised in many African villages among indigenous peoples,[2] can be found in the dancehall. Ritual in the traditional sense has an important link with spirituality. It is the act of communicating with Spirit for healing at the level of the community/village, body and soul. Using particular spaces with planned and unplanned elements, ritual is not an everyday formality but a call to Spirit and the ancestors for transformation and healing through reconnection with purpose. "Ritual is a dance with Spirit, the soul's way of interacting with the Other World, the human psyche's opportunity to develop relationship with the symbols of this world and the spirits of the other" (Somé 1999, 146).

Rather, my concern here is the everyday celebration of the God/self/life/death/anniversary continuum that dancehall presents within its everyday calendar. Though White's insight separates rituals in the traditional African sense from dancehall, dancehall performance can be read as ritual, as "action wrapped in webs of significance (Kertzer 1988, 9) and as a "permanent possibility in social life" (Robert Pelton in Austin-Broos, 1997, 46–47). In this sense, a more open interpretation of ritual is claimed. The experience of dance in this New World context has enabled the rereading of status, cosmos and sense of space especially among dancers, which is tantamount to a counter-invention of the self as a cultural and political strategy (cf. Wynter, 1977, 36). Through ritual events the self can connect to a deep structured and pre-conscious origin. And, through celebrations of life, death, anniversaries, victory and birth, conscious pacts with ancestry in traditional Jamaican dance forms, such as Gereh, Dinki Mini, Kumina and Jonkonnu, as well as contemporary forms, give way to techniques of freedom manifest through the body in an everyday context. Neither the state nor violence deters the rituals, nor is it encumbered by denominational/moral brand names manifest in, for example, the Christian church. As social commentators and creators, dancers and patrons make social, cultural and economic space in real terms.

Turner's (1969) signature concept of *communitas* resonates in this reading of ritual. The concept is Turner's representation of how, in the negation of normal rites and social hierarchy, bonds between people which enable society to exist are able to emerge in ritual contexts. It is the experience of heightened sociality, such as that found in the liminal phase of rites of passages, that is highlighted by Turner and which crucially separates the dancehall event from any other perceived as mere entertainment. Turner saw liminality as by far the most important phase of the ritual process. It involves a prolonged period where the participant is both literally and symbiotically marginalized. During liminality the status of the participant is vague in order to ensure distinctness of the ritual process from normal life. Turner argued that this period of liminality, if prolonged, leads to the development of a transcendental feeling of social togetherness. This is evidenced within dancehall by interviews with patrons in terms of psychological benefits and feelings of attachment. It is this that *communitas* is aimed at capturing – the transcendence of social structure that brings the participant under the authority of the community. The initiate submits to nothing less than the authority of the community.

Popular Jamaican DJ Bounty Killer puts this into sharp focus when he says, "Poor people keep a dance, poor people gather, poor people spend money, poor people make money, we build each other. . . . Poor people do these things for themselves" (CVM TV interview, October 2003). Ritual is therefore to be viewed as everyday potential seen in the liminal spaces through which entities can pass outside the realm of normal or dominant classificatory schemes that serve to ground them in particular cultural/symbolic ordering systems.

This new permanent possibility and place of the liminal in the analysis of New World performance highlights liminality then as "an idiom of performance" (cf. Austin-Broos 1997, 47). This performance is the way social beings reclaim lost rituals and create and recreate themselves and their way of being, and it is how they also remember (Connerton 1989, 22). Significantly, performance rites such as those within commemorative ceremonies, that is, "expressive acts" having "conspicuous regularity" of a formal, stereotyped, stylized and repetitive nature (44–45), are important over time and space and their meaning extends beyond the ritual to "non-ritual actions, to the whole life of a community" (45).

The dance event ultimately represents a celebration of community (see Stanley Niaah 2004d, 2004b). There's a sense in which the dance typifies the sense of community that inner-city dwellers have had to negotiate through shared activities around "yard" and "area" life or "livity", evidenced by the purpose, sociality and character of these events. Early events that epitomized this sense of community were the welcome home dances that celebrated the return of a prisoner to the community, which was popular among the lower classes during the 1930s within the Burru drumming tradition (Hebdige 1997 [1974]; White 1984). Sound systems such as Sir Coxone's Downbeat continued such events that today are expressed particularly in street events emergent around the community corner shop or bar and domino tables as the standard weekend leisure activity.

More recently, major street events such as "Passa Passa", located in the heart of a partisan, politically controlled area and one which is feared by many Kingstonians, becomes a unique example. Passa Passa was initiated in 2003 in Tivoli Gardens (Western Kingston) on Wednesday nights and celebrated its second anniversary on 2 March 2005. It was first dominated by residents of that community and surrounding areas but soon became a novelty because it was declared safe to attend the event in this politically charged and sometimes violence-ridden area. Where this community used to be a sort of ghost town after dark, the dance event has transformed the community, making it a convergence zone for a variety of patrons: local and international, rich and poor, uptown and downtown participants could mingle in a good street dance. On a Wednesday night therefore, the community becomes an open border across which residents of that community and surrounding areas, Asians and other tourists, businessmen and others cross, even during periods of heightened political and gang warfare. The Passa Passa event is an example of the regeneration of community spirit and economic viability, a heightened celebration of life and the redefinition of community for several residents.

There are many other examples of events that constitute a celebration of community. These include the "Backline" event, once held at the corner of Spanish Town Road and Beeston Street (Western Kingston), and the popular vintage music event on Rae Street known as "Rae Town" (Eastern Kingston). The consistency of their occurrence, emergence and impact makes it impossible to ignore their utility and the nature of such celebrations.

THE DANCE EVENT

What then are these rituals and how do they manifest? What is their essential nature and purpose? The dance event has observable rituals: of preparation, arrival, community, birth, death, victory, memorializing, anniversaries, accession or ascension, transcendence/transformation, welcome, competition and fertility.[3] In order to fully understand the importance attached to dancehall, its events and the formality of its performance practice, I wish to explain the importance of names, time and purpose which are all tied up with the ritualistic or commemorative aspects of such events.

Dance events always have a name. Their appeal and consequent power converge around this naming, this rite of celebration, which takes the form of the latest dancehall and/or inner-city *lingua franca*. This is crucial to attracting patrons. Some of these names are song titles or lines and include "Ol' Time Something Come Back Again", "Clean Up Yuh Heart an Come", "Girl's Dem Bashment", "Bruck Out, Bruck Out", "Raw and Rough", "Fully Loaded", "Weh di Gal Dem Want: Vitamin S-E-X", "Gimme di Light" and "Rasta Jamboree" among many others.

Named events spot the nightscape of any given week throughout the calendar year, almost every night, all year round. The most popular period within the calendar year is that between December and September. Dancehall's "liturgical calendar" is noteworthy because it persists regardless of season, state power or sanctions, and presents a challenge to conceptualizations of popular dancehall culture as "carnivalesque" in the Bakhtinian sense, in which the specific carnival period where everyday norms are relaxed suggests a time limit.

Whereas weekend and holiday events were the most popular events in the 1950s and 1960s, by the late 1980s to 1990s (arguably dancehall's first high point) the typical week was:

- Monday: Stone Love sound system at Tropic Club, and Waltham Park Road
- Tuesday: Super D sound system at Top Line Bar (later Southdale Plaza)

- Wednesday: Backline event at Spanish Town Road and Metro Media sound system at Woodford Park
- Thursday: Stone Love at House of Leo
- Friday and Saturday: standard weekend commercial and party events (usually several)
- Sunday: Klassique sound system at Rae Street and Super D at Jamaica Gates

By 2004, Kingston's weekly dancehall calendar had mushroomed into several events characteristic of a highpoint:

- Monday: Early Mondays (at Waterford and Stand Pipe), Hot Mondays
- Tuesday: Kool Tuesday, Asylum Ladies Night
- Wednesday: Asylum Oldies Night, Weddy Weddy Wednesday, Blazing Wednesday, Passa Passa
- Thursday: Early Thursday, Asylum Dancehall Night, Sicky Sicky Thursday, Stress Free Thursday
- Friday: Jiggy Friday, Spooky Friday, Kidz Friday
- Saturday: Crazy Saturday, along with numerous events
- Sunday: Rae Town, Bad Mind Sunday, Asylum Vintage Night, along with popular Sunday events in West Kingston

It should be noted that the emergence of "early" events signal higher levels of coordination among promoters who are successfully reclaiming the total hours during a night: three or more events are now commonplace. Key patrons attend all events and they can be observed moving from one to the other at precise times. This level of coordination is unprecedented and protocols related to the placement of events within the weekly calendar are an area for further study.

What sustains such high levels of performance activity in the face of seemingly diminishing economic and social capital? The answer to this lies in the power of the ritual, the sustenance it affords, its democratic regimes, its tangible structure of rules and codes alongside a highly developed sense of meaning and identity tied to location among its key participants. In this light dancehall differs from carnival and the consequent reading of its liberatory potential according to Bakhtinian carnivalesque analysis. Where a Bakhtinian analysis simply offers a liberatory potential, the daily persistence of dancehall is liberation actualized in the sense of daily celebration of the everyday condition. This study of dancehall acknowledges that even while its *habitus* is marginal, dancehall is sacred space by virtue of the sense in which souls continue to be sustained. Obviously, there is also the matter of importing readings of culture that are decontextualized in their wider application.

Time, whether commencement or termination time, is a significant feature of any dancehall event and it has varied over the past fifty years. The significance of the dark for planning revolts, telling duppy and Anancy stories or dance activities is well documented. Reminiscent of the secret slave meetings of the plantations in the West Indies when massa was asleep, the twenty-first-century dance event warms up at 1:00 a.m. on average, when all society is in a state of slumber. This 1:00 a.m. time contrasts with the

8:00 p.m. time of the 1960s and later 11:00 p.m. in the 1990s. Not all events begin after dark. Stage shows, at the furthest extreme of commercial dancehall practice, particularly those events that occur on the beach, often commence in the mid-afternoon to evening hours.

The average event that is not prematurely ended by the police or other disruption in the 1960s lasted five hours. This average time applies to the late 1990s to present, as the later starting time of events has meant later ending times determined by the time the last patron leaves. Downtown community events end at dawn while events at uptown clubs end earlier. Clubs observe strict ending times because of employment terms, their location within Kingston's business centre and their potential for disrupting rush hour traffic flow.

"The dance" is not just an event; it is a system of rules and codes, an institution. Patrons are aware of the latest dance moves, latest songs, debates and artistes. There are salutations, tributes and paying of respect. Validation is signalled in specific ways – cigarette lighter flashes, gun salutes or saying "pram pram" or "boukaya", for instance, as signs of approval. The audience *participates* in the fundamental themes or moral codes that have been part of the dancehall scene, many of them from its inception. Some of these include "celebrating the community or local area", "friendship and love versus animosity", "power and prowess of the rude boy/badman", "competition and struggle", "sexuality and morality/ethics of the penis and vagina", "celebrating the vagina, women, mother, girls", "celebrating the DJ and/or sound system", "dancing", "the authority and divinity of Rastafari's Haile Selassie and the Christian God", "the essential herb", "colour/class identity", "material culture" and "relationship between state institutions and the people".

These themes are apparent in the music and in the call of selectors who solicit appropriate audience responses. It is not uncommon to hear the selector calling his crowd to respond by showing of hands to, among other liturgical incantations, "from a bwoy nuh badda dan you, han up inna di air" (put your hand in the air if you are the baddest), or put your hand in the air if you "have yu owna man" (have your own man), "if you hole no condemn" (if your vagina is not condemned), "from yuh neva dash weh belly" (from you have never had an abortion), "all who seh ganja fi bu'n" (all who say ganja is to be smoked) and "put up yuh gun finger if you a nuh battyman" (put your gun finger in the air if you are not a homosexual). Similarly, the selector will call for a showing of hands of those who love God and the audience will respond after which a song which typifies the sentiment will be played. There is a particular interaction ritual at hand here in the dynamic relationship between the patrons, selectors' conversations, DJ music and dance.

Events also have norms and codes. Norms of dance, location, fashion and status exist. Women adorn themselves according to the dictates of the current dancehall fashion. Between the 1960s and 1980s women wore platform shoes, bell-bottom pants, dresses below the knees with sleeves and high neckline and Afros; the trend by the 1990s moved through pieces of red or white, this or that, to extremes both of nakedness and glamour. In the early 1990s golden braids, coloured wigs, gold cargo necklaces and earrings, mesh tops with one-inch holes, transparent low-cut blouses, transparent leggings or stockings, g-string panties, gloves, nail extensions and spectacles were common, as opposed to the current trends in athletic jerseys and shoes from, among others, Tommy Hilfiger, Ralph Lauren, Fubu and Nike.

No matter the nationality, weight or reproductive status, individuals are welcomed in the dance and the same codes apply. A fat woman, like the pregnant girl, Japanese girl, and patrons of Euro-American descent like "Medusa" have their place within dancehall's inclusivity and attending dance events makes them aware of important behavioral codes, including the latest dance moves, songs and debates. There are also salutations, tributes, the paying of respect and notions of hierarchy and seniority that patrons will observe.

Crews are essentially social groupings, sometimes gangs, peer groups or persons defined by residence in a particular area, such as the Standpipe crew or the Montego Bay crew as locational identifiers; they have always been a part of the social scene that is amplified within dancehall. The crew is a significant part of a ritual of arrival, reminiscent of shipmate bonds of the enslaved: one would attend the dance with a crew and this is still true today. They may be a community, such as fashion or dancing crews (Ouch or Black Roses crews, respectively), and their identities are defined by any or all of the following attributes: style, place of origin, skill or a combination of these. The crew is not only a sign of social relations but serves important functions such as security. Some would attend the dance with a crew of men only, depending on the security risk determined by whether the dance was being held in a politically volatile area, the sound system being labelled, gang feuds or persistent police invasion. In such a space the crew remains alert and in close proximity to the perimeter of the dance venue or a wall that can be scaled in the case of gunfire or any other act that propels the need for quick exit. As a rule, a crew member who is aware of the security risks involved in attending an event that might prove volatile needs to be able to see the gate (personal interview, Harry T, 24 April 2002).

Once the event's tone and structural elements are set, the purpose takes over. Events are organized around a purpose: a regular session for enjoyment with sale of liquor for profit on a specific night of the week or month, an event at the highest commercial end such as a stage show, or a celebration of old music such as an "oldies" party. Previously, dance events have been identified in music terms – how, why and by whom it is played. For example, Stolzoff (2000, 194) identified two major types of sound system dances, that of the "clash" and the "juggling" events which are distinguished by the competitive versus non-competitive mode of music playing. He also distinguished "performance modes" determined by the selector's performance, such as ritual and sacrifice (210–12). Highlighting the music does not fully take account of the purpose. Because most dance events seek to celebrate an aspect of social life, they reveal a great deal about Kingston's cultural life. For example, the "Christmas dance", which dates back to the experience of enslaved Africans in Jamaica, is the antecedent of all contemporary dances. Oral accounts of dancehall reveal that people looked toward a Christmas dance with great anticipation as a chance to affirm, or "big up", their social identity and cultural experience. By the early 1980s these dance events disappeared. Marcia Davis, businesswoman of Frontline Pub, reported that in the late 1980s her business partner started staging events to bring back the dance spirit that had faded with the decline of Christmas events (personal interview, April 2002).

Similarly, celebration of style is also crucial. Events like "Piece of Yellow" at Rainbow Lawn on 27 September 2002; "Workforce Uniform Party" at Market Place on 5 August 2003; "Red and White Party" on 15 February 2003 at Rainbow Lawn; "Sports Wear and Jersey Dance" at Breezy Castle, 12 April 2003; "British Fashion Party" at Villa Ronai, 24 April 2003; and "Curves: The Ultimate Stretch Jeans Party" at Market Place, 25 December 2002, are all examples of the way in which fashion is celebrated in dancehall. Other celebrations are dance events that bear the name of popular dance moves, such as "Pon di River" and "Higher Level". Such names signal the tempo and emphasis of the event, intended to feature the most popular dancers and moves.

There are characteristic holiday/commemorative events that celebrate not only Christmas but Jamaica's independence, Valentine's Day, Easter and Heroes Day. Other events are dedicated to oldies music such as Merritone Disco's "Old Hits Party", "Grooving on a Friday Afternoon" at Venus Headquarters, 22¾ Waltham Park Road or "Good Times", the biennial oldies party last staged at Mas Camp, 30 August 2003. Lastly, there are other events dedicated to Rastafari culture, the famous Jah Love sound system dances, as well as "Rasta Jamboree", 29 March 2003, at 2 Skibo Avenue, and "Melkam Liddet" on 7 January 2003, at Rainbow Lawn, a celebration of Ethiopian Christmas.

Ultimately, the dancehall facilitates a change in social, psychological and spatial states for the individual and the group. The (rite de) passage from home to the dance, through the dance event, the passage during the event into other states, the passage from non-entity into legitimacy of purpose during the event and, finally, the return home all delineate dancehall as ritual space, especially among its working-/underclass communicants such as a dancehall queen. The persistence of this nightly celebration merges the ritual with the everyday, blurring the boundaries to extend dancehall into daily existence; a different world inside but outside of society. One could also argue based on dancehall's mostly non-seasonal nature that it exists within a kind of social limbo. There is really never incorporation back into the everyday, as the everyday becomes the entire ritual – of preparation, communion, withdrawal and rest, then back to preparation all over again.

MAJOR DANCE EVENTS

The *birthday bash* moves through important stages of ceremony and is by far the most ceremonial of dances. It includes the cutting of a cake, tributes to the celebrated and specially featured artistes. It is an event used by popular and semi-popular dance patrons, DJs and promoters who are able to attract large crowds. Examples of this event include the birthdays of Elephant Man (10 September 2005 at Mass Camp Village), Bounty Killer (It's tha Party, 14 June 2003) and DYCR (23 March 2003 at Hellshire Beach). Others include such personalities as cosmetologist Sherene Birthday Bash (7 July 2002, at Wet n' Wild Roof club), video producer Jack Sowah and John the Dancer (22 May 2002 at New Little Copa Club) and promoter Q45 (6 November 2002 at Stone Love's Burlington Avenue base) who have staged events. There are also generic birthday events like "Taurus Hype: It's a Birthday Affair" (8 May 2002 at New Little Copa), where all taureans are special guests.

Depending on the host or celebrant, birthday events can take the form of a large stage show where there are featured artistes. They can also attract a cover charge or none at all. For example, Bounty Killer's birthday bash at the Caymanas Polo Club featured international acts, the entire "Alliance" (the name of the Bounty Killer fraternity of recording artists or friendship circle), among others, in addition to dancing girls on stage in cages as a new feature within events. Dancehall queen (crowned in 1999) Stacey's birthday bash (8 December 2001 at Mahoe Drive in her hometown of Cockburn Gardens) featured Beenie Man, Spragga Benz, Lukie D, Mad Anju and Cecile, all friends of Stacey who performed at what was a street dance attracting no cover charge.

Memorial dances, such as one to commemorate the death of a don or area leader, include the "Jim Brown Memorial Dance", which has been organized for the past twelve years in February (for example, on 23 February 2003); that of former area leader and member of the Black Roses Crew "Willy Haggart the Great Memorial" (for example, on 18 April 2003, Rainbow Lawn); and Blacka Douge, a businessman killed at the same time as Willy Haggart, whose second memorial called "Missing You" was held 17 April 2003 at Naseberry Pub, 31 Greenwich Road. On the street, dons such as Haggart were known to be involved in illicit activities but were role models who were charged, sometimes inadvertently, with the responsibility of financing the less fortunate in their area or community of de facto control. It could be argued that Lester "Jim Brown" Coke was the don of all dons. He was one of two leaders of the famed west Kingston Shower Posse with strong international links. The posse has been charged with gun and drug related crimes locally and in the United States.[4]

Memorial events typically have family members, DJs, members of Parliament and friends, in addition to regular patrons paying tribute. Observances such as moments of silence are common. This mode of celebration functions as collective memorializing consistent with performance rituals of the folk, especially through wakes. It is important to note that pre-funeral and post-funeral activities can take the form of a dance. There are also beliefs that accompany the organization of memorial dances, that is, how long they should last and when they should commence. For example, it was thought that to continue the memorial events for Jim Brown beyond ten years would bring destruction on the family. And, if memorial events begin in the first year after death it is believed that the event has to be staged every year after that, while if a year passes, memorial events can be planned when it is convenient for the family members.

The *anniversary dance* can celebrate the anniversary of a sound system; Stone Love's anniversary dances on 13 December 2003 and 14 December 2002 at Market Place are examples. Stone Love's anniversary dances started in 1993 when the twenty-first anniversary of its inception was celebrated. Similarly, sound systems like that of Jack Ruby celebrated its twenty-eighth anniversary in 1987 and recently established sound systems like Fire Links (initiator of the Hot Mondays event in 2003) celebrated its anniversary on 19 October 2002 at New Little Copa, Bull Bay. Also, celebrating the anniversary of an event is common. For example, the Passa Passa and Hot Mondays first anniversary events were staged on 25 February 2004, at 47 Spanish Town Road and 20 October 2003, at Market Place, respectively.

The anniversary is sometimes celebrated through a series of events. In the case of Stone Love, notwithstanding the Christmas celebrations, anniversary events often cover the first three weekends of the month of December, with the main anniversary dance as the master event. At a Stone Love anniversary dance it is likely that the event will feature an early juggling session, where each of the sound systems present will play in order of seniority/popularity, after which the start of musical selection by the most senior/popular one will signal the start of the show. The host sometimes remains on stage for the duration of the show, which features performance tributes from amateur and professional DJs.

Anniversary events can also celebrate the existence of a venue, such as New Little Copa's anniversary celebrations (25 May 2002); a newspaper such as *XNews* (8 August 2003); and tenure in a political office, indicating the extensive use of this performance practice as a vehicle for celebration. For example, Jamaica's former opposition leader celebrated his fortieth anniversary as member of Parliament in the West Kingston constituency with a dance on 10 March 2002, in Tivoli Gardens, with sound systems Swatch, Katarock and Stone Love.

The *girls' dance*, like that of "XXX Girls" on 14 August 1994, "Roll Out 2002" on 21 July 2002 (by-lined "the girl's roll call") and "Hot Girls Fiesta" on 2 August 2003, are events dedicated to the girls of dancehall. There are small events and large ones. An example of a large event is that of the Dancehall Queen contest, in which a queen is crowned. Sound system queens have also been crowned and the events constitute varying types of a girls' dance, which combines the importance of fashion, dance moves and attitude, in an event totally dedicated to the women of dancehall. Though the annual Dancehall Queen event has so far been staged in Montego Bay, it is an urban space, and some 70 per cent[5] of the entrants are from Kingston and the surrounding parish of St Catherine. People also travel from Kingston for the event and the idea behind the show was spawned from the popularity of dancehall queen Carlene in the early dancehall highpoint.

Celebrations of gangs are an important part of the liturgical calendar. The annual "Original Spanglers Dance", celebrating the well-known PNP-affiliated Spangler's posse, is an annual event, held, for example, on 27 April 2002 and 26 April 2003, at Rainbow Lawn. This event is always a top crowd-puller of those showing allegiance or affiliation, from DJs booked to perform or just passing through to regular patrons and hosts of vendors. Such an event, different from a street dance, attracts a cover charge and its profit is sometimes given to charity, as well as paying the DJs who are hired to perform.

Stage shows vary in size, duration and appeal and are some of the first events to have put dancehall on the performance map for members of the international community. At its highest expression are events such as the now-defunct Reggae Sunsplash, Reggae Sumfest staged in Montego Bay and Sting, considered the University of Dancehall,[6] staged at the Jamworld entertainment complex on the outskirts of the Kingston Metropolitan Area. Sumfest and Sting are annual events which have long histories: in the case of Sting, over twenty years. Sumfest during its 2003 staging lasted seven nights, with its most patronized "dancehall night" gathering over twenty-five thousand people. Sting is staged on Boxing Day, and features the hottest dancehall acts of the preceding calendar year. Other events like Sashi (25 August 2002, James Bond Beach) lasted three days. One night events like Hot Shots (21 December 2002, Constant Spring Golf Club) featuring Shaggy, Sean Paul, Damian Marley and Bounty Killer, among others, attract cover charges that equate to one night's fee of Sumfest. Events like Hot Shots, usually held at an accessible upscale venue above Crossroads, have to attract a wide cross-section of Kingston's population to be a commercial success. Their commercial significance far outweighs that of any other event in terms of capital investment and potential profit.

Sound clashes have been popular since the inception of dancehall. Beginning with Sir Coxone's Downbeat and Tom's The Great Sebastian sound systems that clashed several times amid others desperately vying for the position of top sound, the event's purpose is to symbolically crown a champion sound. This trend continued and intensified in the early 1990s. Sound systems travelled from Japan and Germany for clashes in Jamaica and vice versa. Events titled "Metro Media versus Bodyguard" or "African Star versus Crystal Disco", typically naming the sound systems and signalling the sound war to ensue, were common. "Specials" (DJ recordings that honour sound systems) were sonic weapons pre-recorded by popular DJs for the sound systems to ensure positive crowd response in signature dancehall salutatory mechanisms, including the gun salute, the cigarette lighter or the cell phone.

Clashes operate at several levels: the symbolic and the real. The real entails violence, which has plagued the dancehall tradition since its inception but particularly in the first highpoint when gun play, gun salutes and gang warfare peaked in the 1960s and 1970s. In particular, clashes at all levels – sound clash, matie wars, political and gang warfare and DJ wars – inspired violence among their supporters. Certain tunes would produce the blazing of guns and others brought about fights. Many events ended in violence or police raids. The owner of Stone Love – Winston Powell – acknowledged that a popularly anticipated clash in the early 1990s was between Stone Love and Killamanjaro sound systems. They met about five times and all ended prematurely with no distinct winner. Clashes are expensive – the sound system has to be in top shape, "specials" are bought and losses are the symbolic or actual death of a sound system through the loss of reputation. Ultimately the clash leads to broken spirits, both of the patrons and sound system operators.

Throughout my research on dancehall from 1999 to the present, the clash was virtually non-existent, possibly because the losses are still thought to outweigh the gains. As the violence reduced tolerance for dancehall, economic liability and decline of dance events reduced the desire for clashes. With dancing as an important site of expression in Jamaica, learning from past mistakes has become necessary to preserve this outlet. However, the clash is still a part of the legacy manifest in dancehall culture in other countries such as Japan and Germany. One of the most recent clashes held in Jamaica involved a German sound system, Sentinel, at the event called "Who Rule the Holy Mountain – War, It's War, War Tonight" held at Cactus Lawn, Middleton (rural St Andrew) on 20 September 2003. It is important to note that DJ wars, also called clashes, remain a staple of the Sting stage show. As recent as the 2003 show, veteran DJ and Sting (stage show) "clash artist" Ninja Man was party to a war of words turned fist fight with emerging DJ Vybz Kartel.

Vintage or Oldies Dance events are different in approach, patronage, speed, appeal and popularity and are epitomized by the Rae Town street dance in East Kingston. At the other level there are stage shows such as Heineken Star time, Stars R Us and Good Times. Smaller events include Sunday Classics at Little Copa (now defunct), Party Party in March of each year at 18 Patrick Drive and Olanzo Hawk's Birthday Bash held on 5 September 2003. Sound systems classified as soul sounds (Soul Shack, Purple Love, Mid Wheel Disco and Merritone among others) are the sonic specialists at these events and the emphasis is on playing musical selections of old from different musical genres such as rhythm and blues, soul and reggae.

Kenneth "Bop" Campbell, who plays regularly on the Mid Wheel Disco, says the oldies event is about bringing back the love, the memory of love, respect, family spirit/stability and relationships among people of all ages. He attributes the lack of respect for life in Jamaica to the lack of love. Campbell explains that "when you go to a vintage dance . . . you see people hugging and dancing, that is what we want back in dancehall. . . . When I go to a dance you hug up . . . it is the love."[7] Vintage events, like their name suggests, have held a strong position on the dancehall calendar because of their appeal to a distinct group that has expanded over time to include folks from the younger generations who cannot appreciate the faster pace of the typical dance.

The Link-Up Dance events include Washington, DC; Philadelphia; Canada/Jamaica; Britain; New Jersey (11 May 2003, La Roose); New York (14 June 2003); Baltimore (23 May 2003, Mas Camp); California (9 August 2003, Rainbow Lawn); and New York/Jamaica/England (6 April 2002, La Roose). The first link-up event I recognized was a Taxi Link-Up in 1999 on Sarah Street, in Central Kingston. As I began my research I found this concept unique and reminiscent of, but more sophisticated than, the usual round robin events at the community level. However, the British link-up is by far the most popular and manifests in a season of events.

The British link-up events illustrate the tangible Jamaican diasporic links that still exist and continue based on this performance practice. Through the events organized, the type of patrons and rituals observed, the British "dance" has come to epitomize the terms "bashment", "bling bling" and "ghetto fabulous", at which the "nicest" girls, best dancers, most prominent dancehall stars, and most expensive clothes, automobiles and beverages are present. These three interrelated terms refer to excitement and an exciting event, hyped possessions and lower-class prosperity, respectively.

The British link-up events began in 1990 when British returning residents, who book their flights very early, usually on a chartered flight, were welcomed home. These events are commonly designated as a "big dance": their character and appeal rival that of stage shows. The dancehall community looks forward to the British events around Easter and Christmas (for example, British Xmas Bash at La Roose, 1998) in Jamaica as well as other events in London (around Jamaica's Independence Day), Canada and the United States. The British events around Easter in Jamaica constitute a season which includes the bus ride, pool party, beach bash, school uniform party and final British link-up dance. There have been other additions to the regular season, such as a fashion party (British Fashion Party at Villa Ronai, Stony Hill, 24 April 2003) and a British Sport Swimwear Affair (Urban Development Corporation beach, Montego Bay, 26 April 2003).

CONCLUSION

This chapter continues the task of unearthing missing texts in the process of historicizing dancehall. Crucially, it separates itself from the "music-mania" that has characterized readings of the performance practice for the past twenty years. An understanding of dancehall as a whole culture must be led by greater exposition of its institutional frameworks, systems, codes and ethics, and most importantly its reclamation and reinterpretation of ritual and manifestation of New World rituals.

By viewing rituals performed through the spectrum of events (celebrating death, birth, life, anniversary, victory and memory), the chapter contributes new ways of understanding "dance" and "community". This approach allows for the expansion of the definition of dancehall beyond a carnivalesque space, a seasonal, fleshly and "escapist" liberatory potential; and for the expansion of its citizenry beyond a worthless, unsophisticated underclass. Tainted by Eurocentric interpretations within dance research and sociology, "dance" and "community" are seen to be deceptive conceptual categories that mask a complex movement system, on the one hand, and a sociocultural system on the other. Through dance, performers define, project and re-engineer their identity, contesting prescribed categories, de-legitimating, expanding, reinventing or absorbing them as desired. Firmly held systems of maintenance and renewal exist in the values, codes, morality, norms, rituals, hierarchies, themes and recruitment criteria that contribute to the high degrees of sociality and senses of community in dancehall culture. The consumption of lyrics in dance halls through bodily movement and around specific themes reveal potent modes of community throughout history, signalling developed forms of commentary, problem-solving and memorializing.

It is another space, process and means of connecting to a higher self as well as the community that dancehall provides outside the everyday routine of survival, especially for the disenfranchised youth within the Jamaican lower class. It is this open-ended enactment of self, community, area, gender and nation, this stylization of everyday life, this performance through the actions of the body within spaces that stand apart from the status quo in the evolution of the New World that is ultimately represented. Dancehall, by virtue of its incorporation of the traditional, stands between the old and new worlds and the concept of limbo, as well as its invoked extension, liminality. Limbo and dancehall symbolize an everyday that occupies shrubs, streets, yards and the cracks and margins, but yielding tremendous power in philosophy, transcendence, and transformation of space.

My conclusion is that dancehall can be understood as a liminal performance space, a sort of crossroads. The crossroads is the meeting place of cardinal points, of loss and gain, the sacred and profane, joy and sorrow (Chevannes 2001, 7)[8] – these being important aspects of Caribbean reality. I propose that liminality is expressed as context (space/place/location), consciousness, history, method and identity between here and there, east and west, centre and margin, conscious and unconscious, Africa and Europe, sacred and profane. In this liminal space, dancehall has been criticized and predictions of its demise publicized. But it is the liminal that occasions its possibilities of articulation and rearticulation through its rituals.

NOTES

1. See Katrina Hazzard-Gordon (1996), who points out that the adaptation of traditional West African patterns to new sociocultural environments involved the role of the sacred being transformed as dance moved from its sacred ceremonial African context to the numerous secularized uses it acquired under slavery.
2. See, among others, Somé (1999) Turner (1967, 1969).
3. Fertility rituals have been highlighted by Cooper (2004), and Ryman (1980) has looked at the importance of the reporoductive process and its influence on traditional and, by extension, contemporary popular Jamaican dance.
4. See Gunst (1995, 42–43) for an explanation of Jim Brown's criminal experience.
5. From field notes, sixth annual Dancehall Queen contest, Pier One, Montego Bay, 10 August 2002. Over 70 per cent of the contestants identified themselves as representing Kingston or St Catherine, the neighbouring parish, of which some of its environs are included in the Kingston Metropolitan Area.
6. Winford Williams, *On Stage*, CVM Television, 20 September 2003.
7. Translated from the Jamaican language in which Campbell spoke to the author in a personal interview in 2003.
8. See his inaugural lecture "Ambiguity and the Search for Knowledge" for an extended look at the importance of the crossroad in Caribbean existence. He noted that liminality implies "ambiguity". It is a part of the everyday life of many cultures, some having gods/deities who preside over it, especially at the crossroad. It is important to note that deities of the crossroad, and by extension the importance of the crossroad as bequeathed to Caribbean experience from West African societies, have survived in the Caribbean within Haitian, Cuban, Trinidadian, Grenadian and Jamaican folk religions.

REFERENCES

Alleyne, M. 1988. *Roots of Jamaican Culture*. London: Pluto Press.

Austin-Broos, D. 1997. *Jamaica Genesis: Religion and the Politics of Moral Orders*. Chicago: University of Chicago Press.

Chevannes, B. 2001. "Ambiguity and the Search for Knowledge: An Open-Ended Adventure of Imagination". Lecture, University of the West Indies, Mona, Jamaica, 22 March.

Connerton P. 1989. *How Societies Remember*. Cambridge: Cambridge University Press.

Cooper, C. 2004. "Lady Saw Cuts Loose: Female Fertility Rituals in the Dancehall". *Jamaica Journal* 27, nos. 2–3: 13–19.

Gunst, L. 1995. *Born fi Dead: A Journey through the Jamaican Posse Underworld*. New York: Henry Holt.

Hazzard-Gordon, K. 1996. "Dancing under the Lash: Sociocultural Disruption, Continuity, and Synthesis". In *African Dance: An Artistic, Historical and Philosophical Inquiry*, edited by Kariamu Welsh-Asante, 101–30. Trenton, NJ: Africa World Press.

Hebdige, D. 1997 [1974]. "From Reggae, Rastas and Rudies: Style and the Subversion of Form". In *Reggae, Rasta, Revolution: Jamaican Music from Ska to Dub*, edited by C. Potash, 121–28. New York: Schirmer/Prentice Hall International.

Kertzer, D. 1988. *Ritual, Politics and Power*. London: Yale University Press.

Ryman, C. 1980. "The Jamaican Heritage in Dance". *Jamaica Journal*, no. 44: 2–13.

Somé, M. 1999. *The Healing Wisdom of Africa: Finding Life Purpose through Nature, Ritual and Community*. New York: Jeremy P. Tarcher/Putnam.

Stanley Niaah, S. 2004a. "A Common Genealogy: Dancehall, Limbo and the Sacred Performance Space". *Discourses in Dance* 2, no. 2: 9–26.

———. 2004b. "Kingston's Dancehall: A Story of Space and Celebration". PhD thesis, University of the West Indies, Mona.

Turner, Victor. 1967. "Betwixt and Between: The Liminal Period in Rites de Passage". In *The Forest of Symbols: Aspects of Ndembu Ritual*, by Victor Turner, 93–111. Ithaca, NY: Cornell University Press.

———. 1969. *The Ritual Process*. Harmondsworth: Penguin.

White, G. 1984. "The Development of Jamaican Popular Music, Part 2. Urbanization of the Folk: The Merger of Traditional and the Popular in Jamaican Music". *ACIJ Research Review* 1:3–15, 24–36.

Wynter, S. 1977. "We Know Where We Are From: The Politics of Black Culture from Myal to Marley". Paper presented at Houston Conference, November, in C.L.R. James Collection, Africana Studies Department, Brown University.

CHAPTER 22

Egúngún in Disguise

The Jamaican Nine Night Ceremony[*]

LENA DELGADO DE TORRES

THIS CHAPTER SEEKS TO MAKE CONNECTIONS BETWEEN JAMAICAN Nine Night rituals and Egúngún ancestral worship within traditional Yorùbá religion and Cuban Lùkùmi, also known as Regla de Ocha, or simply "Ocha". Nine Nights are Jamaican funerary rituals. They are prolonged wake periods that last nine days, hence the name "Nine Night". Despite the strength of orthodox Christianity, syncretic religious forms are also present. These combine Christian and African elements, such as Jonkonnu processions, Pukkumina, Zion Church, Revival and Rastafari. Revival religion and Jonkonnu processions are particularly important to this study. Explicitly Yorùbán-descended religions are also present in Jamaica, in particular, the Nago tradition, practised in the parish of Westmoreland until at least 1979 (Lewin 2000, 184). Nine Nights are ostensibly Christian practices, but like so many other cultural forms in Jamaica, they are combined with African religious practices.

This chapter draws together multiple lines of evidence, including original research and fieldwork dating from 2009 to 2011, anthropological accounts from the 1950s, Ocha and Ifá sacred divination literature known as Odù, and esoteric knowledge culled from practitioners' written and oral accounts, in order to understand the Nine Night's relation to Yorùbá-based ancestral worship. Furthermore, this chapter documents the gradual transition in Jamaican society from Nine Night's older folk cultural forms to a newer culture that draws deeply on the old forms – dancehall. Lastly, the chapter traces the shifts of women's power within the Egúngún societies, in the context of Ọya's significance for women in the dancehall and a feminist reading of Yorùbá and Jamaican ancestral worship.

In order to understand the cultural forms of Yorùbá ancestral worship, we must take a brief journey into the underworld. In the Yorùbá pantheon, Death holds an exalted position among God's creations. He is the final transformer, the Òrìṣà called Ikú. He is also known as Òjiṣẹ́ Ọ́run – heaven's bailiff. He is entrusted with escorting souls from this world to the next, a condition in which dying is likened to a debt all humans must

[*]Previously published in *Journal of American Rootwork* 1, no. 1 (2018).

pay. Ikú is the collector, the grim reaper who harvests our souls. Ikú's ability to transform our loved ones, hiding them from our view, "causes pain, anguish and bewilderment in society" (Mason 1985, 28). Mason argues that it is because of the need to deal with the excruciating pain and confusion resulting from death that the Yorùbá, and their descendants throughout the African diaspora, have developed a "sophisticated and detailed response to the fact of death" (28). This response, Mason argues, is best observed in the Ẹgbẹ́ Egúngún (ancestor society). Egúngún societies were developed by the Ọ̀yọ Yorùbá, who "adapted and added" to masking traditions honouring the ancestors practised by other West African ethnic groups (28). Mason describes "the Ẹgbẹ́ Egúngún as a society of spiritual specialists who oversee the observance of ancestral devotion and come to the aid and comfort of the community when Death strikes in its midst" (28). Egúngún worshippers honour and impersonate the dead through their masking practices.

Mason (1985, 28) notes that Egúngún is the collective of ancestral spirits who live in heaven. They are called Ará Ọ̀run (dwellers of heaven). These spirits are constantly watching their survivors who are still living on earth. Our ancestors have the power to bless, protect, warn and punish us, depending on how we care for them, or whether we neglect them (29). The collective of ancestral spirits protects the community from evil, ensuring its well-being. These spirits can be called on at certain times, either while standing on the graves of the ancestors or at the family shrine. Practitioners of Yorùbá traditional religion, Regla de Ocha or Lùkùmi, as this way of life is known in Cuba, are in constant contact with their ancestors. In fact, the ancestral spirits are thought to be closer to human beings than even the Òrìṣàs, who are the gods of the Yorùbá pantheon (29).

For the Yorùbá, the ancestral spirits may be invited to visit the earth physically through the masquerade, in which they appear in masks. The masked are known as the Egúngún. The appearance of masked characters is a time of festivity and entertainment for the Yorùbá, in which the living intimately associate with the ancestors and rededicate themselves to the family lineage, strengthening ties and loyalties. The parading and dancing of the Egúngún bestows blessings and affirms lineage pride. It is a time when practitioners apprehend the malevolent forces of the universe, meanwhile reassuring themselves of divine protection and guidance. The community is spiritually cleansed through the Egúngún's disclosure of unethical behaviour that has occurred. In this way, warnings, messages and blessings are issued to members of the community. While it is considered dangerous for ancestral spirits to roam unfettered, thereby ruling the daily affairs of the living, the occasional ceremonial appearances of the Egúngún allow the living to commune with the ancestors and to give praise to them, facilitating them to protect rather than harm (Mason 1985, 29).

In Yorùbá traditional religions, Odù are chapters of Ifá literature, in which each Odù has a corresponding sign that appears in divination (Abimbọla 1997, 179). Ogberíkúsa is an Odù that illustrates the origin of Egúngún. Before the creation of the earth, the Egúngún were spirits who dwelled in the heavens (or the underworld). After the creation, the earth became unstable, and try as they may, the Òrìṣà were unable to quell this instability. Only when Olódùmaré, the creator of the universe, sent down the Ẹ́bọ́rá (heavenly spirits) to earth were they successful in bringing any measure of stability to human affairs. The Ẹ́bọ́rá had to disguise themselves in order "to carry necessary rituals to the four corners of the earth" (Mason 1985, 30). After that, the earth became stable. These Ẹ́bọ́rá then came to be called Ṣe *aiyé gún* – those who make the earth stable. According to Mason (1985, 30), this Odù explains the political and social roles of the Egúngún. The communion with Egúngún rids society (and practitioners' lives) of the malevolent forces of instability in human life.

Anthropologist George Eaton Simpson recorded the following Nine Night in Denham Town, a working-class community in downtown Kingston, during 1953. The Revival and Pukkumina religious groups of Jamaica believe that the spirits of the dead can "affect the fate of the living in important ways", and so, "it is essential that they be treated with respect" (Simpson 1957, 329). According to Simpson's research, Nine Nights were presided over by Revival or Pukkumina leaders. Today, it is commonly held by folklore researchers that many Revival practices, musical traditions and beliefs have filtered into the wider Jamaican culture and can be found widely dispersed throughout practices such as Nine Night, as well as the contemporary dancehall culture (Cooper 2004; Nettleford 1993). The following passage describes the Nine Night sequence of events:

> A "set'n up" or wake is held every night until the day of the funeral, which is usually no later than the second or third day. Following the tradition of Christ's resurrection, those who die are believed to rise on the third night. A brief ritual is conducted on this night, and a "rising light" is put outside the house [in which the person died]. Inside the house, a light is kept burning for nine nights. The spirit of a dead person returns to its home on the ninth night after death. (Simpson 1957, 329).

The most important part of the Nine Night ceremony occurs in the room where the person died. Here, an altar is built. The altar is constructed as follows:

> A triple-tiered altar is improvised by placing boxes on a table. An equal number of nine, twelve, or twenty-four black and white candles is placed on each level, but no tier has only black or white candles. One glass of water is placed on each tier, and a vase of flowers is put in the center of the top tier. If a photograph of the dead person is available, it is placed against the flower vase. (Simpson 1957, 329)

The Nine Night ceremony starts after 11:30 p.m. with the designated Leader's lighting of the candles, after which the dead person's good qualities are eulogized, and the decedent's life history is recounted by friends and relatives. At midnight, the dead person's spirit is supposed to appear through the possession of the Leader or another officiant. The ancestral spirit communicates with the family through this possession event in order to resolve any remaining conflicts in the community. After this, the family marches out of the house singing "Jesus, Lover of My Soul" or a similar hymn. Refreshments are served in the yard to all those in attendance, and wine, milk, black coffee, green tea or another favourite beverage of the deceased is placed on the table or altar (Simpson 1957, 330). A saucer of unsalted rice is placed near the drink. It must be unsalted, since no spirit will touch salted food. The rice is sometimes thrown, together with rum, all over the floor of the room to feed the dead. The ceremony goes on until early morning with singing and the playing of dominoes. The candles are allowed to burn down, and after daybreak, the water in the glasses placed on the altar is thrown into the street, away from the house and yard, in order to free the spirit (Simpson 1957, 330).

During a Nine Night dating to the 1950s, which took place in a Kingston working-class community known as Sugartown, anthropologist Edith Clarke notes that a female leader, whom she calls Mrs X, arrives with her sisters to the home of the bereaved family. The women announce that they have come to keep the company of the grieving family and that all arrangements "would be made by them alone" (Simpson 1957, 331). After singing hymns, Mrs X and her sisters address the gathering, announcing that while the Lord has made the deceased's paths straight, the living must straighten their ways since we never know when the Lord may come to take our souls. Then members of the gathering tell stories about others in the community who are wasting their days. Finally, a man in his sixties stands to address the crowd and tells of a woman who practised evil magic, or obeah. He cites her as an example of a person who "has no part with God" (333). The Nine Night, like the Egúngún festival, is a time when admonishments, advice and prayers are dispensed to a community in the wake of trauma. Values and personal ties are reaffirmed during the Nine Night, as human beings attempt to make sense of the chaos of death.

In 2011, I attended a Nine Night in Red Ground, a small community in the rural parish of Westmoreland. The occasion was the celebration of life for Mr Babsie Ryan Reynolds (1932–2011), also known as Bungo, Shecky or Uncle Babsie. The Nine Night is a series of events. It is a period consisting of nine evenings spent doing various activities, including domino playing, music and singing. Early on, the children of the family were organized into a choir in order to learn a hymn to sing at the formal Christian funeral that was to come. The choir practice time became a communal event for the family. Adults would gather and watch the children sing, commenting on their performance all the while. One night, there was a candle-lighting ceremony performed by the family members for the surrounding community. Each family member lit a white candle and placed it alongside the road leading away from the home in which Uncle Babsie died, lining yards of roadside. The candles stretched along the narrow road, lighting the pathway to and from the house. The candlelight was meant to illumine the path of the spirit. Family members testified that this stretch of road was a path the man commonly tread in life. The candlelight signified to those in the area that a member of the community had recently passed on to the next world. The lighting event helped the community to make meaning of the death.

It is widely held that Revival music and dance have filtered into the wider Jamaican culture and can be found disguised in reggae and contemporary dancehall. The same can be said of Nine Night. On the final night before the funeral service, there was a "dance" sponsored by the family, held in the outdoor space surrounding their house. A sound system was constructed, a selector arrived laden with music and a goat soup known as mannish water was served in abundance to all. People came to the dance from miles around, some dressed to the nines in the most elaborate of costumes. Dancehall has replaced many traditional folk practices in Jamaica. As the older folkloric forms fall into disuse for various reasons, dancehall rushes in to fill the cultural vacuum left by their disappearance. Dancehall satisfies people's need for entertainment and spirituality of a non-Orthodox variety. Shortly after midnight, it is still believed that the dead person's spirit should make an appearance. Miss Beverly Reynolds said she heard her Uncle Babsie's familiar cough around midnight, the very cough that had carried him off into the world beyond. But when she looked around to see from whence it came, there was no one to be found. This revelation brought contentment to the family. Through the spirit's appearance, it was confirmed that the soul was free and that the spirit was satisfied with the rites performed in its honour. Through this apparition, the living were reassured that they need not fear a restless soul who wishes to torment the living.

There are many elements of Egúngún worship in the Jamaican Nine Night ceremonies and in the Jonkonnu masquerades; however, they are syncretized with, and disguised by, Christianity. The Egúngún honour and impersonate the dead, and make their appearance as masqueraders covered from head to toe. The principal Odù, or sacred sign, which shows how Egúngún originated is called Otúrúpon Méjì: "It claims that when a . . . [person] dies the corpse is buried but the spirit joins the ancestors to become Egúngún. As the corpse of the deceased is covered head and feet so are the Egúngún in heaven. That is why every Oyó Egúngún is fully costumed, no part of the masquerader can be revealed to the public" (Mason 1985, 30). The patron divinity of the Egúngún, the Òrìṣà Amaiyégún, "sets the world in order" (Mason 1985, 29). He is credited with scaring death away by dressing in a multicoloured costume consisting of swirling swatches of cloth that covered his whole body.

The Egúngún masquerade is thought to have taken new form in Jamaica through the characters of Jonkonnu. These were groups of masked dancers and musicians who would parade through the streets of Jamaican towns during special occasions throughout the year. The Jonkonnu festivities date back to slavery but have fallen into obscurity since the 1950s. The widely popular Jonkonnu character Pitchy-Patchy appears in a similar multicoloured costume as the patron divinity of the Egúngún (Ryman 1984, 57). As we know, the political and social function of the Egúngún is to rid society of all forces of instability due to death (Mason 1985, 30). The Egúngún are considered to be extremely important, and our ancestors are even closer to us than the Òrìṣàs. Thus, it makes sense that Egúngún worship took new forms in Jamaican society.

Jamaican cultural critics Rex Nettleford (1993) and Carolyn Cooper (2004) have likened the contemporary dancehall performers to the Egúngún masqueraders, especially the new wave of male dancers, who often appear in elaborate costumes, covered from head to toe, eyes hidden behind dark sunglasses:

> Among the "people from below" the device of "masking" (in fancy-dress) persists with a vengeance. We still have reason to devise masks to disguise, to create music to affirm, and to assemble dances to celebrate. The ambush of a less than just society under the cover of festive Masquerades has been one way of experiencing control, if only a temporary one. Being King or Queen for a day was a way of having a taste for power, even if it was mock power and fleeting. The actual dress is important. For the costume is a mask helping to transform the persona to

> do wild and uninhibited things – much tulle, dark glasses replacing the old meshwire masks the Jonkonnu characters wore and still do, sequins and costume jewelry, beads, baubles of all kinds, earrings (knobs or droplets), all reminiscent of the pieces of broken mirror on the fancy dress of traditional Jonkonnu! (Nettleford 1993, 16D)

The pieces of flashing, sparkling broken mirrors on the Jonkonnu costumes to which Nettleford refers represent indigenous precedents for dancehall's "bling-bling" aesthetic, in addition to the influence of hip-hop. Of course, since Jonkonnu celebrations were also a cultural mainstay in the US South, there is no reason to rule out the possibility that the bling-bling aesthetic of both hip-hop and dancehall is related to these deeper African diasporic discursive structures of ancestral worship.

In the above citation, Nettleford correlates the wearing of dark glasses in the dancehall with the Jonkonnu meshwire masks. Echoing this assertion, a dancer I interviewed during my research highlighted the importance of wearing sunglasses for his performance:

> Another thing I realized too is when I'm dancing, I always like dance with my shades, cuz you see, when I'm not dancing with my shades, I kinda feel unconfident, and I may not do pretty good, but when I have my shades I know that nobody is seeing my eyes and I actually do better. So like me now, sometimes in the clubs I don't really have confidence but when I have my shades on, I'm fine. Apart from when I'm at work, when I'm at work, it's different stuff, but when I go out . . . yea, you see me. You don't want anybody looking at your eyes, you feel much more comfortable when you have on a glass (sunglasses). Most of the dancers in Kingston – that's how they stay.

For this dancer, the sunglasses give him confidence, because no one can see his eyes. But is there also something else that the glasses lend him, which is the ability to dance beyond the norm? The glasses are his mask, and they give him the ability to do things he would not customarily do and perhaps move into a state of psychic arousal in which he is connected to ancestral spirits.

It is difficult to privilege one African culture in the development of Afro-Jamaican religions and folkways. Lewin (2000) writes of the myriad African influences which have formed Jamaican "folk" cultures, only to be popularized in dancehall culture. Just a few of these folk cultures are Jonkonnu, Bruckins, Revival, Kumina and Maroon; these combined with mento to provide the basis for reggae music. In many of the Afro-Jamaican religions, ancestral worship is central. Ancestral spirits play an important role in the everyday life of these communities. Spirit possession and trance-like states reached through dance are desirable and integral to the ritualistic cleansing offered by dance and music in these religions. "This belief focuses on a view of life wherein the lines of demarcation between what the average person may view as the real, tangible world and that of the unreal world of spirits and gods are in a sense non-existent" (Lewin 2000, 148).

This blurring of the borderlines between real and unreal, reality and fantasy is characteristic of dancehall culture as well. According to Stanley Niaah (2004, 128), it involves a transition through "social, psychological and spatial states for the individual and the group". The passage through preparation during the day, transport to the dance event and back home after daybreak represents one set of transitions. Then there is the passage during the dance into other states, which consecrate the dancehall as a sacred space:

> Especially for key participants such as a Dancehall Queen, the (rite de) passage from home to the dance, through the dance event and the return home, as well as the passage during the event into other states, passage from non-entity into legitimacy of purpose during the event and among its working/under class communicants, delineates in the Dancehall space a sanctified temple. The persistence of this nightly celebration merges the ritual with the everyday blurring the boundaries to extend Dancehall into daily existence; a different world inside but outside society. One could also argue based on Dancehall's mostly non-seasonal nature that it exists within a kind of social limbo. There is really never incorporation back into the everyday as the everyday becomes the entire ritual of preparation, communion, withdrawal and rest, then back to preparation all over again. (Stanley Niaah 2004, 128–29)

The ordinary lives of important personages such as dancehall kings and queens become extraordinary existences in which opulence, spiritual and material abundance become reality. The lucky ones escape poverty and deprivation by earning a living from dancehall; the rest create alternately blessed realities. Just as night blends into daybreak at the dance, the borderlines are blurred between presence of the self and states of spiritual possession. Dancehall creates feelings of ecstasy in its devotees, a sense of being transported outside of the self in rapturous contemplation of the divine. These extraordinary experiences become the everyday lives of the dancers. There is no incorporation back into ordinary everyday life for the dancehall devotee.

The moment of spirit possession achieved through dancing is known as "going into Myal" when it occurs at Maroon, Kumina or Revival ceremonies (Lewin 2000, 191). Myalism was a religious practice of the 1840s, in which spirit possession took the form of violent movements and dancing (190). Myalism and the Native Baptist Movement also aided the development of the Great Revival of 1861. The roots of the Great Revival were African and Christian; however, the means to reach salvation were more African than European. The beginnings of Revival are found in missionary Christianity, especially the Native Baptist church, which has always been more inclusive in terms of its membership (191). In fact, the Revival tune "If I Had the Wings of a Dove" inspired the first ska song (150). Myal, generally understood as good magic or medicine, is to be contrasted with obeah, or evil. In post-emancipation Jamaica, obeah came to be a pejorative term that for many encompassed all the African religious practices and retentions. For others, obeah became magic practised for bad purposes, defined as hurting or manipulating people. The anti-obeah discourse became a way to deal with the wide-scale social transformations and resulting discomforts experienced by the majority of the population during the post-emancipation era. Orthodox Christianity worked to repress the African cultures, condemning all African religious practice as obeah. The Myalist "Medicine Man", or "Obeah-Puller", emerged during the 1840s as a sorcerer able to remove the obeah, disease and disharmony from individuals in the changing society. Today, obeah occupies an ambivalent place in dancehall discourse, at once criticized, feared and respected within selectors' utterances and artists' song lyrics. The orthodox Christian churches continue to condemn obeah, reinforcing the negative association it holds for many Jamaicans, although some people may practice it in secret.

Several scholars have documented the costuming and masquerading of Jonkonnu (Barnett 1979; Lewin 2000; Nettleford 1993; Wynter 1970). Some have acknowledged it as a foundation for dancehall (Nettleford 1993; Stanley Niaah 2004; Cooper 2004). The dancers themselves claim Jonkonnu as an inspiration. A popular dance in 2006 was the "Jonkonnu Dip"; a rendition can be found in Voicemail's video of the song "Wacky Dip", a tribute to the deceased dancer (and ancestor) Mr Wacky, also known as Bogle. Wynter cites Patterson's work which claims three points of origin for Jonkonnu: the Yam festivals of the Ibo, the recreational activities of the Egúngún societies of the Yorùbá and the Homowo harvest festivals of the Ga (Wynter 1970, 37). All three have to do with summoning the ancestral spirits to walk with the participant. The mask, which must cover the entire body and includes the costume, forms an important node in this connection between human and divine. The human and divine are intimately connected through dances in which ancestral spirits fête with the living: "Rhythm is the universal life force. On donning the mask, the dancer enters into this force, the god possesses him, and in a modern Jamaican cult term informed with the same meaning, the dancer '*delivers*' himself by patterning the steps of the gods, or ancestral spirits" (38). Wynter's examination of Jonkonnu is astounding in its historical and critical treatment of a phenomenon that others have studied only empirically or with sentimental romanticism.

Wynter (1970, 34) begins her study discussing the way in which "folk" culture in Jamaica occupies a space of ambivalence, which is the colonial legacy of the Jamaican psyche. There is an insecurity and lack of confidence that coalesces with a widespread shame and embarrassment among many Jamaicans regarding the indigenous folk cultures and their African characteristics (35). This sense of shame was widespread by 1825. Wynter wrote this piece at a time when the shame of African culture was beginning to dissipate. Unfortunately, much of the same consternation regarding Revival traditions and African-derived religious practices persists in the contemporary society.

Wynter (1970, 36) likens folk culture to cultural guerilla warfare. She claims that the enslaved African used "folk" culture to resist the onslaught of the plantation economy and to save their own humanity. She writes that the history of folk culture in Jamaica is the history of this ambivalent relation between two contradictory processes, one as creator of rehumanized Nature through folklore and the other as plough for the conquest of Nature (36). In the beginning of Jamaica's colonial period, Wynter defines the cultural process as indigenization, in which the rooting of the African in the new environment of the Americas commenced. This entailed adapting African cultural processes to the Jamaican context. The drum, horn and dance were integral components of this indigenization period. The Maroons employed all three, using the Abeng horn and drum to communicate and employing dance to reach spirit possession. Wynter calls these the drum scripts, or drum rhythms that form a language. They are a mode of communication among the living and the ancestors. We find that the drum, horn and dance still form a mode of communication within dancehall. The horn sound motif is played by the selector numerous times throughout a dancehall event as the crescendo of intensity builds, transporting participants to various states of consciousness. The drum rhythms are clearly reproduced, except they are now blasted over mega-watt speakers, audible for miles around.

Lastly, there is dance. Although the dancers I interviewed did not candidly admit any involvement in Afro-Jamaican religions entailing spirit possession, certain dancers did state a very clear understanding of the way in which dance formed a language of communication between themselves, their families and their ancestors. These young iconoclasts had a vision of their connection to African performativity:

> Dancer: You see, our tradition is through music, our ancestors and our godparents, through music, it translates by dancing, our drums and instruments.
> Interviewer: What is your opinion of Dancehall culture's connection to Africa?
> Dancer: Well, as you can see, we both got a lot in common, Africans associate by dancing, by all of those beats and different moves, reflex and all of those tings.
> Interviewer: What do you mean that they associate by dancing?
> Dancer: Back in the day, our ancestors used to associate by dancing, it's something like a language that they keep among themselves.
> Interviewer: So it's a way of communicating?
> Dancer: Yeah, you can talk to each other through it.

These dancers, while not explicitly claiming to practise Myalism or Revival, have a very clear understanding of the importance of their ancestors, or the Egúngún. These dancers also acknowledge the importance of dance as a language and means of communication between the past and present. Dance is a unifier within the African diaspora, and dancehall displays a repertoire of body movements comprising a vocabulary.

Numerous scholars have elaborated upon the significant role of women in dancehall, especially the dancehall queen (Bakare-Yusuf 2005; Cooper 2004; Hope 2010; Stanley Niaah 2004). Women are indeed in authority in the dance, but that authority must also be earned. The dancehall queen must get the dance "poppin" in order to lay her claim to authority in the dancehall. The dancehall queens ascended the throne formally in the 1990s. As Stanley Niaah (2004) suggests, Jamaica's queen narrative draws on ancient African and European matriarchal structures and finds a popular manifestation and embodiment in the character of the dancehall queen. Dancehall's primarily male selectors control the pace and flow of the music, which draws the spirits to the dancers. The selector plays a crucial role in egging on the dancers and inspiring them to go into various states of arousal and stimulation. In Afro-Jamaican religions, this is considered going into Myal. In Yorùbá religion, it is known as being mounted by an Òrìṣà divinity or an ancestral Égún. It is important to note however, that going into Myal is a privileged state that few practitioners ever experience (Lewin 2000, 234). There are various shifts in consciousness that precede going into Myal. When the spirit mounts a devotee, it might knock them to the ground. This is akin to the "Drop Dead" dance move, in which the dancer falls to the ground and lies motionless. Niaah describes the high point of the night for Stacey, dancehall queen:

> Her best hour is 5.00 a.m. when she can be seen mounting the ground, dancing on her head top, a tower of speakers or a nearby roof. In her best acts Stacey can be seen making space in between and outside of the conventions of dance movement and the circle or designated dance space, as she pushes the boundary of the "normal" . . . .Of note, at Stacey's Birthday Bash 2001 she was observed dancing on the passing vehicles, sometimes even infiltrating them to "wine" on the male driver and passengers. This act seemed to be a signal to passing cars that they had encroached on ritual space and could not be allowed to pass until properly inducted. (Stanley Niaah 2004, 127–28)

It is clear that Stacey is dancing well enough for "di cars dem weh a pass haffi wine dung window" (to make the passing cars roll down their windows), as sings Elephant Man in the tune "Nuh Linga". Inherent in this moment is the kinesthetic pleasure that the dancehall queen herself derives from dancing, as well as the pleasure of the spectacle, in which dancehall's devotees eagerly partake in the visual consumption of her obvious joy in movement. Stacey's mounting the ground to perform "Head-Top" or climbing a tower of speakers, straddling the roof or the driver of a passing car, demonstrates that she has shifted to another psychic state of arousal that is beyond the "norm" even for most dancehall patrons. Thus, while dancehall's ancestral rituals are widely available to the masses of Jamaicans, the psychic state of the dancehall queen, the heightened kinesthetic pleasure and arousal beyond the norm, the mounting of the ancestral or divine possession inherent in going into Myal, are the privilege of very few. It is the heightened kinesthetic joy and arousal of women that ultimately provides source-energy for other participants' pleasure in the dance.

African-derived religions adapted and incorporated Christianity, but the reverse did not occur. Orthodox Christianity early on assumed a Manichean posture toward the African-derived religious practices of Jamaica, painting all Myalism and African-derived animism as evil. The Jamaican folk culture of the seventeenth and early eighteenth centuries was characterized by Jonkonnu processions, River Mumma dances, the Dahomey Sky Cult, the Death and Rebirth cults and Myalist Doctor Plays (among many others). Eventually, all of these African-derived religious practices coalesced under the unifying rubric of Myalism, which in 1774 was prohibited by the British. The drum, dance and horn of the Myal spelled revolt and had to be outlawed. The British permitted the "secular" Jonkonnu processions, committing the Western fallacy that secular and sacred are dichotomous rather than a unity within West African cosmologies. Jonkonnu became secularized and billed exclusively for entertainment, when in fact it drew on the same Myalist religious practices of spirit possession through dance. Given the history of Jamaica's cultural indigenization, the lines become blurred between African religious practices and "secular" dancehall intended solely for entertainment.

Despite repression, Myal was not to be denied, emerging triumphant in the Great Myal Procession of the 1840s. Erna Brodber's novel *Myal* presents an anti-colonial critique of Christianity. Her marvelous narrative depicts the orthodox Christian intolerance of the Myalist traditions in Jamaica, as opposed to the Native Baptist point of contact with Myalism that formed the Revival cults. These Revival cults relied upon immersion in water, in addition to the Myal spirit possession through dance. Paul Bogle, leader of the Morant Bay Rebellion, preached in a Native Baptist church in his village in the eastern parish of St Thomas (Holt 1992, 290). The symphony of horn and drum was a well-known feature of revolt by the time the Morant Bay Rebellion occurred in 1865 (Holt 1992, 296). Brodber and Wynter's work point to the need for Jamaicans, especially orthodox Christians, to come to terms with this history and the African religious practices that are so foundational to Nine Night rituals and to Jamaican national culture. Pukkumina, Zion and Rastafari religions are harmonious and holistic syncretisms of Afro-Christianity. They represent the opposite reaction to the Manichean stance orthodox Christianity takes toward the African religions.

The construction of the black majority in Jamaica and the dehumanizing system of race, class and colour were built upon slavery. Jamaica is, after all, a "post-colonial" society scarred by deep schisms between haves and have-nots, home to extremes of poverty and wealth. The coloniality of power (Quijano and Ennis 2000) makes itself felt everywhere in Jamaica; it even makes an appearance in the historical development of Jonkonnu characters. Wynter (1970, 39) skilfully historicizes Jonkonnu in terms of power and empire. She describes the acculturation process as one in which elements of the English Morris dances entered the religious aspects of Jonkonnu, as the celebration became increasingly secularized during the nineteenth century. The cultural fusion between the English pagan festival and the African practices of masquerade was the result of the contact between Irish, English and Scottish indentured servants and African people during plantation slavery. It is often cited that mummings rituals of pagan spirit possession among the ancient Germanic tribes and other European cultures contributed to Jonkonnu (Wynter 1970, 37; Lewin 2000). By the nineteenth century, the creolization process had triumphed over the indigenization process with the preeminence of the "Brown" Set Girls. The elegantly dressed Set Girls, housekeepers of the English, Scottish and Irish plantation masters and mistresses, competed against one another, aided by their partisan owners. The African-derived horned characters such as Oxhead became subordinated aesthetically to the Set Girls in the colonial accounts of the European travel writers. The religious aspects of Jonkonnu's "Medicine Man" had become secularized (Wynter 1970, 39–43).

In addition to Jonkonnu's appearance within dancehall's repertoire, ancestral worship has taken new form in the Nine Night rituals. Within the New World Yorùbá religion of Cuban Lùkùmi, ancestral shrines can resemble the Nine Night altar Simpson describes. The following passage tells how to create a New World Egúngún shrine:

> Candles are one of many items to be placed on the shrine. Their inclusion is an example of the possible influence the ritual pageantry of the Catholic Church, had on some aspects of Yorùbá ritual. They are said to provide light and energy for those in the spirit world. We have the choice of placing one, four, five or nine white candles. . . . Next, place a large clear or white glass bowl of cool water on the shrine. Some devotees alternate between one large bowl of water and nine large goblets of water. Nine is also the number associated with transformation, and water is the medium of the spirits. The other items that can go on the ancestral shrine are

> cigars, cigarettes, pipes, tobacco, perfume, cologne, Florida water, wine, liquor, beer, coffee, tea, milk, fruit juice, bread, all foods, and white flowers. . . . Pictures of the family dead and lists with their names should be placed on the shrine. (Mason 1985, 39–40)

The Egúngún shrine bears many similarities to the Nine Night altar. Both feature candles often in multiples of nine. Both feature the placing of food and beverages intended to feed the dead, and the inclusion of a picture of the deceased upon the altar. The importance of the number nine and water is very apparent. Water is the medium of the spirits; this is another reason the water is thrown out after the Nine Night ritual. In this way, the spirits can travel back into the earth through the water.

In Cuban Lùkùmi, Egúngún worship was not recreated to the same extent as it was in Brazil. In Cuba, Spanish colonial authorities' violent repression of the Egúngún masquerade ensured that it passed out of use by the nineteenth century (Mason 1985, 31). The syncretic Espiritismo, a complex mixture of European and African ancestor worship, has influenced the ancestral worship in some houses (Abimbọla 1997, 107). In Espiritismo, *misas* are held in order to communicate with the ancestral spirits. Ancestral altars known as *bobedas*, which feature nine glasses of water, are prominent. At the end of every *misa*, the water from each of the nine glasses placed on the ancestral shrine is thrown out onto the ground outside of the house. Just as in the Jamaican Nine Night, it is crucial that the water is discarded away from the house so that the spirits are free to travel back into the earth through the ground water.[1] In Cuba and the United States, ancestral shrines for the Egúngún are often located in bathrooms, kitchens and basements, close to water or sewer pipes and drains. According to Mason, these waters flow from the house and become one with the river (1985, 31–32).

Not only is Egúngún associated with water and rivers but so is Ọya, the Òrìṣà who is connected to the ancestors and the number nine, hence the Nine Night ceremony. The significance of nine as the number associated with the transformation of death can be found in other Afro-Caribbean funerary settings. Cuba's Novenario and the Dominican Republic's Novena are both Christian syncretic rituals which prescribe nine-day periods of mourning.[2] It is generally assumed that these are Catholic traditions, but when we excavate further, we find that Christian syncretism is only skin deep (Abimbọla 1997, 106). The importance of the number nine in funerary and ancestral contexts within the diaspora is deeply rooted in West African cosmology. In Yorùbán cosmology, nine is the favourite number of Ọya, the powerful Òrìṣà who is said to guard the gates of the cemetery, and the same Òrìṣà who takes away our last breath.

There are various Odù which relate to the birth of Egúngún, linking them with the number nine and Ọya. The Odù, Ọ̀kànràn Ògúndá, further demonstrates the significance of the number nine within the origin of Egúngún and shows the significance of this number for children of Ọya. This Odù explains that Egúngún was the last of Ọya's nine sons. Ọya is also the favourite wife of Ṣàngó. Ọya was barren for many years, until she was asked to use the queen ant as a fertility charm. Ọya was warned, however, that she should deliver the child inside the ant hill. The first eight of Ọya's children were born without incident, but the soldier ants disfigured the face of her ninth child, Egúngún.

Because of this, Egúngún wore a mask to cover his face, and since he could not speak naturally, he was seen as an Ẹ̀bọ́rá, a spirit of the underworld (Mason 1985, 30).

The number nine also figures prominently in Cuban Lùkùmí burial rites, which are now practised among African American spiritual houses in the United States as well. When an Òrìṣà devotee dies, the ritual of *Ìtútù* (coldness) must be performed. This ritual is intended to separate the spirit of the deceased from this plane of existence (Mason 1985, 34). The funeral rites last for nine days and certain ceremonial objects are counted in nines (36).

The Odù, Ọ̀sá Méjì, further demonstrates the connection between Egúngún, Ọya and the number nine. In Ọ̀sá Méjì, all of Ọya's children die at birth. She consults Ọ̀rúnmìlà and is told to make an *ẹbọ* (sacrifice) with cloth of many colours and an ewe. The *ẹbọ* is successful and Ọya gives birth to nine children, the last of whom is born in a caul. Ọya becomes known as Ìyánsàń (mother of nine). Because of this, Ọya is said to be the mother of Egúngún (Mason 1985, 54).

Ọya, the mother of nine, provides a template for women in the dancehall and introduces a feminist reading of the Egúngún societies and ancestral worship. Cooper (2004, 104) asserts that Ọya is not only a river deity but also a divinity of tornadoes and wind. Ultimately, she is an Òrìṣà of masquerades and women's power. Cooper highlights women's use of the mask and disguise within the spectacle of dancehall. In its various forms of costuming, adornment and techniques of the body, dancehall's aesthetics encourage the participant to become another persona. Through the use of sartorial confections, wigs, haircuts, makeup and alterations to the body such as skin bleaching, piercings, tattoos and eyebrow-shaping, dancehall devotees create the masquerade. Dancehall queens aggressively compete with another for preeminence. Ọya is the mother of ancestral Egúngún, as well as the deity who rules over the spectacle of their masquerade (Cooper 2004, 104). Ọya, like her husband Ṣàngó, is known for her wrath (Oyěwùmí 1997, 140). She is portrayed in Òrìṣà literature as fearsome and ruthless. Each Òrìṣà has *oríkì* (poetry) that is sung in praise of them; one line of Ọya's praise poetry says "Obì nrin gbona, okùnrin sa" (females will hit the road, and males will run; everybody flees when she appears) (Oyěwùmí 1997, 174). The concept of femininity as aggressive and bellicose, as embodied in Ọya and the dancehall queen, is markedly different from the Victorian version of femininity, in which "true" women are always submissive (Cooper 2004, 104; Oyěwùmí 1997, 174).

A closer examination of Ọya highlights the power of women in traditional Yorùbá religion. Ọya is the "ultimate feminist" (Owomoyela 1989, 270). Ọya refuses to stay out of spaces that are preempted by male authority. In one Odù, Ọya's husband, Ṣàngó, is challenged by his enemies. In his defence, he sends Ọya to retrieve medicine for thunderbolts from Èṣù. She is to transport the medicine under her tongue to Ṣàngó. She does so, but not before appropriating some of the medicine for herself, first claiming for herself the right to throw thunderbolts (Owomoyela 1989, 270). Ọya is the deity of wind and lightning, the most dangerous and powerful elements of storms, while Ṣàngó rules the sound of thunder. To Ọya belongs the power, to her husband belongs the bluster (Owomoyela 1989, 271).

Perhaps it was the psychic insecurity stemming from women's fundamental power that motivated men to appropriate Egúngún's mysteries. Although it is Ọya, a female deity, who originally gave birth to Egúngún, men have appropriated aspects of the Egúngún societies over the years (Owomoyela 1989, 271). While contemporary Yorùbá Egúngún societies are composed of men and women whose lineages are associated with the masquerade, men exclusively wear masks and costumes. Women do not mask themselves, but they do participate in the chorus, singing praise poems and histories of family lineages. At the same time, it is undeniable that female power is indispensable to the process of nurturing life and enabling human achievement. Despite their theft of the masquerade and appropriation of its secrets, men still acknowledge that when matters become most difficult, "women make more powerful carriers of the mask than do men" (Owomoyela 1989, 271). Egúngún societies are associated with paramount religious matters of state. Notably, women occupy leading positions in the Egúngún societies – that of the *Ato* (Oyěwùmí 1997, 119).

How does the recreation of ancestral worship in Jamaica reflect gender roles in Yorùbá Egúngún societies? Nine Night leaders can be male or female, meanwhile traditional Jonkonnu masqueraders were exclusively men. This changed during the nineteenth century as Jonkonnu became more secularized, and new female characters such as the Set Girls joined the processions. This would seem to reflect a similar appropriation of women's power within early forms of Jamaican ancestral worship but over time shows an African gender flexibility that is in stark contrast to Victorian formulations of gender in the West (Amadiume 1987, 28). We see the preeminence of an assertive women's power apparent in the dancehall's Ọya-inspired Egúngún masquerade, in which women's pleasure is placed at the forefront. Women's kinesthetic pleasure in the dancehall provides the source-energy of the spectacle, which all of the dance's participants visually consume (Cooper 2004; Delgado de Torres 2010).

Erna Brodber (2002) tells us that magical realism is part of the Jamaican way of life, arguing that it is not only in Latin America that the belief in magic, destiny and spirits persist. Although colonized by various European powers, Jamaica, Cuba and the Dominican Republic share funerary customs which revolve around nine days of mourning. Each of these traditions is unique in its own particularity, meanwhile sharing African ancestry. In diversity, there is unity. The ancestors, disguised, continue their masquerade through Jonkonnu, the Nine Night and dancehall. Ultimately, an analysis that places Nine Night funerary rites in their African context is not only anti-colonial but feminist. An examination of Ọya reveals a feminist epistemology that is at times disguised in Jonkonnu and Nine Night, but that is becoming abundantly apparent in the contemporary forms of "secularized" ancestral worship taking place in the dancehall.

NOTES

1. Edwin Mariano, interview by author, Lakewood, New Jersey, 29 August 2011.
2. Mariano, interview; Yohan Vicente, interview by author, West New York, NJ, 16 September 2011.

REFERENCES

Abimbọla, Wande. 1997. *Ifá Will Mend Our Broken World: Thoughts on Yorùbá Religion and Culture in Africa and the Diaspora*. Massachusetts: Aim Books.

Amadiume, Ifi. 1987. *Male Daughters, Female Husbands: Gender and Sex in an African Society*. London: Zed Books.

Bakare-Yusuf, Bibi. 2005. "'I Love Myself When I Am Dancing and Carrying On': Refiguring the Agency of Black Women's Creative Expression in Jamaican Dancehall Culture". *International Journal of Media and Cultural Politics* 1, no. 3: 263–76.

Barnett, Sheila. 1979. "Jonkonnu: Pitchy Patchy". *Jamaica Journal* 43: 18–32.

Brodber, Erna. 2002. "Beyond the Boundary: Magical Realism in the Jamaican Frame of Reference". In *Sisyphus and Eldorado: Magical and Other Realisms in Caribbean Literature*, edited by Timothy J. Reiss, 15–24. Trenton, NJ: Africa World Press.

Brodber, Erna. 1988. *Myal: A Novel*. London: New Beacon Books.

Cooper, Carolyn. 2004. *Sound Clash: Jamaican Dancehall Culture at Large*. New York: Palgrave Macmillan.

Delgado de Torres, Lena. 2010. "Queens, Kings and Swagga: Gender and the Will to Adorn in Jamaican Dancehall". PhD dissertation, Binghamton University.

Holt, Thomas C. 1992. *The Problem of Freedom: Race, Labor, and Politics in Jamaica and Britain, 1832–1938*. Baltimore: Johns Hopkins University Press.

Hope, Donna. 2010. *Man Vibes: Masculinities in the Jamaican Dancehall*. Kingston: Ian Randle.

Lewin, Olive. 2000. *Rock It Come Over: The Folk Music of Jamaica*. Kingston: University of West Indies Press.

Mason, John. 1985. *Four New World Yorùbá Rituals*. Brooklyn: Yorùbá Theological Archministry.

Nettleford, Rex. 1993. "Fancy Dress and the Roots of Culture: From Jonkonnu to Dancehall". *Sunday Gleaner*, 18 July, 1D and 16D.

Oyěwùmí, Oyèrónké. 1997. *The Invention of Women: Making an African Sense of Western Gender Discourses*. Minneapolis: University of Minnesota Press.

Owomoyela, Oyekan. 1989. "Review of *Ọya: In Praise of the Goddess*, by Judith Gleason". *Research in African Literatures: Special Issue on Popular Culture* 20, no. 2 (Summer): 270–72.

Quijano, Aníbal, and Michael Ennis. 2000. "Coloniality of Power, Eurocentrism and Latin America". *Nepantla: Views from the South* 1, no. 3: 533–80.

Ryman, Cheryl. 1984. "Jonkonnu, a Neo-African Form, Part II". *Jamaica Journal* 17, no. 2 (May): 50–61.

Simpson, George Eaton. 1957. "The Nine Night Ceremony in Jamaica". *Journal of American Folklore* 70, no. 278 (October–December): 329–35.

Stanley Niaah, Sonjah. 2004. "Making Space: Kingston's Dancehall Culture and its Philosophy of 'Boundarylessness'". *African Identities* 2, no. 2: 117–32.

Wynter, Sylvia. 1970. "Jonkonnu in Jamaica: Towards the Interpretation of Folk Dance as a Cultural Process". *Jamaica Journal* 4, no. 2: 34–49.

CHAPTER 23

Representations of "Obeah" and "Bad-Mind" in Contemporary Jamaican Dancehall

KATE LAWTON

Dutty mind waan see me drop dead,
Iniquity waan see me drop dead,
Dem no like me, me no like dem,
Obeah workers, lef' Jah Jah's children.
Hoobakaba! Habakaba!
Science[1] again,
. . . Dem a laugh but dem a nuh your friend,
Send a, send a prayer pon dem.
—Vybz Kartel, "Poco Man Skank" (2017)[2]

THE THEMES OF ENVY, JEALOUSY AND ENEMIES DESCRIBED by the Jamaican artist Vybz Kartel are common topics in contemporary Jamaican dancehall music. Almost without exception, its major artists reference "bad-mind", a compound word in Jamaican slang for someone who harbours or displays malicious intent and "obeah", "which encompasses a wide variety of beliefs and practices involving the control or channelling of supernatural/spiritual forces" (Bilby and Handler 2004, 154).

Bad-mind in the dancehall context is often presented as a disease, parasitically destroying intimate bonds of kinship and friendship. The hugely popular dancehall artist Mavado (also known as the "Gully God"[3]) talks about bad-mind people being ready to "grudge da yute dem fi dem tings" (2007).[4] This is echoed by his musical rival Vybz Kartel ("Di Teacha/World Boss"), who extends the motif: "bad-mind get di best of them . . . dem claim seh dem a yuh friend" (2011).[5] Another artist, Blak Ryno, attests to the strength of this intent, "bad-mind wah mi fi lay dung, six foot six under bare ground" (2009).[6] Bad-mind then, within the dancehall narrative, attests to the malicious intention of people to harm others due to envy.

Obeah, in this context, is the practice by which such negative ("bad-mind") thoughts may be given effect, through the conscious manipulation of the external world. As the artist Demarco sings in "Send Dem Home" (2011): "I could ah tell obeah man dem ah work wi, / Bumbohole dat caan stop mi from burst it." And Jah Vinci in "Bad-Mind a Go Fall" (2011): "Lawd, badmind just a wuk di obeah / Nah stop put mi trust inna Jehoveh." Taken together in this context, bad-mind and obeah describe a set of thoughts, practices and beliefs that enable us to consider the cultural expression of envy. And if dancehall is, as some commentators suggest, "a reflection of the lived realities of its adherents" (Hope 2001, 20), then the presentation of these themes within the genre provides an opportunity to consider the influences that have shaped these experiences.

My discussion in this chapter is based predominantly on a textual analysis of the lyrics of dancehall songs released in the last two decades. Although the presentation of these themes is to be found in older popular Caribbean songs in a way that is replicated in contemporary examples,[7] I make a number of observations about the form, frequency and function of these terms which I would suggest are unique to modern dancehall.

The first relates to the sheer number of artists and proliferation of lyrics dealing with this motif in contemporary songs, to the extent that its stylization appears almost as an "obsession" in recent dancehall music, although with the absence of definitive statistics these are my observations as a dancehall enthusiast. The second is that "big name", contemporary artists use fear and generalized accusations about obeah working (because of ostensible bad-mind toward them) to enhance their own reputation, manipulating this cultural complex to their own advantage in order to make it even more clear how successful they are.

In considering this possibility, we must caution against invalidating the artists' perception that they are threatened by material manifestations of bad-mind. On a macro level Jamaican society has been highly divided, with reciprocal violence a feature of the Jamaican political system (Stone 1983). Fear of the intentions and motives of others, expressed through the idea of bad-mind, is palpable and real: "dancehall artists face the potential not only for great acknowledgement and social reward, but also for fierce competition and brutal attacks, such as armed assaults by rival performers and gangsters" (Stolzoff 2000, 8). Many individual artists can attest to the presence of violence in their immediate sphere of experience, either because of, or in spite of, the fact that they are public figures.[8]

"Participants in the music industry are largely products of poor urban communities that were steeped in the democratic socialist values prevalent within the Jamaican State, to a varying degree, from the 1940s up until 1989 when the dramatic ideological shift toward neoliberal capitalism occurred" (Galvin 2014, 7). In offering a possible explanation for the apparent ubiquity of these terms and their possible role in enhancing status, I draw on these socio-economic changes within Jamaican society, since independence from British rule in the 1960s to the 1980s when the genre of dancehall developed into the form recognizable today. This style can be characterized as braggadocio and self-promoting, and its narrative frequently references material accumulation and sexual prowess. An example of this stylization is evident in Beenie Man in "Bad-Mind People" (2014):

Big gold chain and mi rolex weh full a rock
Every weh mi turn up me and mi whole crew a lock
Last year girls get sub fi the newer stock
No matter what unuh full a crap
....
Achieve many gold and more a set
Rich already and still waan more asset
Dem a go turn up the bad mind more a bet
Cause dem still don't have no tour a get
I swear seh mi never work obeah yet[9]

"Big gold chain", "mi rolex weh full of a rock": contemporary artists actively engage in envy-inducing behaviour of the type that could arouse bad-mind (while simultaneously lamenting its existence), in a manner not apparent in older popular songs (and that I would argue is partly a product of the socio-economic changes taking place). Accusations of bad-mind and obeah use within the dancehall arena are made by artists who are demonstrably successful (unlike witchcraft accusations, for example, which in some cases are levelled against someone thought to have caused misfortune to the accuser due to envy), and therefore I argue can serve partly to *reflect*, *highlight* and *enhance* status.

Such "boasy" behaviour is problematic; there are powerful cultural norms of egalitarianism which constrain flaunting difference by those at close rank (Sobo 1993, 104–5). Giving and generosity in Jamaican urban communities are signifiers of "reputation" and "respectability" where other cultural markers (such as education or use of standard English) have been rejected or where access has been denied (Galvin 2014, 25). Since the publication of Wilson's *Crab Antics* (1973), these concepts have provided an important theoretical framework for understanding prestige, and its opposite; times when this is negated and individuals behave like "crabs in a barrel", pulling each down in a competitive effort to get to the top. Bad-mind then, can thus been seen as the articulation of this "crabs in a barrel" sentiment. But if, as I argue, one views such accusations also as a means of reflecting and enhancing status, powerful cultural norms are being transgressed. As a way of overcoming fear of the consequences posed by the desire to be honoured through economic signifiers, I point to evidence that contemporary artists, in some cases, cultivate a narrative of "good" and "legitimate" wealth, helping them to overcome any such transgressions. This analysis supplements the current academic understanding of obeah accusations, which have not explored this as a means of enhancing status or as a cultural complex manipulated by actors. In looking at bad-mind I consider a concept markedly unexplored.[10]

DANCEHALL AS A SITE OF CONFRONTATION

As discussed more fully elsewhere in this volume, the proliferation of dancehall can be seen "as an organic critical response of Jamaican popular culture to the discordant call of the social, political and economic constraints of the 1980s" (Hope 2001, 9) and some of the explanation for its confrontational stance must be located in the development of sectarian politics, garrison communities, political violence and urban warfare which is a reality for many dancehall artists, as it has been (and still is) for many Jamaicans.

The economic and social conditions of the 1980s created both need and opportunity and saw the rise of informal entrepreneurship "driven by an aggressive and creative instinct for survival at all costs . . . encouraged by opportunities that arose in the mish-mash of structural adjustment and market capitalism" (Hope 2001, 8). Dancehall took its place within this expanding informal sector and gave poorer, inner city, lower class men (and women) both the resources and the reason to become vocal.

Yet as well as being a vehicle for reflecting harsh social realities, dancehall also became a medium for creating and articulating social aspiration and status, as defined by the acquisition of wealth and conspicuous consumption. Popcaan, a popular Jamaican dancehall artist, attests to this desire (2010a):

> Every youth waan be di winner
> Every ghetto youth waan own a bimma
> Regular mi never have no dinner
> Growin up life did bitter like vinegar[11]

The dancehall industry today continues to provide a vibrant economic base and the prospect of social mobility connected to it.[12] Dancehall then, in every sense, offers a "magic wand that many individuals from poverty-stricken inner cities . . . use to transform and redefine the subordinate roles and identities ascribed to them by traditional Jamaican society. This makes dancehalls, 'bashment', 'bling, bling' and hype immensely powerful" (Hope 2001, xix).

Alongside consideration of the historical moment which created dancehall and provided its story must be consideration of the form itself. Described as a "true site of contestation as different groups jockey for hierarchical positions in a rigid, class-structured society" (Hope, 2001) confrontation – lyrically, territorially and symbolically – runs through the heart of the genre. This real and symbolic clashing is highly relevant to any explanation as to why the reference to external threats – manifested as bad-mind and obeah – are so prolific.

Dancehall thus reflects, reinforces and recreates the tensions that exist in wider society, whilst also providing a route to success and a platform for articulating it to others. As Popcaan articulates in "Gangster City" (2010b):

> I'm from a place, where dog eat dog
> Mi know bout living hard
> From we born, we see people ah starve,
> Vendor get beat by sarge

Yet "to understand the implications of the clash, it is not simply enough to look at the rising levels of violence in society. The clash first emerged and continues to function as a way for a particular sound system to differentiate themselves and thus clear a space in a crowded sphere of competitors" (Galvin 2014, 9). Clashing in dancehall can be located within a wider tradition of competitive lyrical performance in Jamaica, and Caribbean and African American culture more broadly. Such performance traditions included challenges, toasting (a lengthy rhymed narrative), braggadocio, improvised and ritual exchanges of insults and mocking, deployed as dramatic devices and often characterised by a powerfully obscene language and highly charged vocabulary and with links to an African past (Abrahams 1964, 1993; Wald 2012). As well as a physical event, clashing is also a dramatic device which is a fundamental part of the dancehall experience. Artists flex their lyrical prowess against other artists, rivalry is inherent and there are entrenched (even if purely symbolic) conflicts between singers, deejays and sound systems.

Real and symbolic confrontation, lyrical and performative, is thus a fundamental part of the theatre of dancehall and an important part of a wider tradition of distinguishing oneself in a field of competitors. In the dancehall context this is undertaken by actors who are often precariously placed economically and sociopolitically yet intent on redefining their ascribed roles to claim higher levels of wealth, respect and authority and are thus defensive and protective of their perceived status. The desire to be honoured and the simultaneous fear of the consequences of envy must account for a good deal of the tensions in dancehall narratives and songs about bad-mind and obeah which testify to the presence and will of those who would seek to bring them down.

An explanation for these accusations in modern dancehall can be seen partly as a continuation of wider traditions of lyrical competition in which dramatic devices are used to establish oneself against a competitor. Such denunciations could thus be seen as part of the repertoire of lyrical and symbolic weapons aimed at undermining and discrediting a rival. To be called "bad-minded" is an insult – such people try to spoil or "mash down"[13] others, as Sean Paul sings in "Ovaload" (2017), "Yuh and yuh negativity fi guh overboard, / Yuh too bad-mind, that mi discover / Yuh too narrow mind deh pon overload."

Part of the explanation must also lie in the specific historical conditions in which dancehall was created – the ideological shift to neoliberalist capitalism which has forced an increase in individual self-reliance and resourcefulness. Shrinking resources mean that although the number of artists is increasing, only a handful will ever succeed in a big way. In this sense, the ground has become more fertile for fears of abuse of power through bad-mind. The dancehall industry offers the real potential to accumulate (relative) wealth and attracts ever growing numbers of young people who hope to join the field. This calculus lends itself easy to growing envy with the presence of obeah and bad-mind functioning as its synonyms. However, I assert that we are also partly witnessing the adaptation/manipulation of these older concepts and ideas within a contemporary environment which privileges status as reflected through conspicuous consumption. In such cases these accusations are but mirrors of success.

DESCRIPTIONS OF BAD-MIND AND OBEAH IN POPULAR JAMAICAN MUSIC

There is a need to contextualize the way these terms are used and the purpose they serve.

In the *Dictionary of Caribbean English Usage* (2003), the compound word "bad-mind" is referenced as both a noun and an adjective. As a noun, having a bad-mind denotes malice, animosity and the harbouring of active ill will and is said to originate from a number of African languages, brought with the slave trade, in which "mind" is expressed as the same word for "heart", "chest" and "inside body".[14] As an adjective, bad-mind pejoratively describes negative behaviour, as when Elephant Man sings "you're too bad-mind" in his song "Bun Bad Mind". "Bad-mind" is thus the grudgeful union between psyche and soma and bears a similarity to other Jamaican phraseology such as "cut your eye at/on/after somebody". These Caribbean compounds label behaviours for which the etymological and structural explanations are to be found in their African languages of origin and the historical, social and linguistic developments underway from the seventeenth century.

Reflecting these etymological origins, bad-mind in dancehall is often presented as a disease, infecting the minds of individuals and the bonds within communities. In the song "The Cure (fi Bad-Mind)" (2013), Vybz Kartel says:

> Ah no aids a no diabetes,
> Bad-mind a di worsest disease
> A no syphilis, a no herpes,
> Bad-mind a di worsest disease,
> Mi sure. Hey missa bad-mind come fi di cure,
> Go jump off di twin tower top floor,
> Go drink some gas an light yo throat hole,
> Bet say yo cure[15]

Similarly Beenie Man, in his song "Bad-Mind" (2015):

> Bad-mind disease dem carrying,
> Worser than Genghis, and Hitler and Stalin,
> Another thing when dem see champagne popping,
> Bad-mind a the sinus,
> Mi money a the pollen,
> Money allergies mi not having,
> Base ball mi and mi money a play catching,
> Right round the clock not stopping,
> Ticka, ticka, tock, the golden egg hatching

The use of bad-mind, and in particular its description as a sickness, could be seen as rooted in a wider, distinctly Jamaican ontological framework negotiated in the collision between West African belief systems and a Christian world view brought via colonization. As Austin-Broos (1997, 7) outlines, enslaved Africans brought with them a meaningful set of cultural practices, a sense of personhood and a concept of sin as a corporeal sickness that required healing through ritual acts.[16] A feature of many West African belief systems was therefore the concept of divination rites, which attended to the suffering body in order to restore stability to the disordered world. An aspect of this was "obeah", the term which has come to describe a wide variety of beliefs and practices related to the control or channelling of supernatural/spiritual forces.

Obeah

> "People say mi obeah dem. Mi a cook poison . . . ahh obeah curry goat gi affa dem . . . and all dis foolishness . . . I don't want to go back to those [days] . . . I can't bother wid people everyday say mi obeah dem . . . wah Lord Jesus, have I ever obeah anybody? Inna ma life? What is obeah?"[17]

What is obeah? "No word of African origin which has survived in the New World has taken on such a grim meaning as the word obia in many of the islands of the Caribbean" (Herskovits and Herskovits 1934, quoted in Handler and Bilby 2013, 307). The words of Lady Saw show that this "grim meaning" endures – the dispensing of cooked poison, in this case through curried goat, described as a feature of its practice.[18]

Ever since it was outlawed in Jamaica by the colonial administration in 1761 following a substantial slave rebellion,[19] it has been deployed as an all-encompassing term to refer to a range of beliefs and practices that have not been precisely defined or understood. Although it appears never to have referred to an organized religion, accounts of its practice have a number of commonalities, such as the recitation of spells and the manipulation of material objects with spiritual qualities. Despite often being portrayed to the contrary, there is evidence that it was understood as, and used for, socially benevolent (healing) as well as malignant purposes (Handler and Bilby 2013).

Yet the apparatus of the colonial complex (via which our understanding of obeah is largely received) viewed it initially as a threat to the status quo and later as a fraudulent activity and engineered a stranglehold on its practice. Between 1761 and 1898, when Jamaica's Obeah Act was passed (substantial parts of which remain in effect today), legal provisions were worked and reworked to criminalize the practice of obeah, possession of any items associated with it, consultation with practitioners of it and the publication or distribution of any printed matter that promoted it (Handler and Bilby 2013). Alongside legislative architecture was a religious imperative: waves of missionaries came to the island to Christianize the enslaved population and banish superstition, resulting in a syncretic blending of Christian precepts and West African practices (Austin-Broos 1997).

A feature of many obeah accounts, both academic and first hand, is that its existence provides an explanation for unfortunate events. As Bryan Edwards, a prominent Jamaican planter and member of the colonial assembly writes of the enslaved population in 1794 (2:88): "When, at any time, sudden or untimely death overtakes any of their companions . . . they never fail to impute it to the malicious contrivances and diabolical arts of some practitioner in obeah." Academic accounts which have sought to decolonize obeah from its pejorative associations still emphasize its role as an explanation (albeit a rational rather than a "superstitious" one) for "disease and fear":

> The principle of obeah is . . . like medical principles everywhere, the process of healing/protection through seeking out the source or explanation of the cause . . . of the disease or fear. This was debased by slave master/missionary/prospero into an assumption, inherited by most of us, that obeah deals in evil. In this way, not only has African science been discredited, but Afro Caribbean religion has been negatively fragmented and almost . . . publicly destroyed. (Brathwaite 1974, 74–75)

The characterization of obeah in dancehall has inherited many of the pejorative associations of earlier accounts – perhaps a legacy of an historical process of cultural domination that has reduced it to an antisocial practice intended to harm. It is presented almost exclusively as (1) a phenomenon that is practised for malevolent purposes; (2) practised largely because of jealous or envious motives; (3) is secretive and clandestine; and (4) is largely ineffective either because the intended target is too successful, too powerful or too protected.[20] The final point is revealing: dancehall artists make anonymous accusations from a position of demonstrable success, and this is a considerable departure from the way in which obeah use has previously been understood.

REPRESENTATIONS OF OBEAH AND BAD-MIND IN OLDER CARIBBEAN SONG

Modern dancehall shares many of the characterizations of obeah (and to a certain extent bad-mind) that are present in older popular Caribbean songs. Bilby (2012) provides a number of examples from different styles across the anglophone Caribbean (such as mento, Barbadian spouge and Trinidadian calypso), each of which reflects different aspects of the cultural understanding of obeah and which are also present in the contemporary examples under discussion.

One of the most common themes for the use of obeah in such songs is for "'tying' a lover with spiritual power – rendering him of her incapable of rejecting or leaving the person who does the tying" (Bilby 2012, 52). Obeah use to induce love in another, or as an explanation for the amorous feelings one might experience in the precursors to dancehall music, is echoed in recent songs such as Alkaline's "Obeah" (2014)[21] and Vybz Kartel's "Dutty Angela" (2009) discussed later (and often not considered to be positive).

In other examples, such as the reggae song "Samfie Man" by the Pioneers (1969), Bilby identifies the depiction of obeah workers as charlatans and fraudsters that deceive and take advantage of their clients:

> Woi, samfie[22] man, woi woi,
> You no fe take de man money under false pretence
> Now you're acting so funny just to build a defence
> You go up a Mass Rob fe go get de job
> You dig de hole, sinner man, you plant de pole

Again, such representation of obeah workers can be found in modern dancehall lyrics (although not frequently). In "Behind Curtain", the reggae artist Chronixx[23] sings:

> Because dem evil,
> dutty heart bad mind people
> watch everything that we do,
> sit down and plan fi kill you,
> yeh a good thing say mi know Jah,
> or mi would have been a fallen soldier,
> Mek mi tell you bad-mind cyaa get mi off a da road yah,
> so stop spend yo money pon obeah

The person using obeah because of "bad-mind" thoughts is wasting their time – the implication being that it is ineffectual. This is echoed in Beenie Man's "Fire Burn" (2013), condemning talk not supported by practice: "Fire burn a word without works, / Fire burn up di obeah man shirt." Bilby does locate a number of songs that deal with obeah as a practice with efficacy, or even as a positive force. Of those songs that give credence to the efficacy of obeah, this is sometimes in relation to the control of troublesome duppies[24] and ascribing the obeah man as gifted with positive power.

Given the complex, competing and often contradictory meanings ascribed to the term, this may in some cases be the conscious acknowledgement and projection of an image of obeah as a force to be reclaimed as part of ancestral cultural knowledge, and/or demonstrates that "even in the anglophone Caribbean, one can find songs that clearly demonstrate that obeah was never completely redefined, and that the stigmatization of obeah of as the work of evildoers was never absolute" (Bilby 2012, 60). I have not particularly observed these themes in current dancehall lyrics, but the line of inquiry would be worth some further attention.

It would appear that a far more frequent representation in modern dancehall lyrics and its antecedents is what Bilby describes as "as a kind of anti-social witchcraft or sorcery, used – whether at the request of an obeah-man's client, or out of pure evil mindedness on the part of the practitioner-him or herself – to cause illness, misfortune and general suffering" (Bilby 2012, 50). The majority of contemporary examples I discuss below depict obeah as a service which would be procured by those whose intention it is to cause harm (often represented as against the artist him or herself or sometimes against "the youth"), and at times simply synonymous with evil. It is worth restating that what sets contemporary songs apart from earlier examples is the number of songs that describe accusations being directed against them personally (as a person that is successful). But such charges of bad-mind or obeah use are not directed against a specific offender, nor do they arise in circumstances of demonstrable misfortune or injury. Quite the opposite: many of these artists are locally and internationally successful. Again I would reiterate that these generalized accusations therefore function as a means of signifying status.

"BOMBOCLAAT MUSSI OBEAH YO OBEAH ME TO RAASCLAAT"[25]

This representation of obeah as the conscious manipulation of malevolent forces is perpetuated in dancehall. In "Dutty Angela" (Dirty Angela) (2009), Vybz Kartel tells the story of a woman who talks/gossips about him all the time and consults an obeah practitioner to try and kill him:

> She gone obeah man,
> Fi try to tek weh mi life
> She say a mi she hate she mi wuss and no like,
> She use to beg mi mi things,
> She a real parasite,
> Now she siddung pon mi fucking name day and night
> . . . .
> Mi born a night but mi nuh born last night,
> A red eye you red eye mek you gi mi a fight
> . . . .
> Angela mi jah bless
> You witchcraft caan curse
> Mi know nuff bad-mind you are di worst[26]

The protagonist is too wise ("mi a born a night but mi nuh born last night") and too protected ("mi jah bless") to fall prey to her attempts to threaten him. As Sobo (1993, 294) outlines in her work on the Jamaican body as a medium for the expression of ideas about the social and moral order:

> People who "live good" cannot, ideally, be caught by a socially precipitated sickness: sickness instigated in perceived affronts by an animate being (a neighbour, a demon, God, or a duppy sent by a "science man" hired by a "grudgeful" villager). In an ideal world, a moral, sociable person could never anger anyone enough to attack. And should anyone really want to "sick" a physically and spiritually "clean" person (a "bad mind" individual might), God and his angels provide protection.

Throughout the nineteenth century, obeah was characterized by official discourse as "a social evil based on fraudulent motives" (Handler and Biby 2013, xx), for which, to the missionaries at least, Christianity was the cure. Many dancehall songs reflect the profound influence that the missionary movement had on such West African practices. In "Fall Rain Fall" Mavado (2009) sends out a warning to bad-mind people who are trying to bring him down through working obeah – the modern practice of obeah portrayed in a number of dancehall songs describes protagonists sprinkling oils to cause harm: "Mi send a lightening message to bad mind people overall (yeah, yeah) / Fi all di oil and di powder / Weh dem sprinkle at di stalls."[27] These people are motivated by jealousy: "Dem watch yuh things and dem drink and smoke and get stressed" and he warns the ghetto youth to "watch your step . . . work dem a work yuh fi mek yuh drop and bruk yuh neck". Again, like Kartel in "Dutty Angela", he cannot be stopped because he is too successful:

From mi touch di road there's no turning back
Dem wah mi fi weak,
Walk off and drop,
Dem dying fi hear mi deh inna cell block,
I'm touring! Go check di world map!
How I'm doing? Go ask your girl that![28]

He also has divine support: "Jah wet dem up, Jah wet dem up, / Deh from dem bad mind and corrupt / . . . From a obeah dem a wuk."[29] Omnipotent protection from malevolent intent is a recurring narrative in the presentation of obeah in dancehall, drawing heavily from the Jamaican Christian Revival tradition and appropriating the pejorative hegemonic view of the practice. In Elephant Man's "Bun Bad Mind" (2004), his lyrics and visual imagery invoke religious signs and symbols familiar to many Jamaicans. In the video for the song he parades through the village in a pastor's outfit collecting believers, until a whole congregation is processing behind him. Hands waving, and chanting "you too bad mind, you too bad mind" to the tune of "When the Saints Go Marching In", they exhort Satan to "scoobay" (go away) and the camera moves to a group of parishioners that begin to process with Elephant Man down the road.

Later, in a church, Elephant Man is dressed in white and preaches to a rapturous congregation, who answer at every opportunity, creating the call-and-response pattern so familiar in black religious preaching.[30] "Rebuke dem (alright), Rebuke dem (weh yuh seh), dem nuh like we and we nuh like dem (alright)", he says, drawing heavily from the Christian narrative and emphasizing his protected status:

Every weapon that rise against me shall fall
Brim stone and fire a wey we put over the wall
Father God sey we fi preach it like Paul slew heathen
Like Goliath and Saul (mi can't believe it) small axe mek big tree fall
. . . .
When me see Peter deny/Judas betray di most high
Dat's why mi nuh beg fren and frenship mi nuh buy[31]

Dancehall thus reflects the mish-mash, hybridization and fusion of West African beliefs about personhood, obeah and healing with the various Christian influences on Jamaican society. In raising this tension between good and evil to biblical proportions, the dancehall artist shows that he is protected and tells us something important about how the terms are used.

DANCEHALL AND COMPETITIVE ENVY

Bad-mind and obeah in dancehall are as much about status as anything else. Competitive envy and inducing desire in others through conspicuous consumption or other means is to secure one's status vis-à-vis a competitor or challenger. By referring to the existence of those who are "bad-minded" against them, the dancehall star is establishing and reinforcing their status in relation to another. This is illustrated by Mr Vegas in "I Am Blessed" (2009):

Dem caan stop mi.
I am blessed,
I am blessed
Every day of my life
I am blessed
When I wake up in the morning,
And I lay my head to rest
Every day of my life I am blessed.
Mi seh mi praise God straight,
Mek money straight
Bun haters, straight,
Bun bad mind, straight.
God know seh mi straight
....
A nuff of dem try stop mi
Mi fly past dem straight.
Whole heap of dem a wicked
So a dem mi nuh rate, yuh know
Dem waan box di likkle food from mi plate
But a God ova devil,
A hell fi dem straight[32]

DANCEHALL AND THE NARRATIVE OF LEGITIMACY

Societies differ in the manner in which they deal with the aim to "neutralise, or reduce or otherwise control the dangers they see stemming from envy, and especially their fear of envy" (Foster 1972, 165). In some, social health is based on a notion of shared poverty and people are reluctant to advance beyond their peers because they know the sanctions that will be levelled against them. In others, envy seems to be directed toward a person envied by direct aggression and its functional equivalent – witchcraft.

As Foster outlines in his work on envy, all societies seem to have cultural forms, attitudinal norms and cognitive outlooks which serve to reduce the fear of envy, contributing to the well-being of the group and the psychological well-being of the individual. Foster categorizes these forms as concealment (a prophylactic measure), denial, symbolic sharing and true sharing. But the controlled use of envy may be important for asserting status through which arises the need to deal with its consequences. Societies aim to reduce this contradiction by specifying what occasions are suitable for gaining prestige, and alongside the braggadocio of dancehall culture, a recurring motif is the concept of legitimate gain.[33]

The gangster artist desires to be protected from his foes and slanderers and have the essential justice of his own actions recognized. As shown earlier, this often invokes divine protection, but it also manifests itself in the portrayal of the artist as hero who has overcome a number of struggles to attain his position, making his wealth and associated markers of success thus legitimate. This narrative is extended more broadly to the "ghetto youth", who are overcoming barriers in a society that they feel does not want them to succeed.

In "The Cure (fi Bad-Mind)" (2013), referenced earlier for its portrayal of "bad mind" as a sickness, Vybz Kartel casts himself as the hero in his own drama of persecution. But Kartel cannot let bad-mind stop his ascent:

> Bad mind cyan get mi down,
> Mi cyan stop cah mi don't know how,
> Portmore, down town, up town,
> Bun bad mind, bun bad mind[34]

He reminds the audience he was a "sufferer", authenticating himself as part of the "ghetto" from which he has struggled to attain his position and has a legitimate right to keep it. As an attempt to neutralize any contradiction between flaunting wealth and inducing envy, he describes how he came from nothing:

> You fi stop bad mind,
> You fi happy me happy,
> And if mi nuh happy mi a grab it and clatt it,
>
> A when u did deh when mi a suffa to rawtid,
> When mi a go a school wid one suit of khaki,
> So now si mi a floss and a mash-up di party,
> No grudge mi fi mi fendi and mi isi miakie,
> When hungry a kick kick mi like karate,
> Weh you deh?[35]

His ability to access high-value goods (Fendi and Issey Miyake) is deserved and legitimate. Those that think otherwise are bad-mind. Legitimate gain, in the face of a competitor shows how envy can be used to heighten the status of the individual. No one shows it better than the "King of the Dancehall" himself:

> How you fi dis mi?
> I'm the star of the show,
> I'm a movie star and the world dun know,
> ....
> Mi and mi girls flex through Ontario,
> Drinking Alozade, driving in the limo
> (Beenie Man 2014)

The ubiquity of songs about bad-mind and obeah in dancehall can be located in the underbelly of the free market, with its entrepreneurs and its rising stars. Fermented against a toxic backdrop of violent political sectarianism and criminal gangs, fear, suspicion and mistrust, this creates legitimate reason to fear threats. The economic transformation of the 1980s enabled the acquisition of wealth and the status of a person became increasingly reflected in how that wealth was spent. Neo-liberalist policies shrank the resources and role of the state and individuals had to become resourceful. Yet if capitalism created the desire and the free market created the conditions, dancehall created the stage: vehicles, name-brand clothes, jewellery and trips abroad let society know you were doing well. But rapid wealth accumulation, which dancehall has enabled for a few but created as an aspiration for many, disturbs the status quo. The desire to be honoured and the fear of the consequences mean walking a perpetual tightrope.

Across the world, envy avoidance strategies are deployed to reinforce the stability of the social group and the psychological well-being of the individual. But dancehall is big, brash and braggadocio and respect is a form of social capital. Participants have to find another means of containing this tension. They do so by emphasizing credibility and an authenticity which validates wealth creation and its outward expression as legitimate, deserved and morally sound. But envy avoidance is only part of the story. In part, the accusation of bad-mind should be understood as a prophylactic against attack. Through invidious consumption, participants induce envy as a means of establishing, securing and reflecting their status. Manipulation of envy yields power, reducing others to a feeling of inferiority and the accusation of harbouring bad-mind. Dancehall's recent obsession with referencing the term serves to reinforce its heroes. As Popcaan (2013) says: "Tell them anytime they fight wi, we get stronger, stronger, stronger / And every time them try fi kill wi off wi live longer, longer, longer."

NOTES

1. The words "iniquity" and "science" in Jamaican usage can function as synonyms for obeah (Paton and Forde 2012, 50–57).
2. Pocomania is a "term commonly used to refer to any of the more African-identified forms of Jamaican Revivalism. The etymology of Pocomania is unknown (although the term may be of African derivation)" (Bilby 2016, 219).
3. Gully here refers to an urban residential area in Kingston known as Cassava Piece, which could be termed a ghetto or garrison, and is the place where Mavado was born. Artists representing the "Gully-side" clash with those representing "Gaza", which refers to Portmore, another Kingston garrison.
4. "Resentful of the youth for the things they have." In her study of ideas of embodied sickness and health held by Jamaicans, Sobo reports "grudgeful" people as those who feel others do not deserve their success and therefore such people directly aim to keep you from "lifting up" (Sobo 1993, 98).
5. "Jealousy and envy get the best of people who claim to be your friend."
6. "Bad-minded people want him dead, laying six foot underground."
7. Bilby for example, cites Trinidadian calypso songs from as early as 1930 (Paton and Forde 2012, 51).
8. Many dancehall artists talk about "bad-mind" people because they are intimately familiar

with ghetto life and its attendant violence and are themselves a target for those who want a share of their material wealth. There is thus a legitimate reason to fear attack as just a handful of examples show. Bounty Killer and Munga Honorable have been victims of assault, Mavado's father was murdered in Switzerland and Spragga Benz's son was shot in Kingston. Some artists have also perpetrated violence or are gang affiliated. Vybz Kartel and Ninja Man (Don Gorgon) are incarcerated for murder. Busy Signal and Buju Banton have spent time in jail.

9. "I have a big gold chain and my rolex is full of diamonds / Everywhere I go me and my friends run the place / Girls get given the latest fashions". "Swear seh mi never work obeah yet"; Beenie Man is distancing himself from potential accusations that his success is due to him consulting obeah practitioners.

10. I have been unable to locate many academic explorations of "bad-mind" in the literature with a few notable exceptions. Sobo considers the term in relation to conceptions of embodied health and sickness and kinship held by Jamaicans. Idealized kinship relations are based on support and cooperation, but the anticipation of competition, sabotage and coercion is strong and "resentments, wary manoeuvres to guard resources, and efforts to undermine economic positions are common among non-kin" (Sob 1993, 81). Excessive demands for sharing dissipate or level wealth and so block people from achieving social "uplift", and cultural ideals for altruistic generosity mean that those who try to become "big" are judged greedy or anti-social. Envy and disdain is easily aroused by those who might rise above the rest and this can lead to negative repercussions. Scott Lewis (2014) examines the use of the term among local vendors at a craft market in Montego Bay, Jamaica, who eke out a living selling to tourists. Here, accusations of bad-mind (Scott Lewis notes claims of bad-mind are furtively discussed as gossip, not acts which manifest themselves as in overt displays of resentment) are studied as a culturally informed response to competition. In a country of stagnant economic progress, vendors attribute their economic failing and the conditions that create them to a chronic lack of black Jamaican unity (expressed to Scott Lewis by the vendors as a uniquely black attitude "a so black people stay", explained as a product of slavery and the colonial experience and expressed through the concept of "sufferation"). Bad-mind accusations show that charges of self-interest operate as a mechanism of morality, working as a constraint on, rather than a facilitator of the market. As competition increases, sentiments of bad-mind appear and this leads to a further disincentive to invest, whether financially or emotionally, in the success of the market, creating and reinforcing the view of disunity.

11. "Every youth wants to be the winner, wants to own a BMW. Often we didn't have dinner. Life was bitter."

12. As Stolzoff (2000) outlines, dancehall is big business both locally and globally. A survey of the current status and potential of the music industry was commissioned in 1995 by the Jamaican government.

13. Although the accusations are often generalized and non-specific. As Scott Lewis (2014, 77) notes in the context of a Jamaican market, "actual charges of bad-mind were seldom directly, or publicly raised against an offender, and were instead discussed furtively, almost as a form of gossip".

14. Allsopp and Allsopp (2003, 67) show that, for example, in the Efik language, the native

language of the native people of Nigeria, the phrase *enye enyene idiọk-esit* (he/she has bad chest) means "he is angry/malevolent/grudgeful". In Mende, a major language of Sierra Leone, *lima-nyamu* (bad-heart/chest) means "hatred". Also in Kikongo, the Bantu language spoken in the Congo and Angola, *ntim 'ambi kena wamu* (heart bad he is with) means "he is spiteful". In Yoruba, a language spoken in West Africa, mainly in Nigeria and Benin, the phrase *ni inu buruku* (have bad inside) means "to be malevolent".

15. "Bad-mind is a disease worse than syphilis, herpes etc. Mr Bad-Mind, cure yourself by jumping from a building or light gas in your throat."
16. As Austin-Broos (1997, 7) observes, the formation of a Jamaican ontology is at the nexus between the proselytizers and the proselytized, "a negotiation of meanings, practices, symbols and powers through which people sought to address their environment, both in slavery and in the post emancipation period".
17. Jamaican dancehall artist Lady Saw talking about fellow artist Spice in an interview, July 2015 (Onstage TV 2015). There are many accusations of obeah use between artists, a subject of gossip within the dancehall fraternity.
18. Fear of the use of poison is a long-standing one in Jamaica, with roots in West African traditions, especially for divination (Sobo 1993, 110).
19. Tacky's Rebellion or the Coromantee War started on the Frontier plantation in April 1760 but quickly spread to neighbouring estates. Reports suggested that an "obeahman" was involved in advising the uprising slaves that they could not be hurt by bullets and when the rebellion was quashed the reputed individual was hung up with the feathers and teeth that were said to be the tools of his practice. Legislation titled "An Act to Remedy the Evils Arising from Irregular Assemblies of Slaves" went into effect on 1 January 1761, which pointed to the presence on many estates and plantations of "obeah men and women by whose influence over the minds of their fellow slaves . . . many and great dangers have arisen destructive of the peace and welfare of this island". Its clauses addressed the "practice of obeah . . . the wicked art" of "pretending to have communication with the devil and other evil spirits".
20. The way in which obeah is referred to in the dancehall context may even be different to how the term is used and understood in wider Jamaican society. Information on the contemporary practice of obeah is scarce, but it seems to be referred to as a response to when an individual suffers misfortune ("so and so obeahed me") or something deployed when the individual wants to attain something (a lover, good exam results and so on).
21. "A mussi obeah, you obeah me, to rassclaat, make me inna love with your pussy so / And me don't know wha' yo do to me girl, but everyday me waan fuck you."
22. As Bilby (2012, 52) states, the word "samfai", sometimes spelled "samfie", means con man or trickster but has also been identified as originally also referring to obeah man.
23. Chronixx Behind Curtain, Reggae Festival, 2013. Chronixx is a Jamaican reggae artist who could be characterized as part of a "reggae revival". He is often played in bashment events to an enthusiastic audience.
24. Cassidy and Le Page (1967, 164) define "duppy" as "the spirit of the dead, believed to be capable of returning to aid or (more often) harm living beings, directly or indirectly; they are also believed subject to the power of obeah and its practitioners who can 'set' or 'put' a duppy upon a victim and 'take off' their influence".

25. Alkaline (2014).
26. "She has gone to an obeah man to have me killed. She says she hates me. She used to use me for my things – a real parasite. Now she talks about me day and night. I'm not stupid, you are trying to curse me. Angela, I'm blessed by Jah, your witchcraft cannot curse me. I know many people with bad-mind but you are the worst".
27. See also Assassin (2014).
28. "When I go out there is no turning back, those who want me to get weak, walk off and die, they're dying to hear that I'm in prison. I'm touring, check the map. How am I doing? Ask your girlfriend!"
29. "When they work obeah, God must deal with them". "Wet" could refer to rain washing away the powder said to be sprinkled by obeah practitioners. It is also a slang term for stabbing someone: "to wet someone up".
30. Black religious preaching styles are often characterized by the rhythmic cadence of the preacher who improvises around a theme of sacred and profane. The call-and-response pattern became the way in which the congregation, often less literate and intellectual than the minister, could turn up to any ceremony and know its rules.
31. "I don't beg or buy friendship."
32. "I'm blessed. Many people try to stop me, even steal food from my plate, but God overcomes the devil."
33. This is a narrative found in hip-hop and rap music, as shown in Collins (2006).
34. "Bad-mind can't get me down or stop me, I can't be stopped."
35. "You should stop 'bad-minding' me and be happy for me. Where were you when I was suffering and went to school without a uniform and hungry? So now that I party and show off don't grudge me for my named brands. When hunger kicked me, where were you?"

REFERENCES

Abrahams, Roger, D. 1964. *Deep Down in the Jungle: Negro Narrative Folklore from the Streets of Philadelphia*. Hatboro, PA: Folklore Associates.

———. 1993. *Singing the Master: The Emergence of African American Culture in the Planation South*. New York: Penguin.

Allsopp, Richard. 2003. *Dictionary of Caribbean English Usage*. Kingston: University of the West Indies Press.

Austin-Broos, Diane. 1997. *Jamaica Genesis: Religion and the Politics of Moral Order*. Chicago: University of Chicago Press.

Bilby, Kenneth M., and Jerome S. Handler. 2004. "Obeah: Healing and Protection in West Indian Slave Life". *Journal of Caribbean History* 38, no. 2: 153–83.

Bilby, Kenneth M. 2012. "An (Un)natural Mystic in the Air: Images of Obeah in Caribbean Song". In *Obeah and Other Powers: The Politics of Caribbean Religion and Healing*, edited by Diana Paton and Maarit Forde, 45–78. Durham, NC: Duke University Press.

———. 2016. *Words of Our Mouth, Meditations of Our Heart: Pioneering Musicians of Ska, Rocksteady, Reggae, and Dancehall*. Middletown, CT: Wesleyan University Press.

Brathwaite, Edward Kamau. 1974. "The African Presence in Caribbean Literature". In *Slavery, Colonialism and Racism*, edited by Sidney Mintz, 74–75. New York: W.W. Norton.

Cassidy, F., and R.B. Le Page. 1967. *Dictionary of Jamaican English*. Cambridge: Cambridge University Press.

Collins Michael, S. 2006. "Biggie Envy and the Gangsta Sublime". *Callaloo* 29, no. 3: 911–38.

Edwards, Bryan. 1794. *An Abridgement of Mr Edwards' Civil and Commercial History of the British West Indies: In Two Volumes*. J. Parsons and J. Bell.

Foster, George. 1972. "The Anatomy of Envy: A Study in Symbolic Behaviour". *Current Anthropology* 13, no. 2 (April): 165–202.

Galvin Anne M. 2014. *Sounds of the Citizens, Dancehall and Community in Jamaica*. Nashville: Vanderbilt University Press.

Handler, Jerome S., and Kenneth M. Bilby. 2013. *Enacting Power: The Criminalisation of Obeah in the Anglophone Caribbean, 1760–2011*. Kingston: University of West Indies Press.

Hope, Donna P. 2001. *Inna di Dancehall: Popular Culture and the Politics of Identity in Jamaica*. Kingston: University of West Indies Press.

Onstage TV. 2015. "Lady Saw: How She Killed Sumfest". YouTube video, 19:17. 25 July. https://www.youtube.com/watch?v=Veso-yxVNtU.

Scott Lewis, Jovan. 2014. "Sufferer's Market: Sufferation and Economic Ethics in Jamaica". PhD thesis, London School of Economics and Political Science.

Sobo, Elisa Janine. 1993. *One Blood: The Jamaican Body*: New York: State University of New York Press.

Stolzoff, Norman C. 2000. *Wake the Town and Tell the People: Dancehall Culture in Jamaica*. Durham, NC: Duke University Press.

Stone, Carl. 1983. *Democracy and Clientalism in Jamaica*. Piscataway, NJ: Transaction Books.

Wald, Elijah. 2012. *The Dozens: A History of Rap's Mama*. New York: Oxford University Press.

Wilson, Peter. 1973. *Crab Antics: A Caribbean Study of the Conflict between Reputation and Respectability: The Social Anthropology of English-Speaking Negro Societies of the Caribbean*. New Haven: Yale University Press.

DISCOGRAPHY

Alkaline. 2014. "Obeah". *The Ultimate 2014 (Raw)*. Tad's Record Inc.

Assassin (aka Agent Sasco). 2014. "Dem a Sprinkle Oil". Penthouse Records.

Beenie Man. 2013. "Fire Burn".

———. 2014. "Bad-Mind People". *Happy Hour Riddim*. Chimney Records.

———. 2015. "Bad-Mind". *Opium Riddim*. Payday Music.

Blak Ryno. 2009. "Badmind". *Nuh Fear Riddim*. Head Concussion.

Demarco. 2011. "Send Dem Home".

Elephant Man. 2004. "Bun Bad Mind". *Reggae Hits*, vol. 33. Jet Star Music.

Jah Vinci. 2011 "Badmind Ago Fall".

Mavado. 2007. "Me and My Dogs". *Gangsta for Life: The Symphony of David Brooks*. VP Music Group.

———. 2009. "Fall Rain Fall". *Surivor Riddim*. DJ Frass Production.

Mr Vegas. 2009. "I Am Blessed". Tad's Record Inc.

Paul, Sean. 2017. "Ovaload". ATV Music.

Pioneers. 1969. "Samfie Man". Beverleys.

Popcaan. 2010a. "Dream". *Gangsta City*. Adidjahiem/Notnice Production.
———. 2010b. "Gangster City". *Gangsta City*. Adidjahiem/Notnice Production.
———. 2013. "Born Bad". Young Vibez Productions.
Vybz Kartel. 2009. "Dutty Angela". *Grades Riddim*. Notnice Records.
———. 2011. "The Best of Them". Head Concussion.
———. 2013. "The Cure (fi Bad-Mind)", feat. Russian. *Kartel Forever: Trilogy*. Tad's Record Inc.
———. 2017. "Poco Man Skank". *Money Mix Riddim*. Good Good Productions.

Sample of Songs Referencing "Bad-Mind" and/or "Obeah"

Admiral Bailey, "Mi a God Pickney"
Alborosie, "Bad-Mind"
Alkaline, "Little Harder"
Alkaline, "Nothing but Bad Mind"
Alkaline, "Obeah"
Anthony B, "Bad Mind People"
Anthony B, "Wi Nuh Bad-Mind"
Assassin, "Bad-Mind People"
Assassin, "Dem Bad-Mind"
Assassin, "Dem a Sprinkle Oil"
Beenie Man, "Bad Mind"
Beenie Man, "Bad Mind Is Active"
Beenie Man, "Bad-Mind People"
Blak Rhyno, "Bad-Mind"
Blak Rhyno, "Take Control"
Bounty Killer, "Fed Up"
Bounty Killer and I Octane, "Bad-Mind Dem a Pree"
Capleton, "Bad-Mind a Go Kill Dem"
Capleton, "Dem no Like Me"
Chan Dizzy, "Hello Bad-Mind"
Charly Black, "Bad-Mind a Go Kill Dem"
Cobra, "Teddybears"
Collie Budz, "Blind to You"
Collie Budz, "No Time"
Delus, "Cah Make Bad-Mind Win"
Demarco, "Allergic to Bad-Mind Friend"
Demarco, "Fulla Gyal"
Demarco, "Send Dem Home"
Demarco, "True Friend (Buss A Shot)"
Demarco ft. Ding Dong, "Bad-Mind Energy"
Dennis Brown/Cocoa Tea, "Bad Mind"
Don Andre, "Bad-Mind Friends"
Elephant Man,"Bad Man a Bad Man"
Elephant Man, "Bad-Mind Keep Your Distance"

Elephant Man, “Bless Me More”
Elephant Man, “Bun Bad-Mind”
Elephant Man, “Fuck You Sign”
Elephant Man, “Too Bad-Mind”
Etana, “Bad-Mind”
G Whizz, “Life Soon Sort Out”
Gyptian, “Too Bad-Mind”
I Octane, “Fly Over Bad-Mind People”
I Octane, “Bad-Mind fi di Year”
Jah Vinci, “Badmind Ago Fall”
Jah Vinci, “Remedy”
Jah Vinci, “Watch Ya Friends”
Jah Vinci ft. Aidona, “Bad-Mind Cyaa Stop We”
Konshens, “The Realest Song”
Luciano, “Bun Bad-Mind”
Lutan Fyah, “No Bad-Mind”
Mavado, “Bad-Mind Cyaa Hold Me Again”
Mavado, “Bad-Mind in This Place”
Mavado, “Bad-Mind in This Time”
Mavado, “Cah Tek We Life”
Mavado,“Fall Rain Fall”
Mavado, “Jah Is My Everything”
Mavado, “Me and My Dogs”
Mavado, “Nuh Bad Mind Friend”
Merital ft. Vybz Kartel, “My Money (Ha Ha)”
Mr Peppa, “Talk”
Mr Vegas, “Tek Weh Yuh Self”
Popcaan, “Bad Mind a Kill Dem”
Popcaan, “Bad-Mind People”
Popcaan, “Burn Bad-Mind People”
Popcaan, “Can’t Believe It”
Popcaan, “Dem Sell We Out”
Popcaan, “Dream”
Popcaan, “Only Jah Knows”
Popcaan, “Jah Jah Protect Me”
Popcaan, “Where We Come From”
Samini Scatter,“Bad-Mind”
Sean Paul, “Pepper Pot”
Shatta Wale,“Dutty Bad-Mind”
Shatta Wale, “Mr Bad-Mind”
Shawn Storm,“Bad-Mind”
Singa Blinga & Lenny Mattic,“Look Out fi Bad Mind”
Sizzla,“Parole Bless Up”
T.O.K.,“Imposter (Bad-Mind)”

The Wailers,"Bad-Mind People"
T'Nez, "Bad-Mind Place"
Vybz Kartel,"Bad-Mind"
Vybz Kartel, "Bad-Mind Inna Dem"
Vybz Kartel, "The Best of Dem"
Vybz Kartel, "Bun Out Bad-Mind fi Di"
Vybz Kartel, "The Cure (fi Bad-Mind)"
Vybz Kartel,"Dutty Angela"
Vybz Kartel, "Friends Turn Enemies"
Vybz Kartel, "Mi Nah Guh (Dem Bad-Mind)"

PART 7

ADORNMENT, EMBODIMENT AND STYLE

CHAPTER 24

Fabricating Identities

*Survival and the Imagination in Jamaican Dancehall Culture**

BIBI BAKARE-YUSUF

AN ASSESSMENT OF RECENT WORK ON JAMAICAN DANCEHALL culture reveals the absence of any systematic analysis of the role that fashion and adornment play in the culture. This is surprising given that fashion is a prominent and constitutive part of the culture *and* the site for vigorous debate about lower-class women's morality and sexuality in Jamaica. This failure can only be attributed to the fact that analyses of dancehall culture have generally focused on lyrical content, the sound system and the economic production of music (Stolzoff 2000; Cooper 1993a). I suggest that underlying this focus is the implicit assumption that music equates with interiority, language and "deep" meaning. In contrast, adornment and fashion are considered to elude or even destroy meaning. Therefore, to invest energy on adornment conjures up images of superficial, transient and frivolous activities undertaken only by women (Polhemus 1988; Tseëlon 1997), in contrast to the serious male world of ideas connoted by music production. While undeniably significant for a critical analysis of dancehall culture, a continued over-emphasis on music and lyrical content, to the neglect of other aspects of the culture, unwittingly privileges the activities of men and their interpretation of the culture to the exclusion of women.[1]

In this chapter, I want to shift attention away from lyrical content and a specific focus on dancehall culture to examine the embodied practices that emerged in the late 1980s to the end of the 1990s in Jamaica. I argue that working-class black women in Jamaica use fashion to fabricate a space for the presentation of self-identity and assertion of agency. Through adornment, dancehall women have been able to address creatively the anxiety, violence and joy of daily life. At the same time, they have been able to register historical, cultural, economic and technological changes through their bodies (Breward 1994). Prior to speech or any written manifesto, different modes of adornment are employed to contest

*Previously published in *Fashion Theory* 10, no. 4 (2015): 461–83.

society's representation of and expectations about lower-class leisure activity, morality and sexual expression. In a nutshell, fashion allows dancehall women[2] to challenge the patriarchal, class-based and (Christian and Rastafarian) puritanical logic operating in Jamaica. Of course, the wider context in which this articulation of social relations has taken place is that of socio-political and economic realities, which includes continued anti-black racism, black nationalism and global cultural and economic restructuring. In this sense, far from fashion being meaningless, superficial and unworthy of cultural analysis, it allows working-class black women to invest their everyday lived realities with multiple meanings and processes, which link them to both the spectacular fetishism of global consumerism and mass media semiosis and the African love of ceremonial pomp and pageantry.

The fact that dancehall women most often do not consciously adhere to this critical position in their speech, nor readily perceive their action as jamming the hegemonic syntax, is quite beside the point.[3] Phenomenology teaches us that there is often a gap between intentional action and explicit, self-aware interpretation (Tseëlon 1997). Far from imputing a kind of rational, contestive voluntarism to dancehall women, I suggest that the significance and meaning of their action as a form of contestation is not always available for self-articulation. As such, my account and interpretation of the meaning of fashion and adornment in the culture is not wholly circumscribed by empirical enquiry into conscious explanation, speech acts or verbalized discourse. Rather, my analysis is based on *both* empirical engagement and my own analysis of the expressive body in the culture. This body, its desires and perceptions are seldom fully disclosed within speech; rather, they are made manifest in a variety of bodily practices.

CHANGING TIMES, CHANGING STYLES

Fashion styles are always embodied and situated phenomena, reflecting and embodying social and historical changes. Prosperity, crisis and social upheaval are stitched into the fabric of every epoch. For example, the extraordinary wealth of Renaissance Europe was materially layered into the ornate and elaborate detailing of upper-class clothing. In contrast, in its rejection of the sumptuous and colourful style of the *ancien régime*, post-revolution France adopted a less ostentatious and simple cut in order to reflect new-found freedom (Breward 1994; Connerton 1989). Fashion and bodily practices became a crucial site to both express wealth in the one case and challenge old hierarchies in the other.

Among New World Africans, fashion and bodily practices have also absorbed and expressed key symbolic functions. Starting from the long revolution fomented in the hold of the slave ship, when the enslaved cut their hair into elaborate designs (Mintz and Price 1976), and reaching its apogee in the Black Power movement of the 1970s, bodily practices were as important as political manifestos in the struggle for freedom, agency and assertion of cultural identity. The "natural" Afro hairstyle, dashiki, large-hooped earrings, psychedelic skirts and patchwork miniskirts of the 1960s and 1970s signalled a rejection of European aesthetics. Fashion styles visually represented and extended the ideological affirmation and valorization of blackness and Africanity in circulation during the period. Like their North American counterparts, many Jamaicans adopted Africanized textiles, kaftans and long flowing brightly coloured majestic robes, head-wraps and jewellery made from natural materials such as seashells. However, during this period, the most important challenge to the aesthetic and ethical sensibilities of the Jamaican elite came in the form of Reggae music and the wearing of dreadlocks. Many Rastafarians and Reggae fans adopted dreadlocks and the military uniform of khakis and combat trousers. These motifs not only posed a challenge to the white capitalist and Christian ideology pervasive on the island but they also drew attention to the permanent state of warfare that characterized life in the downtown ghettos of Kingston. Rastafarian fashion, in particular the wearing of dreadlocks, performed a critique of the dominant regime, asserting an alternative cultural, ethical and aesthetic sensibility in its stead.

In the late 1970s, the rise of Edward Seaga's neo-liberal free-enterprise government heralded a new era of increased insecurity, violence and anxiety. This political turn gave rise to a corresponding cultural energy. Popular cultural expression on the island such as music, dance and clothing style moved away from the socialist, pan-Africanist eschatological project associated with the Rastafarian reggae of Bob Marley and Michael Manley's socialist government toward what appeared to be the hedonistic, self-seeking pleasure and excess of dancehall style (Chude-Sokei 1997; Barrow and Dalton 1997). Because the elite found it offensive and it was not initially given airplay on national radio, dancehall music was generally produced and consumed in the open air or indoor spaces designated as dancehalls. Dancehall music or ragga (as it is known in Britain) is reggae's grittier and tougher offspring, making use of digital recording, remixing and sampling while DJs "skank" or "toast" over dubplates (Jahn and Weber 1992). To the ruling elite, the music was considered pure noise, a cacophonous drone that grated the nerves. The lyrics were considered bawdy, guttural and sexually explicit. Finally, the elite considered dancehall (especially female) dress and adornment brash and excessive, reinforcing the view that lower-class black women were sexually permissive. As a whole, the subculture confirmed to the Eurocentrically inclined elite the immorality and degeneracy of the urban poor.[4]

In contrast to this disparagingly reductive view, dancehall culture should be viewed as a complex reminder of the continued relationship between popular expressions, commodification, urbanization, global economic and political realities and historico-cultural memory. For example, in music, older Jamaican styles and practices were revived and brought into conversation with new digital technologies and global flows of information (Bilby 1997). In terms of dance, dancehall unearthed older Jamaican forms such as dinki mini and mento. As the Jamaican choreographer and cultural theorist Rex Nettleford notes, "The movements in dancehall are nothing new; in my own youth I witnessed and participated in mento sessions which forced from executants the kind of axial movements which concentrated on the pelvic region with feet firmly grounded on one spot" (1994, 1C). Dancehall fashion fits into a general "African love of pageantry, adornments and social events" (Mustafa 1998). The African American folklorist Zora Neale Hurston suggested that "the will to adorn" constitutes "the second . . . most notable characteristic in Negro expression" (1933, 294). The will to adorn, she argued, is not an attempt to meet conventional standards of beauty but to satisfy the soul of its creator (1933, 294). I suggest that the desire to "satisfy the soul" and project their own aesthetics onto the world is at the core of dancehall women's sartorial practice.

DANCEHALL FASHION

In a society influenced by Christian puritanism and the sexual conservatism of Rastafarian ideology, dancehall fashion has responded antithetically with bare-as-you-dare fashion. Unlike previous African diasporic youth subcultures, dancehall is unique in that women are highly visible. Although there are a number of prominent female dancehall music performers, women's visibility in the culture centres on their ostentatious, sartorial pageantry. The "session", "bashment" or "dance" is an occasion for visual overload, maximalism and the liminal expression of female agency. Women form "modelling posses" or rival groups, where they compete with each other at a dance event for the most risqué and outlandish clothes. Their consumption practices are largely funded through the informal sector, as higglers (informal commercial traders), petty traders, cleaners, dancehall fashion designers or by having a "sugar daddy". Many of the outfits are designed and made by the wearer or by a local tailor. The style appears anarchic, confrontational and openly sexual. Slashed clothing, the so-called "lingerie look" (such as g-string panties, bra tops), "puny printers" (showing the outline of the genitals), Wild West and dominatrix themes, pant suits, figure-hugging short dresses and micro hot pants infamously known as "batty riders" are favoured. Revealing mesh tops, cheap lace, jeans designed as though bullets have ripped into the fabric and sequined bra tops became an essential part of dancehall women's wardrobe in the 1990s. At the close of the 1980s, the dancehall female body was wrapped in bondage straps and broad long fringes or panels attached to long dresses to accentuate the fluidity of the body's movement in dance. Incompatible materials and designs were juxtaposed – velvet, lace, leather, suede, different shades of denim, rubber and PVC, as well as animal prints such as mock snake, zebra and leopard skin, to produce an eclectic personal statement. Seemingly irreconcilable colours are combined to produce a refreshingly audacious, motile canvas on the dance floor. According to Carolyn Cooper (1993a, 155), the sessions are the "social space in which the smell of female power is exuded in the extravagant display of flashy jewellery, expensive clothes [and] elaborate hairstyles".

Hairstyle, make-up and jewellery are a key part of the dancehall look. In the late 1980s to late 1990s, huge cheap and chunky gold earrings with razor-blade designs, as well as necklaces with dollar signs were worn on the ears, nose, nails, waist and belly button as status symbols. More recently, the style has moved toward "ice" (slang for diamonds) and "bling-bling" (code for expensive jewellery and accessories). Hair is either dyed in bright colours or covered in metallic-coloured wigs, weaves and extensions (platinum blonde, orange, turquoise, aubergine, pink). This style disrupts the Jamaican elite notions of "good" and "natural" hair versus "bad" and "processed" hair. In so doing, dancehall women draw attention to the artifice of African hairstyle (Mercer 1987) and the way "black women exercise power and choice" (Banks 2000, 69). In opposition to the Jamaican elite preference for understated beauty characterized by lightly applied make-up highlighting flawless skin, dancehall women's make-up is deliberately bright, glittery and brash.

Shoe styles continue the sexual fetish theme of the clothes: laced or zipped up stilettos, knee or thigh-length boots in patent leather or "pleather" are favoured for their emphasizing effects on the crotch and thighs. High-heeled strap shoes that coil round the calves toward the knees complete the image (D'Elia 2002).

DISRUPTING BEAUTY, CLASS AND GENDER

Given the intensity of dancehall modes of adornment, the question that arises is how to account for the phenomenon, both in terms of the socio-historical context of Jamaican culture and dancehall fashion's position within a global economy of signs and material flows. Here, I will identify three interwoven processes at work. First, I will point to the ways in which the fashion disrupts Jamaica's elite ideas of black female beauty and norms of appearance, via an overtly sexualized paradigm shift toward what I term the "aesthetics of voluptuousness". Second, I will show how practices of adornment in Jamaican dancehall are women's response to a "limit situation" in which the issues that face them on a daily basis are issues of survival and keeping the terror of daily life at bay. Contrary to the conventional (Western) impulse to assume that "limit situations" necessitate a victim mentality, attenuating agency and expression in the process, I will argue that limit situations can stimulate the collective imagination to heightened states of intensity and excess. Finally, I will show how dancehall fashion is located within a network of global flows and exchanges. Rather than being a uniquely local phenomenon explicable solely in local terms, dancehall fashion demands a broader understanding of how both local and international signifying systems have been adopted and appropriated by Jamaican women, creating the distinctive aesthetic form and self that is dancehall style.

In order to understand the ways in which modes of adornment in dancehall work to disrupt existing conventions of the beautiful and express sexual difference, we need to appreciate the Jamaican upper-class perspective against which it responds. In Jamaica, as elsewhere in the New World, the voluptuous black female body came to embody upper-class anxiety over the moral status of the lower class. According to Carolyn Cooper (2000, 350), it is this body that became the site for "ongoing struggle over high culture and low, respectability and riot, propriety and vulgarity". Just as in late eighteenth- and nineteenth-century Europe, where a distinction was made between the modest and chaste (typically upper-class body) woman and the vulgar and obscene (working-class and African body), a similar bifurcation takes place in the Caribbean. The European upper-class moral ideal also operates on the island with an accompanying aesthetic transfer. The ideal look for elite Jamaican women is essentially a *white* look: slender, restrained, calm, long flowing (straightened) hair and light or brown skin. The continued value placed on skin colour as an important aspect of social mobility still exerts its own peculiar influence and particular form of violence on the psyche of Jamaicans (Douglas 1992; Barnes 1999). Although class is a critically important social vector in Jamaica, it is often articulated "through the idiom of colour shade and can reflect biologized notions of race" (Austin-Broos 1994, 218). Class, colour/race and gender in combination constitute what Austin-Broos has called "Jamaica's discourse of heritable identity" (218). This discourse perpetuates and reproduces the cultural logic of plantation society, where upper-class European values and morality have dominated the sociocultural and economic landscape till the present day. It is the world view of the brown or non-black elite which features most prominently in public arenas such as newspapers, beauty contests and television, and in the political and economic life of a country where 90 per cent of the population is black. Lower-class black women are accordingly derided as vulgar, uncontrollable and dangerous. To the ruling elite, the protruding belly, large dimpled buttocks and thighs squeezed into revealing batty riders marks dancehall women as indecent, morally repugnant and unproductive elements within society. Writing in the *Daily Gleaner*, André Fanon (1988, 14) echoes the views of the ruling class:

> Dance-hall becomes a danger when the dance-hall syndrome is made into a way of life . . . Dance hall . . . under-develops our women who feel that they must learn to "wine" and "cock out" their posteriors as champion bubblers. Dance hall as a way of life emphasises the unproductive elements in society. If not channelled, dance hall will create a class of people which is incapable of doing anything productive.

In their purposely garish coiffure, slashed latex body suits and flashy gold jewellery, the women assert their distance to and non-conformity with the sobriety of Fanon's official culture and all that it represents: formal work and chaste morality. Importantly, these sumptuary practices mark dancehall women out as being unaffected by the lack and poverty that is a characteristic of ghetto life. According to Nettleford, dancehall fashion "all together spells for many a form of personal liberation from the strictures of a humourless existence which the hardships of poverty like the cloying satisfaction of affluence seem to impose on human beings at the opposite ends of the social scale" (1994, 16D). Dancehall women contest the association of material poverty with the inability to care and attend to public self-presentation. As one participant in the culture succinctly puts it, "I may be poor and come from the ghetto, it don't mean I have to look shabby. A woman always has to look good even if it means spending her last dollar. Going to a dance is the time to dress up and let the world really see you as you are." As Paulette McDonald (1993, 10) notes of another dancehall fan, "dressing up in expensive clothes sends a clear message to those who think that ghetto people are the scum of the earth: they can indeed set the fashion pace". Dancehall attire suggests that without engaging in the arduous work of the formal economy, women in the culture still have at their disposal the money and creative resources that enables them to invest and participate in a fashion-based signifying economy. Rather than directing their labour toward the formal, bureaucratic structure, dancehall women work on their body as a "canvas of representation" (Hall 1992, 27) so that the world can see them as they are.

Moreover, against the upper-class slur of idle unproductivity as described by Fanon above, dancehall modes of adornment should be viewed as a form of work in its own right – the work of creative resistance as a product of a playful imaginative and historical retrieval. In the context of a conservative and moralistic society, dancehall adornment invokes a visual subversion by returning to the subterranean sources of Jamaican folk culture, demonstrating a capacity to admit variation as a form of continuation. Of course, as I suggested above, this subversive historical recall does not necessarily conform to an intentional politics of conscious resistance. Dancehall female fans often have an unconscious pre-theoretical response relation to the ideology surrounding them, the variety of ways it is working through them and the responses engendered by it. As the French sociologist Pierre Bourdieu (1977, 79) points out, "It is because subjects do not, strictly speaking, know what they are doing that what they do has more meaning than they know." This unconscious collective agency of bodily action resists theorization in the language of conscious articulation. As elsewhere, the female body in dancehall perceives and responds in its own way to forms of affirmation and negation in the world. Through this unconscious collective response, dancehall women contest Euro-hegemony as it is manifested in Jamaica. Whether or not these resistances and refusals could ever be so well articulated in speech or deemed important is quite another matter.

Indeed, beyond being a form of creative labour, I suggest that the work of the imagination has as its goal the disruptive parody of the Jamaican class structure itself. From a perspective influenced by Marx's theory of commodity fetishism, women's stylistic excess can be decoded as class struggle by other means. The function of creative strategies of adornment in dancehall is to destabilize the field of class distinctions in Jamaica. It is helpful, in this context, to refer to the work by Jonathan Friedman (1994). Friedman adopts and critiques Pierre Bourdieu's analysis of distinction-making in order to show how the Congolese Sapeurs appropriate fashion styles (especially that of European haute couture) in order to disrupt the field of taste distinctions at work in Congolese society. For Friedman, it is precisely through appropriation, repetition and strategies of exaggeration and excess that the Sapeurs destabilize normative conventions of taste. By borrowing modes of dress and aesthetics associated with the economic elite, the Sapeurs (who are mostly poor and urban dwellers) undermine the commodity fetishism and prestige value with which exclusive European clothing was previously invested. His argument therefore borrows from and exceeds that of Bourdieu. For the French sociologist, taste distinction occurs within a field – a horizon of differences that comprise the differential fabric of society. For Friedman, in contrast, the work of adornment among the Sapeurs tears at the social fabric of taste. In a parallel manner, in dancehall culture, a far more destabilizing dynamic is unleashed than that of simple social differentiation. Dancehall women are less concerned about being accepted by or assimilated within mainstream society, or to pretend to be something they are not. Again, they are not concerned to mark out a simple difference in taste. Rather, the overloading of the senses through sartorial extravagance works to deconstruct and jam the field of distinctions itself, through the exaggerated mimicry of conventional conceptions of feminine comportment. In a forceful response to denigration from upper/middle-class sensibilities and the Rastafarian restricted "mother earth" style for women, dancehall women dress to oppose every aspect of "appropriate" feminine comportment, appearance and conduct. Whereas middle-class Jamaican women tend to desire a slender and sleek figure, dancehall women rejoice in an unruly voluptuosity – the joy of being fat. And more troubling, slender women have resorted to using drugs, food and even hormones, the "fowl pill", to get fat as described in one of Lexxus's lyrics.[5] In opposition to the Rastafarian chaste concealment, dancehall women revel in exposed flesh. Where both uptown and Rastafarian women value stylistic restraint (in terms of fabric, fit and colours), dancehall women value riotous colours and sheer maximalism. In this sense, the fetishized commodity of cloth in Jamaica, divided between elite, Rastafarian and poor urban-underclass sensibilities, threatens to break out of a rigidly Marxist perspective of class struggle to include a contestation of what it is to be a woman. Dancehall fashion is considered such a threat by the ruling elite that at the emergency department of the Bustamante children's hospital in Kingston a "dress code" is deemed necessary to restrict dancehall aesthetic from spilling over into such an institution:

> I. Please cover all body parts!!
> II. Please attend to personal hygiene!
> III. No setters in hair!
> IV. NO Dancehall Style! (cited in Cooper 1993b)

Dancehall culture therefore is the site of a contestation of both class and sexual difference, to the extent that neither can be reduced wholly into the terms of the other. While the aim of dancehall style is meant to shock and rebel against the upper- and middle-class and Rastafarian ethos, it cannot be fully understood outside of an attempt to intervene against repressive attitudes toward female sexuality, appearance and comportment. Drawing on motifs of deviant sexuality and symbols of excessive femininity allows dancehall women to express sexual power and affirm their own sexual objectification at the same time. By presenting the fleshy female body as unruly and hyper-feminine, dancehall women show femininity to be a masquerade, a kind of mask. The question then arises about how to theorize this masking process and its intent. In European intellectual history, theories of masquerade can be crudely characterized in three ways: first, the feminist tradition, which views masking in terms of patriarchal scopic economy which hides and stifles the true identity of women (Irigaray 1985; Mulvey 1989); second, the psychoanalytic tradition, which regards the mask of femininity as covering a non-identity, that is, there is no substantive identity to reveal beneath the mask (Riviere 1986; Heath 1986). Both these perspectives view masquerade as absence, superficial, lack and negation. In so doing, they repeat specific assumptions about the relation between surface and depth, inner and outer, masculine and female. In contrast the third, broadly phenomenological, approach holds that identity is constituted *through* the mask itself. In this view (which traces its roots back to Nietzsche), there is nothing behind the mask, except yet another mask and yet another mode of identity imbricated within another potential surface. In this sense, the layerings that constitute the feminine are neither a hidden essence nor a concealment of absence; rather, the mask is resolutely dynamic (see Karim Benammar n.d.). As one layer yields to another, identity-as-essence gives way to identity-as-performance. In this sense, femininity as a masked identity in dancehall is therefore both a performative and a generative space of being, where the binary opposition between the authentic and inauthentic has no traction.

It is important to remember that dancehall fashion operates within a patriarchal economy which positions women as the object of male desire and control. The extent to which the explicit celebration of women's sexuality challenges the power relations between the sexes is therefore limited. Dancehall fashion should, however, be understood as both an expression of female agency *and* the opportunity for male scopic mastery. For Diane McCaulay, a contributor to the *Gleaner*, although dancehall fashion offends her feminist sensibility because it reinforces the image of women as sexual objects, she nonetheless sees it as a statement of female strength and agency. She goes further:

> I have to say mostly, though, because I confess to a certain admiration for the outright defiance of dancehall fashion. Further, dancehall clothes cannot be said to promote feminine weakness; on the contrary, dancehall women are clearly not to be messed with. I am particularly uncomfortable with the inordinate interest shown by the authority figures (usually men) in the way women dress, and the quantum leap of ascribing national moral decline to the popularity of a certain type of female fashion. It is a very short distance from excluding dancehall from festival to not allowing it at all. Who is going to decide? Apart from who decides, how are we going to establish what is unsuitable entertainment? What about carnival? Many members of the middle-class deprecate dancehall as obscene, while embracing the equally lascivious gyrations of soca. . . . But there is clearly no real difference between the display of skin and the drunkenness of carnival revelry, and the outrageousness of dancehall. (McCauley 1994)

Dancehall women therefore expose femininity as a performative and generative construction that calls into question the Eurocentric and patriarchal separation between the Madonna and the whore, life and theatre, real and appearance. The eroticized exposure of ample, black female flesh in revealing clothes thereby disrupts the patriarchal schism between the sexualized female body and the maternal body. Mary Russo (1986) argues that in Western culture, the exposure of the female flesh, especially the aging, fat or pregnant body, is seen as vulgar and grotesque, "making a spectacle of oneself". It is precisely this kind of female corporeal spectacle that dancehall women seek to celebrate, as they reject and complicate the dominant reduction of female identity to a maternal or sexual binarism and the veneration of the slender ideal. With such self-presentations, the dancehall woman "puts distance between herself and her observers" (Evans and Thornton 1991, 55). Evans and Thornton argue that this distance enables women to create "a space in which to manoeuvre and to determine the meanings of the show" (55). Within a subcultural space that both challenges official discourse and yet nonetheless reproduces its patriarchal scopic framing, dancehall women have found a way to intervene through their corporeal styling. Through sartorial eloquence, dancehall women invite the male gaze only to fend off scopic capture. This is due to the extravagant, risqué style of their adornment, their dancing skills and the unsmiling, distant look, which can only be responded to with awed silence by the appreciative audience – both male and female. Therefore, what appears initially as sexual vulnerability or availability becomes a form of defensive armoury in which the women assert their own subject position and an unwillingness to be intimidated by the normative pressures of a passive femininity.

Beyond aesthetics and a jamming of the class syntax in Jamaica, a non-European relation to embodiment and corporeal expression is at work in dancehall. Instead of restraint and a self-confining attitude toward the body, dancehall women call upon alternative traditions available within their culture. In this social space, women push the African love of ceremonial pomp to its absolute limit. The desire for full-bodied women in Jamaica is celebrated by the women themselves. Similar to the punk style described by Dick Hebidge (1979, 108) and others, dancehall fashion exhumes an iconography of sexual kinkiness "from the boudoir, closet and the pornographic film and placed on the streets where they retained their forbidden connotations".

This sexualized expression is taken to the limit, as bulky black flesh folds over figure-hugging slashed tops to exude an air of self-assurance and intimidation. This bold attitude and stance tempers the sexual offering; the "bad, vulnerable girl" image invoking a bodily confidence is characterized by masculine bravado. Here, we find a psychological corollary to the explicit forms of adornment among dancehall women: a strident confidence that again seeks to oppose and disrupt the chaste respectability of the uptown woman.

SURVIVAL AND IMAGINATION

In addition to the extreme oppositional logic combating class oppression and the uptown normative violence of feminine respectability, dancehall fashion speaks of the edgy conditions in which many women in Jamaican ghettos find themselves. Here, we can introduce the metaphor of cultural energy. When a group is pushed to the limit of existence and marginalized from the normative centres of the production of meaning and cultural symbolization, the expressive energy that seeks output from the group cannot be released smoothly and easily. This energy builds up and seeks an outlet, like a blocked pipe. What often emerges between the gaps is an uncontrollable and uncontainable explosion of creative excessive energy, as desire transduces itself into expression. For dancehall women, the maximal intensity of their clothing, jewellery and hairstyle is the body's response to the existential conditions of their lifeworld: the noise, chaos and volatility that surrounds. The body transforms itself into an ocular symphony, an expressive machine competing via visual overload with the sound booming out of the sound system. The loud screams of their clothing, jewellery and hairstyle is a retort against the gutteral tempo of the music. Sartorial excess emerges as a solution to a limit situation: what Jamaicans call "sufferation".

Women's overinvestment in extreme forms of adornment in this culture is therefore an essential aspect of what it means to survive. Against the legacy of plantation slavery, global economic inequality, hetero-patriarchal constraint, the violence of class inequality and religious conservatism, survival entails the transcendence of social death, through an attempt to overcome the horrors and anxieties of daily life. Survival for dancehall women means the attempt to generate meaning and sense in a context of profound meaninglessness and senselessness. In a context where class, patriarchy and colour combine to create a unique blend of violence and erasure, survival finally concerns the search for identity, honour and prestige; the attempt to fuse the metaphysical, the spiritual and the existential in a way that allows the urban poor to "imagine an undominated fruition and to live within existing dominations equipped with a determination to do more than survive" (Simone 1989, 158).

Sartorial excess is the way in which transcendence (however temporary) from the harshness of life in the ghetto is imagined and manifested. Female dancehall fans may live under the threat of daily assault and opportunity-denying poverty; they are, however, the best-dressed poor women. Here, there are parallels with other forms of sartorial baroque practices operating as a survival strategy in different cultural settings. The example of Sapeurs mentioned above is a case in point. Like the Sapeurs, for dancehall women, baroque stylization of the body transcends issue of style toward the fabrication of identities, whereby conspicuous consumption is an aspect of the maintenance of self. Friedman (1994, 106) writes, "Consumption is a life-and-death struggle for psychic and social survival and it consumes the entire person. If there is a fundamental desperation at the bottom of this activity it is perhaps related to the state of narcissistic non-being generated by a social crisis of self-constitution."

The violence, anxiety and vulnerability of daily life are stitched into the designs of the fabric. The culture of gunning and knifing down opponents that characterizes ghetto life is visually woven into the sheered tops and the motif of bullet holes in jeans. This representation of violence has the effect of both foregrounding existential reality and erasing it at the same time. In their reading of Schiaparelli's 1937 "The Tear Dress", Caroline Evans and Minna Thornton have suggested that by combining the motif of violence with sophisticated high fashion, "violence and eroticism are simultaneously displayed and made to disappear; beauty is brought to bear on rupture" (1991, 50). Baroque sartorial practice becomes the very means by which daily violence is tamed.

This examination of the issue of adornment in dancehall sheds light on a specific but ingrained contingent relationship between the question of "survival" and that of the imagination, expression and identity. Here, we find a marginalized majority, impoverished, vulnerable and violated in the midst of an urban and spiritual decay inflicted ultimately by the abstract authority of Western capital and Europeanized class ideology. At this point, we are faced with a puzzle that requires something more than the explanation based on the model of cultural energy referred to above: how can this basic subversion of need in favour of an excessive imaginative expression occur in such extreme circumstances? The expectation is quite the opposite: that it is only in the case of material comfort that questions of need and survival can be forgotten, replaced by the bourgeois recourse to worlds of the imagination. In this case, how can this vigorously unique style fabricate itself within such a crisis-ridden space?

To answer this question, we need to turn the assumption that creative excess follows material abundance (and its inverse, that attenuation follows material depletion) on its head. It is clear that instead of emaciated abjection, dancehall women respond to their socio-political and economic plight through the multitextural imprint of enculturated cloth. In a culture where appearance fixes and positions the agent according to a rigid signifying system, dancehall fashion and adornment actively contests and subverts the system of classification itself. Instead of allowing the body to collapse or be rendered mute and inexpressive inside the anxieties of everyday life, through clothing the body is presented as a voluptuous, radiant transcendence of crisis. The "survival" at work in dancehall conforms to the phenomenological logic of the mask: instead of a fixed order of *necessity* – of the basic physical issues of need and demand – necessity is undercut by the performative subversions of desire and expression:

> Among the "people from below" the device of "masking" (in fancy-dress) persists with a vengeance. We still have reason to devise masks to disguise, to create music to affirm, and to assemble dances to celebrate. The ambush of a less than just society under the cover of festive masquerades has been one way of experiencing control, if only a temporary one. Being King or Queen for a day was a way of having a taste for power, even if it was mock power and fleeting. . . . The actual dress is important. For the costume is a mask helping to transform the persona to do wild and uninhibited things – much tulle, dark glasses replacing the old meshwire masks the Jonkonnu characters wore and still do, sequins and costume jewellery, beads, baubles of all kinds, earrings (knobs or droplets), all reminiscent of the pieces of broken mirror on the fancy dress of traditional Jonkonnu! (Nettleford 1995, 16D)

As with the Sapeurs, survival involves an imagination that refuses to be flattened by the forces of negation at work beyond the frontiers of the ghetto. In this way, a truly radical transgression is in operation: dancehall bears no conformity with even the basic existential/social hierarchies of Western normative assumptions. Dancehall women live in such extreme circumstances – of crossfire, acid attacks, rape, spousal abuse, sole caregiver and negation – that fearlessness itself becomes the only mode of survival. It is the extremity of circumstance – the toughness of a life that has been pushed to the limit and is no longer afraid of death or pain – that enables fearlessness to arise. On the one hand, having nothing to fear can lead to senseless acts of violence; with dancehall women, however, it leads to a refusal to acquiesce to the pseudo-transgressive logic of the carnival which Jamaican elites find more agreeable, where a normative order waits to restore normativity behind the mask. It is precisely in this liminal situation that women finally can lose any anxiety over the social perception of their appearance. Instead of the fear of being called a "skettel" or a tart or seen as obscene, the dancehall woman dresses for herself and her community, without care for Jamaican uptown decorum and respectability.

GLOBAL AND LOCAL FLOWS

At first sight, dancehall fashion appears to be strangely dislocated from the rest of society, an orchidacious subculture extruded from beyond the rim of mainstream culture. Dancehall adornment springs out like an alien life form complete with its own entirely separate dynamics of existence and taste, like fungi on a tree. Dancehall fashion seems to be the very antithesis of conservative restraint and the concealed style of both official culture and Rastafarian gender coding. It appears to be totally divorced from any cultural or historical context or continuity; springing forth with mutant abundance in a flash of audaciously coloured wigs, raucous screech-screaming lamé and sequined tops stretched revealingly across expanses of black flesh. And yet, this dislocated appearance is deceptive. Closer examination of dancehall style reveals deep cross-cultural and historical connections at work in its constitution, demonstrating an attunement with a hybrid array of cultural elements. In an age of transactional flow of bodies, information, goods, mass media and images, cultural eclecticism has become the only response. Jamaica's proximity to North America, with the more than sixty American television channels that beam into Jamaican homes, combined with the large number of Jamaicans in the diaspora, means that cultural influence and exchange is the norm. Like their counterparts in the sonic world, dancehall fashion also favours sampling, cutting and mixing in order to give birth to something different and distinct. Dancehall women have raided the global wardrobe and given it local texture. Odd and incongruous materials, imageries, accessories and patterns are combined to produce dizzying and dazzling layers of material, texture and form. Plastic, lurex, polyester, lycra, nylon are combined with leather, silk, organza lace, velvet, brocade. Late 1960s hot pants ride higher into the buttocks to reveal more than its original ever did; English granny purple-rinse hair styles become an unrecognizable, chromatic sculptured coiffure on youthful bodies; the "cut up" and bondage straps of punk were cleaned up and re-emerged as the "air-conditioned linen summer wear" designed by Sandra Campbell; Vivienne Westwood's 1976 Bondage Collection was hungrily retrieved and stripped of its Nazi associations. Punk girls' fishnet tights became the now classic mesh string vest. Fake chunky 22-carat gold evoked the tradition of goldsmith's art that flourished in the former Gold Coast of West Africa, Ghana, denuded of its royalty and hierarchy and reduced to a kitschy repetition of the original. The bridal nose ring linked to the ear by a fine delicate chain connects dancehall women to a tradition of Bollywood-esque ostentatious display. All these motifs are emblematic of the way in which dancehall women have absorbed and adapted global fashions, goods and images and inflected them with new meanings that have made them refreshingly and uniquely Jamaican. This is what Hudita Nura Mustafa (1988, 22), in her account of changing fashion in Senegal, has termed the "sartorial ecumene". Sartorial ecumene refers to the "incorporation of objects and images of global origins into [local] practices and circulations involving dress and bodily adornment". It is in the surface of adornment that the creative subjectivity and agency of women at the core of dancehall styling should be understood.

The fabric and cut of aspect of dancehall fashion also has a direct lineage to the

Jamaican masquerade tradition of Jonkonnu and "Pitchy Patchy". Here, women are clothed in strips of material gathered together to give the appearance of a jumble of loose layers of fabric. This historical connection enables us to understand a key point about dancehall culture – that it is far more closely connected to the deep fibre of the Jamaican folk tradition than the ruling elite would like to acknowledge: "Old characters like Pitchy Patchy have their counterparts in contemporary dancehall. The best jeans (stone washed or plain) are made to look ragged with designer-looking patches of varying colours, with strategic rips or strips hanging like the organised raggedness of traditional Pitchy Patchy" (Nettleford 1995, 16D). Female adornment is grounded in a dense hybrid matrix of borrowing and repetition, creating a truly diasporic culture of excess that is at once deeply embedded within a Jamaican folkloric tradition as well as a manifestation of cultural borrowing and exchange from outside. Dancehall fashion is therefore a historical palimpsest, providing glimpses into layers of other historical styles, traditions and symbolic systems.

Having prowled through the international circuit of goods and images and woven them back into the local fabric, dancehall women return them to the world of consumption for further restitching. Dancehall fashion has quickly gathered its own international crop of sartorial disciples who raid and absorb the aesthetic reservoir of global streetwear and turn them into high fashion, by changing the context and the price and investing them with a symbolic capital that was missing in the early incarnation. Stripped of its rawness and tamed to suit European high-fashion tastes, dancehall fashion becomes an object of desire that those who are scornful of dancehall (but secretly admire it) can now wear. This is later recirculated among dancehall style aficionados to signify renewed prestige and taste in a complex feedback loop of call and response. For example, as the 1990s drew to a close, dancehall fashion connoisseurs turned to the very couture designers they inspired. Moschino and Versace are favourites among dancehall fashionistas (with their labels hanging out to show that they are wearing the "genuine" article). The issue of "original" and "copy" in reality however have little importance: designs, fabrics and modes of accessorizing are inscribed within a system of incessant borrowing and dialogue to the extent that it becomes futile to fixate on origin. Which came first, Pam Hogg's autumn/winter 1992/93 slashed latex body suit or the slashed t-shirts doing the rounds in Jamaica around the same time? Are Versace's gold-encrusted jeans an original which the dancehall fashion aficionados imitated? The answer to these questions is impossible to resolve. The line of influence of any cultural artefact is often not obvious or explicit; in dancehall the line is a spaghetti sprawl of loops and curves. Origins and originals are the stuff of bourgeois distinction-making and intellectual property rights – elements with no meaning in a world where the distinction between fake and real has little purchase. Rather, the incessant appropriation, reappropriation and expropriation of global/local exchanges reveal the intrinsic mutuality of cultural artefacts and patterns of expression. Through dancehall's sartorial borrowing and transfer, fashion is perpetually caught up within a dynamic of differential repetition that has multiple origins.

In this chapter, I have argued that dancehall fashion and corporeal stylization show how women inured by life in the urban ghettos of Kingston interpret their life world, inflect it with meaning and recycle the different cultural artefacts circulating within a global economy of sartorial signs. Beneath interpretation and a semiotic analysis, however, I have indicated that dancehall styling is ultimately a question of survival, an excessively imaginative response to the class, race and gender-based normative violence of the hegemonic morality of the uptown elite. I hope to have encouraged an appreciation of the ways in which, prior to speech and lyricization, women in dancehall culture exhibit an expressive styling that ultimately should be characterized as a defiant performance of generative identity in the midst of perpetual existential crisis.

NOTES

1. This is not to deny that women do also contribute to the production of music, as is evident with the prominence of female dancehall DJs (such as Lady Saw). However, through sartorial practices a larger group of women can participate and contribute to dancehall culture. Fashion and adornment thus becomes a democratic space which allows different categories of women to participate in the production of symbols and cultural meaning.
2. Not all female participants in the culture dress so flamboyantly, however. Dancehall women therefore refer to those women who spend a considerable amount of their time and resources attending the dancehall events, drawing attention to themselves at any event through their fashion style which stands them out from the rest of the crowd. It is these women known as dancehall "divas" or "donnets" who have aroused interest, fascination and vilification all at once who are the central subject of this chapter.
3. During the fieldwork for this research it became clear that some of the subversive and transformative potential I attributed to dancehall women were not always explicitly shared by dancehall women. Many pointed out that they had not intentionally set out to challenge hegemonic structures. Rather, they were simply dressing for themselves and the dancehall space provided them with the opportunity to express themselves. The gap between how participants understand and explain their action and my own interpretation of their action in no way detracts from the argument. It is important to remember that Jamaican women have a long history of resisting oppressive regimes and articulating their existential positioning using a variety of media. I locate dancehall women's sartorial expression as a continuation of this history of resistance and cultural production.
4. It will be true to say that dancehall music and culture has now become mainstream, but its energy, creativity and reproduction continue to be drawn from the socio-political and economic realities of the marginalized urban poor. Despite being a major Jamaican cultural export, dancehall still occupies an ambivalent place within Jamaican elite cultural imaginary.
5. In "Let Those Monkeys Out", Dancehall DJ Lexxus sings about the use of bleaching cream by dark-skinned women to acquire the browning effect and their increasing use of fattening pills used in industrial chicken-farming to acquire an ample body is so valorized in the culture. A verse from the lyrics goes,

   Me hear some o' them nuh stop take the fowl pill
   MmMm, so me know she them gyal there skill

A take the fowl pill just to impress Phil
When you see them you fi shout, "Dill dill"

REFERENCES

Austin-Broos, Diana J. 1994. "Race/Class: Jamaica's Discourse of Heritable Identity". *New West Indian Guide* 68, no. 3/4: 213–33.

Banks, Ingrid. 2000. *Hair Matters: Beauty, Power, and Black Consciousness*. New York: New York University Press.

Barnes, Natasha B. 1999. "Face of the Nation: Race, Nationalisms, and Identities in Jamaican Beauty Pageants". In *Daughters of Caliban: Caribbean Women in the Twentieth Century*, edited by Consuelo Lopez Springfield, 285–306. Bloomington: Indiana University Press.

Barrow, Steve, and Peter Dalton. 1997. *Reggae: The Rough Guide*. London: Rough Guides.

Benammar, Karim. N.d. "The Mask and Self in Contemporary Japanese Philosophy". Unpublished paper. http://www.plethora.nl/benammar-maskandself.htm.

Bilby, Kenneth. 1997. "From "Jamaica". In *Reggae, Rasta, Revolution: Jamaican Music from Ska to Dub*, edited by Chris Potash, 29–38. London: Schirmer.

Bourdieu, Pierre. 1977. *Outline of a Theory of Practice*. Translated by R. Nice. Cambridge: Cambridge University Press.

Breward, C. 1994. *The Culture of Fashion*. Manchester: Manchester University Press.

Chude-Sokei, Louis. 1997. "Post-Nationalist Geographies: Rasta, Ragga, and Reinventing Africa". In *Reggae, Rasta, Revolution: Jamaican Music from Ska to Dub*, edited by Chris Potash, 215–27. London: Schirmer.

Connerton, Paul. 1989. *How Societies Remember*. Cambridge: Cambridge University Press.

Cooper, Carolyn. 1993a. *Noises in the Blood: Gender and the "Vulgar" Body of Jamaican Popular Culture*. London: Macmillan.

———. 1993b. "Emergency (Un)Dress". *Lifestyle* 27, July/August.

———. 2000. "Virginity Revamped: Representations of Female Sexuality in the Lyrics of Bob Marley and Shabba Ranks". *Black British Culture and Society: A Reader*, edited by Kwesi Owusu, 347–57. London: Routledge.

D'Elia, Susan. 2002. "Women's Fashion in Jamaican Dancehalls". http://debate.uvm.edu/dread library/delia02.html

Douglas, Lisa. 1992. *The Power of Sentiment: Love, Hierarchy and the Jamaican Family Elite*. Boulder: Westview.

Evans, Caroline, and Minna Thornton. 1991. "Fashion, Representation, Femininity". *Feminist Review* 38 (Summer): 49–61.

Fanon, André. 1988. "Is Dance Hall Music a Creative Force?" *Gleaner*, 29 November.

Friedman, Jonathan. 1994. *Cultural Identity and Global Process*. London: Sage.

Hall, Stuart. 1992. "What Is This 'Black' in Black Popular Culture?" In *Black Popular Culture*, edited by G. Dent, 21–23. Seattle: Bay Press.

Heath, Steven. 1986. "Joan Riviere and the Masquerade". In *Formations of Fantasy*, edited by V. Burgin, J. Donald and C. Kaplan, 45–61. London: Methuen.

Hebidge, Dick. 1979. *Subculture: The Meaning of Style*. London: Methuen.

Hurston, Zora Neal. 1933 [1999]. "Characteristics of Negro Expression". In *Signifyin(g), Sanctifyin', and Slam Dunking: A Reader in African American Expressive Culture*, edited by Gena Dagel Caponi, 303–6. Amherst: University of Massachusetts Press.

Irigaray, Luce. 1985. *Speculum of the Other Woman*. Translated by G.C. Gill. Ithaca: Cornell University Press.

Jahn, Brian and Tom Weber. 1992. *Reggae Island: Music in the Digital Age*. Kingston: Kingston Publishers.

McCaulay, Diane. 1994. "Dancehall and Choice". *Gleaner*, 12 April.

McDonald, Paulette. 1993. "The Dancehall Revisited". *Lifestyle* 27, July/August.

Mercer, Kobena. 1987. "Black Hair/Style Politics". *New Formation* 3, Winter.

Mintz, Sidney W., and Richard Price. 1976. *The Birth of African-American Cultures: Anthropological Perspective*. Boston: Beacon.

Mulvey, Laura. 1989. "Visual Pleasure and Narrative Cinema". In *Visual and Other Pleasures*, edited by Laura Mulvey, 14–26. London: Macmillan.

Mustafa, Hudita Nura 1998. "Sartorial Ecumenism: African Styles in a Social and Economic Context". In *The Art of African Fashion*, 13–48. Netherlands and Eritrea/USA: Prince Claus Fund and African World Press.

Nettleford, Rex. 1994. "Dance-Hall, Part of the Jamaican Heritage?" *Gleaner*, 22 July.

———. 1995. "From Jonkonnu to Dancehall". *Gleaner*, [date unknown].

Polhemus, Ted. 1988. *Bodystyles*. Luton: Lennard.

Riviere, J. 1986. "Womanliness as Masquerade". In *Formations of Fantasy*, edited by V. Burgin, J. Donald and C. Kaplan, 35–44. London: Methuen.

Russo, Mary. 1986. "Female Grotesques: Carnival and Theory". In *Feminist Studies/Critical Theory*, edited by Teresa de Leureatis, 213–29. Bloomington: Indiana University Press.

Simone, Timothy Abdoumaliq. 1989. *About Face: Race in Postmodern America*. New York: Automedia.

Stolzoff, Norman C. 2000. *Wake the Town and Tell the People: Dancehall Culture in Jamaica*. Durham, NC: Duke University Press.

Tseëlon, E. 1997. *The Masque of Femininity*. London: Sage.

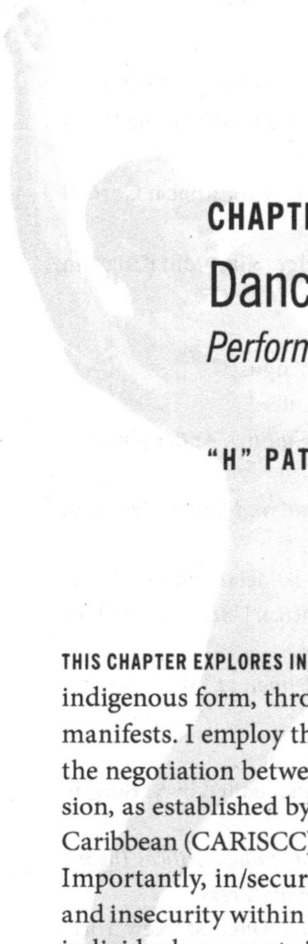

CHAPTER 25

Dancehall Bodies

Performing In/Securities

"H" PATTEN

THIS CHAPTER EXPLORES IN/SECURITY WITHIN THE REGGAE/DANCEHALL GENRE, Jamaica's most popular indigenous form, through the lens of the dancing body and the cultural expression it manifests. I employ the notion of "in/security" drawing from its conceptualization as the negotiation between security and insecurity in the creative navigation of oppression, as established by the Caribbean In/Securities: Creativity and Negotiation in the Caribbean (CARISCC) international research network, funded by the Leverhulme Trust. Importantly, in/security facilitates a redefinition of the lived experiences of security and insecurity within everyday life where the two often clash. Hence, what secures one individual can create insecurity for another.

REGGAE/DANCEHALL AS A TERM

Presenting extracts from a larger work (Patten 2016), this chapter explores reggae/dancehall as a complex phenomenon wherein the transformative nature of dance both reflects and manifests "sonic dominance" (Henriques 2011), that is, the all-engulfing body-penetrating musical "riddim" (rhythm). I use the term "dancehall" in relation to the discrete music and dance genre emerging from the late 1970s onward, as adopted by many Jamaican dancehall participants. The term "reggae/dancehall" signals dancehall as a phenomenon and historical space that incorporates its long genealogical history, its points of connection with Jamaican resistance against oppression and its ties to spiritual African/neo-African music and dance expressions such as Jonkonnu Masquerade, Revivalism and Kumina. The genealogical continuities of these practices remain evident in mento, ska, rocksteady and reggae, dancehall's chronological forerunners.

I argue therefore that through the performance of dance within the dancehall space, marginalized lower-class African/Jamaicans manifest African/neo-African genealogical continuities. Thus, dancehall dance culture forms part of an in/secure contemporary expression representing a unifying and historically contingent survival tactic, both in

Jamaica and among the large numbers of Jamaican settlers in Britain that now form part of dancehall's diaspora. This chapter focuses on in/security in relation to two main themes: (1) dance and what I coin the "corporeal dancing body" in the dancehall space and (2) the functioning of dance for dancehall participants.

THE CORPOREAL DANCING BODY

The corporeal dancing body is central to dance, as it is through corporeality or the body's boundary that communication and knowledge transfer takes place through language, senses, symbolic gestures and kinaesthetic action, enabling the possibility of meaning making. I coin this term "corporeal dancing body" to emphasize intentionally the fleshly physicality of black African dancing bodies to move beyond the exotic gaze. Black bodies embody historical references of "otherness", connected to notions of slavery, oppression and inferiority mapped on them in relation to the white race, thus rendering the body an animated corpse. The black "corporeal dancing body" signals a reflective, spiritual and physical reanimation in the performance of an African/neo-African embodied genealogy. However, up until now, the alternative histories hidden within the vocabulary of reggae/dancehall's "corporeal dancing body", the main focus of my research, have been substantially overlooked within dancehall scholarship.

According to Thomas Fuchs (2003), corporeal movement incorporates the "lived body", the phenomenological pre-reflective integration of the senses and the actions of the physical limbs, with the "corporeal body", which signals a reflective engagement that manifests as emotion. I extend this notion in combining the two, as the "corporeal dancing body" not only reunites the physical body, reason and emotion but also integrates the spiritual coding embodied and mapped within African dancing bodies. L'Antoinette Stines (2005) refers to this spiritual coding as "ancestral data", that is, knowledge passed down both generationally and via departed ancestors. Spiritual coding also resonates with what Carolyn Cooper (1993) terms *Noises in the Blood*. Furthermore, the "corporeal dancing body" includes what Diedre Sklar calls "cultural knowledge" (1991), historically situated constructs that enable cultural continuities both sacred and secular. Thus, "corporeal dancing bodies" facilitate the "cultural memory" of a people handed down over generations as symbolic gestures that emotionally tie a community to its environment (Buckland 2001; Taylor 2003; Meusburger, Heffernan and Wunder 2011). In this instance, the concept of "corporeal dancing bodies" is argued as manifesting "cultural memory" within contemporary in/secure dancehall spaces.

THE FUNCTIONING OF DANCE FOR DANCEHALL PARTICIPANTS: IN/SECURITY IN DANCEHALL

Critical attention regarding reggae/dancehall has primarily focused on slackness (vulgarity) and violence tropes, thus contributing to the perception of dancehall as being an in/secure space. Although slackness and violence is undeniable and therefore a major focus, dancehall scholarship has also explored its lyrical content, rhythmic structure and issues of gender, sexuality and fashion, among other discourses. However, with the exception of Sonjah Stanley Niaah's geographical study "with emphasis placed on the dancers practice and space" (2010, 121), where she foregrounds the body's expansion of the dancehall space, the "corporeal dancing body" and the alternative histories it embodies have been largely neglected.

FEMALE PERSPECTIVES: WINING

The corporeal dancing body within the dancehall space is in/secure from multiple perspectives, as it has always been an essential part of Jamaican popular culture and acknowledged by many as an important catalyst in the progression from mento to ska, rocksteady into reggae and on to dancehall. However, the corporeal body became a central part of dancehall discourse with the emergence of the dancehall queen during the early 1990s. Yet, the queen narrative has a long established genealogy; the Kumina queen, which arguably influenced dancehall through "the matriarchal structure of Kumina" (Torres 2010, 19), stands on the shoulders of Queen Nanny of the Maroons during enslavement, the Red and Blue Queens of the emancipatory bruckins dance, and the "mother" post or functionary within Revivalism and other African/neo-African spiritual practices, including Pentecostalism and the Baptist Christian religions.

Dancehall queens heralded the female *modellers* and *dancers* who extend the dance floor in their execution of spontaneous and choreographed movements, as scholars have noted (Stolzoff 2000; Wright 2004; Hope 2006; Stanley Niaah 2010). Female corporeal dancing bodies employ, as Donna P. Hope describes, "erotic posing and gymnastic and erotic dancing to claim the status of Queens in the dancehall" (2010, 136). These erotic corporeal displays reflect the in/security of the female form as, their "strident confidence . . . oppose[s] and disrupt[s] the chaste respectability of the uptown [ruling class] woman" (Bakare-Yusuf 2006, 15). Female corporeality defies society's moral coding by subverting hegemonic notions of decency and respectability on one hand, while challenging patriarchal structures on the other (Cooper 2004; Stanley Niaah 2010). An example is "whining" or "wining", a signature female dancehall movement that involves circling or rotating the pelvis while rocking it back and forth to produce a tumbling, or as Stines (2009) terms it, a "bubbling" quality. Wining is performed with varying degrees of dynamic athleticism in almost every dancehall event. However, dancehall wining is regarded as slackness by many outside of the genre; therefore, slackness is simultaneously part of the rejection and attraction of dancehall.

For its participants, dancehall is increasingly regarded as a liberating, subversive and transformative ritual expression, which scholars such as Carolyn Cooper (2004) and Beth-Sarah Wright (2004) also argue represents modern female fertility and healing rituals, respectively. Within the "Uptown Mondays" dancehall session held in Savannah Plaza (Kingston), female dancers regularly risk life and limb, challenging each other by inverting themselves precariously on the railings of the plaza's upper open-staircase landing while performing dancehall's contemporary female Head-Top dance – balancing upside down in a handstand while wining, tumbling or bubbling the pelvis, often simultaneously kicking their legs. Stacey Xpressionz exemplifies dancehall in/security, balancing on balcony railings by her shoulders without holding on – she secures her profile by demonstrating her daring and skill. Unfortunately, in/security manifests beyond dancehall dance spaces in the perception of the majority of outsiders to the genre, particularly the Jamaican ruling class, Britain's dominant white society and the aspiring diaspora black middle-classes, who mostly regard dancehall culture as exotic, risqué, vulgar and dangerous.

Similar to Jamaica, within the British context, black African bodies are produced and operate in relation to place and are defined by a dominant culture that negates their agency. As a space in which notions of identity are developed and negotiated, reggae/dancehall is a countercultural space where black African bodies regain physical and emotional agency by manifesting the in/secure, temporal cultural and artistic expression of their "corporeal dancing body". However, female in/security continues in dancehall's maintenance of the patriarchal male gaze, which serves to divert attention from the male body. One exception is during coupling dances such as "grinding", as popularly termed in the United Kingdom, where males and females wining together connect pelvises to create a grinding action. A contemporary version of Cheryl Ryman's (2010, 118) description of the mento dance, "the 'dry grind', 'rent a tile' and 'dub' or 'rub a dub'" forms part of both reggae and the reggae-influenced British lover's rock genre and is simply termed "rub", "dub" or "scrub". Performance of "grinding" often incorporates a dipping action to complement the slow, intimate, full contact of the male and female pelvis rubbing against each other in half or full circles, or scribing a figure-of-eight. Although often characterized as a "soft" style of reggae (Palmer 2011), lover's rock and the "rub" as a coupling dance provide an in/secure, resistant countercultural space. As Lisa A. Palmer (2011, 190) fittingly articulates, "the erotic . . . intimate 'slow wine' dance to lovers' rock music, can be interpreted as an open expression and validation of black male and female sexualities and humanity". However, dancehall's danced continuity of African resistance is explicitly clear on both sides of the Atlantic, within the hip thrusting action of the daggering dance.

The genealogical link to dancehall's African/neo-African antecedents is apparent in the corporeal body's circling of the pelvis during dance, which in both the African and Caribbean contexts represents a symbolic challenge to death in its affirmation of life (Ryman 2010). The pelvis replaces the life that death takes away, so through dance the pelvis constantly signals itself as the life-giving force. Hence, the unification of male and female corporeal dancing bodies is a continuity that runs through mento, rocksteady, reggae and dancehall, but in ska, although pelvises might not lock (touch), the symbolism remains within the pelvic action. Thus, to dismiss wining or daggering is to effectively reduce reggae/dancehall to a mere simulation of sex acts, which fails to recognize the metaphoric rejection of Eurocentric value systems that dancehall symbolizes.

MALE PERSPECTIVES: WARRIORS

African and diaspora masculinity has been in/securely shaped by hegemonic values founded on a Eurocentric patriarchy determined by the white male gaze. A legacy of enslavement and colonialism, as African American theologian Michael Eric Dyson (2004, 224) suitably asserts, is that "black sexuality was cloaked in white fantasy and fear. Black women were thought to be hot and ready to be bothered. Black men were believed to have big sexual desires and even bigger organs to realize their lust."

White fantasy and fear have historically been projected onto African corporeal dancing bodies. This is complicated by the Western perception of dance as being a feminized activity, which from a male perspective carries the stigma of "'effemina[cy]' . . . a code word for homosexual[ity]" (Burt 1995, 12), particularly within the theatrical setting. Therefore, coupled with dancehall's barrage of anti-homosexual lyrics, the erotic or sexual styling of the male body was deliberately avoided within the dancehall genre for some time. A direct effect of Jamaica's high art, low culture class divide, Rex Nettleford (2003), former director of the Jamaican National Dance Theatre Company, outlines insightfully the in/security of the male corporeal dancing body as often being stigmatized, apart from that which takes place within the context of traditional practices such as Kumina and Revivalism. However, the "legsman" era of the 1960s and the rise to prominence of Gerald "Bogle" Levy, creator of the Bogle dance made popular in song by Buju Banton in the 1990s,[1] together with the rise of Bogle's associates, the Black Roses Crew, all served to change perceptions of masculinity in relation to dance. Male dancing within dancehall, although still considered a transgressive activity, now operates relatively free of any perceived stigma, despite constantly pushing the boundaries of both masculinity and hegemonic morality, as recorded over time (Pinnock 2007; Stanley Niaah 2010; Hope 2010).

Importantly, dancehall masculinity is further secured by the manifestation of African/neo-African dance vocabulary within its form. Dances like Pressure Dem by Sheldon "Shelly Belly" Lewis manifest links, both in its aesthetics and its "vibe" (feeling or energy), to the warrior type energy of the Ghanaian Adzogbo dance,[2] particularly the male Atsia section. Atsia involves the backward (contraction) movement of the chest to the beat and its return to the centre (neutral) position on the off-beat. The legs (positioned just over shoulder width apart) maintain relaxed knees, as the ball of each foot swivels alternately, enabling the corresponding heel to touch in (on the beat) and out (on the off-beat). Remarkably, the difference or variation between Pressure Dem and Atsia is solely in the use of the arms and the slightly more upright positioning of the torso.

In/security in relation to male dancers is ever present in the pressure for them to create dance movements that must achieve popularity and success by being adopted and performed by crowds of people within the dancehall space. Orville Hall (personal interview, 2010), artistic director of Dance Xpressionz and resident judge on Jamaican television's *Dancin' Dynamites* dance competition, agrees that the performance of a dance in the absence of its creator(s) secures its status as a legitimate hit. However, the popularity of a dance is always temporary, lasting only as long as the time it takes for the next big dance movement to "buss" (become a hit), thus shifting the focus and "hype" (excitement) from one originator to the next. This is exemplified by the abundance of dances and dancers such as Della Move (Admiral Bailey); Bogle and World Dance (Bogle); Chaka-Chaka and Sweep (Ding Dong and Ravers Clavers); Gully Creeper (David "ICE" Alexander Smith); Signal di Plane and Pon di River (Jonathan "John Hype" Prendergast); Nuh Linga (Marlon "Ovamars" Hardy); Cow Foot and Pressure Dem (Shelly Belly); alongside Big and Nasty and Tender Touch (Dance Xpressionz) that have held dancehall's in/secure centre spot.

The "video light" as coined by Hope (2006) highlights the in/security of the dancer's career path, offering international profile as it captures the dancer's movement, style, elegance and creativity, frequently streaming it across the internet to global audiences. This provides many dancers with an opportunity to enjoy a degree of temporary success. The in/security of this temporary success is all too apparent, as at any moment another artist may rip away the video light mid-performance by performing either better or more daring movements than the previous dancer. Female wining, particularly performed in the bare-as-you-dare dress code, often supersedes the strongest and most intricate of male dance bravado in commanding the video light. Moreover, the video footage, streamed mostly on social media sites, maintains the in/security of dancehall dance artists. While some may gain profile and a degree of exposure, only a fortunate few get work and really earn money from their video appearances. The vast majority receive little or no financial reward from their appearances in dancehall videos. Many are unwittingly exploited daily, as their dance movements, recorded within videos broadcasted across the internet, are used in distant "imagined communities" (Anderson 1983) by numerous individuals who learn, copy, teach and even make in/secure livings from them.

CONCLUSION

As I have argued, in/security is an integral part of the reggae/dancehall genre, but additionally, dance is attractive to its participants, not least due to its entertainment value. A large percentage of dancehall participants are obliged to negotiate the in/security of personhood, gender and identity alongside a whole range of other in/securities, including movement between garrison and home territories in attending the variety of dancehall events on offer each night of the week. A number of high-level negotiations are necessitated between politicians, area dons, individuals, communities, the police, promoters, sound systems and artists, in addition to the various gang and posse members, who all play an important function in the successful and secure running of any dancehall session (Charles 2002; Stanley Niaah 2010). In/security is a key component of dancehall culture and is often a serious consideration for many individuals when choosing whether or not to engage with the dancehall space.

NOTES

1. Gerald "Bogle" Levy has since been credited with creating a succession of popular dancehall dances, including: Urkel, World-a-Dance and Row Like a Boat (Stolzoff 2000, 271n9; Hope 2006, 30; Stanley Niaah 2010, 124).
2. Adzogbo is a ceremonial Ewe dance originating from Dahomey (Benin), which consists of the Kadodo dance (performed by the whole community) and the Atsia dance (performed by the young men) and is connected to the Voodoo religious practice.

REFERENCES

Anderson, B. 1983. *Imagined Communities: Reflections on the Origin and Spread of Nationalism.* New York: Verso.

Bakare-Yusuf, B. 2006. "Fabricating Identities: Survival and the Imagination in Jamaican Dancehall Culture". *Fashion Theory* 10, no. 3: 1–24.

Buckland, T.J. 2001. "Dance, Authenticity and Cultural Memory: The Politics of Embodiment". *Yearbook for Traditional Music* 33:1–16.

Burt, R. 1995. *The Male Dancer: Bodies, Spectacle, Sexualities.* London: Routledge.

Charles, C.A.D. 2002. "Garrison Communities as Counter Societies and the 1998 Zeeks Riot in Jamaica". *IDEAZ* 1:29–43.

Cooper, C. 1993. *Noises in the Blood: Gender and the "Vulgar" Body of Jamaican Popular Culture.* London: Macmillan.

———. 2004. *Sound Clash: Jamaican Dancehall Culture at Large.* New York: Palgrave Macmillan.

Dyson, M. 2004. *The Michael Eric Dyson Reader.* New York: Basic Civitas Books.

Fuchs T. 2003. "The Phenomenology of Shame, Guilt and the Body in Body Dysmorphic Disorder and Depression". *Journal of Phenomenological Psychology* 33, no. 2: 223–43.

Henriques, J.F. 2011. *Sonic Bodies: Reggae Sound Systems, Performance Techniques and Ways of Knowing.* New York: Continuum.

Hope, D.P. 2006. *Inna di Dancehall: Popular Culture and the Politics of Identity in Jamaica.* Kingston: University of the West Indies Press.

———. 2010. *Man Vibes: Masculinities in the Jamaican Dancehall.* Kingston: Ian Randle.

Meusburger, P., M. Heffernan and E. Wunder. 2011. "Cultural Memories: The Geographical Point of View". *Knowledge and Space* 4, no. 1: 3–14.

Nettleford, R. 2003. *Caribbean Cultural Identity: The Case of Jamaica – An Essay in Cultural Dynamics.* Kingston: Ian Randle.

Palmer, L.A. 2011. "'Ladies a Your Time Now!' Erotic Politics, Lovers' Rock and Resistance in the UK, African and Black Diaspora". *International Journal* 4, no. 2: 177–92.

Patten, H. 2016. "Feel de Riddim, Feel de Vibes: Dance as a Transcendent Act of Survival and Upliftment". In *British Dance: Black Routes*, edited by C. Adair and R. Burt, 99–124. New York: Routledge.

Pinnock, A.M.N. 2007. "'A Ghetto Education Is Basic': (Jamaican) Dancehall Masculinities as Counter-Culture". *Journal of Pan African Studies* 1, no. 9: 47–84.

Ryman, C. 2010. "When Jamaican Dances: Context and Content". In *Making Caribbean Dance: Continuity and Creativity in Island Cultures*, edited by S. Sloat, 97–131. Gainesville: University Press of Florida.

Sklar, D. 1991. "On Dance Ethnography". *Dance Research Journal* 23, no. 1: 6–10.

Stanley Niaah, S. 2010. *Dancehall: From Slave Ship to Ghetto.* Ottawa: University of Ottawa Press.

Stines, L. 2005. "Does the Caribbean Body Daaance Or Daunce? An Exploration of Modern Contemporary Dance from a Caribbean Perspective". *Caribbean Quarterly* 51, nos. 3–4: 35–54.

——— 2009. "Spirit Dancing (Daaancing) in Patois: L'Antech as Contemporary Nation Dance Language". PhD thesis. University of the West Indies.

Stolzoff, N.C. 2000. *Wake the Town and Tell the People: Dancehall Culture in Jamaica*. Durham, NC: Duke University Press.

Taylor, D. 2003. *The Archive and the Repertoire: Performing Cultural Memory in the Americas*. Durham, NC: Duke University Press.

Torres, L. Delgado de. 2010. "Queens, Kings and Swagga: Gender and the Will to Adorn in Jamaican Dancehall". PhD dissertation, SUNY Binghamton.

Wright, B.S. 2004. "Speaking the Unspeakable: Politics of the Vagina in Dancehall Docu-Videos". *Discourses in Dance* 2, no. 2: 45–60.

CHAPTER 26

"Born in Chanel, Christen in Gucci"

*The Rhetoric of Brand Names and Haute Couture in Jamaican Dancehall**

ANDREA SHAW NEVINS

> Tight pussy gal no fight over man
> An everybody know say we a name brand
> When me a wind me gi him de wickedest slam
> But me sorry fi di gal dem out deh weh no have no glam.
> —Spice, "Fight over Man"[1]

THIS CHAPTER EXPLORES THE ROLE OF HIGH-END DESIGNER fashion in the reggae dancehall arena and contemplates how fashion in general, but specifically designer wear, is invoked and fetishized within that realm.[2] Given the North American and European origins of high fashion, I am particularly interested in how performers employ their designer-wear discourse and how this discourse relates to the political and social tensions between the Caribbean and the developed world. In "Signal di Plane" (2003), Elephant Man sings:

> Da dance yah make everybody a kick up a storm
> Show Jack Sowah the brand weh you have on
> If a Louis Votorni, Armani, Sean John
> Enjoy yourself, nuh make nobody keep you calm.

In this quite celebratory tune, why does Ellie mention designer Louis Vuitton, whose name Ellie has himself transformed into Louis Votorni? What is it that accounts for the recent proliferation of references to designer name brands in dancehall – the addition of Gucci, Moschino and Dior, among others, to dancehall's lexicon? Perhaps your initial response to this question is the same as mine: an acknowledgment that Jamaicans may simply have too much of a "foreign mind", in this case a love for imported products, especially from North America and Europe. While this observation may be true and

---

*Previously published in *Archipelagos of Sound: Transnational Caribbeanities, Women and Music*, edited by Ifeona Fulani (Kingston: University of the West Indies Press, 2012), 171–90.

perhaps explains the underpinning of dancehall culture's appetite for designer brands, I'm not convinced the answer is quite so simple. Jamaican dancehall fashion has become a distinctive visual signifier of the music after which it is named. This fashion aesthetic took shape in Jamaica during the 1980s, the decade which gave rise to the current epoch of dancehall music, a genre that continues to dominate the Jamaican musical landscape and influence musical styles worldwide. Women's dancehall fashion – often associated with explosive colour, sequins andubiquitous spandex – has been particularly conspicuous in the public visual arena, the clothing's salacious reputation the subject of numerous newspaper editorials and radio talk show discussions.[3]

In a 2008 *Gleaner* article titled "Slackness and More Slackness", the principal of a local high school engaged in a lengthy harangue about the corrosive qualities of dancehall music: "Dancehall dress leaves little of the women's bodies to the imagination. It is this mindset that is now affecting so many of our young people in school. They are following the dancehall culture of 'badmanism', 'hottie girls', 'nuff girls', 'nuff skin' and body parts exposed, 'nuff slackness', public wining and grinding, 'bling and more bling' and every thing else that the culture promotes" (Tyson 2008). As self-appointed arbiters of Jamaican propriety, the middle and upper classes have increasingly voiced "nuff" disdain for dancehall music, which defies and contests traditional notions of decency. Middle- and upper-class ideals also hold similar contempt for dancehall music's rough-and-tumble comrades, including the controversial "daggering",[4] street dances and their attendant "chaka chaka" noise, and, of course, dancehall's extravagant fashion.

Power struggles relating to dancehall fashion have also emerged *within* the dancehall. They play out in the 1997 film *Dancehall Queen* through the challenges facing Marcia, the film's leading character, as she tries to establish herself as a key contender in the dancehall arena (Elgood and Letts 2004). Marcia is a street vendor and single parent struggling to earn a living. After seeing the reigning dancehall queen during the daytime when she is dislocated from the glamorous dancehall space, Marcia realizes that the queen looks quite ordinary without the aid of her elaborate clothing. This revelation regarding fashion's capacity to alter the wearer prompts Marcia to vie for the title of Dancehall Queen, so she can supplement her paltry street-vending income. However, she must compete against numerous other women, and the film reveals fashion's crucial role in capturing attention within the dancehall and improving the opportunity of ascension to queen. Marcia designs her own outfits and begins to bedazzle the dancehall audience, which cannot tell that this queenly woman is Marcia the vendor. In fact, her own daughter can hardly recognize her mother once Marcia is festooned in her fashion creations. Marcia's dancehall outfits, like Cinderella's gown, transform her appearance, indeed her persona, and eventually transform her economic circumstances when she wins the Dancehall Queen title.

Sonjah Stanley Niaah (2010, 134) defines the transformation enabled by dancehall fashion as a form of "masking", associated with historical African cultural practices. In the context of the dancehall, masking is a ritualistic practice which disputes identities associated with the abject poverty faced by Jamaica's black underclass (132). Furthermore, Stanley Niaah argues that dancehall fashion "contests and rewrites historically biased religious, sexual, and class scripts" (134). Dressing in designer wear (the current fashion ideal in dancehall), or approximations of these types of clothing, allows patrons and performers to represent themselves in ways that challenge their social status as underprivileged. According to Stanley Niaah, "masks are aggrandizing tools for the self", and "within such practices as dress (new outfit and hairstyle), the wearing of a different mask at each dancehall event ensures readiness for the video light" (132–33).

Carolyn Cooper (2004, 127) suggests that Marcia is fully aware of "the power of costume to enable the transformation" from vendor to dancehall diva. This transformation process takes on as fantastical an identity as the elaborate costumes themselves. This is because of the "magical" potential costuming provides for the economic transformation that becomes accessible to women who can attract attention in the dancehall as either performers or patrons. Donna Hope (2006, 127) explains: "Dancehall's emphasis on costuming and public performance is organically linked to the development of what I call the 'video-light syndrome' in the dancehall dis/place. This powerful need to be seen, documented, photographed and, in particular, videotaped, has been an important part of dancehall culture since the introduction of video cameras as a regular part of activities in the dancehall." Hope further explains that a number of contests anchored in a dancehall aesthetic, similar to the contest portrayed in *Dancehall Queen*, have been developed (although some may no longer exist), such as Miss Buff Bay, Miss Healthy Body and Miss Go-Go Wine (71–73). The prizes and publicity associated with these contests play a pivotal role in propelling participants to dancehall fame. An actual Dancehall Queen contest, which attracts both local and international contestants, has thrived for well over a decade, and the 2010 winner, Kristal Anderson, took home J$400,000 (approximately US$4,600), a trophy and a variety of gift packages (Frater 2010).

Additionally, women who are not vying for specific dancehall-associated titles like Anderson's and are content with their role as dancehall patrons nevertheless actively compete for attention in the dancehall, and fashion plays a key role in their viability. Hope (2006, 63) describes these women as "hidden queens of the dancehall" and explains that they are economically independent women who "wear elaborate hairstyles and engage in conspicuous consumption of expensive liquor at dancehall events". One such woman Hope references is Sandra Lee, whose family background is in informal commercial trading. According to Hope, Lee frequents dancehall events, where her arrival is usually announced and her image recorded by videographers. Surprisingly, funerals have become another venue where women compete for attention in their dancehall garb.

Over the past two decades, the flamboyance and performativity of the dancehall expressive complex[5] have had a distinct impact on funeral rituals practised by some inner-city Jamaicans. These funerals have become increasingly conspicuous and exhibitionist, generating as much contempt and condemnation as the music and fashion that have influenced them. Annie Paul (2006) explains that "the coffin or casket in particular acquires the expressiveness of a status symbol signifying the importance both of the deceased and the bereaved family or community". She further notes that families spend relatively large sums to acquire these elaborately adorned caskets. The dress and behaviour of funeral participants have also been implicated as elaborate, extravagant and unruly.

In the aftermath of the funeral of dancehall dance legend Bogle, journalist Ian Boyne (2005) commented that the Seventh-Day Adventist Church was reviewing its funeral policies and suggested that this was because of the behaviour of attendees at Bogle's funeral: "The wearing of outrageous dancehall fashion – a tautology – the smoking of ganja, drinking of liquor on church premises and general unruly behaviour at what is traditionally a solemn occasion where the dead is honoured, has been proving too much for the conservative Christian denomination." Doyenne of the Jamaican fashion world Norma Soas proffered a similarly derisive critique of the inner-city don[6] Jim Brown's funeral in 1992, suggesting that the dancehall styles worn by the mourners were vulgar and indecent: "No mini was too short, no tights too tight, no chiffon too sheer, no lace too see through" (quoted in Ulysse 2004, 223). However, dancehall fashion, in all its extravagance, is also a locus of celebration and commercial success for some, including Soas's designer counterparts whose clothing graces the dancehall stage and floor.

Numerous dancehall fashion designers have become pre-eminent on the local fashion scene, including names like Earl "Biggy" Turner, Stanley "Lexxus" Bailey, Paul "Tu-Lox" Gaynor, Garfield Hussey and White Skyy Designs. Furthermore, designers such as Lexx Perry have taken dancehall fashion onto the global stage, designing for celebrities and showcasing clothing at international venues. Dancehall fashion is now routinely included in local fashion events, and organizers of the prestigious 2008 Pulse Model Search fashion show used the dancehall expressive complex as inspiration for their show's set. The backdrop featured zinc fences, ostensibly invoking the inner cities, inscribed with dancehall vernacular like "to the wurl'" and "gully creepa" (Henry 2008).

Dancehall's impact on fashion is a notable one, and fashion itself is a powerful transformative force that betrays cultural desires to belong, escape and contain. The socio-political significance of dress within the new world is evidenced by the politics surrounding it that emerged during the European colonial venture. Perhaps the most foundational component of dress politics that affected Africans in the new world was the requirement that they wear European-styled clothing. In his insightful study *The Language of Dress: Resistance and Accommodation in Jamaica*, Steeve Buckridge (2004, 29) explains that a 1696 law in Jamaica not only specified the items of clothing an enslaved person should have but imposed a fine on slaveholders who did not provide their enslaved people with sufficient garments. This requirement underscored the European colonizers' persistent presumption of a feral and primitive African nature in need of containment. European-styled clothing on the bodies of the enslaved signalled white dominance and legitimated the oppressive enterprise of slavery because it in part resulted in the gentrification of black bodies that may otherwise have been irreverently exposed. In Jamaica and other parts of the New World, osnaburg was the favoured fabric for concealing the enslaved black body; it was cheap and durable but also extremely uncomfortable. In light of this, enslaved people in Jamaica sometimes sold their clothing allotments in order to trade up and purchase better quality garments (Buckridge 2004, 36).

In fact, white men used clothing as currency to reward enslaved women for "sexual favours" (Buckridge 2004, 43). This availability of fashion alternatives for enslaved people led to a range of New World anxieties, and, in some parts of the Caribbean, sumptuary laws were passed, prohibiting enslaved people from wearing fabrics such as silk (31). This restriction reflects the plantation hegemony's fears over the enslaved challenging their status in the plantation hierarchy at the nadir of that society's social ladder. In addition, it demonstrates the fluidity of race, since physiology alone was not sufficient to permanently fix race, and its attendant class presumptions, in place. Similar dress restrictions were enacted in the antebellum South, among these the South Carolina Negro Act of 1735. Leon Higginbotham (1980, 173) explains: "When a slave managed to obtain clothing that might accord him some dignity or prestige, the act declared that when such clothing was 'above' that which a slave should wear, it could be taken from the slave by 'all and every constable and other persons' to be used for his or their own benefit." This act limited slaves to clothing made from "negro cloth . . . osnabrigs . . . coarse garlix or calicoes . . . not exceeding ten shillings per yard" (174). These sumptuary laws were enacted based on hegemonic imperatives to deprive the enslaved people of access to the transformative power of fashion.

Clothing's ability to alter the wearer has long been recognized, and it is at the heart of several popular myths. Cinderella's conversion from a grimy chambermaid into a beautiful maiden is firmly anchored to the glamorous evening gown her fairy godmother conjures up. The Congolese folktale of Umusha Mwaice bears remarkable resemblance to the Cinderella story and tells of a enslaved girl who has exquisite clothing made from leaves. When one of her father's wives takes away her clothes, she climbs into the belly of a cow and emerges with even more exquisite fineries than those she had before (Lupton 1986, 410). Furthermore, when Dorothy becomes stranded in Oz (Baum 2000), in *The Wizard of Oz*, her ability to transform her surroundings and get back home to Kansas is facilitated by magical shoes. Indeed, the transformative effect of clothing is so potent that even the false belief that one is wearing clothes produces an alteration in persona, which occurs in the fairy tale "The Emperor's New Clothes". The emperor marches through town completely naked but with great aplomb because of the confidence he derives from the clothing he *thinks* he is wearing. References to clothing and designer fashion in reggae dancehall lyrics indicate a similar recognition of the transformative power of dress – its impact on the body of the wearer and on the nature of the gaze from the onlooker. Many reggae songs seem to offer up the black female body as the site of transformation and fetishize items of female clothing in response to a male onlooker. In their 1978 hit "Uptown Top Ranking" Althea and Donna (2001) sing the following:

> See mi 'pon the road and hear you call out to me
> True you see me in me pants and thing
> See me in a 'alter back,
> Say me gi' you heart attack.

The woman's halter back outfit threatens to give the male-constructed onlooker a "heart attack", reifying the potency of female dress.

Buju Banton's "Batty Rider" (1993) also celebrates the potency of dress, as he ecstatically acclaims the item of women's clothing after which the song is titled:

Gal you see you batty rider, murder!
You must be waan the DJ charge fa
. . . .
Shorts hitch up on you saddle, ride up on you back
Exposing you property, man a say it fat.

A "batty rider" is a very short pair of women's shorts that exposes the derrière of the wearer. Banton's lyrics imply that because the woman referenced in the song is so overwhelmingly appealing due to her shorts, the song's narrator could end up charged for an offence, presumably some sexually inappropriate behaviour. Reference to the woman's buttocks as "fat" is grounded in an African diasporic aesthetic that recognizes the fleshy woman's body as appealing.[7]

This privileging of the heterosexual male gaze and celebration of clothing that titillates the male gazer is popular in reggae and dancehall. Some songs even go as far as to warn against disappointing the male gaze by not appropriately dressing the female body. In "Deport Them" (2000) Sean Paul warns,

From a gal no up to date we deport them
Can't keep up with the trends we report them
If a no the modelling type we no court them
But if a the big beauty queen we support them.

Sean Paul's use of deportation as the metaphorical punishment for non-compliance with the current fashion trends seems severe, but it aptly reveals the real-life urgency attending the female pursuit of what my mother would call "up-to-date" clothing. Just as deportation from the cities of the United States and Great Britain is often preceded by a reduced access to the economic and educational opportunities represented by these locales, fashion deportation, such as what "Deport Them" calls for, is preceded by a decline in female access to the economic and social opportunities that men provide in exchange for sex. Fashion deportation, an inability to "keep up to the trends" as Sean Paul says, expels women from the realm of sexual viability into a chasm of sexual improbability.

In recent years, however, these lyrical references to clothing have taken on even more distinctive characteristics as attention has turned quite specifically to European and North American designer wear. Elephant Man's "Signal di Plane" (2003), Tifa's "Spell It Out" (2009) and Vybz Kartel's "Start Well" (2004) also tout designer brand names, including Armani, Moschino and Gucci, with a peculiar familiarity that disrupts the conspicuously Jamaican flavour of dancehall yet quite appropriately situates the music within its increasingly global context. Tifa (2009) sings: "Woy, me body full a Armani / Me no wear town G-U-C-C-I / Me have to take first class F-L-Y."[8] She revels in her designer garments, thumbing her nose at fake brand-name products from the local market (she refers to these as "town Gucci"), and suggests that her Armani-clad body is an equivalent status symbol to first class travel.

The song "Fight over Man" is performed by Spice (2006), a female Jamaican deejay, and similarly celebrates designer fashion; furthermore, Spice situates fashion as a metonym for sexual dexterity. The song both applauds and mystifies female sexuality, attributing the narrator's bedroom prowess to her designer clothing and resultant erotic appeal. "Fight over Man" quite specifically identifies its protagonist's "tightness" as the source of her appeal and labels this apparently desirable quality as a designer feature, in effect branding the woman's private parts just as clothing is branded. Girls lacking in "glam" are sentenced to the "deportation" process for which Sean Paul advocates in his song. Spice (2006) sings:

Tight pussy gal no fight over man
An everybody know say we a name brand
When me a wind me gi him de wickedest slam
But me sorry fi di gal dem out deh weh no have no glam.

The narrator in "Fight over Man", however, need not fear being "dipped". Her "name brand booty" not only saves her from exile but gives her access to wealth and social mobility. Unlike other women whose private parts bear a generic label, the narrator, with her designer-brand booty, does not need to compete for male attention due to her superior talents in the bedroom:

Mi know fi do me ting me know fi gauge an pace it
Big buddy deh ya but some woman a waste it
Gal a wind fast like a race she a race it
Me put it on proper him say do make me taste it
Me no have no time fi come a war with Susan
She a fight fi man cause him would give her a two grand
Whole heap a millionaire deh yuh fi pick and choose from
An me know me keep me nooky tight like a clam.

In the chorus of "Fight over Man" Spice sings, "De whole a dem a dead over mi name brand booty / Cause me born inna Chanel an me christen in Gucci". These lines further underscore the songs branding motif and suggest that sexual desirability is conferred through designer wear. Being "born in Chanel and christened in Gucci" now sits alongside being born with a silver spoon in one's mouth, both signifiers of a prestigious social status.

Buju Banton's "Driver A" (2006) presents a masculinized perspective on brand-name fashion that reflects the sentiments in "Fight over Man". "Driver A" features a male protagonist who is ostensibly one of the millionaires the narrator of "Fight over Man" can "pick and choose from" because these men are interested in acquiring sexual favours from her. The song opens with the narrator immersed in anxiety over the delivery of his illicit drug shipment. This "boss man" provides a range of strict "delivery" guidelines for his driver and implores, warns, begs and threatens him to make sure that, no matter what, the delivery arrives safely at its final destination. The boss lists various reasons why the success of this delivery mission is a must, and interestingly, but not surprisingly, among them is his woman's penchant for designer underwear. In the boss man's own words, "A business man a run me no inna no but nor because / My gal waan wear Victoria Secret drawers." This reasoning certainly reflects the sentiments in Spice's song and suggests that one of the aims of Caribbean male labour and its resultant economic benefits is to secure and maintain women who offer designer-brand sexual services.[9]

Like "Fight over Man", "Hotter Than the Rest" from Lady G and Mr Vegas ([1998] 2010) celebrates this transformative power of designer fashion and insists that the female narrator's "hotness" derives from the numerous items of designer clothes and accessories she is able to import. "Hotter Than the Rest" illuminates the global context within which dancehall operates. It highlights the growing significance of imported brands as a legitimating agent for female sexual value, and perhaps nationalistic value as well. "Hotter" emphasizes these importations – the "Moschino and Versace we fling down / You know a Dolce and Gabbana we a bring down" – that commingle with the black Jamaican female body to alter it and to glamorize it in such a way that it becomes "hotter than the rest". Furthermore, the song enunciates a marginalization of non-brand-name fashion. According to the female narrator, "Me no wear no frilla frilla / that a sketel name brand fi make me favour fritters."

Classifying fashion that is not brand-name with the appellation of "sketel name brand" positions these garments and the bodies that wear them as underclass, unrefined and lacking sexual sophistication. "Sketel" refers to a promiscuous woman; this "sketel" class of goods ostensibly includes locally produced garments that do not have the designer-name recognition of, say, Moschino or Versace. The ordinary and unappealing quality of locally produced fashion is further implied when the song invokes fritters in association with "sketel" fashion. Fritters are a popular Caribbean food item, somewhat similar to pancakes. They are not usually perceived as a glamorous or sophisticated dish. In fact, because they can be made relative cheaply – the main ingredient is flour – they are often associated with the poor and working class.

Dancehall enthusiasts who favour brand-name designer fashion that claims its origins in the metropoles of the United States and Europe mark their bodies as sophisticated and Westernized in contradistinction to wearers of "sketel" or "fritter" fashion. This dichotomy, with unsophisticated sketel clothing on one end of the continuum and Moschino or Versace on the other, suggests that the wearer of brand-name designer fashion is part of an expansive global fashion community in which membership is established and validated via one's degree of access to foreign designer clothing. Reinforcing colonially inspired notions that Eurocentric culture and ideals are more desirable than those originating in native, racialized spaces, "Hotter Than the Rest", alongside various other dancehall songs that reference designer fashion, devalues locally made clothing and the bodies that wear those clothes, rendering those bodies and the spaces they occupy unrefined and vulgar.

According to local dancehall fashion designer Earl "Biggy" Turner, this penchant for foreign clothing has had a damaging effect on the Jamaican fashion industry. In a 2006 newspaper article, Turner decries the influx of imported clothes turning up in the world of dancehall fashion. Of the past, he says, the clothing worn to the dancehall "was just the fashion of the people. The people would never be caught out without their specific dancehall fashion. They had something that defined them and that they could identify with" (Anglin-Christie 2006). Turner implies that the "fashion of the people" was clothing conceived and produced in Jamaica by Jamaican design talent. Another local designer, Paul "Tu-Lox" Gaynor further elaborates on this perceived loss of originality: "We were more original, that is number one. The dancehall now is more geared towards the cable look . . . the whole cable thing take away from the dancehall designers" (Anglin-Christie 2006). Gaynor's comment implicates the global mass media as an agent of fashion, and by extension cultural, indoctrination. He also recognizes the ways in which this preference for "cable" fashion privileges the accompanying values associated with the global while disenfranchising those bodies and values associated with the local. He concludes by suggesting that the early dancehall styles have all but disappeared, a consequence of this disenfranchisement: "Dancehall now don't have a dress code, we only have some music. If we don't hold on strong we are not going to have dancehall again" (Anglin-Christie 2006). These fashions initially associated with the dancehall were bright and flamboyant, but they were, most importantly, created by local fashion designers, and despite the current fetishization of imports, some dancehall artists like Beenie Man remain faithful to locally designed fashion. According to Martin Miller of White Skyy Designs, "Dancehall image now is more about brand than fashion. Beenie is the only one right now who has maintained the image of what the dancehall is with his style" (Ellis 2008).

Some sectors of the reggae dancehall expressive complex echo Turner and Gaynor's perception of designer brands as an affront to dancehall, namely the "conscious" reggae performers whose music is tightly yoked to Rastafarian ideology. Capleton is one of these performers, and he addresses the fetishization of designer wear in his song "Bun Dung Dreddie", a diatribe against Rastafarian backsliders who flout Rasta principles. Capleton sings:

> How you fi ras and then you still a eat pork
> How you fi ras and then you still a smoke coke
> Still all a sail pon Babylon boat
> Nuff rent-a-dread a bow pon the north coast.

These lines admonish sexual behaviour by alluding to "rent-a-dreads" (dreadlocked male prostitutes who sell their sexual services to tourists) as well as non-ital (Buckridge 2004, 63) dietary habits and drug use. Further in the song, Capleton includes fashion missteps among his list of infractions, celebrating traditional Rastafarian dress and dismissing designer garments: "Can't see the king if you no royal hot / Royalness a fi the royal flock / Robe and turban fi de royal flock / No Moschini, Versace and dress like ah ah." In keeping with the Afrocentric tenets of Rastafarian identity politics, Capleton rejects dancehall music's current embrace of Western designers like Moschino and Versace. He locates imported fashion as antithetical to Rastafarian principles. By touting a "robe and turban" as idealized garments, Capleton definitively anchors Rastafarian fashion principles in both an African and a religious aesthetic, since the image of a robe and turban evokes both traditional African dress as well as visual interpretations of biblical fashion.

In many respects, the colonial venture in Jamaica set the precedence for favouring imported fashion. According to Buckridge (2004, 93), female European settlers on the island initially ordered all their clothing from Europe. These garments were highly inappropriate given Jamaica's hot climate, but for several generations, European settlers refused to alter their dress customs. This resistance reiterates the cultural function of clothing; it is an expression of the British colonizer's desire to not be subsumed by a Caribbean identity. Among slave women, there was a parallel preference for garments similarly identified as exclusive; consequently, "expensive and elaborate dress" was "often a way of achieving differentiation and social mobility".[10] Eventually "creole" fashion emerged among the slaves, combining elements of both European and African dress. Buckridge (2004, 93) explains, "Creole dress was fundamentally radical because it defied easy categorization" and resisted the white hegemony's efforts to employ fashion as a clear definer of race.

The designer-brand references emerging from dancehall music suggest that the intermingling of designer clothing and the Caribbean female body result in a similar creolization, a blending of black Caribbean bodies and white-identified designer garments. This hybrid status of the dancehall diva who can acquire the appropriate clothing becomes a potent signifier of femininity that renders the wearer of these designer garbs "hotter than the rest", that is to say sexually superior to her counterpart clad in local fashion and deadly to her male conquests. Interestingly, the women who provided working-class Jamaicans with some of the earliest access to brand name clothing, and imitations of that clothing, themselves emerged from the same marginalized space occupied by the dancehall.

Higglers or, as they are more politically correctly referenced, informal commercial importers, are Jamaican, and indeed Caribbean, entrepreneurs who import products for resale. Women predominate in this industry, and during the 1970s they became a conspicuous presence on the sidewalks of popular "uptown" shopping areas in Kingston. They sell a range of products, including clothing, fashion accessories and household goods. Commentary from Jamaican journalist Morris Cargill (1998, 28–29) quite aptly represents the resistance of some of the middle class to their presence. He also refers to these traders and their luggage full of the merchandise destined for Jamaica's sidewalks as a "menace" to other travellers and comments that they "infest" the shopping centres where they sell their goods. He further marginalizes them by implying that their bodies are physiological anomalies: "[F]ew [higglers] seem to weigh less than 250 lbs. They are also a special shape, sticking out back and front simultaneously: huge protruding bottoms and equally huge tops, both of which they use as battering rams" (29).[11]

The shopping centres to which Cargill refers are popularly known as "uptown", a term also used in Jamaica as a distinguisher of class, with implications of race. The price of the products offered for sale in Kingston's uptown shopping areas distinctly marks these venues as middle- and upper-class spaces. Higglers disrupt presumptions of who can legitimately occupy that space while also creating opportunities for "downtown" and other women to engage in "uptown" consumptive practices by giving them access to cheaper variations of previously inaccessible products. As such, higglers bear a very meaningful economic and symbolic relationship to dancehall.

Their forceful entrance into the class-restricted entrepreneurial spaces of Jamaica helped create the means by which inner-city women developed a style of dress that challenges uptown conventions of fashion and attendant values. After historical exclusions of the poor and working class from the opportunities to engage in middle-class consumption patterns, modern-day dancehall divas use dancehall fashion as a way of mirroring those consumptive practices while concurrently resisting them. With increased access to faux and authentic designer wear, inner-city women are able to redeploy middle-class styles in ways that transgress conventional fashion norms. Just as informal commercial importers have emerged as a part of Jamaica's ongoing forays into the commercial global arena, the sustained invocation of brand-name clothing in the dancehall expressive complex globalizes the dancehall space and is perhaps a response to global commentary on both dancehall and blackness – commentary from within and without that suggest the space is vulgar, undesirable and unrefined.

This commentary on dancehall also questions the spending ethics of inner-city women and implicates dancehall as the cause of many an unpaid school fee and empty kitchen cupboard. While it is true that the sartorial extravagance associated with dancehall may compromise some women's financial circumstances and limit their ability to cover other essential expenses, I do not see dancehall as the *cause* of this fiscal imprudence any more than I see the manufacturers of BMW motorcars as the cause of middle-class extravagance and attendant excessive debt, with which many professionals struggle. What the willingness to spend beyond one's means to buy Gucci and Armani demonstrates is that poor money management is an egalitarian ailment, and the attendant criticisms are perhaps informed by the impulse to legislate working-class values and are also a projection of the middle class's anxieties about its own irresponsible spending habits.

In fact, I imagine that some of the wives and daughters of the British colonizers who insisted on "keeping up with the trends" in Europe probably accumulated quite a bit of debt themselves. Just as these women would not have their British identity devoured by a primitive Caribbean space, the desire for exclusive foreign clothing on behalf of modern-day dancehall proponents may represent a similar impulse. By consuming these white-identified garments, the dancehall space and the bodies that operate within are creolized to produce a more palatable black body and perhaps even a more palatable black experience that is not the equivalent of a "sketel name brand" that "favour fritters".[12] Instead, the result is a Moschino, Versace or Dior body that is not subject to the "deportation" of which Sean Paul sings because the exclusivity and desire associated with that body due to the designer fashion in which it is clad is transformative.

Furthermore, the deportation metaphor helps to unravel and expose some of the gender dilemmas created by the Caribbean's dominant patriarchal hegemony, which has persisted from colonial times through to the present. Patriarchal and hegemonic aesthetic imperatives, which undergird hierarchical determinations about female sexual viability, prescribe specific physiological, behavioural and sartorial standards. Ignorance about these prescriptive aesthetic norms or the inability to conform to them has always resulted in a type of metaphorical deportation from the realm of sexual viability. So, in many respects, the colonial white women who imported expensive and uncomfortable clothing from Europe along with present-day underclass black women who insist on sporting Gucci or Dior have formed a sisterhood of sorts, a sorority whose objective is to stand firm in a space where their heterosexual aesthetic appeal is affirmed and the perception of their sexuality as a "designer" brand is unquestioned. While dependency on imported fashion is rooted in patriarchal hegemonic efforts to sustain female anxieties over the value of women's bodies, diverting female attention from the numerous gendered inequities and abuses endemic to a patriarchy, women's collusive role in the entire scheme must be acknowledged. Because without women's ideological embrace of this hierarchical order to determine sexual viability and even more of the specific requirements (such as dressing their bodies in imported garments) that determine designation in that order, anxieties over being "born in Chanel and christen in Gucci" would not be possible.

NOTES

1. The chapter title is a line from the chorus of "Fight over Man" by Spice. The epigraph translates to standard English as follows: "Girls with tight pussies don't fight over men / Everyone knows that we are like a name brand / When I am engaged in sex, I give him the utmost in pleasure / But I'm sorry for the girls out there who are not glamorous."
2. The fetishization of designer wear within the dancehall space bears some notable irony given that space's concurrent demonization and dismissal of homosexuality, metaphorical and otherwise, and the conspicuous presence of gay men in the cadre of North American and European designers. Another occurrence, well worth scholarly pursuit, is the increasing attention that men in the dancehall arena have been giving to their own appearance and the increasing flamboyance of male dancehall fashion. The feminized aesthetic that results from this amplified attention often features dyed hair, plucked eyebrows and hip-hugging, bright-coloured clothing.
3. While dancehall music and hip-hop music have both cross pollinated and influenced each other's development, arguably so have the associated clothing trends. Hip-hop fashion, legendary for its exaggerated jewellery, exposed undergarments and revealing female dress, bears a distinct similarity to dancehall fashion in its subversion of propriety and conventional dress codes.
4. "Daggering" refers to a dance style that involves very aggressive and suggestive sexual movements.
5. My term for the various creative components associated with dancehall, including the music itself, associated dance moves, fashion trends, hair styles, vernacular and so on.
6. "Don" refers to inner-city area leaders who are often presumed to control their territory through illegal activities, including drug trafficking and blackmail.
7. See my discussion of black beauty aesthetics in Shaw (2006, 6–7).
8. "Whoa, my body is full of Armani / I don't wear town Gucci / I have to take first class flights."
9. "Driver A" suggests that male capitalistic desire is fuelled by female consumerism and that women's bodies are culpable for men's risky and perhaps immoral and illegal capitalistic

engagements. This seemingly disingenuous appropriation of responsibility bears a distinct similarity to arguments made in service to the European colonial project. Tillman Nechtman (2006, 10) argues that nabobinas, the female relatives of British men employed by East India Company, became "implicated in domestic conversations about luxury, consumerism, and material opulence. They were suspected of harboring a passion for material consumption that verged dangerously on the edge of immorality." Could "Driver A" also seek to reduce the responsibility for questionable male behaviour by dislodging and relocating it on the site of the women's body?

10. "Ital" is an idiom that derives from Rastafarian culture and refers to something wholesome and healthy. It is usually used in reference to food.
11. See my discussion of higglers in the context of their black and presumably fat bodies in Shaw (2006, ch. 3).
12. For a study of the identity politics affixed to the "uptown" and "downtown" dichotomy, see Ulysse (2004).

REFERENCES

Anglin-Christie, Kavelle. 2006. "Dancehall's Flair Ladies". *Gleaner*, 12 February.

Baum, Frank. 2000. *The Wonderful Wizard of Oz*. New York: HarperCollins.

Boyne, Ian. 2005. "Easter and the 'Money Oh' Culture". *Gleaner*, 27 March.

Buckridge, Steve. 2004. *The Language of Dress: Resistance and Accommodation in Jamaica, 1760–1890*. Kingston: University of the West Indies Press.

Cargill, Morris. 1998. *Public Disturbances: A Collection of Writings 1986–1996*. Kingston: Mill Press.

Cooper, Carolyn. 2004. *Soundclash: Jamaican Dancehall Culture at Large*. New York: Palgrave Macmillan.

Elgood, Rick and Don Letts, dir. 2004. *Dancehall Queen*. USA: Palm Pictures. DVD.

Ellis, Tanya C. 2008. "Dancehall's Trends". *Star*, 5 January.

Frater, Adrian. 2010. "Trelawny's 'Fluffy' Is Dancehall Queen". *Star*, 4 August. http://jamaica-star.com/thestar/20100804/ent/ent6.html.

Henry, Krista. 2008. Dancehall, Fashion Took Centre Stage". *Star*, 9 September.

Higginbotham Jr., A. Leon. 1980. *In the Matter of Color Race and the American Legal Process: The Colonial Period*. New York: Oxford University Press.

Hope, Donna P. 2006. *Inna di Dancehall*. Kingston: University of the West Indies Press.

Lupton, Mary Jane. 1986. "Clothes and Closure in Three Novels by Black Women". *Black American Literature Forum* 20, no. 4 (Winter): 409–21.

Nechtman, Tillman. 2006. "Nabobinas: Luxury, Gender, and the Sexual Politics of British Imperialism in India in the Late Eighteenth Century". *Journal of Women's History* 18, no. 4: 8–30.

Paul, Annie. 2007. "'No Grave Cannot Hold My Body Down': Rituals of Death and Burial in Postcolonial Jamaica". *Small Axe*, no. 23: 142– 62.

Shaw, Andrea Elizabeth. 2006. *The Embodiment of Disobedience: Fat Black Women's Unruly Political Bodies*. New York: Lexington.

Stanley Niaah, Sonjah. 2010. *Dancehall: From Slave Ship to Ghetto*. Ottawa: University of Ottawa Press.

Tyson, Esther. 2008. "Slackness and More Slackness". *Gleaner*, 6 April. http://www.jamaica-gleaner.com/gleaner/20080406 /cleisure/cleisure5.html.

Ulysse, Gina. 2004. *Downtown Ladies: Informal Commercial Importers, a Haitian Anthropologist and Self-Making in Jamaica.* Chicago: University of Chicago Press.

DISCOGRAPHY

Althea and Donna. [1978] 2001. "Uptown Top Ranking". *Uptown Top Ranking.* Frontline CDFL 2023, compact disc.

Buju Banton. 1993. "Batty Rider". *Mr Mention.* Fader 921 503-2, compact disc.

———. 2006. "Driver A". *Too Bad.* Gargamel Music GGML 004, compact disc.

Capleton. 2000. "Bun Dung Dreddie". *More Fire.* VP Records VPCD1587, compact disc.

Elephant Man. 2003. "Signal Di Plane". *Good 2 Go.* VP Records 83681-2, compact disc.

Lady G and Mr Vegas. [1998] 2010. "Hotter Than the Rest". *Best of the Best Volume 1: Roots Culture Dancehall.* Jamdown Records, MP3 download.

Sean Paul. 2000. "Deport Them". *Stage One.* VP Records, VPCD1572, compact disc.

Spice. 2006. "Fight over Man". *Eighty Five (Rhythm).* Mad House, compact disc.

Tifa. 2009. "Spell It Out". *Ward 21: The Brand New Riddims*, Ward 21 Productions, MP3 download.

Vybz Kartel. 2004. "Start Well". *Up 2 Di Time.* Greensleeves GRELCD 275, compact disc.

PART 8

THE DANCEHALL TRANSNATION

CHAPTER 27

Music and Orality

*Authenticity in Japanese Sound System Culture**

MARVIN D. STERLING

ALTHOUGH DANCEHALL HAS BEEN THE MOST POPULAR MUSIC in Jamaica since the 1980s, dancehall culture in Japan has until recently remained largely undiscovered by most mainstream Japanese audiences. But a smaller number of Japanese more in tune with the changes in reggae music have been pursuing dancehall for many years. The members of Mighty Crown had been attending dancehall events in Yokohama since the early 1990s. They had been drawing large crowds wherever they performed in Japan even before 1999, the year they first won the World Clash title. Since word of this victory reached Japan, dancehall in the country, including sound system culture, has been on a steady rise. The first edition of the dancehall free paper *Strive*, published in 2001, confirms the existence of at least 150 sound systems in Japan; its publisher told me she was confident that the number is significantly higher. (Masta Simon of Mighty Crown, which has a close affiliation with *Strive*, recently suggested that there are now about 300 sound systems, a credible number since the 150 figure was suggested before the dancehall boom.) Jamaica's population is only a fraction of Japan's (2.5 million compared to 127 million), but the very safe figure of 150 sound systems remains impressive, since in all of dancehall-saturated Jamaica there are only about three hundred sounds.

Two sound system cultures are present in Japan: one, currently the more popular, is oriented around dancehall music, and the other around dub. (I will focus on the dancehall element of sound system culture in this chapter, briefly touching on the dub aspect later.) In addition to Mighty Crown, the most popular dancehall sound systems are Mighty Jam Rock, Jam Tek, Sunset, Infinity 16, Blast Star, Red Spider and King Ryūkyū. Dub music has recently had little current presence in dancehall-dominated Jamaica but has been a stronger cultural force in Britain. Dub-based sound systems share the digital musical manipulation and MC orality of dancehall even as they tend to retain more of roots reggae's Rasta-influenced message of spiritual uplift. This message is evoked in

*Previously published in *Babylon East: Performing Dancehall, Roots Reggae, and Rastafari in Japan* (Durham, NC: Duke University Press, 2010), 65–78.

the distinct sound of dub's ethereal remixing of previously recorded as well as original roots reggae tunes. Among the major Japanese dub sound systems are Mighty Massa, Direct Impact, Shandi I and Jah Works.

IMMERSION IN THE SOURCE: NEW YORK AND JAMAICA

Dancehall sound system members, DJs and fans became interested in dancehall in a number of ways. Few older roots fans – say, those in their late twenties and older during the initial period of my research, between 1998 and 2000 – have gone on to express interest in the emerging dancehall culture. However, many younger fans grew interested in dancehall after being introduced to roots reggae around the mid- to late 1990s. Other young Japanese people became interested in dancehall culture when their high-school or college friends, eager to impress them with something they had never heard before, loaned them dancehall CDs or took them to local dancehall events. Despite, or perhaps because of, the fact that most young Japanese flock to the familiar J-pop, a few search for novel underground music. Dancehall fits the bill.

Those who go on to become deeply involved in dancehall culture – including, of course, performers – often travel to dancehall's two main international centres, New York and Jamaica. (England represents an important third centre, especially for dub sounds.) A clear pattern emerged throughout my research in which sound system members and DJs reported travelling to these two sites specifically to develop their skills. From Japan they go to New York to establish contact with Jamaican and Jamaican American DJs and sound systems at dancehall events held in such largely Jamaican communities as Crown Heights and Bedford-Stuyvesant. Many stay in New York for months or years, not only to become acclimatized to New York's dancehall scene but also to experience life in general in this city that figures greatly in the popular Japanese imagination of the West. Many earn a living at part-time jobs unrelated to dancehall culture.

From New York, these musicians then make something of a pilgrimage to Jamaica (many, of course, travel directly there from Japan). Depending on their resources, some might stay in Jamaica for only a few days, while others remain for several months, even a year or two. A key form of symbolic capital obtainable in Jamaica is knowledge and possession of many Jamaican dancehall records. Given the huge Japanese interest in roots reggae a few years ago, as well as the more recent interest in dancehall, there is little delay between the release of new tunes in Jamaica and in Japan. Jamaican vendors in New York also sell mix tapes or more recently CDs of new dancehall tunes and events; Japanese artists who happen to be in the city return to Japan with this edge. Japanese entrepreneurs live in Jamaica and ship thousands of dancehall records to Japan each month, feeding the appetites of Japanese consumers who want to hear the most recent Jamaican dancehall tunes as soon as they are produced.

But for the most competitive sound systems, nothing short of immersion is enough. Their members regularly travel to Jamaica or New York to stay on top of the most popular songs at Jamaican dances as well as over the airwaves. In addition to awareness of what is going on in Jamaica musically, the ability to speak Patwa is a second key form of subcultural prestige. Less skilled Japanese MCs and DJs can speak only in Japanese, with a few terms drawn from Jamaican dancehall records and DVDs. The more skilled ones learn Jamaican Creole, particularly the vocabulary of dancehall culture. While in Jamaica, Japanese sound system members often make business contacts with major Jamaican DJs. A primary purpose for this contact is to obtain "dubplates". Dubplates are similar to dub music in that both are versions of songs. (Again, dub music as a genre emphasizes the record producer as artist, who creatively remixes the instrumentation of previously recorded, but sometimes original, songs.) Dubplates are recordings in which the vocal track is stripped from the riddim – the musical element of a tune – and a new vocal track with similar lyrics is overlaid. A Japanese sound system will pay a Jamaican DJ to make a dubplate of one of his popular songs. In the new lyrics, the DJ sings the customized praises of the paying sound system and marvels at the foolhardiness of those rival systems that attempt to compete. In dancehall everywhere, dubplates, especially at sound clashes – competitions between sound systems – are the lingua franca or ammunition of the sound system's subcultural power. Although both the DJs and the sound systems try to keep payment figures secret, a DJ usually makes between a few hundred US dollars to well over a thousand or a couple thousand for a dubplate, depending on his or her fame and relationship with the Japanese sound system. The members of some sound systems have reported to me that they paid reduced prices to DJs with whom they have had long-term relationships; other systems report receiving dubplates at no charge, in exceptional cases.

The Japanese musicians return home from Jamaica, sometimes by way of New York. They then put into play in Japanese dancehall clubs across the country the skills and capital they acquired in Jamaica, New York, London and other expatriate Jamaican communities. Once this primary transnational socialization has been completed, the musicians travel occasionally to Jamaican communities to keep on top of subcultural developments there.

SINGERS AND DJS

While Japanese sounds have recently been enjoying some international success, to date there has been little effort to move Japanese deejaying outside Japan. Nahki, perhaps the most popular DJ in Japan from the late 1980s to the mid-1990s, has been something of an exception to this rule. He speaks Patwa and English fluently, and to my knowledge, he is the only Japanese DJ to have performed in Jamaica's Reggae Sunsplash. I have already mentioned the 2006 performance he, Megaryu and Pang gave in New York; the veteran DJ duo Ackee and Saltfish has performed internationally, including in Jamaica. Sister Kaya has performed at an annual reggae concert in San Diego. Besides these and a few others, there are few established Japanese DJs and singers on the international reggae scene.

Nevertheless, the surge in popularity of dancehall singing and deejaying in Japan has been one of the most noticeable trends in Japanese dancehall over the last few years. DJs like Miki Dōzan, Papa Bon, Papa U-Gee, Chozen Lee, Ng Head, Cone Head, Yoyo-

C, Fireball, Junior Dee, Jun 4 Shot, Lady Q, Machao, H-Man, Rankin Taxi, Hibikilla, Chehon, Ryo the Skywalker and Rude Boy Face; duos and groups like Mighty Jam Rock, Megaryu, and Ackee and Saltfish; and singers like Pushim, Kaana, Moomin, Minmi, Munehiro and Pang are among the well-known performers who at various stages of their careers have achieved some measure of fame in Japanese dancehall culture. Most of these individuals were part of the underground dancehall scene before it boomed.

Stolzoff (2000) provides a useful categorization of the various performance styles, rarely discrete, in which Jamaican DJs and singers perform. These include, among DJs, such categories as the cultural Rasta, rude boy Rasta, gangster/gunman, reality, slackness/loverman, comedian/gimmick and all-rounder. Among singers there are culture singers, lovers rock singers, dancehall style singers, classic singers, combination acts and singjays. While I will not elaborate on the specific meanings Stolzoff attributes to all these categories, Japanese dancehall artists may be similarly grouped, since most artists to some degree define their musical identities – including through their choice of professional names – in relation to Jamaican artists they admire.

The extent to which the performers may not be so categorized, however, is also significant. Japanese sound systems do play at their events a steady diet of Jamaican reality, cultural Rasta and gangster/gunman tunes. However, few Japanese DJs perform in any of these styles, which do not very well reflect Japanese sociocultural, economic or political circumstances. Jamaican reality DJs tend to express concern about crime, hunger and political corruption in Jamaican society (a testament to dancehall's local sensibility); the cultural Rasta voices a revolutionary Afrocentric rhetoric that does not obviously accord with the Japanese situation; and the violent machismo that the gangster/gunman romanticizes seems at odds with life in a comparatively safe Japan. Just as Jamaican DJs must sometimes excise Jamaica-specific lyrics when recording dubplates for Japanese sounds, Japanese DJs have avoided performance styles that do not much reflect the presumed sensibilities of their Japanese audiences. This, of course, is less the case when Japanese DJs travel to Jamaica, New York and London, and feel the need to adjust their performance style to fit what is expected by Jamaican audiences there. Papa Bon, who discusses below his travels to and performances in Jamaica and New York, illustrates this point. I suspect that one of the reasons why Mighty Crown's victory in 1999 was so surprising to many Jamaicans was because it required deep commitment to learning reggae ("tune") in archival depth; to developing a sense of which tune to play based on audience mood; and to learning and wielding dancehall's subculturally particular patois in the bawdy, adversarial manner ("argument") needed to defeat their rivals. When a Japanese MC does not just get by in Patwa but also uses it to ritually question the heterosexual competency of his Jamaican rivals, or to flirtatiously offer "Japanese baby" to his Jamaican female audience members, it is somewhat at odds with assumptions about Japanese civility, as well as with the relative civility actually found in dancehall in Japan.

A category of deejaying worth commenting on here is the slackness/loverman mode. In Jamaica, the loverman is the DJ who proclaims his ability to attract women, his prowess in bed. When such sentiments enter into the realm of the explicitly erotic, they become "slack". In Jamaican society, "slackness" generally refers to moral misconduct of many kinds: a politician's failure to provide for his constituents, for instance, or utility companies shutting off water and electricity frequently and without notice. Especially as used within, as well as by social observers commenting on dancehall culture, "slackness" can also be an emphatically pleasurable openness about matters of sex (while remaining within the limits of Jamaican heterosexual norms). This is an openness both on the part of the DJ, who is specific about what he likes in a woman, and on the part of the woman in the audience whose intentions to attract male attention are similarly clear (such as through erotic dress or, in the case of the small number of female DJs like Lady Saw and Makka Diamond, their own slack lyrics). Slackness within the dancehall, as a certain forthrightness about matters of sex, rather than cause for condemnation or shame, is celebrated: in the skill of the artist able to speak about such matters in an artful way, in reveling in the pleasures of courtship and sex. (Of course, some outside dancehall may have difficulty seeing the artistry involved when DJs – who are not all equally talented – describe women and sexual acts in blunt anatomical detail.)

Among Japanese DJs, slackness tends toward *sukebe* (the mischievously lewd) and is less frequently in the realm of *gehin* (the vulgar), thus readily meshing with traditions of popular humour in Japan. In this way, slackness in Japan is not so seriously about phallic empowerment in the genuinely self-impressed way that it is among slackness/loverman Jamaican DJs. The host of one Shibuya dancehall event I attended was an older man, perhaps in his mid-forties, who appeared onstage in a series of outlandish outfits. One of these was an ostrich outfit, in which the black, feathery body of the ostrich began at the man's crotch, with the bird's neck angled upward so that its head reached the level of the man's chest. While many Jamaican women outside dancehall feel insulted by the vulgar machismo in much slackness/loverman music, young Japanese women at events like the one in Shibuya might only giggle at this silly man.

The Japanese DJ's slackness, in fact, is sometimes linked to another category of deejaying, the comedian/gimmick. Veteran DJs H-Man and Rankin' Taxi are among those who often perform in this mode. An example of this light-hearted reggae is H-Man's "Aketemo Kuretemo (Day In, Day Out)". In the song, H-Man describes his addiction to reggae music, one that afflicts him waking or sleeping. He is giddily tormented by lyrical possibility, of the creative potential that inheres in "connected words, connected sounds":

> Aketemo aketemo kuretemo kuretemo
> Asa kara ban made regee tsuke
> Anata ni au no mo
> Watashi ga aru no mo
> Ima kono shunkan sono okage
> Aketemo aketemo kuretemo kuretemo
> Hiru de mo yoru de mo regee DJ
> Aketemo aketemo aketemo aketemo
> Tsugi naru tobira o mata akete
>
> (Day in, day in, day out, day out,

From morning until night: addicted to reggae.
In meeting up with you
and just being around too,
Right at this moment, that's what it's about.
Day in, day in, day out, day out,
Doesn't matter if it's day, doesn't matter if it's night: I'm a reggae DJ.
Day in, day in, day in, day in:
Open up again [the possibilities of] what comes next.)

Of all the performative modes that have made their way from Jamaica to Japan, perhaps the one that has arrived most intact is the lover's rock singer. These men sing in candy-voiced falsetto, with little explicit sexual content, about their undying romantic love for individual women. Probably the most popular lover's rock singer is Moomin. In addition to his talents as a vocal artist, the international power of love songs and the fact that he is heavily promoted in *Riddim* (owned by Overheat Communications, of which Overheat Records, Moomin's label, is also a subsidiary), Moomin's success might be attributed to the appeal to the Japanese of his soft singing style, as well as to his music's similarity to that of such Jamaican artists as Jimmy Cliff.

NATIONALISM AND AUTHENTICITY IN JAPANESE REGGAE

While Japanese reggae artists adopt a broad range of themes and performance styles, a number of Japanese reggae songs bearing a strong theme of national pride have emerged, especially since 2000.[1] This theme affords perspective on the constitution of an authentic Japanese reggae and the political stakes involved in this effort.

One of the ways in which Japanese reggae artists celebrate Japanese cultural distinctiveness – as seen in foodways, local cultural differences, national treasures, and even, for one mischievous DJ, instant ramen and the so-called shower toilet – is by linking it with the natural world. In the music video for Munehiro's "Japaniizu" [Japanese], the female singer announces that the song is dedicated "to all Japanese Muffins / Yeah, Yeah! / Nippon! Nippon!" Munehiro is dressed in kimono with a parasol, spotlit in red against a black background. Yellow and green spotlights appear, which, combined with the red, complete the Rasta colours. The word "Japanese" appears in katakana[2] script, similarly spotlit in red, yellow and green. This use of colour literally highlights the Japanese through the Jamaican. Its riddim decidedly upbeat, the song is pitched in cultural naturalist qua nationalist terms:

Shiki ga irodoru yutaka na kara
Daichi ga umidasu minori no aka
Mada mada utsukushii shimaguni kara
Wakai ibuki ga hanatsu pawa wa mugendai
. . . .
Taishi idaki habatakou sekai e
China Korea Asia

Te o torimukaou heiwa e
Jidai ga nagaretemo
Uketsugou roots and culture
Saa, mazu wa kono basho kara
Nippon! Nippon!

(Rich colours of the four seasons,
Red of the harvest that the earth bears.
From an island country, still beautiful
The unleashed power of the breath of youth is infinite
. . . .
With ambition, let's fly into the world –
China, Korea, Asia,
Let's join hands, facing peace.
Even as time goes by
Toward roots and culture,
Yes, it starts from this place –
Japan! Japan!)

Especially during the roots boom, but even now, reggae music is closely associated with celebrations of the natural (for instance, reggae is most popularly regarded as "summertime music"). This song couples the beauty of the Japanese natural with that of the Japanese national, celebrating "an island country, still beautiful", resplendent in all its colours. Such an appreciation becomes a base from which Japanese can engage the international – in this song, China, Korea and the rest of Asia. These celebrations of the Japanese natural are nearly de rigueur in patriotic Japanese reggae. Miki Dōzan's "Japan Ichiban" (Japan, Number One), for instance, describes the natural beauty of Japan in "the springtime bloom of cherry blossoms / nights of full moons in the autumn skies / beautiful scenery that makes the heart dance".

Munehiro's song calls for an "original nation" to renew itself – ironically, through a return to its traditions. This is expressed in gendered terms in her video, most explicitly evidenced by her wearing kimono (which young Japanese women generally do not do very often now, except on special occasions). In "Nishi Muku Samurai" (Samurai Facing West), Ryo the Skywalker employs the same gendered logic, this time inflected through a masculinist reference to samurai. Making explicit how gazing westward often invokes self-orientalization, he specifically references the topknot (*chonmage*) and the sword (*kata*) as instruments of a revalorized Japanese masculinity moving confidently into the West. Dōzan's "Japan Ichiban" is among the many other songs bearing this samurai theme. He laments how Western society became enamored of the sword and the topknot just as they were discarded by Japanese. In "Appare Japan" (Honourable Japan), Hibikilla's invocation of the samurai is less ambiguous, referring to Japan as a civilization of "the samurai fighter" and to the sword as "Japan's pride". However, in what may be a reference to the United States, and to Japanese society's imagination of itself as an emissary of postwar world peace, he says: "But there is pride also in throwing away the sword / Those good people over there, they still can't lay it aside?" If "those good people over there" are indeed Euro-Americans, this reference places the song on the list of patriotic Japanese reggae in which the West figures prominently. In "Appare Japan", the distinctiveness of Japan emerges out of numerous influences, including China and the United States.

Chūgoku kara kanji mananda
Kagaku to igaku wa oranda
Our emperor from kudara
Shogaikoku e wasurenu kansha
Sono jūnansa ga hanpa nai

(We learned kanji from China,
Science and medicine was Holland,
Our emperor from [the ancient Korean kingdom of] Kudara.
Don't forget to thank the various foreign countries –
That flexibility is excellent.)

Significantly, given the discrimination against Koreans in Japan, this song celebrates the controversial possibility of the Korean provenance of the imperial line (Watts 2001). Japan is the beneficiary of a writing system from China and of sciences from the West. However, in most of these songs the West is cast in more negative terms. Dōzan's "Japan Ichiban" song comments on what is for him the weirdness of looking at Japanese commercials and fashion magazines and seeing only foreigners, of Japanese aspiring to be like the actors they see in Hollywood films. Like Ryo the Skywalker, who commands his "Japan crew" in Patwa to, "se [say] yu proud to be yellow", Dōzan calls for Japanese to recognize the absolute beauty of the colour of their skin. The song continues:

Machigai nakatta Meiji Ishin
Mazukatta no wa ato no hōshin
Yugande nakushita aikokushin
Conpurekkusu o toriharaou
Nihon wa subarashii kuni mo hito mo

(The Meiji Restoration was not a mistake.
What was bad was the path taken after that:
Distorted, spoilt patriotism.
Let's destroy our complex.
Japan is a wonderful country, its people too.)

The Meiji Restoration, which brought Japan out of a long period of seclusion from the outside world, was a first step toward Japan's becoming an international power. This in itself, and the imperial institution that was "restored" to power in 1868 as a symbol of national unity, are causes for patriotic celebration. However, Dōzan adopts a familiar postwar national rhetoric in which the noble patriotism of the Japanese people is exploited by its warmongering leaders. Assuming continuity between the third and fourth lines, this path of military colonialism is discreetly Western: Japan's inferiority complex toward the West led to Japanese leaders' competing with this West, in Western ways, with ruinous effect.

Even more explicitly critical of the West, and of America particularly, is Nanjaman's poetic, musically subdued yet politically unambiguous "Born Japanese". He sings of Japan as a land of ancient samurai, of a people who fight with all their heart, of a people with *yamato damashii* (Japanese spirit). Japanese fly into the world, Nanjaman quietly intones, in search of something important. They look outward because they sense something amiss at home, as shown in the many people who work hard (a good thing in itself), but only out of an excessive concern for money; in the *usokusai* (reeking of lies) faces of politicians on campaign posters. In the spirit of *jibun sagashi* in its aspect as flight from the petty economics of life in recessionary Japan, Nanjaman – in a gesture similar to those of Ryo the Skywalker in "Nishi Muku Samurai" and Munehiro in "Japanese" – encourages his listener to look across the ocean, to escape in a single bound this flawed Japan. But the international, and the West particularly, are fraught with moral danger:

Amerika
Minna akogareru jiyū no kuni
Amerika
Dakedo Indian o koroshite ubatta Amerika
Kokujin o dorei ni shite ita Amerika
Nihon ni genbaku otoshita Amerika
Otoko to otoko ga kekkon suru Amerika
Iraku ni misairu otosu Amerika
Seigi no mikata no tsumori no Amerika

(America,
The free country everyone yearns for, America.
And yet, it is the America that killed and robbed Indians,
The America that enslaved black people,
The America that dropped the atomic bomb on Japan,
The America where men marry men,
The America that drops missiles on Iraq,
The America that is supposed to be the friend of justice.)

America's offences around the world are not only of the past; indeed, unable to lay aside the sword, its oppression registers in more recent times in such conflicts as the second war in Iraq.[3] These offences do not only evidence themselves around the world but also at home, including in heteronormative terms, given the designation of America as a (clearly sinful) place where men marry men.

In these songs, then, Japanese reggae artists sing and deejay against a Western, and specifically American, hegemony that, despite its destructive nature, makes the Japanese yearn blindly for America. Even with the recent Korean wave (*hanryū*) – the surge of popularity of Korean culture in Japan and elsewhere in Asia (see Hanaki et al. 2007) – it is still remarkable to hear a Japanese artist acknowledge with pride the strong possibility that the emperor's ancestors came from ancient Korea, as well as to hear China acknowledged as a significant source of present-day Japanese culture. The proud invocation of "yellow skin" in Miki Dōzan's and Ryo the Skywalker's songs provides a rare, explicit commentary on race in Japan (here vis-à-vis the international). Nanjaman evocatively articulates postcolonial affinities between American Indians, blacks, Iraqis and Japanese.

However, despite these insights, this nationalistic line of Japanese reggae is problematic. It embraces Asia with little acknowledgment of Japanese militarism and colonialism throughout the region. Dōzan's song refers to past Japanese misconduct, but not very specifically, and only to quickly absolve the Japanese public of responsibility for the war. Without directly acknowledging the past, the celebrations of *yamato damashii* and the desire for an ambitious Japan to embrace its Asian brothers on Japanese cultural terms (as is heard particularly in Munehiro's song) sound eerily similar to the rhetoric of the Greater East Asia Co-Prosperity Sphere, a colonial initiative to unite Asia under Japanese leadership. These songs support Koichi Iwabuchi's (2002) argument that recessionary Japan's popular-cultural embrace during the 1990s of an essentialized, backward Asia – orientalized in this way much as Japan positively orientalizes itself as the naturally resplendent land of the samurai – restores prewar rhetoric of a privileged Japanese nation as being in a unique position of leadership over its Asian neighbours.

I am not saying that Munehiro or any of the other artists are making secret calls for Japan to recolonize East Asia. Their celebrations of Japan are to be more immediately understood as an effort to constitute Japan as an intimate point of departure and therefore a safe place for return from the alluring, but at the same time forbiddingly alien, global (a theme that recurs throughout this book). My point is only that given a lack of specific discussion, however uncomfortable, of how the Japanese colonial legacy is still intensely of issue throughout Asia, calls for Asian unity centred proudly on Japan run the risk of appearing self-serving. Such calls seem too easily to represent the Asian political sphere as a unity most readily achieved with Japan at its centre, rather than what might be seen as an opposite reality, in which the Japanese centre in recent history has actually been a source of regional discontent. This discontent has been voiced in debates surrounding the Japanese military's forcing so-called comfort women from Korean and other countries to be prostitutes for Japanese servicemen during the Second World War (Choi 1997; Min 2003; Stetz and Oh 2001; Yang 2008; Yoshiaki 2000); the visits of Japanese prime ministers to Tokyo's Yasukuni Shrine, where several war criminals are interred (Antoni 1988; Nelson 2003); and revisionist representations of Japanese colonial military aggression in Japanese schoolbooks (Barnard 2001).

In the end, this patriotic line of Japanese reggae emerges from feelings of national pride in the fifth period of Japanese reggae, following Japanese success in international competition. These feelings find a ready audience in many Japanese people inside and outside the subculture. Living in a recessionary Japan, they are ready for a music that speaks to the possibilities of accomplishment overseas, accomplishments that must be marked as specifically Japanese (hence the traditionalist references to geisha and samurai).

This leads to another absence in most of these songs that is of concern in this book:

that of Jamaica. Nanjaman does describe in "Born Japanese", for instance, how black Jamaicans were brought to the island after white people had killed off most the indigenous population. But in general, the Jamaican provenance of the reggae music through which these expressions of Japanese national pride take place is effaced. When Miki Dōzan sings that it does not do to defer too much to foreign countries, one wonders if he means to include not just America (in political terms) but also Jamaica (in musical subcultural terms).

The absence of explicit reference to Jamaica in many of these songs, however, should not be a reason to miss the ways in which Japanese nationalist sentiment remains significantly articulated vis-à-vis the "authentic" Jamaican. The (Japanese) nationalistic sentiment is appropriate to an authentic (Japanese) reggae, since it is common to hear Jamaican reggae musicians express a sense of pride in their own island country in nationalist terms. For instance, Munehiro mobilizes the expression "roots and culture" – a Rasta term that celebrates Afro-Jamaicans' material and spiritual situatedness in the soil, a sense of deep cultural history – with very similar effect in the Japanese context. Ryo the Skywalker admonishes Japanese men without symbolic topknots in a way that recalls the ridicule by Jamaican dreadlocked Rastas of non-Rasta Jamaican men as Westernized "baldheads". Nanjaman's homophobic sentiment is discreetly authorized by similar expressions in Jamaican dancehall; his annoyance at the dishonesty of Japanese politicians helps authenticate Japanese dancehall, given that Jamaicans make the same complaint about their politicians. The call for Asian unity and peace and love may be regarded as authentically (Japanese) reggae since it so directly corresponds to Jamaican reggae calls for pan-African unity and peace and love. The claims of the value of yellow skin are appropriately expressed through a music whose progenitors, also oppressed by the West, assert the value of their black skin. In these ways, then, like the renderings of Japanese people as phenotypically white in Japanese manga, the Jamaican origin of Japanese reggae is rendered as a code that operates below the level of – and richly hybridizes – identification as Japanese. Despite Japanese reggae artists' lyrical and other performative moves to articulate reggae in specifically Japanese terms, in ways that largely efface Jamaica from the music, this Jamaican presence is felt in a generalization of political issues, symbols, themes and rhetorical conventions expressed in Jamaican reggae, permitting them to be applied specifically to Japan. It is largely through a gaze toward and a careful knowing of the Jamaican – an instance of the broader Japanese gaze at the international – that reggae can be articulated as authentically Japanese.

NOTES

1. The journalist Minako Ikeshiro confirmed what were originally my only vague impressions of contemporary Japanese reggae, especially since 2000, as "conservative". I thank her for encouraging me in this way to more fully pursue this route. I am also much indebted to my colleague Shinichiro Suzuki, of Kwansei Gakuin University, for introducing me to a number of songs with this theme, including several discussed here.
2. Katakana is one of the two syllabaries used in the Japanese writing system.

3. As another example of indictments of ongoing American global oppression, the Okinawan duo U-Dou and Platy in some of their music criticize America's military presence in the prefecture.

REFERENCES

Antoni, Klaus. 1988. "Yasukuni-Jinja and Folk Religion: The Problem of Vengeful Spirits". *Asian Folklore Studies* 47, no. 1: 123–36.

Barnard, Christopher. 2001. "Isolating Knowledge of the Unpleasant: The Rape of Nanking in Japanese High-School Textbooks". *British Journal of Sociology of Education* 22, no. 4: 519–30.

Choi, Chungmoo, ed. 1997. "The Colonial Women: Colonialism, War, and Sex". Special issue. *Positions* 5, no. 1.

Hanaki, Toru, Arvind Singhal, Min Wha Han, Do Kyun Kim, and Ketan Chitnis. 2007. "Hanryu Sweeps East Asia: How 'Winter Sonata' Is Gripping Japan". *International Communication Gazette* 69, no. 3: 281–94.

Iwabuchi, Koichi. 2002. "Nostalgia for a (Different) Asian Modernity: Media Consumption of 'Asia' in Japan". *Positions* 10, no. 3: 547–73.

Min, Pyong Gap. 2003. "Korean 'Comfort Women': The Intersection of Colonial Power, Gender, and Class". *Gender and Society* 17, no. 6: 938–57.

Nelson, John. 2003. "Social Memory as Ritual Practice: Commemorating Spirits of the Military Dead at Yasukuni Shinto Shrine". *Journal of Asian Studies* 62, no. 2: 443–67.

Stetz, Margaret D., and Bonnie B. C. Oh, eds. 2001. *Legacies of the Comfort Women of World War II*. Armonk, NY: M. E. Sharpe.

Stolzoff, Norman C. 2000. *Wake the Town and Tell the People: Dancehall Culture in Jamaica*. Durham, NC: Duke University Press.

Watts, Jonathan. 2001. "The Emperor's New Roots". *Guardian*, 28 December.

Yang, Hyunah. 2008. "Finding the 'Map of Memory': Testimony of the Japanese Military Sexual Slavery Survivors". *Positions* 16, no. 1: 79–107.

Yoshiaki, Yoshimi. 2000. *Comfort Women*. New York: Columbia University Press.

CHAPTER 28

Zimdancehall

Jamaican Music in a Transatlantic and African Perspective

ANDREA HOLLINGTON

THE TRANSATLANTIC SLAVE TRADE HAS BROUGHT LARGE NUMBERS of enslaved Africans to the Americas. The African legacy in Jamaica has been studied with regard to language, culture, religion and music, among other domains (see for instance Alleyne 1988; Cassidy 1961; Cassidy and Le Page 1967; Farquharson 2012; Stewart 2005; Warner-Lewis 1977, 1993, 2003, 2007; Bilby 1992, 2005; Lewin 2000; Marshall 2012). While this is undeniably an important field of study which uncovers history and ties it to the present through culture, identity and belonging, there are also influences in other directions, which have taken on many forms. In this regard, I want to emphasize the idea of the Atlantic as a dynamic contact zone which is characterized by multidirectional and multidimensional encounters and entanglements, a perspective which has been taken on most often by studies on music. For instance, Stanley Niaah illustrates dynamic transnational ties, in particular comparing dancehall music with South African kwaito (Stanley Niaah 2008), while White (2002) discusses transatlantic flows of rumba between Cuba and the Democratic Republic of the Congo. In this chapter, I want to bring attention to Jamaican dancehall's reverberation in Zimbabwe. Reggae and dancehall music, as well as Jamaican popular culture (including language practices, films, clothing, hairstyles and much more), enjoy a very high level of popularity in many African societies. Jamaican artists often fill large stadiums and concert halls in African cities. In this chapter I want to argue, following other scholars, that the high profile of reggae and dancehall in Africa is facilitated through established common ground built on shared experiences of colonialism, racism, oppression, life in the ghetto and resistance, among others. Listeners in Africa can often identify with the topics and stories of Jamaican reggae and dancehall songs, and many artists love to use Jamaican expressions and phrases and incorporate Jamaican verbal arts into their lyrics and performances. By showing examples of Zimdancehall, the Zimbabwean version of dancehall, I want to argue that music, especially in the age of digital communication, is an important and driving force in the manifestation of transatlantic relations between

Jamaica and Africa, which are constantly being recreated, negotiated, renewed and strengthened.

The Jamaican-Zimbabwean relations which are manifest in dancehall culture and built on common ground of shared experiences are exemplified in this chapter through material collected through research in Zimbabwe in 2015–16. The fieldwork carried out by the author included participant observation at Zimdancehall events and places (for instance recording studios), interviews with artists, producers and fans, a documentation of locations and emblematic spaces in Mbare, the Zimdancehall stronghold in Harare, as well as collections, translations and analyses of Zimdancehall lyrics.

The second section will introduce Zimbabwe and discuss the country's transatlantic relations to Jamaica, with special regard to reggae and dancehall music. The emergence of Zimdancehall, as will become obvious, is part of a longer history of Jamaican musical influences in Zimbabwe, which started during the country's liberation struggle against colonialism. These result from the pan-African ideology of Jamaican roots reggae and the Jamaican embracing of African culture and identity, which in turn found fertile ground on the continent. The section also sheds light on the Jamaican musical and cultural impacts on Zimbabwe in the era of dancehall and outlines parallels between the two dancehall cultures. The third section looks at the ghetto more closely and discusses emblematic spaces of Zimdancehall in Mbare, while the fourth section looks at two song examples with a special focus on linguistic practices employed by the artists. The music examples are analysed with regard to their combination of Jamaican and Zimbabwean musical and linguistic elements. A sociolinguistic analysis of the lyrics will provide insights into the artists' multilingual practices in their local and transnational context. The chapter ends with a short conclusion which summarizes the discussion.

JAMAICAN-ZIMBABWEAN CULTURAL RELATIONS AND THE EMERGENCE OF ZIMDANCEHALL

Zimbabwe is a southern African country which is known for its rich precolonial history and distinct architecture (most famously "Great Zimbabwe"). While in precolonial times, southern Africa was inhabited by various ethnic and linguistic groups, colonization and the creation of colonial borders turned Zimbabwe into a multilingual state. While English became the language of prestige and power through colonial rule, chiShona, a Bantu language, is the dominant African language and lingua franca in the country to the present day. IsiNdebele, the second largest linguistic group of the country and also part of the large Bantu family, is spoken in the west and southwest of Zimbabwe and is closely related to the isiZulu language, spoken in adjacent South Africa. Apart from those three major languages, a number of other African languages are spoken by smaller minority groups. During the time of colonialism, from the late nineteenth century to 1980, the African population of what became known as (Southern) Rhodesia engaged in various forms of resistance against colonial rule, including several wars that became known as *Chimurenga* (a word from the chiShona language meaning "struggle"). In fact, the term Chimurenga refers to a range of struggles in Zimbabwean history during and after colonialism. The "first Chimurenga" denotes the anti-colonial fight of the maShona and amaNdebele people against the British South Africa Company, which was won by the latter and led to the colonization of the maShona and amaNdebele territories under the name "(Southern) Rhodesia" (after Cecil Rhodes, a white supremacist and major protagonist in colonial administration, appropriation and oppression in southern Africa) at the end of the nineteenth century. In the second half of the twentieth century, anti-colonial ideologies opened the doors to rebellious music from within and outside the country. Reggae music emerged and became popular internationally at the time of the Zimbabwean liberation struggle, often referred to as the "second Chimurenga". The term Chimurenga also denotes a musical style which was created by Zimbabwean musician Thomas Mapfumo during the liberation struggle; it is characterized by a mix of Zimbabwean traditional music with Western instruments such as the electric guitar, and became a strong marker of resistance against oppression in Zimbabwe. From 1966 until 1979, Zimbabweans fought a guerrilla war against the white Rhodesian government and colonial rule. With lyrics about liberation from oppression, reggae music was a motivating force for the liberation fighters and their supporters. In 1979, the final year of the war for independence, Bob Marley released the song "Zimbabwe" in support of the liberation struggle (interestingly, the lyrics of the song contain rhetoric and words incorporated in the concept of Chimurenga, including "revolutionary", "struggle" and "liberation").[1] When Zimbabwe became independent in 1980, Bob Marley was invited to play at the independence celebrations at Rufaro Stadium. This concert, which was epic in its own way and whose more detailed consideration would go beyond the scope of this chapter, marked the beginning of reggae and dancehall culture in Zimbabwe; since then, numerous Jamaican artists have performed in Zimbabwe, filling stadiums. Marley's concert is still remembered as an important event by Zimbabweans, as well as by Jamaican reggae artists. In her book, *Africa in Stereo*, Tsitsi Ella Jaji recalls the night of the concert:

> Two weeks before my fourth birthday, Zimbabwe gained independence after a long and bloody struggle against first British colonialism and then the racist Ian Smith regime. I remember my father and brother going to Rufaro Stadium in Mbare for the independence festivities in April 1980. My brother shared with my grandfather the name *Tafirenyinka* – meaning "we have died for our country" in Shona – and it seemed fitting that he, the youngest member of our family, should witness the fruition of the costly war for independence. I later learned that Robert Nesta Marley had performed that night, celebrating the new nation by singing "Zimbabwe", a song that had been an anthem of global solidarity with the fight against the Rhodesian Front and its allies. (2014, 1)

Mr Mojo, band member of Morgan Heritage, a reggae band that performed in Harare in recent years, said in an interview with a Zimbabwean newspaper (before their concert):

> Zimbabwe means a lot to us as Jamaicans because you embraced one of our biggest ambassadors in Bob Marley when you celebrated your independence. . . . It's a concert that has resonated around the world in the reggae circles. People know of Bob Marley's performance

> in Zimbabwe on Independence Day. It was a legendary performance.... For us as reggae artists, Zimbabwe is a place we always wanted to perform in one day in our career. To see the land that Bob Marley performed in.... (Mojo, quoted in Matongorere 2015)

This transatlantic narrative of Bob Marley's song and performance thus played an important role in shaping Jamaican-Zimbabwean (musical) relations, as well as further developments in the Zimbabwean music scene, marking an epic moment in global reggae history. This particular narrative, as well as many other songs, performances and events that followed, testify to the transformative power of music, not only in terms of musical developments but also with regard to society at large. The musicologist Jacques Attali wrote in 1985 about the prophetic role of the musician and the potential of music to change the world:

> Poet laureate of power, herald of freedom – the musician is at the same time within society, which protects, purchases, and finances him, and outside it, when he threatens it with his visions.... When he is reassuring, he alienates; when he is disturbing, he destroys; when he speaks too loudly, power silences him. Unless in doing so he is announcing the new clamor and glory of powers in the making. A creator, he changes the world's reality. (1985, 11)

While Zimbabwe has developed its own reggae and dancehall scene and the genre Zimdancehall, Jamaican reggae and dancehall artists continue to enjoy high popularity in the country, and numerous artists and bands from the island have performed in the southern African country since the famous Bob Marley show, such as Jimmy Cliff, Culture, Gregory Isaacs and Shaba Ranks to name just a few. The connections have increased during the recent era of Zimdancehall and in the last years, many Jamaican artists have been invited to perform in the country, among them Beenie Man, Morgan Heritage, Shaggy, Sean Paul, Busy Signal, Jah Cure, Romain Virgo, Christopher Martin, Charly Black and I-Octane. Some of these artists have also recorded songs in local Zimdancehall recording studios during their stay in the Zimbabwe (Kahvu 2017), for instance Busy Signal and I-Octane, who recorded songs at Chill Spot Records. The visits of Jamaican artists shape the music scene in Zimbabwe and the country's relation to Jamaica in many ways. While Zimbabwean dancehall artists such as Ninja Lipsy state that local artists learn from their Jamaican colleagues, who are often seen as role models, the shows also have economic benefits for both sides. In an interview, Chill Sport Records producer Fantan states: "The Jamaican reggae artistes are coming into Zimbabwe because of the good deals they are being offered, where there is money there is a 'drive'. On the other hand, their coming indirectly promotes Zimdancehall music globally" (Kahvu 2017).

As mentioned above, Zimbabwe has also developed its own reggae and dancehall scene, bringing forth new realities in the newly independent country. The first Zimbabwean reggae bands, such as the well-known Transit Crew, evolved in the course of the 1980s. The rise and international popularity of dancehall has had a strong impact in Zimbabwe and has also influenced the establishment of Zimdancehall over the past decade. Zimdancehall is currently the most popular music genre in Zimbabwe, with well-known artists such as Winky D, Soul Jah Love, Lady Squanda, Bounty Lisa, Empress

Shelly, Killer T, Ras Pompy, Tockey Vibes, Da Ruler and Ras Caleb, among many others. As these artist names reveal, there are male and female protagonists in Zimdancehall culture. While male artists seem to dominate the scene in terms of popularity and playing as headliners at shows, there are numerous rising female voices in the Zimdancehall. However, producers, engineers and promoters are usually male which shows that, to this date, the production and marketing of the music is basically a male business.

The actual musical practices show strong parallels to Jamaican dancehall culture and Zimdancehall has adopted many characteristics known from Jamaican music, such as riddim[2] and sound system[3] culture, deejaying[4] (for more information on these cultural practices and their historical development in the context of Jamaican music see for instance Habekost 1993). Moreover, the use of (elements of) Jamaican language, as well as distinct clothing, hair and dance styles, became part and parcel of Zimdancehall.[5] While some of these elements may look like direct imitations of Jamaican role models, the processes involved here are more complex and Jamaican practices are not merely copied but also transformed and developed as they are interpreted in Zimbabwean context. For instance, a Zimdancehall artist may have dreadlocks and use Rastafari rhetoric without embracing the *livity* and ideologies of Rastafari. This shows that while there are obviously many parallels, Zimbabweans also make their own sense out of the elements they adopt from Jamaican reggae and dancehall culture. These processes of cultural contact and translocal music creation will be discussed by employing the notions of the "Black Atlantic" (Gilroy 1993) as a cultural space and "mimesis" (Taussig 1993) as a creative space when analysing examples of Zimdancehall.

Another general parallel in Jamaican and Zimbabwean cultural practices can be seen in Stanley Niaah's (2010) perspective on the dancehall as a "status-granting institution". This is particularly relevant for youths from the ghetto, who have the chance to gain respect and prestige through the dancehall, although they are otherwise marginalized in Zimbabwean society. An article on Zimdancehall published in *Panorama Magazine* (Pano 2014) states, for instance: "Many of these dancehall artists feel marginalized and have constructed a new symbolism of the ghetto, successfully portraying it as a space to organize and assert themselves in a quest for justice and equality." Given this large spectrum of parallels that transgress any borders between reggae and dancehall, there are also many similarities in terms of the lyrics of dancehall songs in Zimbabwe and Jamaica: Zimdancehall songs can sometimes be conscious rebel music to fight down oppression or criticize social injustice, as well as "party tunes"; they can express ghetto life experiences as well as slackness, ghetto rivalry or rivalry between artists. The reception of lyrics promoting slackness, drunkenness or violence also reveals similar discourses in both countries: like in Jamaica, in Zimbabwe many voices criticize and accuse Zimdancehall for having a negative influence on youths' behaviour and blame it for the decay in moral standards (see Stanley Niaah 2008 for the Jamaican context, Pano 2014 for the Zimbabwean context).[6] However, these parallels also testify to common experiences of life in the ghetto and hardship, which present a further stage of shared history following colonialism and oppression. Dancehall culture, in this regard, gives agency to marginalized (young) protagonists, who, by expressing and celebrating their daily life, make visible their lifestyles and struggles which are otherwise not acknowledged or accepted by mainstream society. This also includes the practices, images and language of excess and transgression which characterize dancehall culture. While all too often stigmatized, such practices also push at the boundaries of society and challenge established norms.

EMBLEMATIC SPACES OF ZIMDANCEHALL IN THE GHETTO OF MBARE

The previous section has highlighted some of the general parallels between Zimdancehall and Jamaican dancehall music and culture by showing which practices have been adopted and adapted from Jamaica. This section will take a further step by looking more closely at the aspect of space. As briefly mentioned, Zimdancehall is strongly tied to the ghetto as its locus of origin. The role of the ghetto as the creative hub of Zimdancehall can be explored with regard to what I will refer to as "emblematic spaces". While several ghettos in and around Harare feature Zimdancehall spaces and host artists and studios, in this section I will focus on Mbare, which is the largest and oldest ghetto in Zimbabwe's capital city and which must be regarded as a major stronghold of Zimdancehall culture. The origins of Mbare go back to the early twentieth century, when the ghetto was established as a so-called high-density area during colonialism. At that time, the area was called Harare and served as a housing area for labourers who came both from Zimbabwe and from other neighbouring countries to build the city of Salisbury, founded by the white settlers. After independence, Salisbury was renamed Harare and the former Harare, located in the south of the city, became Mbare.

Figures 28.1 to 28.6 present photos of Zimdancehall spaces in Mbare, which show various aspects, persons and institutions of Zimdancehall culture, such as recording studios, artists and street art. The photos show the creative adoption of further cultural, linguistic and spatial elements of Jamaican dancehall culture, including the two infamous factions "Gaza" and "Gully".

FIGURE 28.1. Producer Levels at Chill Spot Records

FIGURE 28.2. Po po po

FIGURE 28.3. Zimdancehall artists

FIGURE 28.4. Gully Syd

FIGURE 28.5. Gaza

FIGURE 28.6. Mama Gaza's car

As the figures illustrate, the ghetto of Mbare features many sites that display the spatial-material construction of Zimdancehall identity. These material and spatial acts of identity include art, language and the presence of personae, as well as musical practices (here exemplified through the recording studios): there is street art which includes the use of emblematic colours (red, yellow, green and black which index Rastafari as well as the Zimbabwean flag in several of the figures), a Rastaman with turban (figure 28.5), a ganja leaf (figure 28.6), a spliff (that is, a joint, figure 28.5) and a lion (figure 28.4); there are persons who identify as Zimdancehall personae through their clothing style and hair (figures 28.3 and 28.2); and there is Jamaican language use common in dancehall rhetoric and music in written forms, including "po po po" (a sound symbolism for gunshots, figure 28.2), "Gully Syd" (Gully Side) and "Gaza" (figures 28.4, 28.5 and 28.6), "ghetto upliftment", "gaza commander" and "an empire for ghetto youths" (figures 28.5). These iconic and indexical signs, which come together and combine to creative and complex units, mark spaces which become recognized and cherished places of Zimdancehall history in the making and serve as emblematic markers. Stanley Niaah (2008, 2010) explores the dimensions of space with regard to dancehall (as well as raggaeton and kwaito) and their rootedness in the ghetto. She uses the concept of "performance geography", which she defines as "an integral and unexplored dimension of cultural studies and cultural geography that expands the definitions of cultural geography and performance studies to include the ways in which people living in particular locations give these locations identity through certain acts" (2010, 32). People come together in these recognized spaces to live and produce dancehall culture, which also creates a community feeling, or a community of practice (Eckert 2000). Figures 28.1–28.6 illustrate the use of many signs adopted from Jamaican reggae and dancehall culture, as well as those of Zimbabwean origin which result in new creations and reflect identity processes that are characteristic not only of a Zimdancehall culture but also as part of "Black Atlantic culture" which links Africa and its diaspora. The concept of the "Black Atlantic" here serves to address shared transnational history and heritage of colonialism and the transatlantic slave trade and in particular relates to a common black identity that was created based on those shared experiences (Gilroy 1993). This identity and the cultural productions underlying have been acts of resistance to racism in the making of modernity and constitute strong transnational cultural ties (Gilroy 1993). The examples outlined here reflect that the ghetto, in this context, constitutes a "common space" (Stanley Niaah 2008) in which Black Atlantic music culture can flourish (Gilroy 1993), producing new creative forms and serving as a tool for identity formation. As Stanley Niaah (2010) sums up, these practices reveal "common genealogies, the common space linking the Old World with elements of the New World. Here, distance is inconsequential and space is about flows, with the local and the global, temporal and spatial influences all feeding each other" (179). The adoption of Jamaican elements in Zimdancehall is of particular significance here and links Africa and diaspora in a new postcolonial creation reflecting the multilayered and complex Black Atlantic: the anthropologist Michael Taussig, in his seminal work *Mimesis and Alterity* (1993), wrote about the power of replication and the way mimetic practices serve as a creative strategy in postcolonial contexts. I want to argue that shared experiences of colonialism, oppression and a struggle for self-determination enable the flow and translation of cultural, musical and linguistic practices and encourage Zimbabweans' strong appreciation for Jamaican music and popular culture. Mimesis, in this context, becomes a complex process with far deeper roots than the simple act of imitation can tell: scholars like Taussig (1993) and Bhabha (1994) have developed theories of mimesis or mimicry in colonial contexts, whereby the act of imitation is more than simply that, but a powerful tool of changing reality and even resistance that the colonized employed when appropriating and remaking the culture of the colonizer. In the transatlantic postcolonial context, mimesis also serves as a tool of building pan-African relations and exploring entangled futures of shared histories. In this regard, Zimdancehall features a double-inverse relationship with historical depth: While Jamaican reggae and dancehall music have been influenced and inspired by the island's African heritage, Jamaican music and culture now continue to impact the Zimbabwean (as well as other African) popular music scenes. This reflects that the Atlantic is a dynamic contact zone with multilayered complexity whose entanglements inspire the creation of mimetic cultural productions which are also acts of identity. Jaji (2014) makes a similar point in her analysis of the role that African diaspora music from the Americas plays on the African continent. For instance, discussing the impact of Bob Marley's song "Buffalo Soldier" in Zimbabwe, she explains that not all aspects of the song's meaning were taken up in Zimbabwe, but states that "what came across the airwaves loud and clear was that the 'dreadlock rasta[s]' fighting for survival shared with us a legacy of resistance – Chimurenga in the Shona language – that had yielded our independence" (Jaji 2014, 2). The author takes this a step further by regarding transatlantic entanglements and influences as a manifestation of pan-African solidarity.

This and the previous section have discussed parallels in the Jamaican and Zimbabwean dancehall cultures and their emblematic spaces. In the next section we will turn to the language, which shows Zimdancehall artists' versatile linguistic creativity and their ways with Jamaican language practices. These do not only add a distinct flavour to Zimbabwean dancehall music but also further illustrate the points made in this and the previous sections regarding mimesis as creative formation of postcolonial identity.

CREATIVE LANGUAGE PRACTICES

As the discussion has so far established, while Zimdancehall adapts numerous elements from Jamaican dancehall culture, there are also typical Zimbabwean aspects and new ways and contexts in which Zimdancehall artists rearrange Jamaican resources and combine them with Zimbabwean practices. The most obvious is the combination of heavily Jamaican-influenced riddims with lyrics in the chiShona language, the main African lingua franca of the country. Additionally, the Zimdancehall riddims may also exhibit Zimbabwean musical elements, such as the infamous and award-winning Zimbo Flavor Riddim, produced by Levels/Chill Spot Records. Zimdancehall also developed in the context of other Zimbabwean and southern African popular music genres, such as sungura and kwaito, and is strongly related to urban groove, a Zimbabwean version of hip-hop, which dominated the country in the first decade of this millennium. In this section, we will take a look at two Zimdancehall songs, which illustrate various aspects of the creation of Jamaican-Zimbabwean music culture. As these examples will show, language is an important factor in Zimdancehall, as the artists, most of whom are young, draw from large multilingual and often transnational and global repertoires, using their linguistic resources creatively to compose songs that are in vogue and express urban identities that are both local and global, addressing issues of young Zimbabwean lifestyle while at the same time expressing transatlantic relations and finding their place in global dancehall culture.

The first song I want to discuss is "Satan Sejampa Amafence" by Qubella and Mido Killa, a combination of artists that illustrates the multilingual nature of the Zimbabwean state, as the two artists sing in isiNdebele and chiShona, respectively, the two major African languages spoken in the country. It should be noted here that Zimdancehall, based in Harare, which is the country's capital and also the urban centre of Mashonaland, is mostly chiShona-dominated, and the majority of artists use the chiShona language (alongside English and Jamaican linguistic resources). This reflects the political situation of the country, which recognizes chiShona as the dominant language used in various official domains, especially in Mashonaland. Matabeleland, the western and southwestern region where the isiNdebele language is predominantly spoken, is strongly influenced by other popular music genres such as South African House and does not host much Zimdancehall. Therefore, isiNdebele is not a language that is often used in Zimdancehall. However, the song "Satan Sejampa Amafence" constitutes one of the few examples of Zimdancehall songs which feature the isiNdebele language. The artist Qubella is concerned with bringing isiNdebele into Zimdancehall and proudly refers to himself as "Ndebele King". In the course of time, it seems likely that more local Ndebele artists will emerge on the Zimdancehall horizon which might change the picture in the future. Example 1 presents parts of the lyrics of the song and illustrates the creative multilingual practices of the artists. The song is concerned with the misappropriation of funds in churches by pastors and deacons, and the ways in which churchgoers are cheated.

Example 1: "Satan Sejampa Amafence"[7]

Chorus	
u*satan*i se*jamp*a ama*fence*	Satan is now jumping over fences
Ubugqili sebugewele ema*church*	cheating is now full in churches
sebesidla imali zomnikelo	they are eating money for offerings
bethenga izimota logetsi	buying cars and electricity
bayabhadabhada ngama*verse*	They cover up (lit. "smear layers") with verses
budlubu i*double* i*cash*	eating double cash
bazalwane liqaphele	church people be careful
ayi ngifuna liqaphele ayeha	ayi I want you to be careful ayeha
Verse	
Qubella wapedza ipapo	Qubella you finished there
wataura *shuwa*	you said the truth
ma*dikon*i arikunova mari	deacons are spending money
hazvisi zveguwa warikutora mari	it's not gossip they are taking money
mu*church* votenga mota magetsi	from church buying cars and electricity
hunhu wavo hwakashata saka	their behaviour is bad so
vanhu vasatani	people of Satan
Mido ama*pastor* lenzinsuku	Mido pastors these days
asisaba*trust*i	we don't trust them

Musically, the track sounds like a typical dancehall riddim in terms of the beat and the bassline, but with an electronic *mbira* melody which adds a Zimbabwean flavour to the riddim. This riddim is quite typical of the more strongly Zimbabwe-influenced Zimdancehall riddims and is very similar to the above-mentioned Zimbo Flavor Riddim. There are other Zimdancehall riddims which do not show Zimbabwean elements so obviously and sound very much like Jamaican dancehall riddims. The lyrics of the song "Satan Sejampa Amafence" show a combination of isiNdebele (unmarked) and chiShona (underlined), with many words derived from English (in italics). The artists smoothly combine resources from their multilingual repertoires and adapt English words to African Bantu phonology and morphology: they combine English words with chiShona and isiNdebele noun classes (for example, *ama-fence, ma-dikoni, mu-church*), add "*-a*" to English verbs ending in consonants (because Bantu verbs end in "*-a*" in indicative mood, for example, *sejampa*, derived from "jump") and manipulate the pronunciation of English words in order to fit into Bantu phonology (for example, *shuwa* for "sure"). These creative multilingual practices illustrate the fluid nature of language and the agency of the speakers, as exemplified by the concept of "translanguaging" (García and Li Wei 2014). Jamaican techniques are also employed by the artists and include the art of deejaying (see note 4 to this chapter), the calling of the other artist's stage name at the beginning of the deejay part (which creates a kind of "big-up effect" and expresses respect for the fellow artist, marked in bold in the example above), and the use of the autotune effect,[8] which has long been established in the Jamaican dancehall. The creative musical bricolage as well as the translanguaging practices illustrate creativity beyond mimesis: mimetic practices are incorporated into complex transatlantic creations which combine Jamaican and Zimbabwean elements and produce a distinct version of Black Atlantic music culture.

The second song to be discussed here is Bounty Lisa's "Basa Rangu", a song in the chiShona language in which the artist incorporates numerous Jamaican linguistic elements. Bounty Lisa chose her name in recognition of the Jamaican deejay Bounty Killer,[9] to whom she listened as a teenager. In the lyrics of her song "Basa Rangu" she makes direct reference to other Jamaican artists, namely Tanya Stephens and Tommy Lee Sparta. Example 2 presents parts of the lyrics of the song.

Example 2: "Basa Rangu"[10]

Intro 1:	
mi name **Bounty Lisa**	my name is Bounty Lisa
representing **Chillspot Records**	representing Chillspot Records
bigup **Propa Bless**, *bigup* **Jusa**	bigup Propa Bless, bigup Jusa
outa dehya . . . yuh see mi?	outta there . . . you see me?
Intro 2:	
mi name **Bounty Lisa**	my name is Bounty Lisa
anotimisa tomupisa	who steps up – we will burn them
gore rino tirikutyisa	this year we are scary
Big up **Jusa**, yo **Proper Bless**	Big up Jusa, yo Proper Bless
eh yo **Tanya Stevens**	eh yo Tanya Stevens
yo big up **Sparta** *blame di yutes*	yo big up Sparta blame di yutes
ayo lecoo kaboom	ayo lecoo kaboom
Yo **Levels**, **chillspot** *tell dem seh*	Yo Levels, chillspot tell dem seh

Chorus	
Ibasa rangu **Bounty** ndiro zita rangu	it is my work, Bounty is my name
Musandivhiringidzira pabasa rangu	don't disturb me at my work
Mondivengera mangoma kubasa kwangu	you hate me? Music is my job
One to dem kutaura wevavengi vangu	one to dem: talking to my haters
Verse 1	
Rega ndiva*tip*ire matsaga mabonga	let me tell them matsaga mabonga
Ndima*tipe* **Bounty Lisa**	I tell them Bounty Lisa
ndini ndaakutonga	I am the one who is ruling
Rangu itarenda, haridi mushonga,	Mine is a talent, it doesn't need witchcraft
kubva kare muchizviona makapenga	from way back you saw yourself off the hook
Bounty Lisa Duppy Lady zita ndatora	Bounty Lisa Duppy Lady the name that I took
tiri pa **Chillspot** ne*gang*a chakatyora	we are at Chillspot with the gang chilling
zvekuimba *steady* ne *lyric* rinotyora	to sing steady with lyrics that will break you
Ayo **Sparta**, mira ndima*tipe* magora	Ayo Sparta let me tell those haters
ndipe *mix* ne *leaf* ndimbosunga chamba	give me the mix with leaf I roll a blunt of weed
zvangu zvauya vavengi	my time is here the haters
motojamba jamba	tremble (jump up and down)
ndiri kuvava kunge tea yawanda masamba	I am bitter like tea with many tea leaves
wese wekuMbare imombe yemudanga	everyone from Mbare is a cow from the kraal
wakaita dzungu murukova vokunhonga	if you are confused in the stream they will pick you up
flow rangu rinonyudza kunge rukova	my flow is deep like a river
hatikwate ndinenge lacto ndakakora	we are not afraid, I am thick milk, I am thick
Murivapfanha ndokutumai	you are small kids
kunotenga *Koka Kora*	I can send you to buy Coca Cola
. . .	

In the lyrics of this song, Bounty Lisa employs a translanguaging technique by creatively combining linguistic resources from chiShona (unmarked), English and Jamaican (both in italics). She also makes direct reference to artists, producers and promoters (names in bold) in order to express respect, which is a common practice in (Zim)dancehall songs. The intro, in particular, is full of Jamaican speech forms, which in the Zimbabwean context also serve as markers of authenticity due to Jamaican's status as the international language of reggae and dancehall. Around the globe, we can witness the emergence of reggae and dancehall songs in local languages as well as in Jamaican. It is important to note that Zimdancehall artists, as well as many other youths in Zimbabwe and other African societies, invest a lot of time and effort in learning Jamaican through music and the internet. While Jamaican also has a high impact on youth language practices in places like the United Kingdom (which has influenced recent sociolinguistic approaches to those new youth varieties as "multiethnolects"), the situation is different from that in many African societies. In the United Kingdom, Jamaican linguistic practices have come into existence basically through the presence of a large Jamaican diaspora in the United Kingdom, whose youths have a great impact on mainstream youth culture and language in those societies. With regard to Africa, however, with a few exceptions such as parts of Ethiopia, there is no significant Jamaican community and thus the impact of Jamaican cultural and linguistic practices is based on a high prestige awarded to Jamaican practices, especially among African youths. Music plays the most important role in this regard and must be seen as the major driving force in the dissemination and spread of the Jamaican language and other social practices. In this regard, the role of Jamaica's cultural productions must be highlighted, as the island's music, culture and language are not only important subjects of mimetic processes "back home on the continent" but also have such a great impact that local youth in Zimbabwe invest time and effort in learning the Jamaican language through music and the internet. This results in the creative combination of Jamaican and local languages in Zimdancehall and situates the music in a local and global context simultaneously; it also helps the youths of Zimbabwe to express a transatlantic global urban identity which is at the same time uniquely Zimbabwean.

CONCLUSION

While Zimdancehall artists adapt many Jamaican practices, including language and music styles, they do not merely copy cultural meanings; instead the mimetic practices reveal that they use Jamaican resources in new ways and new contexts, reflecting the creativity and bricolage of Zimdancehall. This chapter has shown that Jamaican music has had a great impact in Zimbabwe ever since the time of Bob Marley's legendary performance in the country. The development of Zimdancehall illustrates new transatlantic creations which combine Jamaican and African practices in Zimbabwean contexts and express an identity that is part of a new Black Atlantic culture. The mimesis and enacting of Jamaican cultural, music and linguistic practices in the local dancehall space testifies to the impact of Jamaican music on the African continent in general, and Zimbabwe in particular. As argued in this chapter, these transatlantic cross-fertilizations are facilitated through shared and common experiences of colonialism and oppression in the ghetto. With regard to the latter, we have seen that the ghetto – in Zimbabwe as in Jamaica – constitutes a creative breeding of dancehall and that several emblematic spaces have been produced which serve as locations of identity practices. Zimdancehall thus presents a prime example of the flourishing Black Atlantic music culture, which is characterized by transatlantic flows and pan-African solidarity (Stanley Niaah 2010; Jaji 2014).

ACKNOWLEDGEMENTS

I am indebted to the Zimdancehall community of Harare, in particular the Chill Spot Records family in Mbare, for their support and for sharing their knowledge and insights with me. Moreover, I am grateful to the Global South Studies Center who financed my research. I also want to express my gratitude to the organizers and participants of the Global Reggae conference 2017 in Kingston, Jamaica, for the opportunity to present my research and for the stimulating feedback. Finally, thanks are due to Mary Chambers for proofreading and copy editing the manuscript.

NOTES

1. It is worth pointing out that the song "Zimbabwe" is connected to the African continent in another way: according to the oral history of the Rastafari community in Shashemene, Ethiopia, repatriate brother Flippins helped to write the song during Bob Marley's visit to Shashemene at the end of the 1970s.
2. A "riddim" is the instrumental version of a song. These versions used to be pressed on the b-sides of 45 record singles. Deejays (see below) would "talk over" or "toast" (that is, sing in a distinct speech-style) on the riddim in the dancehall while it also became common that a riddim would be "voiced" by various artists in the studio, which means that different artists would record their song versions on the same riddim.
3. A "sound sytsem" is like a mobile discotheque, operated by "selectors" (who select and play the songs and versions) and "deejays" (or MCs) who talk over the music and animate the audience. For more information see for instance Habekost (1993)
4. "Deejaying" denotes a distinct singing speech-style that deejays in the dancehall and artists employ as they deliver their lyrics to a riddim.
5. The names of these Zimdancehall artists also reflect Jamaican influences in naming practices and especially an adoption of titles and terms of address used in Rastafari, such as "Ras" and "Empress". For more details on Zimbabwean and Jamaican titles and stage names see Hollington (2018)
6. These demonizations of Zimdancehall also include dance practices.
7. In this excerpt of the lyrics, unmarked parts are in isiNdebele, while English and borrowings from Englsh are in italics and parts in chiShona are underlined. Moreover, both artists call out their fellow artist's name at the beginning of their deejay parts, which is marked in bold here.
8. Autotune is a pitch-altering audio processor which is commonly used as a sound effect in music production of popular music.
9. See http://www.pindula.co.zw/Bounty_Lisa.
10. In this excerpt of the lyrics, chiShona is unmarked and English and Jamaican parts are in italics. The artist frequently calls out the names of fellow Jamaican and Zimbabwean artists and protagonists as well as the name of the record label, which is marked in bold.

REFERENCES

Alleyne, Mervyn C. 1988. *Roots of Jamaican Culture*. London: Pluto Press.

Attali, Jacques. 1985. *Noise. The Political Economy of Music*. Minneapolis: University of Minnesota Press.

Bhabha, Homi. 1994. *The Location of Culture*. London: Routledge

Bilby, Kenneth. 1992. *Drums of Defiance: Maroon Music from the Earliest Free Black Communities of Jamaica*. Washington, DC: Smithsonian Folkways.

———. 2005. *True Born Maroons*. Gainesville, FL: University of Florida Press.

Cassidy, Frederic G. 1961. *Jamaica Talk: Three Hundred Years of the English Language in Jamaica*. London: Macmillan.

Cassidy, Frederic G., and Robert B. Le Page. 1967. *Dictionary of Jamaican English*. Cambridge: Cambridge University Press.

Eckert, Penelope. 2000. *Linguistic Variation as Social Practice: The Linguistic Construction of Identity in Belten High*. Oxford: Blackwell.

Farquharson, Joseph T. 2012. "The African Lexis in Jamaican: Its Linguistic and Sociohistorical Significance". PhD dissertation, University of the West Indies, Mona, Jamaica.

García, Ofelia, and Li Wei. 2014. *Translanguaging: Language, Bilingualism and Education*. London: Palgrave Macmillan.

Gilroy, Paul. 1993. *The Black Atlantic: Modernity and Double Consciousness*. Cambridge, MA: Harvard University Press.

Habekost, Christian. 1993. *Verbal Riddim: The Politics and Aesthetics of African-Caribbean Dub Poetry*. Amsterdam: Rodopi

Hollington, Andrea. 2018. "Transatlantic translanguaging in Zimdancehall: Reassessing Linguistic Creativity in Youth Language Practices". *Mouth* 3: 105–23.

Jaji, Tsitsi Ella. 2014. *Africa in Stereo: Modernism, Music, and Pan-African Solidarity*. Oxford: Oxford University Press.

Kavhu, Sharon. 2017. "Jamaican Artists' Shows in Zim: A 50–50 Deal for Zimdancehall". *Southern Times*, Zimbabwe, 1 September. https://southernafrican.news/2017/09/01/jamaican-artistes-shows-in-zim-a-50-50-deal-for-zimdancehall/.

Lewin, Olive. 2000. *Rock It Come Over: The Folk Music of Jamaica*. Kingston: University of the West Indies Press.

Marshall, Emily Z. 2012. *Anansi's Journey: A Story of Jamaican Cultural Resistance*. Kingston: University of the West Indies Press.

Matongorere, Nigel. 2015. "Zim Is Home of Reggae: Mr Mojo". *Daily News*, Zimbabwe, 19 November. https://www.dailynews.co.zw/articles/2015/11/19/zim-is-home-of-reggae-mr-mojo.

Pano. 2014. "Revisiting ZimDancehall". *Panorama Magazine*, 15 November. http://www.panorama.co.zw/revisiting-zimdancehall/.

Stanley Niaah, Sonjah. 2008. "A Common Space: Dancehall, Kwaito and the Mapping of New World Music and Performance". *World of Music* 50, no. 2: 35–50.

———. 2010. *Dancehall: From Slave Ship to Ghetto*. Ottawa: University of Ottawa Press.

Stewart, Dianne M. 2005. *Three Eyes for the Journey: African Dimensions of the Jamaican Religious Experience*. Oxford: Oxford University Press.

Taussig. Michael. 1993. *Mimesis and Alterity: A Particular History of the Senses*. London: Routledge.

Warner-Lewis, Maureen. 1977. "The Nkuyu: Spirit Messengers of the Kumina". Pamphlet, University of the West Indies, West Indies Collection.

———. 1993. "African Continuities in the Rastafari Belief System". *Caribbean Quarterly* 39, nos. 3–4: 108–23.

———. 2003. *Central Africa in the Caribbean: Transcending Time, Transforming Culture*. Kingston: University of the West Indies Press.

———. 2007. *Archibald Monteath: Igbo, Jamaican, Moravian*. Kingston: University of the West Indies Press.

White, Bob W. 2002. "Congolese Rumba and Other Cosmopolitanisms". *Cahiers d'Études Africaines* 42, no. 168: 663–86.

CHAPTER 29

Black Music, Popular Culture and Existential Capital

The Relationship between Appropriation and Originality

BRUNO BARBOZA MUNIZ

THIS CHAPTER IS CONCERNED WITH THE RELATIONSHIP BETWEEN appropriation and originality in music production. I revise empirical material collected in the last eight years of research with producers, musicians and dancers. These artists appropriate elements from other artists and are most of the time conscious of doing so. However, they also value originality. How is this possible?

Since 2010, I have conducted ethnographic research and interviewed agents involved with *baile funk* music. Baile funk is a style of electronic music associated with the favelas, areas of Rio de Janeiro marked by segregation and lack of services. Before this research on baile funk, I conducted interviews with producers remixing traditional music for a project called *Mauritsstadt Dub*, an album composed of two compact discs. The first CD contains traditional music from Pernambuco, Brazil, while the second one contains dub remixes of these songs. My objective when analysing this material collected during previous research with popular music was to find a common theme cross-cutting the interviews. With this objective in mind, I noticed that debates on the conflict between copying and creativity raised very fruitful conversations with different creative agents. Producers, musicians and dancers revealed during semi-structured interviews their opinions about the relationship between appropriation and creativity. The idea that appropriating aesthetic elements created by others is a creative and valid strategy was evident in most interviews. Curiously enough, interviewees who used or appropriated elements to create music or dance had their own notions of originality as well. In sum, there is evidence that appropriation and the praising of originality can coexist in the same musical scene.

In order to understand how they interrelate, it is important to pay attention to music making and how cultural repertoires and practices are processed, mediated and dislocated. In the first section, I introduce the historical moment when dub appeared and discuss the influence it had on electronic music and consequently baile funk music.

This discussion about dub music serves to situate baile funk music inside the Black Atlantic tradition described by Gilroy (1993). Following this historical discussion, this chapter analyses the notion of existential capital and how it aids the comprehension of the relationship between appropriation and originality. Stealing as a creative practice is also discussed through the contributions of the musician Siba and hip-hop producer Rodrigo Brandão. After this debate, DJ Marlboro provides an interesting example of how the position occupied in the market by the agent affects the judgement of appropriation and copying. The last empirical material discussed in this chapter is about the *passinho* dance, a style of dance that has gained visibility in Rio de Janeiro. Passinho is based on a collage of different steps. However, as will be shown, dancers also had their own conceptions regarding originality.

DUB AND CULTURAL SHIFTS

Stuart Hall and Cornel West identify three different "coordinates" – or one could say, historical changes – happening during the last century. First, one should consider the "displacement of European models of high culture" (Hall 1996, 468). Second, the United States emerges as the "centre of global cultural production and circulation" (Hall 1996, 468). Lastly, both authors mention the "emergence of decolonized sensibilities" (Hall 1996, 469). Hall uses as examples the struggles for civil rights and the black movement. When developed by Bourdieu (2010), the term "cultural capital" had a strong connection with high status symbols and the necessary skills to enjoy highbrow art. Nevertheless, according to Hall, the definition of culture itself has changed. How does one account for the value of popular culture today? I refer to the concept of value in the broader sense proposed by Bourdieu, considering the articulation of social, cultural and economic variables. Cornel West (2000), however, argues for an existential reading of the term cultural capital, proposing the term "existential capital".

Since Hall's article was first published in 1996, the three coordinates mentioned in the first paragraph of this section suffered modifications. However, some of Hall's (1996) qualifications about Cornel's coordinates gained, in my opinion, growing relevance. One must pay attention to the ambivalence in the relationship between popular culture and European high culture. For instance, originality is still an important guiding principle to judge culture, even popular culture. Many producers interviewed for this chapter still seem to support this statement, even though those same producers recognize that stealing ideas from others is necessary to create.

Ambivalence seems to be an inescapable word when it comes to comprehending popular culture. This is the main reason why Hall (1996, 471) prefers to depart from "grand counter-narratives" by focusing on strategies. He criticizes the assumption that "the system always wins", which is according to him a protective strategy, employed by some "American cultural critics" against occasional defeats (471). The ambivalence of popular culture brings a range of difficulties regarding its sociological analysis. Value is "contingent and situational" and mediated by very different processes, such as labour and affect (Skeggs, 2010, 35). The shift from modernism to postmodernism brought new strategies and opportunities in the popular culture field, meanwhile old hierarchies have lost centrality (Hall 1996).

At the same time, Hall argues that even though there is more space for differences (for example, cultural, sexual and racial), this fascination might simply mean the desire to experience a touch of the exotic, while those understood as the "other" remain silenced. There is indeed a new movement reconfiguring geopolitics (Gilroy 2010). Some inequalities remain the same while new forms of repression emerge, including a change in racialized structures established since the nineteenth century. According to Gilroy (2010, 4): "The north Atlantic no longer lies at the centre."

In this context of change, one artist gained immense relevance in the last half-century: Bob Marley. In Paul Gilroy's (2010, 88) words: "Politically and culturally, it embodies a decisive shift away from US centred discourses on blackness and its limits. Marley's stardom therefore represents a move into what might be termed a 'Third World' mode of freedom struggle." The contradictions involving Bob Marley's appropriation by capitalist interests, especially after his death, is accompanied by an almost "saintly quality" (91) acquired by him during that period. I mentioned Bob Marley for two reasons. First, it shows how a rebellious ideology can be voiced worldwide, while putting Jamaica at the centre of the entertainment industry. Second, Marley's stardom helped to shed light on a range of different innovations occurring in Jamaica, including a very influential but less noticed trend – dub music.

In Jamaica during the 1970s, it was extremely common for reggae songs to be released on 16-inch vinyl records; one side of the record contained the original song and the other side contained the dub version. These were the so-called dubplates. A dub version is a reconstruction of an original song, normally a reggae song, which is stripped of most of its instruments. The bass and the drums remain as structuring elements, even though one or the other might be momentarily taken out as part of the dynamics of the track. In a dub remix, the elements that were initially removed (such as horns, voice and guitars) are not absent all the time and might phantasmagorically come back processed by reverbs and delays. These audio effects are employed to create a dream-like environment that contrasts with the precision of the drum and bass section. Curiously, much earlier than the term "drum and bass" appeared to designate an electronic music style, the two words already appeared together in 16-inch records from Jamaica as a reference to the dub version of a reggae song (Veal 2007).

Different authors have noticed a conflict between dub music and copyright. Scholars have discussed the challenge dub poses to the conception of the artist as an originator (Hitchcock 1993). The category "producer" is not exactly easy to delimitate and the activities one producer can engage in are quite vast. The widespread use of this category reveals changes in the music business and it stresses the emergence of new aesthetic practices. One of the foundations behind the emergence of the producer as a key aesthetic character lies in Jamaica. King Tubby and Lee Perry represent two producers and sound engineers that gained recognition and are praised as important influences in dub. Tubby and Perry profoundly influenced electronic music.

If one analyses the context of music production in Jamaica at the 1970s, dub music inaugurated many of the conflicts that emerged afterwards regarding copyright in songs using loops or citations. Producers and owners from studios would record musicians and reuse the material without paying them again (Veal 2007). For a time, dub music was not played on the radio in Jamaica because the musician's union was legally fighting to receive the copyright revenues. However, the dub versions were played during sound system parties and they had enough power to popularize songs and create their own market. One important use of the dub version was in the sound system party. Since the vocals were removed, an empty space was created for the toaster to improvise talks and melodies over the beats (Veal 2007). In hip-hop and baile funk music, the MC has a similar function.

Working with repetition also has to do with an emphasis on the process, on the moment, instead of trying to preserve the artistic object. Veal (2007) argues that a West African tradition called Mbari and associated with the Igbo people might have influenced the fluidity of certain performances already outside the African continent, including dub. Copyright pushes in a different direction, since it aims to preserve the value of artistic creations, which are taken as finished objects that should be admired. In this context, "when the product is preserved or venerated, the impulse to repeat the process is compromised" (Achebe 1984, ix).

Dub music had the producer or engineer as a central reference and represented an analogic precursor of contemporary electronic music, including hip-hop and baile funk. The centrality of the bass and the drums as well as the use of effects to create a psychedelic environment were already aesthetic strategies employed by producers in Jamaica back in the 1970s. The use of effects, tracks, loops or repetitive rhythmic structures to create a live collage and the emphasis on the beat are characteristics baile funk have in common with dub and hip-hop. The lower frequencies are also important in baile funk. A person attending a baile will feel that the physical presence of the sound affects your body as a whole. During a baile funk in Rocinha, I could not stay next to the large speakers, even though I saw many people standing there and dancing. Nevertheless, the term "bass culture" (Henriques 2010) is not completely precise to describe baile funk music. In reggae and dancehall, the bass line is extremely relevant to identify the beat or riddim (Veal 2007). Yet, in funk, the high-pitched sounds have a defining role regarding the beat.

Since the 2000s, funk has incorporated more and more rhythms from the Afro-Brazilian tradition. For example, one funk beat was given the name *tamborzão* and it has many similarities with a traditional beat called *maculelê* (Sobrinho 2013). Similar to capoeira, an Afro-Brazilian art form practised across the world, maculelê is a mixture of dance and fight. The player crosses swords (*grimas* or *esgrimas*), which are normally represented by wooden rods, making a noise that accompanies a beat. A person playing a drum called an *atabaque*, made of wood and rawhide, produces the beat.

THE VALUE OF POPULAR CULTURE AND EXISTENTIAL CAPITAL

Traditional Bourdieusian approaches consider how agents use different forms of capital to obtain better positions within a certain field. One can use this Bourdieusian idea to understand how music producers compete using social connections, status and taking advantage of the positions they occupy. Literature has associated cultural capital with high-status practices (Lamont and Lareau 1988). Therefore, how could one discuss styles such as hip-hop, baile funk and dancehall using this concept if they are all originally associated with low-status symbols? Mediations might translate the music coming from underprivileged groups in a way that it becomes a symbol of high status. Bourdieu (2010) already noticed this possibility regarding art more broadly. However, hip-hop, baile funk, dancehall and other scenes did not prosper only because of mediations allowing their consumption by privileged groups. It is crucial to acknowledge the value emanating from communities and specific localities or events.

The idea of existential capital serves as an instrument to understand how popular culture creates collective value. Proposing the concept of existential capital depends on a critical stance toward Bourdieu, as well as toward many later readings of his work that focus on the vocabulary of capitals and field theory (Nettleton 2013). For the purposes of this chapter, two critiques developed by Born (2010) are necessary. First, in Bourdieu, there is almost a refusal "to address the art object and its aesthetic properties, and to allow them to play a part in the unfolding analysis" (Born 2010, 178). Second, he seems to explain social processes exclusively in competitive terms. Agents are constantly waging war, struggling or competing to obtain a privileged position in any given field (Born 2010).

Affective and embodied interactions are as important, if not more so, than rationality or classifications in order to assess how people relate to music. Trying to understand affect means analysing what people share and not only how they compete for resources. Nettleton (2013, 205) used the concept of "existential capital", an embodied capital marked by non-instrumental characteristics, to describe a kind of value that is "appreciated for its own sake" (207). She argues that looking at passionate relations instead of "instrumental and calculative" strategies allows us to understand what "people share in common" (197).

Cultural practices, common experiences and memories all create collective value and the term "existential capital" serves to describe it. Many people in Rio de Janeiro love baile funk and funk generates existential capital based on what people share, spaces, moments in life, memories, neighbourhoods and skills. People that may not have met face-to-face share preferences, affects and forms of knowledge. Those engaging with baile funk music create new ways of dressing, moving and talking (Essinger 2005; Mizrahi 2010; Muniz 2016).

According to Childs (2000, 37), existential capital "is the name given to those assets we desire and require as human beings to secure our needed sense of belonging and of self-esteem". Existential capital allows us to see fields as "passionately defined" (Nettleton 2013, 197). This possibility leads the way to an affective reading of Bourdieu (Wacquant 2015; Muniz 2016). It allows the comprehension of how value can be collectively created and used. But if in Nettleton's analysis of fell running sports can dilute inequality, according to Childs, "there is existential capital to be gained from adherence to racist ideologies" (Childs 2000, 37).

White supremacism also mobilizes existential capital. As Cornel West (2000, 264) has noted when introducing the term, "many Western peoples get much existential capital from racist illusions, from ideologies of Race". Therefore, the concept of existential capital should not be employed to promote the idea that Brazil is in any way a racial democracy in which collective value supersedes racism and inequality. In fact, the criminalization of baile funk music in Rio de Janeiro exemplifies very explicitly the divisions established by racist structures (Lopes 2012).

STEALING AS A CREATIVE STRATEGY

Appropriation in music is driven by affect. In electronic music, for example, samplers are a very common way to provoke reactions in the audience. Remixes, short citations, sounds and talks from movies, all those alternatives can be introduced during a song to provide a connection between the people listening to it and a certain year, place or time of their lives.

Rodrigo Brandão, a hip-hop producer from São Paulo who also presented a television show on MTV, told me that he was making an effort to give a Brazilian identity to his beats. Sampling was a good strategy for him, serving to reinforce a certain sense of belonging or connectedness:

> I was talking to a friend of mine: "I think I'm going to sample a lot of things, no shame." Because these days, to be sued by someone, "that guy sampled my music and stuff", the guy has to have sold many copies. The guy has to have made some money out of it. And if one day I get to that point. Cool! . . .
>
> It's not exactly the same thing, but more important than if it's legal or not is that a certain piece of music made me very emotional and I'm going to make another song from it myself. I will not stop doing it because the law is saying that it's irregular. Fuck the law in that sense, right?

One can only use the word "stealing" when considering cultural practices from the perspective of private property and originality. Reproducing themes and patterns is not exclusive to recent electronic popular culture, even though it seems almost common sense to say that lowbrow practices loot while high-status cultural practices seek originality. Those discourses regarding popular culture emerge when one analyses culture from a hierarchical perspective. Words such as "lowbrow" or "highbrow" serve to describe this hierarchy.

If one looks at popular culture through the lenses of existential capital, the abovementioned difficulty in understanding authorship within popular culture is attenuated. First, the concept of existential capital aims to overcome the hierarchy between high and low and presupposes the idea of cultural capital, which is associated with originality and individual creativity. Second, and most importantly, talking about existential capital allows for the comprehension of popular culture's value by acknowledging its collective and affective importance, including the role it plays in creating affective communities (Gandhi 2006).

Playing with patterns is not a recent practice in music. The fact that turntables and digital equipment do the job does not change completely the basic aesthetic idea of working with repetition and referencing present in many different cultural contexts. Nevertheless, for legal reasons, it is not always so simple to work based on those two principles, since many phonograms are copyrighted. In this context, the narrative of stealing might gain a political edge. Stealing music as a form of composition seems to instigate an interesting question: is creativity also about taking from others? Many musicians and producers believe that a certain extent of "stealing" is important to be creative and interesting; debates occur when they reveal the extent they think one can take from others and the strategies employed to "cheat". For instance, one can be inspired by another melody and change only a few notes to create a new one. DJs often use effects and change the phonogram in order to create a new unrecognizable version of a small loop extracted from another song. Producers create completely new songs based on this process.

Siba, a musician from Pernambuco in the northeast of Brazil, who has different projects involving *maracatu*, *ciranda* and other styles, told me during an interview:

> We're always robbing each other, right? But the fool does not exist only from the top to the bottom. Everyone is always somehow taking advantage of the access to information. That's it. In principle, people are always robbing each other in some way, artists are even worse. Even in classic art forms, or the so-called classic and so-called popular, we are always appropriating elements that interest us that you saw from another person somewhere. The limit between this and the actual unfair use is very tenuous. It is very hard to say exactly where the line goes. It involves ethics, relationships.

Siba introduces two elements to what it means to steal in music making: trust and the relationship between artists and communities. In this sense, one could deduce that if you break an agreement you are being unethical. This point is easy to understand, even though the content of the contract can also be disputed. Other elements such as ethnicity, race, class and place of dwelling cannot be ignored. All those variables are mediated by an affective sense of belonging, which is crucial to explain how freely people appropriate/steal/take from "others". The idea itself of otherness is also an affective one.

During the interview, Siba stressed two processes. First, the extent of the changes you make in the original material you took as a source. Second, the agreements and contracts between those involved. In the first case, you are allowed to copy because no one will be able to link the source to the final result. However, in this case, you are not referencing but actually producing something new. When the idea is to reference another song, you will have to deal with either the author or the publisher. In this case, the freedom to create will be affected, since the producer might have their access to the phonogram denied.

COPYRIGHT AND APPROPRIATION

DJ Marlboro lives in Mangaratiba, a touristy location with rainforest and beaches, part of the so-called Costa Verde (Green Coast). I drove two hours from Rio de Janeiro and arrived at his house at 10:00 a.m. I waited by the pool talking to an employee. When he appeared, we went to the studio to have the interview, and his children followed him. The studio had two floors. On the first floor, he had his DJ equipment and a long-play records collection. On the second floor was the recording studio.

DJ Marlboro released one of the first long-plays of baile funk music, called *DJ Marlboro Apresenta Funk Brasil* (DJ Marlboro Introduces Funk Brazil). After this first LP he released many other albums, becoming one of the most important producers of funk music; many MCs, the singers in the baile funk scene, became famous or gained recognition by singing on one of his records. He manages a record label, a publishing company, an *equipe de som* (sound system) and a video-production firm. He also has a radio show (Ariza 2006).

DJ Marlboro enjoys a privileged and well-established place in the scene of funk music production. This position certainly interferes in his opinions regarding copying. According to him, using the music from other artists was justifiable at the beginning of the baile funk scene but now doing the same is "out of place". Taking beats and melodies from other contexts was a very common strategy in the end of the 1980s at the beginning of baile funk music. North American hip-hop was one of the favourite influences. DJ Marlboro's first hit, called "Melô da Mulher Feia", was an adaptation from the 2 Live Crew song "Do Wah Diddy".[1] In DJ Marlboro's case, he was actually adapting a version created by the crowd, singing their own lyrics during the baile together with the original version in English. The lyrics narrated the sexual activities of an ugly woman but the lyrics were too heavy to be played on the radio. DJ Marlboro provided a politically correct version of the words sung in baile funk. This story shows us the contradictions and different perspectives one person can have along a professional trajectory in the music business, but it also shows the importance of the baile funk as an event. One can say that it was not DJ Marlboro or any other producer who created baile funk. Funk was actually created in the dance floor.

The experiences of various producers considered in this study, and data produced by the Getúlio Vargas Foundation in 2008,[2] demonstrate funk market's relative independence from big labels and recording companies. Eighteen per cent of MCs interviewed in the survey had contracts with recording companies. Even though numbers suggest that funk production is a relatively informal activity, the majority of MCs register their songs: 96 per cent compose their own songs and 76 per cent "always" register them.

The defence of copyright is normally based on the economic argument that it helps to secure the market for original and innovative work by protecting it from plagiarism. However, other authors have pointed out that creativity relies a lot on taking from others: "all authorship builds upon pre-existing expression" (Netanel 2008, 58). According to Netanel, the copyright system became so pervasive that it has begun to constrain creativity and therefore it might have the opposite effect defended by economists, since it negatively affects a kind of creativity that depends on taking from others. Moreover, signing a contract many times prevents the artist from using their own work, and this is the reason why many MCs resent signing in the first place. At the same time, DJ Marlboro complains about artists who sign exclusive contracts with different people or companies. He said that this attitude creates distrust and that the MCs are only "creating problems for them in the future".

AFFECTIVE COMMUNITIES AND COPYING IN PASSINHO DANCE

In the funk scene, copyright generates a range of conflicts mentioned in this chapter and elsewhere (Ariza 2006; Facina 2005). After analysing the problems affecting the production of music, I want to focus on another practice, the passinho, a dance that emerged in the last decade in Rio de Janeiro. According to DJ Marlboro, dancing has been a crucial element of the baile funk scene since the beginning. Nevertheless, in the last decade, a new trend developed in which dancers articulate different styles, such as breakdance, popping, frevo, samba and so on. They create choreographies that have in common a basic step: passinho, or "little step". This basic step involves quick and vigorous leg movements while the upper part of the dancer's body remains straight.

Two dancers who are pioneers in the passinho dance, Cebolinha and Baianinho, told me the same story about the day they first met. Baianinho, for example, provided an interesting account on how dancing funk can produce affective connections, stimulate the development of artistic skills and connect different parts of the city:

> Cebolinha went to Jacaré, but I was already very renowned for doing shows with my former group Os Atraentes [The Attractives], and I was late for the *baile*. The other guys had that thing of running to me every time there was someone new dancing in the *baile*. I'm from Jacaré, there is someone in Manguinhos, someone in Complexo do Alemão, someone in Rocinha, I'm the best in Jacaré, but each community has it own best dancer. But if this guy comes here I have a duty to protect the community, and to continue to be the best one there. That day Cebolinha came to Jacaré, I arrived at the show and they all came to me, "Look that guy is duelling with everyone." I arrived, very humble, he was even with his girlfriend, and I started dancing. Who wants to duel, don't arrive calling for a duel, just start dancing, and provoke, that's what I do. Today I don't duel anymore. I start to dance and a circle opens in the crowd, every time I dance it happens.... For many people it was a draw, for others I won, it doesn't matter, I don't care. But it was good to meet him, today I have him as a brother. I love that guy from my heart.

The competition described above occurring spontaneously in baile funk is completely different from organized competitions of passinho. For instance, in Batalha do Passinho, an institutionalized dance competition, two dancers have a limited amount of time to show their skills and impress three judges. The duels occur in a big square stage in front of a crowd. One of the organizers of Batalha do Passinho recognized the difference between passinho as an art that occurs inside the baile funk and the duels from Batalha do Passinho. Rafael Dragaud, one producer involved in Batalha do Passinho, acknowledges that the dance is a "choreographic art happening momentarily at the *baile*, it is not something you can grab and put up on the stage". He also says that Batalha do Passinho is just a "byproduct, not in a pejorative sense, of *passinho*". Therefore, for him, passinho is a broader encompassing set of practices, and "his objective is to help those guys [dancers] to create new byproducts", fostering the creation of a "creative economy" surrounding it.

This difference that Rafael Dragaud noted between the two contexts – passinho in the *baile* and passinho in Batalha do Passinho – is extremely relevant to understanding this art not only from an aesthetic perspective but also vis-à-vis the production of existential capital. Passinho as an art form cannot be dissociated from *baile funk*. It can happen in other spaces and it can be danced in a stage, but passinho gains dynamism and mobilizes affective communities on the dance floor of parties, where the youth meet, compete and interact. This statement does not intend to raise purist interpretations. The idea is not that by changing passinho's context one is necessarily destroying it or corrupting it. I simply want to stress the importance of the exchange of affects occurring in a given moment and space, which allows a singular aesthetic experience and sense of connectedness to emerge.

The meeting between Cebolinha and Baianinho described above exemplifies how *baile funk* is an event that stimulate the development of social and artistic skills. The media and its racist narratives normally represent *baile funk* occurring in *favelas* as a place of sexual promiscuity and consumption of drugs (Herschman 2005). Despite all the stigmatization, attending a *baile funk* can be a way of acquiring existential capital. However, going to a specific nightclub or being a frequent guest of a specific cultural event does not necessarily result in the production of existential capital. The production of existential capital is associated with the affective effects of cultural practices being developed in meetings and events occurring in different localities and articulating existing cultural resources.

The discussion about copying in passinho is an interesting one. The style itself is a collage of different dance steps extracted from completely different contexts. In this case, appropriation is not a top-down process, but quite the reverse. Even though appropriation is also a creative strategy for passinho dancers, among dancers there are also conflicts regarding originality. This reinforces the idea being proposed in this chapter – that aesthetic practices can use copying as an important resource, even though the creative minds behind it still value originality. The conflicts emerging from this state of affairs do not reach the courts. However, creators find other means of regulating originality.

Dancers started adapting dance steps from North American artists. Those that managed to dominate those steps before popularization in the passinho scene gained status. In this context, copying steps from another passinho dancer instead of bringing them from outside the scene was judged as lack of originality. Copying the general style of another dancer was also a source of critique. During my fieldwork in Rio de Janeiro, according to dancers interviewed for my research, many young dancers were copying Gambá, who popularized the so-called gay way of dancing passinho. Gambá won one edition of Batalha do Passinho's competition occurring in 2011, and this led to the proliferation of dancers using the same style. The objective is not to take for granted these critiques but to understand how in passinho, which is basically a dance collage, being original is still a value. Originality in this case is not a transcendental value but a situated one. The dancers impress by dancing on the right rhythm, by being charismatic – but also by introducing new steps.

Dancers use, consciously and unconsciously, YouTube as a learning platform (Pereira Sá 2014). Moreover, they also use steps from Brazilian and local dance traditions such as frevo, samba and capoeira. Therefore, one could say that in order to be innovative or original, dancers expanded the range of traditions and styles they used to draw inspiration from.

CULTURAL APPROPRIATION AND BLACK MUSICS

It is important to distinguish between cultural appropriation and the appropriation of elements or copying. The individual appropriation of elements might be part of a broader structured process of cultural appropriation or not. Therefore, to understand the relationship between originality and appropriation, one has also to take power dynamics into account. One important work on cultural appropriation is Said's book *Orientalism* (2006), in which he analyses the exotic and colonial representations of the East created by Western countries. The fact that different European countries took ritual and political objects from their colonies, only to present and sell them in metropolitan centres, has helped to shape the understanding of art in the West (Güner 2017). According to Güner, these objects profoundly influenced European artists, even helping them to be "more confrontational". Two famous examples are Picasso and Matisse. Understanding the development of European art considering colonialism makes the perspective introduced so far more complex, since existential capital is not the only factor involved.

One problem associated with power imbalances and popular culture, especially "traditional" non-Western popular culture, is the assumption of anonymity. The assumption is that those creations emerge from the community and hence have no author. Structural racism and inequality allow certain individuals or institutions to appropriate cultural practices without even attributing authorship, either collectively or individually. However, ignoring the collective creativity of popular culture is also a mistake.

Discussing cultural appropriation using examples like *baile funk* music, dancehall or hip-hop involves necessarily dealing with ambiguities and contradictions, since appropriation strategies are central to these styles. More importantly, these strategies are not simply a way of cheating or being dishonest but part of the artistic procedure itself. Hip-hop, dub, *baile funk*, all musical strands discussed in this chapter, use samplers and repetition and somehow involve using the music of others by recycling sounds. At the same time, in the theoretical arena, debating cultural appropriation in a context where anthropology has defined culture as something impure and "consisting of heterogeneous elements *ab initio*" (Schneider 2003, 217) seems like participating in cultural essentialism. However, the empirical evidence introduced in this chapter shows that appropriation and originality do coexist and it is not so simple to discard the critique of appropriation based only on accusations of essentialism. The producers of culture themselves appropriate while trying to protect their own creations from being copied. One can argue that this behaviour has to do with self-interest or egoism, but this is a very incomplete answer.

Schneider discussed the concept of cultural appropriation, adopting the following definition: "the taking – from a culture that is not one's own – of intellectual property, cultural expressions or artifacts, history and ways of knowledge" (Ziff and Rao 1997, 1). However, the author himself already pointed out a problem in this definition: some artists "appropriate culture which at the same time are and are *not* regarded as their own" (Schneider 2003, 218). The author also points out that the definitions of culture and appropriation are constantly shifting according to "context". However, the problem is not only that the definition of culture is changing but also that the sense of otherness is also affectively and existentially constructed. In this context, one important question regarding appropriation is: What kind of value does one appropriate?

Unless one accepts originality and cultures as enclosed entities, sociological and anthropological accounts of appropriation should consider that appropriation is to a certain extent positive to foster creativity (Netanel 2008). However, cultural appropriation is also an act that should be understood together with power and social structure. Originality is mostly regarded as a European value emerging during the Renaissance. Necessarily, different cultural practices that were not associated with European highbrow culture were judged from this perspective. Copyright is one example of how originality is enforced.

Paul Gilroy (1993) gives an account of "black musics" in his book *The Black Atlantic* that helps us to understand the contradictory relationship between originality and appropriation in *baile funk* music. According to him, the power of black music derives from its "unsteady location simultaneously inside and outside the conventions, assumptions, aesthetic rules which distinguish and periodise modernity" (73). Therefore, to understand black music one has to depart from a focus on textuality and start to pay "careful attention to the structures of feeling which underpin black expressive cultures" (77). In order to analyse, for example, dub, hip-hop or *baile funk* music, the concept of cultural capital is incomplete, since it relies on typically Western and modern assumptions, such as the division between high culture and popular culture.

The notion of existential capital seems more adequate to understand black cultural practices and the strategies of appropriation employed by musicians, producers and dancers. Herbie Hancock's answer to Feld's questioning regarding the copying of a melody from the pygmies found in ethnomusicological recordings from Simha Arom and Geneviève Taurelle exemplify this claim. Hancock simply stated: "It's a brothers kind of thing" (Feld 1996, 6). In other words, he feels entitled to use a melody recorded on another continent by people that he has never met because he feels affectively and musically connected to them.

The theme of diaspora and dislocation is central to understand the sense of community that leads black music to have specific qualities. Gilroy's words can be helpful here once again: "Dislocated from their original conditions of existence, the sound tracks of this African-American cultural broadcast fed a new metaphysics of blackness elaborated and enacted in Europe and elsewhere within the underground, alternative, public spaces constituted around the expressive culture that was dominated by music" (1993, 83). The fact that many populations removed from the African continent shared similar experiences of racial segregation, memories of slavery and religious references contributed to a sense of affective connection through music. Therefore, one should note that different practices of appropriation exist and they should not all be equated to postmodern pastiche.

It is central to the argument of this text that practices of appropriation should be situated. The possibility of appropriating cultural practices while retaining an aura of originality has to do with the possession of existential capital. "Making the past audible in the present" (Gilroy 2010, 127) involves referencing but it also involves connectedness to a certain history and communal cultural practices. As the case of passinho exemplifies, if you are not inside the affective community, appropriation acts might not be recognized as original because they lack a specific kind of value that can only be produced by togetherness.

CONCLUSION

All the different sets of music practices discussed in this chapter – dub techniques, hip-hop, *baile funk* music and passinho dance – use the appropriation of repertoires as a central creative strategy. Cultural appropriation occurs when existential capital is appropriated, when the ways of living of communities are used to sell products, foster stereotypes and to convince people of a line of action or social policy. This critique to cultural appropriation does not entail an essentialist view, since references to originality can be situated and provisional; references are constantly translated, reworked and mediated through artistic processes.

To imitate is also to create, and the critique should focus on processes. It is more about *how* and less about *what*, since basically any element can be charged with the affective potential of creating mobilization and raising emotions. One example is how producers use the term "stealing". They recognize the copyright ownership and assume the risk of copying it while generating an image of rebelliousness. The process of appropriation itself becomes a challenge to the status quo. And in passinho dance, dancers take steps from other contexts but have their own standards regarding the evaluation of originality based on personal style and introduction of unseen and innovative steps. In other words, copying is allowed but if the dancer is not participating in that community, they will not know the right steps to impress the crowd, their peers and judges in dance competitions.

Even if a certain cultural practice is based upon the use of elements from different contexts, the procedure of making this mediation can be very specific and complex. Analysing music, dance or any other art form using the parameters set by copyright law means reducing the importance of forms of creation that do not rely on the respect to the originality of specific elements within the performance but on sophisticated mimetic processes, as passinho dance and dub music exemplify. In *baile funk* music the use of collage and other forms of mimetic practices dwell with claims of originality. This occurs because, very commonly, in different musical scenes, forms of appropriation are allowed while other forms are repressed either by artists and the audience or by copyright owners.

Comparing how dancers defend and promote originality differs from discussions regarding the use of sounds and melodies. In passinho, there is no formal regulatory framework imposed on dance moves, the judgement of originality remains largely aesthetic and non-institutionalized. Copyright partially transfers the social enactment of originality and the control of aesthetic exchanges to an institutionalized order. The word "partially" serves as a reminder that imitation remains a practice one can use to produce music, even under the limitations imposed by the law.

NOTES

1. Curiously enough, the case *Campbell v. Acuff-Rose Music, Inc.* (1994), a paradigmatic one in the history of North American copyright legislation, involved a parody produced by 2 Live Crew of the song "Oh! Pretty Woman" from William Dees and Roy Orbison. The court decided in favour of 2 Live Crew, arguing that US law, in order to balance creativity and protection, should take into account fair use.
2. The Getúlio Vargas Foundation interviewed 381 professionals working with funk, including 114 MCs.

REFERENCES

Achebe, Chinua. 1984. Foreword. In *Igbo Arts : Community and Cosmos*, edited by Herbert M. Cole and Chike Cyril Aniakor. Los Angeles: Museum of Cultural History–University of California.

Ariza, Adonay. 2006. *Electronic Samba: A Música Brasileira no Contexto das Tendências Internacionais.* São Paulo: Annablume.

Born, Georgina. 2010. "The Social and the Aesthetic: For a Post-Bourdieuian Theory of Cultural Production". *Cultural Sociology* 4, no. 2: 171–208.

Bourdieu, Pierre. 2010. *Distinction: A Social Critique of the Judgement of Taste.* London: Routledge.

Childs, James. 2000. *Preaching Justice: The Ethical Vocation of Word and Sacrament Ministry.* Harrisburg, PA: Trinity Press International.

Essinger, Silvio. 2005. *Batidão: Uma História do Funk.* Rio de Janeiro: Record.

Facina, Adriana. 2014. "Cultura Como Crime, Cultura Como Direito: A Luta Contra a Resolução 013 No Rio de Janeiro". In *Anais Da 29a Reunião Brasileira de Antropologia.* Natal.

Feld, Steven. 1996. "Pygmy POP: A Genealogy of Schizophonic Mimesis". *Yearbook for Traditional Music* 28: 1–35.

Gandhi, Leela. 2006. *Affective Communities: Anticolonial Thought, Fin-de Siècle Radicalism, and the Politics of Friendship.* Durham, NC: Duke University Press.

Gilroy, Paul. 1993. *The Black Atlantic: Modernity and Double-Consciousness.* Cambridge, MA: Harvard University Press.

———. 2010. *Darker than Blue: On the Moral Economies of Black Atlantic Culture.* Cambridge and London: Harvard University Press.

Güner, Fisun. 2017. "Folk art from Africa and the Pacific Changed the Modern World by Pushing Western Artists to Be More Confrontational, Writes Fisun Güner". 18 August. http://www.bbc.com/culture/story/20170818-how-a-small-african-figurine-changed-art.

Hall, Stuart. 1996. "What Is This 'Black' in Black Popular Culture?" In *Critical Dialogues in Cultural Studies*, edited by David Morley and Kuan-Hsing Chen, 468–78. London: Routledge.

Henriques, J. 2010. "The Vibrations of Affect and their Propagation on a Night Out on Kingston's Dancehall Scene". *Body and Society* 16, no. 1: 57–89.

Herschmann, Micael. 2005. *O Funk e o Hip-Hop Invadem a Cena.* Rio de Janeiro: Editora Universidade Federal do Rio de Janeiro.

Hitchcock, Peter. 1993. "'It Dread Inna Inglan': Linton Kwesi Johnson, Dread, and Dub Identity". *Postmodern Culture* 4, no. 1: 1–25.

Lamont, Michèle, and Annette Lareau. 1988. "Cultural Capital: Allusions, Gaps and Glissandos in Recent Theoretical Developments". *Sociological Theory* 6 no. 2: 153–68.

Lopes, Adriana Carvalho. 2012. "Cidade Do Funk: Expressões Da Diáspora Negra Nas Favelas Cariocas Funk Music City: The Expressions of the Black Diaspora of Rio de Janeiro's Favelas". *Revista do Arquivo Geral da Cidade do Rio de Janeiro*, no. 6: 193–206.

Mizrahi, Mylene. 2010. "A Estética Funk Carioca: Criação e Conectividade em Mr Catra". PhD dissertation, Universidade Federal do Rio de Janeiro.

Muniz, Bruno. 2016. "Quem Precisa de Cultura? O Capital Existencial Do Funk e a Conveniência da Cultura". *Sociologia & Antropologia* 6, no. 2: 447–67.

Netanel, Neil. 2008. *Copyright's Paradox.* Oxford: Oxford University Press.

Nettleton, Sarah. 2013. "Cementing Relations within a Sporting Field: Fell Running in the English Lake District and the Acquisition of Existential Capital". *Cultural Sociology*, 7, no. 2: 196–210.

Pereira de Sá, Simone. 2014. "Apropriações Low-Tech no Funk Carioca: A Batalha do Passinho e a Rede de Música Popular de Periferia". *Fronteiras* 16, no. 1: 28–37.

Said, Edward. 2006. *Orientalism: Western Conception of the Orient.* London: Penguin.

Savage, M. 2013. "A New Model of Social Class? Findings from the BBC's Great British Class Survey Experiment". *Sociology* 47, no. 2: 219–50.

Schneider, Arnd. 2003. "On 'Appropriation'. A Critical Reappraisal of the Concept and Its Application in Global Art Practices". *Social Anthropology* 11 no. 2: 215–29.

———. 2006. *Appropriation as Practice: Art and Identity in Argentina.* New York: Palgrave Macmillan.

Skeggs, Beverley. 2010. "The Value of Relationships: Affective Scenes and Emotional Performances". *Feminist Legal Studies* 18, no. 1: 29–51.

Sobrinho, Pedro. 2013. "O Que o Funk Tem em Comum com o Maculelê". 25 March. http://www.blogsoestado.com/pedrosobrinho/2013/03/25/o-que- funk-tem-em-comum-com-o-maculele/.

Veal, Michael. 2007. *Dub: Soundscapes and Shattered Songs in Jamaican Reggae.* Middletown, CT: Wesleyan Press.

Wacquant, L. 2015. "For a Sociology of Flesh and Blood". *Qualitative Sociology* 38, no. 1: 1–11.

West, Cornel. 2000. *The Cornel West Reader.* New York: Civitas Books.

Ziff, Bruno, and Pratima V. Rao, eds. 1997. *Borrowed Power. Essays on Cultural Appropriation.* New Brunswick, NJ: Rutgers University Press.

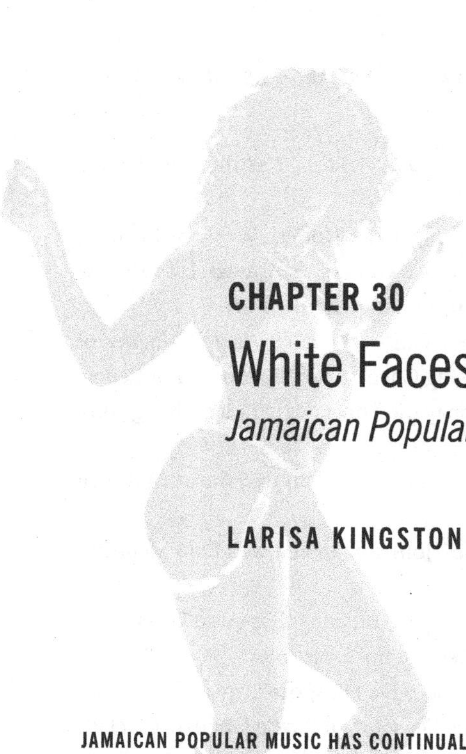

CHAPTER 30

White Faces in Intimate Spaces

Jamaican Popular Music in Global Circulation

LARISA KINGSTON MANN

JAMAICAN POPULAR MUSIC HAS CONTINUALLY ENGAGED WITH GLOBALLY networked media technologies, from the eras of vinyl records, cassettes and CDs circulating across the island and the world. However, street dances, a vital element of Jamaicn popular music's creative energy, have remained centres of cultural authority that are resolutely local, not only to Jamaica but specifically to the urban poor in whose neighbourhoods the dances flourish best. The fact that street dances occur primarily outside of elite neighbourhoods, in places where the urban poor have a measure of informal social authority, has tended to maintain urban poor Jamaicans' culture at the centre of Jamaican popular music even as the music has become a global phenomenon. In the dances, audiences, as well as DJs and soundmen, vet new artists, new music and new methods of musical engagement (including dancing and fashion).[1] Newly networked technologies for circulating visual media in global networks are reshaping how Jamaicans perform identity in these spaces. These technologies also affect street dances' social function, reinforcing existing and historic inequalities of race and gender, while reshaping and limiting street dances' traditional function as a site of autonomy and resistance to colonial inequality.

THE GLOBAL EYE: THE RISE OF THE VIDEO LIGHT

Video cameras have become a regular feature at street dances. I regularly observed "video men" traversing the space with a bright light affixed to the camera, often trailing a cable connected to the sound system power supply. DVDs of these official video recordings sell all over the world, online, and in music and video stores. Sound system owners often split a percentage of the sales with the person who duplicated them. Meanwhile, amateur videographers, using smaller cameras or cell phones, also permeate the space and upload recordings to personal websites, social networks and music-oriented websites. Sometimes these amateurs are compensated directly for their work; others indirectly enhance their own reputations as scenesters and documentarians. Audience members and sound system operators also see being featured in a DVD, or in even amateur reporting, as a chance to enhance one's reputation. Jamaican musickers have always been aware that being seen, especially by foreign audiences, is important to financial advancement, but the heightened struggle for the video light reveals a new interest in being seen, as global media circulation makes it possible to imagine oneself on an even broader stage than was previously available. Dancers' vigorous, even violent pursuit of the video light, pathologized by scholar Donna Hope in her term "video light syndrome" (2006, 135), highlights the perceived value of potential exposure ("Women Fight for Video Light" 2008).

The eye of the video light now represents the gaze of a much broader, whiter and more remote audience. Musickers seeking to capitalize on it are incentivized to satisfy, at least in part, the cultural desires and interests of non-Jamaicans in new ways.

New technology has made it easier for international audiences to have access to the street dance. Cameras, in particular, have shrunk in size and cost and are increasingly embedded in popular devices such as mobile phones, enabling anyone present in a space to document images as well as sounds. The increased presence of networked audio and video devices parallels the rise of the video light as a subject of popular song and marks the beginning of a newly visual and differently global dynamic in Jamaican music media circulation. As cameras have shrunk, increasing bandwidth has enabled Jamaican and international news and music websites to invite people to upload recordings from music events. These uploads also reach social media networks, YouTube and other sites that can circulate images from local events farther than ever before and also remove contextual information that used to accompany CDs, personal photographs or home videos and shape their reception.

One of these dynamics is the changing set of expectations in relation to appearance. Jamaican popular culture has always been filled with pressures to look good, of particular importance in the context of colonial inequality wherein people risk being judged "uncivilized". Upper-class Jamaican culture judges bodies themselves, as well as their movements, as excessive and uncivilized if they do not conform in shape and skin tone to Eurocentric standards (Hobson 2003). Crossover success in the global pop market also reflected similar pressures. Broadly speaking, many traits associated with the poor decreased artists' ability to reach a mass audience at the global level. Use of standard English instead of Patwa, as well as light skin, while not always predictors of crossover success, are often correlated with artists' success at the global level. Thus, directions from Mr Vegas and Lexxus (2002) to "video light girls" to "Tall-u up inna di video fah yuh cute gal" (Stand up tall in the video because you are cute, girl) also include increasing pressure to define "cute" in line with global tastes for lighter skin. Jamaican songs about bleaching go back at least to the 1980s, but the early 2000s saw a rise in songs discussing skin bleaching, often linked with the presence of the video light. In "Video Light" (2002), the group T.O.K. asserts: "Some gal bleach good some gal bleach bad, some gal bleach you wudda check say dem mad [you would think they were crazy], gal nah bleaching cream face get sad [a girl who doesn't use bleaching cream on her face gets sad]." Elsewhere, singer Elephant Man (2006) uses the phrase "two colour face" to describe the uneven skin tone that bleaching creams can cause and also links these bleaching practices to the video camera's evaluating gaze: "two colour face gal nuh ready fi di video yet" (not ready for the video yet). The song's chorus and title "Nuh Ready fi di Video Yet" present bleaching as feminine preparation (here incomplete) for the video light.

Song lyrics discuss bleaching as such a feminine practice (Hope 2011) that it is used to insult men by (sexist) association: Mavado, in his ongoing feud with Vybz Kartel, sang that "Addi di teacha [another name for Vybz Kartel] bleach out like Latisha [a woman's name]". However, ethnographic evidence illustrates a complex relationship between discourse and practice. Despite a long-standing popular discourse of women competing for (male) attention on the dance floor, I observed male dancers actually dominating the video light. Female singer Macka Diamond decried this situation in her song "Too Much Bull", wherein she demanded women get their fair share of the video light. Female dancers publicly supported Diamond's claim ("Macka Diamond" 2010). This development corresponded with a public anxiety over whether it was proper for men to be the subject of an evaluating gaze (Hope 2010). Ricky Blaze's tune "How Mi Look?"(How Do I Look/How Is My Look?) (2009) spurred an online controversy that revealed anxiety about the changing power of male performers. "SINCE WHEN MAN AH ASK MAN HOW MI LOOK?" (Since when do men ask men how they look?) thundered one commentator in all-capital letters at dancehallreggae.com (Marshall 2008). Blaze's willingness to subject himself to evaluation suggests there may be new pressures on male performers, a perspective also demonstrated by Vybz Kartel's evaluation of his options as a performer described at the beginning of this chapter. This change in male performers' position is most usefully read not in relation to female performers, but instead, in relation to all performers' experiences in the broader media landscape. A reduction in Jamaican male autonomy does not correlate with an increase in Jamaican female autonomy but instead may be a reduction across the board since both operate in a white supremacist context.

Digital Media as Digital Surveillance?

In Jamaica, globally networked technologies of media circulation are increasingly ubiquitous in daily life, and they are consciously sponsored by state and local programs of information and communications technologies for development as well as by foreign aid, charity and investment actions of technology companies. Many in Jamaica have celebrated the chance to increase musicians' access to potential markets and audiences, as well as audiences' access to recordings. The increased transparency of local musicking can provide opportunities for promotion, but it has its dark sides. Some studies of information and communications technologies for development in the Global South suggest that the fastest-growing trend is to use this technology for tracking, identifying and categorizing people for the purpose of political repression (Korac-Boisvert and Kouzmin 1994). In Jamaica, political repression via technology has not been a major concern, but at the same time, surveillance and tracking is appealing to copyright owners in ways that do not necessarily advance Jamaican interests, especially those of the poor.

Copyright ownership overall is still concentrated in the Global North, and the prevalence of local practices that contradict copyright makes enforcement a mixed benefit for Jamaican musickers. "Infringement" is often defined by US record labels and does not necessarily relate to non-US legal or cultural traditions. Legal threats from foreign companies against Jamaican musickers over copyright infringement have not yet led to lawsuits, but such demands serve as a warning to would-be international artists about practices unwelcome in the (legal) global music arena.

Global digital media networks can enforce this warning automatically; many media platforms such as YouTube embed technologies that ban, filter, flag or remove "infringing" materials. Thus, communities of particular practices face copyright-based surveillance technology that could exclude them based on their choices of creative practices (Cohen 2006; Cohen 2011). Jamaicans closest to Jamaican popular musicking traditions would be most disadvantaged by this surveillance. Surveillance can also involve decontextualization, fetishization and defamation. Hypervisible black bodies can be used to reinforce negative stereotypes of black sexuality and aggression, which can affect black communities' participation in media, autonomy and access to resources. Outsiders' ability to gaze into sites of cultural intimacy breaks down some of their nurturing power, increasing the pressure to conform to white definitions of beauty. Rewards that come from being seen are allocated in ways that disadvantage or exploit stereotypes of blackness.

Poor Jamaicans are often invited to enter into a system of globally networked technology and media that can require them to alter or abandon their creative practices and connections to their communities. These practices and connections, however, have long been a site of struggle toward autonomous practices that resist the norms and institutions of a still-colonial system. Currently, most platforms for engaging with media poorly address these historically established inequalities of ownership, authority and control over culture and body, which form the basis of individual and community autonomy. Although Jamaicans can choose not to participate, there are strong incentives to do so, especially for the poor.

Exilic Spaces, Policy and Technology

International technological and legal regimes transform the terms on which Jamaican performers can engage with audiences. This transformation has the potential to reshape Jamaican performances and Jamaican bodies. Technology can allow entry by people whose traditions developed outside of the purview of previous industry institutions, but it also can limit their ability to alter their communities' social position in relation to power. As a matter of policy, whose interpretation of the law and which social norms ought to be embedded in these transnational media platforms? This question cannot be answered without deciding on a set of values related to access and intimacy.

Best (2008) has suggested that the "lag time" between digital technologies' proliferation in different regions is a crucial "strategic space" in which local (and specifically Caribbean) communities can develop their responses to new technology. My work here suggests that the strategic value of such space depends on its capacity to be exilic and foster cultural intimacy. Until the values generated by these characteristics can be guaranteed or the structuring colonial inequalities can be addressed, strategic space may be better occupied than ventured out of.

The pressures of a white supremacist media landscape require a solution that engages with the politics of representation. However, there are few working legal solutions to the harms of recontextualization or other insults to dignity and autonomy. Addressing those concerns from a legal perspective would require rights to be redefined to include protection from new kinds of cultural harms, perhaps tied to international human rights of dignity and cultural survival. In the meantime, legal constructs like Creative Commons do allow for some tailoring of rights definition to local interests for artists entering global digital media networks. Technical remedies or preventions for certain kinds of misuse could be implemented as well. The same technologies that currently enable copyright owners or media companies to shut down sites or block particular actors or activities remotely on media sharing platforms could be used differently in the hands of marginalized communities. Watermarking could prevent tagged videos from being reposted on pornographic sites and could allow people to track down possible offenders and speak back to them in a public or private way. Technologists and policy-makers that account for these concerns could thus better serve the interests of marginalized communities, especially those in the Global South.

EXILIC SPACES AND CULTURAL INTIMACY AS CONDITIONS FOR AUTONOMY

Street dances have particular characteristics that create and maintain values relating to autonomy and practices central to the street dance that could not occur in more formal, regulated spaces. Many of the creative practices of Jamaican musicking contradict copyright law. The most popular sound systems violate zoning laws. The wildest dance moves can threaten the politics of respectability that privilege upper-class culture or can be reinterpreted to justify racist and sexist stereotypes. Performers seeking fame bet on being rewarded for capitalizing on these stereotypes, as Kartel's skin-bleaching choice dramatizes.

Given the potential risks of new exposure in a hostile media and cultural landscape, what are the responsibilities of those designing and shaping the platforms and technologies available to Jamaicans and others in the Global South? Accounting for cultural intimacy and exilic space[2] in technology and policy design would better foster the values of Jamaican musicking and creative practices and better facilitate resistance to exploitative and demeaning treatment in the global media landscape.

NOTES

1. Musicking, a term coined by musicologist Christopher Small (1998), describes the full range of activities by which people engage with music and give it meaning; this includes playing instruments, singing and deejaying/selecting but also dancing, posing, cheering, providing food and drink at a musical event, and so on.
2. The term "exilic social space" was coined by Gray (2004, 93) to describe a social space that can provide refuge for people who are held, by formal systems of society and the state in in a condition of "social dishonour". The term describes how Kingston's poor urban areas are neither wholly open to nor dependent on state power. This "exile" actually allows people living there to craft lives, worldviews and political identities less dependent on the dominant social order, in such a way that they can negotiate from a position of some strength. Gray focuses on political power, but this independence is reflected and nurtured in cultural practices, including the music that is generated in poor urban communities.

REFERENCES

Best, Curwen. 2008. "Caribbean Cyberculture: Towards an Understanding of Gender, Sexuality and Identity within the Digital Culture Matrix". In *Constructing Vernacular Culture in the Trans-Caribbean*, edited by Holger Henke and Karl-Heinz Magister, 377–98. Washington, DC: Lexington.

Cohen, Julie E. 2006. "Pervasively Distributed Copyright Enforcement". *Georgetown Law Journal* 95: 1–44.

Cohen, Nicole S. 2011. "The Valorization of Surveillance: Towards a Political Economy of Facebook". *Democratic Communiqué* 22, no. 1: 5–22.

Gray, Obika. 2004. *Demeaned but Empowered: The Social Power of the Urban Poor in Jamaica*. Kingston: University of the West Indies Press.

Hobson, Janell. "The 'Batty' Politic: Toward an Aesthetic of the Black Female Body". *Hypatia* 18, no. 4 (2003): 87–105.

Hope, Donna P. 2006. "Passa Passa: Interrogating Cultural Hybridities in Jamaican Dancehall". *Small Axe* 10, no. 3: 125–39.

———. 2010. *Man Vibes: Masculinities in Jamaican Dancehall*. Kingston: Ian Randle.

———. 2011. "From Browning to Cake Soap: Popular Debates on Skin Bleaching in the Jamaican Dancehall". *Journal of Pan African Studies* 4: 165–94.

Korac-Boisvert, Nada, and Alexander Kouzmin. 1994. "The Dark Side of Info-Age Social Networks in Public Organizations and Creeping Crises". *Administrative Theory and Praxis* 16, no. 1: 57–82.

"Macka Diamond, Female Dancers Defend Their Video Light". 2010. *Star*, 16 October. http://jamaica-star.com/thestar/20101016/ent/ent1.html.

Marshall, Wayne. 2008. "The Anxiety of Influence". *Wayneandwax* (blog), 2 October. http://wayneandwax.com/?p=529.

Small, C. 1998. *Musicking: The Meanings of Performing and Listening*. Middletown, CT: Wesleyan University Press.

"Women Fight for Video Light: Three to Be Sentenced after Brawl at Dance". 2008. *Star*, 12 August. http://jamaica-star.com/thestar/20080812/news/news1.html.

DISCOGRAPHY

Blaze, Ricky. 2009. "How Mi Look". *Ragga Ragga Ragga 2009*. Greensleeves.

Elephant Man. 2006. "Nuh Ready fi di Video Yet". *Gully Slime Riddim*. Natural Bridge.

Mr Vegas and Lexxus. 2002. "Why (Video Light Girl)". *The Biggest Ragga Dancehall Anthems 2002*. Greensleeves.

T.O.K. 2002. "Video Light (Medley)". *Ragga Ragga Ragga 16*. Vol. GRELCD268. Greensleeves.

PART 9

TRIBUTE TO BOGLE

CHAPTER 31

"Bogle ah di Order fi di Day"

*Dance and Identity in Jamaican Dancehall**

SONJAH STANLEY NIAAH

WHAT DO THE NAMES KID HAROLD, BASKIN, PAM Pam, Persian the Cat, Labba Labba, Bogle, Carlene, Stacey, Keiva, Craigy Dread, Mad Michelle, Sample Six, Ravers Clavers, Ice, Colo Colo, Shelly Belly and Black Blingers have in common? All have made indelible marks on the popular dance repertoire and performance style of Jamaica from the 1930s in dance events at Marcus Garvey's Edelweiss Park to present day venues such as Weekenz. Creators of dance moves such as the Bogle (Gerald "Bogle" Levy a.k.a. Mr Wacky), Gully Creepa (David "Ice" Smith) and No Linga (Marlon "Overmars" Hardy of Ravers Clavers) – these individuals continue the task of dancing their way into local, regional and global performance histories.

The dance is a distinguishing feature of the Jamaican dancehall space. In dancehall dancers and other patrons take on the toil of ridding their mind of daily troubles, becoming devotees, not in a capitalist (post)modernity that disenfranchises, but in a somatic and kinaesthetic sense. As if they were "slaves to the rhythm" that beat around them and inside them amid the social ills of everyday Jamaica, in the way Grace Jones (1985) suggests in her song of the same name, the exerting body on the contemporary dance floors of Jamaica literally and symbolically replaces those on the plantations that preceded them. Here is the body that, through contestation, exploitation, discrimination and oppression, has preserved itself through performance to tell the tales of history, while dance venues become de-localized for just a moment when they transcend time and produce the inevitable "congregational kinesis" (Brathwaite 1995, 46). The dance is therefore linked to old and new ways of toiling for freedom, creating space through rhythm.

This chapter examines some of the central and arguably, underexposed creators of dance moves and by extension their personhood within dancehall. Their voices have,

*Previously published in *LT1: Gender and Sexuality in Jamaica*, edited by Sachiyo Morimoto (Zentsūji, Japan: Mighty Mules, 2008), 87–109.

to a large extent, been mediated through the practice of the deejay, selectors of music and singers, but dancers have not been silent. Their expressions are mostly through movement as a tool of celebration, and with the body as their instrument, they make their mark on Jamaican history, politics and nationhood, as well as the world. While much public debate about dancehall moves has revolved around evaluative judgements of the dancers' practice, in this chapter I am interested in the manifestations of gender identity, politics and transgression in Jamaican dance performance. Using Bogle as the main case, I traverse Jamaican dance history to make statements about old and new stories in the tapestry of identity negotiation in a postcolonial context.

FROM KID HAROLD TO BOGLE

Following a long tradition of performers including itinerant songster troubadours and street preachers, male dancers such as the "legs man" have imprinted themselves on the Jamaican dance landscape, aesthetic and catalogue. Male dancers of one kind or another have been considered dancehall stars. An important example is Kid Harold (c. 1911–85), who was a part of the comedy team Harold and Trim, one of Jamaica's top show groups, and leader of the Butterfly Troupe of dancers. Known for his tap dancing, he was personally recruited by national hero Marcus Mosiah Garvey for performances at Edelweiss Park and to help the dance trainer/coordinator on staff, Gerardo Leon. He also appeared in plays at Edelweiss Park that were written and produced by Ranny Williams (Hamilton 1988, 87–111). It is notable that dance styles in the dancehall came from diverse traditions, including from rhythm and blues moves of the 1950s, jazz, Afro-Cuban/Brazilian styles, as well as the traditional Jamaican forms such as brukins, mento, gerreh and folk religions such as Kumina. So the shuffle, bebop and jitterbug could be seen in the dance halls. Such movement patterns propelled the creation of indigenous moves that coexisted with American popular moves. The modelling of dances (from feature films) by the likes of Kid Harold and Pam Pam (White 1984, 72) existed alongside purely "blues moves" such as "legs". Other local moves were developed and include the "Shake-a-Leg", "Going to Town", "Rocksteady" and "Reggae" (74). By the 1970s, famous dancers from the ghetto included Needle, Clifford Strokes, "Persian" the Cat, Bop (Mr Legs), Sparkie, Pam Pam and Baskin, who appeared at major dance events and stage shows.

White (1984, 72–73) proposes that dance practitioners should be considered "culture heroes" for creating a celebratory ethos, as well as facilitating the development and tempo of Jamaica's popular music industry and performance practice. The experienced dancer was and still is like a "god"; if one couldn't dance they were definitely seen as a lesser being. Dance and dancers have a paramount role in dance halls and remarkably many of the famous dancers recorded in the history of dancehall culture, since the 1950s in particular, have been males. Further, the ability to execute dance movement was an indication of one's class membership and it has been established that there is a strong link between both gender and class identity in the context of the dance (White 1984, 75; Stanley Niaah, 2004).

I want to focus here on one male dancer who embodies the title "culture hero", but who up until the time of his death was never proclaimed that. Media coverage in January 2005 when Bogle was tragically slain by gunmen centred on whether he was an icon, which led entities such as the Jamaica Gleaner Company to publish articles that only in death acknowledged Bogle as an icon.[1] After all, citizens from the underclass, despite their achievements and contribution to national identity and development, have historically had difficulty in being proclaimed official icons or heroes. Debate about Bogle as a cultural icon rings similar to that of Bob Marley being named a national hero. On the one hand, Bogle has created more dancehall dance moves than any other figure and, on the other, Marley has catapulted Jamaica into world fame through reggae music. Arguably both have received recognition disproportionate to their acclaim and contribution in their spaces of operation.

Who was Bogle and what was the nature of his oeuvre? Was he an icon? The *Cambridge International Dictionary of English* defines "icon" in relation to holy paintings (such as those of Jesus Christ), a computer symbol or representation. The reference is to a famous person or thing considered as representing a set of beliefs or a way of life. Examples of this include Elvis Presley, Marilyn Monroe or the skyscraper as American icon. Despite the lack of consensus about his status as an icon, Bogle's death allowed for important reflections on his place as a dancehall celebrity/dancer/choreographer, and his role in the creation and proliferation of dancehall culture.

DANCE MASTER BOGLE

The title Dancehall King was reserved for the legsman of yesteryear. Today there is a new breed of legsman best illustrated by the unnamed king, Bogle. Bogle constitutes the twenty-first-century legsman whose dance repertoire reflects twenty-first-century politics, lifestyle and tensions. Bogle was born in 1966 in Trench Town, West Kingston. At the community level, Bogle's image is tantamount to that of a popular cultural hero. Originating in humble beginnings, he recalled that his mother's house was wooden (a semi-permanent structure) until the family moved to a concrete housing development in the 1970s. Though he grew up in the area referred to by residents as Jungle, he says he never carried the "jungle" with him. Bogle's secondary education started at Charlie Smith All Age, after which he spent a short time at St George's College.

After being unable to fully take advantage of the school system, he decided to go with what God seemed to be telling him, "you are star", so his decision was to be a star. "All of my life a dancing me know 'bout . . . or else me woulda mix up", is how Bogle described his life's dedication to dance. He received a copious amount of flogging from his mother, who had no faith in that vocation. Bogle explained that while growing up he had thoughts of becoming a lawyer, doctor, teacher or civil servant as those were the respected professions, but dancing prevailed as his preferred occupation. He started early and by the 1970s he was appearing on the Louise Bennett Saturday morning show *Ring Ding* televised on the Jamaica Broadcasting Corporation, and in the 1980s, the Saturday evening programme *Where It's At* on the same station. By the early 1990s Bogle and his Black Roses Crew from the (in)famous Roses Corner, later designated by Bogle as the "Dancehall Dimension", were prominent dancehall phenomena, successfully shaping and changing the image of popular Jamaican dance.

It is the feet, not the mind that Bogle privileged in the dance creation process and it was for this reason that Bogle admitted he never knew what he was going to create; creations just came. "Nuff time when I dance, I don't listen to the music, I listen to my foot bottom. Most people don't know that." In respect of the Pelpa for example, he was just at the Asylum nightclub "and the vibes just touch me and mi seh to me colleagues dem 'tek style' and me just go into the Pelpa" (Allen 1998). Bogle said he could create a dance anytime as he was consumed by the power of the dance so much so he abandoned a promising football career. Essentially, he spoke through his feet, supporting the idea that the feet, indeed the entire body communicates through dance, which is itself a language communicating concrete ideas, value systems and cultures for centuries.

No other person has been credited with creating and popularizing as many dance moves as Bogle. These include

1. Zip It Up
2. Log On
3. L.O.Y.
4. Pelpa
5. Pop the Collar
6. Pick It Off
7. Genie
8. Gwanie Gwanie
9. Mission Impossible
10. Hot 97
11. Erkel
12. Flip
13. Butterfly (Carlene also claims to have originated this dance)
14. World Dance
15. Imitation Bogle
16. Bogle
17. Wave
18. Row Like a Boat
19. Jiggy
20. Back to Basics

Bogle often released the dances to the media before exposing them on the dancehall stage. He was also present at many events promoting the moves: sometimes he was dancing, sometimes he was on the microphone given by a selector to entertain the audience. Previously, he thought of becoming a deejay but didn't pursue this up until near his death, when he released the single "All Dem Deh" (Bogle 2005) and proclaimed to newspaper reporters that he would be spending a lot of time at the recording studio where he had already recorded four songs which were shortly to be released. This did not materialize, and Bogle's sojourn in the studio came forcefully in the recordings about him that constitute proclamations of his place in dancehall. From Beenie Man to Elephant Man, Buju Banton and Voicemail, Bogle has been acknowledged by his peers in the following way:

> Bogle a di order fi di day
> Di wickedest dancer from outa JA
> (Buju Banton 1992)
>
> Mr Wacky a di teacher . . .
> Roses have di flow dem . . .
> Wacky set di trend fi dem
> (Elephant Man 2008)
>
> Black Roses time
> Well yuh dun know,
> a di return of di greatest dancer of all time, Fadda Bogle
> (Beenie Man, 2004)

Members of the dance fraternity such as former dancehall queen Denise "Stacey" Cumberland (crowned 1999) have also praised his contribution: "Bogle set the trend, Bogle a elder, Bogle a di real ting."

Dancing was Bogle's forte, however, and his motto "to dance or die" was borne out in the amount of time he dedicated to his career and the number of dance moves he created. In his words, "a mus dance alone mi think bout all these years to create so many dance. Mi couldn't think about nothing else. . . . What else could I think about? The dance wouldn't come good. The dance wouldn't come clean!" Bogle suggested that he embodied the very essence of dancehall. "Because of me. . . . Everybody wanna dance! Everybody wanna dance right now." In Bogle's opinion, the "dance don't change until Bogle come. . . . You never see any difference in the dance until Bogle come." And, he was confident about his ability to allow any deejay to reap success from their songs if only Bogle were to create a dance for it. Bogle took credit for the success of such deejays as Beenie Man, Bounty Killer, Buju Banton and Junior Reid who have songs describing Bogle's dance styles or built on Bogle's lyrical suggestions. There are phrases such as "Mr Mention" used by Buju Banton for his album and single of the same name that have sprung from Bogle's fountain of creativity. These have gone unacknowledged and Bogle was very concerned about the way his intellectual property was used without appropriate recognition, benefits or royalties. Apart from deejays who used his phrases in their song lyrics, others forgot to mention or pay tribute to his creativity by acknowledging his place as dance creator. One such example is the single "Log On" about the dance of the same name, where, instead of Bogle, the deejay named Keiva, who purportedly has a "dancing school" to which she should take those in need of dance tutelage. The deejay in this case is Elephant Man, who built his career on recording songs about dance moves. In addition to the Log On, Elephant Man has recordings about numerous dance moves, including the Online, Signal di Plane, Pon di River Pon di Bank, Chaka Chaka, Hot Fuk, Limbo, Willie Bounce, Gangsta Rock, Nuh Linga and Gully Creepa, among others.

Bogle's contribution gained significant international exposure as well. One of his famous dances – the Wave – was created in the United States during a period of self-imposed exile. Bogle explained that "it is not easy to create a dance in America . . . only Michael Jackson" can do that. Bogle created the dances and "fedexed them out to Jamaica". Bogle's style had been to "bus" or release the dances in Jamaica and "fedex" (short for the worldwide courier Federal Express) or courier them to the United States. In the case of the Wave, he reversed the process. This dance was released in the United States where it became popular, after which it went to Jamaica. It was called "Wave" in Miami and "Super Bowl" in New York. Perhaps the most visible international platform precipitating increased popularity for Bogle was the medium of the music video. Beyond appearances in local music videos by a range of artists that gain international exposure through rotations on cable channels, including Tempo and BET in particular, there were appearances in music videos of international acts such as Foxy Brown as just one manifestation of the rewards produced by Bogle's hard work His success was not limited to dancing either, as he was to be found in acting roles within films such as Hype Williams's *Belly*.

"Jamaica caan pay me fi dance", he said, specifically referring to the importance of his role within dancehall culture internationally, especially after the Sashi stage show which signalled his return to Jamaica from his self-imposed exile in 2002 where he performed as an act in his own right. He was clear that "a some big open land to start teach people fi dance . . . dem ting deh mi waan do now. . . . So many products in Jamaica [but we] don't know how to put them in play." Bogle explained that he was a big product, an international dancer as evidenced by his appearances with Stone Love at Disney World, various Caribbean and international destinations, his music video, and movie and other television appearances, all of which Jamaica does not understand how to honour. Bogle's importance to the dancehall space has not gone unnoticed, however, because his moves have circulated within the more prestigious dance theatre companies within Jamaica. Dancer, artistic director and choreographer of the National Dance Theatre Company Rex Nettleford, in commenting on the new dances within dancehall, observed however that "new dances are hard to study because they disappear as soon as they appear in the dancehalls" ("Different Tune Same Dance", *Star*, 15 February 2001, 11). He also acknowledged the common genealogy among folk dances and those within the contemporary dancehall space.

Bogle felt that he contributed immensely to the dance/music industry but did not reap commensurate rewards or attain the recognition he deserved. It was clear to him that dancers had reaped rewards from the public and the dancehall arena in contrast to him. For example, Carlene Smith was accorded the title of Dancehall Queen by media proclamation even though she did not create dance moves. In an interview with Chicagoreggae.com,[3] Bogle asked, "You ever heard of Carlene creating a dance in Jamaica? . . . Who create all of the dance in Jamaica? . . . You ever hear them crown me King?" To these questions the interviewee answered "No." Bogle is not just a dancer but a creator and ethno-choreographer and he was concerned that there was no proclamation that "Bogle is the King". Arguably, dancing skill had less to do with Carlene's ascension to the throne of Dancehall Queen than her brown complexion in as much as Bogle's colour/class positioning in Jamaica determined the ceiling of his acclaim. Bogle was concerned for example about the way people treated him because he was a resident of a lower-class community. He remarked about the way people responded with surprise on hearing him speak due to their perception that citizens from lower socio-economic backgrounds cannot speak standard English fluently. Bogle summarized his position by concluding that "people always check where you are from, not where you are going".

Class identity and its link to political identity created barriers to dancehall performance which are highlighted through Bogle's experience. Being a citizen of the People's National Party (PNP)–affiliated Jungle and mostly residing in the PNP-affiliated Arnett Gardens, Bogle was seen to be a PNP supporter. Added to this, his support for the sound system Stone Love, branded as a "PNP sound" from its liaisons with PNP-affiliated communities such as Jones Town, had inadvertently created spatial and political borders for Bogle in respect of performance. One which was not as easily surmountable was the Jamaica Labour Party's political stronghold on the garrision community of Tivoli Gardens. The Passa Passa event which has been staged in that community since 2003 is one Bogle did not attend up to time of my last interview with him. He did not feel that he could step into that space without permission from the area leader. Anything might have happened and he was not willing to put the future at risk for past events. By April 2004, I witnessed Bogle at Passa Passa and he informed me that he was making an impact there. Though the boundaries of class, community and socio-economic status are sometimes surmountable, evidenced in the international reach as well as economic gains and transition to middle- and upper-class lifestyles for some artists, Bogle remained a resident of Arnett Gardens and there were obvious boundaries within the boundless "enjoyment" that could be experienced within the performance practice. He still did not receive the recognition or rewards befitting his de facto status as king of the dancehall dance.

GENDER DEMARCATIONS AND NEGOTIATIONS IN DANCE

Around the 1990s when Bogle rose to popularity, dance practice in dancehall stood outside the boundaries of scrutiny by the "regulators" of gender identity, its display and possibilities for transgression in post-1990 Jamaica. There was thus no explicit anxiety about males in what has become a female dominated practice, or contradiction perceived about "feminine" display of male dancing bodies in contrast to the standards of macho, aggressive and tough masculinity prescribed by the Jamaican social context. Further, perceptions about male dancers in dancehall did not attract labels of homosexuality or feminized performance which has intensified since 2003 when male dancers and dancing crews began to proliferate and, in their emergence, upstaging female dancers in visible competition for stage, street and video spotlight. Therefore, to a large extent, Bogle and those inspired by him have remained outside these perceptions and have expressed brands of masculinity within dancehall akin to that of the 1960s legsman. These include non-aggressive modes of being, centring on the improvisational nature of the individual, and increasingly, group creative dance process. Males dance with males, females with females, as well as males with females within both group (crews) and couple modalities. Arguably, there is less emphasis on sexuality and more on expanding the space and performance of dance styles. This does not mean that macho masculinities are not also performed by dancers, but this has always been less visible in male dancers' performances and in contrast pronounced in that of the male deejay.

An important dynamic in the post-2000 dance scene is that women were noticeably attending events on their own and there was less emphasis on partner dancing, as distinct from the 1990s. A contributing factor is, arguably, the degree of independence some women achieved as a result of economic activities such as "higglering" (vending). One male dancer observed that in the late 1980s and early 1990s, "girl just give you a dance and any amount a dance" (girls just give you a dance, any amount of dances) due, among other things, to "personal" security. Another male dancer revealed, "If dance a keep, wi go to get a girl." In an acknowledgement of the mid-1990s shift, female dancers admitted that they did not attend dance events with male partners but rather with girlfriends, because attending the event with one's partner reduced the degree of freedom the dancer could exercise in terms of dance moves executed and choice of dance partners. The 1990s then could be said to have ushered in an element of free play among women, in particular as new levels of economic and social independence were reached.

While male and female heterosexual identities are visible in partner dancing through amorous display and sexually provocative or explicit dance styles that in many cases simulate sexual intercourse, perceptions of males dancing in crews began to gain visibility when associations were made with a homosexual identity. Anxiety about male dancing surfaced in dancehall around 2003 when male dancers adopted fashion trends consistent with a feminine aesthetic reminiscent of performers such as Prince and Michael Jackson who reigned supreme over the disco era of the 1980s. Such trends include, among others, tight pants, pink and/or pastel colour clothing, accessories such as scarves, shaped eyebrows and make-up that go against the grain of normative dress for men in the West.

What is more pronounced is that associations are made with homo-/trans-sexual modes of dress, one which finds no comfortable dwelling place in the minds of some Jamaicans who arguably construct the image of Jamaica as one of the most homophobic societies in the world. Entertainers have been explicit not only about their intolerance of homosexuality in Jamaica and dancehall specifically but also about the way the feminine character of the dance, dress and attitude of some males have now overshadowed female presence in the dance. For example, deejay/selector Tony Matterhorn of the Bembe Thursdays DJ Squad highlighted that the event was initiated to bring back females to dancehall and the dance arena generally. Males were thought to be dominating the dance floor, male dance moves overshadowed those created by females and the dancehall was overrun by a new male aesthetic that ran counter to normative social constructions of gender identity. It was not "gender appropriate" for men to upstage women on the dance floor. Statements by other deejays have revolved around sentiments such as "tight pants a woman supp'n [something]" or "badman nuh dress like girl", among a range of criticisms about men trying to take the spotlight away from women in dancehall.

It is important to note that some dancehall actors enjoy the ability to transgress modes of dress, action and perceptions about normative gender roles and expectations. For example, there are perceptions about deejay Elephant Man's embodiment of queer aesthetics with an over-emphasis on the characteristics of drag queen/transvestite modes of dress, including, other among elements, hair extensions, hair dyes, scarves and shaped/shaved eyebrows featured in his characteristically extravagant sartorial creations. However, his song lyrics often belie his presentation of self due to an emphasis on the gangsta/badman lifestyle, and in the history of his career, there have been no public clashes about his fashion choices or sexuality.

Dance and gender are also intertwined in terms of kinesthetic emphasis which inadvertently invites classification according to the sex of performers. In discussing his creations, Bogle acknowledged that the Bogle dance move was really for men while the Butterfly was created with women in mind (Reyes 1993, 48). While many dances were performed by women, those such as the One Foot Skank, Legs, Cool an' Deadly, Get Flat and, more recently, the Chaplin, Bad Man Forward and Gangsta Rock were performed mostly by men. A larger number of the dance moves were performed by both sexes. These include the World Dance, Bogle, Tatti, Screetchie, Angel, Tall Up Tall Up, Higher Level, Curfew, Log On, Row Like a Boat, Wave, Parachute, Blazay, Signal di Plane, Tek Weh Yu Self and the Gully Creepa. Classically, female dances are generally those in which the essential point of articulation is the rotation or thrust of the pelvic girdle, while male dances emphasize complex leg and hand-coordinated movements. Moves performed by both sexes are multidimensional in nature. The latter are not centred on the pelvic girdle or hand/leg coordination; they emphasize individual memory rather than dance skills and the entire community can execute these moves, therein maintaining the characteristic sociality of dancehall culture. Everyone can participate.

On the other hand, dance moves such as the head top, body basics, sketel, bike back position, and the various "wines" – Wine an' Go Down, Go Go Wine, Bruk Wine and Beyonce Wine – have been created by and for women. Here, the skill of "wining" is a central component – winding the waist in a smooth, generic "bubble" or rotation of the hips, "wining" like a go-go dancer (exotic dancer), or "wining" on the head top. There are various songs that encourage wining and a developed wining skill. Elephant Man's "Wining Queen" (2002) asks the question: who is going to be the next wining queen, the next wining machine? His "Fan Dem Off" (2003) encourages the dancer to "don't stop wine up your body like a snake in the vine, wine it up 'cause you inna you prime". Captain Barkey's (1996) song "Go Go Wine" sings of the dancers wining their waistline, their chest and their rumps because they have no problem: they have fed their children, and they are hotter than the competition. Patra's "Bruk Wine", Early Black's "Stuck", Shabba Ranks' "Girls Wine" are all similar "wining" incantations to the dancer. A crucial component of the "wining" capacity dancers must have is control of the buttocks. In various body positions, the dancer's buttocks can shimmy, thrust, rotate, release and contract, push, press and pump, in a light, heavy, frantic, sharp, fluid or jerky manner. Moves such as the bike back, position and sidung pon it are examples: not only do they require fluid movement of the hips, they also feature a particular aesthetic of the buttock. The large derrière which is celebrated in dancehall and more widely in Jamaican culture matters in such a move and it is a dancer with a posterior that can be manipulated who will command attention: the larger and more flexible the derrière, the better.

Bogle created one of the most popular female dance steps and the movement pattern illustrates the characteristic points of emphasis for female dancers. The Butterfly was the most popular dance in 1992. The dance simulates the flapping of the butterfly's wings using the outspread legs and arms. The Butterfly is danced with bent knees, a characteristic feature of African and diasporic movement patterns, with the feet flat to support the dynamic displacement of the hips, shoulder girdle and legs. The knees, which open and close fluidly on a horizontal axis, mimic the flapping of the butterfly's wings in flight. While the Butterfly has clear connections with the Charleston, its North Atlantic cousin which has roots in an Ashanti ancestor dance, with its quick spreading and crossing of hands on the knees (Jones 1968, 17; Eskamp and de Geus 1993, 60), there are differences. For example, the forward and backward thrust of the hip which supports the opening and closing of the legs allows for increased degrees of variation on the movement style, while emphasizing the hips and buttocks.

MR WACKY "TO DI WORLD"

Because of Bogle's presence in the dance, there has been an increase in the number of popular male dancers and financial opportunities for advancement, albeit with Bogle himself not benefiting in ways that he envisioned. These include John Hype, who received a contract with Skocking Vibes promotions (former managers of DJ Beenie Man), Blazay, nickname of the dancer that developed the Blazay Dance, Shelly Belly, Ding Dong, Craigy Dread, Shortman, Spongebob, and Ice, as well as the male crews such as Cadillac, Sample Six, Ravers Clavers, Black Blingers, Colo Squad, and Sadiki and the Crew. These dancers have risen to prominence at a time when the stage had already been set for appreciation of dancehall dance and are popular features not just at stage shows and dance events but also on national platforms such as national independence celebrations (August 2008), or homecoming celebrations to honour outstanding Jamaican athletes after their success at the Beijing Olympic Games (October 2008). They also gain international exposure in the songs that highlight their names as well as show appearances. Most importantly, Bogle has (re)created a platform for other male dancers, some of whom testify to dancehall's life-saving role, many of whom exist in political hotbeds, but because of their practice can be singled out in many a dancehall anthem rather than as a statistic in the evening news. This phenomenon supports the idea of a resurgence of "other kinds of masculinities" within dancehall, paralleled by the legsman whose dance skills found no contradiction with the macho, aggressive and tough masculinity prescribed by the Jamaican social context. Despite perceptions about Jamaica as a homophobic society, and male dancers as stereotypically homosexual because dance falls within the realm of female pursuit and aesthetic, Bogle and those inspired by him occupy a space in which they can express new brands of masculinity, often outside social deviance, as mentioned earlier. This does not mean that macho masculinities are not also performed by dancers, but this is less visible among male dancers' performances than it is of the male deejay.

Bogle's impact is evident in the way artists have built professional reputations based on his contribution. No other artist deserves mention in this category more than Elephant Man. It is remarkable that Elephant Man's career was largely built on songs about dance movement, of which many were created by Bogle, but he has not appropriately acknowledged Bogle's role in his career. For example, this is the same deejay who chose to highlight the dancer Keiva as having a dancing school but remained silent on Bogle's legacy. Emerging first as a member of the Monster Shock Crew with his self-designated soubriquet "Energy God", Elephant Man is well known for selections such as "Gangsta Rock", "Bad Man Anthem" and "Gully Creepa". The success of Elephant Man's solo career is directly related to the emphasis on dance moves which have captured regional and international attention evidenced in the rotation of his music videos on international cable channels such as BET, Tempo and MTV. Musical collaborations with international artists such as Busta Rhymes, Ying Yang Twins, Rihanna, Kat Deluna, Jho Jho and Wyclef Jean have also facilitated the crossing of musical boundaries and markets, engineering greater success. By far the most telling moment was the 2008 Beijing Olympics when Usain Bolt danced in celebration of his sprint sweep of three gold medals and three world records. Usain Bolt allows us to consider deeper dimensions of a despatialized dancehall with Bogle and his dancing disciples as major pillars. There are significant stories of performance and display at the 2008 Olympic Games, but also of Jamaican identity and geopolitical and cultural distinctiveness. When Usain Bolt performed, among others, the popular 2008 No Linga and Gully Creepa moves during his victory laps on Chinese soil at the Beijing games with several millions watching, the Jamaican dance floor became delocalized in its transplantation to Asian soil, where several million spectators were momentarily participants recorded in the critical journey of largely underclass dance pioneers such as Baskin, Persian the Cat, Pam Pam and Bogle, who did not achieve world fame on their own but through time in the performance of Usain Bolt. Images of the way Bolt used dance as part of his athletic training routine as well as recreation are locked into web pages such as sponsor Puma's "Chasing Bolt".[4] Among others, this site features the video entitled "Time to Dance: Usain vs Asafa" using footage from the Puma-hosted final Olympic party to celebrate Jamaica's success. Highlights included Usain and Asafa Powell in a dance-off, both of them skilfully executing the chosen dance moves in addition to Bolt controlling the DJ booth. With fans eager to take photos and interact with Bolt, he was moved to ask for two hours in which dancing alone would be the focus to achieve the heightened celebration after the hard work of training for and succeeding in the Olympics. Sealing his place as a Jamaican ambassador-at-large, Bolt succeeded in "tekking" the Jamaican dance repertoire and performance aesthetic "to the world" to millions of viewers.

Arguably, Bolt represented many ancestors, indeed cultural heroes, including the late Bogle as well as national hero Paul Bogle, who fought for the poor black population. Neither Bogle got the chance to celebrate the honour of being one of Jamaica's dance kings, on the one hand, or celebrate victory prior to his hanging for leading the 1865 Morant Bay Rebellion against the repressive local post-emancipation government, on the other. Metaphorically then, Bolt's performance, which was received as the work of a hero for many Jamaicans, can be read as the fulfilment of national pride and agency especially for the poor who have been creators of rebellions and performance cultures alike. Bolt represents the bodies that, through contestation, exploitation, discrimination and oppression preserve themselves to tell survival tales, tales of history and agency when they transcend time in their link to old and new ways of toiling for freedom while creating space and identity through performance on local yet transnational dance floors.

Bolt's performance at the 2008 Olympics and in the homecoming celebrations following the games with national and international impact was consistent with Bogle's vision: like Bogle, Usain listened to and responded with his feet to maintain dancehall dominance through dance. Bogle wore the attitude of dancehall, and so does Bolt who has extended Bogle's relevance through his performance of dances created by Bogle and his protégés such as Ice, who created the Gully Creepa.

CONCLUSION

Dancehall is the progeny of reggae and through music and dance they have put Jamaica more indelibly on the world map. In this chapter I have explained Bogle's milestone contribution to the repertoire, aesthetic and training in dancehall dance, and I have looked at the historical antecedents through actors such as Kid Harold and the place dancers occupied as cultural heroes. Undoubtedly, Bogle has left a legacy that even in this time stands unprecedented. Bogle distinguished himself as the "life" of the proverbial "dancehall party" with his presence at every major event. Dancing was his middle name – it kept him out of a life of badness and many have emulated his example. Most notably, his dance creations, alongside the rhythms created, sustained increased levels of popularity and interest in dancehall during the two highpoints between 1989 and 1994 and 1999 and 2004. He was and is the quintessential dancehall spirit: that which is going to be expressed by any means necessary as long as music and dance are its media. In the words of one who commented on Bogle at his funeral: "Fi mi, Bogle nuh gawn, because im stan' up pon di foreparents back, im leave a legacy."

NOTES

1. See http://www.jamaica-gleaner.com/gleaner/20050123/ent/ent1.html.
2. The information on Bogle presented here was received during personal interviews with him in June 2002 and 2003, as well as secondary sources.
3. Interview published as "The Uncrowned King of the Dancehall: Montana Interviews Bogle", 31 October 2001, http://www.chicagoreggae.com/bogle.htm.
4. See http://www.pumarunning.com/#EN/running/content/ main/chasingBOLT.

REFERENCES

Allen, I. 1998. "Bogle Demonstrates the 'Pelpa' Dance on the Black Roses Corner, While Members of the 'Pelpa Crew' Look On". *Gleaner,* 23 February, C4.

Brathwaite, Kamau. 1995. *History of the Voice: The Development of Nation Language in Anglophone Caribbean Poetry.* London: New Beacon Books.

Eskamp, Kees and Frank de Geus. 1993. "The Pelvis as Shock Absorber: Modern and African Dance". *Journal of Popular Culture,* 27, no. 1: 55–65.

Hamilton, Beverley. 1988. "Marcus Garvey and Cultural Development in Jamaica: A Preliminary Survey". In *Garvey: His Work and Impact,* edited by R. Lewis and P. Bryan, 87–111. Kingston: University of the West Indies.

Jones, Leroy. 1968. *Blues People: Negro Experience in White America and the Music That Developed from It.* New York: William Morrow.

Reyes, Carla. 1993. "Investigation into Dancehall". Research paper in Dance and Theatre Production. Jamaica School of Dance, Edna Manley College for the Visual and Performing Arts, Jamaica.

Stanley Niaah, Sonjah. 2004. "Kingston's Dancehall: A Story of Space and Celebration". *Space and Culture* 7, no. 1: 102–18.

White, Garth. 1984. "The Development of Jamaican Popular Music, Part 2. Urbanization of the Folk: The Merger of Traditional and the Popular in Jamaican Music". *ACIJ Research Review* 1:3–15, 24–36.

Contributors

SONJAH STANLEY NIAAH is Senior Lecturer in Cultural Studies and Director of the Institute of Caribbean Studies, the University of the West Indies, Mona, Jamaica. Her publications include *Reggae Pilgrimages: Festivals and the Movement of Jah People* and *Dancehall: From Slave Ship to Ghetto.*

BIBI BAKARE-YUSUF is an independent scholar, and co-founder and publishing director of Cassava Republic Press (www.cassavarepublic.biz).

ZACHARY J.M. BEIER is Lecturer, Department of History and Archaeology, the University of the West Indies, Mona, Jamaica. His publications include the co-edited collection *British Forts and Their Communities: Archaeological and Historical Perspectives.*

JOSHUA CHAMBERLAIN received his PhD in cultural studies from the University of the West Indies, Mona, Jamaica. He was a founding board member of the Jamaica Sound System Federation.

LOUIS CHUDE-SOKEI Professor of English, George and Joyce Wein Chair in African American Studies, and Director of the African American Studies Program, Boston University. His publications include *The Last Darky*, *The Sound of Culture*, and *Dr Satan's Echo Chamber and other Essays*, and he is the editor-in-chief of the *Black Scholar.*

ROBIN CLARKE is Senior Lecturer and Communications and Public Relations Officer, Excelsior Community College, Kingston, Jamaica, and Adjunct Lecturer, Institute of Caribbean Studies, the University of the West Indies, Mona, Jamaica.

CAROLYN COOPER is Professor Emerita, the University of the West Indies, Mona, Jamaica. Her publications include *Sound Clash: Jamaican Dancehall Culture at Large*; *Noises in the Blood: Orality, Gender and the "Vulgar" Body of Jamaican Popular Culture;* and the edited collection *Global Reggae.*

LENA DELGADO DE TORRES is Lecturer, Bloomfield College, New Jersey.

NADIA ELLIS is Associate Professor of English, University of California, Berkeley, and the author of *Territories of the Soul: Queered Belonging in the Black Diaspora.*

JULIAN HENRIQUES is Professor in the Department of Media and Communications, Goldsmiths, University of London. His publications include *Sonic Media: The Street Technology of the Jamaican Sound System* and *Sonic Bodies: Reggae Sound Systems, Performance Techniques and Ways of Knowing* and he is writer-director of the film feature *Babymother.*

AUDENE S. HENRY is Lecturer in the Faculty of Education and Liberal Studies, the University of Technology, Jamaica.

RAY HITCHINS is Lecturer, the Institute of Caribbean Studies, the University of the West Indies, Mona, Jamaica. His publications include *Vibe Merchants: The Sound Creators of Jamaican Popular Music.*

ANDREA HOLLINGTON is Senior Researcher, the University of Cologne, Germany.

DONNA P. HOPE is Professor of Culture, Gender and Society, the Institute of Caribbean Studies and the Reggae Studies Unit, the University of the West Indies, Mona. Her publications include *Man Vibes: Masculinities in the Jamaican Dancehall; Inna di Dancehall: Popular Culture and the Politics of Identity in Jamaica;* and the edited collection *ReggaeStories: Jamaican Musical Legends and Cultural Legacies.*

DENNIS HOWARD is Director of Research, the Institute of Cultural Policy and Innovation, and Adjunct Lecturer, the University of the West Indies, the University of the Commonwealth Caribbean, and the Media Technology Institute, Kingston, Jamaica. His publications include *Rantin Inside the Dancehall* and *The Creative Echo Chamber: Contemporary Music Production in Kingston Jamaica.*

KATE LAWTON works in the public sector. Her research interests include Jamaica and the Jamaican diaspora, Caribbean history and religious syncretism from a multidisciplinary perspective.

ERIN C. MacLEOD teaches Caribbean Literature at Vanier College, Montreal, Canada. Her publications include *Visions of Zion: Ethiopians and Rastafari in the Search for the Promised Land.*

LARISA KINGSTON MANN is Assistant Professor of Media Studies and Production, Klein College, Temple University.

PETER MANUEL is Professor of Ethnomusicology, John Jay College and the Graduate Center of the City University of New York. His publications include *Caribbean Currents: Caribbean Music from Rumba to Reggae; Cassette Culture: Popular Music and Technology in North India*; and *Tales, Tunes, and Tassa Drums: Retention and Invention in Indo-Caribbean Music.*

WAYNE MARSHALL is Assistant Professor of Music History, Berklee College of Music. His publications include the co-edited volume *Reggaeton.*

BRUNO BARBOZA MUNIZ is Post-Doctoral Researcher, the Centre for Social Studies, the University of Coimbra, Portugal.

ANDREA SHAW NEVINS is Professor and Assistant Dean for Academic Affairs in the College of Arts, Humanities and Social Sciences, Nova Southeastern University, Florida. Her publications include *The Embodiment of Disobedience: Fat Black Women's Unruly Political Bodies* and *Working Juju: Representations of the Caribbean Fantastic.*

"H" PATTEN is a performer, choreographer, filmmaker and university lecturer at Canterbury Christ Church University and IRIE! Dance Theatre, University of Roehampton.

JOSEPH PEREIRA, now retired, lectured in Spanish at the University of the West Indies, Mona, Jamaica, where he was also Director of the Institute of Caribbean Studies and Deputy Principal.

ANNA KASAFI PERKINS is Senior Programme Officer, Quality Assurance, the University of the West Indies, Mona, Jamaica, and Adjunct Faculty, St Michael's Theological College, Kingston, Jamaica. Her publications include *Justice as Equality: Michael Manley's Caribbean Vision of Justice*; *Is Moral Dis-ease Making Jamaica Ill? Re-engaging the Conversation on Morality*; and the edited collection *Quality in Higher Education in the Caribbean.*

AGOSTINHO PINNOCK is completing a PhD at Loughborough University, England.

TRACEY SKELTON is Associate Professor, Department of Geography, National University of Singapore. Her publications include the edited book *Introduction to the Pan-Caribbean.*

MARVIN D. STERLING is Associate Professor of Cultural Anthropology, Indiana University, Bloomington. His publications include *Babylon East: Performing Dancehall, Roots Reggae, and Rastafari in Japan.*

NORMAN C. STOLZOFF is President (and founder) of Ethnographic Insight, a research, training and strategy firm. He is the author of *Wake the Town and Tell the People: Dancehall Culture in Jamaica* and director of the documentary *Louder than Words.*

KRISTA THOMPSON is the Mary Jane Crowe Professor Art History at Northwestern University, Chicago, Illinois. Her publications include *An Eye for the Tropics* and *Shine: The Visual Economy of Light in African Diasporic Aesthetic Practice.*

GARTH WHITE is a reggae historian and scholar.

